Exchange Rates and International Finance

We work with leading authors to develop the
strongest educational materials in business and finance,
bringing cutting-edge thinking and best
learning practice to a global market.

Under a range of well-known imprints, including
Financial Times Prentice Hall, we craft high-quality print and
electronic publications that help readers to understand
and apply their content, whether studying or at work.

To find out more about the complete range of our
publishing, please visit us on the World Wide Web at:
www.pearsoned.co.uk

Fifth Edition

Exchange Rates and International Finance

Laurence S. Copeland

Prentice Hall

FINANCIAL TIMES

An imprint of **Pearson Education**
Harlow, England • London • New York • Boston • San Francisco • Toronto • Sydney • Singapore • Hong Kong
Tokyo • Seoul • Taipei • New Delhi • Cape Town • Madrid • Mexico City • Amsterdam • Munich • Paris • Milan

Pearson Education Limited
Edinburgh Gate
Harlow
Essex CM20 2JE
England

and Associated Companies throughout the world

Visit us on the World Wide Web at:
www.pearsoned.co.uk

First published 1989
Second edition published 1994
Third edition published 2000
Fourth edition published 2005
Fifth edition published 2008

ISBN: 978-0-273-71027-1

British Library Cataloguing-in-Publication Data
A catalogue record for this book is available from the British Library

Library of Congress Cataloging-in-Publication Data
Copeland, Laurence S.
  Exchange rates and international finance / Laurence S. Copeland. –
5th ed.
        p. cm.
  Includes bibliographical references and index.
  ISBN-13: 978-0-273-71027-1
1. Foreign exchange rates. 2. International finance. I. Title.
  HG3821.C78 2008
  332.4′56–dc22

                                        2008003822

10 9 8 7 6 5 4 3 2 1
11 10 09 08

Typeset in 10/12.5pt Times by 35
Printed and bound in Great Britain by Ashford Colour Press Ltd, Gosport, Hampshire

The publisher's policy is to use paper manufactured from sustainable forests.

Contents

Preface to the fifth edition

This book is now almost 20 years old, and the international economy has changed beyond recognition in those decades. In fact, re-reading the preface to the fourth edition makes it plain that the outlook has changed dramatically even in the past three years. In particular, I think it is clear that we are not going to have a world 'divided into two blocs – a dollar bloc encompassing the USA and most of Asia other than Japan, and a euro bloc . . .' The renminbi is certain to become a major currency as soon as it becomes convertible, a move that is in preparation, to judge from the plans already underway to establish derivatives markets in Shanghai. At the very least, it seems likely to be at the centre of a Greater China bloc comprising the Hong Kong dollar (if the two are not actually integrated at some point), and probably the New Taiwan dollar. Moreover, unless the rise of the emerging economies is reversed (which would be both surprising and tragic), there are likely before long to be two or three or even more newly important currencies, the most obvious candidates being the rupee, the rouble and the real.

I am unsure whether these momentous events require any substantial change in the subject matter of a textbook such as this. In the end, it seems probable that the new players on the world economic scene will develop their financial markets along lines broadly similar to those in the 'old world', in which case there is room to hope that the models covered in this book will remain as relevant as ever.

Target readership

The caveats I included in the preface to the first edition are still valid. This is not intended to be a reference book of published research on international finance or macroeconomics, and nor is it a manual for currency traders or for treasurers of multinational corporations, though it may well be of interest and use to them both.

In terms of its level of difficulty, the centre of gravity of the book, its 'expected reader' as it were, is a third-year economics undergraduate or possibly a non-specialist graduate on an MBA international finance module. In other words, although the first few chapters may well be covered in a first- or second-year course, some of the topics in the later chapters are more likely to find a place in a specialist postgraduate degree. The progression is not entirely monotonic. In particular, Chapter 10 probably contains the hardest (and most up-to-date) material, but it belongs naturally in the middle of the book because it is essentially non-stochastic. As edition succeeds edition, there is a tendency for the proportion of more advanced material to increase because in most cases the new chapters cover research that previously seemed too recondite for inclusion.

The more difficult sections of the book have been signalled by a star *. In some cases, starred sections have been preceded by simplified versions of the analysis, so as to offer an alternative to the 'high road'. Wherever possible, I try to manage without relying on mathematics, though it is unavoidable in places.

Throughout the book, the emphasis is on delivering the *intuition* behind the results. Rigour is available in abundance in the original literature, references to which are provided at the end of each chapter (updated on the book's website). In order to preserve the clarity of the argument, I include only the absolute minimum of institutional detail and mention the mechanics of trading only when absolutely necessary. For the same reason, the empirical work is covered briefly, with only the most important methodological issues addressed (hence, econometrics is not a prerequisite), and the literature survey is limited in most cases to one or two seminal contributions.

Instead, the aim in the sections on empirical results is to give a concise summary of what we know (or think we know) on the topic and some indication of which questions remain open. If my own experience is typical, students and laymen often have difficulty understanding why economists find it so hard to answer apparently straightforward questions such as: *Does purchasing power parity hold? Is there a risk premium? Are expectations rational?* Wherever possible, I have tried to explain the main problems faced by researchers in this field, while always bearing in mind that the overwhelming majority of readers have no desire to lay the foundations of an academic career.

The book will have achieved its objective if, after finishing a chapter, the reader is able to understand the economic argument in the published literature, even if the technicalities remain out of reach. It is to be hoped that ambitious readers will be stimulated to approach the learned journals with sufficient enthusiasm to overcome the technical barriers to entry.

New to this edition

In addition to the usual running repairs and updating graphs and tables, I have made a number of major changes in this edition:

- I have included a new chapter, Chapter 14, to give the reader a taste of the microstructure models that have been developed over the past few years. The new material is not especially difficult, but it will be best appreciated by readers who have some background in basic microeconomics.
- I have added a paragraph or two in Chapter 12.
- I have rewritten the concluding chapter for the first time.

Web page support

A new web page is now up and running at www.pearsoned.co.uk/copeland. The intention is to use this page as a supplement to the text, providing a more up-to-date bibliography, occasional comments and useful links, especially to data sources, as well as references to current news items and controversies.

Acknowledgements

Each successive edition has benefited from the comments of colleagues, friends and students. Fred Burton, Martyn Duffy and Ronnie MacDonald read parts of the first edition; Sheila Dow commented on the first draft of the chapter on currency unions; Sugata Ghosh and Laurian Lungu commented on the third edition; and the fourth edition benefited from the recommendations of the publishers' own reviewers, as well as research assistance from two Cardiff PhD students, Zhao Tianshu and Zhu Yanhui. For the current edition, I owe a major thankyou to Nicholas Rau, not least for prodding me into removing most of the references to the European legacy currencies, and a smaller thank you to Sergio Lagoa for pointing out an error in Equation 15.11 (as it appeared in earlier editions). The burden of this time-consuming exercise (yet another reason for being unenthusiastic about EMU!) mostly fell on Zhu Yanhui again. Over the years, I have learnt a lot from students – both my own and others whom I have never met but who send me occasional emails with comments and questions that I usually have no time to answer but that I am glad to receive nonetheless. Finally, at Pearson, I wish to record my gratitude to Justinia Seaman, who set this edition in motion, to Ellen Morgan who has now replaced her, and to Pauline Gillett. Unfortunately, being a recidivist, I have had to call on their patience with this edition as much as with the last.

As always, the author keeps the copyright to his own errors, but whatever failings remain would have been far worse without the contribution of the people acknowledged here.

Laurence S. Copeland
September 2007

A note on language: For reasons of simplicity, the pronoun 'he' is used to relate to both male and female throughout the book.

Publisher's acknowledgements

We are grateful to the following for permission to reproduce copyright material:

Table 1.3 UK Balance of Payments, 1998, from the Office for National Statistics; reproduced under the terms of the Click-Use Licence.

We are grateful to the Financial Times Limited for permission to reprint the following material:

Table 1.1 Exchange cross rates, © *Financial Times*, 16 September 1999; Table 1.2 FT quotations from 'Pound spot forward against the pound' and 'Euro spot forward against the Euro', © *Financial Times* 20 February 1993.

1 Introduction

Introduction

Until a few years ago, it might have been necessary to start a book such as this by asking the question 'Why study exchange rates?' and then giving an answer in terms of academic curiosity, the design of macroeconomic policy, international trade and so on.

Nowadays, surely, there is no need to justify devoting a book to the subject. Exchange rates are no longer an arcane interest confined to a handful of economic specialists and traders. They are simply ubiquitous, to the point where it almost seems that whatever the subject under discussion – the outlook for the domestic or world economy, stock markets, industrial competitiveness at the level of the firm or the industry, even the outcome of the next election – the answer almost invariably turns out to revolve around the exchange rate. The days when exchange rates could safely be ignored by the vast majority of decisionmakers are long gone and there is at the moment little prospect of them ever returning.

To some extent, the increased importance being attached to exchange rates is a result of the internationalization of modern business, the continuing growth in world trade relative to national economies, the trend towards economic integration (in Europe, at least), and the rapid pace of change in the technology of money transfer. It is also in large part a consequence of the fact that exchange rates are not only variable but also highly volatile. The attention given to them can be traced to the role they play as the joker in the pack: the unpredictable element in the calculations that could turn a profitable deal into a disastrous lossmaker, or make an attractive investment project into the albatross on the company's balance sheet, or push the cost of your family holiday way beyond your budget.

However, it would be dishonest to claim that the reader will learn from this book how to make reliable forecasts of future exchange rate movements. Neither the author nor anyone else really knows how to do that – and the chances are that anyone who *does* know how will never tell the rest of us. (Guess why.)

Instead, the objectives of this book are to enable the reader to understand:

- Why exchange rates change – at least, in so far as economists know why they do.
- Why it is so difficult to forecast exchange rate changes.
- How exchange rate risks can be hedged.
- The main research questions: what we know and what we do not yet know.
- How to evaluate critically the comments on the exchange rate found in the financial press, brokers' circulars, speeches by bankers and politicians, and so on.
- The main issues of policy with respect to exchange rates – in general terms (floating versus fixed rates, international monetary reform, and so on) and in particular instances, for example, the European Monetary Union (EMU) membership controversy in the UK.
- How to interpret new research results.

Notice what is *not* claimed. The book will not enable the reader to embark on original research. To see why, take a quick glance at one of the technical references in the reading guide at the end of one of the later chapters. It will immediately be obvious that the prerequisites for undertaking serious research in what is already a well-worked area include:

- A thorough knowledge of the existing literature on exchange rates.
- A good grounding in general macro- and microeconomics and modern finance.
- A reasonable competence in the specialized applications of statistics to economic models, a discipline known as econometrics.

Now this book aims to provide a starting point for the first of these prerequisites. As far as the second is concerned, it tries to take as little for granted as possible, though inevitably some knowledge of economics has had to be assumed at various points in the book. Certainly, the coverage of topics outside the field of exchange rates can be nowhere near sufficient to equip the reader who wants to generate his own research results. As far as the third requirement is concerned, the decision has been taken to avoid almost completely any discussion of econometric issues or research results, and to limit the commentary to '. . . evidence was found to support the view that . . .' and so on. The reasoning behind what will appear to some readers a perverse decision is that covering the econometrics would make the book inaccessible to the many readers who lack the relevant background, while not really helping those who do, since surveys of the empirical literature are available in a number of different places (as will be made clear in the reading guide at the end of each chapter and on the book web page **www.pearsoned.co.uk/copeland**). In any case, after having finished the chapter here, the reader who can cope with econometrics should be in a position to go on and read the literature without hesitation.

Instead, the emphasis in this book will be on conveying *at an intuitive level* the main propositions in the literature. As a result, the reader with little economics background will be able to grasp propositions that would otherwise have been completely inaccessible. For the professional or academic economist coming to the subject fresh from other specialist areas and wanting to get to grips with the exchange rate literature in the shortest possible time, the coverage (particularly in the later chapters) is intended to offer a flying start.

This introductory chapter clears the ground for what is to come, starting with an explanation of what we mean by the exchange rate – bilateral, trade-weighted, spot or forward. In Section 1.2, we look in general terms at supply and demand in the currency markets, an exercise that provides the essential framework for analysing how exchange rates are determined. In the process, we see what is involved in fixing an exchange rate. The next section provides, for those readers who need it, an explanation of the balance of payments and its relationship to events in the currency markets. Section 1.4 looks at the conventional wisdom on exchange rates and the balance of payments – a worthwhile exercise if only because, for some purposes, what people believe to be true can be as important as the truth itself (even if we knew it). Section 1.5 contains a potted history of the international monetary system since World War II – essential to understanding the present situation in world financial markets. Section 1.6 gives an overview of the rest of the book, while the last two sections contain, as in all the other chapters, a summary and a reading guide, respectively.

1.1 What is an exchange rate?

The first thing to understand about the exchange rate is that it is simply a *price*. Or, putting it the other way round, prices as we normally understand the term are themselves exchange rates: the UK price of this book is the exchange rate between a particular good (the book) and pounds sterling. Suppose that it is quoted as £30, which means a book sells for £30, or can be bought at that price. It changes hands at an exchange rate of 1 book = £30.

Notice, as far as the bookseller is concerned, that means 'money can be bought' at the rate of £30 per book. From the bookseller's point of view, the price of £1 is 1/30th of a copy of this book. If its price were £31, the shop would need to supply only 1/31th of a copy in order to earn £1. So a *rise* in the price of the book, from £30 to £31, is the same as a *fall* in the price of money, from 1/30th to 1/31th of a book.

In the same way, an exchange rate of £1 = €1.50 means that the price of a euro in UK currency is £(1/1.50) = £0.66. To a German or Italian, a pound costs €1.50. In general, the exchange rate of currency A in terms of currency B is the number of units of B needed to buy a unit of A.

Unfortunately, although it is normal to talk of the (money) price of books rather than the (book) price of money, there is no *normal* way to express an exchange rate. Both £1 = €1.50 and €1.00 = £0.66 are acceptable ways of expressing the same exchange rate. Strangely enough, both the British and the Germans usually choose the former. In general, the continental Europeans and the Japanese tend to think of exchange rates as the price of foreign currency: *direct quotations*, in market jargon. The British (invariably) and the Americans (usually, though not always) prefer to think in terms of the purchasing power of the pound or dollar[1] respectively – nobody in currency markets seems very concerned to make life simple for the textbook reader (or writer).

We had better make our choice here at the start of the book and stick with it. So:

> **Convention 1.1** Throughout the analysis, the exchange rate (symbol S) will be defined as the domestic currency price of foreign currency. So a rise in S_t means a rise in the price of foreign exchange at the time t, hence a relative cheapening of the domestic currency, or a *depreciation*. Conversely, a fall in S implies a reduction in the number of units of domestic currency required to buy a unit of foreign exchange; that is, a rise in the relative value of the home country's money, or an *appreciation*.

The only exception is that when we look at the facts (which we try to do after each new dose of theory), we sometimes talk in terms of dollars per pound, simply because it is so much more familiar. On all other occasions in this book, we follow continental European practice, as in Convention 1.1 – which also happens to be much the more popular choice in the exchange rate literature.

1.1.1 Bilateral versus trade-weighted exchange rates

Suppose, one day, I hear the pound has depreciated against the US dollar – in other words, the price of dollars has risen. Does that mean the pound's international value has fallen? Or would it be more accurate to say that the value of the US currency has risen?

From a purely bilateral perspective, the two amount to the same thing. However, for many purposes, a two-country view is far too narrow. For example, suppose we wish to explain *why* the bilateral exchange rate has moved against the pound and in favour of the dollar. Plainly, if we have grounds for believing that it is the US currency that has strengthened rather than the pound that has weakened, we ought to look at developments in the USA rather than the UK to explain the change in the exchange rate, and vice versa if we believe the pound to have weakened and the dollar to have remained unchanged.

The problem is exactly the same as trying to explain a rise in the price of, say, beef. Our first step ought to be to decide whether it is the *relative* price of beef that has risen, in which case the explanation is presumably to be found in changes in the beef market, or whether, on the other hand, it is the price of goods *in general* that has risen (that is, inflation), which would suggest a macroeconomic cause.

Notice that when the price of a single good or class of goods goes up, while all others stay the same, we say the price of beef or meat or whatever has risen. When the price of beef rises, *at the same time as all other prices*, we say the value of money has fallen.

In the same way, if the (sterling) price of dollars goes up, while the (sterling) price of all other currencies is unchanged, we say the US currency has strengthened. On the other hand, if all exchange rates move against the pound, then the pound has weakened. The difference is not purely semantic. If the pound suddenly weakens against *all* other currencies, one would intuitively expect to find the cause in some change in the UK rather than the American or German economies, and vice versa if it is the dollar that has risen in value.

All of which should serve to illustrate why, for some purposes, it will suffice to look at the exchange rate between two countries only, while for other purposes this narrow approach could be completely misleading. So far, we have have thought of exchange rates only in a two-country context. To be more precise, we need the following definition:

> The **bilateral exchange rate** between, say, the UK and the USA, is the price of dollars in terms of pounds.

So, what has been said is that a change in the UK–US bilateral exchange rate in favour of the dollar could be indicative of *either* a decline in the international value of the pound *or* a rise in that of the dollar – or both, of course. How can we be sure which? How can we get some indication of what has happened to the *overall* value of the pound or the dollar?

One way would be simply to look at how both UK and US currencies have moved against the euro – which would involve looking at two bilateral exchange rates for the UK (£/$, £/€) and two for the US ($/£, $/€). To give a real-world example, look at Table 1.1, which is taken from the currencies page of the *Financial Times* of 14 September 2007, and shows cross rates – to be explained shortly – for the previous day.

Look at the bottom row, labelled USA. The numbers in that row, starting 1.033, 5.371, 0.721, 115.1, . . . are the number of Canadian dollars, Danish kroner, euros,

Table 1.1 Exchange cross rates

14 September		C$	DKr	Euro	Y	NKr	SK	SFr	£	$
Canada	C$	1	5.201	0.698	111.4	5.448	6.477	1.152	0.481	0.968
Denmark	DKr	1.923	10	1.342	214.2	10.48	12.45	2.215	0.926	1.862
Euro	Euro	1.432	7.449	1	159.6	7.804	9.276	1.650	0.689	1.387
Japan	Y	0.898	4.668	0.627	100	4.890	5.813	1.034	0.432	0.869
Norway	NKr	1.835	9.545	1.281	204.5	10	11.89	2.114	0.883	1.777
Sweden	SKr	1.544	8.030	1.078	172.0	8.412	10	1.779	0.743	1.495
Switzerland	SFr	0.868	4.514	0.606	96.71	4.729	5.622	1	0.418	0.840
UK	£	2.077	10.80	1.450	231.5	11.32	13.45	2.393	1	2.012
USA	$	1.033	5.371	0.721	115.1	5.627	6.689	1.190	0.497	1

Danish kroner, Norwegian kroner and Swedish kroner per 10; yen per 100.

Source: *Financial Times*, derived from WM Reuters.

yen, etc. that could be bought with $US1.00 in the currency market at the close of business on the day in question. The row ends with 0.497, the number of pounds bought with a dollar, and 1, the number of dollars per dollar. For the same reason, there are 1s along the diagonal of the table. The final column of the table starting 0.968, 1.862, 1.387, 0.869, . . . gives exchange rates in terms of dollar prices; it costs $0.968 (or 96.8 cents) to buy a Canadian dollar, $1.862 to buy 10 Danish kroner, $1.387 to buy 1 euro, and so forth, which are just the reciprocals of the numbers in the bottom row.

Now let us pick another entry in the table, for example the fourth number in the third row, which tells us that €1.00 = yen 159.6. Ask yourself the question: is this telling us anything we could not have worked out for ourselves simply from knowing the numbers in *either* the USA row *or* the USA column alone? Obviously, we ought to have:

$$\text{Yen price of euros} = \frac{\text{dollar price of euros}}{\text{dollar price of (100) yen}}$$

$$159.6 = \frac{1.387}{0.869/100}$$

otherwise there would be a profit opportunity waiting to be exploited.

Question Suppose the euro/yen exchange rate actually stood at 159.2? Or at 160.0? What would you do in order to profit from the situation? What problems might you face in the process?

So, most of the 81 numbers in the matrix are redundant. In fact, all the rates can be, and in practice actually *are*, calculated from the nine exchange rates in the US dollar column. If we introduce the following definition:

A **cross-exchange rate** is an exchange rate between two currencies, A and B, neither of which is the US dollar. It can be calculated as the ratio of the exchange rate of A to the dollar, divided by the exchange rate of B to the dollar.

we can then say that, given N currencies including the numeraire (the dollar), there will be $N(N-1)/2$ cross rates. In Table 1.1, we have $N = 9$ currencies, so there are 8 (that is, $N-1$) dollar rates, and $(9 \times 8)/2 = 36$ cross rates – the remaining entries are either 1s or the reciprocals of the cross rates.

Now suppose that we were to look at the cross rates and find that the pound has *depreciated* against the US dollar but *appreciated* against the yen. Is the net effect on the pound a rise (appreciation) or fall (depreciation) in its international value?

There is no completely adequate answer to this question. The nearest we can get to a satisfactory solution is to apply the same logic we use in dealing with changes in the domestic purchasing power of money. In situations where some (goods) prices are rising and others are falling, we measure changes in the price of goods *in general* by computing a price index.

In the same way, we can arrive at some indication of what has happened to the price of foreign currencies *in general* by looking at an index of its international value, defined as follows:

> The **effective or trade-weighted exchange rate** of currency A is a weighted average[2] of its exchange rate against currencies B, C, D, E, . . . The weights used are usually the proportion of country A's trade that involves B, C, D, E, . . . , respectively.

Notice that the effective exchange rate is *multilateral* rather than bilateral. Furthermore, as is the case with the Retail Price Index, there is no meaning to be attached to the absolute level of the effective exchange rate – it all depends on our choice of base year. So, for example, the fact that the effective exchange rate of the euro stood at 115.44 on 19 March 2008 meant that its average value against the world's other major currencies was just over 15% above its average level in the base period, the first quarter of 1999.

This is no place to discuss at length the question of when to use effective and when to use bilateral exchange rates. All that needs to be said is that the theoretical literature sometimes looks at the relationship between the economies of two countries, the domestic and the foreign, so that the conclusions naturally relate to the bilateral exchange rate. In other cases, it tries to explain the value of a single country's currency relative to other currencies in general, so that the obvious interpretation in terms of real-world data is the effective exchange rate. None the less, even in the latter case, we can always handle the theory as though the exchange rate being determined is the one between the domestic economy and another all-enveloping country – the Rest of the World (ROW).

To simplify matters and to clarify the exposition as far as possible, whenever the analysis takes place in the context of a two-country world, we shall keep to the following:

> **Convention 1.2** Unless otherwise specified, the 'home' country is the UK and the domestic currency is the pound sterling. Likewise, the 'foreign' country is the USA, and the foreign currency is the US dollar.

1.1.2   Spot versus forward rates

All of the exchange rates we have referred to so far have had one thing in common. They have all related to deals conducted 'on the spot' – in other words, involving the delivery of currency more or less immediately when the bargain is struck. In the jargon, we have been dealing with *spot rates*.

However, there are many deals struck in currency markets that involve no immediate exchange of money. Contracts that commit the two parties to exchange one currency for another at some future date at a predetermined price – the forward or futures exchange rate, as the case may be – will play an important part in the later chapters of this book and will be explained then. To avoid confusion, we shall stick to the following convention:

> **Convention 1.3** All exchange rates are *spot* rates, unless specified otherwise.

1.1.3 Buying versus selling rates

There is one more complication to deal with when looking at exchange rate quotations. It arises out of the fact that in the currency market, as in so many other markets, most transactions involve intermediaries who act as temporary buyers for agents wishing to sell, and vice versa for those who want to buy. Of course, the intermediaries are not motivated purely by charity. In some cases, they may charge a fee or commission for the service of, in effect, matching buyers and sellers. For major transactions, however, the source of their profit lies in the gap between the price at which they buy a currency and the price at which they are able to sell it. As usual, there is specialized jargon to cover this situation:

> The **bid rate** for currency A in terms of currency B is the rate at which dealers buy currency A (sell currency B). The **offer** (or **ask**) **rate** is the rate at which dealers sell currency A (buy currency B). The **(bid/ask) spread** is the gap between the offer and bid rates.

For example, the *Financial Times* of 14 September 2007 contained the rates for the pound and euro quoted in London shown in Table 1.2.

The top half of the table shows rates for the pound and the bottom half for the euro. The first column, labelled 'Closing mid-point' gives the average of the bid and ask exchange rates (currency per pound or euro) at the close of business on the day in question. 'Change on day' in the next column is the difference between today's closing rate (i.e. the rate given in the previous column) and the level at the end of yesterday's trading. So, for example, looking at the Hong Kong row, the pound bought $HK15.6678 at the end of the day in London, which represented a fall of $HK0.125 over 24 hours. In other words, the pound closed at $15.5428 (= $15.6678 − $0.125), a depreciation against the Hong Kong dollar of 0.8%[3] – one of the more turbulent days in the market, but by no means without precedent.

In the 'Bid/offer spread' column, we find the Hong Kong dollar quoted as 654–701, meaning that the currency could be bought with pounds at £1 = $HK15.6654 and sold for pounds at £1 = $HK15.6701, a bid/ask spread of (0.0701 − 0.0654)/15.6678 = 0.0003 or 0.03%. The spread is tight because this is a heavily traded currency pair. In fact, for the pound/US dollar rate, the spread is even smaller. On the other hand, for Slovak koruna, it is (0.0857 − 0.0049)/48.9453 = 0.17%.

A point worth noting is that since one can only *buy* one currency by simultaneously *selling* another, it follows that the ask price for currency A (in terms of currency B) is the reciprocal of the *bid*, not the ask price, for currency B (in terms of A). In other words, whereas in the absence of transaction costs, we can simply say that:

$$S(\text{£ per \$}) = 1/S(\text{\$ per £}) \tag{1.1}$$

this is no longer the case when we allow for the spread between bid and ask rates. Instead, if we write $S^b(A/B)$ to denote the bid price for currency B in terms of currency A, S^a(A/B) for the ask price of B in terms of A, and similarly S^b(B/A) and S^a(B/A) are bid and ask for A in terms of B, then the following relationship holds:

$$S^b(B/A) = 1/S^a(A/B) \quad \text{and} \quad S^a(B/A) = 1/S^b(A/B) \qquad (1.2)$$

One implication of this is that in practice the relationship between cross rates is not quite as simple as it was made to appear in Section 1.1. In fact, it turns out that cross rates can show inconsistencies in proportion to the bid/ask spreads on the currencies involved.

Obviously, dealers require a spread on all transactions, whether spot or forward. As we saw by comparing the Hong Kong dollar and the koruna, the less frequently traded currencies are associated with higher spreads, other things being equal, since dealers may have to keep these currencies on their books (that is, in stock) for far longer than the more heavily traded currencies.[4]

For the most part in this book, we shall regard the distinction between buying and selling rates as merely a technicality affecting precise calculations of the profitability of deals, but not in principle changing our conclusions regarding the basic mechanisms at work in currency markets. With the exception of Section 3.3, and more importantly Chapter 14, which is in part about the way dealers set the spread, we shall ignore the distinction between bid and ask rates from now on. In fact, we impose the following:

> **Convention 1.4** Unless specified otherwise, all exchange rates, forward and spot, are to be understood as mid-market rates – that is, averages of bid and offered rates.

Continuing with the explanation of Table 1.2, the two columns labelled 'Day's mid' simply give the range of variation over the day (sometimes called the trading range), so that readers can tell how volatile the exchange rate was over the day. So we find that at some point during 14 September 2007, the pound was quoted as high as $HK15.7541 and at another point as low as $HK15.6249 against the Hong Kong dollar.

Forward exchange rates have already been mentioned. Table 1.2 gives rates for 1-, 3- and 12-month forward delivery, which were quoted as $HK15.6502, $HK15.6027 and $HK15.4414, respectively. Note the '%PA' column, computed as $[(15.6678/15.6502) - 1] \times 12 = 1.35\%$ for the monthly rate, $[(15.6678/15.6027) - 1] \times 4 = 1.67\%$ for the three-month rate and $[(15.6678/15.4414) - 1] \times 4 = 1.47\%$ for the annual rate. In other words, these percentages indicate the extent to which the pound buys fewer Hong Kong dollars for 1-month, 3-month and 12-month delivery. The fact that these numbers are all positive is expressed by saying the pound was at a discount (and the Hong Kong dollar at a premium) of 1.35% in the one-month forward market. By contrast, the pound was more expensive forward than spot in the case of the Turkish lira, hence the negative numbers in this column for Turkey. The reasons for these differences will be discussed at several points in this book.

Finally, the last column of Table 1.2 gives the level of the effective exchange rate for those currencies for which the Bank of England computes a trade-weighted index in the way described earlier.

Table 1.2 *Financial Times quotations for pound and euro*

14 September		Closing mid-point	Change on day	Bid/offer spread	Day's mid		One month		Three months		One year		Bank of England Index
					High	Low	Rate	%PA	Rate	%PA	Rate	%PA	
Europe													
Czech Rep.	(Koruna)	39.8155	−0.2941	837–472	40.0260	39.7780	39.7126	3.1	39.5176	3.0	38.9294	2.2	–
Denmark	(DKr)	10.8042	−0.0736	014–069	10.8574	10.7900	10.7862	2.0	10.7540	1.9	10.6480	1.4	108.3
Hungary	(Forint)	368.964	−1.8329	647–282	370.860	367.680	369.345	−1.2	369.926	−1.0	373.065	−1.1	–
Norway	(NKr)	11.3188	−0.1149	132–244	11.4398	11.2970	11.3093	1.0	11.2916	1.0	11.2656	0.5	105.8
Poland	(Zloty)	5.4818	−0.0408	781–854	5.5128	5.4693	5.4745	1.6	5.4598	1.6	5.4329	0.9	–
Russia	(Rouble)	50.9867	−0.4452	744–989	51.3062	50.8866	51.0006	−0.3	51.0154	−0.2	51.1358	−0.3	–
Slovakia	(Koruna)	48.9453	−0.2940	049–857	49.1320	48.8830	48.8628	2.0	48.6614	2.3	48.0244	1.9	–
Sweden	(SKr)	13.4547	−0.0709	493–601	13.5124	13.4272	13.4302	2.2	13.3799	2.2	13.2369	1.6	81.9
Switzerland	(SFr)	2.3933	−0.0158	924–942	2.3998	2.3850	2.3857	3.8	2.3707	3.8	2.3182	3.1	107.8
Turkey	(Lira)	2.5358	−0.0252	336–379	2.5598	2.5282	2.5590	−11.0	2.6043	−10.8	2.7989	−10.4	–
UK	(£)												102.9
Euro	(Euro)	1.4505	−0.0100	501–508	1.4577	1.4485	1.4481	2.0	1.4438	1.8	1.4287	1.5	97.30
SDR	–	1.3044	−0.0091										
Americas													
Argentina	(Peso)	6.2936	−0.0495	903–969	6.3297	6.2828	6.3350	−7.9	6.4261	−8.4	6.8127	−8.2	–
Brazil	(R$)	3.8158	−0.0393	134–182	3.8567	3.8053	3.8252	−2.9	3.8414	−2.7	3.9326	−3.1	–
Canada	(C$)	2.0775	−0.0170	767–782	2.0939	2.0655	2.0754	1.2	2.0711	1.2	2.0550	1.1	110.5
Mexico	(New Peso)	22.3449	−0.1076	391–507	22.4795	22.2922	22.3645	−1.1	22.4016	−1.0	22.7021	−1.6	–
Peru	(New Sol)	6.3133	−0.0628	094–171	6.3171	6.3094	6.3090	0.8	6.2987	0.9	6.2869	0.4	–
USA	($)	2.0116	−0.0158	113–118	2.0225	2.0063	2.0101	0.9	2.0069	0.9	1.9909	1.0	87.5

Pound spot forward against the pound

Pacific/Middle East/Africa

Australia	(A$)	2.3908	−0.0267	899–916	2.4210	2.3836	−0.3	2.3927	−0.3	2.4135	−1.0	96.1
Hong Kong	(HK$)	15.6678	−0.1250	654–701	15.7541	15.6249	1.3	15.6027	1.7	15.4414	1.4	—
India	(Rs)	81.3873	−0.6292	671–075	81.7760	80.9940	−0.9	81.5295	−0.7	81.9564	−0.7	—
Indonesia	(Rupiah)	18868.3	−193.8195	620–747	19005.9	18823.1	−1.1	18909.4	−0.9	19063.1	−1.0	—
Iran	(Rial)	18744.6	−129.9994	292–600	—	—						—
Israel	(Shk)	8.2353	−0.0648	282–423	8.2916	8.2142	2.3	8.1943	2.0	8.1437	1.1	—
Japan	(Y)	231.459	−2.5682	400–518	233.300	230.270	5.5	228.307	5.4	220.164	4.9	120.4
Kuwait	(Dinar)	0.5658	−0.0041	656–659	0.5684	0.5641	1.3	0.5644	1.0	0.5603	1.0	—
Malaysia	(M$)	7.0052	−0.0449	993–111	7.0319	6.9920	2.8	6.9557	2.8	6.8358	2.4	—
New Zealand	(NZ$)	2.8251	−0.0021	237–264	2.8561	2.8119	−2.2	2.8408	−2.2	2.8948	−2.5	107.7
Philippines	(Peso)	93.2152	−0.9958	835–469	94.3908	92.8745	−0.4	93.2486	−0.1	93.3814	−0.2	—
Saudi Arabia	(SR)	7.5441	−0.0592	428–453	7.5846	7.5252	1.7	7.5168	1.4	7.4488	1.3	—
Singapore	(S$)	3.0411	−0.0185	401–420	3.0564	3.0341	3.8	3.0118	3.8	2.9424	3.2	—
South Africa	(R)	14.4017	−0.0559	898–135	14.5417	14.3712	−4.0	14.5503	−4.1	15.0768	−4.7	—
South Korea	(Won)	1867.93	−20.9567	709–876	1882.59	1863.14	2.0	1857.02	2.3	1832.55	1.9	—
Taiwan	(T$)	66.5290	−0.5206	157–423	66.9071	66.3885	3.4	65.9451	3.5	64.3338	3.3	—
Thailand	(Bt)	68.9559	−0.4707	071–047	69.2440	68.8160	2.7	68.4839	2.7	67.4177	2.2	—
U A E	(Dirham)	7.3865	−0.0597	851–879	7.4265	7.3685	1.5	7.3596	1.5	7.2831	1.4	—

Euro locking rates: Austrian schilling 13.7603, Belgium/Luxembourg franc 40.339, Finnish markka 5.94573, French franc 6.55957, German mark 1.95583, Greek drachma 340.75, Irish punt 0.787564, Italian lira 1936.27, Netherlands guilder 2.20371, Portuguese escudo 200.482, Spanish peseta 166.386. Bid/offer speads in the euro spot table show only the last three decimal places. Bid, offer, mid-spot rates and forward rates are derived from the WM/Reuters closing spot and forward rate services. Some values are rounded by the FT.

Table 1.2 (Cont'd)

14 September		Closing mid-point	Change on day	Bid/offer spread	Day's mid high	Day's mid low	One month Rate	One month %PA	Three months Rate	Three months %PA	One year Rate	One year %PA
Europe												
Czech Rep.	(Koruna)	27.4505	−0.0120	350–660	27.5120	27.4350	27.4244	1.1	27.3701	1.2	27.2482	0.7
Denmark	(DKr)	7.4489	0.0010	487–490	7.4528	7.4452	7.4487	–	7.4483	–	7.4529	−0.1
Hungary	(Forint)	254.380	0.5000	220–540	255.140	253.430	255.059	−3.2	256.213	−2.9	261.123	−2.7
Norway	(NKr)	7.8037	−0.0248	016–057	7.8566	7.7968	7.8099	−1.0	7.8206	−0.9	7.8852	−1.0
Poland	(Zloty)	3.7794	−0.0019	777–810	3.7920	3.7748	3.7805	−0.4	3.7815	−0.2	3.8027	−0.6
Russia	(Rouble)	35.1524	−0.0624	445–603	35.2177	35.1029	35.2196	−2.3	35.3336	−2.1	35.7919	−1.8
Slovakia	(Koruna)	33.7450	0.0315	250–650	33.7880	33.6458	33.7433	0.1	33.7032	0.5	33.6141	0.4
Sweden	(SKr)	9.2763	0.0154	747–778	9.2827	9.2580	9.2745	0.2	9.2670	0.4	9.2650	0.1
Switzerland	(SFr)	1.6501	0.0006	498–503	1.6516	1.6430	1.6475	1.9	1.6420	2.0	1.6226	1.7
Turkey	(Lira)	1.7483	−0.0052	468–497	1.7609	1.7430	1.7671	−13.0	1.8037	−12.7	1.9591	−12.1
UK	(£)	0.6895	0.0048	893–896	0.6904	0.6860	0.6906	−2.0	0.6926	−1.8	0.7000	−1.5
Americas												
Argentina	(Peso)	4.3391	−0.0039	369–413	4.3489	4.3335	4.3748	−9.9	4.4508	−10.3	4.7685	−9.9
Brazil	(R$)	2.6308	−0.0087	292–324	2.6597	2.6239	2.6416	−4.9	2.6606	−4.5	2.7526	−4.6
Canada	(C$)	1.4323	−0.0018	318–328	1.4375	1.4256	1.4333	−0.8	1.4345	−0.6	1.4384	−0.4
Mexico	(New Peso)	15.4056	0.0327	018–093	15.4486	15.3799	15.4443	−3.0	15.5155	−2.9	15.8901	−3.1
Peru	(New Sol)	4.3527	−0.0130	501–552	4.3630	4.3446	4.3568	−1.1	4.3625	−0.9	4.4004	−1.1
USA	($)	1.3869	−0.0012	867–870	1.3895	1.3850	1.3881	−1.1	1.3900	−0.9	1.3935	−0.5

Euro spot forward against the euro

Pacific/Middle East/Africa

Australia	(A$)	1.6483	−0.0069	477–488	1.6618	1.6451	1.6514	−2.3	1.6572	−2.2	1.6893	−2.5
Hong Kong	(HK$)	10.8021	−0.0110	006–035	10.8235	10.7832	10.8076	−0.6	10.8065	−0.2	10.8081	−0.1
India	(Rs)	56.1120	−0.0436	989–250	56.2040	55.7730	56.2471	−2.9	56.4679	−2.5	57.3645	−2.2
Indonesia	(Rupiah)	13008.7	−42.9574	045–128	13047.2	12989.4	13041.5	−3.0	13096.8	−2.7	13343.0	−2.6
Iran	(Rial)	12923.4	0.1507	130–338	12936.0	12910.0						
Israel	(Shk)	5.6778	−0.0052	730–825	5.6970	5.6680	5.6761	0.3	5.6755	0.2	5.7001	−0.4
Japan	(Y)	159.578	−0.6574	540–616	160.220	158.830	159.111	3.5	158.127	3.6	154.102	3.4
Kuwait	(Dinar)	0.3901	−0.0001	899–902	0.3905	0.3893	0.3903	−0.7	0.3909	−0.9	0.3921	−0.5
Malaysia	(M$)	4.8297	0.0026	257–337	4.8348	4.8219	4.8263	0.8	4.8176	1.0	4.7847	0.9
New Zealand	(NZ$)	1.9477	0.0120	468–486	1.9603	1.9390	1.9544	−4.1	1.9676	−4.1	2.0262	−4.0
Philippines	(Peso)	64.2667	−0.2383	458–875	64.8220	64.0100	64.3954	−2.4	64.5846	−2.0	65.3613	−1.7
Saudi Arabia	(SR)	5.2012	−0.0047	004–019	5.2110	5.1927	5.2023	−0.3	5.2062	−0.4	5.2136	−0.2
Singapore	(S$)	2.0967	0.0018	960–973	2.1002	2.0931	2.0935	1.8	2.0860	2.0	2.0595	1.8
South Africa	(R)	9.9292	0.0303	211–372	10.0060	9.9086	9.9788	−6.0	10.0777	−6.0	10.5529	−6.3
South Korea	(Won)	1287.83	−5.4639	727–838	1293.11	1286.02	1287.77	0.1	1286.19	0.5	1282.67	0.4
Taiwan	(T$)	45.8680	−0.0399	596–764	45.9720	45.7940	45.8132	1.4	45.6741	1.7	45.0297	1.8
Thailand	(Bt)	47.5412	0.0057	083–741	47.5974	47.4884	47.5136	0.7	47.4324	0.9	47.1882	0.7
U A E	(Dirham)	5.0926	−0.0057	917–935	5.1026	5.0857	5.0945	−0.4	5.0973	−0.4	5.0977	−0.1

Euro locking rates: Austrian schilling 13.7603, Belgium/Luxembourg franc 40.3399, Finnish markka 5.94573, French franc 6.55957, German mark 1.95583, Greek drachma 340.75, Irish punt 0.787564, Italian lira 1936.27, Netherlands guilder 2.20371, Portuguese escudo 200.482, Spanish peseta 166.386. Bid/offer spreds in the euro spot table show only the last three decimal places. Bid, offer, mid-spot rates and forward rates are derived from the WM/Reuters closing spot and forward rate services. Some values are rounded by the FT.

Source: Financial Times, derived from WM Reuters.

1.2 The market for foreign currency

What determines exchange rates? What factors can explain the wild fluctuations in currency values that seem to occur so frequently nowadays?

Answering questions such as these will take up most of this book. However, at the simplest possible level, we can give an answer in terms of elementary microeconomics – one that is not in itself very illuminating but that provides an essential framework for thinking about exchange rates.

As with any other market, price is determined by supply and demand. Look at Figure 1.1(b), ignoring for the moment Figure 1.1(a) to its left. The upward-sloping supply and downward-sloping demand curves will look reassuringly familiar to anyone who has ever had any previous encounter with microeconomics. However, we need to be a little careful in interpreting these curves in the present case.

First, note the price on the vertical axis: it is the variable we are calling S, the exchange rate measured as the price of a dollar in domestic (UK) currency. On the horizontal axis we measure the quantity of dollars traded, because the dollar is the good whose price is measured on the vertical.

(Notice that since the sterling price of dollars is the reciprocal of the dollar price of pounds, the vertical axis could have been drawn for $1/S$, the dollar price of pounds. To be consistent, we would have had to plot on the horizontal axis the quantity of *sterling* changing hands.

All of which serves simply to illustrate an obvious but important point: in a bilateral context, *any supply of dollars is equivalent to a demand for sterling*, and vice versa. So the whole of the supply and demand analysis that follows could be carried out in terms of the market for sterling instead of the market for dollars.[5])

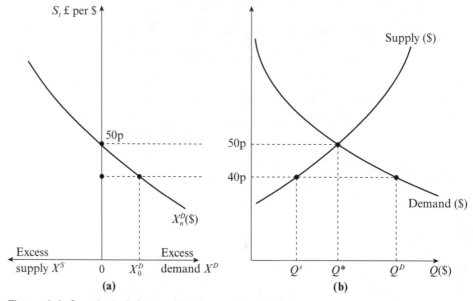

Figure 1.1 Supply and demand in the market for foreign currency

Now consider this question: what is the motivation behind the demand and supply curves in Figure 1.1(b)? What kind of agents supply or demand foreign currency?[6] For the present purposes, we can divide them all into one of three categories:

■ *Exporters* supply goods to foreign buyers. In return, they either receive foreign currency directly or are paid in sterling that has been purchased by the overseas importer with foreign currency. In either case, the net effect must be an associated *supply* of foreign exchange – dollars, if the exports were sold to the USA, or to any of the many other countries that use dollars for their foreign trade. Symmetrically, *importers* buy goods from foreign suppliers, paying with dollars bought for the purpose in the currency market, or occasionally with sterling, leaving the recipient in the USA or wherever to convert the pounds into dollars. Hence, imports are associated with the *demand* for foreign currency.

■ *Foreign investors* buy sterling so as to purchase assets such as office blocks in the City, shares in UK companies or estates in Scotland. *British investors* exchange pounds for dollars so as to buy holiday homes in Florida or shares in IBM, or, perhaps via their pension funds, to snap up real estate in Texas.

■ *Speculators* will be regarded for present purposes simply as economic agents who operate in currency markets so as to make themselves a profit from the activity of buying or selling foreign exchange.[7] For the most part, their activity takes the form of the purchase of short-term assets, typically deposits of one form or another in UK or US financial institutions.

Next, ask yourself this question: how will these three kinds of agent be influenced by the exchange rate?

As far as importers and exporters are concerned, there are a number of reasons to suppose that the demand for dollars will be greater and the supply smaller, the lower the price – in other words, the higher the relative value of the pound. The reason is that when the dollar is cheaper and the pound more expensive, a given sterling price of UK output translates into a higher dollar price. *Other things being equal*, this is likely to reduce the volume of exports from Britain and increase the volume of relatively cheap, dollar-priced imports. The net effect in the market for dollars must be to increase the demand and decrease the supply.[8]

A similar argument applies to what have been called long-term investors. It is not that exchange rates will necessarily be the dominant factor in their investment decision. All we can say is that the cheaper the dollar and the higher the value of the pound, the more dollars are required to buy any asset in Britain – hence, the less likely it is that the prospective investment will satisfy the decision criteria of the American investor, whether an individual or an institution. At the same time, a cheap dollar means that UK investors and the institutions that manage much of Britain's wealth will find US assets attractively cheap to buy with sterling. The result must be that when the dollar is cheap and the pound relatively dear, at the lower end of the graph in Figure 1.1(b), the demand for dollars to buy US assets is great, and the supply, by Americans wanting to buy assets in the domestic economy, is small.

Finally, as we shall see, where speculators are concerned, the main consideration is prospective capital gain. Now there are a number of assumptions one could make about how they arrive at their forecasts of the likely capital gain, and we shall have a lot to say on this point in the course of the book. For the moment, if we ignore these issues and take speculators' expectations as given, we can say with some confidence that the higher the pound's international value, the less attractive it will be to hold, and vice versa.

In total then, whichever kind of agent we consider, the conclusion is the same: the lower the price of dollars, S, the greater the demand and the smaller the supply. Conversely, when the dollar is expensive, there will be a smaller demand and greater supply. At some exchange rate – $1 = £0.50 in the diagram – the demand and supply will be equal. Below this equilibrium price level, demand is greater than supply; above it, the opposite is true.

In Figure 1.1(a), excess demand is plotted, sloping downwards from left to right.

Now, of course, any demand and supply diagram can be redrawn in terms of excess demand alone. However, this approach is particularly appropriate in the present instance, because of the peculiar nature of supply and demand in the currency markets. In the textbook model of the market for a consumer good, supply is the outcome of the optimal behaviour of firms, while demand results from utility maximization by households. By contrast, in currency markets, not only is there a complete symmetry between the supply and demand – exporters and importers, inward investment and outward investment, and so on – but also the agents involved on both sides are of broadly the same kind. In fact, one can go further and say *the suppliers and demanders will often be the very same individuals or institutions.*

This is unlikely to be true of exporters and importers, in the short term at least. By and large, exporters do not switch to importing when exchange rates are unfavourable, and vice versa.[9] Some types of investor can and certainly do switch from being buyers of a currency to sellers – particularly where the assets being bought are financial. Thus, a US mutual fund may be a net purchaser of shares in London when the exchange rate is $1 = £0.70, but a net seller out of its UK portfolio if the value of the pound rises to $1 = £0.40. What is certainly true is that the third category of agent in the currency market – the one we have called, for want of a better name, the speculator – is completely flexible, demanding dollars when he perceives the pound's value as too high and supplying them when he thinks it is too low.[10]

Now it has become almost a truism to say that modern currency markets are dominated by speculators, whose trading volumes completely swamp those of other types of agent. It follows that, for all practical purposes, the distinction between supply and demand is irrelevant. There is no intrinsic difference between the two. We may as well think solely in terms of the *net* demand for a currency.

For this reason, much exchange rate theory can be seen as concerned only with the question of what determines the slope and position of the excess demand curve in Figure 1.1(a), rather than the underlying supply and demand curves in Figure 1.1(b).

1.2.1 Floating rates

Now consider Figure 1.2. Starting from an initial equilibrium at $1 = £0.50, suppose that for some reason or other the excess demand schedule rises, from X^D to $X^{D'}$ – whether as the result of an upward shift in the demand curve or a downward shift in the supply curve is immaterial. The impact effect is to create an excess demand for dollars of X_1^D (at point B).

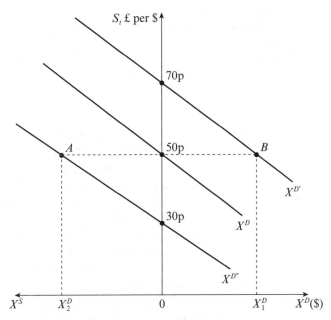

Figure 1.2 Shifts in the excess demand for foreign currency

In practice, the excess demand for dollars (and associated excess supply of pounds) would manifest itself to traders in a build-up of their sterling positions beyond normal or desired levels, and a fall in their dollar holdings. Orders to exchange pounds for dollars would be greater in volume than orders to buy pounds with dollars. Given the speed with which currency markets move nowadays, traders would need to change the price immediately in order to be able to carry on doing business. The direction of the change is obvious. The excess demand for the dollar means that its price must rise, and the excess demand for sterling dictates the need to reduce its relative price.

It follows that, in the absence of any impediment, the price of dollars will rise from $1 = £0.50 and carry on rising until the excess demand has been eliminated, at the new equilibrium rate of $1 = £0.70. As we have seen, it is difficult to think of a reason why this process should not be very rapid indeed – more or less instantaneous, in fact.

Should there be an opposite change in market sentiment, pushing the excess demand schedule down to $X^{D''}$, then the excess supply of X_2^D (at point A) would drive the dollar's relative price down more or less immediately to $1 = £0.30.

In this kind of regime, the exchange rate is determined by market forces alone. We define:

> A *completely flexible or (purely or freely) floating exchange rate* is one whose level is determined exclusively by the underlying balance of supply and demand for the currencies involved, with no outside intervention.

For the most part, we shall be concerned with the behaviour of floating exchange rates in this book. In fact, to avoid any possible confusion:

> **Convention 1.5** Unless specified otherwise, the analysis assumes a freely floating exchange rate.

1.2.2 Fixed rates

Now it is not difficult to see why exchange rate fluctuations such as those illustrated in Figure 1.2 are widely regarded as very damaging indeed for the economy of the country or countries concerned.[11] We are all familiar with the problems created for British tourists when there is a sudden change in the value of the pound. Of much more importance to the economy is the fact that exchange rate uncertainties make it very difficult for exporters and importers to enter into long-term commitments to supply or buy goods at a price fixed in advance. Worse still, the risk of unfavourable movements in the exchange rate adds to the uncertainties involved in international investment decisions: where to site new production facilities, which markets to expand into and which to abandon, and so on.

For example, a US motor manufacturer thinking of building a new plant will be faced with the problem that, given production costs in the two countries measured in pounds and dollars respectively, the new facility will be best sited in the UK if the pound's relative value is low, and in the USA if the dollar is relatively cheaper. The trouble is that the decision to build the plant has to be taken several years in advance, and in the interim the exchange rate may change so as to make what looked the more cost-effective alternative completely uncompetitive by the time production starts.

From agreeing that exchange rate volatility is damaging, it is only a short step to arguing that 'the government must do something'[12] – for example, fix the exchange rate at an 'acceptable' level, whatever that may mean. How can this be achieved?

One way would be to announce the fixed exchange rate and impose it by placing legal restrictions on dealings. For example, the authorities could insist that, henceforth, all sales or purchases of foreign currency must be made via the central bank only. Or, going further still, private holdings of foreign currency could be banned altogether or permitted only with official consent.

Even today, restrictions such as these are, sadly, more or less the norm across the world – particularly in developing countries but sometimes in the industrialized world too. Their effect[13] is to make it possible for the authorities to peg the exchange rate without operating via the market. In the jargon, currencies subjected to controls such as these are said to be *inconvertible* or *not fully convertible*.

However, where the authorities wish to fix the exchange rate while preserving convertibility, the situation is a great deal more complicated.

Suppose that the UK authorities wished to peg the pound/dollar rate at the level $1 = £0.50. As long as the supply and demand curves are in the same position as in Figure 1.1(b), there is no problem – the market rate is acceptable and there is no need for the authorities to do anything but sit on the sidelines.

But, as we have seen, if market conditions change, and there is a sudden upward shift in the excess demand curve to X^D in Figure 1.2, then the impact effect will be to create an instantaneous excess demand for dollars (excess supply of pounds) of X_1^D. If the market is left to its own devices – under a pure float – the upward pressure on the price of dollars will cause their price to be bid up to $1 = £0.70 – in other words, a fall in the value of the pound.

How can the exchange rate be kept from moving? In order to prevent a depreciation, the government[14] could supply the additional dollars in order to satisfy the excess demand – or, in other words, buy up the excess supply of sterling before its impact is felt in the market. If it does this, the market will remain in equilibrium at the fixed rate $1 = £0.50. For all practical purposes, the authorities will have completely neutralized the shift in the underlying market excess demand schedule.[15]

If this seems simple, so it should. There is no difference in principle between fixing an exchange rate and fixing any other price. In order to fix the price of eggs, say, all that is required is for *somebody* – it need not necessarily be the government – to stand ready to enter the market, offering cash to buy up any excess supply that threatens to drive down the price, or supplying eggs to satisfy any excess demand that would otherwise cause the price to rise. The only prerequisite is a buffer stock – or, more precisely, two buffer stocks: one of eggs, for supplying when there is excess demand, and one of cash, for using when there is excess supply.

Put like that, it should be clear why governments prefer, by and large, to live with the vagaries of demand and supply in the egg market, rather than attempt to fix the price.[16]

Not only would the government have to bear the day-to-day cost of managing and financing a buffer stock of eggs, but also it would also have to deal with the perennial problem facing all such intervention systems: what happens when there are long periods of excess demand or supply? In the former case, it has to keep on supplying eggs to the market, so that at some point its buffer stock is likely to be exhausted. The latter case is slightly different. If it faces excess supply situations day after day, it will need to have access to a large stock of cash. For the monetary authority, printing additional money is always a feasible option – but it is impossible to reconcile with any monetary policy. Or more precisely, it means monetary policy has to be targeted on fixing the price of eggs.[17]

Exactly the same type of problem arises in the case of a fixed exchange rate system, where the nation's reserves of gold and foreign currency act as the buffer stock. As long as short periods of excess demand for dollars (as at point *B* in Figure 1.2) alternate with periods of excess supply (point *A*), the system can be sustained. The central bank takes dollars into the reserves at times when the pound is strong and allows the reserves to run down at times when it is weak, so that over any period the level of the reserves is more or less steady.

However, if at some stage market sentiment should undergo a longer-lasting change, the reserves will be subject to a sustained rise or fall, depending on whether the new mood is in favour of the pound at the expense of the dollar, or vice versa.

There is an asymmetry here. If the pattern in the market is a sequence of excess demand situations (as at *B*, in Figure 1.2), then the trend of the reserves will be downward. The situation is unstable, since it carries the threat of complete exhaustion of the reserves, an event that the market will almost certainly anticipate, and thereby hasten, as we shall see in Chapter 17.

On the other hand, there is nothing to stop the central bank printing money at zero cost to satisfy an excess demand for pounds (excess supply of dollars) at points like *A* in the diagram – nothing, that is, as long as the government cherishes no other objectives for its monetary policy (for example, keeping its money stock constant, so as to prevent inflation).

The reader (along with many politicians and economic commentators) might be forgiven for thinking that it ought to be simple to sidestep this dilemma. After all, persistent excess supply or demand is, by definition, evidence of fundamental disequilibrium. So, the argument runs, a fixed exchange rate regime is quite feasible, provided that the authorities make no heroic attempts to resist *long-run* changes in the equilibrium exchange rate. The prescription is simple: neutralize *temporary* excess demand or supply, so as to reduce the noise in the system or if possible eliminate it altogether, but move the fixed rate up or down in response to *permanent* changes in equilibrium.

Unfortunately, in practice, it is usually impossible to distinguish between temporary and permanent disturbances to equilibrium *at the time they occur*.[18] A temporary disturbance emerges unexpectedly, and as days turn into weeks, and weeks into months of disequilibrium, it gradually becomes apparent that the change in market sentiment is permanent, or at least far too long-lived to be resisted without either exhausting the reserves or leading to massive monetary expansion.

The difficulty is alleviated only slightly by the fact that fixed exchange rate systems are invariably operated in a somewhat less rigid fashion than is described here.[19] Typically, instead of announcing a completely fixed exchange rate, a 'parity value' is established, around which a predefined amount of variation will be permitted. For example, the UK authorities might decide to allow the pound to fluctuate freely within a band of 2% on either side of the fixed rate of $1 = £0.50 – that is, between a ceiling level of $1 = £0.51 and a floor of $1 = £0.49. This modification, known as a target zone (see Chapter 17), has the advantage of allowing the central bank more time to respond to market disequilibrium. On the other hand, it has the disadvantage that a currency that is seen to be bumping along its floor is even more obviously overvalued, and vice versa when it is pushed against its ceiling.

Although we are concerned primarily with floating rates in this book, we shall have more to say about the implications of operating a fixed exchange rate regime in Chapters 5 and 6.

1.2.3 Managed floating

From considering a fixed rate with fluctuation bands, it is easy to envisage a system, or rather a non-system, where the authorities manipulate the exchange rate to suit their own (usually unannounced) objectives,[20] sometimes intervening to fix the rate, sometimes staying on the sidelines. This type of compromise is known as a 'managed' or 'dirty' float. In fact, it characterizes the behaviour of most of the major exchange rates during the so-called floating rate era of the 1970s and 1980s. As proof, one need only cite the fact that the announced foreign exchange reserves of all the major countries fluctuated quite substantially over this period (see Section 1.4).

In general, then, exchange rate regimes could be classified by their implications for the foreign currency reserves. Under a pure float, the reserves are constant – in fact, there is no need for the monetary authority to hold any reserves at all. Under a managed float, the reserves fluctuate on a day-to-day, month-to-month basis, but around a broadly constant level. With a fixed exchange rate, however, the reserves must carry the full burden of adjustment to disequilibrium in the currency markets and can be expected therefore to be far more volatile, probably exhibiting long swings up or down.

1.3 The balance of payments

Consider the problem of drawing up an account of all the transactions conducted between the UK and the ROW. It would serve as a kind of index of the flow of demand and supply for the pound over any period. This is precisely the purpose of a balance of payments account.[21]

Table 1.3 presents a summary of the UK balance of payments for 2006,[22] with the components of the current account in the top half, followed by the capital account. The data given are net, i.e. the excess of credits over debits over the year.

1.3.1 The current account

As the name implies, the current account covers transactions that create no *future* claim in either direction, involving simply an exchange 'here and now'. The account

Table 1.3 UK balance of payments 2006

	£000m		
Goods and services		**−54.4**	
Goods	−83.6		
Services	29.2		
Current income		**18.5**	
Employees' income	−0.8		
Investment income	19.3		
Transfers		**−11.9**	
Government transfers	−9.6		
Non-governmental transfers	−2.3		
Current account			**−47.8**
Capital account			**0.8**
Financial account			**32.7**
Direct investment	7.4		
Portfolio investment	−43.5		
Financial derivatives	7.4		
Other investment	61.0		
Reserve change	0.4		
Errors and omissions			**14.1**

Source: National Statistics website: www.statistics.gov.uk. Crown copyright material is reproduced with the permission of the Controller Office of Public Information (OPSI).

is itself divided into sections, in order to give a broad indication of the contribution of the different types of transaction involved.

Goods and services

The goods account, as the name suggests, covers all current transactions between the UK and the ROW involving the purchase or sale of *goods*[23] for *current*[24] purposes. In practice, this coincides for the most part with items cleared through customs, so that reasonably accurate data are available within a few weeks of the end of the month in question. As can be seen from Table 1.3, in 2006 the UK imported goods worth £83.6bn more than the value of its exports, making it one of the largest trade deficits in the world at the time. To some extent, this was offset by a surplus on services of nearly £30bn.

Which is more important: the trade in goods or in services?

In fact, there is no economically meaningful answer to this question. The only valid reason for distinguishing the two sorts of item is the frequency (and probably the accuracy) with which the two items are measured. Just as in a domestic context there is no significant distinction between transactions in services and transactions in goods, the same is true in balance of payments terms. In the same way the American importer of Scotch whisky has to buy sterling with dollars, so the US Public Broadcasting System has to do the same in order to buy the rights to screen British TV productions. Conversely, a British company assembling US-designed aircraft has to buy dollars to pay for the service it imports in the form of a production licence from the USA, so that the effect is qualitatively the same as if it had imported the aircraft in complete form.

The services account covers the whole spectrum of international transactions like these. In the case of the UK, the major invisible items are tourism (in deficit) and insurance, shipping and banking (all three heavily in surplus). The result is a very substantial surplus: Britain sold services to a value £29.2bn greater than those it bought from the ROW.

Apart from trading goods and services, there are two other ways countries can earn flows of foreign currency without changing their net capital position. Both involve the sale of the services of factors of production, labour and capital. Current labour transactions occur whenever UK citizens sell their labour to foreign-based firms, or conversely UK firms pay salaries to foreigners – hence the line labelled 'Employees' income'. For the UK, a much larger item is generated by capital as investment income, sometimes known as 'capital service', which was worth £19.3bn in 2006. In so far as British capital is employed by foreigners, payments made for its use are earnings of the UK economy, and vice versa. For example, if IBM rents a house in England to accommodate its executives, then the rent payment to the (British) landlord represents the export from the UK of housing services, and furthermore serves to swell the demand to exchange dollars for pounds. Less obviously, the interest earned by a British company on its deposit in a New York bank amounts to a payment by Americans for the use of British-owned funds – again, an export of capital services. Similarly, profits or dividends earned by UK residents or British-registered companies from their holdings of shares in US companies count as exports from Britain and imports by the USA, and vice versa.

Other things being equal, the balance on capital services will be greater (that is, more positive) the larger the domestic country's capital stock. The latter, *in the international context*, is the country's net asset position vis-à-vis the ROW. The more the country has accumulated (net) claims on foreigners, the greater is likely to be the (net) flow of income it receives from overseas as payment for the use of its assets.

For example, the Industrial Revolution in Britain generated wealth that was, to a large extent, invested overseas: in development projects in the Empire, in building railways in the Americas, in developing oil fields in the Middle East, and so on. The result was to create a situation where the UK had a very large surplus on capital service, and for a variety of reasons this situation has persisted through the twentieth century to the present day.

The third component of the current account is the item known as transfers. It consists of unrequited payments made to the UK by foreigners, and vice versa – in other words, payments made without any specific offsetting transfer of goods or services. Governments make these kinds of unilateral transfer to cover the country's subscriptions to international 'clubs' of one description or another (EU, IMF, UN agencies, and so on) and its bilateral aid donations, adding up to a total net cost for the UK of nearly £10bn. Private citizens make transfers as gifts of one kind or another to foreigners. Since most private transfers involve remittances by people working to families overseas, this item is still relatively small for the UK, with a deficit of £2.3bn in 2006.[25]

Current account balance

The overall current account surplus or deficit is for many purposes the most important single figure in the balance of payments. There are a number of ways of expressing what it signifies. From one perspective, it serves as an indicator of the balance of demand and supply within the domestic economy. So the UK current account deficit of £47.8bn indicates the scale of excess demand for goods and services in the British economy during the year.

Putting the matter slightly differently, it is easy to show[26] that the current account deficit or surplus is identically equal to the total saving net of investment in the economy – public plus private sector. Hence, in the same way that an individual who saves over any period adds to his net worth, a country running a current account surplus accumulates net assets, and one running a deficit reduces its assets or increases its liabilities. In 2006, then, the UK's net credit position in the world deteriorated by nearly £50bn.

Is the current account deficit large? There are two sorts of answer to this question. On the one hand, for the UK it amounts to less than 5% of gross domestic product (GDP), which is high but not unprecedented, and comparable to that of a number of other rich countries, including the USA.

On the other hand, the deficit is quite small compared with the value of the inflows and outflows involved. Exports and imports of goods and services alone totalled around £400bn in each direction, so that the two-way trade on current account was equivalent to well over three-quarters of GDP. It follows that what looks like a dramatic improvement or deterioration in the current balance can result from a purely marginal change on the credit or debit side of the account – or, of course, from one of the frequent revisions of the data that sometimes occur years later.

This last point is worth emphasizing, because it needs to be borne in mind at all times when looking at balance of payments data. With modern computerized record-keeping, there is no reason why statistics on exports and imports of goods should not be accurate and easily accessible with little or no delay. The same may be true of government transfers. For all the other categories in the balance of payments, it is hard to see the statistics as anything more than rough estimates, based as they often are on incomplete data, surveys and samples, questionnaires, etc. It is important to understand that this is not simply a matter of incomplete data collection, because there are often questions of principle involved that cannot be answered straight-forwardly. For example, take the employees' income item. If a UK citizen is paid by a foreign resident individual or company, then we register a credit under this heading. But what is a foreign company? Is it simply a foreign-registered company, which may at the same time be based in Britain for all other purposes? Or a company that, wherever it has chosen to put its registered office, is actually British-owned? And in any case, what does British-owned actually mean, in the case of a company quoted on the stock exchange, for example? Who knows the nationality of the shareholders who own the company?[27] Moreover, it is residence rather than nationality that is said to be the criterion for making these decisions, and residence is often even harder to establish than nationality.

Problems of interpretation such as these have existed ever since balance of payments statistics were first published, but the advent of the so-called global economy has made them far more acute, so that while, from a historical perspective, the technology for collecting the data has advanced by leaps and bounds, the figures produced are arguably less irrelevant today than ever before.

1.3.2 Capital account

How far did this reduction in the UK's net assets take the form of an increase in the debts owed by the UK public sector to the ROW? Or did it take the form mainly of an increase in private sector liabilities? To what extent did it involve, instead, the running down of UK assets overseas? Were the assets involved short-term or long-term? Financial or non-financial? Portfolio assets or direct holdings?

In principle, the capital account gives the answer to all of these questions. In practice, however, the data are grossly inaccurate and in any case very difficult to interpret. For that reason, the net amounts have been presented in Table 1.3 under only five headings, so as to give the reader a flavour of the kind of difficulties involved.

Before going on to examine the capital account, however, it needs to be remembered that balance of payments concepts follow the conventions of modern double-entry bookkeeping, under which every credit generates a debit, and the overall balance is zero. To be consistent with this principle, we have to interpret a capital account surplus as borrowing, i.e. an increase in net indebtedness or a reduction in assets needed to finance a current account deficit.

The first and second categories in the capital account are best explained together. The difference between direct and portfolio investment is that the latter refers, as the name implies, to assets purchased purely as additions to international portfolios of equities, property, bonds and so on – mainly held by financial institutions of one kind or another. Thus, the UK's £43bn deficit on this item is probably indicative of the fact that foreign financial institutions – US hedge funds, Asian and Middle Eastern investment groups, and so on – bought smaller quantities of UK equities and gilt-edged securities for their portfolios than the amount purchased by their British counterparts in foreign markets over the year.

On the other hand, direct investment in the UK occurs when, for example, a foreign company increases the scale of its operations in the UK, either by buying a British company or by expanding an existing subsidiary, or, for instance, when a foreign resident buys a home in London. In principle, direct investment occurs when the asset buyer takes a managerial interest in the assets purchased. In practice, however, the distinction between this item and portfolio investment is somewhat nebulous. There are many cases where the difference between portfolio and direct investment is more or less arbitrary, often based more on convention than on any broadly justifiable criterion.[28]

The 'Financial derivatives' item reflects the change in the value of the positions held by British institutions in the markets for futures and forwards, swaps and options. As such, its contribution to the balance of payments is too large to ignore, at £7.4bn, but not very illuminating for reasons that cannot be explained at this stage.[29]

The next heading, 'Other investment', consists mainly of net lending by agencies other than the UK government: banks, non-bank institutions and individuals. A net increase in indebtedness of £60bn implies that the UK deficit was funded largely by borrowing, probably mostly short-term.

The most important item in the capital account is the one labelled 'Reserve change'. As we saw in Section 1.2.1, in a pure float this item would be identically zero – by definition, the reserves are constant under a regime of pure floating, leaving the exchange rate free to move so as to generate a capital account balance just sufficient to offset the current account deficit or surplus.

On the other hand, if the exchange rate is to be prevented from moving, then the burden of adjustment must fall on the official reserves. The fact that the Bank of England's reserves changed during the year is proof that the exchange rate was being managed. As can be seen, the charge in the reserves was very small during the year – a change of £0.4bn is tiny relative to the scale of the other items in the balance of payments.

The 'Errors and omissions' term of £14.1bn is a balancing item. It arises because, by definition, the balance of payments must balance: the measured deficit (surplus) must be equal to net asset sales (net asset accumulation) during the period, in exactly the same way that an individual's spending in excess of his income must be identically equal to the increase in his liabilities or decrease in his assets.

However, since the data on current and capital accounts are collected from completely independent sources, any inaccuracies show up in a non-zero overall balance, which by convention is presented as a separate item of the size and sign required. The balancing item of £14bn for is non-negligible – it is twice the size of the net direct investment in the UK, for example. Moreover, this is not a one-off situation. The balance of payments error has been substantial almost every year for at least the past two decades, often being substantially larger than the current account deficit. In general, this item above all casts doubt on the value of the data as a whole, especially as it is matched by an even more mysterious hole in the balance of payments of the world as a whole.[30]

2006 was not in this respect exceptional. For example, in 1984, 1985 and 1986, the balancing item amounted to £5.0bn, £4.5bn and an amazing £12.2bn, respectively – figures so large as to dwarf the current account balance and raise questions about the value of the whole exercise.[31]

1.4 The DIY model

In a well-known series of lectures,[32] David Henderson referred to what he called the 'do-it-yourself model', as a useful summary of the conventional lay 'wisdom' – the common-sense, man in the street's misguided view of how the economy works.

The exchange rate is perhaps not as obviously a subject for amateur economists as, say, the rate of inflation or unemployment. None the less it is quite possible to define an 'economic correspondent's' model, one that seems to lie behind the opinions of media commentators, politicians and intelligent laymen – if not *quite* the man on the proverbial Clapham omnibus. Perhaps, instead of a DIY model, it ought to be called a 'mongrel model', since it contains elements of a number of models found in the typical undergraduate syllabus in the 1960s and 1970s – when many of today's commentators were economics students.[33]

The DIY model of the exchange rate consists, at the minimum, of the following propositions:

- *The higher the level of economic activity and/or the more rapid its growth rate, the lower the value of the domestic currency and/or the greater the current account deficit.* The proposition is rationalized by the argument that, at high levels of activity, the demand for imported consumer goods is high, other things being equal, and the incentive for domestic producers to export rather than sell on the home market is reduced. Furthermore, cost pressures build up in the domestic economy when output is buoyant, thereby eroding the competitiveness of local production (see Chapters 5 and 6).

- *Devaluation improves the competitiveness of the devaluing country's output, thereby increasing its current account surplus or reducing its deficit* (see Chapter 5).

- *The higher are interest rates in any country relative to the ROW, the greater the value of its currency* (see Chapter 3 and beyond).

In each case, these propositions will be shown to be not strictly wrong but certainly incomplete and usually misleading.

Perhaps an analogy from outside economics would be useful here. Consider the following proposition: strenuous activity often triggers heart attacks. As it stands, this may well be supported by facts. None the less, the statement is potentially misleading, since it ignores the more fundamental causes of heart attacks (smoking, obesity, and so on). Furthermore, if we base our forecasts on the proposition, we will be hopelessly wrong (for example, we will expect to see marathon runners dropping like flies), and as a basis for policy decisions, it seems to imply we should stop all exercise immediately.

1.5 Exchange rates since World War II: a brief history

It will help to provide a backdrop to some of the discussion in the remainder of the book if we present a very brief overview of the post-war history of the currency markets. It may also help the reader to understand the incessant calls for reform of what is sometimes called the international monetary system, though it is hard to think of foreign exchange markets as being part of any kind of system. At various points in later chapters, we shall have reason to recall the episodes summarized in this section.

1.5.1 The Bretton Woods system: 1944–68

The world of international economic policymaking at the end of World War II was dominated by two preoccupations: first, to facilitate the reconstruction of European economies; and second, if possible, to prevent a return to the competitive devaluations and protectionism that had characterized the 1930s. To that end, the British and American governments established the International Monetary Fund (IMF), which was intended to police a system of fixed exchange rates known universally as the Bretton Woods system, after the small New Hampshire ski resort where the agreement was signed in 1944.

Under the Bretton Woods system, countries undertook two major commitments: first, to maintain convertibility; and second, to preserve a fixed exchange rate until unambiguous evidence of 'fundamental disequilibrium' appeared, at which point they were expected to devalue or revalue, as the case may be – in other words, to announce a new ('fixed') parity. Convertibility turned out to be more a pious intention than a realistic objective – it was always more honoured in the breach than the observance, with only the USA among the major economic powers ever permitting full freedom of capital movements.[34]

As far as fixity of exchange rates was concerned, however, the Bretton Woods system was a success. Changes in the major parities were few and, when they did prove unavoidable, tended to be relatively small scale, at least by comparison with the wild swings that took place in the 1970s and 1980s. Until the process of breakdown began, in the late 1960s, there were only really two marked trends: the decline in the value of the pound, with two devaluations, in 1948 and 1967, and the rise of the Deutschmark, as the German economy recovered and the competitiveness of US trade decreased.

The Bretton Woods system worked on a principle known as the Gold Exchange Standard, which amounted to a kind of nineteenth-century Gold Standard by proxy. Under this arrangement, the USA operated a fully fledged Gold Standard – in other words, it pledged to keep the dollar price of gold fixed irrevocably (at the price of $35 per ounce), by standing ready to exchange gold for US currency on demand via the so-called Gold Window.[35] Notice that the requirements for fixing the dollar price of gold are similar to those for fixing the dollar price of foreign currency – the will and the resources to exchange dollars for gold or vice versa *in whatever quantity market conditions may demand.*

Other countries then fixed their currencies in terms of dollars, devaluing or revaluing as necessary in order to counteract disequilibrium, whether it was deemed to originate in their own deviant behaviour or in that of the USA. In other words, the USA anchored the system as a whole, by virtue of the fixed dollar price of gold. Other countries then had to accommodate themselves by changing their exchange rates when required.

1.5.2 The breakdown of Bretton Woods: 1968–73

Much has been written about how and why the Bretton Woods system broke down. For present purposes, and in view of the fact that we have yet to look at even the simplest model of exchange rate determination, it will suffice to explain the breakdown in terms of the elementary supply and demand framework covered in Section 1.2.2. Broadly, the net demand for dollars shifted downwards progressively throughout the 1950s and 1960s, for the following reasons:

- The parities established at the outset (including the gold price) reflected the world as it was at the end of the war, with the USA overwhelmingly the world's major economic power, possessor of virtually the entire stock of gold, and with industries that for the most part faced no international competition at all. As the rest of the industrial world recovered, the initial parities were bound to become increasingly inappropriate. In the event, they did so to an extent that could hardly have been foreseen, particularly as the process was exacerbated by the relatively sluggish rate of growth in US productive capacity, compared with the rapid expansion in the continental European economies and the explosive growth in Japan.

- Instead of the deflation, which had been feared by the participants at the original Bretton Woods conference, the 1950s and 1960s witnessed steadily accelerating worldwide inflation – slow, at first, but quite rapid from about 1967 onwards. This had the effect of raising the price of all commodities other than gold, leaving gold increasingly undervalued in terms of all the major currencies.

- What was probably the decisive factor in bringing about the collapse was the willingness of the US authorities to print money in the second half of the 1960s so as to finance war on two fronts: domestically, on poverty (the Great Society), and overseas, on North Vietnam. The result was, on the one hand, to make the dollar seem overvalued relative to other hard currencies, particularly the Deutschmark, whose value was protected by the ultraconservative monetary policies of the Bundesbank. On the other hand, in so far as monetary expansion pushed up the dollar prices of other goods, including raw materials, it made $35 per ounce of pure gold look more and more of a bargain offer.

- With diminishing economic hegemony came a weakening in the political and moral force of the USA. In particular, the Gaullist French administration recognized no obligation to refrain from hoarding gold and began an ostentatious programme to substitute gold for dollars in its reserves, further increasing the excess supply of US currency and excess demand for gold.

- As with all fixed exchange rate regimes, the more they are expected to disintegrate, the greater the pressure on them.[36] Thus, as the prospect of breakdown came ever closer, buying gold – preferably with borrowed dollars – became more and more of a one-way bet, since there was every prospect of being able ultimately to sell the gold at a profit and repay the debt in devalued US currency.[37] That, in turn, increased the demand for gold and supply of dollars, so that it became possible to extrapolate to the point at which Fort Knox would be emptied.[38]

In the event, the disintegration came in stages, starting in 1968 with the inception of an unofficial free market in gold, from which central banks were barred. What this meant was in effect a two-tier gold price, which had the effect of making absolutely transparent the extent to which the official price of monetary gold was unrealistic. Putting the matter differently, it made it possible to calculate the extent to which dollar holders were subsidizing the USA.

The system finally broke down on 15 August 1971, when President Nixon announced the closing of the Gold Window. After a six-month hiatus, there followed an attempt to patch up the fixed exchange rate system, known as the Smithsonian Agreement, which increased the price of gold from $35 to $38 and set a new, more realistic grid of parities in terms of the dollar. Unfortunately, as was perhaps inevitable, the Smithsonian System was never more than a museum piece, and it broke down in less than 12 months, mainly as a result of upward pressure on the Deutschmark.

It should be pointed out that although the end of the Bretton Woods system was entirely a matter of *force majeure*, it did none the less come as the culmination of more than 20 years of debate within the economics profession over the relative merits of floating compared with fixed exchange rates. In the 1950s, while the fixed exchange rate system was at its most robust, the advocates of floating were relatively few, though they included the formidable figure of Milton Friedman. In the late 1960s, however, as national inflation rates began to diverge and the inconsistencies in Bretton Woods became increasingly obvious, floating appeared more and more attractive as a possible solution to the problems created by the incompatible macroeconomic policies of the major industrial countries.

In particular, the argument that a floating exchange rate country behaves like a closed economy (for reasons to be explained in Chapter 5) seemed convincing to many economists. A corollary of this view was that fears that floating exchange rates would be highly volatile were largely groundless.

1.5.3 The floating rate era: 1973 to date

The period since the beginning of 1973 has been characterized by a number of attempts to reinstate fixed exchange rates, all of which have failed for one reason or another. However, apart from the European Monetary System (EMS) period (see the following section and Chapter 10), the major rates have floated to a more or less managed degree for the whole period, as can be seen in Figure 1.3.

The floating exchange rate era has certainly not delivered anything approaching the degree of stability its advocates had hoped to see. Ever since the end of the initial honeymoon period in the mid-1970s, currency values have been subject both to wild day-to-day fluctuations and to long-run swings into apparent over- or undervaluation. In general, the 1970s and 1980s were dominated by the dollar's cycle: initial decline during the mid-1970s, followed by a 50% resurgence to a peak in 1985 and a decline to its 1990 level, from which point it has been reasonably stable (see Figure 1.4). Notice the amplitude of the movements in the dollar's trade-weighted

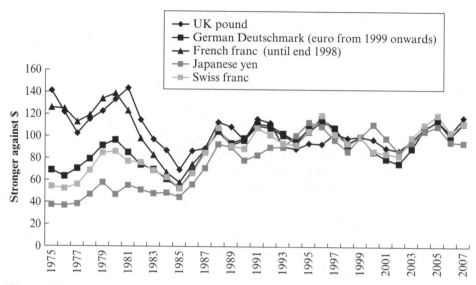

Figure 1.3 Exchange rates against the US dollar, 1975–2007 (1999 = 100)

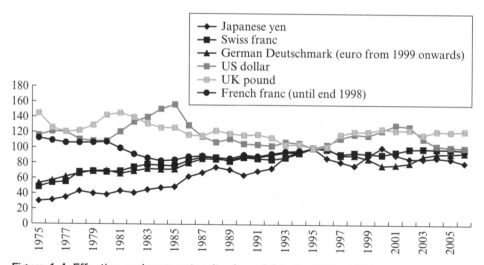

Figure 1.4 Effective exchange rates (trade-weighted), 1975–2006

value – and, of course, the variation in bilateral exchange rates was even greater (as can be seen in the case of the pound from the comparison in Figure 1.5).[39]

On the other hand, when account is taken of the shocks to the world's financial markets over the period, it becomes clear that no straightforward comparison of the fixed and floating exchange rate periods can reasonably be made: the 1970s and 1980s were far more turbulent in a number of respects than the Bretton Woods period.[40]

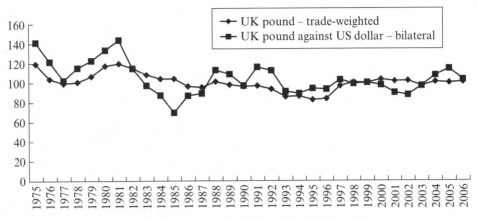

Figure 1.5 The pound (trade-weighted and bilateral), 1975–2006

The main features of the floating exchange rate period so far have been:

- A large US current account deficit, reaching well over $100bn by the end of the 1980s, whose domestic counterparts were a very low savings ratio in the private sector and federal overspending of the same order of size as the external deficit (the so-called 'twin deficit' problem). By contrast, both Japan and West Germany enjoyed large surpluses for most of this period.

- Two massive increases in the price of crude oil, engineered by the (OPEC) cartel – in 1973–4 and 1979. Broadly speaking, the first shock was accommodated by the fiscal and monetary policies of the oil-importing countries and therefore led to accelerated inflation. The second shock, by contrast, was not accommodated and was associated with a short, sharp recession in the USA and a more prolonged slump in Europe. The consequent decline in relative oil prices lasting from 1984 until the end of the 1990s attracted far less attention, partly because it was masked to some extent by the fall in the value of the dollar (in which oil prices are fixed). None the less, its impact on world financial markets, though indirect, was probably substantial, particularly via its effect on the stability of the US banking system.

- A deepening international debt crisis. The massive OPEC oil surpluses of the 1970s and early 1980s had found their way, in large part, into short-term deposits in Western commercial banks, whence the latter had recycled them into (mostly dollar-denominated) loans to governments of developing world countries ('sovereign loans'), particularly in Latin America. However, for reasons that are not yet clear, as inflation decelerated in the early 1980s, nominal interest rates stayed high.[41] The consequent high *real* interest rates combined with the rising exchange rate of the dollar and other aggravating factors (falling primary product prices, political instability, and so forth) all served to create a situation in which a large number of countries were unable to service their debts. The effect of insolvency on a global scale is still being felt in financial markets.

- The problems of sovereign lending were exacerbated further by a crisis in the US financial system in the 1980s. Whatever the root cause or causes, the symptom was a growing number of failures among banks lending to Latin America, the local US agricultural sector, high-cost oil producers, and so on, and, perhaps most serious of all, increasing insolvencies in the savings and loan (that is, housing loan) sector.

- A perceptible acceleration of post-war trends in terms of the balance of economic power. By the mid-1980s, Japan was in most respects the world's largest trading nation (though the EU is the major trade bloc). Japan was also the greatest creditor nation. In many respects – the scale of its equity market, its financial institutions and the funds they manage – it had come to dominate the world's financial markets. In the 1990s, however, this trend was somewhat overshadowed by the rising importance of the other East Asian economies: Hong Kong, Singapore, Taiwan, Thailand, Malaysia, Korea and, above all, China.

- Much greater international capital mobility, brought about by technological advance, increasing internationalization of commerce and industry, and deregulation of capital markets in all the major financial centres.

- Greatly increased volatility in most financial markets – whether as a result of the developments already mentioned or for other reasons is not yet clear. The volatility of currency markets will be a recurring theme of this book. But it should be borne in mind that increased, in some cases unprecedented, volatility also characterized other financial markets – most spectacularly, equity markets in the period surrounding the worldwide stock market crashes of October 1987, and lesser sharp falls in the years since then.

- As a result of the last two developments mentioned, the 1980s and 1990s saw an astonishing expansion in the trade in derivative financial instruments. Not only was there a vast increase in the volume of trade in existing derivative securities – that is, forward and future contracts – but also the past few years have witnessed the introduction of a bewildering variety of new instruments, in particular a large and still-expanding range of different types of option contract: options on spot rates, options on forwards, bond options, stock-index options, and so on. With the increasing variety of available instruments has come increased sophistication on the part of the more important agents in currency markets, particularly multinational corporations, for whom the Treasury Department is nowadays expected to hedge a large proportion of its currency risk and possibly generate a profit too.

1.5.4 The European Monetary System: 1979–93[42]

In 1979, the member countries of the EU, with the exception of the UK, fixed the values of their currencies against each other in a so-called parity grid, specifying central rates for each exchange rate, along with maximum ranges of fluctuation. During the early years, the EMS had two major advantages. In the first place, it involved only two major currencies, the Deutschmark and the French franc, of which the former carried far more weight in international trade and finance. By comparison, the other currencies were relatively minor, so that the central exchange rate was overwhelmingly the franc/Deutschmark rate. Second, this key exchange rate was kept stable to a great extent by capital controls in France, as well as some of the other countries in the system.

Even with these advantages, there were strains, most notably in 1981 when the new Socialist government in France was initially unwilling to accept the constraints of EMS membership. As the worldwide recession took hold in France, it tried to reflate the French economy. The resulting devaluations of the franc (in 1981–83) made the constraints plain for all to see, and no country subsequently attempted to go it alone.[43]

As so often seems to happen in financial markets, what appears inevitable ultimately happens, but not necessarily at the expected time. In the late 1980s, the EMS seemed to be becoming more and more stable, thanks to a broad consensus on the need for coordinated monetary policy and a consequent convergence of inflation rates and, to some extent, interest rates across the EMS. A future of permanently fixed exchange rates leading to full monetary union appeared to beckon.

A number of developments at the end of the 1980s proved fatal, however:

- The removal of the remaining restrictions on capital movements into and out of France meant the franc was for the first time completely exposed to changes in market sentiment.

- The entry of the UK on 8 October 1990, the culmination of years of increasingly frantic lobbying, introduced another major currency into the system, as well as an economy with a post-war history of (by European standards) highly volatile financial markets.

- The last straw that broke the system's back was the reunification of Germany in the early 1990s.[44] The burden of raising standards of living in the former Democratic Republic to equality with those in the West caused the German budget deficit to mushroom. Given the refusal of the Bundesbank to contemplate printing money to finance the additional expenditure,[45] the effect was to raise German interest rates and hence those of other EMS countries – even those that were impeccably conservative in their fiscal policies. As the business cycle turned down in the aftermath of the late 1980s' boom, the burden of high interest rates became increasingly onerous.

The EMS disintegrated in two stages. The first crisis resulted in the departure of the UK and Italy on 16 September 1992. The final agony came nearly a year later, when the French authorities gave up the battle to prevent the franc falling below its floor against the Deutschmark.[46] We shall return to this example in Section 18.2.2.

1.5.5 European monetary union: 1999 onwards

The conclusion drawn by many from the collapse of the EMS was that, in a world of free capital movements and electronic trading systems, fixed exchange rate regimes were doomed to failure. Rather than reconciling themselves to floating, however, EU policymakers seized the opportunity to argue the case for full monetary union with a single currency for all member countries. The details were finalized at the Maastricht Conference of December 1991, which set a start date of 1 January 1999 for the translation into the new currency of all wholesale dealing, i.e. almost all transactions excluding only small-scale, mostly cash business involving members of the

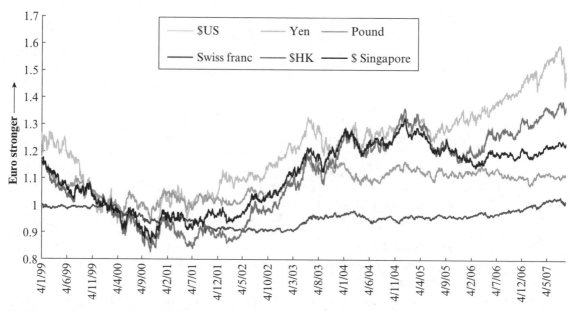

Figure 1.6 The euro since 1999: currencies per €

Note: each exchange rate is the daily closing mid-price of €1.00. For US$, the data are unscaled. The other five exchange rates are scaled so that 25/01/00 = 1.0, to match the $US, which actually stood at €1.00 = $1.0008 on that day.

public. Member countries would need to satisfy strict pre-entry convergence criteria (see Section 10.3.4), which in the event were relaxed to such an extent that only Greece was denied membership. The UK, Sweden and Denmark were granted the right to opt out of the union, on an ostensibly temporary basis.

To the surprise of almost all observers, both the transition to EMU and its inception proceeded without a hitch, in spite of the turmoil in world financial markets in the second half of 1998 (see Section 1.5.6). The only problem in the first few months of EMU was the 10% decline in the value of the new currency, though this brought the short-term benefit of a much needed improvement in European competitiveness (see Figure 1.6). From the start, however, the new European Central Bank faced a familiar dilemma: the predictable clash over how to frame a monetary policy suited to the divergent needs of all the member countries, with some of the peripheral countries (notably Ireland) patently growing at unsustainably high rates while others (especially Germany) stagnated. At the time of writing, the problem remains unresolved, and it seems likely to get worse in the immediate future as the ongoing fall in the dollar has reversed the euro's weakness, to the point that the core European economies, particularly Germany, seem likely to slip further into the recession from which they have never really escaped for the past decade. However, it is also true that the monetary policy problem seems to have been completely overshadowed by the more complicated (and politically sensitive) issue of how to preserve fiscal policy freedom in EMU.

The pros and cons of monetary union are discussed with particular reference to EMU in Chapter 11.

1.5.6 Crises in Asia, Russia and Brazil: July 1997 to August 1998

The final years of the twentieth century were dominated by a series of overlapping crises, resulting in the most turbulent financial markets seen since the 1930s. The Asian crisis will be analysed in somewhat more detail in Section 18.3.1, and so only the most important events are noted here.

The background to the crisis is simply stated. In the wake of Japan's rise to world economic leadership in the 1970s and 1980s, the so-called *Asian tigers* had been regarded as models of how to transform poor, underdeveloped countries into advanced capitalist economies in the space of only two generations, thanks to fiscal rectitude, high rates of saving and investment (especially in education), cumulative balance of payments surpluses translated into large foreign currency reserves and consequently high levels of international competitiveness.

The crisis that is normally regarded as having started on 2 July 1997, when Thailand devalued its currency, the baht, caught almost all observers by surprise. Thanks to the structure of its economy, the crisis in Thailand could never have been restricted to its foreign sector, and the ensuing banking crisis spread the problems throughout its economy. For reasons that are not yet entirely clear, the crisis conditions were also rapidly transmitted to other countries in the region, particularly Malaysia, Indonesia and Korea, where in addition to bank insolvencies they were also accompanied by political problems of varying degrees of seriousness, which further exacerbated the economic difficulties. Countries that had previously been magnets for foreign investment suddenly witnessed unmanageable outflows, as confidence in their ability to restore their economies to stable growth evaporated.

To the relief of Western governments, the crisis seemed at first to be confined to Asia, with no sign of long-term repercussions in the world's major capital markets. However, with the Asian economies apparently stagnating, the situation actually took a turn for the worse at the end of August 1998, when, for reasons that were primarily domestic, the Russian government defaulted on its debts. The resulting turmoil caused the collapse of one of the world's biggest hedge funds, Long Term Capital Management, an event so threatening that it forced the US authorities to organize a bailout, without which the damage to the whole international monetary edifice might have been fatal.

1.5.7 The twenty-first century

The turn of the century saw more crises in Latin America, the most damaging by far being the collapse of Argentina's currency board system, accompanied as it was by the largest debt default ever seen and an implosion of the local economy. Within three or four years, economic activity seemed to have recovered to a great extent, though it remains to be seen whether the recovery can be sustained, given the current susceptibility of so many Latin American countries to antideluvian economic policies.

The start of the twenty-first century also saw a dramatic fall in stock markets worldwide, the result of the bursting of a bubble that had seen truly insane valuations placed on so-called tech stocks, especially in the USA, but increasingly in other countries too. As the bubble deflated in early 2000, the Fed – in spite of its chairman's warnings three years earlier about the dangers of 'irrational exuberance' – felt it had to act, and it did so decisively, if unwisely, by reducing interest rates and making credit easily available. Perhaps, having felt impelled to act so as to prevent a dramatic fall in asset values, Chairman Alan Greenspan might subsequently have been inclined to reverse the move when prices recovered. We shall never know, because before a recovery could get properly under way, the terrorist outrage of 11 September 2001 set off the next world crisis. This time, the Fed lowered short-term interest rates progressively to the lowest seen in modern times, only just above 1% in 2003, with predictable results in terms of flows of spending:

- Massive excess demand in the US economy, as evidenced by all-time high (and growing) current account deficits, *but*
- Near-constant prices for manufacturers and very low overall retail price inflation worldwide, *as*
- China (and to some extent other Asian countries) supplied the excess demand for goods at constant prices (and a fixed exchange rate), increasing their industrial labour force as required by simply sucking in more workers from among the underemployed millions in the countryside and generating an export-led boom in Asia and GDP growth in China of around 10% per year.
- High saving rates in the Far East meant that the increased wealth inevitably boosted prices in whichever asset class it was invested – which, for the most part, meant dollar assets.

In other words, the situation could be caricatured by saying that China and Japan have granted Americans the loans to buy their exports, which can therefore be viewed as being supplied on trade credit. The result is that although China and Japan own an increasingly large share of the world's dollar assets and are increasingly looking beyond financial securities to real estate, corporate assets and other forms of wealth, the USA is increasingly indebted.

The situation has been greatly exacerbated by the fact that the enthusiasm of Asians for dollar- and, to a lesser extent, sterling-denominated assets has kept interest rates low, which in turn has triggered a worldwide boom in residential housing, especially in the English-speaking world: the USA, the UK, Australia and Ireland, as well as parts of Europe popular with British buyers.

The situation described here has seemed unsustainable to some of us for a number of years, and at the time of writing (mid-September 2007) we do appear to be witnessing the final breakdown of this money machine, relying as it does on lending more and more money to borrowers who as yet show not the slightest sign of changing their spending patterns so as to pay off their debts. By the time this book goes on sale, much will have changed, no doubt, and the crisis may already have been resolved.

However, as a hostage to fortune, and in order to demonstrate to readers the folly of economic prophesy, I hazard the following guesses as to the likely outcome once the dust has settled:

- A lower (maybe far lower) exchange rate for the dollar
- A further series of revaluations of the Chinese currency, the RMB
- At some point, though possibly after a delay of a few months, a far stronger yen
- Falling house prices in all the countries that have witnessed a boom

- Recession in the USA and UK, which could be prolonged
- Possible recession in Asia, but of short duration (as in 1998).

Readers' judgement on the accuracy of these forecasts should be tempered by a reading of Chapter 12!

1.6 Overview of the book

The remainder of the book is divided into three parts. Part I deals with the important preliminaries, with two chapters on the basic arbitrage relationships in an open economy, starting with the goods market (Chapter 2), and then the market for securities (Chapter 3). Chapter 4 covers the macroeconomic foundations for exchange rate determination, extending the basic aggregate supply and demand model to accommodate an external sector. Most readers will be familiar with some of the material in these chapters, in which case they may choose to skip this part of the book. In any case, it may be convenient to be able to refer back to it during later chapters.

In Part II, we get down to business, with an examination of a number of well-known models of exchange rate determination, starting with the very simplest examples of the genre, the flexible price monetary model (Chapter 5) and the fixed price Keynesian model (Chapter 6), and going on to analyse a more complicated extension that takes account of the fact that goods and labour markets (the 'real sector') are slower to react to disturbances than are financial markets (Chapter 7). Chapter 8 introduces two additional complications in the form of markets for domestic and foreign currency bonds. Chapter 9 concentrates on the phenomenon of currency substitution in situations where economic agents are free to hold foreign as well as domestic money balances. The next two chapters have a different flavour from the others in this block. In Chapter 10, instead of concentrating on the money market, we zoom out, in order to take a general equilibrium view of the exchange rate as part of the broader macro-economy. Chapter 11 takes a political economy perspective to consider some of the issues relating to currency unions, with particular reference to the EMU, which began in 1999.

The third block, Chapters 12–15, contains more difficult material. The unifying theme of these chapters is exchange rate uncertainty: its implications for the market and for individual economic agents, and how to modify our earlier conclusions to cope with it.

Chapter 12 deals with the meaning and implication of the concepts of rational expectations and market efficiency. Both play a large part in the succeeding chapter, which relates these ideas to the volatility of currency markets. Chapter 14 takes a magnifying glass to currency markets to examine the way they work in more detail than in the rest of the book, while the following chapter focuses on an analysis of individual behaviour under uncertainty, looking at the way the market rewards risk-bearing. Chapter 16, which is more technical, looks at the possible implications for exchange rates of non-linearity, and in particular of the class of processes usually called chaotic.

Chapters 17 and 18 both deal with questions related to how fixed exchange rate regimes work in practice. As already pointed out, fixed exchange rate systems usually involve setting a target zone, and the implications of this type of arrangement are analysed in Chapter 17. Chapter 18 discusses how fixed exchange rate regimes die. Suicide? Homicide? Natural causes? The chapter analyses the way death occurs and looks at the evidence.

Chapter 19 stands on its own. It concludes the book by looking at some of the issues – theoretical, empirical and institutional – not touched upon in the book, as well as listing some of the many questions about exchange rates left unanswered in the research literature to date.

Summary

- A *bilateral spot exchange rate* is simply the price of foreign exchange (dollars) measured in units of domestic currency (pounds). For some purposes, we need to look at a broad index of the value of a currency, measured against a basket of other currencies – the effective or trade-weighted exchange rate.

- In the market for foreign currency, the demand is smaller and the supply greater when the price rises. This is because when the foreign currency, the dollar, is relatively expensive (and the pound relatively cheap), imports and foreign investments are less attractive and, given market expectations, so is speculation on a rise in the price of dollars. Conversely, exporting and investing in the UK are more profitable than at a low dollar price.

- Under a *pure float*, the exchange rate is determined by demand and supply, so that spontaneous (in the jargon – endogenous) fluctuations in supply or demand schedules are reflected in variation in the exchange rate. Under *fixed exchange rates*, the authorities are committed to preventing any variation in currency values. In the absence of controls on transactions in foreign exchange, they can achieve this only by direct intervention in the market, to buy up excess supplies of pounds with dollars, when necessary, and conversely to supply additional sterling when there is an excess supply of dollars. Fixing the exchange rate therefore implies surrendering control of the domestic money stock. A system where the government intervenes at its own discretion is known as a managed or dirty float.

- The *balance of payments* is an account of the flow of demand and supply for the domestic currency over a year or quarter. The *current account*, covering goods and services, factor incomes and transfers, deals with the country's flow of net earnings from overseas, resulting from sales of goods and services less purchases thereof. The difference between current sales and purchases is the current account surplus or deficit. The *capital account* keeps track of changes during the period in the country's net assets (assets less liabilities). It shows how the deficit was financed (by net asset sales) or the surplus allocated to net asset purchases. Under a floating exchange rate regime, the capital account consists entirely of endogenous capital movements. Under fixed exchange rates (or dirty floating), there will be an exogenous item: changes in the total of *official reserves*, resulting from intervention by the authorities in the currency markets.

- In the popular view (the *do-it-yourself model*), the pound is weaker and the balance of payments more likely to be in deficit when national income is high and interest rates low.

■ The post-war history of the international monetary system consists of two phases, the first being the fixed rate era, known as the *Bretton Woods* regime, which broke down in 1971, and the floating rate period since then. For reasons that are not yet clear, floating rates have proved extremely volatile, with violent short-term fluctuations and longer-run swings to apparent over- and undervaluation characterizing all the major currencies, including the dollar. Among the notable features of the international financial scene in recent years have been the US 'twin deficit' problem, two OPEC oil shocks in the 1970s and a steeply falling price in the 1980s, a gathering crisis in international and US domestic debt, the rapidly increasing importance of Japan and concomitant decline in the relative weight of the USA in world markets – all accompanied by an unprecedented degree of volatility and rapid innovation, both in the technology of executing transactions and in the range of financial instruments actually traded.

Reading guide

The subject matter of Sections 1.2 and 1.3 is amply covered in most textbooks about economic principles, all of which also provide more than enough microeconomic background material, for example, Begg, Dornbusch and Fischer (1987). For more detail, see specialized texts such as Kindleberger and Lindert (1978) or Grubel (1977). Section 1.1.3 is a little different in orientation. A fuller coverage is given in most international financial management texts, which typically also explain more of the jargon of the currency markets.

The trouble with books on the institutional background is that they date very quickly, as a result of the speed with which trading patterns in currency markets evolve nowadays. They are also frequently rather personalized in their approach – as may be the treatment here, too. Good examples are McKinnon (1979) and Williamson (1983), both of which contain excellent accounts of the Bretton Woods years. Perhaps the most useful guide to the intricacies of foreign exchange market operation is Grabbe (1986), which also starts with a fuller history than is given in Section 1.6 above and which will be of particular interest to any reader wanting more detail on the mechanics of the EMS.

For a summary of the facts of floating exchange rate life that need explaining, see Mussa (1979). Running commentaries are available in a number of different places, for example the *Bank of England Quarterly Bulletin*.

The references to the debate on the relative merits of fixed versus floating rates in Section 1.6.3 may be difficult for the reader to understand at this stage. It might be worth looking back at these passages after reading Chapters 2 and 5. At any rate, the classic statement of the case for floating exchange rates is Friedman (1953). Dunn (1983) argues against floating. On the economics of the EMS, see the readings in Artis (1984).

Web page: **www.pearsoned.co.uk/copeland**.

Notes

1 To complicate matters further, it is common to refer to quotations against the dollar either as in European terms (that is, non-US currency per dollar) or as in American terms (dollar per currency). The reader, having been warned of the complications awaiting in the market, would be best to avoid them for the moment, by sticking with the conventions set out in this chapter.

2 In general, a weighted average of three numbers, X, Y and Z, is calculated as:

$$w_1 X + w_2 Y + w_3 Z$$

where the weights w_1, w_2 and w_3 are proportions so that we have:

$$w_1 + w_2 + w_3 = 1$$

The reader may easily verify that what is known as 'the average' in everyday usage – the arithmetic mean, to give it its correct name – is simply a special case of a weighted average: one where the weights are all equal and so can safely be ignored.

3 This may not seem very much until it is realized that we are talking about a variation of nearly 1% in one single day. As an annual rate (that is, if repeated day after day for a whole year), it amounts to an astronomic range.

4 Of course, even for major currencies, spreads are far from negligible for small trades, as can be verified by consulting the table of tourist exchange rates published in newspapers or displayed in the window of any bank or travel agent with a bureau de change. However, the impact of tourists' purchases and sales on the exchange rate is very small, and so we concentrate on the activities of the large traders here.

5 It would be a worthwhile exercise for the reader to redraw Figures 1.1(a) and 1.1(b) in terms of the market for pounds rather than dollars.

6 A trivial answer would be foreign exchange traders, since the vast majority of currency transactions are carried out between professionals in the specialized currency markets in London, New York, Tokyo, Zurich, Frankfurt, and so on. However, traders either act on behalf of other economic agents, in which case we prefer to deal with the actual decisionmakers rather than their representatives, or behave as principals in their own right, in which case they count as speculators or arbitrageurs themselves.

7 A more precise definition of speculation will be given later in the book. For the moment, note that there is emphatically no intention whatsoever to make moral distinctions between speculators and non-speculators, or indeed to pass moral judgements on any type of activity carried out in the currency markets. It so happens that, in the author's opinion, there are no moral grounds for passing judgement, and even if there were the fact would be irrelevant to the analysis.

All of which will probably not stop some readers from wanting to divide the currency markets into 'goodies' and 'baddies', the former consisting of the meek in spirit ('genuine' traders – that is, exporters and importers, long-term investors and so on – for the most part multinational corporations), and the latter corresponding to what were once called 'the gnomes of Zurich' – traders interested only in short-term gain: wealthy, cynical and, worst of all, foreign!

8 This is not to say, of course, that the exchange rate will be anything like the only, or even the major, factor affecting the volume of trade in the two directions – hence the qualification in italics, which will be familiar to readers who have had even the briefest encounter with elementary microeconomics. The subject is, in any case, one about which a lot more will be said later in the book, especially in Chapter 2.

9 In the long run, however, they may well switch sides. This is particularly true of multinational corporations (for whom a change from exporting to importing may simply involve diverting production from a subsidiary in the home country to one overseas) or indeed, of the international trading companies peculiar to the Far East.

10 Far from matching the free-wheeling 'cowboy' image of popular imagination, the speculator is most likely to be operating on behalf of an international bank that has reached the conclusion – with more or less help from the economic model on its computer – that the exchange rate is 'out of line'.

11 Notice the potential asymmetry: volatility in the pound/dollar rate creates difficulties for many UK decisionmakers but is in most cases of peripheral importance to their opposite numbers in the USA.

12 A short step, though not necessarily a sensible one – after all, cold weather is often damaging, but we only expect the government to help people live with the consequences, not to stabilize the temperature!

13 Apart, that is, from distorting the real sector of the economy, fostering the creation of 'parallel' (that is, black) markets, with a consequent growth in criminal activity of one kind or another

and an erosion of respect for the law, as well as abridging the freedom of the citizen in the countries in question – marginally, perhaps, by the restrictions themselves, though much more seriously by the measures taken to enforce the restrictions.

14 The task of actually operating in the currency markets so as to fix a country's exchange rate is usually assigned to another institution (often its central bank), which is not always strictly an arm of government. For example, while the Bank of England is an agency of Her Majesty's government, the US Federal Reserve Bank is independent of the federal government in Washington, DC.

For our purposes, these subtleties are ignored, and at no point in the book will any attempt be made to distinguish between the policies and responsibilities of the government and the central bank.

15 In fact, traders may not even be aware that the central bank has been operating in the market. Very often they may only observe 'business as usual', with brisk two-way trading and no tendency for positions to accumulate on either side of the market. Where the markets do get wind of intervention, it is often because the authorities intend the news to emerge.

Of course, in the end, it all 'comes out in the wash' – in the UK and USA, at any rate – with the publication of the monthly figures for the change in the reserves. But by then, the information is of more or less historical interest only.

16 Except, that is, where the authorities are able and willing to impose a price by decree – as happened in the Communist bloc, for example. In such cases, what is needed is not a buffer stock but either a docile populace willing to accept queuing as a way of life or a secret police capable of preventing the market from reasserting itself – preferably both.

Notice that this scenario is simply the equivalent in the egg market of inconvertibility in the currency market – with about the same moral authority.

17 Since originally writing this chapter, reality has caught up with this particular example in the form of the UK salmonella scandal at the end of 1988, when the British government was actually forced to buy up a sudden excess supply of eggs in order to prevent the price falling.

18 And often long afterwards too. For example, it is still unclear, even now, whether the rise in the dollar in the mid-1980s was, in fact, an equilibrium or disequilibrium phenomenon. What is clear, of course, is that it could never have been prevented by intervention in the currency markets alone.

19 In practice, fixed exchange rate mechanisms tend to be highly complex arrangements, specifying in such detail the obligations and entitlements of the countries involved. It would take a whole book to describe them fully. The objective here is, as always, simply to allow the reader to understand the general principles underlying the institutional arrangement.

20 This non-system has the dubious attraction that it maximizes the discretionary power of the monetary authority.

21 More generally, the relationship of balance of payments accounting to the analysis of exchange rate determination is the same as that between national income accounting and (closed economy) macroeconomics or, for that matter, financial accounting and corporate finance theory.

22 It must be emphasized that balance of payments accounts are subject to a margin of error that is wide even by the standards of economic data. It is highly likely that the 2006 accounts will be subject to revision for some years to come, and when they are eventually allowed to settle down the final figures may well bear little resemblance to those given here, particularly as far as the capital account is concerned.

23 As someone once described them: items that hurt when you drop them on your toe!

24 There is an uneasy compromise here between what is feasible and what is ideally desirable. Strictly speaking, if the distinction between transactions on current and capital accounts is to be preserved, then imports of durable goods (for example, motor vehicles, aircraft, computers) ought to be treated as the purchase of assets rather than imports of (consumer) goods, and similarly for exports of durables. However, as is often the case with data on domestic aggregate consumption, separating the two is impractical.

In the context of the balance of payments, the result is that if a British firm purchases a piece of equipment in the USA and brings it into the UK, it is deemed to have imported on current account. On the other hand, if for any reason the equipment remains abroad – leased back to its original owners or used by the British company for its operations in the USA or elsewhere outside the UK – then the purchase, if it is picked up at all by the statistics, will be included in the capital account. From our standpoint, all that matters is that in both cases, the result of the transaction is (a) an addition to the UK's productive capacity and (b) an increase in the net demand for foreign currency by sterling holders.

25 For some countries, the transfer item is far from negligible, relative to the balance of payments as a whole. For example, most of the countries of southern Europe have substantial foreign currency income in the form of remittances from emigrants working abroad to their families at home. Some developing countries have considerable receipts of aid that come under this heading. Likewise, reparations paid by Germany after the world wars appeared as transfer payments in the German balance of payments and as credits in those of the recipient countries.

26 See the chapter on the circular flow of income or national income accounting in any economic principles textbook, or Section 5.1.1 of this book.

27 Note that the register of shareholders is often not much help in this regard, since many shares are held by nominees, rather than the ultimate owner, or simply by investment vehicles such as mutual funds on behalf of the owners.

28 For example, suppose that (American company) A buys 10% of the equity of (UK company) B in a 'dawn raid' on the London Stock Market. Does that count as portfolio or direct investment in the UK? Presumably, if it increased A's holding in B to 51% (in other words, if A previously owned 41%), then the answer would be unambiguous, since for all practical purposes (that is, in terms of control of the target company), it would be as good as 100% ownership. But what if A's move had only raised its stake in B to 30%?

It is worth pointing out that capital account presentation used to focus much more on the distinction between short-term and long-term investment than it does today. The case for this distinction rested on the assumption that long-term investment was inherently less sensitive to market sentiment with respect to the currency than short-term investment, which in the limit was nothing more than so-called 'hot money'. This distinction was probably never clear enough to warrant separating the two types of investment in this way in theory, let alone in practical statistical terms.

29 The numbers under this heading tell us very little for a number of reasons. First, the value of a derivative security depends on marking to market, which is often based mainly on judgement alone (and, alas, sometimes on a large measure of wishful thinking). Second, the value of instruments as volatile as derivatives can change dramatically in a few minutes, and so the relevance of this data, given that they are published several months in arrears, is minimal.

30 The deficits of all the countries in the world ought to add up to zero, as long as there are no transactions with Mars. Unfortunately, there is often a large deficit. Among the explanations offered have been underrecording associated with crime (e.g. drug dealings) and with an increasing tendency to hide transactions for tax avoidance or evasion purposes, as direct and indirect taxation levels are pushed ever higher, as well as increasing Internet usage for all sorts of business.

31 It is usually assumed that the main source of inaccuracies lies in the capital account. However, other evidence suggests that there may well be enormous errors in the current account data too.

For example, as long as there is no trade with Mars, then the sum total of all the world's current account balances must obviously equal zero – one country's surplus must be another's deficit. Unfortunately, instead of adding up to zero, the world's current account has in recent years been in apparent deficit by as much as $60bn – a staggering figure that is greater, for example, than West Germany's surplus during the 1980s. If this underrecording were shared out in proportion to each country's proportion of world trade, then the UK's current account position would have been transformed throughout the 1980s into one of embarrassing robustness.

32 The BBC's 1985 Reith Lectures, published in *The Listener*, from 7 November 1985 onward.

33 It owes most to the orthodox Keynesian models current at that time, which is ironic in the light of Keynes' own famous and prophetic comment at the end of his General Theory that: 'Practical men, who believe themselves to be quite exempt from any intellectual influences, are usually the slaves of some defunct economist.'

34 Broadly speaking, from about 1958 onwards, the major European currencies offered current account convertibility – that is, were freely usable for financing trade – but were either com-

pletely unavailable or were subject to serious restrictions where the purchase or sale of foreign assets was concerned.

35 Strictly speaking, however, this amounted to less than full convertibility, since only banks were allowed access to the Gold Window. Neither in America nor Europe were private citizens allowed to hold gold. It is interesting to speculate how much sooner the system would have broken down if private holdings of gold had been permitted.

36 Recent years have seen the growth of a literature analysing mathematically the process whereby fixed exchange rate regimes collapse. Its starting point is the insight that the market will not look on passively as a country's reserves run out. Instead, it will anticipate the point at which the reserves are exhausted, and in the process hasten the collapse (see Chapter 18).

37 Something that is often forgotten by people discussing the merits of fixed exchange rates is that even a relatively small probability of a devaluation (or revaluation) may be enough to attract a speculator, *if the chance of an adverse movement can be totally discounted*, as it often can under fixity. The one-way bet situation is usually exacerbated by the fact that governments often delay parity changes, particularly devaluations, until far too late.

38 In fact, even as early as 1960, foreign central bank holdings of dollars were estimated to be greater than the US stock of gold, valued at the official price of $35 an ounce.

39 The graphs also mask the variability because they plot annual average exchange rates. End-of-year data, for example, would exhibit greater variability. Of course, higher frequency data would show still more variation.

40 No attempt is made here to cover the debate on the merits of floating versus fixity (recently rejoined in the UK, with fixed rate fans wearing first EMS and then EMU colours). The interested reader should see the references in the reading guide.

Readers ought to be warned, however, that there is more at issue than simply the desirability or otherwise of fixed rates. It is also a question of the feasibility of fixing exchange rates. Too often, the debate centres on the first question alone, ignoring the second. If fixity is unachievable then its attractiveness is irrelevant. This author suspects that there is no force on earth which could have anchored the major dollar exchange rates in the 1980s, given the domestic macro-economic policies pursued by the protagonists, particularly the USA. Of course, proponents of fixed rates argue for coordination of domestic economic policies. But that is a political issue, related more to Utopian visions of world government than to economics. Many of these issues appear again in the discussion of currency unions in Chapter 10.

41 For readers unfamiliar with this very important distinction: the *nominal interest* rate, for example for 12 months, is the interest rate actually observed at any time for 12-month riskless loans. The *real interest* rate is the nominal interest rate less the inflation rate that the market expects will apply over the 12-month life of the loan.

$$r^N = R^e + \mathrm{D}^e$$

In the absence of inflation, the nominal rate would equal the real rate (see Section 3.6).

We can, therefore, say that in the absence of taxation, the real rate is the return on a loan after allowing for the effect of inflation on the value of the debt. Alternatively, the nominal rate at any time reflects the amount needed to compensate the lender for the decline in the value of money and still give a return equal to the real rate.

42 In theory, the so-called exchange rate mechanism described here was only one component of the EMS. However, since it was by far the most important feature of the system, we follow common practice in this chapter, using the EMS to refer to the exchange rate mechanism alone.

43 Though there was another franc devaluation in 1986.

44 Of course, it is a matter of conjecture whether the system would have survived without the geopolitical upheavals that occurred at the end of the 1980s. It is the author's view that fixed exchange rate systems are as prone to accident as they are to death from natural causes. On this view, if it had not succumbed to the problem of the German budget deficit, then some other *deus ex machina* would no doubt have wrecked the EMS. Thus, if the UK had joined the EMS at its inception in 1979, it seems highly doubtful that it would have proved possible to keep sterling within its permitted limits in the face of the upward pressure generated by the oil price rise in 1980 and 1981.

45 The situation was exacerbated (albeit to an extent that cannot be quantified) by the fact that the German currency was being used widely in the newly liberated countries of Eastern Europe. This meant that the growth rate of the German money stock probably substantially underestimated the degree of monetary stringency over the period.

46 Strictly speaking, the system remained in operation, with 15% rather than 1% fluctuation bands – which meant it was alive in the same way as the parrot in the famous Monty Python sketch.

PART I

The international setting

The next three chapters cover some very important preliminaries, setting the scene for what is to follow in Parts II and III. We start in Chapter 2 by looking at the price of goods and services in an open economy and introduce the concept of purchasing power parity (PPP), which plays a vital part in many theories of what determines exchange rates. The implications of capital mobility for interest rates are considered in the next chapter, where we encounter another parity relationship – interest rate parity. In the process, we explain what is meant by a forward exchange rate. The final chapter in this part gives an overview of the textbook aggregate demand and supply model, extended to take account of the fact we are dealing with an open economy.

2

Prices in the open economy: purchasing power parity

Introduction

In one form or another, purchasing power parity (PPP) doctrine is almost as old as paper money itself. In fact, it has been traced back as far as sixteenth-century Spain. Its revival in modern times, however, is attributable mainly to the work of the Swedish economist Gustav Cassel in the period between the two world wars.

Today, although there are severe doubts about how well it holds in practice, an understanding of the basic notion of PPP is essential if we are to be able to get to grips with more sophisticated models of exchange rate determination. That is why we choose to cover it first, starting in Section 2.1 with what is perhaps the most fundamental law in economics, the law of one price, and introducing, via a number of examples, some very important ideas such as arbitrage, transaction costs and so on. In Section 2.2, we go on to consider the law of one price in the international context. Section 2.3 contains a useful digression: a simple exposition of what is meant by a price index. It can easily be skipped by anyone who is already familiar with the basic concept. Section 2.4 introduces PPP proper, and the problems of reconciling it with the evidence are briefly discussed in the following section. The story is brought up to date in Section 2.6, which covers extensions and modifications of the simple PPP relationship intended to match the theory and the facts more closely.

2.1   The law of one price in the domestic economy

In the context of the domestic economy, the *law of one price* states simply that:

> If two goods are identical, they must sell for the same price.

This looks a harmless, somewhat uncontroversial statement. It is, in fact, just the kind of blindingly obvious statement that sceptics complain about in economics. However, the same sceptics would almost certainly change their tune if they were to consider the implications of the law of one price. On the contrary, they would probably dismiss economics as a collection of very dubious propositions indeed.

In order to illustrate the kinds of issue involved, let us take a look at a number of more or less everyday examples to which we can refer back in later sections.

2.1.1   Example 1

Imagine that Robbie Williams is giving a concert at Wembley Stadium in London, a fortnight from now. All the tickets have been sold at face value through the usual distribution channels across the UK, but excess demand has created a black market, operating outside ticket agencies, in pubs, on street corners, in discos, in the classified ads columns of local newspapers and, of course, on the Internet.

Now suppose that you are told that tickets for seats in a particular part of the stadium are on offer on the black market in Birmingham for £50. What would you expect an identical ticket to cost in, say, Manchester? By the law of one price, the answer has to be £50 and, in practice, under these circumstances, you probably would find tickets of the same category on sale at more or less the same price in different towns.

Why would this tend to be the case? To see why, ask yourself what would be likely to happen if the law did not hold in this example. Suppose, for argument's sake, that the price of a ticket were £5 lower in Manchester than in Birmingham. Then anyone in Birmingham who wanted to go to the concert would buy the ticket in Manchester, while no one in Manchester would buy in Birmingham. So, sellers in Birmingham would be unable to sell any tickets as long as there were any on sale at a cheaper price in Manchester.

You may object that in reality ordinary Robbie Williams fans in Birmingham would be unlikely ever to find out that tickets were on offer at a lower price on a street corner in Manchester, in the small ads pages of Manchester newspapers or on some obscure website somewhere in cyberspace.

That is almost certainly true. At the very least, it might take some days or even weeks before word reached Birmingham, by which time it would be too late – the big day would have come and gone.

Do we then conclude that the law of one price might well break down in this, the first case we have examined?

We might do so, were it not for the well-known fact that there are people who make a living out of exploiting just such situations. What they do is to watch out for price divergences like these. In the present case, they would simply buy up as many tickets as they could in the cheap location (Manchester) and sell them immediately in the dear location (Birmingham). In the process, they would be doing three things: making a tidy profit for themselves, driving up the price of tickets in Manchester from £45 and driving down the price in Birmingham from £50. On each ticket they trade, a profit is made that is equal to the price differential. The larger the price differential, the greater the profit and hence the greater the incentive to trade. As they bid up the price in Manchester and push down the price in Birmingham, the gap narrows and their profit falls from £5 per ticket to virtually nothing, so that the incentive to trade is progressively reduced. Obviously, the process tails off and stops altogether when prices in the two cities are brought into equality at some price between £45 and £50, say £47. At this point, profit opportunities have been exhausted.

People who make a living by trading rock concert (or football match) tickets on the black market are usually called 'touts' or 'scalpers', although touts also operate in the black market in another way. More generally, and more relevant to the subject matter of this book, the process of moving goods from one market to another so as to take advantage of a price differential is referred to as *arbitrage* and those who make a living in this way are called arbitrageurs. As we shall see, they have a number of important roles to play in the currency markets and, in fact, throughout the financial sector of the economy, so the following definition is given here for future reference:

> **Arbitrage** is the process of buying or selling something in order to exploit a price differential so as to make a riskless profit.

The word 'something' is intentionally vague. For the present, we are concerned with arbitrage in goods and services, but in Chapter 3 we shall be concerned with arbitrage in securities. The expression is a completely general concept and is also frequently encountered in markets for equities, commodities and currencies themselves.

Now let us return to our example. Consider the following question: given the existence of arbitrageurs, albeit in the somewhat unsavoury form of ticket touts, are there any factors that could prevent the law of one price prevailing?

Lack of information has been ruled out as unlikely, simply because the touts will make it their business to know about any price differentials that exist and, in any case, nowadays the Internet serves to spread the word extremely rapidly. Their livelihood depends on their keeping their ears to the ground. They specialize in gathering this type of information.

Similarly, they are unlikely to be hampered very seriously by the actual cost of trading. The costs might involve a few trips between the two cities carrying their precious cargo, possibly the price of a small advertisement or two, no doubt some long-distance phone calls, some postage, a few drinks to close valuable deals and oil the wheels, and so on.[1] However, these costs are likely to be small, probably negligible, relative to the value of the transactions involved.

As we shall see in subsequent examples, the costs of actually transacting will not always be so insignificant. For now, it will be useful to have a definition to hand:

> **Transaction costs** are all the costs associated with a transaction, over and above the cost of the item that actually changes hands.

Table 2.1 The ticket tout's profit

Costs	
Buy 100 tickets in Manchester @ £45 each = total outlay of	£4500
Transaction costs (buying + selling)	£10
Total cost	**£4510**
Revenue	
Sell 100 tickets in Birmingham @ £50 each = revenue of	£5000
Profit	
Revenue less total cost	£490

As a specialist trader in large blocks, the scalper's transaction costs are minimal. A scalper who knows that a consignment of, say, 100 tickets can be bought and sold with transaction costs of only £10 will still be able to exploit the £5 per ticket price differential between Manchester and Birmingham. The profit from the purchase and sale of 100 tickets is shown in the calculation in Table 2.1.

Obviously, profit is reduced by the amount of the transaction cost (£490 instead of £500), but the deal is none the less well worthwhile. Notice that the profit per ticket sold has fallen from £5 to £4.90. Why? This is because although the selling price of each ticket has remained the same, the all-inclusive cost of the average ticket has risen by the amount of the transaction cost *per ticket* – that is, £0.10 (= £10/100).[2]

As arbitrage proceeds, however, we have seen that the price differential is progressively reduced. At what point will arbitrage no longer be profitable? In the absence of transaction costs, the answer was: when the price differential was completely eliminated. Will this still be true, now that we are allowing for the fact that simply buying and selling involves a cost?

Looking at the calculations in Table 2.1, it is plain that our previous conclusion has to be modified to read: arbitrage will cease to be profitable when the price differential is no greater than the transaction cost per item. Instead of ending up with a situation where a price of £47 reigns in both towns, the arbitrage process will come to a halt when the price differential has narrowed to £0.10. You can see this for yourself if you repeat the calculation with a price of £47.10 in Birmingham and £47 in Manchester. You will find that at these prices arbitrage profits are zero.

For future reference, we will describe this equilibrium in symbols as follows:

$$P^B = P^M + C \tag{2.1}$$

where P^B is the price of a ticket in Birmingham, P^M is the price in Manchester and C is the transaction cost.[3]

Before going on to look at a very different example, there are one or two more points worth noting. Notice that our conclusions relate to the price of tickets outside London, where the concert is to be held. Since London fans have so much shorter a distance to travel, it could reasonably be expected that the demand for tickets will be greater at any price level there than in the provinces. Does this mean the price in London will be higher than elsewhere in the UK?

A moment's consideration will show that, under our assumptions, we can rewrite Equation 2.1 with P^L on the left-hand side (that is, the price in London). In general, throughout the country, arbitrage will have smoothed out the price variations that might otherwise exist due to localized excess demand (or supply) situations.

To see what loose ends remain in our analysis of this example, let us briefly recap. It was concluded that it would be unrealistic to expect price equality to prevail, because of the existence of transaction costs. Taking them into account, however, led us to the conclusion that the modified version of the law of one price in Equation 2.1 could be expected to assert itself, thanks mainly to the activities of ticket touts specializing in arbitrage operations.

Now, are there any other factors we have neglected that may prevent even our modified law of one price from asserting itself? One obvious fly in the ointment is the unfortunate fact that ticket touting, whatever its economic benefits, is more or less illegal. In fact, legal barriers to arbitrage are not uncommon, even in much less racy sectors of the economy, particularly those sectors involving international trade and investment. Their effectiveness in preventing arbitrageurs from trading varies enormously, depending on the nature of the commodity, the type of market, the ser-iousness with which law breaking is treated, and so on. In the present case, it seems the legal barriers would probably have very little effect – the law of one price would almost certainly prove stronger than the law of the land.[4]

As a matter of fact, we can claim to have taken at least some account of the legal barrier to trade in our Equation 2.1. Our transaction cost, C, will be substantially affected by the fact that the business deals involved may amount to a crime. Perhaps, for example, the choice of relatively expensive marketing channels (selling in pubs, small ads, and so on, and in small batches of ones and twos) is dictated by the need to evade the long arm of the law. Perhaps the £0.10 per ticket also includes an ele-ment of reward for the risks of arrest and subsequent fine by the courts, or it may even incorporate an allowance for legal costs.

One important point to note is that risk of arrest is the *only* risk involved. In a pure arbitrage transaction, there are no trading risks in the normal sense. The arbitrageur takes the opportunity of a near-riskless profit. Arbitrageurs can be regarded as sell-ing their tickets in Birmingham almost at the same time that they buy in Manchester, so that their actual trading risk is zero. The absence of risk is a distinguishing feature of arbitrage.

Because arbitrage involves no trading risk it might seem that there is always likely to be a ready supply both of arbitrageurs and of funds to finance their operations. As the present example illustrates, however, this will not always be the case. Reputable financial institutions will not be willing to make loans to ticket touts, even though they stand to make a riskless 'killing'. This is not simply because the funds are required for an illegal activity. Even if they can invent a respectable reason for want-ing an advance, ticket touts will probably not be in good enough standing with their bankers to be able to raise very large loans. The possibility arises, then, that the law of one price could be frustrated simply by the fact that the supply of arbitrage funds is too small to eliminate the price differential.

Mention of borrowing and lending raises the question of interest rates. Ought there to be an interest charge included in our transaction cost term, C? The answer has nothing whatever to do with the question of whether a ticket tout borrows or uses his own funds as working capital. (Why not?)

In principle, there is no interest cost to pure arbitrage for the same reason that there is no risk: if buying and selling are instantaneous, then the working capital needed is nil. In practice, there may be a cost of financing stocks of tickets for, say, one day prior to sale, but we shall regard this as negligible.

Finally, it will be helpful if we use this example to compare and contrast the two classes of market agent who have already been mentioned with a third type of agent. Recall that we introduced the arbitrageur into the story only after concluding that the price in different towns was unlikely to be equated simply by the interaction of bona fide Robbie Williams fans who are buying tickets with the concert organizers who are selling them. Does this mean their activities are completely irrelevant to the determination of market prices?

Certainly not. The interaction of what we could call normal traders – fans wanting to attend the concert and the organizers supplying the seats – is the ultimate determinant of the equilibrium, 'central' (say, London) price. We can then think of the operations of arbitrageurs fixing the Manchester and Birmingham prices in the way we have analysed in this example.

In cases like this, however, the equilibrium price may also be affected in the short run by the activity of a different species of ticket scalper – one who holds on to tickets *in expectation of higher prices later*. From now on, we shall use the following name for this form of enterprise:

> **Speculation** is the activity of holding a good or security in the hope of profiting from a future rise in its price.

Notice that, unlike arbitrage, speculation is inherently risky, since the price rise may fail to materialize. The speculator–tout buys tickets and holds on to them so as to sell them when the time is right – typically, outside the stadium immediately before the concert starts. He backs his judgement. If, however, he miscalculates, and there turns out to be an excess supply on the day of the concert, he loses money.

To summarize, in any market, we may potentially have three different kinds of agent at work:

- *traders* (in our example, the fans, whose tastes condition their demand, and the organizers, whose costs determine the supply)
- *arbitrageurs* (touts who exploit local price variations)
- *speculators* (scalpers who hold on to tickets in the hope of making a 'killing').

Although we shall deliberately ignore the moral and legal distinctions between the activities of these three classes of market agent, we shall often have cause to treat them separately in our analysis of other markets in Chapters 3, 6 and 7. The theoretical distinctions are clear. However, we must not forget, particularly when thinking about policy measures, that in practice it is often virtually impossible to separate the different classes of transactor. In our example, there may be no feasible way to tell the tout from the genuine rock music fan, let alone the arbitrageur–tout from the speculator–tout. Certainly, a legally convincing distinction may be elusive, which is precisely the problem faced by law enforcement agencies.

This case has been analysed in some depth because it illustrates many of the issues surrounding the functioning, or non-functioning, of the law of one price, as well as providing a first encounter with some of the concepts that are central to the material in the rest of the book. The remaining examples will be dealt with more briefly.

2.1.2 Example 2

The down-to-earth subject of this example is the price of potatoes. Could the price in Manchester ever deviate from the price in London? Plainly, this is a straightforward application of the modified law of one price, as in Equation 2.1. The transaction cost, C, may be quite substantial in this case, simply because potatoes are costly to move from one end of a country to the other. Provided that we allow for this fact and make sure we are looking at the same quality of potato in each case, we are likely to find that prices in the two cities are very close to each other.

Notice that the question of where the potatoes have been grown is irrelevant. Note also that we need not rely on the existence of arbitrageurs. (Anyway, whoever heard of potato arbitrageurs?) As long as retailers are competitive, they are likely to keep price deviations within the margins set by the costs of transporting potatoes. Or, to put the point another way, genuinely competitive distributors (wholesalers or retailers) will themselves act as arbitrageurs.

2.1.3 Example 3

Take a typical manufactured good, for example a folding umbrella made in China. Can we be sure that its price will be uniform across the UK?

At first glance, you might think that the answer was no – the price even varies from shop to shop in the same town. That's why we shop around, isn't it?

Not really. We shop around for two reasons mainly: first, because we like to compare different makes of goods and, second, to compare different models produced by the same manufacturer. However, *the law of one price relates only to identical goods*. Where manufactures are concerned, products made by different firms are rarely, if ever, regarded as identical. Even though the objective differences may be small, products are almost always differentiated in the mind of the consumer, if only as a result of the efforts of the advertising industry. So the fact that two products with different labels do not carry the same price tag has no bearing whatever on the law of one price.

Even so, don't prices vary even for genuinely identical goods – same model, same producer, same label? Yes, they do, if we look in different shops. Why? The reason lies in large part in the fact that a shopper buys not only the umbrella but also the services of the retailer who sells it. If the shop itself supplies a retailing service that is above average in prestige, in convenience, in friendliness or in helpfulness, or even in length of opening hours, then it will be able to sell its service at an above-average price, which will take the form of a premium on some or all of its wares. The umbrella will cost more if bought in a smart city store than in an unprepossessing discount warehouse out in the suburbs. Likewise, try buying an umbrella at four o'clock on a Sunday morning when it is pouring down. If you can find anywhere to buy one, do not expect a bargain.

The failure of the law of one price in the case of a typical manufactured good, for instance an umbrella, may for these reasons be only apparent. If we are sufficiently strict in defining identical goods, we may well conclude that the law of one price holds reasonably well.

2.1.4 Example 4

Compare the price of houses in the north (Manchester) and the south (London). Where do you start? How can we find two genuinely identical houses in two different cities? Even if we are careful enough to choose a given type of house for comparison (say, semi-detached, three bedrooms, garage, and so on), we cannot avoid the problem that a house in Manchester is simply *not* the same asset as a house in London. The difference is attributable in the first instance to local market conditions. However, it is sustained by one obvious fact: houses cannot be moved from one end of the country to the other. The transaction cost is not simply high; it is infinite – at least in the short run.

Since arbitrage has to be completely ruled out in this case, does it follow that the price of houses in the two locations can diverge without limit forever? There is no clear answer to this question, but it is certainly possible that there exist forces likely to prevent prices diverging indefinitely. At some point, the relative price of housing in Manchester will become so cheap that it will start to attract Londoners whose work situation allows them to move. People may even start to commute from Manchester to London so as to exploit the cheap housing in the north. By the same token, builders will be tempted to divert resources from other areas, particularly cheap housing areas, to sites in London, thereby increasing the supply and reducing the excess demand.

In the long run, therefore, there may well be a kind of law of one price operating even here, the only difference being that, in this case, it is the relative price of houses in the two locations that is kept constant, at a level where prices in London are, say, 1.75 times higher than those in Manchester for otherwise comparable accommodation. Even then, remember that we are only forced to talk in terms of a *relative price* because of the fact that we are comparing two intrinsically different commodities.

For a final example, we consider a totally different item, but with similar conclusions applying.

2.1.5 Example 5

A haircut. To avoid the problems of comparability already encountered in previous examples, it had better be a standard haircut, of the kind favoured by old-fashioned men (like the author).

Remember, first of all, that nothing in economics relies on a distinction between the market for goods and the market for services. For the purposes of economic analysis, it makes no difference at all whether we are talking about a tangible, visible good or an intangible, invisible service. This fact should be borne in mind throughout the book.

Now, can the price of a haircut in London deviate from that in Manchester? Plainly, the answer is yes, and substantially so. Even if demand is similar, the cost of the main hairdressing inputs (wages, rent, and so on) is greater in London, and so the supply curve is further to the left.

As before, arbitrage in the normal sense is ruled out, so that the short-run price differential can be enormous. This fact has led many writers in the international economics literature to describe services such as hairdressing, motor vehicle repairing, plumbing, medical services, and so on, as well as some goods (such as houses), as *non-traded goods*. For future reference, let us introduce the following definition:

> **Non-traded goods** (or **non-tradeables**) are items (usually services) for which interregional price differentials cannot be eliminated by arbitrage.

Notice that the definition does not refer to goods, if any such exist, for which price differentials can *never* be eliminated. All we mean is goods that, for sound practical reasons, cannot be moved from place to place so as to exploit price differences. As we saw in the previous example, and as is plainly true in the case of haircuts, there may well be other, less direct mechanisms than arbitrage that will ultimately drive London and Manchester prices into equality. For anyone who is not completely bald, haircuts figure in the cost of living in the same way as housing does and, in the long run, there may well be forces tending to eliminate price deviations over broad categories of services, as we shall see in Chapters 5 and 7. None the less, since arbitrage is impossible, haircuts and so on must be regarded as non-traded goods and the law of one price cannot be expected to apply automatically.

Put differently, we can say that the transaction cost in the case of a haircut is near infinite – not in absolute terms, as was the case with houses, but because, relative to the cost of the commodity itself, the transaction cost per unit amounts to several hundred or thousand per cent (that is, the cost of travelling between Manchester and London, relative to the price of the haircut itself). With this sort of argument in mind, we could view the vast range of goods and services produced in a modern economy as spanning the whole spectrum from most to least tradeable. At one end would be homogeneous commodities with negligible transport costs (financial assets, tickets for rock concerts, and so on) and at the other end would be personal services and real estate, with all other goods and services ranged somewhere in between these two extremes.

Now that we have examined in some detail a number of examples of the working or non-working of the law of one price in a closed economy context, moving over to the open economy will turn out to be quite simple.

2.2 The law of one price in the open economy

In this section, we have the task of answering the same kinds of question as in Section 2.1, with one vital difference. What if the two cities involved are not London and Manchester, but London and New York? What changes have to be made in our conclusions?

There turns out to be only one significant change required, and it will be encountered as soon as we return to our first example.

2.2.1 Example 1

The Robbie Williams concert again. An enterprising New York travel agent is selling tickets for the concert – mainly to attract customers for his cut-price trips to London.

If you make him an offer, however, he will sell the concert tickets separately. How will the price that he can get for them compare with the price of £50 that rules on the free (that is, black) market in London?

The first and most obvious point is that, in the window of the New York travel agent, the price will not be shown in pounds at all. It will be in dollars, of course. We cannot directly compare the price in London and New York in the way that we could compare the price in London and Manchester.

Let us be a little pedantic about the reason why we cannot compare prices on opposite sides of the Atlantic. Strictly speaking, it is *not* just because the UK and USA are two different countries. It is because they use different currencies. Quite frequently, there are situations where countries, for one reason or another, share a common currency, officially or unofficially.[5] Where two countries do indeed share a common currency, we can compare prices directly and, for purposes of the law of one price, we may as well be dealing with a closed economy.

Where there is no common currency, however, we have to translate dollar prices into pound prices, or vice versa, so as to allow us to make a comparison. It is a problem familiar to anyone who has ever been on holiday abroad. Unfortunately for our purposes, holidaymakers often buy their foreign currency, traveller's cheques, and so on before setting out on their trip, so that they do not always see the connection between the two relevant prices: the price of the goods they buy abroad and the price of the currency.

Now put yourself in the position of an enterprising London ticket tout who has just heard from some American tourists that tickets are on sale at, say, $100 each in New York. Is it worth making a transatlantic call to order tickets for resale in London? For every ticket he wants, he will have to buy $100 and then send the US currency to New York. Let us ignore transaction costs for the moment. (When all is said and done, if it doesn't pay to do anything when we ignore transaction costs, it certainly won't pay when we take account of them.)

The best way to look at this deal is to regard it as involving what we might call a 'compound purchase': first buy the dollars, and then use the dollars to buy the tickets. In the closed economy context, we exchange domestic money directly for goods. When buying from another country, we first have to exchange domestic money for foreign money, and then exchange the foreign currency for the foreign goods.

In this example, the price paid by the London tout for US dollars is, of course, the sterling/dollar exchange rate. For convenience, we repeat here our definition of the exchange rate:

> The **exchange rate** is the price of a unit of foreign currency, measured in units of domestic currency.

Remember from Section 1.1.1 that our definition reverses the way we are used to seeing the sterling exchange rate quoted. Instead of the dollar price of pounds (for example, $1.25 = £1), we are following the practice of most countries other than UK and USA, which is units of domestic currency per unit of foreign currency ($1 = £0.80, and so on).

The advantage of doing things this way round should be clear when we work our way through the arithmetic of our imaginary international arbitrage in concert tickets.

Whenever you undertake a compound purchase, buying an item for cash, and then using that item to buy a second, the overall price you will have paid will be the product of the two prices. In the same way, the sterling price that the London tout will have to pay for the New York tickets will be the product of the price of each dollar and the dollar price of the tickets.

Suppose, on enquiry, that the exchange rate turns out to be $1.00 = £0.80. In other words, the price of a dollar is 80p. Obviously, it will cost 100 times 80p (£80) to buy the $100 asked for by the New York travel agent for each ticket. The £80 is the result of the following calculation:

Sterling price of a dollar × dollar price of a ticket = sterling price of a ticket

If we use the letter S to denote the exchange rate (remember that this is defined as the pound price of a dollar) and P^{NY} for the price in dollars advertised in New York, then the overall price to a Londoner is SP^{NY}.

We have now found out how to translate foreign prices into domestic currency prices. To put it differently, we have converted ticket prices into a common currency. Sterling was chosen because we were putting ourselves in the place of a Londoner, who was interested only in his profits measured in pounds, for the obvious reason that almost all of his spending was in pounds. As will be made clear, we would reach exactly the same conclusion if we looked at things from the American point of view.

You will be glad to know that we have now finished the most important task in this section. From now on, it will be downhill all the way. All we need do is apply exactly the same logic to our translated prices as we did in Section 2.1 to our UK domestic prices.

Will it be worth paying £80 for a ticket from New York? Certainly not – they can be bought for £50 in London, remember? What is more, as soon as New Yorkers find out that they are better off waiting to buy tickets when they get off the plane in London, the demand in New York will tail off. In fact, there is every chance that an enterprising competitor of our American travel agent will steal a march, by jetting over to London and buying a consignment to take back to New York. For each ticket wanted, the competitor will need to buy £50. Each pound will cost $(1/0.80) = 1/S$ dollars – that is, $1.25. The total outlay will be $1.25 × 50 = $62.50 per ticket. It follows that, if we continue to ignore transaction costs, the competitor can afford to undercut the competition by $37.50.

We can shorten the story somewhat, thanks to our analysis of the closed economy example. At some point, it is likely that the forces of normal trade and probably of arbitrage as well will eliminate profit opportunities. This will have been achieved when the price in New York stands in such a relation to the price in London that, when translated into a common currency the two prices are equal; in other words, when the price in New York has fallen to just $62.50 (assuming the New York market is, in this case, negligibly small relative to the market in the UK, where the concert is actually taking place).

To represent the equilibrium symbolically, look back at Equation 2.1. Replace P^B and P^M with P^L and P^{NY}, the London and New York prices. Now, on the left-hand side we have the London price (in pounds). On the right-hand side, we must have the equilibrium New York price (in dollars) multiplied by the price of a dollar, which is $62.50 × 0.80 = £50.00$, or $P^{NY} × S$. For good measure, we will add the transaction cost, C, just to remind ourselves that in practice there will be room for some divergence from the strict law of one price, so we have:

$$P^L = SP^{NY} + C \qquad\qquad (2.2)$$

as our open economy version of the law of one price.

All the other points made in the closed economy example follow in obvious fashion. There is one significant extension that needs to be made, however, and it relates to the activities of speculators in the present context. It is simply this: if there are a significant number of tickets in the hands of New Yorkers, then the London speculator runs an extra risk, over and above the one borne by the speculator in a closed economy context. Not only must he gamble on the underlying demand for tickets, but he must also take a chance on the exchange rate. For example, suppose in the last few days before the concert that the dollar weakens (that is, the price of a dollar falls). Since that will initially raise the equilibrium New York price, it may damp down demand by Americans and reduce the total demand for tickets, even though nothing has happened to affect the popularity of the concert itself. We shall not follow up the implications of this fact at the moment, although we shall have cause to refer back to it in Chapters 8 and 14.

We now proceed to examine the remaining examples from the previous section.

2.2.2 Examples 2 and 3

Let us take the two cases together, potatoes and umbrellas. Can we simply apply Equation 2.2, without further ado? Obviously, transport costs are likely to be even higher in an international than an interregional context. Is that the only difference between the open and closed economy as far as this example is concerned?

It is not, because, in addition to the difficulties involved in trading goods within a country, there will usually be man-made or rather government-made barriers to cross-border trade.

In the first place, there will often be tariffs, which are a barrier to trade that are familiar to most tourists under the name of customs duty. A general definition would be as follows:

A **tariff** is a tax levied on goods crossing an international border.

Nothing has been or will be said in this book about the method used to calculate the size of the tariff payable on goods. Suffice to say, the level of tariff varies with the importing country, the broad category of goods, sometimes the destination of the goods, as well as a host of other factors. The calculation is sometimes so complicated as to be incomprehensible to all but dedicated industry professionals. (An example of this occurs with the import of wines and spirits into the UK.)

The question of the impact of a tariff on the price of a good is one that would fill several chapters in a history of international trade theory. For our purposes, we need note only that it represents another factor likely to drive a wedge between foreign and domestic prices. Strictly speaking, where it is levied at a flat rate per unit, it can be regarded simply as inflating the value of our transaction portmanteau term, C. More frequently, it consists of a more or less *ad valorem* tax – in other words, one levied in proportion to the price per unit.

In the case of agricultural products, particularly, there may be other barriers to international trade. Some countries impose quotas that are more or less rigid limits on the quantity of a good that may be imported or, occasionally, exported.

Furthermore, this is not all. If you try carrying potatoes through UK customs, you may encounter more problems than simply a slipped disc. There are actually prohibitions on bringing into the UK a variety of agricultural products, animals, domestic pets, and so on. These non-tariff barriers, as they are called, are sometimes put in place in order to protect the health of a country's human or non-human residents. There are also restrictions on the import of manufactured goods of certain types – dangerous toys, weapons, and so on – as well as on the export of strategic goods, art treasures, and so forth. Often the restrictions amount to little more than red tape, especially for the large firms that conduct most of the world's international trade. On other occasions, they amount to an intentional or unintentional trade blockage, designed specifically to prevent the law of one price from asserting itself in the way described in the closed economy case.[6]

We can conclude, then, that the simple relationship described by Equation 2.2 is likely to hold only as an approximation. It is a reasonably accurate one for some goods but a very distant one for others. If these are our conclusions with regard to traded goods, what can we expect of non-traded goods?

2.2.3 Examples 4 and 5

In the case both of housing and of services such as haircuts, the closed economy arguments apply with somewhat greater force. As with interregional trade, it would be overstating the case to argue that the law of one price will always be completely inoperative. For example, many UK estate agents advertise homes in foreign holiday resorts such as Spain, Florida, and so on alongside their domestic properties. Now obviously a holiday home on the Gulf of Mexico is hardly a substitute for the typical semi-detached house in a London suburb. Nonetheless, *at the margin*, it may well compete directly with a holiday home in a UK resort (fortunately, not everyone likes the sun). These kinds of consideration may place a limit on the degree to which prices can deviate internationally, even for housing.

Remember also that, in the case of so-called non-tradeables, the man-made barriers to trade such as tariffs, quotas, red tape, and so on are often fewer than for tradeables.[7] That being the case, the only obstacles are usually the physical ones that apply equally in a closed economy. It follows that the price of a service such as a haircut in New York may turn out to be almost as close to the price in London as it is to the price in Los Angeles.

In the end, the question of how closely the (international) law of one price fits the facts cannot be settled by theory. Ultimately, the answer can be found only by examination of the evidence, in other words by a careful comparison of prices of individual goods and services across different countries. The evidence will be discussed later in this chapter.

It is worth finishing this section, however, with a warning about a specious argument often encountered in discussions of the law of one price and, indeed, in many other areas far removed from international trade issues or even from economics. In the present case, it goes something like this: 'It is a fact that only a tiny percentage of sales of this type of good (or service) involve exports (or imports). So, with no arbitrage between the domestic and foreign markets, there can be very little relationship between prices at home and abroad.'

To see the fallacy here, imagine that the death penalty were introduced for the crime of drunken driving (as it once was in the USSR). And suppose that it worked. Now consider the following argument: 'There were no executions last year, and so the new get tough policy on drinking and driving must have failed completely.'

It is obviously nonsense. In the same way that the threat of the death penalty presumably deterred drivers from drinking, so the threat of losing markets to foreign competition, particularly when enterprising arbitrageurs are around, may well have a decisive impact on prices *without any trade taking place at all*.[8] From this point of view, it might be preferable to talk of 'tradeables' and 'non-tradeables', rather than 'traded' and 'non-traded' goods.

> **Question** *Has the proportion of tradeable goods and services gone up or down in the past 10 or 20 years?*

2.3 A digression on price indices

So far, we have been concerned with the price of individual, identical goods. If we are to make any progress, however, we are going to have to turn our attention at some point to the price of goods in general, in other words to the general price level. In order to do that, we will have to introduce the concept of a price index. In doing so, no attempt will be made to go into details – they are in any case readily available elsewhere (see the references at the end of this chapter; readers who are already familiar with the concept of a price index are invited to skip this section).

First, for future reference, a definition:

> A **(consumer) price index** is a weighted average of individual product prices, with weights determined by expenditure shares.

To see why we need a price index, imagine the following scenario. You open the newspaper one day to read these sensational headlines:

Price of salt to double! Petrol also up by 3%!

As soon as you recover from the shock, you want to know what this means for your cost of living. Clearly, just because the price of salt has doubled, it does not follow that your cost of living has doubled. How can we take simultaneous account of the fact that the price of salt has gone up by 100% and the price of petrol by 3%, while everything else has remained unchanged?

One answer would be to take a simple (that is, unweighted) average of the price increases:

$$(100\% + 3\%)/2 = 51.5\%$$

or perhaps:

$$(100\% + 3\% + 0\%)/3 = 34.33\%$$

in recognition of the fact that the price of everything else besides salt and petrol has stayed constant.

Both answers are highly unsatisfactory. The first calculation gives us a figure that is halfway between the price change for salt and that for petrol, thus implying that each of the two prices is equally important, an assumption that is nonsensical. Why? Not because salt is somehow less of a necessity than petrol; neither is the opposite true of course.

To see why these calculations are absurd, look at the second of them. Where does the 3 in the divisor come from? A moment's thought will show that it is totally arbitrary. It is not simply one other good whose price has remained unchanged; it is *all* other goods. In that case, should the divisor be 3, 30 or even 3000 for that matter?

In general terms, the calculations are misleading because they contain the hidden assumption that all products, or product categories, are equally important. For most purposes, however, they are *not* all equally important, particularly when we are concerned to answer a question such as: how great an increase in my salary, in my pension or in my student grant do I require in order to compensate for this latest round of price increases? Imagine your employer's reaction if you show them these newspaper headlines and tell them that it means you need a 51.5% rise to compensate.

The way economists (and nowadays governments) deal with this problem is by weighting the price increase for each individual product by a fraction equal to its proportionate contribution to the average household's total expenditure. Now it so happens that most governments in industrialized countries find that they need to collect information on how households spend their income for a variety of different reasons, apart from compiling a retail price index. It is, in principle at least, a relatively simple affair to use this information to compute budget shares for most of the goods and services in the typical family's shopping basket. Once the weights have been calculated, they can be updated at reasonable intervals (annually, in the UK). Using these weights, information gathered during any month on prices in shops, restaurants, pubs, and so on can be translated rapidly into a price index.

For example, in the article that follows the newspaper headlines, the newspaper's economic affairs correspondent warns readers that the grave news in the headlines amounts to a rise in the cost of living of 0.25% (or, one-quarter of 1%) or, in the jargon, it will add a quarter point to the retail price index. The way the calculation is arrived at is by looking at the official statistics to find the weight attached to each of the two goods. Suppose weights of 0.1% for salt and 5.0% for petrol are found (which are more or less the correct figures for the UK). Then the calculation is simply:

$$(0.001 \times 100\%) + (0.050 \times 3\%) = 0.1\% + 0.15\% = 0.25\%$$

Notice that, although its price rose by so much less than that of salt, the relatively small petrol price increase contributes more to the rise in the index than does the doubling in the price of salt. Note, also, that there is a hidden third term in the calculation, which is the one for all other prices. It has been suppressed, because it would read:

$$(0.949 \times 0.0\%) = 0.0\%$$

The weight on all other goods is calculated as $(1.0 - 0.001 - 0.050)$, since the sum of all the expenditure proportions must be unity. In other words, the newspaper correspondent has implicitly assumed that all other prices will remain constant.

That is not all that has been assumed, however. It has also been taken for granted that expenditure shares will remain constant. Now this is a very reasonable assumption to make in the circumstances of our imaginary example, but the same will not always be the case. In 1979, for example, when world crude oil prices were raised almost overnight by 200%, it was only too easy to take that year's expenditure weights for petrol of 3.3% and extrapolate to the conclusion that the cost of living in the UK would rise by $0.033 \times 200 = 6.6\%$, and many commentators who ought to have known better did just that. In the event, of course, the quantity of petrol consumed fell drastically across the industrialized world, so that the ultimate rise in the cost of living was far less than this calculation would suggest.[9]

Those readers familiar with the microeconomics of consumer demand theory will recognize the problem as one relating to the household's budget line. When the price of one good increases, the budget line pivots inward, making the household worse off. How much worse off? That depends on where along the budget line the household operates – the more it consumes of the good whose price has remained constant, the less important is the increase in the price of the other good. In the limit, if it does not consume the good whose price has risen anyway, the household is completely unaffected, so we ought to allocate a weight of zero to it in our index calculation.

There is a snag, however. When we talk about where the household operates along the budget line, do we mean before or after the price increase? Since the post-increase equilibrium will usually involve a fall in consumption of the good that has been marked up in price, and rise in consumption of the other good, the expression 'where the household operates' is ambiguous. For small price changes, for example a 3% rise in the price of petrol, we can ignore the problem, but not when the price rises by 200%.

A lot of theoretical and empirical work has gone into the analysis of this question, without any practical solution being in sight. For our purposes, it will be sufficient to note the following conclusion: as long as price index weights remain fixed, price level comparisons will be valid only for small price changes.

One final point needs to be made with respect to the concept of an index. Our definition refers to an average price, whereas all our numerical examples referred to price changes. The reason is that no unambiguous meaning can be attached to an average of prices for different goods. What meaning can we attach to the statement that the average of the price of salt and the price of petrol was £10 in February 1986? Apart from anything else, the figure will be unit-dependent; in other words, if you use the price of a litre instead of a gallon of petrol, you will substantially change your price average.

If, instead, we look at percentage rates of price increase, we will be dealing with common units (per cent) and the weighted average will have an obvious interpretation, which is the rise in the price of the typical good or service during the period in question.

We then face another problem: it is a rise in price, but since when? A price that has fallen by 2% in the past year may have fallen by 60% in the past two years but *risen* by 400% over the past 10 years. The only solution to this particular problem is to bear in mind that the choice of the period to be used for comparison, called the *base period*, is always arbitrary. Depending on the use to which the index is put, you may get a completely different impression if you change the base period.[10] (Note that, by convention, the value of the price index for the base month or year is usually set equal to 100.)

Subject to all of these caveats, there is no reason in principle why an index cannot be compiled to keep track of movements in the price of any commodity or set of commodities. For our purposes, we shall confine ourselves to considering the general level of prices. This means, in practice, the Retail (or consumer) Price Index (RPI), which is based on a sample of prices in shops and other retail outlets, and the Wholesale (or producer) Price Index (WPI), which measures prices 'at the factory gate'. The former measures prices from the point of view of the household sector, including indirect taxes and distributors' margins, and so on, and covers all goods and services in the typical consumption basket, whether imported or domestically produced. The WPI, by way of contrast, is intended to be a guide to the underlying price level of inputs coming into and output leaving the firms in the corporate sector of the economy.

2.4 Purchasing power parity

Now, at long last, we are in a position to be able to understand the notion of PPP. The basic proposition will be seen to be very simple, although its ramifications are potentially much more complex. We shall build the theory by putting together the components we have assembled in Sections 2.2 and 2.3.

To start with, suppose that we are dealing with two countries, the UK and the USA. Assume transaction costs such as transport, tariffs, and so on are negligible, so that the law of one price applies to all goods and services consumed. Under these circumstances, let us rewrite Equation 2.2. Instead of the superscripts L and NY for London and New York, we shall nominate one country, the UK, as the home country and leave its variables unsuperscripted, with asterisks as superscripts for the other, foreign, country.

Now, remembering that C is zero, because we are assuming away transaction costs, we have:

$$P_i = SP_i^* \quad i = 1 \ldots N \tag{2.3}$$

Notice the Ps have acquired subscripts, to show that they relate to the good or service number i. We had no need of a subscript in Sections 2.1 and 2.2 because we were always referring to a particular case of a specific good. Now that we have introduced the notion of a price index, we have to distinguish carefully between individual and general price levels. Equation 2.3 states that the law of one price holds with respect to the relationship between the domestic and foreign prices of good number i. We happen also to be assuming that Equation 2.3 holds with respect to *all* the goods (and services) consumed in the two countries. So, if there are N such goods, Equation 2.3 could be repeated N times over, with a different subscript each time, which explains the term $i = 1 \ldots N$.

Now ask yourself the question: what can be said about the price index for the domestic country (UK) compared with that of the foreign country, for example the USA?

In general, not much – unless we make an additional assumption. One possibility would be to assume that *the weights used in compiling the respective price indices are identical*. In other words, suppose that, for each one of the N goods, we can say that its share in total US expenditure (and hence its weight in the US price index) is exactly the same as its share of UK expenditure. Under these circumstances, we can be confident that Equation 2.3 will apply equally to the general level of prices, so that we can write:

$$P = SP^* \tag{2.4}$$

where P and P^* (without a subscript) refer to the home country's and foreign country's price index, respectively.

This is the simplest possible version of the PPP hypothesis, and we shall return to it a number of times in one form or another throughout the rest of this book. To be more precise, Equation 2.4 is a statement of what is sometimes called the *absolute purchasing power parity* doctrine, which amounts to the following proposition:

> **Proposition 2.1** The general level of prices, when converted to a common currency, will be the same in every country.

The remainder of this chapter will be spent exploring its implications, its shortcomings and its ability to explain the facts.

Notice that we are dealing with a theory that predicts equality between national price levels translated, via the exchange rate, into a common unit of account. Nothing has so far been said about the mechanism that brings about this result. Now the drift of this chapter so far might seem to offer an obvious answer to this question. After all, if the prices of individual goods are aligned according to the law of one price, as a result of either arbitrage or the normal competitive trading processes, then it is to these forces that one should look for an explanation of how PPP asserts itself. According to this microeconomic view, then, the PPP hypothesis is a natural consequence or a by-product of the law of one price, reflected at aggregate level.

This, however, is by no means the only way to arrive at a PPP equilibrium. It is equally possible to argue in favour of what we might call a *macroeconomic* approach – one that was hinted at indirectly in Sections 2.1 and 2.2. Suppose, instead of the prices of individual goods and services being equated internationally, it is the general price levels themselves that are brought directly into the relationship predicted by PPP. Those readers who have done some macroeconomics before now may well be familiar with simple models of how the price level is determined in a closed economy; in any case, the subject will be covered in Chapter 4. For present purposes, let us simply assume each national price level is determined by that country's macroeconomic policy in the same way it would be if the economy were completely closed. Then, given these independently determined national price levels, the exchange rate could move to satisfy PPP.

There are three points to note about this macroeconomic view of PPP. First, notice that it amounts to treating Equation 2.4 as one that determines the exchange rate. In fact, it is a simple version of what we shall later call the *monetary model of the exchange rate* (see Chapter 5).

Second, it follows that this scenario presupposes a floating exchange rate. In periods when the exchange rate is fixed, PPP either fails to work or is assumed to function in a different way, which is precisely the subject of the so-called monetary model of the balance of payments, also covered in Chapter 5.

Third, note that, in principle at least, this approach does not rely on the law of one price. However, it might still apply, even if there were wide divergences between countries in the price of individual goods and services. As was suggested in Section 2.2, even if there is no mechanism to equate the price of, say, haircuts internationally, there may well be forces generating a broad equality between the cost of living in different countries.

In a sense, then, we would not require the law of one price to hold in each and every case – it might never hold for any good or service and, as we saw, the existing evidence is far from reassuring. It would be sufficient that upward deviations from the law of one price in the case of one good were offset by downward deviations in another case. For example, as between the UK and the USA, it might be that relatively high prices for some UK services (hotels, restaurant meals, and so on) are compensated for by relatively low prices for clothing, healthcare, and so forth.

Notice also that, in this interpretation, we do not require equally weighted price indices. What we do require is no less restrictive, however: that if one good with a weight of 1% is *over*priced by 50%, contributing $(0.01 \times 50\%) = 0.5\%$ to the general price level, then there has to be another good contributing exactly -0.5%, for example one carrying a 5% weighting *under*priced by precisely 10%. This may seem unlikely, but, as with the law of one price, its plausibility or otherwise is ultimately an empirical question. In other words, the proof of the pudding is in the eating.

One final point about the interpretation of PPP. We have chosen to approach the subject by way of the real-world concept of a price index, for the essentially pedagogic reason that it is one with which the reader should be familiar and one that is going to crop up in Chapters 5 and 7. But this is not the only way that PPP can be viewed. At the very least, most economists would agree that none of the published price indices is anything like a perfect measure of the appropriate price level for PPP purposes. In part, the shortcomings may be the same ones that make the Retail Price Index, for example, an imperfect measure of the cost of living: problems of accounting for differences of quality between products, problems of sampling prices actually paid rather than listed prices, and so on. In other cases, the shortcomings may be of the kind that are really significant only in an open economy context, like the fact that different tax regimes and differing degrees of provision of public goods make international cost-of-living comparisons highly questionable.

Since it is virtually impossible to remedy these deficiencies, you may have concluded by now that PPP is a dead duck, in advance of looking at the evidence. Apart from being premature, the judgement is also misguided, for the following reason: Even if there does turn out to be little empirical support for PPP, it is at least possible that, because we are dealing with price level measures that are so imperfect, PPP is in fact alive and kicking in the real world. In other words, Equation 2.4 may be completely valid, but only with the 'true' price level variables that are *unobservable* and related only very distantly to what we actually observe – that is, the *published* UK and US price statistics.

In that case, you may think that PPP is untestable, because it relates to unobservable variables and is not of much practical use for the same reason. As we shall see in Chapter 5, that conclusion does not necessarily follow either. If the true price levels (in other words, those relevant to PPP) are in fact related to other observable variables, then the PPP hypothesis becomes fully operational. Of course, that does not make it any more likely to be true.

Whether true or not, PPP is an important benchmark for the analysis of exchange rate movements, particularly in so far as they impinge on international competitiveness. If the general level of prices is a reasonably accurate index of the cost of production in a country (and this is almost certain to be the case), then the ratio of price levels for any two countries will serve as a measure of relative competitiveness.

Notice that if PPP could be relied on to obtain at all times, then competitiveness measured in this way would not only be constant but also in some sense be equalized across different countries. No country would have a price advantage over another, at least in terms of the broad spread of goods and services represented by the general price level. In practice, as we shall see, international competitiveness has been far from constant in the post-war world. For this reason, economists often wish to measure deviations from PPP, and the concept most often used for this purpose is the so-called real exchange rate:

> The **real exchange rate** is the price of foreign relative to domestic goods and services.

Formally, it is measured by:

$$Q = SP^*/P \tag{2.5}$$

Notice that an alternative interpretation would be to say that it amounts to the exchange rate as we have so far understood it (that is, the *nominal exchange rate*, S), corrected for relative prices, P^*/P.

If PPP holds, then the value of Q ought, in principle, to be 1, as you can see from Equation 2.4. In practice, however, no meaning can be attached to the absolute size of Q, for the same reason that the absolute level of a price index is meaningless, as we saw in Section 2.3.

To see that this is the case, suppose that at some point in time the UK price index is 200, while the US index stands at 250 and the exchange rate is £0.80 = $1.00. (Check that PPP holds and $Q = 1$ for these figures.) Now recall that the choice of base year for an index is completely arbitrary. Choose a different base period for an index and you will always end up with a different figure, unless by chance the index in the new base period is the same as in the old. So rebasing either or both of the price indices in our example will disturb the apparent equilibrium. Moreover, it will not help to base both UK and US price indices on the same period, as all that does is to arbitrarily set both price levels to equality (at 100).

For this reason, it makes more sense to think in terms not of price levels but of rates of change. In this form, the *relative purchasing power parity hypothesis* states that:

> One country's inflation rate can be higher (lower) than another's only to the extent that its exchange rate depreciates (appreciates).

To reformulate our PPP Equation 2.4 in terms of rates of growth requires a little elementary calculus. First, take logs of Equation 2.4. Using lower-case letters to denote logs, this gives us:

$$p = s + p^* \tag{2.6}$$

Now if we take the derivative of a natural logarithm, we arrive at the proportional rate of change, that is $d(\log P) = dp = dP/P$, and so on. In the present case, differentiating in Equation 2.6, we have:

$$dp = ds + dp^* \tag{2.7}$$

This equation says only that the home country's inflation rate, dp, will be equal to the sum of the foreign inflation rate, dp^*, and the rate of currency depreciation, ds.

It might be more illuminating, perhaps, to rewrite Equation 2.7 as:

$$dp - dp^* = ds \tag{2.8}$$

which says that the domestic country can run a higher rate of inflation than the foreign country only if its exchange rate falls pro rata. One way of interpreting this relationship is simply as an extension of the familiar idea that when prices rise, the value of money falls. The more rapidly prices rise, the faster the value of money falls. In a two-country context, the more rapidly prices rise in the home economy *relative to the foreign country*, the more rapidly domestic money loses its value relative to foreign money – or the more its exchange rate depreciates.

Notice that the reformulation in terms of rates of change avoids all the difficulties of choosing a base for the price index. There is no problem in defining unambiguously the rate of inflation or the rate of exchange rate depreciation – at least, no problem of the kind involved in making the absolute PPP hypothesis operational. That is why, although absolute PPP often figures in theoretical models, it is only relative PPP that can actually be tested by an examination of the evidence.

Before going on to do just that, there is one important loose end to be tidied up. When discussing the law of one price, it was freely admitted that allowance would need to be made for transaction costs such as transportation, tariffs, non-tariff barriers, and so on. Surely these costs ought to figure somewhere in our PPP equations, if PPP follows from the open economy version of the law of one price?

Rather than deny this obvious fact, the economics literature copes with the problem in one of the following ways:

- For some purposes, where nothing very important hinges on the way it is specified, economists have tended to use the unadorned versions of absolute or relative PPP, as in Equation 2.4 or Equation 2.7 on the grounds that transaction costs are small enough to be negligible.

- If not negligible, it could be argued that most of the main elements in the total cost of trading vary in proportion to the value of the goods in question. For example, as already noted, tariffs are often charged *ad valorem*, transportation charges may frequently be related to the value of goods shipped, and items such as insurance premiums will almost invariably bear some more or less fixed relation to price per unit.

  This being the case, if we make the assumption that all these costs are proportional to price, then it is easy to see that they will not figure at all in our relative

PPP Equation 2.7. Look back at the steps on the way from Equation 2.4 to Equation 2.7. Retrace them, starting with an absolute PPP equation modified to take account of transaction costs:

$$P = K(SP^*) \qquad\qquad (2.4')$$

where K is a constant, greater or less than unity, covering the total cost of conducting international trade. As before, take logarithms:

$$p = k + s + p^* \qquad\qquad (2.5')$$

From here, it is easy to see that we end up with the same result for relative PPP as before, simply because when we differentiate Equation 2.5, the cost term will disappear. (Remember that the derivative of a constant such as k is zero.) Intuitively, the reason is that under these circumstances, transaction costs have the same effect as a once-over rescaling of prices – they have no effect on the (relative) rate of inflation itself.

■ For a more agnostic view, if neither of the previous assumptions is acceptable, one possibility is, as we shall see, to fall back on an equilibrium real exchange rate, usually one that obtains only in the long run. Obviously, this amounts to assuming that relative PPP applies in some kind of steady state, with deviations permitted in the short run.

■ Finally, we could make use of the distinction already introduced between traded and non-traded goods to reformulate PPP in terms of tradeables alone. In other words, divide the economy into two sectors: one to which PPP applies and another where prices are determined domestically. Although this approach has the advantage of providing a degree of realism, it has the drawback already noted – that, in fact, it may well be that a rigid division of the economy into traded and non-traded goods sectors is no more realistic than the original assumption that all goods are potentially tradeable.

As will be seen in Section 2.6, these are issues that have been addressed at various times in the published literature, but before going any further we take a brief look at the facts about price levels and exchange rates.

2.5   Purchasing power parity – the facts at a glance

To illustrate the extent to which PPP appears to have broken down in the industrialized countries, look at Figures 2.1 to 2.4. The first two figures show the way that real exchange rates have fluctuated over the years since 1970, relative to the base value in 1995.

First, notice the similarity between the patterns for the five countries (the UK, Switzerland, France, Germany and Japan). This reflects the fact that all the exchange rates have moved in a broadly similar fashion relative to the dollar. Thus, all five currencies appreciated relative to the dollar in the late 1970s (the yen spectacularly, the others less markedly), and then depreciated sharply in the 1980s as the dollar rose to a peak in 1985. The dollar then declined as rapidly in the second half of the 1980s. The 1990s have seen far less volatility, helped by the convergence of European economies. What we see in the graphs, then, is the outcome of developments specific

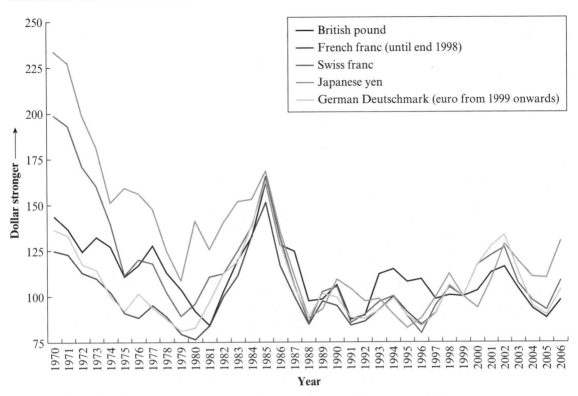

Figure 2.1 Real exchange rates, 1970–2006 (consumer prices) (1995 = 100)

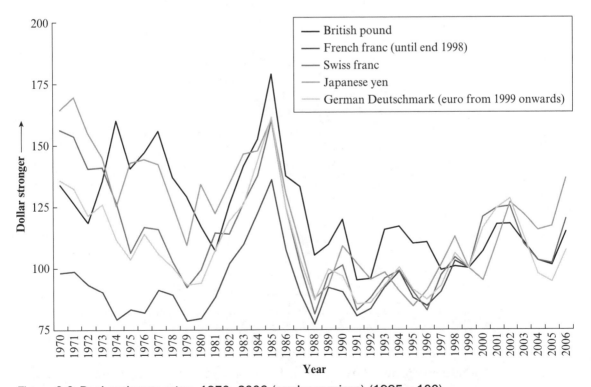

Figure 2.2 Real exchange rates, 1970–2006 (producer prices) (1995 = 100)

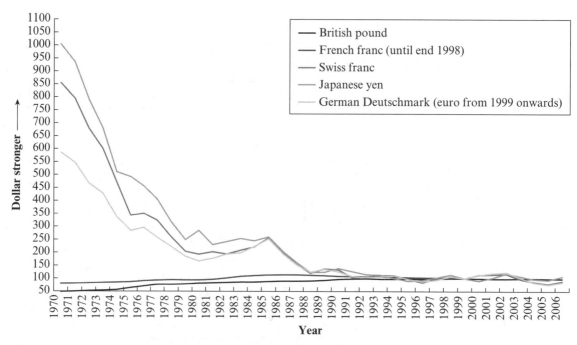

Figure 2.3 Purchasing power parity exchange rates, 1970–2006 (consumer prices) (1995 = 100)

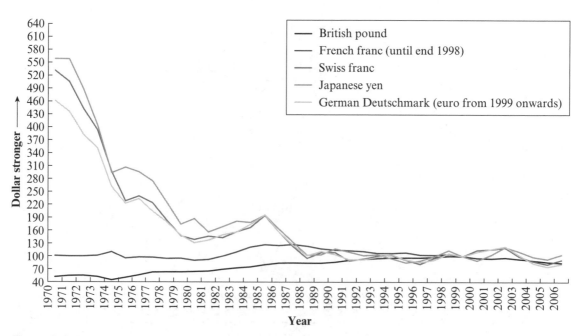

Figure 2.4 Purchasing power parity exchange rates, 1970–2006 (producer prices) (1995 = 100)

to each country with, at the same time, developments affecting the relative value of the dollar.

Second, and most important of all, note the amplitude of the fluctuations in what should, under PPP, be flat graphs. For example, the pound appreciated (in other words, UK competitiveness fell relative to the USA) by nearly one-third in real terms between 1976 and 1980, and then fell by around 60%, recovering much of the ground at the end of the 1980s, only to lose it again on exit from the ERM. Since its initial post-exit fall, however, it has more than made up the lost ground. The other currencies have been only a little less volatile.

In fact, Figures 2.1 and 2.2 could almost be said to track the movements in *nominal* exchange rates shown in Figure 1.3, a feature that serves merely to illustrate the point made earlier on that, except for highly deviant inflation rates, exchange rates fluctuate to an extent that swamps variations in relative price levels.[11]

Figures 2.3 and 2.4 present the facts in a different form. What is labelled there the PPP exchange rate is the nominal exchange rate against the US dollar required to preserve the same *real* exchange rate (that is, the same level of competitiveness) as in 1980. In other words, it is the (1980) nominal exchange rate adjusted for changes in the price ratio. In Figures 2.3 and 2.4, the PPP exchange rate is shown as a ratio of the average spot rate actually observed over the year in question (multiplied by 100). Thus, when this ratio is above 100, the exchange rate is overvalued relative to the dollar – assuming it was at its PPP level in the base year, 1980.

It may be tempting to view Figures 2.3 and 2.4 as reflecting a protracted convergence on current equilibrium levels of competitiveness. There are at least two problems with this optimistic interpretation. First, it is to some extent an optical illusion. If we use a different base year, we end up with a very different picture. In the first two editions of this book, for example, the base year was taken as 1980, which resulted in the currencies seeming to converge smoothly on an equilibrium level of 100 in that year, subsequently diverging without any apparent limit. Second, there is no reason to suppose that fluctuations in the value of the pound, yen and Swiss franc in years to come will not take them far from their present levels.[12] Why should we believe that the real exchange rate will now settle down to its long-run level? The graphs can be more plausibly read as implying that although the cycles of over- or undervaluation do tend to reverse themselves eventually, there is no sign that the process of correction stops when equilibrium has been reinstated, a fact that has led some economists to conclude that exchange rates have an inbuilt tendency to overshoot, as we shall see in Chapter 7.

We can summarize the evidence by saying that, on the face of it, there appears to be no obvious tendency towards PPP. It is not even clear that producer prices fit the hypothesis any better than retail prices, which may be a sign that the distinction between traded and non-traded goods emphasized by some researchers is not very important in practice.

Notice that, in terms of volatility (about which we shall have a lot more to say in Chapters 5, 7 and 12–14), it is unquestionably true that exchange rates have varied far more than prices. Look back at Equation 2.8, which shows how an exchange rate moves according to the relative PPP doctrine. On the left-hand side is the relative inflation rate. Now relative inflation rates between industrialized countries vary somewhat from year to year. A 5% gap may narrow to, say, 3% or 4%, or possibly widen to 6% or 7% or even 10% by the time a year has elapsed. But when we look at exchange rates, we find fluctuations of this magnitude, 1% or 2% or more, *within the space of a single day's trading*. In fact, even looking at monthly data, the volatility of exchange rates is often twice as great as the volatility of price levels.[13]

Any summary of the evidence needs, however, to mention one broad class of exceptions to these otherwise negative conclusions. If we look at situations of very rapid ('triple-digit') inflation, notably in Brazil, Argentina, Chile and Israel in the 1980s, we find PPP maintained to within fairly narrow margins. Not surprisingly, the same is even truer of hyperinflations, that is, inflation at astronomic rates (Germany in 1923–24 being the classic case). The reason seems to be that in this type of hothouse environment, the cost of being wrong about any price is potentially so great that agents are forced to invest considerable effort and expense in gathering information. Furthermore, there tends to be a progressive collapse in the kind of institutional and legal arrangements that in normal times serve to make prices sticky, such as long-term contracts, price controls, and so on. In particular, attempts to fix the exchange rate are soon swamped. The end result is that both prices and the exchange rate move smoothly along their PPP paths.

A more scientific approach to testing PPP might of course yield different conclusions and over the past 20 or 30 years researchers have investigated PPP in great depth. Their results of that research programme will be summarized in Section 2.7, but first we examine some of the explanations offered for the apparent failure of the law of one price and/or PPP.

2.6 Purchasing power parity extensions

If ever there were a theory that ought to work, PPP – or the law of one price, at least – should do so. That, at least, is the feeling of many economists. Its evident failure has motivated a number of extensions of basic PPP theory, in addition of course to the numerous data-related explanations already mentioned. Notice, however, that it is purely a matter of semantics whether we regard these extensions as 'fixes', allowing us to maintain PPP as a viable working hypothesis, or as theoretical explanations of why PPP fails.

2.6.1 Traded versus non-traded goods: Balassa–Samuelson

As long ago as the 1960s, Balassa and Samuelson offered an explanation that sounded plausible then and still does, although the evidence is actually rather mixed.

Their analysis is based on the observation that, at least in the industrialized world, productivity increases are far more rapid in the traded than in the non-traded goods sectors of the economy. One may speculate about the reasons for this bias in technical progress, but identifying traded goods with manufactures and agricultural products, and non-traded goods with the service sector of the economy, it does seem that the benefits of automation are exploited more easily in the former than in the latter. In any case, if this observation is correct, then the implication is that wages in the traded goods sector will tend to rise more rapidly than in the non-traded goods sector, as employers seek to exploit the benefits of higher productivity per worker by expanding output, in the process competing for labour and driving up the wage rate. If there is an integrated labour market, then, in the long run at least, wages will be bid up to the same level in the services sector, *even though productivity growth there has been slower*. This in turn means that prices in the services sector will have to rise relative to those in the traded goods sector, so as to maintain profitability, other things being equal.[14]

2.6.2 Trade costs and adjustment to purchasing power parity

Although the cost of actually moving goods around the world might seem an obvious place to look for an explanation of deviations from PPP, the details are more problematic. In practice, there are many costs that are either fixed or at least unrelated to the value of the goods being shipped – freight costs are normally based on weight or volume, management and administrative expenses are largely fixed, and so on. To this extent, the effect is likely to be the creation of a neutral zone in international price differentials, within which deviations from the law of one price can persist more or less indefinitely. On this view, only when deviations exceed the 'threshold' do prices finally react.

Now consider the implications as we move from individual prices to indices and from the law of one price to PPP. Bear in mind that the fixed costs of trade will vary from product category to category. Starting from a hypothetical PPP equilibrium, a shock that causes a sudden jump in the exchange rate will generate deviations from the law of one price – and hence arbitrage opportunities – in some product markets and not others. In general, the larger the shock to the exchange rate, the greater the number of arbitrage opportunities created. In the absence of barriers to arbitrage, therefore, the larger the shock to the exchange rate, the more likely it is to be rectified. This type of logic has motivated a number of researchers to test models that relate movements in the exchange rate non-linearly to the previous period's deviation from its equilibrium level, with the relationship being stronger the larger the size of the deviation. The result is a model of the form:

$$q_t - \bar{q}_{t-1} = f[(\bar{q}_{t-1} - q_{t-1}), z_{t-1}]\varphi(\bar{q}_{t-1} - q_{t-1}) \quad 0 < f_1 < 1 \tag{2.9}$$

In this equation, q_{t-1} is the log of the real exchange rate at $t-1$ (i.e. in the previous month, quarter or year) and $\bar{q}_t$ is its equilibrium level at t – theoretically 1.0 under the simplest version of PPP, but in practice varying over time, as we have already seen. The term z_t summarizes a list of other factors that may affect $\bar{q}$, typically involving other macroeconomic variables along lines implied by the more complex exchange rate models covered later in this book. The function f, which takes values between 0 and 1 in each period, measures the extent to which a gap between $\bar{q}_{t-1}$ and q_{t-1} is eliminated by the next period's change in the exchange rate. The greater is f, the more rapidly the gap is closed. Since f is assumed to be increasing in the gap itself, the implication is that larger deviations cause the exchange rate to react more. In other words, small deviations from PPP equilibrium are eliminated slowly, and large deviations rapidly. Allowance is often made for f to depend on other variables that may affect adjustment speeds.[15] Notice that one of the attractive features of this model is that it is consistent with the contrasting evidence from low- and high-inflation countries. If PPP is rapidly reinstated under hyperinflation, deviations may never be observed, at least at the monthly or quarterly data frequency typically available. On the other hand, for low-inflation countries, sluggish adjustment may mean that even a period of a century or more may cover very few completed cycles of return to PPP.

2.6.3 Trade costs: iceberg model

If transaction costs are related linearly to the value of the goods shipped, then it might appear that the outcome is more straightforward. Even here, however, there are still complications to overcome, which will come as no surprise to anyone who has ever worked with balance-of-trade statistics. For example, is the value of a country's exports to be understood as including or excluding shipping costs? In any case, is the exporter or the importer assumed to pay?

Assuming importers pay for transportation, insurance, wastage, and so on, a possible formulation is the so-called iceberg model, which assumes that a proportion τ of every unit of goods shipped internationally is 'lost' or consumed in the form of shipping costs, so that the importer only receives the remaining $1 - \tau$ that survives the voyage. This means that goods will sell at different prices, depending on where they originate. Consider first the case of a foreign product imported into the home country. If its price in its country of origin is P_F^* and its price at home is P_F, then the two prices will be related as follows:

$$P_F = P_F^*/(1 - \tau) \tag{2.10}$$

To understand why, imagine the product is a perishable foodstuff, for example feta cheese imported from Greece into France. If $\tau = 0.25$, it is as if 25% of the cheese goes rotten en route and is unsaleable in France. The French importer therefore has to buy $1/(1 - 0.25) = 1.33$ kilograms in order to have 1 kilogram available for sale. If he can get the cheese (or similar) cheaper than $P_F^*/(1 - \tau)$ in another country, whether in the form of a lower basic price for the produce or because of lower transport costs, then he will do so.

If, on the other hand, the cost of transporting Camembert to Greece involves a similar degree of wastage, then its price will be lower in France than in Greece by 25%:

$$P_C = (1 - \tau)P_C^* \tag{2.11}$$

and so a kilo of Camembert will cost only 75% as much in France as in Greece.

Now consider the price of feta relative to Camembert. The mechanism just described plainly drives a wedge between the relative prices of the two cheeses in France and Greece. From the ratio of Equations 2.10 and 2.11, we can see that:

$$\frac{P_C}{P_F} = (1-\tau)^2 \frac{P_C^*}{P_F^*} \tag{2.12}$$

so, relative to feta, Camembert will be only 56% as expensive in France as in Greece.

Notice that nothing has been said here about the exchange rate. As it happens, both France and Greece currently use euros, but the preceding story would be essentially unchanged if prices in the two countries were still quoted in francs and drachma. The only change needed would involve converting to a common currency, for example by multiplying the right-hand side (Greek) prices by the franc price of drachma.

It has been claimed by some authors (notably Obstfeld and Rogoff (2000a)) that this distortion of relative prices may have far-reaching consequences in a number of critical areas of open economy macroeconomics, sufficient to explain some of the apparent anomalies in the pattern of international payments. For the moment, however, it is simply worth noting that this is yet another possible explanation for the failure of PPP. In this scenario, even if the index weights in the two countries are identical, price levels will still differ, without necessarily representing any arbitrage opportunity.

2.6.4 Incomplete pass-through and pricing to market

In the past ten years or so, interest in international pricing has broadened out to cover issues related to industrial structure, which according to standard closed economy microeconomics ought to have an important role to play in this context. In general terms, the conclusion of this literature is easily stated: exchange rate movements will not necessarily be reflected fully and instantaneously in the prices at which exports are sold in foreign markets. A 10% devaluation will not necessarily cause exporters to cut their prices by 10%, at least immediately, and neither will a 10% revaluation make them raise prices at once by the full 10%. In the standard jargon, we should not necessarily expect 100% pass-through, at least in the short term. Instead, we might expect to witness something like, say, 30% immediate pass-through (i.e. a 3% fall in export prices following a 10% devaluation), 75% after six months and 100% only after two years.

Why might there be less than 100% pass-through? To understand what is involved, take the case of an importer buying goods from an exporter, for sale in the importer's home market. It makes no difference whether the importer is an independent specialist whose only business is importing and wholesaling products to local retailers, whether the importer is itself a retailer, or whether, as is often the case nowadays, the importer is a local subsidiary of the multinational company that originally produced the goods. Whatever the situation, as far as the importer is concerned, exchange rates are a cost just like any other. When the currency used to buy the imports rises in value, the importer's costs rise, and vice versa when the currency gets cheaper. Viewed from this angle, the question at issue is simply a matter of judging how the typical importer deals with an increase in its costs – in other words, a suitable case for microeconomic analysis.

Note the obvious point that, even if it is determined to keep its profit margin constant, a firm need only adjust its export price in proportion to the *net* impact of an exchange rate change. For example, suppose at some point the euro appreciates by 5% against the dollar. In practice, the effect is to raise the cost of supplying French wine to the USA by somewhat less than 5%, other things being equal, because the typical French winegrower will rely on inputs – diesel fuel and spare parts for his tractors, fertilizer, possibly computing and telecommunications hardware and software, and so on – some or all of which may be priced in dollars or dollar-linked currencies. If only 75% of costs are in euros, then the no-arbitrage PPP price will only rise by $3^3/_4\%$, with the remaining $1^1/_4\%$ accounted for by a fall in the euro price.

In practice there are a number of reasons why firms may be reluctant to adjust export prices even to this extent in the short run. In the first place, exchange rate movements are high-frequency events. They are certainly far higher frequency than changes in production costs, such as wages, taxes and domestically produced raw materials and intermediate inputs and probably higher frequency than demand fluctuations. Daily exchange rate changes of 1% or 2% are not at all exceptional. It would plainly be ridiculous for firms slavishly to adjust their export prices on a day-by-day basis in response to each day's exchange rate movement. Raising prices immediately may be difficult, especially where customers either have a supply contract or believe they have an unwritten agreement from the importer to keep prices fixed. Moreover, a firm may well have explicit long-term contracts to supply products at fixed prices, in which case it must absorb currency volatility in its profit margins unless it has hedged (i.e. insured) in the forward market or elsewhere (see Chapter 3).[16] Over and above all these considerations is the cost of actually publicizing price changes – costs of printing, advertising, informing customers, and so on.

In summary, changing prices is an activity that itself involves costs. These costs – *menu costs* in the jargon of economics – may be greater or smaller, depending on the circumstances, but will in any case provide an incentive for importers at least to try to smooth price changes.

In addition to these factors, a behavioural explanation for the stickiness of traded goods prices is widely accepted by policymakers and many researchers. For example, suppose the French winegrower has incurred heavy setup costs in establishing a presence in the US market – perhaps recruiting sales staff and advertising in the USA, spending on public relations, forging links with American importers, satisfying federal and state regulatory requirements, and so forth. These costs can be regarded as an irreversible investment whose payoff is the flow of future net profits the firm hopes to earn from US sales. Under these circumstances, the French company may decide to keep the dollar price of its wine fixed when the euro appreciates, rather than raise it and risk losing market share to such an extent that, if the exchange rate returns to its previous level, it will be unable to re-establish itself in the USA without incurring some or all of the setup costs all over again.[17]

All this presupposes that firms are actually able to sustain a policy of *price discrimination*, at least in the short run. In other words, it requires that firms be in a position to set different prices for their output in home and foreign markets. As is well known from elementary microeconomics, any firm able to discriminate in this fashion will normally be able to profit from exploiting the opportunity.[18] But can firms actually seal off their export market from their domestic market? Can they prevent arbitrage leakage of products from the cheaper to the more expensive market? Obviously, the answer varies from country to country and from case to case. In reality, we observe that the most effective barriers to prevent agents from exploiting deviations from the law of one price are invariably created by governments for one reason or another. Cars (especially in the minority of right-hand-drive countries), airline tickets and pharmaceuticals would be classic examples of industries where short-run arbitrage is almost completely out of the question, although even in these cases recent developments have made price discrimination far harder to sustain than a decade ago.[19] Again, the question can be answered only by empirical research.

2.7 Empirical research

PPP is one of the most heavily researched topics in economics. In the first phase, through the 1970s and 1980s, the emerging consensus based on univariate regressions seemed to point to the gloomy conclusion that, even in the long run, there was no evidence to support PPP. On the contrary, the real exchange rate appeared to be what statisticians call a random walk, in other words a process that changes only as a result of purely random disturbances:

$$q_t = q_{t-1} + u_t \tag{2.13}$$

where u_t is a zero-mean random shock unrelated to any previous history.[20]

To understand the implications, consider the situation starting from a position of PPP equilibrium. Now suppose that one Monday something happens to disturb the equilibrium, for example some kind of political upheaval causing a 10% overnight depreciation and, of course, having exactly the same impact on the real exchange rate, since the price level has so far remained unchanged. So, for that Monday only, u_t in Equation 2.13 is 10%, making q_t 10% higher at the start of the next day, Tuesday. However, since it is a random walk, there is no reason to expect u_t to be negative, let alone the −10% required to offset the positive disturbance from the day before. In fact, Tuesday's disturbance is just as likely to be positive, taking the real exchange rate even further from equilibrium, as negative, taking it back towards equilibrium. Moreover, the same is true of Wednesday and Thursday. To say that the real exchange rate is a random walk amounts to saying that there is no reason to suppose that the 10% shock will ever be reversed. Instead, after absorbing Monday's shock, the best forecast is that the real exchange rate will remain at its new level indefinitely – with no time limit on the domestic economy's improved competitiveness.[21]

Of course, this is not to say that we expect no further change. It is simply saying that any further change will be as unpredictable as was the original shock – equally likely to be positive or negative, and equally likely to move the exchange back towards equilibrium or even further away. In general, however overvalued relative to its PPP level a currency may appear to be, it is as likely to rise as fall in subsequent periods.

Although this conclusion seems negative, it can be reconciled with a form of PPP under certain circumstances, as we shall see at the end of the next chapter. Nonetheless, its implications for the stability of a floating exchange rate system are far from encouraging.

Over the past decade, with the help of powerful new econometric methods and ever faster computing, researchers have more or less rescued PPP as a theory of long-run behaviour. In the first place, a number of ways have been found to remedy the problem of a shortage of data points for estimation purposes.[22] A number of researchers have used panel data regressions, i.e. simultaneous analysis of a number of different countries over a relatively short data period. Others have found sources of annual price and exchange rate data for a few countries going back to the nineteenth century and beyond. Powerful new techniques for time-series analysis have also played an important part in generating a new consensus that deviations from PPP have a half-life of between 3.5 and 5 years, depending on the currency pair, the type of price index, the sample period, and so on.[23] This is still uncomfortably long in many respects, but it is not entirely implausible, especially when account is taken of some of the possible explanations as summarized in the previous section.

The new approaches to PPP have also served to refocus attention of the research community on the law of one price.[24] Thirty years ago, in perhaps the most influential of the early studies, Isard (1977) had found evidence of substantial deviations on the basis of regression tests of an equation based on Equation 2.3:

$$p_i^* + s = a + bp_i + u \qquad\qquad (2.14)$$

If the law of one price works as expected, the intercept, a, should be zero and the gradient, b, should be insignificantly different from 1.0. Instead, it turned out that, in most cases, these conditions were clearly not satisfied. More recent work has tended to confirm the negative conclusion in a variety of ways. A particularly eye-catching piece of research compared deviations from law of price (LoP) within states and regions of the USA and Canada with deviations between North America and other countries. If international markets are truly integrated, then any deviations from LoP ought to be attributable mainly to the distance goods have to travel. Once allowance is made for distance, deviations should on average be no greater between countries than between regions or cities in the same country. Instead, the authors found vastly greater international failures in LoP, which they summarized in the dramatic finding that an international border has the same effect as would an additional 75 000 miles between cities in the same country.

2.8   Conclusions

We have seen that there are persuasive reasons for supposing that, in principle at least, PPP ought to be a good approximation to the truth. Unfortunately, however, the facts would appear to provide little support in the short run, and the evidence on the long run is at best mildly supportive.

One plausible explanation that has already been mentioned is the possibility that PPP applies to the true, unobservable price levels. If, instead, we look at what factors determine price levels in a domestic context (particularly the money stock), then PPP will dictate what *ought* to be the relationship between them and the exchange rate. This is precisely what we shall do in Chapter 5.

However, it appears more likely that the true explanation is to be found in the importance of speculative influences in currency markets. Given the scale and volatility of capital account movements in the 1980s and 1990s relative to the comparatively small (and stable) flows of international trade in goods and services, it seems hardly surprising that the link between the current account and the exchange rate is almost invisible. The other side of the coin is the persistence of massive current account surpluses and deficits, even in the face of quite substantial movements in exchange rates. (It is precisely because the capital account is very much the tail that wags the dog in the floating rate era that we shall have very little to say about the factors that influence international trade.)

This, of course, is an observation about relative volatility, not an explanation. How can we reconcile the slow adjustment of real exchange rates and the high volatility of nominal exchange rates? After all, the fact that prices may be slow to react is in this sense irrelevant. Sticky prices do not, of themselves, prevent adjustment to PPP, if the nominal exchange rate moves freely to reinstate equilibrium after a shock. In other words, we can accept the sluggishness of goods markets as unavoidable and plainly explicable, for all the reasons mentioned in this chapter, while still asking: why do exchange rates move so much, but not (systematically and reliably) towards PPP equilibrium? If there is a market failure, then it appears to be in the currency markets first and foremost. PPP failure is primarily a nominal, not a real exchange rate problem.

There is one final point that should be made on this topic, and it concerns the future of PPP. How is the advent of electronic trade going to affect the situation?

On the one hand, it might be thought likely to reinvigorate the LoP. After all, the Internet puts at the disposal of anyone who has a personal computer a whole new universe of information about products and services available anywhere on earth. It is as easy to download software from a site on the other side of the world as from the site owned by one's local computer shop, school or university. Some readers may even have bought this book from an Internet bookshop. Why? Presumably because it is cheaper, quicker or more convenient than visiting their local bookshop. If more people follow this route, then local bookshops will be forced to charge the same prices as those offered by the cheapest Internet bookshops, wherever they are nominally based. In that respect, a bookshop on a street corner in a London suburb will be in competition not only with other bookshops in the same suburb or even with other London shops, but also with the Internet sites selling books online at the click of a mouse button. Of course, the playing field will not be completely level. Buying on the Internet means paying extra for packing and posting, and bookbuyers may in any case be willing to pay a premium for the opportunity to browse in the comfort of a high-street bookseller, with coffee, bagels and music as accompaniment. But many of the other home advantages will be eroded or eliminated altogether. For example, the Internet may make it almost impossible for governments to impose tariffs or even domestic indirect taxes,[25] let alone quotas or other barriers to trade.[26] In general, we may well be facing a quantum leap in the competitiveness of product markets. Location, and in particular *national* location, is bound to become a negligible factor, as markets that were previously more or less closed to consumers, with imports being supplied by specialist entrepreneurs, become open at the point of sale.

On the other hand, although the direction of change in the goods and services markets is clearly towards far greater competitiveness, it is not obvious that modern technology will ultimately have the effect of reinstating PPP exchange rates. The reason is that although the electronic age makes trade in goods and services vastly more efficient, it also makes it possible to move enormous sums of money around the world's banking system with far greater speed and at far lower cost than ever before. To some extent, of course, this change has already occurred: the currency markets have been dominated by electronic trading for 20 years or so. But this particular trend still has some distance to go. In particular, with the advent of Internet-based accounts with banks, stockbrokers and derivatives dealers, it is becoming democratized. We are all potential currency speculators now.

The first effect may tend to push exchange rates towards their PPP levels, while the second makes the current account more irrelevant than ever. The net effect is difficult to foresee.

Summary

- The *law of one price* states that two identical goods must sell for the same price. In the context of the domestic economy, if we allow for *transaction costs*, this relationship can be expected to hold, because it pays entrepreneurs to exploit any price divergences that emerge temporarily, by buying large quantities of the good in the cheap market and selling it immediately in the expensive market, until the price differential is eliminated. This form of riskless trading is known as *arbitrage*. By contrast, *speculation* involves buying something in the hope of being able to resell it later at a higher price.

- The importance of transaction costs will vary from good to good. In some cases, they are a negligible factor and the law of one price might be expected to hold almost exactly. In others, transaction costs drive a substantial wedge between prices in different markets. In the extreme case (*non-traded goods*), transaction costs are so high relative to the price that arbitrage becomes prohibitively expensive.

- In an open economy context, the law of one price states that two identical goods must sell for a price that is the same when translated into a common currency. In order to translate the price in terms of one country's money into the price in terms of another's, one needs to make use of the relative price of the two currencies or the exchange rate. Hence, the open economy version of the law of one price states that the domestic price of a good must be equal to the foreign price multiplied by the domestic currency price of foreign exchange.

- The barriers to international trade and the transaction costs involved are likely to be, for the most part, of the same nature as those in domestic markets, but they will usually be more substantial. In particular, there will frequently be *tariffs* (taxes on cross-border trade) as an additional obstacle to arbitrage.

- In order to measure the level of prices in general, rather than the price of individual goods and services, we need to use a *price index*, which is simply a weighted average of the component prices, with weights corresponding to the relative importance of each product in total expenditure.

- Under certain circumstances, what is true of the prices of individual goods and services in different countries will also be true of the level of prices in general. In other words, (*absolute*) *purchasing power parity* (PPP) will apply; that is, the level of prices in the home country will be equal to the product of the foreign country's price level and the exchange rate, measured as the (domestic currency) price of foreign exchange. Depending on our interpretation of the PPP mechanism, this may or may not presuppose among other things that barriers to trade, including all incidental costs, are negligible.

- In practice, since no meaning can be attached to the absolute level of a price index, it is sensible to consider the PPP hypothesis as it relates to *changes* in price levels (inflation rates). Then, *relative purchasing power parity* states that two countries' inflation rates will diverge by the extent of the change in their bilateral exchange rate.

- Deviations from PPP, where they occur, will normally be associated with changes in a country's relative competitiveness. For that reason, it is often useful to look at the *real exchange rate*, which is the (nominal) exchange rate corrected for changes in relative prices. Among the explanations offered for PPP and LoP failures have been more rapid technological change in the traded goods sector of the typical economy, the impact of trade costs that may introduce threshold non-linearities into LoP relationships and/or cause systematic differences between countries in the relative price of traded goods, and phenomena such as pricing to market.

- Examination of the facts suggests that exchange rates probably do have a long-run tendency to gravitate towards their PPP levels. In the short run, however, PPP is almost completely irrelevant. PPP only really fits the facts well when one of the countries has an inflation rate so high that price adjustments become more or less continuous and the cost of deviating from PPP is therefore prohibitive.

Reading guide

The early research on PPP and the law of one price is quite easy to understand without very much mathematics or econometrics. The influential LoP paper mentioned above is Isard (1977).

The most detailed summary of early work on PPP is Officer (1976). See also Kravis and Lipsey (1971) and Katseli-Papaefstratiou (1979). Magee (1978) dissents from the view that PPP does not hold, attributing apparent deviations to inaccurate price measurement. Two studies supportive of PPP, for the 1920s at least, were published by Frenkel (1978, 1980). The same author, by the same token, charted the 'collapse of PPP during the 1970s'.

Although somewhat out of date by now, it is still worth reading Mussa (1979), which attempts to summarize the facts on PPP, as well as on other aspects of exchange rate movements.

The idea that changes in the real exchange rate are essentially random is due to Roll (1979), although see also Adler and Lehmann (1983).

The recent resurgence of interest in PPP has prompted a number of excellent survey articles, of which the most influential was Rogoff (1996). Sarno and Taylor (2002) bring the story up to date. For discussion of the iceberg model, see Obstfeld and Rogoff (2000a). Pricing to market dates from Krugman (1987), but a lot more work has been done in the context of the new open economy macroeconomics, as will be seen in Chapter 10 of this book. A good example of research on the ESTAR model is Taylor, Peel and Sarno (2001). The first among the many papers uncovering long-term (often *very* long-term) PPP relationships was Diebold, Husted and Rush (1991), but see also Cheung and Lai (1993). On the Balassa–Samuelson hypothesis, see Engel (1999).

Web page: **www.pearsoned.co.uk/copeland**.

Notes

1 Note that an important element in these expenses is likely to be the cost of actually collecting information on price divergences. Nowadays, the process is made much simpler by the Internet.

2 Of course, as the example should make clear, there are substantial cost savings to be made by trading in large quantities. The cost of arbitrage in blocks of 1000 tickets is likely to be far less per ticket than for a block of only 100, because most of the components of the transaction cost, particularly those involved in information gathering, are likely to be the same irrespective of the size of the deal. In the jargon of microeconomics, there are substantial economies of scale to be exploited in arbitrage, and this fact explains why it pays for some individuals or agencies to specialize in the activity.

3 Strictly speaking, Equation 2.1 ought to be written as an inequality:

$$-C^* \leq P^B - P^M \leq C$$

where C and C^* are the transaction costs of arbitrage from Birmingham to Manchester, and vice versa. Assuming the costs are the same in both directions, then the price differential cannot exceed C. For simplicity, we assume it is as great as is permitted by this relationship.

4 In any case, it appears that ticket touting is actually on the margins of legality, depending on all sorts of conditions of sale, contract terms, and so forth.

5 In the modern world, inflation is the most frequent explanation of this phenomenon. The Israelis, for example, coped with triple-digit inflation in the early 1980s by quoting all 'big-ticket' prices such as houses, cars, and so on in US dollars. And, of course, US dollars are used widely alongside local currency in Canada.

6 A notorious example occurred when the French authorities relocated customs clearance facilities for imports of 'cheap' Japanese video cassette recorders from a large Paris office to a small, patently inadequate provincial office. The resulting queues, delays, and so on amounted to a non-pecuniary tariff intended to deter importers, while at the same time avoiding the political problem of having to defend the imposition of an overt tariff increase.

7 It is interesting to speculate why this is the case. No doubt in some cases the volume of cross-border trade is regarded as too small to warrant government interference. In other cases, it is probably more a result of the fact that trade in services is, for some reason or other, less politically sensitive than trade in manufactures. Thus, for some reason beyond this author's understanding, the majority of British and American politicians seem convinced that a nation's economic prowess requires it to have a large positive balance on trade in motor vehicles but see nothing wrong with a deficit in tourist services – the outcome, presumably, of an unholy marriage between mercantilism and Stalinism.

8 For an example of what happens when people fall into this particular logical trap, one could not do better than to look at the US and UK car industries. Back in the 1960s, the same specious argument was used widely in both countries to support the view that foreign prices (especially those for Japanese and German cars) were irrelevant, since imports were a negligible proportion of sales anyway. Those were the days!

9 In fact, by 1981, UK consumption had fallen by about 20% in volume terms from its 1979 level – a repeat of what had happened in the two years following the 1973 OPEC price rises.

10 A fact that, in the case of share prices, is widely exploited by unit trust salesmen.

11 Furthermore, this statement becomes even more obviously true when we examine higher-frequency (for example, quarterly or monthly) data. The data used in the charts are also biased in favour of PPP in so far as it relates to average exchange rates over the year. End-year or mid-year rates would be considerably more volatile, whereas, by contrast, taking averages over a whole year tends to smooth out some of the fluctuations.

12 The Deutschmark and the French franc will, of course, cease to exist when EMU reaches its final stage.

13 The actual ratio depends on the way volatility (standard deviation) is measured, the definition of prices (CPI versus WPI) and, most important of all, the data frequency. Notice that price

levels are only published monthly, and so no comparison is possible at higher frequency. Of course, the fact that no price indices are published on any particular day does not mean that the true unobservable price level is constant.

14 More formally, faster technological progress in traded goods production will raise the marginal product of labour in traded goods more rapidly than in non-traded goods. If money wages are to be the same in the two sectors, then the result will be that the relative price of traded goods will have to fall so as to raise the product wage in the sector, relative to the product wage in services. This analysis presupposes that the weights of the two sectors in the price index are constant. Note also that there is no attempt to claim that productivity levels (and hence the product wage) will actually be higher in the traded goods sector, but simply that productivity will rise more rapidly in the open sector. Of course, with the passage of time, this might be expected to result in higher levels, other things being equal.

15 In fact, in the most up-to-date and convincing form of the theory, the function is assumed to be exponential, with a quadratic exponent – the so-called exponential smooth transition autoregressive (or ESTAR) model. Additional lags of the disequilibrium term $(\bar{q}_{t-2} - q_{1-2})$ may be required, especially when fitting the model to higher-frequency data. A more attractive formulation, in my view, would have the *nominal* exchange rate on the left-hand side, since it is the currency markets that react (or overreact) to relative prices.

16 In principle, the importer's customers can hedge against volatility. In practice, hedging will normally be a lot cheaper for the international trader than for the domestic retailer or consumer, for whom it may be totally impractical.

17 Notice that this is emphatically not a case of sunk costs. If there is no prospect of the company ever wishing to re-enter the US market, then setup costs are irrelevant to the decision. The point here is, rather, that the French company's continuing presence in the USA reduces possible future costs and hence raises future profits, other things being equal. For those familiar with the topic, this is an example of a real option to sell in the USA, purchased by incurring setup costs and also by keeping dollar prices low. Note also that the argument may or may not be symmetric. When the value of the euro falls, a European exporter may decide not to cut his price, so as to offset the long-term effect on profits of periods of underpricing.

18 Strictly, this is true only if the elasticity of demand in the two markets is not the same, so that marginal revenue and marginal cost would be equated at different prices (see any microeconomics textbook). Conventional wisdom seems to be that demand elasticities tend to be higher in export than in a firm's domestic markets, albeit with some well-known exceptions, for example the UK car market.

19 The most significant driving forces have been deregulation (or the attempt to standardize regulation, which has the same effect) in all three cases, overcapacity (in cars and air transport) and the Internet (most noticeably in air travel, but to some extent in the other markets too).

20 In econometric terms, u_t has no autocorrelation structure.

21 Chapter 11 deals with these issues in more detail.

22 Remember that the standard sources of monthly price index data go back no further than 60 years for most industrialized countries, and usually far less. Moreover, the further back in time one goes, the greater the variations in price index weights. As far as exchange rates themselves are concerned, one would at the very least like to be able to examine the possibility that adjustment speeds changed in 1972, at the start of the floating era. All these factors reduce the available number of observations. Note, however, that although common sense (and basic econometrics) support the idea that more observations yield better estimates, a higher frequency is no substitute for a longer data period if we are concerned, as we are here, with a process that may be drawn out over several years.

23 The half-life measures the number of years required for the exchange rate to move sufficiently in order to eliminate 50% of the PPP deviation caused by a sudden disturbance. If any readers are wondering why we deal in half-lives, it is because the mathematics of the fitted models allows for the effect of a shock to diminish with the passage of time, like the ripples on a pond, but never to be totally eliminated. The total life is therefore infinite, but for any reasonable parameter values we can say that at the end of twice the half-life (i.e. seven to ten years in the present case), the remaining effect of a disturbance will be negligible.

24 Most recently, a new impetus has been given by the increasing availability of EPOS data – actual transactions from retailers' electronic records of point-of-sale records, created by barcode readings and so forth.

25 As a matter of fact, most countries impose no tariffs or other taxation on books, but the comment applies to most other goods and many services too.

26 It will become difficult, if not impossible, for governments to police the flow of goods and services, and so restrictions on trade in, for example pornography, politically sensitive material, illegal arms, and so on may all be far more difficult to enforce. Whether desirable or undesirable, these changes all seem likely to increase competitiveness and hence make deviations from the law of one price less sustainable.

3

Financial markets in the open economy

Introduction

In Chapter 2, we saw how the fact that an economy was open to trade with other countries meant that there were certain relationships that could be expected to apply between domestic and foreign prices, though we also found that, in reality, they rarely hold very closely. In this chapter, we shall look at the markets for financial assets rather than goods, and at the relationships one can expect to find linking domestic and foreign asset prices.

We have already looked at one good that had some of the properties of a financial asset: tickets for a rock concert are like assets, in so far as they yield a future return, in the form of entertainment, and also because, being easy to transport and more or less homogeneous, arbitrage is likely to go a long way in order to eliminate price differentials.

Here, we shall be concerned with a more conventional asset. For simplicity's sake, let us pick a single, standard security and stick with it throughout the chapter. The best asset to choose for present purposes will be a 12-month time deposit; that is, a deposit for a fixed term of one year, paying an annual interest rate at maturity and nothing before then. We shall ignore other short-term assets in order to highlight the relationship between the UK and US interest rates on this standard type of deposit.

We shall be concerned with the alternatives open to a representative investor[1] with a large stock of wealth in liquid form. In fact, the investor could actually be a bank or a multinational company with liquid funds. In any case, the choice with which we shall be concerned is between two otherwise identical deposits, one in a UK bank and the other in a US bank.[2] For the most part, we shall view the alternatives as seen from the UK, though symmetrical arguments will apply to US-based investors. We shall also assume that there are no barriers to international transfers of funds, an assumption that is fairly realistic as far as today's currency markets are concerned, and that our investor is exempt from all taxes that might affect the choice of where to deposit.

3.1 Uncovered interest rate parity

To start with, put yourself in the position of a UK resident on 1 January with some funds that he wishes to leave on deposit for one year on the most favourable terms possible. It will simplify matters without changing our conclusions if we assume that the amount involved is just £1. We shall compare two alternatives (call them the UK and the US strategies, respectively) in terms of the sterling return they promise. As an aid to understanding the mechanism involved, we shall make use of Figure 3.1 and Table 3.1, which deal with the general case in terms of symbols, side by side with the numerical examples in Tables 3.2 to 3.4.

3.1.1 The domestic strategy

If the appropriate UK interest rate (expressed as a decimal) is r, then £1 deposited for 12 months in a UK bank will have attracted £1 $\times$ r of interest by the end of the period. The £1 will therefore have 'grown' to:

$$£1 + (£1 \times r) = £(1 + r)$$

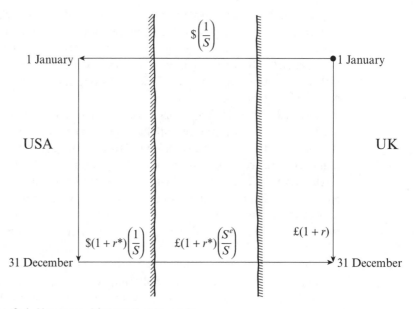

Figure 3.1 Uncovered interest rate parity

Table 3.1 Uncovered interest rate parity – general case (assuming no risk premium)

	UK strategy		US strategy	
	Action	*Yield*	*Action*	*Yield*
1 January				
12-month interest rate		r		r^*
Available for deposit		£1		£1
Exchange rate (£ price of $)				£S
			Buy $ @ £S each:	$(1/S)$
	Place on deposit:	£1	Place on deposit:	$(1/S)$
31 December				
	Liquidate deposit:	£$(1 + r)$	Liquidate deposit:	$(1 + r^*)(1/S)$
Expected exchange rate				£S^e
(£ price of $)				
			Convert back to £	
			Sell $ @ £S^e each:	£$(1 + r^*)(S^e/S)$

Conclusion: If £$(1 + r) >$ £$(1 + r^*)(S^e/S)$: *deposit* in UK
If £$(1 + r) <$ £$(1 + r^*)(S^e/S)$: *deposit* in USA
If £$(1 + r) =$ £$(1 + r^*)(S^e/S)$: *equilibrium*

Table 3.2 Uncovered interest rate parity – case 1 disequilibrium (assuming no risk premium)

	UK strategy		US strategy	
	Action	*Yield*	*Action*	*Yield*
1 January				
12-month interest rate		5%		6%
Available for deposit		£1.00		£1.00
Exchange rate (£ price of $)				£0.50
			Buy $ @ £0.50 each:	$2.00
	Place on deposit:	£1.00	Place on deposit:	$2.00
31 December				
	Liquidate deposit:	£1.05	Liquidate deposit:	$2.12
Expected exchange rate				£0.60
(£ price of $)				
			Convert back to £	
			Sell $ @ £0.60 each:	£1.27

Conclusion: *Deposit* in USA

Table 3.3 Uncovered interest rate parity – case 2 equilibrium (assuming no risk premium)

	UK strategy		US strategy	
	Action	*Yield*	*Action*	*Yield*
1 January				
12-month interest rate		25%		5%
Available for deposit		£1.00		£1.00
Exchange rate (£ price of $)				£0.50
			Buy $ @ £0.50 each:	$2.00
	Place on deposit:	£1.00	Place on deposit:	$2.00
31 December				
	Liquidate deposit:	£1.25	Liquidate deposit:	$2.10
Expected exchange rate (£ price of $)				£0.60
			Convert back to £	
			Sell $ @ £0.60 each:	£1.25

Conclusion: *Equilibrium*

Table 3.4 Uncovered interest rate parity – case 3 equilibrium (assuming no risk premium)

	UK strategy		US strategy	
	Action	*Yield*	*Action*	*Yield*
1 January				
12-month interest rate		15%		5%
Available for deposit		£1.00		£1.00
Exchange rate (£ price of $)				£0.40
			Buy $ @ £0.40 each:	$2.50
	Place on deposit:	£1.00	Place on deposit:	$2.50
31 December				
	Liquidate deposit:	£1.15	Liquidate deposit:	$2.63
Expected exchange rate (£ price of $)				£0.44
			Convert back to £	
			Sell $ @ £0.44 each:	£1.15

Conclusion: *Equilibrium*

by 31 December, as we can see from the downward-pointing arrow on the right-hand (UK) side of Figure 3.1 (or in the middle column of Table 3.1). Note that this outcome is available with complete certainty. The only possible risk would be of bank failure, and we shall rule out that eventuality as being too improbable to be worth considering.[3]

For example, if the interest rate in the UK is 5% per annum (or 0.05), then £1 will earn £0.05 of interest, so that the end-of-year value of the deposit will be £1.05, as we can see from the middle column of Table 3.2. The alternative, on the other hand, is a little more complicated.

3.1.2 The foreign strategy

This consists of the following three operations: convert the pound into dollars, then deposit the dollars with a US bank and, finally, at the end of the year convert the proceeds back into sterling. To calculate the return to this strategy, follow the route round the other three sides of the rectangle in Figure 3.1, or down the right-hand column of Tables 3.1 and 3.2.

Stage 1

Convert the £1 into dollars so as to 'cross the Atlantic' to the USA (the top arrow in Figure 3.1). One pound buys $1/S$ dollars, and so this is the amount available for deposit with the US bank.

For example, if the exchange rate is $1 = £0.50, our investor will have $2.00 available for deposit in the US bank (Table 3.2, right-hand side).

Stage 2

Leave the balance on deposit in America for 12 months. How much will it earn? That will obviously depend on the US interest rate, which we will call r^*. So $\$1/S$ left on deposit at the US interest rate r^* will earn $\$(1/S)r^*$ by the end of the year. Hence, the deposit will, by the end of the year, have grown to $\$(1 + r^*)1/S$.

Continuing our numerical example, if the US interest rate is 6%, then the $2.00 deposited will have grown to $2.12 by 31 December.

Before moving on to the final stage, note that from the standpoint of our imaginary UK investor, the *dollar* proceeds of depositing in the USA are known in advance, on 1 January. All the elements in the calculation of the dollar returns can be taken as known at the start of the year, when the choice of where to deposit is made. The US interest rate is known, in the same way that the UK rate was known. The exchange rate at which dollars can be bought for Stage 1 is equally available, on application to any bank or currency dealer.

Now the crucial point in understanding the process is not to forget that the next stage takes place 12 months later than the first two stages. What concerns our UK investor is the sterling value of the deposit. This is obviously true if the investor is a UK resident. However, even if he is a member of the international jet set, with a lifestyle that involves spending in more or less equal amounts in all the major currencies, or if, more prosaically, he is treasurer of a multinational corporation, *it is only by converting into a common currency that a valid comparison with the domestic deposit strategy can be made*, and we are assuming the common currency is the pound sterling.[4]

Stage 3

On 31 December, liquidate the US deposit and convert the proceeds from dollars into sterling at whatever happens to be the exchange rate on the day in question.

Now, as of 1 January, that exchange rate is unknowable. All the investor can do to arrive at a decision is to make his own forecast of the exchange rate that seems likely to prevail at the end of the year. Call this forecast of the end-of-year exchange rate S^e.

Given his forecast of the exchange rate at which it will prove possible to convert the dollars back to sterling, we can close the circle or, rather, the rectangle in Figure 3.1. A dollar will buy £S^e on 31 December, if the investor's guess turns out to be correct. So the $\$1/S(1 + r^*)$ that the investor will have on 31 December if he decides to follow the US deposit route will buy £$(1 + r^*)S^e/S$ when converted back into sterling (in mid-Atlantic, on the bottom arrow in Figure 3.1).

In terms of our numerical example, if the investor expects the sterling exchange rate to have deteriorated to £0.60 = \$1, then the investor will be able to convert his dollar deposit of \$2.12 into £1.27 (the bottom line of Table 3.2).

3.1.3 Equilibrium: the bottom line

We are now in a position to compare the attractiveness of the two strategies. What should we expect to find? Remember that we are dealing with deposits of the same kind, for the same period, in banks of the same type. Can we then apply the law of one price and conclude that the return from the two strategies must be equal in equilibrium, otherwise arbitrage profits will exist?

Not quite. Recall that, from the point of view of the UK resident, the domestic strategy is riskless. It requires no forecasting, no guesswork and no danger of unpleasant surprises. The calculated return does not rely on expectations that may turn out to be wrong, possibly by a large margin.

The US deposit strategy, by contrast, involves making a guess about the future exchange rate, which is a hazardous business at the best of times. To this extent, the US deposit is not the same asset as the UK deposit. In general, we might expect economic agents either to avoid running risks or, more likely, to demand a reward for doing so. We shall have more to say on the general subject of risk later in the book, especially Chapter 15, but at this stage it is worth introducing one or two concepts that will enable us to sidestep the problem without ignoring it altogether. First:

> The **risk premium** is the reward, usually in the form of an anticipated excess return, that an economic agent gets in order to persuade him to bear risk.

Why do agents usually require an incentive in order to undertake risky projects? The answer given by economic theory relies on the nature of people's preferences when faced with choices between uncertain prospects. It is assumed that, for the most part, individuals prefer riskless to risky investments, other things being equal. This feature of preferences is what explains why risky investments usually yield a higher return than riskless ones. Not that tastes are always such that people demand a risk premium. There are some instances where agents seem content to run risks for no reward, or even in some cases to pay for the privilege of bearing risk. The following definitions are useful in this context:

> **Risk averters** are economic agents who require a (positive) risk premium in order to persuade them to hold risky assets. By contrast, **risk lovers** are willing to pay a premium for the privilege of bearing risk, while **risk-neutral** agents are willing to do so in return for a zero-risk premium.

For the most part, one would expect to find that people are averse to risk, at least in their attitudes to purely economic decisions. None the less, allowing for uncertainty in economics makes analysis very difficult indeed, which is why we are going to defer any consideration of the problems associated with risk until Chapter 15. For present purposes, we shall make the following simplifying assumption:

> From now on and until further notice, we shall be assuming that economic agents are broadly risk-neutral.

Notice this means that we are assuming they are, on balance, neither risk averters nor risk lovers – they are indifferent between an investment yielding a completely secure return, on the one hand, and one offering the prospect of an identical return on average, but with the possibility of a much higher or lower return, on the other. In other words, we assume they are concerned only with average returns.

For the moment, we shall suspend consideration of how realistic this assumption is in practice and note only that it allows us to ignore the risk premium. In the present case, it permits us to jump to the following simple conclusion about the relative attractiveness of UK and US deposits:

> In equilibrium, the domestic and foreign strategies will have to yield the same sterling return.

In other words, in equilibrium the investor must be indifferent between deposits in the two countries. Otherwise, if returns were not equal, our investor would be faced with a 'one-way bet'. Given the investor's expectations, and that he is risk-neutral (that is, indifferent to risk), the question of whether to deposit in the UK or the USA will have a clearcut answer, and it will be one shared by anyone who holds similar expectations. If there is anything approaching a consensus in the market, then there will be a flood of investment either into or out of the UK banking system, depending on which of the two strategies has the higher payoff.

Look at the bottom line of Table 3.2. The US alternative yields £1.27 while the UK deposit pays only £1.05. Plainly, under these circumstances no one would deposit in the UK. Given the level of the exchange rate and its future expected value, and given our assumption of risk neutrality, either the UK interest rate must be higher or the US interest rate lower in order for depositors to be indifferent between the two alternatives.

In general, then, for equilibrium (that is, a situation where there is, on balance, no tendency for funds to move into or out of the UK from the USA, and vice versa), we require that the return from depositing £1 in the UK, £$(1 + r)$, be just equal to the return on a US deposit, £$S^e/S(1 + r^*)$. The steps in the reasoning are summarized in Table 3.1, where we can see from the bottom line that equilibrium requires that the following relationship hold:

$$(1 + r) = (1 + r^*)S^e/S \qquad (3.1)$$

Now with a little manipulation, this equation can be rewritten in a simpler form. First, notice that the term S^e/S has a simple interpretation: the numerator is the exchange rate expected to prevail at the end of the year, and the denominator is the actual exchange rate at the time the decision is being made, that is 1 January. Hence, the ratio of the two, S^e/S, will be greater than 1 if the price of foreign currency is expected to have risen by 31 December. For example, if the exchange rate is expected to be 50% higher by the end of the year (in other words, if the price of foreign currency, S, is forecast to rise by half), then the ratio S^e/S will be 1.50. It therefore makes sense to use the following redefinition:

$$S^e/S \equiv 1 + \Delta s^e \qquad (3.2)$$

where Δs will be referred to as the rate of depreciation (of the domestic currency) or the rate of increase in the price of foreign currency over the period in question, with, as before, the superscript e to remind us that in the present case we are concerned with the *expected* rate of depreciation.

Now use Equation 3.2 in place of S^e/S in Equation 3.1 and multiply out on the right-hand side to give:

$$\begin{aligned}(1 + r) &= (1 + r^*)(1 + \Delta s^e) \\ &= 1 + r^* + \Delta s^e + r^*\Delta s^e\end{aligned} \qquad (3.3)$$

Notice, first, that we can subtract 1 from both sides. Next, consider the final term, $r^*\Delta s^e$. It is the product of two rates: the rate of interest and the expected rate of depreciation. Unless we are dealing with a case of very rapid deterioration in a currency (in a hyperinflation, for example), this cross-product term is likely to be of the second order of smallness and, as such, can safely be ignored.[5] We are left with:

$$r = r^* + \Delta s^e \qquad (3.4)$$

This is the form in which the *uncovered interest rate parity condition* (UIRP) is normally stated. In words:

> The domestic interest rate must be higher (lower) than the foreign interest rate by an amount equal to the expected depreciation (appreciation) of the domestic currency.

The reasoning should by now be clear. First, look back at the numerical examples.

In the example in Table 3.2, the price of a dollar is expected to rise from £0.50 to £0.60; that is, the pound is expected to depreciate at the rate $(0.6/0.5 - 1.0) = 0.2$, or 20%. If UK and US interest rates were equal, then no economic agent, wherever domiciled, would keep his wealth in the UK if there were the alternative of depositing in the USA. In order to persuade the economic agent to hold pounds, the interest rate on sterling deposits would have to be higher than on dollar deposits by 20%, so as to compensate for the fact that repayment at the end of the year is in devalued currency (as in Table 3.3).

Conversely, suppose the pound had been expected to appreciate against the dollar. Then no UK resident would have wished to deposit in the USA (and every US citizen who could do so would want to hold sterling deposits) – unless the UK interest rate were low enough to neutralize the attraction of being repaid in currency that had risen in value over the year.

The reasoning behind the interest rate parity relationship has been covered in somewhat exhaustive detail, not only because it will have an important part to play in some of the models we shall be examining in Chapters 7–12 but also because it has important implications in its own right. To see what some of those implications are, look back at Equation 3.4 and ask yourself the question: which of the three variables involved is exogenous, and which endogenous?[6] To put the question more simply, what causes what? Do increases in the expected rate of depreciation cause the UK interest rate to rise or the US rate to fall? Or do changes in the interest differential, $r - r^*$, cause expectations to change?

The answer to each of these questions depends on the structure of the economic model that we choose to believe, and we shall have a lot more to say on these issues in Part III of the book. For the moment, however, it is worth sketching an *ad hoc* answer that will provide a first insight into the linkages between the different national capital markets.

At a casual level, if we take the expected rate of depreciation first, one would guess that operators in foreign currency markets form their own view, or use the services of professional forecasters. Whether arrived at formally (by using the tools of economics, statistics, and so on) or informally (by guesswork, casual impressions, rumour or astrology), these predictions are unlikely to be amenable to direct influence by the authorities. There is no way in which a government or central bank can decree a change in agents' expectations. From a policy point of view, they may as well be taken as given, at least in the very short run.

What of the US interest rate? As far as the British authorities are concerned, the level of US interest rates is simply a fact of life, a feature of the environment that they must accept and to which they must accommodate their policy. This is a consequence of the obvious fact that the UK is a small economy relative to the USA (notice that the converse is not necessarily true).

We have reached the conclusion that, viewed from the UK, both of the terms on the right-hand side of Equation 3.4 may be taken as given. It follows automatically that the left-hand side, the domestic UK interest rate, must be given. A small country, such as the UK, cannot control its own interest rates. Given the state of expectations, its interest rates are determined on the money markets of New York or, possibly, in the corridors of power in Washington.[7]

3.2   Covered interest rate parity

The process of moving capital around so as to exploit uncovered interest rate differentials, along the lines described in Section 3.1, is often loosely referred to as arbitrage. If we are to be consistent, however, we cannot do the same here. Look back at the definition of arbitrage given in Section 2.1 of Chapter 2 – the crucial words are 'riskless profit'. Although we sidestepped the issue by assuming risk neutrality for purposes of deriving the UIRP condition, there is no avoiding the fact that, in practice, making a deposit in a foreign country involves risk. It is, therefore, an activity more like speculation than arbitrage.

It so happens that there is one way of eliminating all risk from a transaction like the one dealt with in Section 3.1. To see what is involved, recall first that, for the UK resident, the risk in depositing in the USA originates in the uncertainty surrounding the future exchange rate, S^e. The dollar proceeds of the US strategy only become available for reconversion to sterling on 31 December. As of 1 January, when the decision has to be made, the would-be depositor is forced to hazard a guess as to what that rate will be at the end of the year.

Look back at the first of the numerical examples (Table 3.2) and ask yourself how much would be yielded by a deposit in the USA if the exchange rate on 31 December actually turned out to be not £0.60 = $1.00 but rather £0.45 = $1.00. Under those circumstances, even the 1% higher interest in the USA would be insufficient to compensate for the fall in the relative value of the dollar, and the outcome would be not only less attractive than holding a sterling deposit but also an actual loss on reconversion to UK currency. (Of how much?)

Now consider the following remedy: instead of waiting 12 months to reconvert the dollar proceeds of a US deposit to sterling, enter into an agreement with another economic agent to exchange the dollars for pounds in advance. (Remember that the depositor knows at the outset exactly how much US currency he will have for conversion on 31 December, because that depends only on the interest rate on dollars quoted on 1 January.) The agreement will of course specify an exchange rate at which the dollars will be converted to pounds in 12 months' time, and that rate will not normally be the same as the exchange rate prevailing on transactions conducted immediately (or 'on the spot'). The following jargon is used in currency markets:

> The **spot (exchange) rate** is the rate figuring in agreements to exchange one currency for another more or less immediately.

In other words, we have until now been dealing with the spot rate, as we always will be, unless we explicitly specify otherwise. On the other hand:

> The **(1-, 3- or 12-month) forward (exchange) rate** is the rate that appears in contracts to exchange one currency for another 1, 3 or 12 months in advance of the actual transaction.

Notice that no currency actually changes hands between the parties to a forward contract at the time it is signed. All that happens is that both parties contract to exchange one currency for another, at the specified forward rate, at some time in the future (the 'maturity date').[8]

Returning to our example, suppose the depositor in Case 1 of Table 3.2 is able to sell the dollar proceeds of his US deposit 12 months in advance, on 1 January. Furthermore, let us suppose that he is able to do so using the exchange rate entered in Table 3.2 as the expected rate, that is $1.00 = £0.60 (we shall have more to say later about whether the forward rate will in fact be equal to the expected rate). Exactly the same procedure is followed as before, the only difference being that, on 31 December, instead of taking pot luck in exchanging his dollars in the spot market, the depositor is able to enjoy the benefit of the forward contract, which allows the depositor to force the other party to the contract to buy the dollars at the rate agreed at the start of the year.

Put in that way, the advantage of the deal ought to be plain. It is not that the return is any greater than the £1.27 yielded by a spot transaction, because we are assuming that the forward rate is exactly the same as the rate the depositor expected to see prevailing in the spot market on 31 December. Rather, the advantage lies in the fact that, using the forward market, the depositor can *guarantee* a return of £1.27. In other words, the transaction can be made completely riskless – the whole deal is wrapped up on 1 January, at a known US interest rate and a known forward rate. In this sense, the investor is 'covered' or insured against the risk in the interest rate arbitrage process.

Notice that, by locking in the exchange rate via the forward market, the depositor is insured against any nasty shocks – but in doing so the chance of benefiting from any pleasant surprises is sacrificed. Not only does a forward purchase serve to hedge against a lower dollar value than anticipated, but it also means giving up any additional profit that might have been made.

As far as the market as a whole is concerned, since we are now dealing with riskless transactions (arbitrage in the proper sense of the word), it is even less likely that a gap between the sterling yield on UK and US deposits could persist for any length of time. In other words, this time we can conclude that the return from depositing in the USA must be the same as that from depositing in the UK, irrespective of whether potential depositors are risk-neutral or not. Thus, the law of one price can legitimately be invoked.

In the same way that we derived Equation 3.1 by assuming the dollars were converted (spot) at the rate expected to prevail on 31 December, S^e, we now allow for them being sold in advance on 1 January at the 12-month forward rate available at that date. For present purposes, where there is no possibility of confusion over the maturity date, let F denote the forward exchange rate (that is, the sterling price of US dollars) prevailing on 1 January for US currency to be delivered on 31 December.

Then, since all other features of the transaction are unchanged from the previous section, we can simply write F in place of S^e in Equation 3.1 to give:

$$(1+r) = (1+r^*)\frac{F}{S} \qquad (3.5)$$

as the precise form of our covered arbitrage condition. Again, we can manipulate the formula to yield a more intelligible relationship by rewriting F/S, as follows:

$$\frac{F}{S} \equiv 1 + f \qquad (3.6)$$

where f is defined as follows:

> The **forward premium (discount)** is the proportion by which a country's forward exchange rate exceeds (falls below) its spot rate.

In Case 1 of Table 3.2, for example, if $1 = £0.60$ is the 12-month forward rate prevailing at the start of the year, when at the same time the spot rate is $1 = £0.50$, it follows that there is a forward premium of 20% on dollars (and a forward discount on sterling), because dollars to be delivered in 12 months cost 20% more than dollars to be delivered on the spot; so, rewriting Equation 3.6:

$$f \equiv \frac{F}{S} - 1 = \frac{0.60}{0.50} - 1 = 0.2 \tag{3.7}$$

In general terms, then, we can rewrite our equilibrium condition by following the same steps as in the previous section, this time with f in place of Δs^e:

$$\begin{aligned}(1 + r) &= (1 + r^*)(1 + f) \\ &= 1 + r^* + f + r^*f\end{aligned} \tag{3.8}$$

As before, we would expect r^*f to be of the second order of smallness, so that we end up with:

$$r = r^* + f \tag{3.9}$$

This is the normal formulation of the *covered interest rate parity hypothesis* (CIRP), which states that:

> The domestic interest rate must be higher (lower) than the foreign interest rate by an amount equal to the forward discount (premium) on the domestic currency.

3.3 Borrowing and lending

At this point, it is worth pausing for a moment to adopt a slightly different perspective on the arbitrage process discussed in this chapter so far. Let us go back to the example in Table 3.2. The UK and US interest rates are 5% and 6%, respectively, and the exchange rate is expected to change from $1 = £0.50$ to $1 = £0.60$ over the next 12 months. In each of our hypothetical scenarios, the individual was assumed to have a sum of money in pounds (in fact, just £1) available for investment. Although this simplification may have helped to make the process easier to understand, it also had the effect of making the power of arbitrage mechanisms appear weaker than it actually is.

Suppose our hypothetical investor had no money available for deposit either in the UK or in the USA. Does this rule out the possibility of profiting from arbitrage? Plainly, no. As long as the investor can borrow pounds, he can exploit any opportunities offered by deviations from interest rate parity. To see how, go back to the numerical example illustrated in Table 3.2 and rework the calculations on the assumption that the investor borrows £1 on 1 January.

Table 3.5 Uncovered interest rate arbitrage with borrowing

	UK strategy		US strategy	
	Action	*Yield*	*Action*	*Yield*
1 January				
12-month interest rate		5%		6%
Position taken	Borrow short sterling (£1.00)	£1.00	Borrow short sterling (£1.00)	£1.00
			Buy $ @ £0.50 each:	$2.00
Position taken	Place on deposit: i.e. lend long sterling (£1.00)	£1.00	Place on deposit: i.e. lend long dollars ($2.00)	$2.00
Net position during year	**Nil (long − short = 0)**		**(Short £1.00)**	
			(Long $2.00)	
31 December				
	Liquidate deposit:	£1.05	Liquidate deposit:	$2.12
			Convert back to £	
			Sell $ @ £0.60 each:	£1.27
	Repay loan:	£1.05	Repay loan:	£1.05
Net profit		**£0.00**		**£0.22**

The result is that making a deposit in the USA generates a profit of £0.22 per £1 borrowed, whereas the UK deposit simply breaks even (remember we are ignoring transaction costs both for borrowing and lending and for currency conversion). This outcome should come as no surprise. It is clearly no more than would have been expected from the computations in Table 3.2.

For present purposes, however, it is useful to view the process in terms of the investor's asset position in each currency, which is precisely what has been presented in Table 3.5.

As far as the first step is concerned, in borrowing pounds the investor deliberately incurs a liability in sterling. Currency market jargon is helpful here:

An investor who has a **liability** (an **asset**) denominated in a specific currency is said to have a **short** (**long**) **position** in that currency.

So the investor starts by taking a short position in sterling.

Now as far as the UK strategy is concerned, depositing the proceeds of the loan creates an asset denominated in pounds too – that is, a long position in sterling of exactly £1. The *net* effect is to leave the investor with a balanced position in pounds. Moreover, this net zero balance is maintained throughout the year, as the value of the long position increases with the accumulating interest on the deposit and the size of the debt simultaneously rises at the same rate.

By contrast, the US strategy involves converting the £1 to dollars and depositing it in the USA, thus creating a long position in dollars. Now although it is true that initially, on 1 January, the two positions offset each other – the investor's long position in dollars and short in sterling are both valued at exactly £1 – the situation of exact balance will not be sustained. If the dollar weakens in February, say, then the value of the investor's dollar holding will decline while the sterling debt increases.

In other words, the risk associated with the uncovered arbitrage transaction arises from changes in the net position as exchange rate fluctuations alter the value of the position in the two currencies. The problem never arises in the case of the UK strategy because the two positions – borrowing and lending, short and long in pounds – are perfectly matched. Any change in the value of the pound will have offsetting effects on the value of the short and long positions, respectively.

Here, we are assuming that the exchange rate ends the year at $1 = £0.60, which means the value of the long position in dollars appreciates to £1.27 by the time it is liquidated, while the short position has risen as a result of accumulated interest on the borrowing to only £1.05, leaving a net profit of £0.22.

Before going on to look at covered interest rate parity from this perspective, there are a number of lessons to be drawn from the computations in Table 3.5.

- It pays to borrow (be short in) a depreciating currency and lend (be long in) an appreciating currency.[9]

- Since speculation can be achieved by an agent who actually owns no sterling, UIRP does not need to rely on the existence of UK depositors with international perspectives and an inexhaustible supply of funds. In fact, the representative investor/arbitrageur need be neither a UK nor a US resident. Typically, in fact, the agent in question will be a multinational financial institution based in London or New York or one of the major currency trading centres of continental Europe or the Pacific Basin.

- Currency risk arises whenever an investor's net position in a currency is non-zero. When a long position is matched by an equal and opposite short position in the same currency, the investor is said to have a (fully) hedged or covered position in the currency.

Consider hedging the arbitrage in the present example. We saw in the last section that this can be achieved by the simple expedient of selling the dollar proceeds of the US deposit on the forward market on 1 January. The impact on the investor's asset position is traced out in Table 3.6.

The otherwise unbalanced position at the start of the year that introduced the element of risk into the US strategy disappears, because the investor who covers in the forward market has zero net exposure throughout the year. This outcome is achieved as a result of the fact that the forward contract can be viewed as involving two simultaneous transactions: a claim against the counterparty to collect pounds (hence, a long position in sterling) and a commitment to deliver dollars (a short position in dollars). Together, the two transactions undertaken in signing the forward contract offset precisely the initial short position in pounds and long in dollars that arose when the investor borrowed sterling to deposit in the USA. We can therefore add the following conclusions to those we have already deduced in this section:

Table 3.6 Covered interest rate arbitrage with borrowing

	UK strategy		US strategy	
	Action	*Yield*	*Action*	*Yield*
1 January				
12-month interest rate		5%		6%
Position taken	Borrow short sterling (£1.00)	£1.00	Borrow short sterling (£1.00)	£1.00
			Buy $ @ £0.50 each:	$2.00
Position taken	Place on deposit: i.e. lend long sterling (£1.00)	£1.00	Place on deposit: i.e. lend long dollars ($2.00)	$2.00
			Sell $/buy £ forward @ $1.00 = £0.60	$0.60
Position taken			Long sterling (£1.00) Short dollars ($2.00)	
Net position during year	**Nil (long − short = 0)**		**nil (long − short = 0)**	
31 December				
	Liquidate deposit:	£1.05	Liquidate deposit:	$2.12
			Sell $ @ £0.60 each:	£1.27
	Repay loan:	£1.05	Repay loan:	£1.05
Net profit		**£0.00**		**£0.22**

> A forward sale of x dollars against y pounds (a forward purchase of y pounds with x dollars) is equivalent to lending (being long in) the present value of y pounds and borrowing (being short in) the present value of x dollars.[10]

Seen from this point of view, the CIRP relationship between spot and forward exchange rates and interest rates is less surprising. The commitment to exchanging future claims (borrowing and lending) in the two currencies via the forward market must result in the same payoff as exchanging current claims in the spot market. Hence, any difference in the exchange rate at which the two transactions occur must reflect differences in the interest rates on the two currencies.

Putting the matter in hedging terms, the proceeds of the dollar deposit could be hedged without recourse to the forward market by borrowing $2 at the start of the year, converting to sterling on the spot and leaving the £1 on deposit for 12 months. At the end of December, the £1 will have grown to £1.05 – just enough to repay the initial loan – and the $2 borrowing on which $2.12 will be owed can be repaid from the original deposit in the USA.

Clearly, however, what is being described here involves no more than putting the original borrowing/lending mix into reverse, thereby *unwinding* the original position so as to eliminate the risk. It so happens that the type of exchange of claims described here is very common in currency markets, under the following guise:

> A **(plain) currency swap deal** involves two parties in the exchange of principal and interest payments on a loan in one currency for principal and interest payments in another currency.[11]

3.4 Covered interest rate parity – the facts

In the previous three sections, the covered and uncovered interest rate parity conditions were derived by identical routes, using the same examples modified very slightly. In formal terms, the results were, not surprisingly, very similar, as you can see from Equations 3.4 and 3.9. However convenient it may be to approach the two relationships in parallel, as we have done here, it is important to emphasize the differences as well as the similarities between covered and uncovered parity. In this section, we shall compare them and, in the process, have a first encounter with the important concept of market efficiency.

The first thing to notice is that the covered parity condition is unlike most of the relationships in elementary economics, in so far as it relies on very few assumptions about the behaviour or tastes of the agents operating in the market. We do not require that agents maximize utility, we make no assumptions about how they form expectations and, as already noted, since the transactions involved are riskless, we need say nothing about their attitude to risk. All that is required for covered interest rate parity to hold is that three rather weak (and, to some extent, overlapping) conditions apply.

First, there must be sufficient speculation funds available – in other words, one or more potential arbitrageurs with access to enough free resources to drive the respective rates into equilibrium. By 'free', we mean not only liquid, in the normal domestic sense of the term, but also unconstrained by restrictions on international capital movements.

Second, we need the foreign exchange markets, spot or forward, to be organized, with well-defined and well-publicized rates freely available to a group of informed traders who are committed to exploiting any profit opportunities that crop up. In fact, these conditions are almost certainly fulfilled in the markets for the main hard currencies, where a number of financial institutions and specialist foreign exchange traders, as well as the treasury departments of multinational companies, make it their business to watch for profit opportunities that appear temporarily on the banks of visual display units in their trading rooms.[12]

Third, we need it to be true that transaction costs are low enough to be negligible. Otherwise, the possibility arises that rates may deviate from CIRP to the full extent of trading costs. Again there is every reason to suppose that, in this type of highly competitive environment, dealing costs will be extremely small, particularly for the large, professional participants responsible for most of the trading – which is why we have ignored them so far in our theoretical treatment.

None the less, if we wish to proceed to examine the evidence on interest rate parity, we cannot continue to neglect the issue of transaction costs altogether. In fact, as far as covered interest rate parity is concerned, most researchers interpret the question to be investigated as follows: has the gap between international interest rate differentials and the respective forward premium been within the bounds one would expect to find, given the size of dealing costs?

In other words, where (as is usually the case) Equation 3.5 does not hold precisely, is the difference between the left- and right-hand sides of the equation too small to represent an unexploited profit opportunity, after allowing for transaction costs? In formal terms, the question is whether the following inequality is satisfied:

$$\left| (1+r) - (1+r^*)\frac{F}{S} \right| < c \tag{3.10}$$

where c is the cost of carrying out the transaction, and the left-hand side is the absolute value (that is, ignoring the sign) of the gap between UK and US interest rates, adjusted for the forward premium.

The key question, then, relates to the scale of the relevant dealing costs. Estimating costs might appear to be a simple task. In practice, there are a number of complications. For example, do we restrict our attention to arbitrage using own (that is, unborrowed) funds, or do we also consider the transaction costs of borrowing in the UK in order to lend in the USA, when US interest rates are above their forward parity level?[13]

Fortunately, differences over the measurement of transaction costs have not prevented a fair measure of agreement emerging on this issue. In a major study of the subject, Levich (1979) concluded that:

> Overall, the evidence supports the view that . . . there are few unexploited opportunities for risk-free profit in covered interest arbitrage.
>
> (Levich, 1979b, p. 49)

The evidence to which Levich refers relates to the years 1962–75, a period of broadly fixed exchange rates, and certainly very different from the environment of the 1980s and 1990s. If anything, the progressive liberalization of international financial markets in recent years is likely to have tied interest rates even more closely together. Indeed, in cases where interest rates have deviated from CIRP during the 1960s and 1970s, there seems every reason to suppose the cause to have been exchange controls, actual or threatened.[14]

3.5 Efficient markets – a first encounter

If CIRP seems to fit the facts reasonably closely, what of UIRP? It might appear that we can proceed directly to an examination of the evidence in support of this condition too. Unfortunately, there is an immediate obstacle to this approach. Look back at Equation 3.4 and ask yourself the question: are all the variables observable? The answer is plainly no. The expected rate of depreciation is certainly not an observable variable – expectations are not easily quantified, and they are in any case inherently subjective.

This is not to say that there are no assumptions one could make about the nature of market expectations – there are any number of superficially plausible guesses one might make about how agents forecast exchange rate movements. For example, one might formulate a hypothesis that the market always expects the same rate of depreciation in any period as it experienced in the previous period. Or, by contrast, one might postulate that it always expects any change in the rate to be reversed in the next trading session, or that it expects an outcome that is some kind of moving average of the outcomes for the past three days, or five days or three months; or instead of any of these mechanistic rules, one might hypothesize that, as a (very) rough approximation, the market always guesses correctly what the actual change in the exchange rate will be.

Any assumption that allows us to substitute an observable, quantifiable data series for the term Δs^e in Equation 3.4 will serve to extricate us from the impasse of not being able to test the UIRP condition; this is subject to one major drawback, however, which we shall henceforth refer to as the *joint hypothesis problem*. To understand the nature of the difficulty, consider a simple example. Suppose we made the rough and ready assumption that the market always expects the existing exchange rate to stay unchanged over the next period, in other words assume (*temporarily*) that $\Delta s^e = 0$. Looking back at the UIRP condition, Equation 3.4, we would have in that case:

$$r = r^* \tag{3.11}$$

If, relying on this assumption, we then examined the two interest rate series and found there were apparently significant deviations between the UK and US rates, could we then conclude that UIRP was not supported by the facts? Obviously not – the failure of the data to accord with Equation 3.11 could be explained *either* by the fact that UIRP does not hold *or* that our assumption about how market expectations are formed is at fault, *or both*. In other words, we would be simultaneously testing a theory about the relationship between observable variables (interest rates) and a theory about how the market arrives at its predictions or expectations. That is, we would be testing a joint hypothesis.

For this reason, we shall defer any attempt to consider how well the facts accord with uncovered parity until Chapters 11 and 12, by which stage we shall be in a position to take fuller account of expectations, as well as of the determination of the risk premium. For the moment, it is worth simply taking note of the fact that we have made our first encounter with the ubiquitous problem of market expectations.

There is an important link between uncovered and covered interest parity, and it is one that involves the concept of market efficiency. Recall that, in introducing the idea of hedging in the forward market in Section 3.2, the assumption was made that the forward rate on 1 January was equal to the spot rate expected to prevail on 31 December. In order to illustrate what was meant by covered arbitrage, some value for the forward rate had to be assumed, and the expected spot rate was certainly convenient, since it allowed us to use the same numerical examples in both cases.

Look back at the formal analysis in Equations 3.5–3.8. Nothing there required us to have $f = \Delta s^e$ (or $F = S^e$). Covered interest parity could therefore still apply, even if we did not have the forward rate equal to the expected spot rate.

None the less, it is obvious from comparing Equations 3.4 and 3.9 that the condition $f = \Delta s^e$ is far from arbitrary. In fact, since Equations 3.4 and 3.9 together imply that $f = \Delta s^e$, it is obvious that covered and uncovered parity cannot both apply unless we also have equality between the forward rate and the expected spot rate. Putting the matter differently, as long as we continue to assume risk neutrality, if the forward rate is not equal to the expected spot rate, then either covered or uncovered parity has broken down, or both.

Now consider for a moment the situation of an individual market agent who, on 1 January, confidently expects the spot rate at the end of the year to be at a level different from the one currently obtaining for forward foreign currency. Suppose, for example, that the 12-month forward rate is $1.00 = £0.50, and the agent is quite convinced that the rate at the end of the year will be $1.00 = £0.60.

If he is confident in his judgement, he will see himself as having the opportunity to profit by a simple transaction in the forward market. All he need do is buy dollars forward, in other words sign a contract to buy dollars at the end of the year at the current forward price of £0.50 each, which he is so convinced will seem a bargain price on 31 December. If he is correct in his forecast, then 12 months later, when he fulfils his promise under the terms of the forward contract to buy the dollars at £0.50 each,[15] he will be in a position to resell them immediately at the end-of-year price prevailing in the spot market, £0.60 each – a profit of £0.10, or 20% per dollar bought.

Of course, this strategy is risky, and so if the investor is not risk-neutral he will require a risk premium to persuade him to undertake the transaction, and £0.10 per dollar may not be sufficient. However, if we maintain the fiction that investors are risk-neutral, we can say that anyone who expects the spot exchange rate at some future period to be different from the forward rate currently quoted for that period can profit by backing his judgement – that is, by speculating.

If we can generalize the argument to the market as a whole, or, in other words, if we can treat the market as if it were a single individual, then it follows that equilibrium will entail a forward rate equal to the consensus view of the future spot rate. Otherwise, there will be a net excess demand or supply of forward exchange, which will itself tend to move the rate towards its equilibrium level. We shall henceforth make use of the following definition to describe this situation:

> **Unbiasedness** applies when the (3-, 6- or 12-) month forward rate is equal to the spot rate that the market expects to see prevailing when the contract in question matures.[16]

What we are talking about here is a particular example of a very general concept indeed: market efficiency.[17] For the moment, we shall take the opportunity to introduce the following definition:

> **Efficient markets** are ones where prices fully reflect all the available information. There are, therefore, no unexploited opportunities for profit.

The definition seems a little vague, and, in a sense, so it should. What are we to understand by 'fully reflect' all information? That depends on the model of the market in question, and its properties. By contrast, unbiasedness is a very clearly defined state and is in that sense a special case of market efficiency. Unbiasedness implicitly assumes a particular market model, where the following conditions apply:

- There are an adequate number of well-funded and well-informed agents in the currency markets, with broadly similar views about likely future developments.[18] Market prices are well-defined.

- There are no barriers to trade in the markets (that is, no exchange controls) and no costs to dealing (no transaction costs).

- Investors are risk neutral.

3.6 Purchasing power parity revisited*

We can now take the opportunity to tie up a loose end from the previous chapter relating to the link between IRP and PPP. However, since the link is via another parity relationship, we need first to deal with the analysis of how inflation impinges on interest rates in the domestic economy.

3.6.1 Real interest rates and the Fisher equation

We start with an apparent digression on the mechanism underlying individual savings decisions. Our initial standpoint is that of an individual economic agent in the setting of his domestic market making a choice, again involving two periods – the present and next year. In this stylized market, claims[19] to future consumption baskets are exchanged for an identical basket for immediate consumption, in a ratio that reflects demand and supply at each date, now (period 0) and next year (period 1). The question we consider is: how much should the individual consume this period, and how much consumption should he be willing to defer to next year? In other words, what determines the willingness to save?

In its most basic form, this simple question in applied consumer choice theory was settled by Irving Fisher in the early twentieth century. The analysis shows that, subject to the standard assumptions of elementary choice theory,[20] and in particular assuming that prices are constant, the consumer will select a consumption-savings pattern that is determined, other things being equal, by the rate at which the market allows him to exchange consumption between the two periods. Other things being equal, the greater the future sacrifice required per unit of present consumption, the less he will choose to consume this period and the more next. The critical ratio[21] is the number of units of future consumption offered in the market in exchange for a unit of current consumption, which will be denoted by $(1 + R)$. For example, if at some point in time R is 5%, market conditions mean consumers have to sacrifice 1.05 units of consumption next year, in period 1, in order to secure an extra unit for immediate consumption. R is therefore the market premium current consumption commands over future consumption. (Notice that we can be more or less certain that R is always positive.)

By now, it should be clear that R is actually an interest rate – in fact, the *real interest rate*. It is real precisely because it is measured in units of consumption.

To appreciate the importance of inflation, or its absence, consider how R is determined. Plainly, as usual in these models, the market price is the outcome of aggregating the choices of consumers as a whole.[22] If R is 5%, then it follows that it is possible to satisfy borrowers in aggregate only if savers are offered the reward of a standard of living 5% higher next year to compensate for the sacrifice required of them this year. If R were lower than 5%, then there would be insufficient goods available for current consumption, i.e. unsatisfied borrowers, because of an inadequate flow of savings. If R were higher than 5%, then there would be too great a supply of 'sacrifice', i.e. an excess demand for future consumption and excess supply of current consumption by unsatisfied savers only too happy to defer satisfaction until next year.

Now consider how this constant-price scenario would be affected by inflation at the rate of, say, 3% per annum. The answer is not entirely straightforward, because there can be no inflation without money, and so far there has been no money in the analysis. Inflation is by definition a rise in the price of goods relative to money, whereas the only price that matters in this model is the price of period 0 goods in terms of period 1 goods. (Since the whole analysis is in terms of physical units of consumption, it is often described as a barter model.)

However, since R is determined by the preferences of individuals, there is no reason to expect it to change simply because prices rise (or fall) – unless preferences are actually affected in some way by the money units in which consumption is measured. We shall assume here that people are immune to this particular form of irrationality, known as *money-illusion*. In other words, we take for granted that agents are ultimately concerned only with their access to real goods and services, and not with the number or denomination of the banknotes involved in transactions.[23]

In order to cope with the introduction of inflation, imagine that what changes hands between borrowers and savers in the market is not consumption goods directly, but claims on goods – in other words, some form of money, e.g. pounds. The sum of money, £P_0, buys a unit of current consumption, while £P_1 buys a unit of consumption one year from today, at period 1. How much of a premium per pound will savers need to be promised at period 1 in order to persuade them to sacrifice sufficient current consumption to satisfy borrowers? In other words, how many more pounds will they need to be offered in order to keep their behaviour unchanged? In physical terms, the answer remains the same: 5% more consumption, because, as has been explained already, there is no reason for the 'exchange rate' between current and future goods to have moved up or down. But the key point is that, however many pounds were required to buy 1.05 units of consumption next year when we were assuming zero inflation, the number of pounds required in the presence of inflation will be greater by 3%. This is the case because, if P_1 is 3% greater than P, equilibrium requires an exchange ratio of $1.05 \times 1.03 = 1.0815$. In other words, the premium on current consumption in money terms, known as the *nominal interest rate*, must be the product of 1 plus the real rate and 1 plus the inflation rate:

$$1 + r = (1 + R)(1 + dp) \tag{3.12}$$

where dp denotes the inflation rate[24] over the year: $(P_1 - P)/P$. Again, unless the inflation rate is extremely high,[25] we can simplify the relationship to:

$$r = R + dp \tag{3.13}$$

which means that in the numerical example, the equilibrium nominal interest rate is approximately 5% + 3% = 8%.

There is, however, one important modification needed to make the hypothesis realistic. In the light of what has been said in the earlier sections of this chapter, the reader should not need convincing that the inflation rate in Equation 3.13 ought to be replaced by the *expected* inflation rate, since in practice the future price level, P_1, is unknown and unknowable in the current period when the consumption-saving decision has to be made. So the Fisher equation, as it is known to economists, can be written:

$$r = R + dp^e \tag{3.14}$$

which says that the nominal interest rate – the only one we actually observe directly – is the sum of the real interest rate and the market consensus expected inflation rate.[26]

Notice that although the Fisher equation is supported by an undeniable logic, its empirical validity is impossible to ascertain, because attempts to test it against the facts run headlong into the joint hypothesis problem in its most acute form. Both the right-hand side variables in Equation 3.14 are usually unobservable. Survey data have on occasion been used as a measure of expected inflation, though they are often unsatisfactory for the purpose,[27] and there are few direct measures of the real rate.[28] None the less, and perhaps because, unlike PPP, it is so difficult to refute, the Fisher equation tends to be accepted by default in economics.

3.6.2 Purchasing power parity and the real exchange rate

This brings the digression to an end. To see why it was worthwhile, suppose Equation 3.14 applies to the domestic economy, while a similar Fisher equation applies to the foreign country:

$$r^* = R^* + dp^{*e} \tag{3.14'}$$

Notice we are allowing for the possibility that any or all of the variables are different in the foreign country. Clearly Equations 3.14 and 3.14' imply that the interest rate differential is given by:

$$r - r^* = (R - R^*) + (dp^e - dp^{*e}) \tag{3.15}$$

But unless there is something to prevent arbitrage between the securities markets of the two countries, we know from UIRP in Equation 3.4 that, with risk neutrality, the observed or nominal interest rate differential on the left-hand side of Equation 3.15 is equal to the expected rate of depreciation. It follows that:

$$ds^e = (R - R^*) + (dp^e - dp^{*e}) \tag{3.16}$$

which tells us that the rate of depreciation of, say, the dollar against the pound over any time period (e.g. one year) is the sum of the difference between UK and US *real* interest rates for one-year loans and the difference between UK and US inflation rates during the 12 months.

Now consider the real interest differential. Suppose, given my (and the market's) expectations with regard to inflation rates in the UK and USA, I believe the real interest rate to be higher in America. If I can possibly capture the higher real rate in the USA by lending to American borrowers (buying US securities, etc.), I will do so.

The opposite will be the case if I believe that real rates are higher in Britain, i.e. if $R > R^*$. These statements can be made with confidence because, as we have seen, for risk-neutral agents real rates are the ultimate determinants of savings behaviour, since they measure the reward for saving in the ultimate currency: real consumption units or standard of living.

This argument can lead to only one conclusion. In the absence of barriers to cross-border capital movements, real rates should be the same in both countries, so that $R = R^*$ and we are left with the proposition that:

$$ds^e = dp^e - dp^{*e} \tag{3.17}$$

This is sometimes called PPP in expectations. Its implications are straightforward. It says that PPP applies not to actual exchange rates and relative inflation rates but to the market's *expectations* of these variables. According to this view, PPP is a relationship between unobservables, rather than observables, so that any apparent failure to fit the facts can always be interpreted as the outcome of using the wrong measure (or model) of the expected rate of depreciation on the one hand or the expected inflation differential on the other.

Note that we can rewrite Equation 3.17 in terms of the (log of the) expected real exchange rate. By definition, since $d(\log Q) = dq = ds + dp - dp^*$, Equation 3.17 implies

$$dq^e = 0 \tag{3.18}$$

so that the change in the expected real exchange rate is zero, or q is expected to remain constant. In time series terms, Equation 3.18 obviously means that:[29]

$$q_{t+1}^e = q_t \tag{3.19}$$

so the typical agent in the market expects tomorrow's real exchange rate to be the same as today's. This conclusion is more dramatic than it might look at first glance.[30]

In terms of time series statistics, there is a whole class of models consistent with Equation 3.19, in particular the so-called random walk process mentioned in Section 2.7. This argument persuaded a number of researchers that the apparently random nature of the real exchange rate movements they observed was not such a gloomy conclusion after all, but simply a consequence of UIRP on the one hand and real interest rate parity on the other. An alternative rationalization of Equations 3.17 and 3.19 would be to say that if trade in goods takes time, then arbitrageurs will operate not on the basis of actual price differentials but on the basis of their forecasts of price differentials when they complete their trades.

There are two apparent weaknesses in this argument. First, deviations from PPP have far too long a life to be rationalized in this way. As we have seen, recent research suggests a half-life of three or four years, which is long even by the standards of physical capital, let alone consumption goods. Second, for reasons too far removed from the subject of this book to be covered here, real interest rates are likely to be determined by more than simply consumer tastes, such as the return on capital in each country, and all the many factors that affect it.[31] The process by which real interest rates are equated is therefore likely to be more complex than is suggested here, and almost certainly anything but instantaneous. In fact, it is not at all obvious that it will be any faster in practice than the process of arbitrage in the goods market, and it may be substantially slower.

Finally, it is to be hoped that by this stage the relationship between IRP, PPP and the Fisher equation is clear in one respect at least. Suppose, as a benchmark case, all economic agents know the future price levels in the two countries and next year's exchange rate with absolute accuracy. Then, in this unlikely scenario, the two Fisher equations mean we can replace Equation 3.15 with:

$$r - r^* = (R - R^*) + (dp - dp^*) \tag{3.20}$$

and using UIRP (for this reason often called the open Fisher equation) gives, in place of Equation 3.16:

$$ds = (R - R^*) + (dp - dp^*) \tag{3.21}$$

or:

$$dq = R - R^* \tag{3.22}$$

from which we can see that movements in the real exchange rate reflect changes in the real interest rate differential. If we are happy to rely on real interest rates being driven into equality by the international capital markets, then we can go one stage further and say that the real exchange rate must be constant – that is, PPP must apply. In other words, we conclude with the following theorem: *in a world where (i) expectations are correct, (ii) each country has the same real interest rate and (iii) agents are risk-neutral, any two of the following relationships implies the third: the Fisher equation, UIRP and PPP.*

Summary

- If we consider the typical investor faced with the choice between holding a dollar deposit in America or a deposit in pounds in Britain, what will concern him will be the difference between UK and US interest rates, after allowing for any expected change in the exchange rate over the period of the deposit – the *uncovered interest differential*.

- If investors are *risk-neutral*, and all share broadly the same expectations, equilibrium will require that the uncovered differential be zero; that is, that the gap between UK and US interest rates be *just equal* to the consensus view of the likely change in the exchange rate over the relevant time period (uncovered interest rate parity). Otherwise, funds will flood out of one of the countries and into the other.

- Since a British investor, for example, can eliminate the currency risk involved in depositing in the USA by the device of contracting to sell the dollar proceeds on the forward market, it follows that riskless profits will accrue to international interest rate arbitrageurs *unless* covered interest rate parity obtains. In other words, the law of one price requires that, in equilibrium, the gap between UK and US interest rates be *just equal* to the difference between the forward and spot exchange rates at the date when the decision is taken (the forward premium or discount).

- If both covered and uncovered parity hold, then it follows that the forward rate must be equal to the market's expectation of the future spot rate. It is possible to list a number of superficially plausible assumptions that would imply just this proposition, even without recourse to interest rate parity conditions.

In any single country, the nominal (or observed) interest rate can be decomposed into the real rate and the expected inflation rate (the Fisher equation). Comparing any two countries, the difference between their nominal interest rates (equal by UIRP to the expected rate of exchange rate depreciation) must reflect the sum of differences between real rates and differences in their inflation rates. If in addition we impose the condition that international real rates are equal, we are left with PPP in terms of expectations. If expectations are always correct, agents are risk-neutral and real rates are indeed driven to equality, then PPP, UIRP and the Fisher equation are not independent relationships, in the sense that any two imply the third.

Reading guide

On the theory of covered interest rate parity, the classic work is Tsiang (1959). More recently, influential work has been that of Aliber (1973), Frenkel and Levich (1975) and Levich (1979a and 1979b). See also Deardorff (1979).

Taylor (1987) on CIRP is meticulous but still easy to read.

For references on UIRP see Chapter 12. The argument in Section 3.6.2 derives from Adler and Lehman (1983) and Roll (1979).

Web page: **www.pearsoned.co.uk/copeland**.

Notes

1 We are using the word 'investor' to denote an institution or individual with wealth available for allocation to one or more forms of asset holding. This is the way that the term is used in business life, and indeed the way that it is used in finance. For the benefit of those who have followed a basic macroeconomics course, however, this is precisely the way the term 'investor' should not be used. In the jargon of macroeconomics, we are concerned here with a 'saver' or with an institution acting on his behalf.

2 We shall discuss the choice as though it involved actually depositing in Britain in pounds or, alternatively, in America in dollars. In practice, it is nowadays quite simple (and legal) for a British citizen to take sterling to a high-street bank anywhere in the UK and ask to open a deposit in US dollars, and similarly for US citizens. For the most part, in doing so, the retail banks are simply acting as intermediaries – channels through which the man in the local high street can have access to another country's money market. In other words, the UK citizen's pounds, when used to open a dollar deposit in a bank somewhere in England, usually end up by one route or another in a New York financial institution – without the Briton either knowing or caring when or how the transfer takes place. However, the doubting reader may work through an imaginary scenario to convince himself that the conclusions reached in this chapter would be unchanged if we dropped the fiction that the respective deposits are made directly in the UK or the USA.

3 It is sufficient to assume simply that the probability of the UK bank defaulting is the same as that for the US bank. In reality, deposits in both countries are guaranteed by the monetary authorities.

4 It would be a useful exercise for the reader to try replicating Tables 3.1–3.4 for the case of a US investor, or possibly for a Japanese investor faced with the choice between depositing in London or New York.

5 In fact, the reader who attempts to check the results in Tables 3.3 and 3.4 – a computer spreadsheet program such as Excel is ideal for the purpose – will find that the results have been fiddled so as to satisfy Equation 3.4. For example, the last figure in Table 3.3 should be £1.26 (2.10 × £0.60) and not £1.25. The difference of one penny is precisely the cross-product term: the rate of depreciation multiplied by the US interest rate: $0.20 \times 5\% = 1p$.

6 For those unfamiliar with this particular piece of jargon, variables endogenous to any relationship are ones that are assumed to be determined by the relationship or model in question. On the other hand, an exogenous variable is one whose value is taken as a datum, because its value is assumed to be determined outside the model – that is, by some other relationship that is beyond the scope of the analysis being undertaken or even, in some cases, beyond the scope of economics altogether.

7 It is on the basis of considerations such as these that some people in the UK and other European countries charged the USA with keeping world interest rates at what they regarded as damagingly high levels in the 1980s. There is, of course, far more than this to the question of whether world interest rates have been too high in recent years and, if so, why. For the most part, the issue lies beyond the scope of this book. However, the point is raised in the text at this point simply to illustrate the relevance of interest rate parity to questions of national and international economic policy.

8 In reality, things are not quite so simple. For a start, forward contracts are usually conducted through foreign currency dealers, who are specialist intermediaries – in other words, who make it their job to match agents who wish to buy a currency forward with those who wish to sell it at the same maturity. Not only will they charge a commission but they will also quote differing rates for buying and selling ('bid' and 'offer' rates). They may also insist on a 'margin' from a would-be buyer of a forward contract – that is, a sum of money up front as a guarantee of the individual's ability to cover any loss on the deal.

   As far as the maturity date is concerned there is no reason in principle why there should not exist a market in forward contracts of all maturities – from one day up to one century. In practice, a high-volume market exists only at maturities of 30 and 90 days, and then only in the major hard currencies.

   Similarly, there is no reason in principle why forward contracts should not be traded in any type of goods or services. In practice, explicit forward contracts exist only across a narrow range of mostly financial assets. None the less, implicit forward prices often play a part even in the most mundane transactions. For example, it is not unusual to see items such as houses and foreign holidays offered at a 'guaranteed' price to buyers willing to commit themselves immediately to a 'forward' contract.

   Note that a forward contract is almost but not quite the same thing as a futures contract.

9 This obvious point applies not only to currencies. For example, where they can, oil companies borrow dollars and promise to repay lenders in crude oil when they expect the (dollar price of) oil to fall on world markets. Similarly, stock market traders aim to be long in shares that rise in price and short in those that fall. They therefore hope to own and/or lend shares about which they feel bullish and borrow those about which they feel bearish.

10 The present value of a cashflow of, say, $5000 arising 12 months from now is that sum that, if deposited immediately, will yield just $5000 with accumulated interest at the end of the year. In other words, it is the value of a future sum of money in terms of its worth at the present time, allowing for the fact that wealth in the future is of less use than wealth here and now and must therefore be discounted to an extent measured by the appropriate interest rate. For present purposes, the interest rate used should be the rate on 12-month deposits in the currency in question, that is US dollars.

11 There are in practice a number of other wrinkles in the details of currency swaps. For example, swaps typically commit the two parties (usually large companies or financial institutions) to exchange interest payments over a number of years. (See the references in the reading guide.)

12 In particular, financial markets are nowadays characterized by a considerable volume of program trading – that is, trading triggered automatically by computers programmed to generate buy or sell orders whenever an arbitrage relationship such as Equation 3.9 is violated.

13 See Section 3.3 of this chapter. A related question concerns which of the alternative routes arbitrageurs choose to take and, in particular, whether they operate on the spot or forward markets. See Deardorff (1979) for a discussion of these and related issues.

14 See Aliber (1973). It is none the less surprising to see that the Bank of England was still reporting a covered differential between interest rates on Eurodollar and UK local authority deposits of up to one-quarter of 1%, and even higher for interbank sterling deposits. The transaction costs on large deposits must surely be far smaller than this.

15 Notice that he cannot back out of the deal. Having taken on the forward contract at the start of the year, he has no choice but to buy the dollars at the specified price, even if, in the event, he turns out to have guessed wrongly (say, if the pound appreciates to $1.00 = £0.40 by 31 December). This is precisely the difference between a forward contract and an option. The advantage of buying an option rather than a forward contract is that it confers the right (the 'option') to deal at the prespecified price, without any obligation (see Chapter 15).

16 This is not quite complete as a definition of unbiasedness. It also ought to be the case that market expectations are, on average, correct predictions of the future spot rate. However, we defer consideration of these questions until Chapter 11.

17 The notion of market efficiency was originally developed by researchers in finance, particularly Eugene Fama. It has become so well established that it nowadays crops up quite frequently in stockmarket commentary in the newspapers. As you will have already noticed, it forms the subject matter of Chapter 11.

18 The vagueness is again intentional. It can be shown that, under certain circumstances, we do not need all market operators to share exactly the same view of the future exchange rate. We can also have some investors better informed than others. Again, these issues are beyond the scope of the discussion at this point.

19 In the spirit of a stylized model, we assume all claims are default-free.

20 See any microeconomics textbook.

21 Which readers with a grounding in basic microeconomics will recognize as being represented by the gradient of the intertemporal budget line.

22 Note that, by assumption, we are dealing with an exchange economy; that is, we concentrate on the consumption-saving choice, to the exclusion of production. In this simplified scenario, supply and demand both arise from the decisions of consumers to consume now or in the future. Market equilibrium simply requires that consumers in aggregate optimally choose to consume the available quantity in each period (the total 'endowment'), so that those who consume less than their endowment (savers) release sufficient resources to satisfy those who wish to consume more than their endowment (dissavers or borrowers).

23 Expressed in this way, the absence of money illusion looks obvious. However, observation of labour markets or, for example, UK experience with indexed state pensions suggests it is anything but a truism.

24 The notation is consistent with that of Section 2.4, because $dp = \log P - \log P_0$ is approximately equal to $(P_1 - P)/P$.

25 The real interest rate will never be very high.

26 In fact, economics has seen decades of debate on the correct formulation and interpretation of the Fisher equation. We ignore most of these issues here, noting only that Equation 3.14 implicitly assumes risk neutrality. With risk aversion, agents may require an inflation risk premium to compensate them for errors in forecasting the future price level.

27 For example, they usually do not match the interest rate horizon, as the theory would require.

28 Indexed government bonds provide a real rate for some countries and time periods, but even they are subject to a number of distorting factors.

29 Strictly, Equation 3.19 requires that Equation 3.18 be reformulated in finite difference terms, but we skip between differential and difference equations here so as to avoid introducing more notation. Notice also that the right-hand side of Equation 3.19 is just plain q_t, on the assumption that the only unknown is next year's real exchange rate. This year's is known, so $q_t^e = q_t$.

30 The reader will find it straightforward to verify that the conclusion is qualitatively unaffected by the introduction of a constant risk premium in UIRP.

31 See any intermediate macroeconomics textbook. Notice these factors were excluded from the analysis in the earlier part of this section by the device of assuming a pure exchange economy.

4 Open economy macroeconomics

Introduction

So far in this part of the book, we have been dealing with international linkages between macroeconomic variables. As such, we have looked at these relationships in isolation – the so-called partial equilibrium approach. In this chapter, we step back from the fine detail to consider the overall context within which open economy relationships operate to determine the exchange rate.

The general equilibrium model here will look familiar to most readers, since it is simply an extension of the closed economy aggregate supply and demand framework found in most modern undergraduate textbooks. Nonetheless, an understanding of this apparatus is essential to what follows in Chapters 5, 6 and 7, when it will be used to present three important models of exchange rate determination.

We start in Section 4.1 with an introduction to the open economy version of the IS–LM model of aggregate demand. It will be seen that, as far as the IS curve is concerned, allowing for the openness of the economy involves introducing an additional shift variable, the real exchange rate. The LM curve needs no modification at all to accommodate a floating exchange rate. With a fixed exchange rate, however, allowance needs to be made for the endogeneity of the money stock, a task undertaken in Sections 4.2.2 and 4.2.3.

The remainder of the chapter is concerned with the aggregate supply curve, in its classical and Keynesian forms. It is assumed here that openness makes no difference to the supply side of the economy model,[1] and so the analysis is identical to that found in macroeconomics texts.

4.1 IS–LM model of aggregate demand

4.1.1 IS curve

In an open economy, the national income identity can be written as follows:

$$y \equiv C + I + G + B \tag{4.1}$$

where y is (real) national income, C and I are expenditure on consumption and investment, respectively, G is net government purchases of goods and services, and B is the surplus on the current account of the balance of payments:

$$B \equiv exports - imports \tag{4.2}$$

that is, the excess of the country's exports over its imports.

If we subtract C, I and B from both sides of Equation 4.1, we have:

$$Savings - I - B \equiv G \tag{4.3}$$

where we have made use of the fact that savings are, by definition, income less consumption.

Now Equation 4.3 is simply an accounting relationship; as it stands, it can tell us nothing about what determines the level of aggregate demand. In order to reach any conclusions about the determination of aggregate demand, we must make some assumptions about what factors actually impinge on the components of aggregate demand.

Start with saving, which, for simplicity's sake, we can identify with the unspent income of the household sector.[2] What kinds of element are likely to have the most significant impact on the household's savings decision? As far as the individual household is concerned, it seems obvious that the higher its income, other things being equal, the more it will save.[3] Aggregating households, then, total private sector saving is likely to depend positively on the (planned) level of economic activity.

However, that is not all. At any given level of income, it seems probable that a rise in the level of interest rates in the economy will stimulate savings. This is likely because when interest rates are high, the incentive to save (or refrain from consuming) is great and vice versa when interest rates are low. In fact, the interest rate can be viewed as the premium set by society on present relative to future consumption. At a zero interest rate, one might expect saving to drop to zero.

Investment spending by the corporate sector[4] will depend on a comparison of the cost of funds for the purchase of equipment and so on with the profits to be expected from the investment. Now although, in practice, this calculation is bound to be hedged in with uncertainties surrounding the prospective cashflows to investment projects, there is one statement that can be made with reasonable confidence: other things being equal, the higher the interest rate in the economy, the greater the cost of capital and, hence, the less likely it is that any given prospective investment will appear profitable to the decisionmaker. In general, therefore, aggregate investment will vary inversely with the interest rate.

Notice that we have concluded that savings will increase as interest rates rise, while investment falls, so that the difference (savings less investment) will be *related positively* to interest rates.

Government spending will be taken as exogenously given – determined outside the model by factors (political, social, technological, and so on) beyond the scope of a mere economist. That is not to say we assume it never changes. On the contrary, we shall be very much concerned with analysing the effect of a change in fiscal policy. We are only saying that we shall not be concerned with questions of *why* or *how* fiscal expenditure changes.

Finally, but most important of all for present purposes, we come to the current account of the balance of payments. What are likely to be the main influences here? Among the many factors that affect the demand by UK residents for other countries' products and, conversely, the demand by foreigners for goods from Britain, there is almost certain to be one overriding consideration: the competitiveness of domestic relative to foreign output.

In a way, the issue is one that has already been covered in Chapter 2, where the PPP hypothesis was discussed, compared with the facts and appeared to fail. It was concluded there that, whether because of deficiencies in the way that price indices are calculated, because different countries produce different goods or because of the failure of the law of one price, PPP did not apply other than in the very long run. At the same time, it was also argued that it would be grossly implausible to go to the opposite extreme of supposing trade volumes to be completely unaffected by relative prices.

Consider a compromise to take account of the obvious fact that, invariably, the composition of one country's exports differs from that of another, so that country A's exports are only an imperfect substitute for those of country B. For example, the UK exports relatively little in the way of agricultural products, whereas a significant proportion of US exports consist of wheat, rice, soya beans, fruit, and so on, and thus cannot be said to compete with UK output.

Moreover, as was pointed out in Chapter 2, even where similar types of good are concerned, product differentiation means that direct, head-on competition in international trade is quite rare: a Cadillac is by no means a perfect substitute for a Jaguar, and neither is Bourbon for Scotch. Even where international trade in services is concerned, *Dallas* is not the same soap opera as *Coronation Street* or Disneyworld the same kind of attraction as Tower Bridge.

The conclusion reached in Chapter 2 was that indirect international competition between imperfect substitutes would mean that PPP would not necessarily be obtained as an equality at all times, but that, instead, *there would be an equilibrium price ratio fixed by the market at any moment*. In other words, there is an equilibrium relationship between the price of Bourbon and the price of Scotch, which is not necessarily one of equality. It might be, for example, that one bottle of Scotch equals one and a half bottles of Bourbon. If the price of Scotch were to rise to double that of Bourbon, then consumers in both countries would switch in increasing numbers to Bourbon.

What this implies for price levels in general is that it is relative competitiveness, that is, the *real exchange rate*:

$$Q \equiv \frac{SP^*}{P}$$

that determines the state of a country's current account. Recall that the numerator of Q is the price of foreign- (that is, US-) produced goods, measured in pounds. The greater Q is, therefore, the more competitive is domestic output. It follows that, *at higher levels of Q,* the *current account surplus is likely to be greater or the deficit smaller than at low levels.*

There is one other macroeconomic factor likely to influence the current account balance. Just as consumption of domestically produced goods and services rises with national income, the same is bound to be true of expenditure on imports, at a rate determined by the country's *marginal propensity to import.* The higher the income, the smaller is likely to be the surplus (or greater the deficit) on external trade, *other things being equal* – in other words, at any given real exchange rate. Notice that symmetry requires *our* (UK) exports to be greater when *their* (US) national income is higher, so that our external balance depends on the level of economic activity in the USA – which is one of the major channels through which booms and slumps spread from one country to its trading partners. However, since US national income is very much exogenous to a model of the UK economy, we ignore this relationship here.

We now look back at Equation 4.3 and incorporate our conclusions about how the components of aggregate demand are determined. To keep the analysis simple, suppose the relationship takes the following simple form:

$$by + zr - hQ = G_0 \qquad\qquad (4.4)$$

where b, z and h are behavioural parameters, the coefficients of the unknowns in the equation and are all positive. The first term on the left-hand side summarizes the dependence of savings and imports on the level of economic activity, the second incorporates the positive relationship between interest rates and the private sector's saving net of its investment, and the third represents the current account as a function of the real exchange rate. On the right-hand side is the exogenous policy variable, G, fixed initially at the level G_0.

Now Equation 4.4 represents the equilibrium condition in the goods market. In other words, it shows the relationship that must hold between the three variables, y, r and Q, for there to be no excess demand for goods and services.

We shall proceed by taking a given value of Q, say Q_0, allowing us to rewrite the equation as follows:

$$by + zr = G_0 + hQ_0 \qquad\qquad (4.5)$$

which reduces it to a relationship between y and r, for the given values of G and Q on the right-hand side.

Obviously, there are an infinite number of possible combinations of y and r that satisfy Equation 4.5. Consider plotting them on a graph, with r on the vertical axis and y on the horizontal.

Start by picking any arbitrary value for the interest rate, say r_0 (Figure 4.1), and ask yourself the question: at that level of the interest rate, what would have to be the level of national income if we were to have equilibrium in the product market? The answer is, of course, given by the value of y that solves Equation 4.5, when r takes the value r_0. If that value is y_0, then the combination (r_0, y_0) at the point A in Figure 4.1 is the first point we have found on the curve that we set out to plot. In other words, one possible solution of Equation 4.5 is given by:

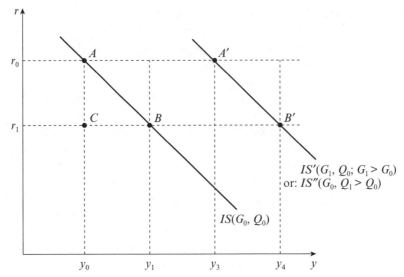

Figure 4.1 The IS curve

$$by_0 + zr_0 = G_0 + hQ_0 \tag{4.5a}$$

To generate more points on the curve, we simply repeat the process, starting from a different interest rate, say r_1, lower than r_0. Now, at r_1, the term zr_1 will be smaller (remember that z is positive, as are all the parameters) so, at the previous value of y (that is, y_0), the left-hand side of Equation 4.5 will be smaller than before and hence smaller than the right-hand side. In terms of the economics, at the lower interest rate, the volume of saving will be smaller and the volume of investment spending greater than at A. Therefore, since A was an equilibrium, with saving net of investment just sufficient to finance the given deficits in the public and external trade sectors of the economy (as in Equation 4.3), net saving must be inadequate at the point C. In other words, there must be an excess demand for goods and services. The crucial point is that the *additional savings will only be forthcoming if the level of national income is greater than y_0, say, y_1*. B will be the next point on our locus of solutions to Equation 4.5 if it happens to be the case that by_1 is just great enough to offset the impact of the lower value of zr (that is, zr_1), so as to leave the left-hand side unchanged. In that case, y_1 will be the level of economic activity that stimulates a flow of savings sufficient to offset the otherwise reduced level of net saving associated with the lower interest rate, so that Equation 4.5 is satisfied at point B by:

$$by_1 + zr_1 = G_0 + hQ_0 \tag{4.5b}$$

We see from this argument that the curve we are plotting, which is universally known as the IS curve, will be downward-sloping, always associating lower levels of the interest rate with higher levels of y.

Note, however, that the exercise we have just undertaken involved seeking solutions of Equation 4.5, for a *given value* of the right-hand side of the equation $G_0 + hQ_0$. For this reason, we have taken care to label the IS curve with the values of G and Q to which it relates. Obviously, an increase in net government spending, G, would make this term larger. So also would a rise in the real exchange rate, Q (that is, a real devaluation), since, as we have already seen, h will be positive, reflecting the fact that the UK current account will have a larger surplus (or smaller deficit) the more competitive are British prices relative to those of the USA. Conversely, a lower value of Q will reduce the right-hand side of Equation 4.5, by making UK output less competitive.

Now consider the effect of an increase in the right-hand side of Equation 4.5 on the solution values for r and y. For example, go back to the interest rate r_0 and repeat the question: what would the value of y have to be were we to have equilibrium in the product market at this interest rate, now that the right-hand side of Equation 4.5 has increased? With a larger right-hand side, the left-hand side of the equation will need to be greater than before. In other words, where previously we saw that y_0 was the answer to our question, making the left-hand side into $by_0 + zr_0$, we must now have a greater value of y, say y_3. Similarly, when the interest rate is at the lower level, r_1, equilibrium now requires y_4 instead of y_1.

The logic of these conclusions is easy to follow. The right-hand side of Equation 4.5 is the sum of the public sector deficit and the foreign sector surplus. This represents the total finance required out of net saving by the domestic private sector. An increase in that requirement can be satisfied only by a change in y and/or r that serves to increase net savings in the economy. The change could be a rise in y, stimulating greater saving by households, or a rise in r, which would have the same effect but which would also cause a fall in investment by the corporate sector or a rise in both.

We conclude that the IS curve will shift to the right whenever there is any change that increases the right-hand side of Equation 4.5, whether a rise in net government spending, G, or an improvement in UK competitiveness (increase in Q).

Before proceeding, we summarize our conclusions about the open economy IS curve.

- The (open economy) IS curve is a downward-sloping line joining all combinations of the interest rate and the level of income, such that the flow of net savings is sufficient to cover the total financing requirements of the public and foreign sectors.

- It is drawn for given values of net government spending, G, and the real exchange rate, Q. Any increase in either G or Q or both will shift the IS curve outwards.

4.1.2 Money market

We now turn to a consideration of the conditions necessary for equilibrium in the money market. Before we go ahead, however, there is an important question to be settled: what do economists mean by the term 'money'?

The problem arises from the fact that 'money' is another of those words such as 'demand', 'supply', 'scarce' and a number of others used both by economists to mean something very precise and by non-economists to refer vaguely to something rather imprecise. Readers who are unfamiliar with the distinction will find it difficult to understand what is meant by concepts such as the 'demand for money', because in laymen's terms money is often a mere synonym for wealth or even, on occasion, for income.

From now on, we shall restrict ourselves to using the word in the way that economists do:

> **Money** refers to the asset or assets that are commonly used as a means of payment.

In other words, money is the name given to the assets used to finance transactions such as to pay for goods and services, to discharge debts and to make loans.

There are a number of things to notice about this definition. In the first place, nothing has been said about which assets actually *are* used as a means of payment, for the simple reason that this will vary from country to country and from one period to another. In medieval Europe, for example, gold and silver were the only widely accepted means of payment. Nowadays, at least in industrialized countries, transactions are conducted using either coins or banknotes or, most frequently, by cheque or electronic funds transferred directly between bank accounts.[5] In the last case, it is the actual bank deposits that serve as the means of payment.

Notice also that this definition does not exclude the possibility that money assets may have other important properties, in addition to their usefulness as means of payment. Typically, money will also serve, to some extent at least, as a store of value, particularly in situations where short-term considerations are paramount. However, this feature of money is, of course, one it shares with all other assets (this is precisely what we mean by the word 'asset'), and so it can hardly be used to distinguish money from non-money assets. In fact, money is a small part of total wealth, both for typical individuals and for the economy as a whole.

In the context of wealth in general, it is not only the case that money has, to some extent at least, the same property as other assets – that is, its usefulness as a store of value. The opposite is also true: other assets may to a greater or lesser degree share the essential characteristic of monetary assets, functioning as a means of payment. Obviously, some assets (for example, real estate, capital equipment, and so on) are virtually useless for conducting transactions. On the other hand, many short-term financial assets other than bank current account deposits are so easily realized, so 'liquid', as to be strong candidates for inclusion in the definition of money – for example, deposits in building societies (savings and loan associations in the USA) and time deposits in banks.

Not surprisingly, a number of different operational definitions of money can be and have been used in practice: the narrowest, known as $M0$, or the monetary base, is currency in circulation, $M1$, which is simply $M0$ plus demand deposits, and, broader still, $M3$, which includes time deposits, and $M4$ more recently in the UK, which adds deposits in building societies as well as some wholesale deposit instruments.[6] How far one should stretch the definition of money to embrace near-money assets is essentially an empirical question and not one that is directly relevant to the subject of exchange rate determination. None the less, in so far as the reader may, on occasion, find it a help in understanding what follows, it is worth specifying more or less arbitrarily a particular measure of the money stock. That being the case, it is suggested that all statements in this book about the demand for or supply of money be interpreted as relating to the total of currency in circulation plus demand deposits ($M1$ in the official statistics) unless otherwise specified.

Demand for money

Perhaps no subject in macroeconomics has received as much attention from researchers as the demand for money, and so what follows can only be a greatly simplified overview of this vast literature. (See the reading guide for further references.)

Start with the following fundamental (and deceptively simple) question: why do people hold money? Why not hold all one's wealth in the form of other, non-money assets? Remember that currency earns no interest at all and neither, until very recently, did cheque accounts.[7]

The answer obviously relates to the special qualities of money already mentioned. Other assets can be used to execute payments, but nowhere near as easily as money. No other asset can offer as attractive a collection of characteristics as money: near-universal acceptability, portability, storability. Money as an asset is easily realized (that is, converted into other assets) and its value, although variable, is usually a lot easier to assess than it is for other assets, with the result that the transaction costs of using money are lower than for other assets. In general, to use an expression that summarizes all these features, we say that money is the most *liquid* of all assets.

It follows that, in holding a proportion of their wealth in the form of money, people are able to enjoy the advantage of liquidity. The greater their money balances, the more of this intangible, immeasurable, but very real benefit they enjoy. The less they hold, the more frequently they have to realize other assets such as stocks or bonds, life insurance policies, real estate, and so forth, in order to pay for transactions.

We can state, then, with complete confidence that *liquidity is always an inherently desirable property*. The statement is virtually a truism. Why then do people ever choose to hold illiquid assets? Why not hold all wealth in its most liquid form – money?

The obvious answer is that non-money assets offer a counterattraction to the liquidity of money. In exchange for the sacrifice of liquidity, non-money assets offer as compensation a return, which appears in a number of different guises: interest (on savings deposits, for example), yield (on bonds), dividend and, possibly, capital gain (on shares), rent (on property), and so on. Sometimes the reward for illiquidity is completely intangible – like the psychological benefit in the peace of mind given by risk insurance or the satisfaction of owning a prestige make of motor car. In other cases, it may be an 'own' return, such as the benefit of having a roof over one's head, which is part of the return on house ownership, or the cooling services yielded by an air conditioner. In the case of physical assets, the returns are often part pecuniary, part non-pecuniary. A painting hanging in one's home, for example, may yield an intangible return every time one sees it. It may also yield a capital gain when sold. Similarly, a house may yield pecuniary and/or non-pecuniary benefits.

Note that since there is a rental market for houses and for many consumer durables, it is possible to put a reasonably accurate value on the services they yield simply by seeing how much people are willing to pay in order to rent them.

In general, then, illiquidity is rewarded by the return on an asset. There is another way of putting the same point: liquidity involves sacrificing the return that could have been earned by holding a less liquid asset. In particular, holding money means sacrificing the return that could be earned on non-money assets. In the jargon of monetary economics:

The **opportunity cost of holding money**[8] is the return that could have been earned by holding a asset less liquid than money.

Notice that, in principle at least, there are as many possible measures of the opportunity cost as there are non-money assets. In particular, in an open economy context, the alternatives may include foreign securities or currency, as we shall see in Chapters 8 and 9.

We can now see the broad outline of how the demand for money mechanism works. On the one hand, economic agents need a stock of money balances in order to transact efficiently. The more transactions they want to conduct, the more money they would like to hold, other things being equal. On the other hand, holding one's wealth in the form of money involves a sacrifice, in the form of a forgone return. The choice as to how much money to hold involves a trade-off between the benefit in terms of transactions convenience and the opportunity cost.

So we have a theory stating that, broadly speaking, the demand for money will be greater the larger the volume of transactions and will be smaller the higher the return on non-money assets. All that remains at this stage is to make the theory operational by specifying, if possible, observable macroeconomic variables to act as indicators of the volume of transactions and of the opportunity cost.

Take the volume of transactions first. A transaction, for present purposes, is any activity where money normally changes hands – either in exchange for goods and services or in exchange for repayment at a later date.

Consider the relationship between transactions and the level of economic activity. Macroeconomics uses as its index of economic activity the aggregate known as national income, which includes only those transactions involving the generation of value added. National income thus excludes, among other things, purchases of raw materials, loans, gifts, government transfers, gambling, and so on, because they involve no net output in the domestic economy. However, all these activities are likely, at some stage, to involve the transfer of money balances and they are all therefore potentially relevant to the demand for money. Neither is that the only problem.

Even where transactions are properly associated with national income, factors such as money transfer technology, established payment practices, the structure of the economy, and so on are likely to influence the relationship between the number of transactions in the economy and the use of money balances. For example, other things being equal, the more infrequently employees are paid, the higher their *average* money balances will need to be.[9] Similarly, any change in the acceptability of near-money assets or in the efficiency with which money balances can be used (because of increased availability of credit cards, for example) would also be likely to affect the demand, for any given volume of transactions.

It follows that we can neither take national income as an infallible indicator of the volume of transactions nor rely on a completely fixed relationship between transactions and the demand for money.

However, suppose that the structure of the economy is fairly stable over some period. In particular, suppose that the kinds of institutional and technological factor that determine the way money is used in the economy are fairly stable and that the structure of the various industries is such that the volume of transactions bears some stable relationship to national income. It may then be reasonable to assume that there would be a stable relationship between the level of economic activity and the volume of transactions.

If we ignore the opportunity cost argument for the moment, what we have arrived at is a relationship between the demand for money and national income, which could be summarized as:

$$M^d = kY \quad k > 0 \tag{4.6}$$

where M^d is the demand for money and Y is national income, both measured in *nominal* terms,[10] and k is a positive parameter.[11] The reason why M^d and Y are both defined in nominal terms should be obvious. Other things being equal, one would expect, say, a 10% increase in the real volume of transactions to have the same effect on the demand for money as a 10% increase in the price level at which the transactions are conducted. In fact, if we define:

$$Y \equiv Py$$

which just says nominal income, Y, is by definition the product of real income, y, multiplied by the price level, P, at which it is traded, then we can rewrite Equation 4.6 as:

$$M^d \equiv kPy \tag{4.7}$$

This formulation is known as the Cambridge quantity equation. The quantity theory, of which it is one version, was the orthodox approach to what we now call the demand for money until well into the twentieth century. It is characterized by a concentration on the role played by the volume of transactions, to the exclusion of any other variables, in particular the return on non-money assets.

The corollary of ignoring the return on other financial assets is that we implicitly assume that economic agents choose between money and goods in general, and not between money and near-money assets. In this sense, Equation 4.7 is oversimplified. None the less, there will be occasions in the next chapter (Sections 5.1 and 5.2) when it will be convenient to make use of this formulation, because of its simplicity and because, very often, it is sufficient as it stands to generate important insights.

Before moving on, notice that by dividing both sides of Equation 4.7 by P, it can be rewritten as follows:

$$\frac{M^d}{P} = ky \tag{4.8}$$

which is, for some purposes, a more useful way of looking at the quantity equation.

The left-hand side is the demand for real money balances, in other words the quantity of purchasing power that the agents in the economy wish to hold in the form of money. The right-hand side is the constant k multiplied by the real income generated in the economy. Now if, as was often assumed by the classical economists, the level of economic activity can be regarded as fluctuating more or less randomly in a fairly narrow region around its long-run equilibrium level, then it follows that the right-hand side of Equation 4.8 must be reasonably stable and hence the demand for real balances must equally be stable.

To see why this is so important a conclusion, consider the effect of an increase in the money supply in this context.

Equilibrium in the money market involves a situation where the demand for money is equal to the supply. So, in the aftermath of an increase in the stock of money by, say, 10%, equilibrium can occur only when the demand has risen by the same amount.

Now look back at Equation 4.8. With the right-hand side broadly constant, the demand for real balances must, as we have seen, be more or less fixed – once the dust has settled, at least. And the demand for *real* balances will be constant only if the 10% rise in the demand for *nominal* money, M^d, is offset by an increase of equal proportions in the price level, P, thereby keeping the ratio M^d/P constant. In other words, each increase in the money supply generates an equiproportionate rise in the price index.

Not only that, but the converse is also true: in a quantity theory world, no increase in the general level of prices can occur without an accommodating rise in the money stock. Hence Milton Friedman's famous assertion, albeit on the basis of a far more sophisticated version of the quantity equation, that 'inflation is always and every-where a monetary phenomenon'. With the real demand fixed, the real money stock must be pegged, which, in turn, means the numerator and denominator must move in parallel.

The power of these conclusions all stems from one critical simplification, which is the assumption, already mentioned, that agents choose between holding money and goods, rather than between money and bonds (or long-term deposits, savings accounts, and so on). It follows that money balances can be reduced only by spending, creating a direct transmission mechanism from excess money supply to additional demand for goods, which, with output fixed, must drive up the price level. Conversely, excess demand for money can be satisfied only by reducing spending on goods and not by selling other financial assets. Hence, excess demand for money is directly associated with excess supply of goods, as agents in aggregate attempt to replenish their balances. The result must be a fall in goods prices, on average at least.

It turns out that these conclusions all have to be modified as soon as we take account of the opportunity cost of holding money.

In order to decide how to measure the opportunity cost, one has, in principle, to decide first what are the relevant assets competing with money for a share in eco-nomic agents' portfolios. Again, at this theoretical level, any or all other assets are potential candidates such as savings deposits, bonds, stocks and shares, real estate or even consumer goods held as inventories (assuming they are not perishable). Much research and not a little controversy has centred on this issue, but it is for the most part not directly relevant to exchange rate determination,[12] and so we shall not open up this particular can of worms.

Instead, make the following assumption: suppose that whenever the return on one non-money asset goes up by 1%, all the other rates of return do the same, other things being equal. This is not as unrealistic an assumption as it might at first appear. Broadly speaking, the difference between the yield on, for example, government long-term securities and the same kind of paper issued by a private sector company is determined by factors unrelated to macroeconomics, and so there is no reason to expect it to change simply because interest rates in the economy rise. In general, if the relative liquidity of the various assets is unchanged, one would expect the returns they offer to stay the same. In fact, changes in the returns on different assets are so closely correlated that it is very difficult in practice to identify a separate impact on the demand for money for more than two assets.

The advantage of making this assumption is that, if it holds good, it makes little difference which rate of return we choose in order to measure the opportunity cost of holding money. The simplest way to proceed, then, is to take an easily observable interest rate (the yield on treasury bills, for example) and refer to it from now on as *the* interest rate. If we do that, we can modify Equation 4.8 as follows:

$$\frac{M^d}{P} = ky - lr \quad k, l > 0 \tag{4.9}$$

The equation now expresses our contention that the demand for real balances will increase with the volume of transactions, but decrease with the opportunity cost, as measured by the interest rate, r.

Notice that our simple quantity theory conclusions about the impact of money supply changes no longer apply, unless interest rates can be assumed to remain constant, which is unlikely.

Moreover, if over some period the price level can be regarded as constant, an increase in the nominal money supply must amount to a rise in the value of real balances in the economy and this, in turn, must cause an increase on the right-hand side of Equation 4.9. Again, if changes in real income are ruled out this must imply a fall in r, so as to reduce the damping effect of the opportunity cost on the demand for real balances.

We can summarize the implications of this more sophisticated demand for money equation as follows. It states that the impact of an increase (or decrease) of $x\%$ in the supply of money will be either to cause the price level to rise (fall) by $x\%$ if the interest rate is unchanged *or* to push the interest rate down (up) if the price level is constant *or some combination of the two* – that is, a price change of less than $x\%$ in addition to an interest rate change.

Government budget constraint and money supply

In order to understand how the supply of money is determined, it will be helpful to start by making a detour to consider the mechanics of government budget finance.

Suppose that in some year the government decides to spend more than it receives in tax revenue. In other words, suppose the government wants to run a budget deficit. How can it finance spending in excess of its tax revenues?

Essentially, the answer to this question is that, just like you or I, a government can live beyond its means (that is, spend more than its income) only by reducing its net assets, in other words by borrowing from others, thereby increasing its liabilities, or by running down its accumulated assets ('borrowing from itself', so to speak). Since governments rarely have much in the way of accumulated assets with which to finance spending,[13] we shall assume any budget deficit is financed by borrowing of one form or another. Let us summarize this fact in the following identity:

$$G - T \equiv the\ budget\ deficit \equiv total\ government\ borrowing$$

where G is government expenditure on goods and services during the year and T is government tax revenue during the year.

Now there are many different forms in which a government can borrow, as indeed there are for an individual, depending on whether the borrowing is long- or short-term, secured or unsecured, indexed or unindexed, in negotiable or non-negotiable instruments, and so on. With one vital exception, we shall not be concerned with the particular form that government borrowing takes.

The single exception is that governments have one borrowing option open to them that is not available to the ordinary individual: they can issue, via the agency of the central bank, a kind of security that the public is willing to accept as money. The fact that some of the state's liabilities are universally acceptable in order to settle debts between parties outside the government sector gives the authorities another degree of freedom, an additional avenue for financing overspending that is not open to any other agency.[14]

In recognition of this fact, we can rewrite the identity, breaking down the right-hand side into components that reflect government borrowing in money and non-money terms:

$$G - T \equiv \Delta MB + \Delta B^s$$

where MB is the quantity of currency in existence, B^s is the quantity of non-monetary government debt in existence ('bonds')[15] and Δ is, by convention, an operator denoting the change in a variable over any period.

This identity is usually given a special name:

> The **government budget constraint** is the identity that expresses the fact that all government spending over any given period must be financed by taxation, by issuing currency or by issuing non-money securities (typically, long-term debt, called from now on 'bonds').

Although it is an identity, in other words a truism, the government budget constraint is important because it summarizes the necessary relationship between fiscal policy, affecting net expenditure on the left-hand side of the equation, and monetary policy, determining the way in which spending is financed on the right-hand side.

Armed with an understanding of the broad outline of the government's funding problem, we can now proceed to a consideration of the money supply mechanism.

Supply of money in an open economy

The first thing to notice about the supply of money is that it is not really a supply at all – at least, not in the sense we use the term in elementary microeconomics. What we mean by the supply of money is nothing more than the quantity of money in existence in the economy at a particular point in time. It is not very helpful for present purposes to think of money actually being *supplied* to the market. Rather, think of the supply process as being simply a mechanism whereby the stock of money (currency plus demand deposits) gets determined.

It turns out that, in order to understand the process, we need to take a look at the structure of the banking system. The fine detail of the institutional framework is, for most industrial countries, bewilderingly complicated and characterized by all sorts of peculiar features, some attributable to legal or regulatory constraints, others

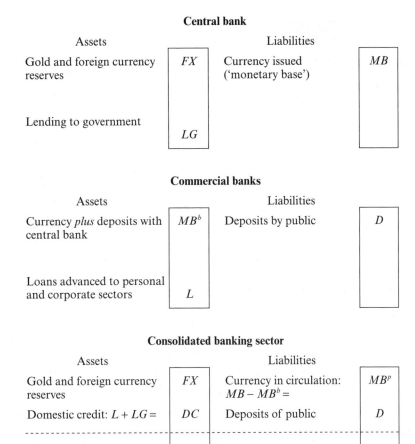

Figure 4.2 Balance sheet of the banking system

to custom and practice. To make matters worse, the whole subject is often shrouded in a fog of esoteric jargon.

We shall avoid most of the complications by dealing with the banking system in broad outline only, avoiding much of the fine detail or relegating it to footnotes that the reader can safely ignore without losing the thread of the argument.

One notable simplification made here and throughout the book, with the exception only of Chapter 9, is to ignore foreign holdings of domestic currency. As far as money supply control is concerned, it is hard to see why foreign holdings of sterling balances should create a problem. Certainly, any difficulties caused are likely to pale into insignificance beside those resulting from demand instability – or even beside the problems the authorities have created for themselves in the past.

Look at Figure 4.2, which lays out in schematic form the balance sheets of two kinds of institution.

The first balance sheet is for a central bank such as the Bank of England, the Federal Reserve Bank of the USA, the Bank of Japan or the People's Bank of China.[16]

Now, although it is the linchpin of a country's financial system, most people's only perception of their central bank is as the issuer of the banknotes they use. Certainly, serving as the bank of issue is an important function,[17] but it is by no means the only one performed by the central bank. In the first place, the central bank has the job of holding the nation's reserves of gold and foreign currency[18] – hence the first entry on the asset side in the table, labelled *FX*. Second, and most important of all, the central bank differs from a commercial bank in having one large customer, the government, to whom it is forced to provide the main banking services of facilitating transactions and, inevitably, providing credit.[19]

At this point, we are back to the question of how the government funds its deficit spending, but this time we concentrate on the mechanics of the process. Suppose a government decides to spend £100m, without raising any additional taxation. Suppose, furthermore, that it intends to do so without borrowing from the non-bank public – in other words, it is determined to avail itself of the option to increase the money supply in order to pay for its spending. The first step in the process involves the government approaching the central bank for a loan, which is granted more or less automatically. In return, we can think of the treasury being compelled to sign IOUs, promising to repay the central bank at some uncertain future date. These IOUs (government securities) are then locked away in the vaults of the central bank.

This transaction is represented on the asset side of the accounts by the item 'Lending to government', consisting of the accumulation of government securities held by the central bank. The form the loans take is the printing of currency, which can then be used by the government for its additional expenditure. Notice that currency printed counts as a *liability* of the central bank, although neither the Bank of England nor the Federal Reserve Bank is actually obliged to redeem banknotes in any meaningful sense at all.[20]

Notice, also, that it is the supply of *currency* that is increased when the government borrows in this way from the central bank, and not the money supply in any but the narrowest sense. The notation ΔMB in the government budget constraint refers to the change in the quantity of currency issued or, as it is sometimes called, base money.

However, this is not the only way the monetary base can be changed. Just as you or I sometimes borrow in order to spend (or consume), we may also, on occasion, take a loan so as to buy another asset. In effect, we voluntarily take on a liability (the loan) in order to purchase an asset, such as a house, perhaps, some shares or a partnership in a business. In the same way, the government sometimes borrows in order to spend, as we have seen already, but may also at other times decide simply to raise a loan from the central bank in order to buy assets. Typically, the government may use the loan to buy back its own IOUs (mainly gilt-edged securities or bonds) from their holders among the non-bank public.

In the jargon of central banking, this type of activity is known as an *open market purchase* to distinguish it from transactions conducted behind closed doors – that is, between the government and the Bank of England.

As far as the impact on the monetary base is concerned, the effect will be to cause an expansion just as if it had used the loan to finance increased spending. Conversely, the government could decide to reverse the process, by issuing debt unnecessarily so as to raise cash direct from the non-bank public (an open market sale). If it subsequently spends the proceeds, the effect on the monetary base is nil. If, by way of contrast, it uses the proceeds so as to repay its debts to the central bank (reducing *LG*), it effectively retires money, reducing *MB*.

Now consider the commercial banking sector.[21] Start this time on the liabilities side of the balance sheet. There is only one major item here, deposits by the public with the banks, D. Clearly, your deposit with the bank in the high street is an asset to you. However, it must equally be a *liability* of the bank, since it represents an obligation on the part of the bank to repay a fixed amount on demand.[22] Thus, that part of the money stock that consists of demand deposits is in fact a liability of the commercial banking system.

What do banks do with the funds deposited with them by the public? If they are to be able to pay any interest on deposits, or indeed cover their costs,[23] they must put the funds deposited with them to work. The way they achieve this is, of course, by lending, mainly to corporate borrowers, although often also to private individuals. At any rate, the important thing to note is that these loans constitute *assets* of the banking system, since they are obligations by the non-bank sector of the economy to repay debts to the banking sector.

Now it would be very helpful, from the bank's point of view, if it could put out on loan every last penny it received on deposit. Unfortunately, it would also be grossly irresponsible, since it would be left with nothing in the till with which to repay depositors who wanted cash. As far as the public is concerned, it is on the under-standing that they can liquidate their deposits for cash on demand that they agree to deposit in the first place. An inability to meet a demand for cash would almost certainly precipitate a crisis of confidence and a run on the bank. Prudence requires, therefore, that a significant proportion of the funds deposited with the banks be held as a cash reserve in order to cover demands for withdrawals.[24]

Hence, the first item on the asset side of the commercial banks' balance sheet, MB^b, which represents precisely these precautionary reserves. Currency in the commercial banks' vaults is kept at a manageable level by regular trips to deposit cash at the central bank – hence the armoured vehicles cluttering up the roads outside our high-street banks. By convention, no balance sheet distinction is made between the currency actually in a commercial bank's till at any moment and the amount it has available on deposit with its bank, the central bank. The total cash reserve is the commercial bank's share of the monetary base, MB^b in the figure.

The bottom third of Figure 4.2 contains a consolidated balance sheet for the banking sector as a whole, commercial banks plus central bank. To see how that is derived, we need to write the balance sheets of the central bank and the commercial banks respectively as equations. First the central bank:

$$FX + LG \equiv MB$$

Then the commercial banks:

$$MB^b + L \equiv D$$

Now, if we add the two balance sheet equations, we get:

$$FX + MB^b + (LG + L) \equiv MB + D$$

The term in parentheses represents the total of the consolidated banking sector's lending, both to the government and to the private, non-bank sector. It is known as *domestic credit*, DC for short. If we rewrite the equation making use of this definition and also taking MB^b away from both sides, we get:

$$FX + DC \equiv (MB - MB^b) + D$$

On the right-hand side, in parentheses, we have the total monetary base, MB, net of that part that is in the coffers of the banks themselves, MB^b. Obviously, currency not in the banks must be in circulation with the non-bank public. Call this part of the monetary base MB^p. Thus, we can rewrite our equation as:

$$FX + DC \equiv MB^p + D$$

The right-hand side now consists of the total of currency in circulation plus deposits in the banks – which is precisely how we defined the money stock at the beginning of Section 4.1.2. We can therefore conclude that:

$$FX + DC \equiv M^s \tag{4.10}$$

In words: the money supply is identically equal to the sum of the domestic credit generated by the banking system plus the value of the country's reserves of gold and foreign currency held at the central bank.

There are a number of points worth noting about this very important equation. Notice that it is an *identity*, in other words a relationship that is true by definition. It cannot be disputed or disproved. What, if anything, does it tell us? If we regard the left-hand side as showing the ultimate process by which the money stock is generated or backed, it tells us that every unit of domestic money must originate either in lending by the banking system (domestic credit) or in the reserves of foreign money. In terms of an expansion of the money stock, it says that each additional unit of domestic currency must have been generated by an expansion of domestic credit or, alternatively, by an increase in the reserves of gold and foreign exchange.

Now these two kinds of asset are qualitatively different. For present purposes, the essential difference is in the way they are created. As far as domestic credit is concerned, it is all directly or indirectly amenable to control by the home country's monetary authorities. To see that this is the case, look back at its two main components: central bank lending to the government and commercial bank advances to the non-bank sector. The former is self-evidently within the control of the authorities – it is determined by the government's budget constraint in conjunction with any central bank open market operations that may be undertaken.

As far as commercial bank lending is concerned, the situation is not quite as clearcut.[25] Recall the discussion of how commercial banks were forced to keep reserves broadly in proportion to their liabilities. This amounts to saying that their lending is constrained by the available reserves of cash. We shall assume that, either by virtue of its control of the quantity of base money printed, or via its ability to fix, legally or otherwise, the relationship between commercial banks' lending and their till money (that is, the ratio MB^b/L), the authorities can determine the total domestic credit in the economy, DC. In other words, we shall assume that domestic credit is an exogenous, policy variable.

By contrast, we cannot possibly regard the foreign exchange reserves as a policy variable. For one thing, the Bank of England may not print US dollars or yen to put in the reserves – that is the prerogative of the Federal Reserve and the Bank of Japan respectively.

To understand this important distinction, recall what was said about the function of the reserves in Chapter 1. They represent a buffer stock of international money available, when necessary, to purchase the domestic currency so as to support the exchange rate. Their size is determined by the accumulation of gold and foreign currency bought by the central bank on previous occasions to support other countries' currencies relative to the domestic.

Changes in the reserves therefore come about as a result of imbalances between the endogenous demand and supply in the currency markets. If there is an excess supply of the domestic currency (that is, excess demand for the foreign currency), a fall in the domestic country's exchange rate can be prevented only by using some of the reserves to buy the domestic currency, thereby satisfying the demand for foreign money. Conversely, the reserves will increase when there is an excess supply of foreign currency that must be bought with domestic money in order to prevent an appreciation.

Two conclusions follow. First, and most obviously, there is no point in a country's hoarding reserves if it does not intend to peg its exchange rate. At the very least, if it is content to see its exchange rate determined in the freely operating currency markets, it need never use its reserves. Second, since the balance of payments accounts represent, at least in principle, an analysis of the flow supply and demand in the currency markets, a deficit in those accounts will need to be offset by reductions in the reserves and vice versa for a surplus. Thus, whatever factors determine the balance of payments also determine the change in the reserves.

To see the importance of these conclusions, go back to our open economy money supply identity, Equation 4.1, and rewrite it in terms of discrete changes:

$$\Delta FX + \Delta DC \equiv \Delta M^s \tag{4.11}$$

The change in a country's money supply is identically equal to the sum of the change in the volume of domestic credit issued by its banking system *plus* the change in its stock of international reserves.

Now, if the country's authorities either have no reserves or choose not to use them, in other words if they are happy to see the value of their currency determined in world markets, then the first term in Equation 4.11 is always zero and changes in the domestic money stock originate exclusively in domestic credit expansion or contraction. Putting the point in terms of the balance of payments account, under these circumstances the balance for official financing is kept at zero.

It follows from all this that we can rephrase the definitions given in Chapter 1:

> A (**pure** or **cleanly**) **floating exchange rate regime** is one such that the balance of payments for official financing is identically zero, because the monetary authority either holds no foreign currency reserves or never uses them to intervene in currency markets.

This is not all, however. Since, in this case, any changes in the money supply are due entirely to domestic credit expansion or contraction, we can add the following to our definition of a floating exchange rate:

> Under a floating exchange rate, the domestic money stock changes only as a result of changes in the **lending behaviour of the domestic banking system**. Since the volume of lending can be controlled by the authorities, so can the money stock. In this sense, the money supply is a policy instrument at the disposal of the home country's monetary authority.

By contrast:

> A **fixed exchange rate regime** (including a '**managed**' or '**dirty**' **float**) is one such that the balance of payments for official financing is *not* identically zero, the surplus or deficit being covered by the domestic monetary authority's use of the foreign currency reserves to intervene in currency markets.

The implications of fixed exchange rates for the money stock have already been mentioned in this section.

Under any form of fixed exchange rate, the domestic money stock may change either as a result of a change in the volume of bank lending or as a result of a change in the foreign currency reserves (that is, a balance of payments deficit or surplus for official financing) – *or both*. Since the change in the reserves cannot be directly controlled by the domestic monetary authority, neither can the change in the domestic money stock.

It follows that, under a fixed exchange rate regime, the money supply cannot be regarded as a policy variable but instead will be an endogenous variable determined by whatever factors influence the balance of payments.

In a nutshell, then, under a floating exchange rate regime, the balance of payments surplus and the consequent increase in the reserves are fixed at zero, making the money supply exogenous and leaving the exchange rate to be determined endogenously by market forces. Under fixed exchange rates, the balance of payments, the change in the reserves and in the money supply are all endogenous. Only the change in the exchange rate is exogenously fixed at zero.

It follows that, in an open economy context, the term 'monetary policy' has two different meanings. Under floating exchange rates, 'monetary policy' means exactly the same thing that it does in textbook models of a closed economy – that is, the management of the money supply. By contrast, under fixed exchange rates, 'monetary policy' means control of the banking system's lending – in other words, what we have called *domestic credit*.

LM curve

Equilibrium obtains in the money market when demand is equal to supply. Combinations of income and the interest rate consistent with equilibrium are plotted along the LM curve.[26] Looking back at Equation 4.9, this means when:

$$\frac{M^s}{P} = \frac{M^d}{P} = ky - lr \quad k, l > 0 \tag{4.12}$$

where we bear in mind what was said in the last section about the determination of the money supply and its relationship to the exchange rate regime.

Now, if the money stock is fixed initially at the level M_0^s, Equation 4.12 is a single equation in three unknowns: r, y and P. To proceed, take a given level of prices, say P_0. If we do that, we are left with the equation:

$$ky - lr = \frac{M_0^s}{P_0} \quad k, l > 0 \tag{4.13}$$

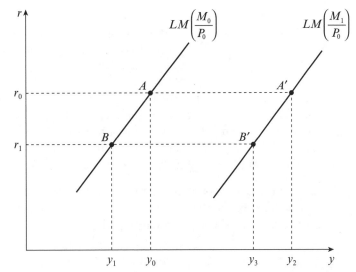

Figure 4.3 The LM curve

as the condition necessary for the money market to be in equilibrium – in other words, for the demand for money to be equal to the supply.

Notice that Equation 4.13 now has the same general form as Equation 4.5, the equation of the IS curve. The right-hand side is given, as before, and we can again generate the equilibrium conditions by picking an interest rate at random and asking ourselves the question: if the interest rate is r_0, what must be the level of y if the money market is to clear? The answer, y_0,[27] is the first point we have located on our LM curve, because it is the first combination of r and y we have found that generates a demand for money just equal to the given supply (point A in Figure 4.3).

Now consider a lower interest rate, r_1. The implication of a lower interest rate is a smaller penalty for holding non-interest-bearing assets and hence less of an incentive to economize on money holdings. It follows that, at r_1, the demand for money would be greater than the supply at the previous level of activity, y_0. Equilibrium therefore requires the lower interest rate to be offset by a lower level of activity, so as to damp down the demand for money for transactions purposes and thereby compensate for the reduced incentive to make money balances 'work harder'. It follows that money market clearing requires a lower interest rate (like r_1) to be associated with a lower level of real activity (like y_1).

We conclude that the LM curve drawn for a given level of real money balances must be upward-sloping.

As before, consider a change in the right-hand side of Equation 4.12. Clearly, an increase in the supply of real money balances could come about as the result of a *rise* in the nominal money stock or a *fall* in the price level at which it is valued. In fact, as we saw, the impact of, say, a 10% rise in the numerator, M^s, would be identical to that of a 10% fall in the price index, since it would have an identical effect on the ratio M^s/P. Anything that leaves the ratio unchanged, for example a 25% increase in both the nominal money stock and the price level, will have no effect on the LM curve.

From whatever source, an increase in the real money stock will mean that previous equilibrium combinations of r and y are now associated with an excess supply of real balances. At any given interest rate, say r_0, there will have to be a compensating change in order to increase the demand. Clearly, this must mean a higher level of activity than at the previous equilibrium. y_0 will no longer be associated with a high enough transactions demand. An income level like y_2 will be required. Putting the same argument somewhat differently, at any level of activity (and associated transactions demand), the larger real money stock makes possible a lower interest rate, because it reduces the required equilibrium opportunity cost of money holding.

We can summarize our conclusions about the LM curve as follows:

- The (open or closed economy) LM curve is an upward-sloping line joining all combinations of the interest rate and the level of income, such that the demand for real money balances is exactly equal to the supply.

- It is drawn for given values of the nominal money stock, M^s, and the price level, P. Any increase in the ratio M^s/P, whether associated with a rise in the nominal money stock, M^s, or a fall in P, will cause an outward shift in the LM curve and vice versa in the case of a fall in M^s or rise in P.

4.1.3 Aggregate demand

Figure 4.4(a) combines the IS and LM curves so as to generate a unique solution to the two simultaneous Equations 4.5 and 4.13. In other words, the value of y at A, y_0, is the answer to the question: what would be the equilibrium level of income if government fiscal spending amounted to G_0, the money supply were set at the level M_0^s, the price level were P_0 and the real exchange rate were Q_0?

However, the term 'equilibrium income' has to be interpreted with care in this context. It means nothing more than 'the level of income consistent with equality between planned spending and income, on the one hand, and also consistent with equality between the demand for money and the supply, on the other'. While this may seem quite a mouthful, it is not yet sufficient for a complete equilibrium. What is missing is some consideration of how the output y_0 relates to the productive capacity of the economy – it might, for example, be way beyond maximum potential output levels. Conversely, it might be so low as to imply mass unemployment of labour and/or capital.

These considerations lie behind the determination of the aggregate supply schedule, which will be dealt with in Section 4.2. For the moment, in recognition that the value of y that corresponds to equilibrium in the IS–LM model may not be the output actually produced, we shall refer to it as aggregate demand, denoted y^d.

Now ask yourself the question: suppose that aggregate demand is greater than the economy's productive potential – what is likely to happen? The intuitively obvious answer is that the price level will rise – and, on this occasion, the intuition is correct. How will a rise in the price of goods and services affect aggregate demand? The answer is given by the aggregate demand schedule, which plots how aggregate demand changes as the general price level changes.

In Figure 4.4(b), aggregate demand is plotted against the price index, taking G, M^s and SP^* as given. Hence the equilibrium at A in the IS–LM diagram is associated with the point on the aggregate demand curve labelled a.

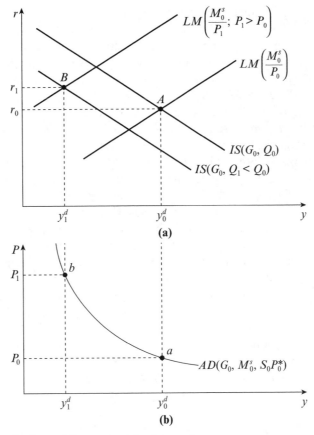

Figure 4.4 Derivation of the aggregate demand curve

The remainder of the points on the aggregate demand schedule are derived simply by varying the price index upwards or downwards from P_0. Take, for example, the higher price level, P_1. As far as the LM curve is concerned, we have seen that a higher price level reduces the value of the given nominal money stock, because it must be the case that:

$$\frac{M_0^s}{P_1} < \frac{M_0^s}{P_0}$$

if P_1 is greater than P_0. It follows that the LM curve for P_1 is further to the left (that is, higher up) than for P_0.

What about the IS curve? The only effect of a higher price level on the IS curve arises via the international relative price term, Q. *Other things being equal*, and, in particular, assuming that neither the nominal exchange rate nor the foreign price level changes, the higher domestic price level reduces the competitiveness of UK production, pushing the IS curve downwards and to the left.

Since both shifts are to the left, the outcome must be a lower level of aggregate demand, say y_1^d instead of y_0^d.[28] Plotting the outcome on to the bottom diagram we conclude that the aggregate demand curve will be downward-sloping, for given values of the money stock, fiscal expenditure, the nominal exchange rate and the foreign price level.

The aggregate demand curve AD_0 was drawn for given values of G, M^s and SP^*. Now consider the effect of changes in each of these variables in turn.

At any given price level, an increase in the nominal money supply will, as we have seen, shift the LM curve outwards, moving the equilibrium down the IS curve to the southeast, in the direction of higher aggregate demand and lower interest rates. It therefore follows that it will shift the aggregate demand curve outwards, accommodating higher demand at all price levels.

An increase in net government expenditure has effects that are similar, but not identical. As we have already established, a fiscal expansion shifts the IS curve outwards, other things being equal, so that the new equilibrium involves a higher level of both the interest rate and aggregate demand in the economy. The greater the rise in interest rates, the smaller the increase in aggregate demand. On the one hand, interest rates have to rise so as to persuade agents to economize on money balances so as to finance the new, higher volume of transactions. On the other hand, the more interest rates rise, the lower the level of private sector expenditure in the new equilibrium. To the extent that the net outcome is a smaller increase in demand than would have taken place had interest rates remained unchanged, private sector expenditure is said to have been *crowded out* by the additional government spending.

Most important, consider the effect of an increase in SP^*, the home currency price of foreign products. At any given domestic price level, P, an increase in SP^* translates directly into a rise in $Q = SP^*/P$ – in other words, an improvement in UK competitiveness. This is the case whether the change is brought about by a rise in S (sterling devaluation) or in P^* (foreign inflation). Hence, a rise either in S or in P^* leads, via the increase in Q, to a rightward shift in the IS curve and consequent rise in aggregate demand, other things being equal. The aggregate demand schedule is therefore moved to the right by the change.

To summarize our conclusions about the aggregate demand curve:

- The aggregate demand curve shows how the level of income that clears the goods and money markets (that is, the equilibrium level of income in the IS–LM curve context) varies as the (domestic) price level changes. It is downward-sloping because, as the domestic price level rises, other things being equal, the real money stock is reduced in value and also the competitiveness of UK output falls, at given levels of S and P^*.

- The aggregate demand curve is drawn for given levels of government spending, G, the nominal money supply, M^s, the nominal exchange rate, S, and the price of foreign output, P^*. An increase in any of these variables will shift the schedule outwards, since they will induce greater aggregate demand at any domestic price level.

4.2 Aggregate supply

The exposition given here of the underpinnings of the aggregate supply curve is brief in the extreme. A fuller explanation taking account of the possibility of short-run output variations can be found in almost any undergraduate macroeconomics textbook.

As a starting point in the derivation of the aggregate supply curve, assume that the quantity of equipment, plant and machinery, and so on (the economy's capital stock) is given at any moment in time. The implication is that, with one factor of production fixed, output depends only on the manpower employed.[29]

Now consider the situation in the labour market.

4.2.1 Flexible prices

A profit-maximizing firm will demand labour up to the point at which the value of its marginal product is just equal to the money wage;[30] that is, up to the point where the last man hour adds just as much to revenue as it does to costs. If marginal product diminishes as labour utilization increases and if employers are competitive in the labour market, then, subject to the usual provisos with respect to aggregation conditions, the demand for labour across the economy will be a decreasing function of the nominal wage at any given price level.

For example, at the price level P_0, the demand for labour will be given by the downward-sloping line labelled $n^d(P_0)$ in Figure 4.5(a).

Clearly, if the price level were 20% higher, firms would seek to employ the same amount of labour at a money wage 20% greater than previously because, other things being equal, the marginal man hour would result in a proportionately greater addition to revenue than previously. Hence, the demand curve would shift vertically upwards so as to associate with any given employment level a nominal wage 1.2 times higher.

By way of contrast, households are presumed to be intent on choosing a utility-maximizing combination of work and leisure. If they are able to do so *in freely competitive labour markets*, they will offer their services up to the point at which the monetary benefit (in terms of consumption) they derive from the last man hour supplied, as measured by the wage rate, is equal to their subjective assessment of its leisure value.[31] The marginal utility of leisure can safely be assumed to increase as the number of hours worked rises and leisure time is reduced. It follows that, at any price level, the quantity of man hours supplied will be an increasing function of the nominal wage, as can be seen from the line marked $n^s(P_0)$ in Figure 4.5(a).

Again, at a higher price level $P_1 = 1.2P_0$, any given money wage buys 20% less consumption. The household will therefore be in equilibrium supplying any given number of man hours at a money wage 20% higher than before.

At the initial price level, the combination of a downward-sloping demand for labour with respect to the nominal wage and an upward-sloping supply of labour guarantees a unique equilibrium level of employment, C, and a corresponding real wage, $I_0 = S_0/P_0$. Following the accepted jargon, we shall call these market-clearing values the equilibrium or *natural* real wage and rate of employment.

At the higher price level $P_1 = 1.2P_0$, as can be seen at point B in Figure 4.4(a), the equilibrium money wage is 20% higher, but *both the real wage and the level of employment are unchanged*.

If the labour market clears with employment equal to C, what will be the level of output? Given the level of the total capital stock, the quantity of equipment per worker will be given, at any employment level. Assuming a given state of technology,

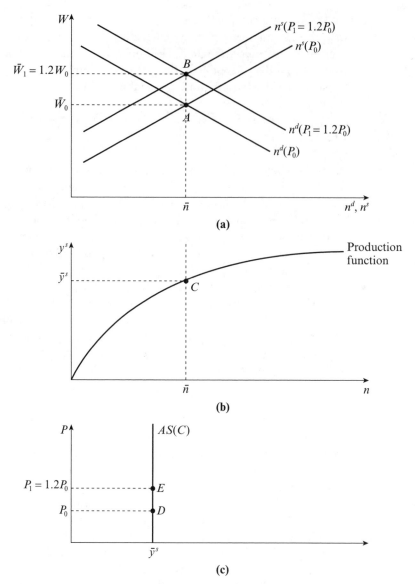

Figure 4.5 Derivation of the classic aggregate supply curve

it follows that the productive capacity of any quantity of labour will be determined. The functional relationship between the quantity of labour utilized and the output produced is normally called the short-run production function (Figure 4.4(b)). In particular, the employed labour force, C, will produce the output, J^s, which we can, in turn, regard as the equilibrium or natural level of real national product.

Now what does this analysis imply for the aggregate supply function? Recall that, symmetrically with the aggregate demand schedule, we are looking for the relationship between aggregate supply and the price level in the economy.

It is plain from what has already been said that the price index has no part to play in determining equilibrium output, since both the demand for labour and the supply depend on the *real* wage. As long as the corporate sector's demand for labour and the household sector's supply are both unaffected by price level changes (as long as neither side suffers from money illusion), the aggregate supply curve will be a vertical line at the level J^s, so that the actual output produced in the economy will be independent of the price level (Figure 4.4(c)).

Notice the implication: if there is no connection between the price level and the aggregate supply, the latter cannot determine the former. It follows that the price level must depend on aggregate demand alone. In other words, any of the factors that have been shown to shift the aggregate demand curve upwards cause the price level to increase, and vice versa for a price level decrease.

One point that should be absolutely clear from this brief analysis is that the role of price and wage flexibility is absolutely critical. If money wages rose by more (or less) than 20% as the price level rose from P_0 to P_1, the outcome would be an increase (or decrease) in the real wage and consequent fall (rise) in employment and output. Everything hinges, therefore, on the smooth functioning of the labour market.

Now since a faith in the ability of markets to adjust rapidly to shocks is the hallmark of classical economics,[32] we conclude:

> The classical or flexible-price aggregate supply curve is vertical at the long-run capacity output level of the economy. This is because, as the price level fluctuates up or down, the money wage adjusts to keep the real wage constant. Hence employment and output never vary and the price level itself is determined by aggregate demand.

4.2.2 Fixed prices

Now consider what would happen if money wages were fixed.

This situation might arise in a number of ways. It could be regarded as the very short-run reaction to a sudden change in the price level – after all, money wages can hardly respond overnight. In fact, wages may be fixed over a longer horizon by the existence of employment contracts, explicit (in other words, written) or implicit (unwritten, but none the less binding). In many cases, the contracts might be between employers and employees represented by trade unions, in which case the mechanism for adjusting money wages is likely to be even more cumbersome.[33]

In any case, the implication is that the *effective* labour supply curve is horizontal at the current fixed money wage, $\bar{W}_0$. Assuming firms continue to react to price changes in the way described in Section 4.2.1, it follows that employment and output are no longer constant (Figure 4.6). A rise in the price level is associated with a fall in the real wage and a consequent increase in employment from $\bar{n}_0$ to $\bar{n}_1$ and output from $\bar{y}_0^s$ to $\bar{y}_1^s$. The result is the upward-sloping aggregate supply curve labelled $AS(\text{K})$ in Figure 4.6(c).

In the limit, if wages form the bulk of the corporate sector's costs or if non-labour costs are constant, competitive producers will never raise prices. Firms will react to higher demand for their output by simply taking on more labour at the fixed money

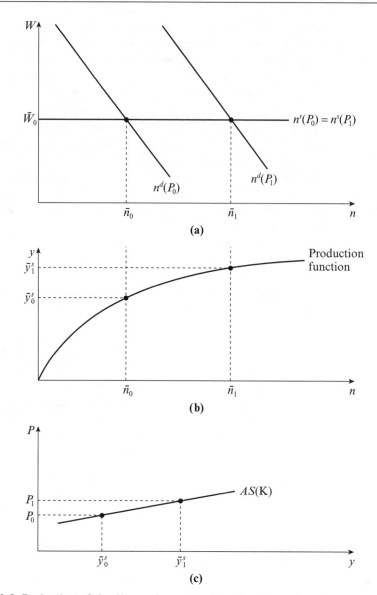

Figure 4.6 Derivation of the Keynesian aggregate supply curve

wage and scaling up production at constant unit costs. The outcome will be a completely flat aggregate supply curve.

Now nobody believes this scenario to be the complete truth about aggregate supply in the long run as; after all, it would imply that a policy of demand expansion (for example, by printing money) could lead to a permanent increase in employment and output. None the less, the account given here will serve as a conveniently simplified description of a commonly held view of aggregate supply in the short run, one we shall henceforth refer to as Keynesian or fixed price.

We conclude:

> The Keynesian or fixed-price aggregate supply curve is flat at the currently given price level, reflecting the fact that demand fluctuations are associated with equal and opposite variation in the real wage. Hence, with fixed prices, employment and output are demand-determined.

With the price level fixed in this scenario, we need concern ourselves only with aggregate demand and the position of the IS and LM curves – which, as we shall see in Chapter 6, is exactly the focus of the Mundell–Fleming model.

4.2.3 A compromise: sticky prices

If the flexible wage model seems an implausible description of the very short-run reaction of labour markets, while the fixed wage alternative is equally unrealistic as a description of long-run behaviour, consider a compromise between the two extremes.

Suppose the assumptions underlying the Keynesian model apply to the short run, while wages and prices are completely flexible in the long run, as in the classic model. In other words, suppose the aggregate supply curve is flat in the immediate impact phase, but gets steeper as time elapses, ultimately becoming vertical in the steady-state equilibrium.

According to this scenario, the economy passes through three phases in the aftermath of a disturbance. Take, for example, the case of an increase in demand from AD_0 to AD_1 (Figure 4.7).

The impact effect is felt purely on output and employment. Workers willingly supply more labour at the going wage, whether because they are unsure how long the increased demand will persist, or because they are bound by fixed wage contracts, or simply as a result of very short-run inertia. The economy therefore moves more or less immediately from point E to point A, with an increase in output from $\bar{y}_0^s$ to $\bar{y}_1^s$.

As time passes, however, contracts (implicit or explicit) are renegotiated and money wages are progressively bid up as employers seek to increase output. In turn, the corporate sector recoups the rise in labour costs by raising output prices, thereby giving added impetus to the wage inflation, as households seek to increase their pay to take account of the higher cost of living. The adjustment phase is therefore characterized by rising prices and falling output, as the aggregate supply curve tilts towards the vertical. At each stage of the adjustment process, we can think of the economy being in a temporary equilibrium, like B in the diagram, with output at y_2^s still above its initial long-run level and the price index somewhat higher, at P_2.

Eventually, the economy reaches its long-run steady state at C, where all real quantities are back where they started. The price level is at its new long-run level of $\bar{P}_s$, but since the money wage has increased pro rata, the real wage and hence employment are unchanged. Output is back at its natural level.

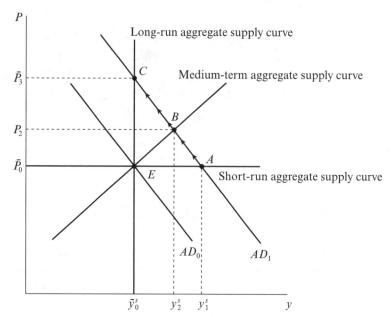

Figure 4.7 The sticky price aggregate supply curve

We can summarize this model as follows:

> The sticky price model of the supply side of the economy is one where the aggregate supply curve is instantaneously flat, becoming steeper as time passes and eventually vertical. It follows that the reaction to an increase in aggregate demand involves initially an expansion in output with no inflation. As time passes, the price level rises and output falls back towards its long-run level.

This compromise provides the background to the Dornbusch model, which will be the subject of Chapter 7.

4.3 Conclusions

For those readers who are familiar with the basic textbook model of the closed economy, this chapter will have contained only two new features. First, the introduction of the real exchange rate into the IS curve. The higher the real exchange rate, the more competitive domestic output on world markets and hence the greater the demand in the economy, other things being equal.

The second innovation is in the treatment of the determination of the money stock. Under a fixed exchange rate regime, the money supply is no longer a policy variable, because, as we saw, it contains a component that is the direct counterpart of the country's foreign currency reserves. Since the latter are clearly not within the direct control of the *domestic* monetary authority, it follows that the money stock can no longer be regarded as simply a policy lever that can be operated at will by the governor of the central bank or the minister of finance.

With the end of this chapter, we can now proceed to the analysis of models of exchange rate determination, the subject matter of Part II of the book.

Summary

- The open economy IS curve links combinations of the interest rate and income consistent with equilibrium in the market for flows of goods and services. It is downward-sloping. Increases in the real exchange rate (real devaluation) or in government net expenditure cause it to shift to the right.

- *Money* means the asset or assets that are usually used as means of payment. For most purposes, it consists of currency in circulation *plus* demand deposits (cheque accounts).

- The *supply of money* is equal to the sum total of the domestic credit created by the central bank in its lending to the government and the commercial banks by their advances to the public *plus* the country's reserves of gold and foreign exchange, if any.

- Increases in the supply of money can arise from policy decisions to permit increased domestic credit or from growth in the reserves. The latter are the result of maintaining a fixed exchange rate under conditions of balance of payments surplus. It follows that, under a fixed exchange rate, changes in the money stock are not necessarily the result of policy decisions. Only under a freely floating rate is the money stock an exogenous variable, since, in that case, the whole of the money stock (or, at least, the whole of any change in it) consists of domestic credit.

- The *demand for money* is to be construed as the demand to hold a stock of purchasing power in the form of monetary assets. It is, therefore, a demand for real balances. As such, it will be greater, other things being equal, when national income is higher, since then the volume of transactions to be financed is larger and it will be smaller the higher are interest rates in the economy, because higher rates of return on non-money assets mean a higher *opportunity cost of holding money*.

- The LM curve links combinations of income and the interest rate consistent with equilibrium in the money market. It is upward-sloping. An increase in the real money stock, whether originating in one of the components of the nominal supply or in a fall in the price level, causes the LM curve to shift to the right.

- The aggregate demand curve shows how the IS–LM equilibrium value of national income ('aggregate demand') varies as the price level changes, holding everything else constant. Since, at higher price levels, a given stock of nominal balances represents a lower real money supply, the aggregate demand curve slopes downward.

- On the supply side of the economy, the demand for labour is a downward-sloping function of the money wage, at any given price level.

- If households are concerned only with the real value of any wage offer, then their labour supply will be homogeneous in prices and wages. If all prices adjust smoothly, it will follow that the level of employment and output are constant, other things being equal, and in particular independent of the price index. Hence the (classic) aggregate supply curve is vertical.

■ If households behave as though subject to money illusion – whether as a result of long-term contracts, inertia, misinformation or simply delays in reacting – real wages will not be invariant and hence both employment and output will fluctuate as the price level changes. Hence the (Keynesian) aggregate supply curve will be upward-sloping. In the limit, it could well be horizontal.

■ It could be argued that the classic aggregate supply curve is a plausible picture of the long-term behaviour of the economy, while the Keynesian version relates to the short term. A compromise would therefore be to take the aggregate supply curve as flat in the immediate term, pivoting upwards as time passes in the aftermath of a demand disturbance, until ultimately the economy returns to its steady state along the vertical long-run supply curve.

Reading guide

The closed economy aggregate demand–supply framework is covered in practically all modern textbooks, though the extensions given here are harder to locate. Among the most widely used macroeconomics texts are Mankiw (2007) and Blanchard (2005), both of which cover these and many other topics.

The approach taken to the demand for money in this section is by no means the only one possible, nor even the most plausible in some respects. Interested readers, and for present purposes that includes all those with ambitions to progress beyond this book in the study of exchange rates, would be well advised to consult Laidler (1985) on the demand for money, and the more important references given therein.

There are a number of channels through which the external sector might impinge on the supply side of the economy – for example, via a cost of living index with a significant import component. However, the result of incorporating these linkages is usually to complicate matters very substantially. The adventurous reader with sufficient mathematical background might like to look at the different approaches taken by Daniel (1982), Bruno and Sachs (1982), Marston (1982) and Copeland (1983).

Web page: **www.pearsoned.co.uk/copeland**.

Notes

1 See the reading guide for references to research on the implications of openness for aggregate supply.

2 In reality, the corporate sector saves by not distributing profits. We shall ignore this fact, without running any risk of its affecting our conclusions.

3 Notice that it is not being claimed that, as a household's income rises, it will actually save a higher proportion of its income, although that may also be a reasonable conjecture. All that is being asserted here is that a household's savings will be greater in absolute terms, the higher its income.

4 For simplicity, we assume investment is an activity exclusive to firms, which means ignoring investment by other sectors of the economy.

5 It should be noted that, even in industrialized countries, there can arise situations where the normal means of payment are no longer universally accepted, either as a result of bank failures or, more frequently, as a result of a lack of confidence in the internal or external purchasing

power of the currency. In such circumstances, the spontaneous response may be to return to a commodity money (cigarettes, gold, silver, and so on), as in the German hyperinflation of 1923, or, in some cases, to adopt a foreign currency as an unofficial means of payment (for example, Israel in the early 1980s). The latter phenomenon is known in the literature as 'currency substitution', and its implications will be examined in Chapter 9.

6 For the sake of simplicity, the definitions given here ignore a number of the less important financial instruments. For a detailed description of how these aggregates are computed in the UK, where $M4$ and $M5$ money supply definitions are also given, see the *Bank of England Quarterly Bulletin*, May 1987.

7 Until, say, the early 1970s, it was almost universally true that demand deposits earned no interest. In fact, there was some debate in the profession as to whether one could regard this as an intrinsic feature of money or whether it was simply a result of the way the banking system had developed, the monopoly power of banks, low inflation rates, and so on. During the 1970s and 1980s, the increased competition in banking, combined with higher inflation rates, led to a situation where explicit interest payments were frequently made to holders of demand deposits. What is even more common, however, is implicit interest on cheque accounts. This involves paying interest by the back door: offering depositors 'free' banking by refunding any charges they would otherwise incur for normal banking operations, such as cheque clearance, use of automated teller machines, and so on. This amounts to paying interest in kind – the bank pays its customers in units of its own output – banking services. Economists refer to this type of arrangement as the payment of an 'own rate' of interest.

8 In general, opportunity cost is the term used by economists to refer to the cost of a resource, viewed as the loss incurred by not employing it in its best alternative use.

9 To see why, compare two employees, one paid monthly and the other paid the same annual salary once a year. Suppose they both spend their income at a smooth rate throughout the year. The monthly paid employee would have an average balance over the year equal to one-half the monthly wage, while the second employee's average money balance would be one-half the annual wage or six times the monthly wage.

10 The distinction between nominal and real values is very important. A real variable is one that measures a physical quantity or volume of goods or services. A nominal variable is one that is valued in money terms. So a nominal value rises when prices rise and falls when they fall, while a real variable changes only when the quantities it measures change. In practice, real variables are computed by taking the values we actually observe – which are always nominal magnitudes – and deflating them by an appropriate price index. For example, if Y is nominal national income and P is the relevant price index (called, in this case, the 'GNP deflator'), then real income, also known as income in volume terms, is given by $y = Y/P$.

11 Strictly speaking, k is the product of two factors of proportionality: one relating national income to the volume of transactions, and the other relating the demand for money to transactions. In fact, k is the reciprocal of what is known as the (income) velocity of circulation. The demand for money is presented here in linear form, for simplicity. In fact, researchers nowadays tend to favour a demand for money equation that is linear in logs, as we shall see in Chapter 7.

12 Broadly speaking, Keynesian monetary theory tends to emphasize substitution between money and other financial assets (typically bonds) while monetarists are more inclined to concentrate, at least in theoretical argument, on the margin between money and real assets, such as physical capital and consumer goods. In practical applications (that is, empirical work), these issues have proved hardly worth the controversy (see Laidler (1985)). The only aspect of this question relevant to exchange rates is, as has already been mentioned, the possibility that the appropriate opportunity cost involves foreign assets (see Chapters 8 and 9).

13 Although governments often have enormous physical assets, they are rarely willing to use them to finance budget deficits, except as part of privatization programmes undertaken, ostensibly at least, for different reasons altogether. Incidentally, readers in the UK will note that, for once, British jargon is particularly appropriate in referring to the budget deficit as the public sector borrowing requirement.

14 The power to print money is referred to as seigniorage.

15 From now on, we shall use the term 'bonds' as a shorthand to refer to all non-monetary financial instruments issued by the authorities.

16 What's in a name? Not a lot, in this instance – not the Bank of Scotland, the Royal Bank of Scotland or even the Bank of America is a central bank, whatever their names may suggest.

17 But not one that is always the exclusive preserve of the central bank. The Scottish commercial banks, for example, are permitted to issue their own banknotes. They do so, however, under licence to the Bank of England. For our purposes here, we shall ignore such complications and assume that the central bank is the sole issuer of currency.

18 A point to note with regard to jargon: in the context of the open economy, the reserves can be taken to refer to the reserves of gold and foreign currency. However, as we shall see shortly, in the context of domestic banking, we often need to refer to a very different type of reserve, the precautionary cash (that is, domestic currency) reserves kept by commercial banks in their vaults. Since it is only in the present section that any possibility for confusion could arise, the convention will be followed in this chapter and throughout the rest of the book that 'the reserves' when unspecified always means the stock of gold and foreign currency held by the central bank.

19 The word 'forced' probably overstates the case somewhat, at least for some countries. Suffice to say that the degree of independence of the central bank depends entirely on constitutional considerations and/or custom and practice in the country in question. The whole issue of the feasibility and desirability of central bank independence is an extremely vexed one and is related to a number of questions regarding monetary and fiscal policy that will crop up at various points in what follows.

   For present purposes, we shall treat the central bank as simply an arm of government, so that transactions between it and the rest of the government are a purely formal, bookkeeping exercise.

20 Under the old Gold Standard, banknotes could in principle be exchanged for gold on demand, although by the time the system collapsed (in August 1971, in the case of the USA), the right to do so was restricted almost exclusively to foreign central banks. British banknotes still carry the meaningless legend: 'I Promise to pay the Bearer the Sum of . . .', signed, it should be noted, not by a minister or government official but by the cashier of the Bank of England.

21 A commercial bank is best thought of as the kind of financial institution with which we are all familiar: the retail or high-street bank, which takes deposits from the public at large and lends the proceeds to local businesses. For present purposes, we can safely ignore the existence of the wholesale banks, discount houses and other quasi-banks as unnecessarily complicating factors.

22 Only in the case of demand deposits (that is, current or cheque accounts). For time deposits ('deposit accounts') and the like, the balance may not have to be repaid on demand. However, in order to keep matters simple we shall restrict our attention to demand deposits, as is consistent with the definition of the money stock we chose at the beginning of Section 4.1.2.

23 The costs of running a bank are covered in two ways: through explicit charges and through the gap between the interest rate that the bank earns on its assets and the rate it must pay on its deposits (which is often zero in the case of cheque accounts).

24 Not only prudence. In some countries, and at times in the UK, the authorities have fixed the proportion of cash the banks are required to hold, not because they mistrusted the banks' judgement but as an alternative means of controlling the volume of bank lending. In other words, instead of controlling the quantity of cash in existence, they control the ratio of cash to loans.

   Another complication we shall ignore is that banks are often allowed to include some types of highly liquid earning assets (for example, treasury bills) in their precautionary reserves. Another fact of banking life over which we draw a veil is that, in addition to making provision for the repayment of deposits to normal, solvent customers, banks also have to set aside a reserve in order to cover bad debts. Finally, we also choose to ignore the possibility that banks can (and do) issue shares and use the proceeds to expand their balance sheets.

25 In fact, in a closed economy context, control of domestic credit is all there is to money supply control. Nevertheless, there have been long, acrimonious debates about how far it is possible to control the money stock, even in a closed economy. The issues, which revolve around the minutiae of the institutional arrangements for control of the banking system, need not concern us here. It should suffice to say that it is certainly possible to imagine a banking system such that control of domestic credit would be possible to 100% accuracy. Whether it is desirable to have

such a system is another matter, as indeed is the question of whether domestic credit can be controlled under the regimes actually in force in, say, the UK or the USA today.

26 So called because it joins points at which the money stock is equal to the demand for money, originally denoted by the letter L, in deference to Keynes' name for it: liquidity preference.

27 Not, of course, the same y_0 as in Figure 4.1.

28 And, almost certainly, a higher interest rate, since the effect of the upward shift in the LM curve is unlikely to be offset by the downward shift in the IS curve.

29 Ignoring other textbook factors of production such as land, managerial expertise, and so on. Notice also that employment ought, in principle, to be measured in man hours of homogeneous labour.

30 Strictly speaking, the product wage. We assume that the distinction can be ignored, at least at the aggregate level. We also make all the usual assumptions necessary to guarantee a downward-sloping marginal physical product curve.

31 Viewed either as the marginal utility of leisure or (the negative of) the marginal disutility of work. We assume leisure is, in the jargon of microeconomics, a normal good.

32 Known nowadays as new classic economics.

33 It is not our concern here as to why or how money wages might be fixed. The original Keynesian view was that money wages were not so much constant as 'downward invariant' – that is, incapable of being pushed down, even in the aftermath of price deflation, but quite easily pushed upward. This asymmetrical money illusion was held to be, at least in part, a cause of the mass unemployment of the 1930s.

PART II

Exchange rate determination

Having covered the preliminaries, we are now in a position to progress to looking at some models of exchange rate determination. We start in Chapter 5 with the simplest (and oldest), the monetary model, which is founded on the assumption that prices are completely flexible, so that PPP obtains at all times. By contrast, Chapter 6 examines a model that takes the price level as absolutely fixed and allows for variations in national income. The Dornbusch model (Chapter 7) offers a compromise with sticky prices and financial markets that compensate in the short run by overadjusting. The next two chapters expand the perspective to take in a richer specification of the menu of assets: domestic and foreign bonds are included in the portfolio balance model (Chapter 8) and the implications of allowing for domestic holdings of foreign currency are examined in Chapter 9. By way of contrast, the models covered in Chapter 10 broaden the perspective in another direction, considering exchange rate determination in the context of equilibrium in the macroeconomy as a whole. Finally, Chapter 11 looks beyond theory to the question of optimal currency zones, a topic in applied exchange rate economics that has loomed large in international political economy since the early 1990s, especially in Europe.

5

Flexible prices: the monetary model

Introduction

5.1 The simple monetary model of a floating exchange rate

5.2 The simple monetary model of a fixed exchange rate

5.3 Interest rates in the monetary model

5.4 The monetary model as an explanation of the facts

Conclusions

Summary

Reading guide

Notes

Introduction

There are a number of reasons why we choose to look at the monetary model first. For one thing, it was the earliest approach to explaining the related phenomena of exchange rate variations on the one hand and the balance of payments on the other. It also had a brief renaissance in the early 1970s. More importantly, it represents an obvious benchmark for comparing the other approaches to modelling exchange rate determination, many of which themselves grew out of the monetary model. Finally, while it is completely inadequate in explaining the wild day-to-day, month-to-month gyrations seen in recent years, it none the less provides some useful insights into the broader picture of long-run trends.

What we now call the monetary model is rooted in an approach to the balance of payments that dates back at least as far as the work of David Hume in 1741. It will be seen to consist of two basic building blocks: the purchasing power parity (PPP) relationship, familiar from Chapter 2, and the demand for money, which was covered in Chapter 4.

In the first section, these two relationships will be incorporated in a particularly simple version of the aggregate demand and supply model, which will then be used in succeeding sections to analyse the effect of increases in the money supply, income and foreign prices on a floating exchange rate. In Section 5.2, we examine the implications of the same disturbances for the balance of payments under a fixed exchange rate regime. Section 5.2.4 analyses the effect of devaluation. Section 5.3 looks at the role played by interest rates. The final section provides a brief survey of the evidence for and (mostly) against the monetary model.

5.1 The simple monetary model of a floating exchange rate

We start by setting the scene. The model to be set out in this section is very much a simplification, but it will suffice none the less to generate the conclusions typical of international monetarism.

5.1.1 Setting

The monetary model rests essentially on three assumptions: a vertical aggregate supply curve, a stable demand for money and PPP. We shall examine these assumptions in that order.

> **Assumption 5.1** The aggregate supply curve is vertical.

Two points should be remembered in this regard from Chapter 4. First, this does *not* imply that output is constant – simply that it can vary only as the result of a change in the productivity of the economy, broadly defined; that is, through technical progress, the accumulation of capital, growth in the labour force or its educational level, and so on.

Second, a vertical supply curve presupposes perfect price flexibility in all markets.

> **Assumption 5.2** The demand for real money balances is a stable function of only a few domestic macroeconomic variables. In fact, for the moment and until further notice, we shall work with the Cambridge quantity equation (Equation 4.7):
>
> $$M^d = kPy \quad k > 0$$
>
> where y is real national income and k is a positive parameter.

This particular formulation simplifies matters considerably. Consider what it implies for the aggregate demand schedule. Given a money stock, M_0^s, equilibrium means we have:

$$M_0^s = kPy = kY \tag{5.1}$$

It follows that nominal income, Y, must be constant along the aggregate demand curve, since it is drawn for a given value of the money stock.

Look at Figure 5.1. The nominal national income $Y = Py$ associated with any point on the curve labelled $AD_0(M_0^s)$ is simply the area of the rectangle between it and the axes, for example OP_0Ay_0 at A and OP_2Dy_1 at D. If these areas are to be equal, then it must follow that, as we move from A to D, the fall in the price level is of the same proportion as the rise in income.[1]

More important for present purposes, consider the effect of an increase in the nominal money stock. As we saw in Chapter 4 this change shifts the aggregate demand

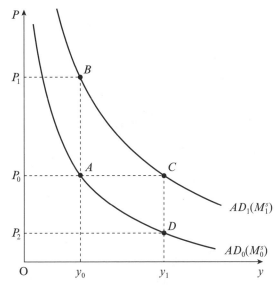

Figure 5.1 Aggregate demand with the quantity equation

curve upward and to the right. By how much, in the present case? Compare points A and B. Obviously, P_1 must be greater than P_0 by the same proportion as M_1^s is greater than M_0^s.

For example, if the change in question is a doubling of the money stock, then the outcome has to be a doubling of nominal demand. At any given real income, y_0, that implies a doubling of the price level.

> **Assumption 5.3** Purchasing power parity (PPP) obtains at all times.

Remember from Chapter 2 (Equation 2.4) that the PPP hypothesis stated that given a domestic (UK) price level of P and a foreign (US) price level of P^*, equilibrium would be obtained when the two price levels stood in the following relationship:

$$SP^* = P$$

so that nothing could be gained by shipping goods from one country to the other. Remember also that this is equivalent to stating that the purchasing power of each country's currency must be the same whether spent on the domestic market or converted into foreign currency and spent abroad.

Now consider Figure 5.2(a), where the vertical axis plots the domestic price level and the horizontal axis plots the sterling price of US dollars. The line drawn out from the origin is the locus of all combinations of S and P that satisfy Equation 2.4 – call it the PPP line. Plainly, it has a gradient equal to P^*. Points above and to the left of the line are those where the UK economy is uncompetitive (the domestic price level is too high), so that it is worth importing goods from the USA in place of relatively expensive UK products. The opposite is true below the line.

In terms of the *real* exchange rate (look back at the definition in Section 2.4, if necessary), above the PPP line a real depreciation is required in order to restore equilibrium and, below it, the opposite is true.

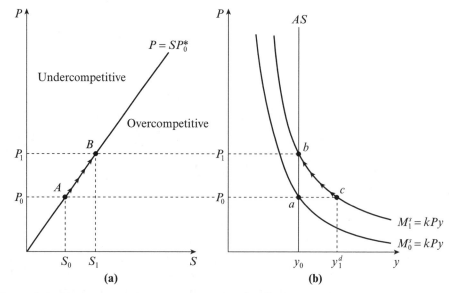

Figure 5.2 Money supply increase under floating rates

5.1.2 Equilibrium

In Figure 5.2(b), the aggregate demand and supply curves are plotted for given values of the money stock and output capacity. With an initial money supply of M_0^s, P_0 is the 'closed economy' equilibrium price level – that is, the one consistent with conditions in the domestic economy.

In fact, P_0 is still the equilibrium price level, even in this open economy model. Furthermore, *its value is determined without any reference to conditions in the external sector of the economy.*

However, in the external sector, PPP requires that a price level of P_0 be associated with an exchange rate of S_0. A lower value of S would leave domestic output uncompetitive on world markets and hence result in an excess supply of the home currency, and vice versa at a higher level of S.

We can see the nature of equilibrium formally by combining Equations 2.4 and 5.1 to give:

$$M_0^s = kPy = kSP^*y \qquad (5.2)$$

so that we can solve for S as:

$$S = \frac{M_0^s}{kP^*y} \qquad (5.3)$$

So the exchange rate in this ultra-simple model is the ratio of the money stock to the demand, measured at the foreign price level. Whatever serves to raise that ratio, in other words to increase the numerator or decrease the denominator, will cause the price of foreign exchange to rise (the domestic currency to depreciate).

Now consider the effect on this equilibrium of three types of disturbance: a monetary expansion and a rise in real income, respectively, in the domestic economy, and an increase in the world price level.

5.1.3 Money supply increase under floating exchange rates

Start with an expansion of the money stock to a new level, M_1^s. Assume the other exogenous variables (real income, y, and the foreign price level, P^*) are unchanged.

At the old price level, P_0, there is clearly an excess supply of money, which will cause economic agents to increase spending in order to reduce their money balances. (Recall that the quantity theory is based on the assumption that the only way for agents to reduce their money balances is by buying goods and services.) The counterpart of the excess supply of money is therefore an excess demand for goods, as measured by the distance $(y_1^d - y_0)$ in Figure 5.2(b).

Given our assumption of a fixed real income and output, the extra spending must drive up prices (hence the arrows between points c and b, and points A and B). As the price of goods rises, the price of dollars must increase (the pound depreciates) in order to keep domestic output competitive – in other words, to prevent a flood of relatively cheap US output into the UK economy in response to the real exchange rate appreciation.

It is easy to see how great a depreciation is required to restore equilibrium. With domestic prices higher in proportion to the monetary expansion and the US price level unchanged, preservation of PPP implies an increase of the same proportion in the price of dollars.

We have reached the first important conclusion in our analysis of the monetary model:

> **Proposition 5.1** In the monetary model, a given percentage increase in the domestic money supply leads, other things being equal, to a depreciation of the same proportion in the value of the domestic currency.

Box 5.1 | **Proof of proposition 5.1**

Formally rewrite Equation 5.1, taking logs of both sides, and then differentiate, to give:

$$\frac{dM}{M} - \frac{dP}{P} = \frac{dy}{y}$$

remembering that for any variable X, $d(\log X) = dX/X$. Since we are assuming that y is constant for present purposes, the right-hand side is zero. Hence, the domestic price level has to change in proportion to the money stock.

Now treat the PPP equation in the same way, to give:

$$\frac{dS}{S} + \frac{dP^*}{P^*} = \frac{dP}{P}$$

Since P^* is assumed constant, this says that the exchange rate must depreciate in proportion to the rise in UK prices.

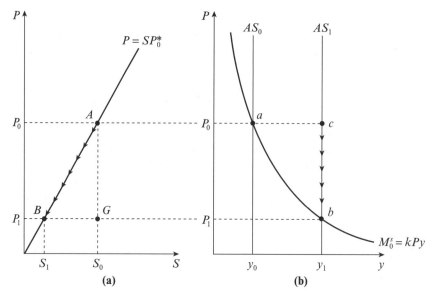

Figure 5.3 Income increase under floating rates

5.1.4 Income increase under floating exchange rates

Now consider the effect of an increase in real income, from y_0 to y_1, with no change in the money stock (Figure 5.3).

At any price level, higher real income implies a greater demand for money. Put differently, with a given money supply we must have constant *nominal* income, Py. So, the higher the real income, the lower must be the price level.

Since nominal income has jumped to $P_0 y_1$ (at point c in Figure 5.3(b)), the impact effect must be to create an excess demand for money and an excess supply of goods equal to the gap $(y_1 - y_0)$ at the original price level, P_0. As we have already seen, real balances can be replenished only by reducing spending.

The result must be deflation, bringing the price level down from P_0 to P_1. In the new equilibrium, at b, both money and goods markets clear, with the same demand and supply as before the income increase and with the same nominal income.

In the open sector of the economy, however, the exchange rate must have fallen (that is, the pound appreciated) from S_0 to S_1. Otherwise, the fall in domestic prices (depreciation in the real exchange rate) would have made the UK overcompetitive, causing a massive excess demand for sterling (as would have been the case at G, for example). PPP is preserved by appreciation, so that the fall in the price of UK output is offset by a rise in the price of sterling relative to the dollar.

We conclude, then, as follows:

> **Proposition 5.2** In the monetary model, a rise in domestic real income leads, other things being equal, to an appreciation of the home currency.

Notice that we associate an increase in real income with an *appreciation* of the currency. This conclusion flatly contradicts the wisdom of the DIY model that, as income rises, the domestic economy tends to suck in imports, causing a depreciation in a floating exchange rate.

The reason we have the opposite result here is that the monetary model concentrates on the impact of an income increase on the demand for *money*, rather than goods. Since it swells the demand for money, it must cause a contraction in the demand for goods, which in turn must lead to a fall in the domestic price level.

5.1.5 Foreign price increase under floating exchange rates

An important feature of the model is its conclusion regarding the effect of a change in the remaining exogenous variable, $P*$, the foreign price level.

Concentrate on the PPP line in Figure 5.4(a). How will it change when $P*$ increases? Since its gradient is $P/S = P*$, it will become steeper, so that the original UK price level P_0 is associated with a lower price of US dollars – in other words, a higher exchange rate for the pound.

The reason for this result should be obvious by now. With higher US prices, UK goods are overcompetitive at the old exchange rate. The demand for sterling by potential US importers of cheaper UK goods is overwhelming and drives the pound's value up until US competitiveness is restored.

In the new equilibrium, the fact that US output is priced higher in dollar terms than previously is offset by the higher relative price of the UK currency. We conclude:

> **Proposition 5.3** In the monetary model, a rise in the foreign price level, other things being equal, is associated with an appreciation of the domestic currency (that is, a fall in the price of foreign exchange, S) and no other change in the domestic economy.

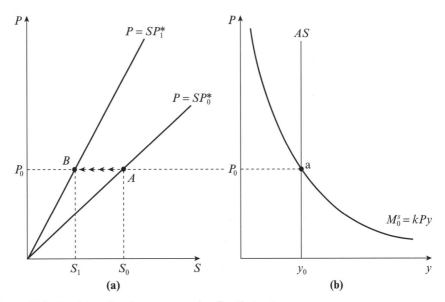

Figure 5.4 Foreign price increase under floating rates

From the point of view of macroeconomic policy, this proposition is highly significant. It suggests that world inflation need have no impact on the domestic economy. The UK price level is determined in UK money markets in exactly the same way that it would be if the rest of the world never existed. The floating exchange rate acts like a valve, continually sliding up or down as required to preserve PPP in the face of disturbances originating in either country's (or both countries') domestic money markets.

The implication is that the sovereignty of each country's macroeconomic policy is preserved by exchange rate flexibility. Each can independently choose its inflation rate[2] without regard to the actions of the other. If national independence is to be regarded as a desirable feature of an international monetary order, then the floating exchange rate system appears highly attractive on the basis of the analysis in this section.

Notice that, in arriving at Proposition 5.3, we had no need to consult Figure 5.4(b). Does that mean the money markets are irrelevant to the outcome?

There are two reasons why the money markets are certainly not irrelevant. First, it is the fact that money market equilibrium is unaffected by the change in US prices that keeps the domestic price level fixed at its initial level P_0 and forces the burden of adjustment on to the exchange rate.

Second, ask yourself the following question: what can have caused the US price level to rise?

5.1.6 Two-country model of a floating exchange rate

The obvious answer to the previous question is something that has caused an excess supply to appear in the US money market, for example an increase in the US money stock or a fall in US income. In fact, if you think about it for a moment, the way the US price level is determined is likely to be the same as the way the UK price level is determined – that is to say, in the local US money market.

Look back at our analysis of the effect of a monetary expansion in the domestic economy (see Section 5.1.3). Why should we not apply the same argument to the USA as was applied to the UK?

An increase in US money supply would cause an excess supply in local money markets, causing Americans to spend more, other things being equal, in order to reduce their balances. The outcome of their attempt to spend more would ultimately be to drive up their own price level, P^*, thereby causing the dollar to depreciate in order to prevent the US being flooded with what would otherwise be cheaper imports.

We can formalize this symmetrical model by writing the US version of our quantity equation (Equation 4.7) as follows:

$$M^{d*} = k^*P^*y^* \tag{5.4}$$

which simply says the US demand for money, M^{d*}, is proportional to US nominal income, P^*y^*. Notice the factor of proportionality is k^*, to allow for the possibility that the US demand for money may be *quantitatively* different from that of the UK, even though it is *qualitatively* similar (that is, of the same functional form).

Now assume that, just as UK money stock is initially M_0^s, US money supply starts off at M_0^{s*}. Divide the UK demand for money equation (Equation 4.7) by Equation 5.4 and set the respective demands for money equal to supply in each country, to give:

$$\frac{M_0^s}{M_0^{s*}} = \frac{kPy}{k^*P^*y^*} \tag{5.5}$$

Since, under PPP, we have $P/P^* = S$, it follows that we can rewrite Equation 5.5 as:

$$\frac{M_0^s}{M_0^{s*}} = \frac{kSy}{k^*y^*} \tag{5.6}$$

Now if we solve for S, we have:

$$S = \frac{M/M^*}{ky/k^*y^*} \tag{5.7}$$

This says the exchange rate equals the ratio of the numerator (relative money stocks) to the denominator (relative real demands). Therefore, anything that tends to increase the UK money stock relative to the US or diminish UK demand for money relative to the US will cause the pound to depreciate (S to rise).

To see how we must modify our previous conclusions, rewrite Equation 5.7 more simply, as follows:

$$S = \frac{\tilde{M}}{\tilde{k}\tilde{y}} \tag{5.8}$$

where the convention has been introduced (and will be followed wherever necessary throughout the book) that a tilde (~) over a variable denotes the ratio of its domestic to foreign value, so $\tilde{M}$ means M/M^*, and so on.

Now remember that a 10% increase in the UK money supply relative to the US, $M/M^* = \tilde{M}$, can come about *either* from a 10% rise in the UK money stock, from a 10% fall in the US money stock, *or*, more likely, from some combination of both, say a 15% increase in UK money supply, with a 5% rise in US money.

It follows that although we can stick to our original conclusion (Proposition 5.1) that an increase in UK money supply, other things being equal, leads to a depreciation in sterling (rise in S) of the same proportion, we now recognize that *the same is true of anything that changes relative money stocks*. Thus, for example, a 10% fall in US money while the UK money stock remained constant would cause a 10% depreciation in the pound's exchange rate, other things being equal.

Similarly, it is *relative* real income that counts in determining the demand for one country's money relative to another, so an increase in US income has the same impact as a fall in UK income and we know from Proposition 5.2 that the latter causes a rise in the relative price of dollars.

It follows, then, that we can generalize both Propositions 5.1 and 5.2 by substituting for the domestic variables their value relative to the same foreign variables.

5.2 **The simple monetary model of a fixed exchange rate**

Now consider a situation where the exchange rate is not allowed to move. The analysis here is slightly more complicated, so it will help if we start by clarifying which variables are being taken as exogenous and which endogenous.

Real income, y, is assumed to be given by factors outside the scope of our model, as before, and the foreign price level, P^*, is determined by foreign money supply, income, and so on, and hence is also taken as given.

Recall the discussion of the money supply in Section 4.1.2 (Equation 4.10). Under a fixed exchange rate regime, we concluded that the money supply was *not* an exogenous variable. Instead, the policy variable was domestic credit, DC, and we could write:

$$FX + DC \equiv M^s$$

so that the burden of adjustment to changes in the exogenous variables fell on the foreign currency reserves, FX.

The only remaining exogenous variable is the exchange rate itself, which is fixed by the decision of the authorities at some level, $\bar{S}$.[3]

5.2.1 Money supply increase under fixed exchange rates

Now look at Figure 5.5, which shows the effect of an expansionary monetary policy – in other words, an increase in domestic credit, from an initial level of DC_0 to a higher level, DC_1.

Start with Figure 5.5(c), which plots levels of the money stock (vertical axis) against levels of the foreign exchange reserves, FX (horizontally). Measure off the

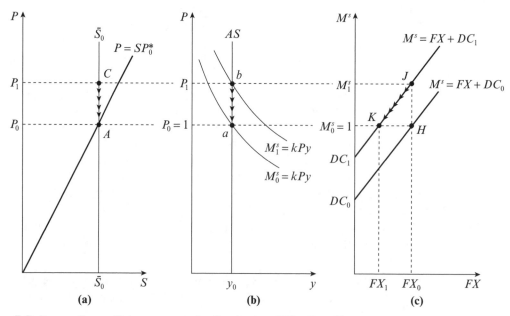

Figure 5.5 Domestic credit increase under fixed rates ($M_0^s = P_0 = 1$)

quantity DC_0 on the vertical axis, and from that point extend a 45-degree line. That ray then shows how the money stock increases with additions to the reserves, given the initial quantity of domestic credit, DC_0. For example, if the reserves were nil, then the whole money stock would be credit. As we move to the right, each additional pound of reserves increases the money stock by one pound exactly.

If we start with reserves of FX_0, the money stock must be:

$$M_0^S = FX_0 + DC_0 \qquad (5.9)$$

so that the starting point in that diagram is at H.

Now let us set the initial value of the money supply and the price level at unity. In other words, assume we happen to have $ky_0 = 1$. This device is for purposes of illustration only. It has the advantage that it allows us to translate the money stock value on the vertical axis of Figure 5.5(c) directly into the implied price level in Figures 5.5(a) and (b).

Exploiting this fact, the initial price level given a money stock of M_0^S must be P_0. Hence, the economy starts off at point a in Figure 5.5(b). Notice that as far as aggregate demand and supply are concerned, the diagram is unchanged, since at this stage we have no reason to believe that the private sector's behaviour will be any different under fixed rather than under floating exchange rates.

As with Figure 5.4, the left-hand diagram (Figure 5.5(a)) plots the PPP line. However, with the exchange rate pegged at $\bar{S}_0$, the economy must at all times be restricted to points that lie along the vertical line. Since, as before, equilibrium requires that the domestic price level be at purchasing power parity, it follows that the system must start off at A, at the intersection of the PPP line with the fixed exchange rate line. Put formally, we must have:

$$P = \bar{S}_0 \bar{P}* \qquad (5.10)$$

where the bars over the right-hand side variables remind us that both S and $P*$ are fixed exogenously.

The economy is in full equilibrium initially, because the PPP price level defined in Equation 5.10 is precisely the one consistent with the (endogenous) money stock and hence with equality of aggregate supply and demand at the point a in Figure 5.5(b).

Now suppose the initial equilibrium illustrated by points A, a and H is disturbed by a monetary expansion.

With the expansion of domestic credit, the 45-degree line in the money supply diagram Figure 5.5(c) shifts upwards by the amount of the expansion, so that, with the foreign exchange reserves still at their previous level of FX_0, the money stock has now swelled to M_1^S, as we can see at point J.

Following the line across from J, we see that the new money stock implies a price level of P_1 (at b), thanks to an upward shift in the aggregate demand schedule. From the PPP line in Figure 5.5(a), it is clear that the higher price level has made the domestic economy uncompetitive, since, given unchanged foreign prices and the fixed exchange rate, it amounts to a real appreciation. At C, there is an incentive for domestic entrepreneurs to import from abroad and none for foreigners to buy locally produced goods.

The obvious outcome must be a deficit on the balance of payments[4] as the economy responds to the changed terms of trade. The situation is unsustainable. It would cause an immediate depreciation if the authorities permitted one. However, by assumption, they avoid that outcome by using the foreign exchange reserves to buy the domestic currency or, to put it differently, to finance the ongoing payments deficit. The result is that *the reserves start to fall*.

Each successive reduction in the reserves tends to reduce the money supply, pushing the economy along the arrowed paths in the three quadrants, so that the system moves from J to K, from b back to a and from C down to A. The process ends with competitiveness restored and the balance of payments deficit reduced to zero, back at A on the PPP line, with the price level restored to its old level of P_0 (at the point a). The reinstatement of the original equilibrium is possible because the money supply has contracted, to the point where it is once more at its initial level, M_0^S.

To understand why we get this result, recall from Equation 4.7 that our demand for money, given PPP, must equal:

$$M^d = kPy = k(\bar{S}\bar{P}^*)\bar{y} \tag{5.11}$$

The final term is the demand for money. Notice that all its components are exogenously given variables. It follows that, under our assumptions, nothing the domestic monetary authority does can affect the demand for money. If the market is to clear, then it follows equally that the money supply must automatically find its way back to its pre-expansion level.

Equating demand and supply:

$$M^d = k\bar{S}\bar{P}^*\bar{y} = M^s = FX + DC \tag{5.12}$$

so that solving for FX gives us:

$$FX = k\bar{S}\bar{P}^*\bar{y} - DC \tag{5.13}$$

Equation 5.13 tells us that the foreign currency reserves, FX, must be exactly equal to the gap between the given demand for domestic money and the supply generated by the local banking system, through the process of domestic credit expansion. It follows that the more sparing the domestic authorities are in their credit creation, the greater will be the shortfall that has to be made up by the reserves.

In terms of *changes*, we can state that:

> **Proposition 5.4** Under fixed exchange rates in the monetary model, starting from a position of equilibrium, domestic credit creation will be neutralized, other things being equal, by a fall in the reserves as a result of a temporary balance of payments deficit. Conversely, domestic credit contraction will cause a temporary balance of payments surplus and a consequent offsetting rise in the reserves.

Notice that, as always in the monetary model, the mechanism involved here could be expressed purely in terms of the excess demand for money.

The right-hand side of Equation 5.13 is the excess demand for money balances. It is this excess demand that is satisfied by the supply of international currency. An increase in domestic credit from an initial equilibrium generates an excess supply of money balances in the local market. As in the closed economy context (see Section 4.1.2), the effect is to cause domestic residents to run down their excess money balances by spending. With real income fixed, however, the consequent inflation makes foreign products relatively cheaper and the home country's exports more expensive. The external deficit is a by-product of the private sector's attempt to substitute goods for excess money balances. As reserves flow out, the foreign component of the money stock falls along with domestic prices until equilibrium is reinstated.

Notice that since it is *stocks* of money that count in this model, the *flow* of reserves in or out of a country can be only a temporary phenomenon, as the money stock adjusts over time to the demand. In other words, balance of payments deficits or surpluses are viewed as inherently transient by-products of the adjustment mechanism. Once that process is complete and the money market is back in equilibrium, the deficit or surplus will have evaporated.

If the money supply, price level and balance of payments all return to their previous level, what has changed in the new equilibrium?

Compare points K and H in Figure 5.5(c). Although the money supply is unchanged at K, its *composition* has altered as a result of the cumulative impact of the balance of payments deficit that persisted throughout the period of adjustment. The new money supply is made up as follows:

$$M_0^s = FX_1 + DC_1 \tag{5.14}$$

In other words, the net outcome is that the money stock now consists of more domestic credit and less foreign exchange than previously. What has occurred is a kind of debasement of the currency – a dilution of the international asset backing of the domestic money supply. Obviously, the process has a well-defined limit – at the point when the reserves have fallen to zero and the entire money stock is composed of domestic credit.

Sterilization of reserve changes

Notice that the process described here amounts to a type of automatic stabilization. In fact, this is broadly the mechanism relied on to guarantee the stability of both the pre-World War I Gold Standard and the Bretton Woods system (see Section 1.5.1). With a fixed exchange rate, flows of reserves act automatically to adjust the money stock so as to reinstate equilibrium. Government monetary policy is not only impossible but also unnecessary.

In particular, viewed from this standpoint, balance of payments deficits (or surpluses), far from requiring remedial macroeconomic policy, are actually the channels through which disequilibria are spontaneously rectified.

None the less, a government that wishes for whatever reason to resist these stabilizing forces might in principle be able to do so, temporarily at least. To see how this can be achieved, go back to the situation facing domestic policymakers at the start of what has been called here the adjustment phase, in the aftermath of the initial destabilizing domestic credit expansion, when the economy is at points C, b and J respectively in Figures 5.5(a) to (c).

At that juncture, the UK is running a balance of payments deficit and is therefore losing reserves (as first seen in Equation 4.11). In other words, the UK money stock is falling because, in the identity:

$$\Delta FX + \Delta DC \equiv \Delta M^s$$

the first term is negative. Since the second term is constant (the once-and-for-all increase is assumed to have already taken place), the money supply is falling. Hence, it is only a matter of time until the cumulative effect of the continuing deficits reduces the money supply to its pre-disturbance level.

Now suppose the authorities decided to try to prevent the money stock falling by further expanding domestic credit. It would appear that, in so doing, they could pre-empt the fall in the money supply. If they increased credit enough to offset the fall in the foreign currency reserves in each period, it looks as though they could neutralize the deficits completely.

The following piece of jargon is commonly used:

> **Sterilization** is the process of neutralizing the effect of a balance of payments deficit (surplus) by creating (retiring) enough domestic credit to offset the fall in the foreign exchange reserves.

There has been a great deal of debate, among both researchers and policymakers, about how far sterilization is actually feasible. Even its most enthusiastic advocates would not claim it can work for very long. Whether it can work at all in today's currency markets is extremely dubious.[5]

To see why its usefulness is likely to be limited, we need to follow through the implication of the second-stage increase in domestic credit. Obviously, the effect of an increase in domestic credit starting from the situation at J in Figure 5.5(c) will be to move the money supply line even further up the vertical axis. The result will be to further dilute the foreign currency backing of the UK money stock.

Neither is that all. We have already established that, as long as the money stock is above its equilibrium level, the UK will be haemorrhaging reserves. Clearly, anything that prolongs that situation will reduce the reserves below what they otherwise would be in the absence of any attempt at sterilization.

It follows that sterilization is likely to prove a treadmill. Each expansion of domestic credit will prolong the reserve loss and hence generate the need for further credit creation. At each stage, the domestic credit component of the money stock gets larger and the reserve component smaller.

In theory, at least, there will come a stage when the reserves are exhausted and the game will be over. In reality, the limit to this process is likely to come some time before the country's reserves are actually exhausted, simply because currency markets will anticipate the evil day and thereby hasten its arrival by rushing to sell pounds at the current exchange rate while they still can,[6] as we shall see in Chapter 17.

5.2.2 Income increase under fixed exchange rates

As far as changes in real income and the world price level are concerned, the analysis involves a straightforward application of the results from the floating rate case.

With the price level unchanged, an increase in real income amounts to a rise in the demand for real money balances, other things being equal. Starting from a position of equilibrium, then, the impact will cause domestic residents to spend less, so as to raise their balances to a level commensurate with their new, higher volume of transactions.

In doing so, they force the price level down, which with a fixed exchange rate makes the home country's output overcompetitive on world markets, leading to a balance of payments surplus and consequent rise in the reserves. This process will come to an end only when the domestic money stock has grown sufficiently to match the new, larger demand.

So, as the reader may confirm by redrawing Figure 5.5 and shifting the aggregate supply line to the right, we can state the following:

> **Proposition 5.5** Under fixed exchange rates in the monetary model, starting from a position of equilibrium, the result of a rise in (the domestic country's) real income will be to cause an increase in the reserves as a result of a temporary balance of payments surplus, other things being equal. In the new equilibrium, the domestic money stock will have risen and the home price level will have returned to its PPP level.

Again, note the contrast with the DIY model (Section 1.4).

5.2.3 Foreign price increase under fixed exchange rates

As for a rise in the world price level, the effect under a fixed exchange rate is directly to increase the home country's competitiveness, causing a payments surplus and consequent rise in the reserves. (In terms of Figure 5.5, the impact effect is to cause the PPP line to become steeper.) This in turn brings about a rise in the money stock, pushing up the home country price level until it reaches parity with that of the outside world, at which point PPP and external balance are restored. So, for completeness:

> **Proposition 5.6** Under fixed exchange rates in the monetary model, starting from a position of equilibrium, the result of a rise in the rest of the world's price level will be to cause an increase in the reserves as the result of a temporary balance of payments surplus, other things being equal. In the new equilibrium, the domestic money stock will be greater and the home price level will have risen to its PPP level.

Note the implication: a country that pegs its exchange rate has ultimately to accept the world price level. In the common jargon of the 1960s and 1970s, it is forced to import inflation from the rest of the world. The fact that it cannot control its own money supply means it cannot choose its price level or inflation rate independently of developments beyond its borders.

Hence, an important conclusion of the monetary model is that, subject to one qualification we shall deal with in a moment, *a country cannot follow an independent monetary policy under fixed exchange rates – neither, as a consequence, can it choose a price level or inflation rate different from that of the rest of the world.*

To see the qualification that needs to be added to this statement, ask yourself the following question: what determines the world price level, P^*? What causes world inflation – at any rate, in this simple model?

The answer must be that world prices rise when the world's money stock increases faster than world demand. Also, world money supply and demand are simply the sum of the supply and demand in all of the countries in the world. It follows that, when we analyse the effect of, say, an increase in the home country's money stock, *we can treat the world price level as exogenous only if the additional money creation is of negligible significance to the world as a whole.* In other words, we have to be able to safely ignore the impact of the home country's money supply increase on the rest of the world's money markets and hence on world prices. Obviously, this assumption makes sense only if the domestic country is small enough in economic terms relative to the world economy for us to be able to ignore the repercussions of its policy measures on the world economy.[7]

5.2.4 Devaluation under fixed exchange rates

Before leaving the analysis of fixed exchange rates, there is one special case that merits attention, because it provides a particularly clear insight into the nature of the monetary model.

No fixed exchange rate is fixed forever. Sooner or later the authorities find themselves forced to move the rate to a new level, higher or lower. That is why a fixed exchange rate regime is sometimes referred to as an adjustable peg. What happens when the peg is adjusted?

Figure 5.6 shows the effect of a devaluation – an announced, once-and-for-all rise in the price of foreign currency. It must be emphasized that the analysis is applicable only to a devaluation that is an isolated event, and perceived as such, and not one that generates the expectation of further devaluation (or revaluation) to come.

Following the pedagogic convention in economics, we start the analysis from a position of equilibrium, which is somewhat unrealistic in this case because countries usually alter a fixed exchange rate only when absolutely necessary to correct an obvious disequilibrium. None the less, it is easy to see how the conclusions could be modified to deal with an initial balance of payments deficit.

The economy starts off in equilibrium at points A, a and G in the three diagrams in Figure 5.6, with, as before, an exchange rate of $\bar{S}_0$, a price level under PPP of P_0, and a money supply of M_0^s, made up of domestic credit in the quantity DC_0 and reserves of FX_0.

The home country then devalues, raising the price of foreign currency to $\bar{S}_1$.

The overnight impact effect is to move the economy instantaneously to a point like C. In other words, with a given foreign price level and, as yet, with no time for domestic prices to change (suppose the devaluation took place over a weekend, as became the fashion in the European Monetary System), the home country is now *over*competitive. Had it started off from a position of being uncompetitive (that is, above the PPP line), the impact effect would have been to move it to the right, making it more competitive than previously, which would, presumably, have been the object of the whole exercise in the first place.

The interim verdict has to be: so far, so good. With both domestic and foreign prices unchanged, it is the *real* as well as the nominal exchange rate that has been devalued. Foreign goods now cost more, while domestic goods are unchanged in

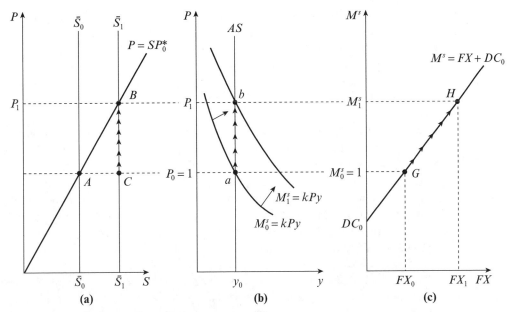

Figure 5.6 Devaluation under fixed rates ($M_0^s = P_0 = 1$)

price. The result must be a tendency for home country consumers to buy more domestically produced output than previously and fewer imports. Conversely, foreigners find the home country's products more attractively priced, on average, than before the devaluation.

Starting from equilibrium, the outcome has to be a balance of payments surplus. If we had started, more realistically, from a position of deficit, we would have been able to assert only that the result would be a less unfavourable foreign balance.

The story of what happens during the next stage, as the economy adjusts to the devaluation, can be told in several different ways, each focusing on the adjustment process in a different sector, and all leading inexorably to the same conclusion.

First, consider what is happening to the money supply when the economy is 'bounced' over to C.[8] With its balance of payments in surplus, the country must be accumulating reserves – hence, the arrows on the path from G to H in the money supply diagram (Figure 5.6(c)). Since the volume of domestic credit is unchanged, the money supply must be growing, shifting the aggregate demand schedule upwards. In terms of the money market, with real income and output constant, and hence an unchanged demand, the price level must be bid up as agents attempt to reduce their excess real balances by buying additional goods. As the price level rises, of course, the competitive advantage and consequent external surplus is eroded, until the new equilibrium is reached at B in Figure 5.6(a).

In terms of the goods market, if output is pegged at y_0, the increased demand by domestic residents (for cheaper import substitutes) and by foreigners (for the home country's exports) cannot be satisfied. The excess demand must simply generate an inflation, which persists until enough of the additional demand has been priced out of the market in order to restore equilibrium.

The version of this process that gained wide acceptance in the early 1970s, particularly in the UK, emphasized the reaction of labour markets to devaluation. It was argued that a key role would be played by wage inflation, induced *either* by a cost–push process, as workers reacted to the higher price of imports by demanding compensating wage rises, *or* by a demand–pull mechanism, as employers bid up the wage rate in an attempt to satisfy the excess demand for goods by recruiting more labour.

Whichever of these processes is the dominant one, there can be no doubt about the conclusion. Ultimately, the economy ends up at *B*, with PPP restored and the real exchange rate back where it was before, thanks to domestic inflation.

What has changed, if anything, compared with the pre-devaluation situation? Obviously, the higher price level is supported or sustained by a larger money stock, M_1^s, made up of the same level of domestic credit plus a larger stock of foreign currency reserves – the accumulation of the intervening weeks, months or possibly years of balance of payments surplus. So:

> **Proposition 5.7** Under fixed exchange rates in the monetary model the result of a once-and-for-all devaluation will be a temporary improvement in the competitiveness of the home country and, consequently, a balance of payments surplus, leading in turn to a rise in its foreign currency reserves. However, the ensuing inflation will, as time passes, erode the country's price advantage, until the economy finds itself back where it started, with a higher price level, greater reserves and a larger *nominal* money stock, but the same *real* money supply.

From a policy point of view, the good news is that, if the monetary model's message is to be believed, devaluation works. It does indeed generate a balance of payments surplus or at least reduce the deficit of a country that starts off in disequilibrium. Devaluation replenishes the reserves or slows down the rate of reserve loss for a deficit country.

The bad news, on the other hand, is that its beneficial effect is temporary. It cannot permanently affect competitiveness. It causes inflation, thereby ultimately neutralizing the benefits that it is supposed to confer. How long the adjustment takes is an empirical question, to which the answer would probably vary from country to country and from case to case.

In any case, there may well be a delay before the balance of payments effect of a devaluation appears. It is often argued that the immediate impact of a devaluation is to worsen rather than improve the situation. The logic is as follows.

If trade flows are usually invoiced in the currency of the exporting nation, then a devaluation of the pound will reduce the average dollar price of UK exports but have no effect on the (dollar) price of our imports. Furthermore, if the very short-run elasticities of demand for exports and imports are negligible (because of inertia in consumer tastes, difficulty in switching production, and so on), then the immediate outcome will be unchanged trade volumes priced less favourably for the home country. Each unit of exports will now earn fewer dollars, while each import still costs the same. The result will be a deterioration in the UK balance of payments, which will be rectified only with the passage of time, as trade volumes react to the new relative price.

If this analysis is correct, devaluation will be followed by an initial increase in the current account deficit, reversing itself gradually, until it surpasses its former position and carries on improving, the so-called *J-curve effect*.

While the J-curve is often regarded as a problem, it is obvious from what has just been said that it relates exclusively to the current account.[9] So, if the objective of devaluation is to improve the current account, the possibility of a J-curve effect may be a worry. Conceivably, the cost pressures generated in the domestic economy by the devaluation could be felt even before the supposed benefits appear. If, however, the aim of devaluation is to replenish the reserves, then there is no obvious reason why the benefits should await an improvement in the current account.

5.3 Interest rates in the monetary model

Until now, we have made use of a particularly simple form of the demand for money, the Cambridge quantity equation. In Chapter 4 (Section 4.1.2), however, it was argued that a plausible view of the demand for money would include a role for interest rates as a key determinant of the opportunity cost. We now proceed to examine the implications of incorporating interest rates into our simple model of exchange rates (Figure 5.7).

Our first approach will be naive, or rather myopic, because we shall temporarily ignore the important conclusions we reached in Chapter 3.

Look back at the formulation of the demand for money in Equation 4.9. As we have already seen, it implies that the demand for real balances will be lower, at any given level of income, the higher are interest rates. In other words, at any price level, the nominal demand will be smaller at a higher interest rate r_1 than at a lower interest rate r_0.

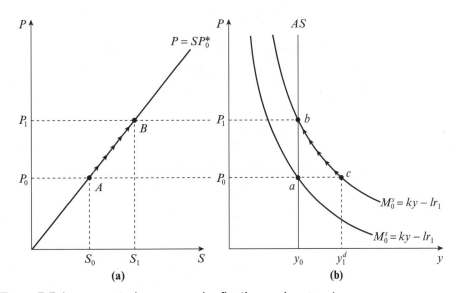

Figure 5.7 Interest rate increase under floating exchange rates

It follows that, with an unchanged money stock, the effect of a rise in UK interest rates is to create a temporary excess supply of money and excess demand for goods. Hence, in Figure 5.7(b) the aggregate demand schedule shifts to the right[10] at the initial price level, P_0, generating immediate excess demand equal to $(y_1^d - y_0)$ and consequent inflation. As the price level rises, the economy moves up its new aggregate demand curve from c to b.

Translating the argument into money market terms, at point c the higher opportunity cost induces agents to economize on real balances by attempting to spend more. In the process, they drive up prices until the real money stock has been reduced sufficiently to reinstate equilibrium at the new, higher interest rate. When equilibrium is reached, at the new price level, P_1, nominal income has increased so as to generate a transactions demand great enough to offset the impact of the higher opportunity cost.

Switching attention to Figure 5.7(a), if the exchange rate is floating, the higher interest rate must be associated with a higher value of S – in other words, a more expensive dollar and a cheaper pound. Furthermore, it is easy to see that a similar logic would apply to a change in the foreign interest rate. Hence, as before, since increased US interest rates mean a cheaper dollar, other things being equal, and higher UK interest rates imply a cheaper pound, the net effect on the exchange rate depends on *relative* interest rates.[11] We appear to have arrived at another general proposition:

> **Proposition 5.8** According to the monetary model, with given nominal money stocks and real incomes, a rise in domestic interest rates relative to those in the foreign country will be associated with a depreciation in the domestic currency.

Again, note the contrast with the DIY model.

However, this proposition is not as simple as it seems. Look back, if necessary, at the conclusions we reached in Chapter 3. In particular, recall the discussion of what determines the interest differential between two countries: under interest rate parity, we came to the conclusion that it would reflect the expected rate of currency depreciation.

What Proposition 5.8 says, then, is that if something occurs that causes agents to expect the exchange rate to depreciate more rapidly, then the domestic country's interest rates rise and the exchange rate does indeed depreciate – *immediately*. In other words, in an international context, we can view the opportunity cost of holding a currency as the rate of change in its international value – that is to say, its command over goods in world markets.

A caveat is in order, however. Consider for a moment the question of what determines the market's expectations with regard to currency movements. Answering this question fully will take up a large slice of the remainder of the book (see Chapters 12 and 13). For the moment, we will be content to sketch a vague outline of the kinds of factor likely to play a part in influencing market perceptions.

It is highly likely, we assert, that currency speculators will base their predictions of future exchange rate movements on their forecasts of what is going to happen to those variables that they believe are the ultimate determinants of long-run exchange rates. In other words, they first forecast the 'fundamentals', and then form their expectations as to the exchange rate accordingly.

What this implies, of course, is that interest rate changes are not exogenous events: they don't just happen but are very much the outcome of changes in expectations.

But now ask yourself another question: what kinds of factor are these 'fundamentals' likely to be?

It is very probable that the fundamentals will turn out to include, among others, the very variables that figured in the simple monetary model that we sketched in Section 5.1 – relative money stocks and income. Changes in the market's anticipations with regard to these fundamentals will trigger reassessments of the future outlook for exchange rates and this, in turn, will cause instantaneous fluctuations in the demand for the different currencies and hence in their international values. So we may well have a situation where an event that is seen as foreshadowing a change in the domestic money stock, for example, brings about an immediate adjustment in the interest rate and a simultaneous movement in the exchange rate.

This type of 'bootstrap' situation is one that will be familiar to anyone who has ever observed the behaviour of a typical financial market when the price of an asset, whether foreign currency, share, bond or commodity, is expected to rise at some point in the future, but the rise occurs *not in the future, but right now*. The very fact it is expected to rise pushes it up immediately.

This type of feedback mechanism will be examined at length later (see Chapter 13). For the moment, all we can do is to note that the association between interest rates and exchange rates is complicated by the fact that, unlike money and income, interest rates cannot seriously be regarded as exogenous variables. Our conclusions in this case, therefore, ought to be viewed as provisional.

5.4 The monetary model as an explanation of the facts

Before going on to look at the question of how well the monetary model explains the facts, it is worth pausing to try to guess the answer, because we already have a clue from Section 2.5. Remember that we concluded then that, for all the plausibility of the PPP hypothesis, it came nowhere near to explaining the wide fluctuations in exchange rates in the 1970s and 1980s. Since the PPP hypothesis is one of the two central building blocks of the simple monetary model, need we bother to go any further? Surely, if the foundations are rotten, there is no need to go on and look at the rest of the edifice?

This is certainly a persuasive argument. At the very least, it is hard to be anything other than extremely pessimistic about the prospects for using the monetary model to explain the facts. None the less, it is worth proceeding – just about. It is still possible (although unlikely) that the monetary model might work for the following reason.

Suppose the reason for the apparent failure of PPP to explain the facts is that the tests use the wrong price index. Suppose furthermore that the 'true' price index (the one that actually measures the prices that agents face) is unobservable. As long as that same unobservable price index figures in the demand for money, we could end up finding that the monetary model fitted quite well in spite of the failure of PPP.[12]

If this seems a forlorn hope, the reader can comfort himself with the thought that sooner or later, in a book of this nature, we would have to take a look at the broad

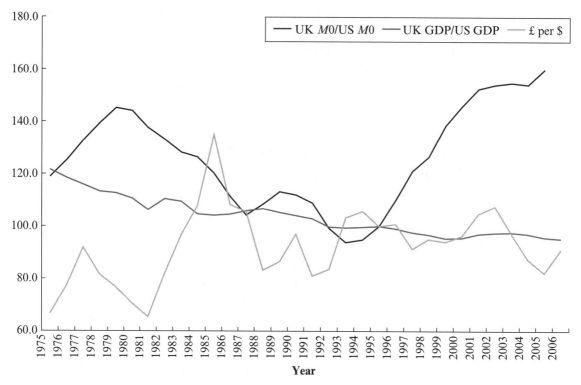

Figure 5.8 UK money, income and exchange rate, 1975–2006 (1995 = 100)

outline of what has happened to relative money stocks and incomes in recent years. Now is as good a time as any.

Figures 5.8–5.10 illustrate graphically the recent history of the UK, West Germany and Japan in this regard. In each case, the variables plotted are domestic $M1$ and GDP, relative to the USA, and the exchange rate, in home currency per dollar. All have been scaled so that 1995 = 100.[13]

The first thing to notice is that all three exchange rates are considerably more volatile than money stocks and incomes, and this is a conclusion that would have been even more forcefully illustrated in the monthly or weekly data, had we presented them.

For the UK, for example, while relative money stock had a range of 55% and relative GDP only 17% (as measured by maximum over minimum), the value of the pound fluctuated by more than 80%. For Germany and Japan, the disparity is even more marked. In both countries, relative money stocks varied by 50% and GDP by just over 20%, while exchange rates moved up and down across a range as wide as 140% in the case of the Deutschmark and just under 400% in the case of the yen. If anything, this understates the extent of the disproportion, which would be even more obvious if we examined monthly, weekly or daily data. At these higher frequencies, we would find the comparatively slow trend changes in income, and even the somewhat more volatile money stock statistics, completely swamped by the sharp day-to-day, week-to-week movements in exchange rates.

Next, look at the trends in the data (where there are any). There was a spectacular rise in UK $M1$ relative to that of the USA in the late 1970s, followed by a long

Figure 5.9 German money, income and exchange rate, 1975–99 (1995 = 100)

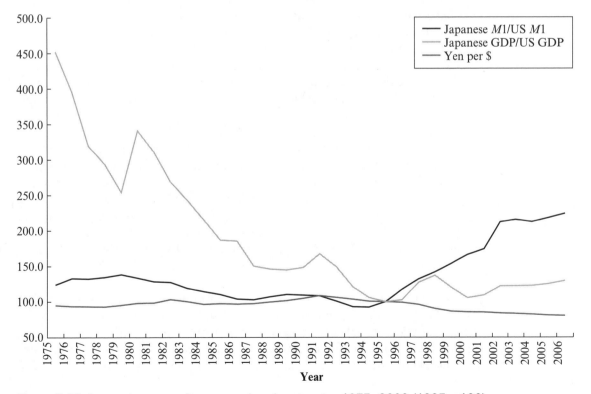

Figure 5.10 Japanese money, income and exchange rate, 1975–2006 (1995 = 100)

fall through most of the Thatcher years of the 1980s, and yet in those 15 years the exchange rate went through two distinct cycles for which there is no apparent explanation here. More recently, the UK money stock has again risen sharply, and yet the exchange rate against the dollar has been more stable than at any time since the start of the floating rate era in 1972.

Japan and Germany are in some respects even more problematic. Both the yen and the Deutschmark enjoyed a long-term appreciation throughout the first 20 years of the period, broken only by the dollar's rise in the early 1980s. Yet neither currency's strength was justified by monetary or real factors. In fact, the changes in the two countries' relative income were so small as to be within the likely margin of error for aggregate data such as these, while monetary growth differentials could justify appreciation of no more than 30% for Japan and 20% for Germany at the absolute maximum.

The evidence presented here is not, on the whole, very encouraging. All that can be said in favour of the monetary model (and it is not something to be dismissed altogether) is that it does appear to explain the facts over the very long run, at least in broad outline. This is particularly true of fixed rate periods.

For example, until the 1980s, the West German economy consistently enjoyed more rapid growth than either the UK or the USA. It also stuck to a monetary policy that was markedly less expansionary than most other industrialized countries. As predicted by the models we have examined in this chapter, the outcome was a balance of payments surplus and reserve accumulation, as well as long-term appreciation of the Deutschmark, whether in forced realignments, when a fixed rate regime was in force, or more gradually, when floating.

Conversely, for most of the post-World War II period until the late 1970s, the UK suffered from relatively slow economic growth, while its policymakers permitted a rapid expansion in the UK's money stock – or at least in its domestic credit component. Again, the result was as predicted – declining reserves and a depreciating currency.

At the same time, Japanese growth averaged several percentage points more than that of the UK or the USA, while its money supply expanded at a moderate rate, causing mounting balance of payments surpluses and an appreciating international value for the yen.

Perhaps unsurprisingly, the more marked are the divergences between rates of monetary growth (and hence inflation), the better the monetary model fits the facts. If we were to examine a currency under conditions of hyperinflation (inflation at rates of, say, 100% per annum and above), we would find its rate of depreciation against any of the hard currencies more or less equal to the difference in rates of monetary growth. However, as was noted at the end of Chapter 2, this is simply a reflection of the fact that in these pathological cases PPP has to be broadly maintained, at least to within limits that are narrow compared with the gap between inflation rates.

However, economists are not in the habit of drawing conclusions on the basis of this kind of cursory examination of a small amount of data. There is a wealth of additional evidence that could be used to cast light on the viability of the monetary model as an explanation of exchange rate changes, and there are sophisticated statistical and econometric techniques that could be brought to bear on the detailed data.

Researchers have, in fact, left no stone unturned in searching for evidence on the validity or otherwise of the monetary model. They have examined annual, quarterly and monthly data.[14] They have looked at trade-weighted as well as bilateral exchange rates. They have used narrow measures of money ($M0$ and $M1$) and broad measures ($M3$, and so on). They have extended and complicated the simple model to take account of adjustment delays ('lags') of all types and they have used state-of-the-art econometric techniques to test the theory.

By and large, their conclusions have been similar to ours. For example, in a series of influential publications, Meese and Rogoff found little support for the monetary model[15] in the period since 1973. Studies of individual exchange rates, particularly the pound/dollar and the Deutschmark/dollar, but also of a number of other hard and soft currencies, lead to similar conclusions.

Even where a clear pattern associating monetary growth with depreciation can be found, the relationship is rarely anything like the strict proportionality predicted by Proposition 5.1. It is often even harder to find a link between a country's national income and the value of its currency (Proposition 5.2), although in some cases this may be the result of the use of inadequate proxy measures in place of GDP.

Worst of all, such relationships that do appear tend to be unstable, with apparently satisfactory results over one period either reversing themselves or disappearing altogether in the next period.

5.5 Conclusions

The monetary model combines the quantity theory of the demand for money with purchasing power parity to generate unambiguous conclusions about the effect of changes in exogenous variables on a floating exchange rate, or on the balance of payments, as the case may be. It remains an important benchmark with which to compare other models – not least because, as we shall see in Chapters 6–9, its predictions accord in most cases with their long-run equilibrium results. Moreover, the analysis in Chapters 13, 16 and 17 takes the monetary model as its starting point.

Unfortunately, as an explanation of the facts, the monetary model must be regarded as grossly inadequate in anything but the very long run, which is hardly surprising given the failure of PPP. If a model that assumes perfect flexibility of prices cannot explain the facts, then we direct our attention in Chapter 6 to one that starts from the assertion that the price level is constant.

Summary

- The monetary model of a *floating exchange rate* predicts that the domestic currency will *depreciate* when any of the following occurs:
  - the domestic (foreign country) money stock increases (decreases);
  - domestic (foreign) national income falls (rises);
  - the foreign price level falls.

  The depreciation will be proportionate to any increase in the relative money stock.

- The monetary model of a *fixed exchange rate* predicts that the balance of payments will *deteriorate* and the home country will lose reserves when any of the following occurs:
  - the home country's domestically generated money stock (that is, domestic credit) increases;
  - domestic (foreign) national income falls (rises);
  - the foreign price level falls.

- *Devaluation* of a fixed exchange rate results in a period of balance of payments surpluses, which comes to an end when the home country's reserves have risen sufficiently to restore the value of the *real* money stock to its pre-devaluation level. Once this has happened, the *real* exchange rate is back at its former level (that is, PPP is reinstated) and the temporary competitive advantage enjoyed by the home country as a result of the devaluation has been completely eliminated by inflation.

- Since higher interest rates mean a smaller demand for money, other things being equal, they also imply a higher price level and therefore a lower value for the home country's currency. However, this conclusion must be qualified by our finding in Chapter 3 that interest rates, far from being an exogenous variable, are likely to reflect the market's expected rate of currency depreciation or appreciation. A firmer conclusion must await the analysis of how market expectations are determined in Chapters 12 and 13 of this book.

- Since PPP does not fit the facts of the 1970s and 1980s very well, it is not surprising that the monetary model turns out to be able to explain the facts only very weakly and even then only over the long run. A cursory examination of annual data for the UK, West Germany and Japan since 1975 is not encouraging, and this is broadly the conclusion reached by most researchers in detailed scientific studies of the data.

Reading guide

On the monetary model, the starting point (well worth reading) is Hume (1741). The simplest modern statement of its basic propositions is in Johnson (1977). Other influential work was by Mussa (1976) and Bilson (1979). The analysis of devaluation is due to Dornbusch (1973).

Influential empirical work has been carried out by Frenkel (1976) and Frankel (1979), among others. The last (empirical) word on the monetary model appears to have been said by Meese and Rogoff (1983), which also contains a useful bibliography.

On exchange rates under hyperinflationary conditions, see Frenkel (1977).

Web page: **www.pearsoned.co.uk/copeland**.

Notes

1 In the language of microeconomics, the aggregate demand curve has unitary elasticity in this special case. It is, in fact, a rectangular hyperbola.

   Note that in the present case, the LM curve is vertical, since the demand for money is unaffected by the interest rate. It follows that we are concerned only with the extent to which it shifts horizontally when the real money stock changes. We are also able to ignore the interest rate because the IS curve is implicitly flat, with saving and investment being equated by the interest rate alone, independently of income.

2 Of course, in this simple model the inflation rate is the only variable left for the government of either country to choose.

3 We ignore another complication here, which is that, in practice, countries running so-called fixed exchange rates invariably allow some measure of freedom for the rate to move up or down from the central parity (see Section 1.2). The consequences of this will be the subject of Chapter 16.

4 The monetary model is normally seen as dealing with the balance of payments rather than the balance of trade alone. In the present context, the distinction hardly matters.

5 The issue is clouded by all kinds of other problems, for example the apparent instability of the demand for money in the UK and the USA, interest differentials (see Section 5.1.3) and risk premiums (Chapter 14), and many others.

6 The sterilization mechanism is also likely to prove self-defeating because of its impact on interest rates.

7 It is an awkward question, of course, to decide how small is small enough for present purposes. On the one hand, the USA, the EU and Japan are obviously far too large to be able to ignore the feedback effects of their policies on the world economy. On the other hand, the vast majority of countries in the world are clearly small relative to world money markets. But what about medium-sized economies such as the UK and Canada, for example? The answer is not obvious.

Those readers who are familiar with elementary price theory will recognize a similarity here with the simple model of the perfectly competitive firm. Remember the paradox there was that market price was unaffected by the typical small firm's output decisions. Although the perfectly competitive firm acting alone cannot influence market price, the small firms in aggregate determine the price by their independently taken decisions. By the same token, we assume here that the small country cannot on its own have an impact on the world economy, but the monetary policy of small countries in aggregate (together with the large countries) determines the world price level.

8 We ignore the second-order effect on the money stock of the rise in the sterling value of the UK reserves when the pound is devalued.

9 In fact, it dates back to arguments about whether devaluation could improve the current account even in the long run. Thus, economists afflicted by 'elasticity pessimism' in the 1950s believed that the J-curve was all tail and no upswing.

10 In IS–LM terms, the upward shift in the horizontal IS curve cuts the unchanged LM curve further to the northeast.

11 A formal demonstration of this fact would be a little messier and more complicated than was the case in Section 5.6 with relative money stocks and incomes. The reason is to be found in our formulation of the demand for money that is linear in natural numbers. Fortunately, there is more or less universal support among researchers for a log linear formulation. In this case, it turns out that exchange rates depend on relative values of all variables, provided that income and interest elasticities are the same in each each country.

12 The possibility referred to here would also imply that demand-for-money studies using the standard price index were misspecified and should be expected to fit poorly. In fact, they fit reasonably well – certainly far better than PPP models (see the reading guide).

13 The pictures would look very similar if we defined money as $M3$ ($M1$ plus time deposits); although recalculating on a different base year would change the pictures superficially, it would not alter the general nature of our conclusions. There are, in any case, no sound reasons for preferring one definition of money to another in the present context or any overwhelming arguments in favour of any particular base year.

14 Higher-frequency data exist only for the US money stock and for financial variables (exchange rates and interest rates). Even then, there are no monthly data on national income, and so most researchers have used the index of industrial production as a proxy.

15 Although they also reached similarly negative conclusions with respect to all the other models they tested. It should be repeated that researchers have usually tested versions of the monetary model that were a good deal more complicated than the one presented in this chapter.

6 Fixed prices: the Mundell–Fleming model

Introduction

In Chapter 5, we looked at the way in which the exchange rate is determined when the price level is perfectly flexible. In this chapter, we look at the opposite extreme. What happens when the price level is completely fixed?

The Mundell–Fleming (M–F) model adheres to the Keynesian tradition that it is aggregate supply that takes the passive role of fixing the price level, while aggregate demand variations determine the level of economic activity.[1] It was highly influential in the 1960s, particularly in policymaking circles, not least because it focuses mainly on normative questions relating to the optimal combination of monetary and fiscal measures for demand management in an open economy.

At the time that the M–F model was developed, the Bretton Woods system was still more or less unchallenged, in the currency markets at least (although it had never enjoyed universal support in academic circles). Not surprisingly under the circumstances, most attention was focused on its conclusions about fixed exchange rates. In this chapter, we look at the M–F analysis of both fixed and floating rates.

As we shall see, the distinguishing feature of the M–F approach is in the emphasis placed on the different conditions determining the current balance on the one hand and the net capital inflow on the other. The outcome is an uneasy stock-flow equilibrium – not too implausible a description of the short-run response of a small open economy, but becoming less and less realistic the longer the time horizon involved.

In Section 6.1, the scene is set and the assumptions made explicit; in the succeeding section, the initial equilibrium is described. The next four sections analyse the results of the following policy experiments: a monetary and a fiscal expansion under floating rates and the same exercises in a fixed rate regime. Section 6.7 compares and contrasts the M–F model with the monetary model in the last chapter.

6.1 Setting

The M–F model is set in the context of a macroeconomic model that is simply the special case referred to as Keynesian in Chapter 4. For that reason, we shall limit the exposition here to a brief recap.

6.1.1 Domestic economy

We start with the supply side of the economy, where it is assumed that:

> **Assumption 6.1** The aggregate supply curve is flat.

Remember that this implies that the burden of adjustment to aggregate demand fluctuations falls on the level of economic activity – y,[2] in the notation used here – rather than on the price level, P. In fact, with the latter fixed, we might as well simplify matters by setting $P = 1$, so that, for the duration of this chapter, M signifies both nominal and real money stocks.

What this means in terms of the analysis is that we can concentrate on the demand side of the economy. In fact, since output adjusts passively, we need only consider the IS–LM framework (see Section 4.1) within which aggregate demand is determined.

6.1.2 Balance of payments

The distinctive feature of the M–F model is in the specification of the external sector of the economy. In particular, the current balance is determined independently of the capital account, so that the achievement of overall balance requires adjustment in the domestic economy.

Current account

As far as the current account is concerned, the starting point is the following assumption:

> **Assumption 6.2** PPP does not hold, even in the long run. Instead, the size of the current account surplus depends positively on the (real) exchange rate and negatively on (real) income.

This is essentially no more than was assumed when the IS curve was introduced in Section 4.1.1. It amounts to asserting that the current account surplus, B, is given by:

$$B = B(y, Q) = B(y, S) \quad B_y < 0 \; B_S > 0 \qquad (6.1)^3$$

The second equality is possible because, given both domestic and foreign price levels, the real and nominal exchange rates are identical.

The part played by income is the familiar one: the higher income is, the greater is the demand for imports and hence the smaller the surplus or the greater the deficit.

It would be possible at this stage to give a symmetrical role to foreign income, allowing for it to have a positive impact on the current balance, via the US propensity to import. For the sake of conciseness it is ignored here. It should be easy for the reader to deduce what effect an increase in US income would have on the value of the pound.

There are a number of other exogenous shift factors that could be incorporated into Equation 6.1: shocks to international tastes, shocks to export demand, and so on.

Capital account

The role of interest rates is absolutely central to the M–F model. In the case of the balance of payments, the reason why this is so is to be found in the following two assumptions:

> **Assumption 6.3** Exchange rate expectations are static.
>
> **Assumption 6.4** Capital mobility is less than perfect.

In Chapter 3, we examined the implications of perfect capital mobility. The analysis there presupposed perfect capital mobility, in the sense that even the smallest deviation from interest rate parity was assumed to be pre-empted by a potential flood into or out of domestic money markets.

In the M–F context, perfect capital mobility is regarded as a special case. In general, international interest rate differentials are assumed to provoke *finite* flows into or out of a country.

As we saw in Chapter 3, one possible rationalization for imperfect capital mobility would take as a starting point the limited supply of arbitrage funds.[4] More plausibly, it could be argued that, given risk aversion, the flow of funds into the home country will be an increasing function of the risk premium offered on securities denominated in the domestic currency, and vice versa for outward flows.

In other words, if we define r^*, the exogenously given foreign interest rate, to include any expected depreciation of the domestic currency, then we have:

$$K = K(r - r^*) = K(r) \quad K' > 0 \qquad (6.2)$$

This simply says that the UK's net capital inflow, K, is an increasing function of the extent to which the domestic interest rate is greater than the one ruling in the USA, inclusive of any depreciation expected in the value of the pound.

Balance of payments locus

Balance of payments (BP) equilibrium obtains when the flow of capital across the exchanges is just sufficient to finance the current account deficit or absorb the surplus. Of course, by definition, under a pure floating exchange rate regime, the *overall* balance of payments[5] must be in equilibrium at all times. This means that the sum of the surplus on capital and current account must be zero; in other words, a surplus on one account must be balanced by a deficit on the other.

If we add Equations 6.1 and 6.2 for the current and capital accounts respectively, a pure float requires the following condition to apply at all times:

$$B(y, S) + K(r) = 0 \tag{6.3}$$

or, more compactly when necessary:

$$F(y, S, r) = 0 \quad F_y < 0, \; F_S > 0, \; F_r > 0 \tag{6.4}$$

This relationship is plotted twice in Figure 6.1.

In Figure 6.1(b), the *BP* lines plot the combinations of y and r consistent with balance of payments equilibrium for different values of S. The lines are upward-sloping

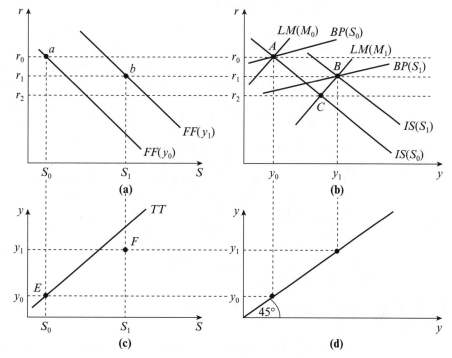

Figure 6.1 Monetary expansion under floating rates in the Mundell–Fleming model

because, as income increases at any given exchange rate, the current account deteriorates as import demand grows. To preserve equilibrium, the capital account must improve. There has to be an improvement in the net inflow across the exchanges, which can be achieved only by an increase in UK interest rates. It follows that higher income must be associated with higher interest rates for balance of payments equilibrium.

The extent of the interest rate increase required to offset a small rise in income (the gradient of the line) depends on the interest elasticity of net capital flows. The greater this elasticity, the flatter the line. In the limit, with perfect capital mobility, an imperceptibly tiny interest rate increase is sufficient to stimulate an infinite inflow, so that the BP line is completely flat.

On the other hand, a rise in S (depreciation of the pound) means a larger current account surplus or smaller deficit at any level of economic activity, and hence requires a more modest net capital inflow, and consequently a lower interest rate. Thus, increases in S shift the BP line downwards and to the right. The exception is when the line is flat, in which case it is unaffected by changes in the exchange rate.

Figure 6.1 also keeps track of the balance of payments explicitly in diagrams (a) and (c). The line labelled TT simply plots Equation 6.1. Notice the superficial similarity to the PPP line of Chapter 5. However, in the present case the price level is constant. In the same way that, in the domestic economy income carries the burden of adjustment previously borne by the price level, so in the external sector it is income that, along with the exchange rate, now determines the current account balance. The higher it is, the greater must be the exchange rate (that is, the lower the value of the pound) for the current account to balance.

> Notice that even in a pure float, the economy does not have to settle on the TT line, because we do not require the current account to balance – neither in short- nor long-run equilibrium. We insist only that any current account deficit (surplus) be offset by a capital account surplus (deficit) of the same size.

Figure 6.1(a) simply plots Equation 6.4 in (r, S) space. Balance of payments equilibrium associates higher interest rates (a more favourable capital account) with a lower price of foreign currency (and hence a less competitive foreign sector). It follows that the FF line slopes downward for a given income level. As income increases, it shifts to the right, since equilibrium requires depreciation to compensate for the additional import demand.

Again, the FF line is flat if capital is perfectly mobile and hence there is no horizontal shift when income increases.

6.2 Equilibrium

For the sake of convenience, we start off in equilibrium in Figure 6.1 at the points A, a and E.

At interest rate r_0 and exchange rate S_0, the balance of payments is in equilibrium, as can be seen from the fact that points a and A lie on the FF and BP lines respectively. Furthermore, at the associated real exchange rate, the product market clears along the curve marked $IS(S_0)$, so that the combination (r_0, y_0) is consistent with general equilibrium in the domestic economy.

Furthermore, tracking the level of income from y_0 down via the 45-degree line in Figure 6.1(d) over to the TT line, we see at E that there is a zero current account deficit at this exchange rate–income combination, with no net tendency for capital to leave or enter the country.

6.3 Monetary expansion with a floating exchange rate

Now consider the effect of expansionary monetary policy, for example a doubling of the money stock. The first point to note is that since the price level is fixed by the flat aggregate supply curve, the increase in the *nominal* money stock is equivalent to a pro rata rise in the *real* money stock. Hence, referring to Figure 6.1(b) the LM curve moves permanently rightwards, so that the interest rate has to fall.

How far must it fall? At first glance, the answer appears to be as far as r_2. But this cannot be correct for a number of reasons. C cannot be an equilibrium because, in the first place, with a lower interest rate the net capital inflow is smaller than it was before the money stock expansion. Furthermore, at the higher level of activity, the current account balance must have deteriorated. For both reasons, the combination at C must involve substantial balance of payments disequilibrium.

Obviously the exchange rate must depreciate. It is tempting to conclude that the pound's value needs to fall far enough to bring the current account into balance. This is not true, however. Remember, it was purely for analytical convenience that we chose to start from a zero current account balance – nothing requires this condition to apply in equilibrium.

Instead, as the (nominal and real) exchange rate depreciates, the competitiveness of domestic production improves and demand for UK output increases, shifting the IS curve outwards to $IS(S_1)$. The boost to demand has the effect of pushing interest rates part of the way back to their original level of r_0.

Ultimately, the economy settles at B, where the interest rate is at the level r_1, and the UK's external payments are back in balance, as evidenced by the line marked $BP(S_1)$. The external sector is returned to equilibrium by two mechanisms: the partial climb back by the interest rate has the effect of reducing the capital account deficit to a level where the current account surplus created by the depreciation in the currency is sufficient to cover it.

Notice that the current account surplus at F is the net outcome of a positive influence, the rise in S, and a negative influence, the increase in y. Thus, the former effect must be assumed the stronger of the two.

In the limiting case of perfect capital mobility, no fall in the interest rate is possible, so that the full burden of external adjustment falls on the exchange rate. The outcome is a greater increase both in income and in the price of dollars.

We conclude:

> **Proposition 6.1** In the M–F model of a floating exchange rate, a money supply increase causes:
>
> ■ a depreciation in the exchange rate
>
> ■ an increase in income
>
> ■ a fall in the interest rate, provided capital is not completely mobile
>
> ■ an improvement in the current account of the balance of payments.

Notice the first conclusion is *qualitatively* the same as in the monetary model, although there is no reason here to suppose that the depreciation will be in proportion to the money supply increase. Likewise, the income increase is unsurprising. It is simply the counterpart of the price rise that would take place with a classical aggregate supply curve.

As has already been mentioned, however, the focus of the M–F work, published as it was in the heyday of demand management, was mainly on policy implications. In this respect, it was regarded as highly significant that the net effect of expansionary monetary policy on the level of economic activity could be shown to be unambiguously positive – even allowing for the crowding-out effect of the increase in demand induced by the fall in the exchange rate.

Furthermore, as we have seen, if the *BP* line were flat – in other words, if there were perfect capital mobility – the interest rate would be completely fixed, eliminating secondary crowding out altogether and resulting in the maximum expansionary impact on aggregate demand.

6.4 Fiscal expansion with a floating exchange rate

By contrast, Figure 6.2 illustrates the effect of a pure fiscal expansion – in other words, an increase in government expenditure (from G_0 to G_1) *with an unchanged money stock*.

In this case, with a fixed money stock and constant price level, the LM curve of Figure 6.2(b) is unmoved. By the same token, as we have seen, fiscal expansion shifts the IS curve to the right, via a direct injection into the flow of expenditure. However, if printing money is ruled out, as we are assuming here, the government can finance its extra spending only by borrowing more. Since the money and credit markets were in equilibrium at the outset, significant additional borrowing is possible only at the cost of a higher interest rate. It follows that the impact effect of the policy is to increase income and the interest rate.

Point C of Figure 6.2(b), where $IS(G_1, S_0)$ cuts the original LM curve, is inconsistent with equilibrium in the external sector, however. A higher interest rate implies an influx of funds into London, which in turn means, starting from an initial balance on external payments, an emerging excess demand for pounds. Neither is the deterioration in the current account caused by the increase in income likely to be enough to offset it.

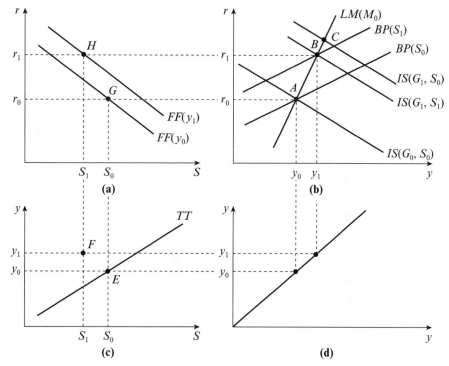

Figure 6.2 Fiscal expansion under floating rates in the Mundell–Fleming model

The pound must therefore appreciate, as Americans join the rush to lend to the British government at the newly attractive interest rate, in the process converting dollars to sterling and bidding up the exchange rate. As the exchange rate rises, UK goods, as distinct from UK securities, become less attractive to foreigners, shifting the IS curve back down to the left and pushing the interest rate some of the way back to its pre-expansion level.

The process comes to an end when the combination of exchange rate and interest rate is such that domestic equilibrium is restored at B, on the line marked $IS(G_1, S_1)$ of Figure 6.2(b). In the external sector (Figure 6.2(c)), the outcome at F is a current account deficit, thanks both to the increase in income and, particularly, to the rise in the value of the pound.

The case of perfect capital mobility is particularly interesting. When the BP and FF curves are flat, the IS curve cannot move other than temporarily. The reason is simply that, with both BP and LM curves unaffected by the disturbance, the equilibrium income–interest rate combination cannot change – the system must remain at the point A in the IS–LM diagram (Figure 6.2(b)). Put in terms of the money market, with the interest rate pegged by external factors, and the real money stock unchanged, there is a unique level of income consistent with equilibrium. It follows that the exchange rate must move so as to keep the IS curve unchanged – that is, enough to offset the expansionary effect on demand of the increase in government spending.

Hence, with perfect capital mobility, crowding out is complete. The whole of the increase in government expenditure is neutralized by the consequent equal fall in demand from the external sector of the economy. In other words, with the interest rate pegged *de facto* by international capital markets, the burden of adjustment falls entirely on the exchange rate, which has to appreciate by enough to generate a current account deficit as great as the increase in fiscal spending that started the process off. In flow of funds terms, in this limiting case, the whole of the increase in government expenditure is funded by borrowing from overseas. Therefore, each pound spent by the government adds one pound to the capital account surplus and equilibrium requires that it be offset by the same amount of net imports of goods and services. Demand is therefore pushed back to its original level, and the impact of fiscal spending on output is nil.

We conclude:

> **Proposition 6.2** In the M–F model of a floating exchange rate, fiscal expansion causes:
>
> ■ an appreciation in the exchange rate
> ■ an increase in income, provided capital is not completely mobile
> ■ a rise in the interest rate, provided capital is not completely mobile
> ■ a deterioration in the current account of the balance of payments.

Notice that, as far as policy considerations are concerned, the result is that the ultimate expansion of demand (and hence activity) is smaller than would be predicted purely on the basis of a closed economy analysis. The reason is that the closed economy mechanism, whereby a rise in the interest rate crowds out some of the injection of autonomous spending, is supplemented in the present context by the rise in the value of the domestic exchange rate, which further crowds out spending – this time by foreigners on UK (net) exports.

For policy purposes, then, the conclusion drawn from the M–F model was that, in a floating exchange rate regime, monetary policy is more powerful than fiscal policy and, furthermore, this was more true the more elastic was the net supply of capital.

6.5 Monetary expansion with a fixed exchange rate

We now switch our attention to fixed exchange rate regimes, to see how far our conclusions need to be changed.

In Figure 6.3(b), the initial equilibrium at *A* is the same as in the floating rate case. To remind us of the difference, a vertical line has been drawn at the fixed exchange rate Q in both Figures 6.3(a) and (c).

Now consider the effect of a once-and-for-all monetary expansion or, more precisely, of an expansion of domestic credit from DC_0 to DC_1.

The impact effect of the increase in the total money stock has to be the downward shift in the LM curve in Figure 6.3(b). Notice that the new curve has been labelled $LM(DC_1, FX_0)$. The new equilibrium at *B* is the outcome of an increase in the domestic component of the money supply with an as yet unchanged quantity of foreign currency reserves.

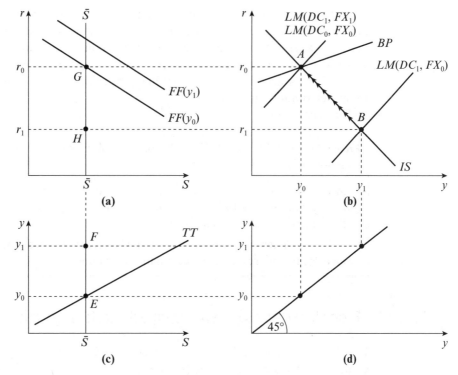

Figure 6.3 Monetary expansion under fixed rates in the Mundell–Fleming model

The sequence of events from this point onwards is clear. Starting from balance of payments equilibrium, as we did, the fall in the interest rate (from r_0 to r_1) must worsen the capital account balance. At the same time, the increase in income (from y_0 to y_1) with an unchanged exchange rate causes a deterioration in the current account, as we can see at point F in Figure 6.3(c).

It follows that the new situation can only be a temporary resting point. The overall balance of payments deficit and associated excess supply of sterling means that the fixed exchange rate can be preserved only by running down the reserves. As we saw in Chapter 5, in the absence of further action by the authorities, the inevitable outcome is a gradual reduction in the foreign currency component of the monetary base. The process ends only when the money stock and hence the LM curve are back where they started.

In the new equilibrium, everything is as before: interest rate, income and the balance of payments are all back at their pre-disturbance level. The only difference is in the composition of the money stock, which is now made up of a lower quantity of foreign currency (FX_1 instead of FX_0) and a greater quantity of domestically generated assets (DC_1 instead of DC_0).

In the limiting case, with perfect capital mobility it must be assumed that any fall in the interest rate is ruled out (even in the short term) since it would provoke an immediate run on the foreign currency reserves. So, in this case, the adjustment process would be more or less instantaneous, with the new money draining straight out of the country across the foreign exchanges.

As long as capital movements are not completely elastic, the possibility exists, in principle at least, of sterilizing the induced outflows of reserves. However, as we saw in Chapter 5, it is hard to believe that the policy could work other than in the very short term, since it ultimately relies on the currency markets being completely myopic in their acceptance of an ever falling stock of reserves, with no sign of an end to the deterioration in view.

The conclusion is:

> **Proposition 6.3** In the M–F model of a fixed exchange rate, a money supply increase causes:
>
> ■ in the short term, and provided capital is not completely mobile, the interest rate to fall, income to increase and the balance of payments to deteriorate on both current and capital account
>
> ■ in the long term, a fall in the foreign currency reserves, but no change in income, the interest rate or the balance of payments.

6.6 Fiscal expansion with a fixed exchange rate

Finally, consider the effect of government spending financed by borrowing in the context of a fixed exchange rate (Figure 6.4).

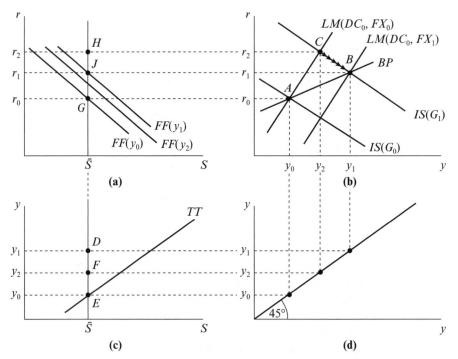

Figure 6.4 Fiscal expansion under fixed rates in the Mundell–Fleming model

Starting from point A of Figure 6.4(b), the impact effect is to shift the IS curve upwards. The interest rate must rise as the authorities try to expand their borrowing from financial markets that are already satisfied with their holdings of government paper. The new IS curve cuts the unchanged LM curve at C.

However, C is not a situation of long-run equilibrium, as evidenced by the fact that it lies above the BP line. The higher interest rate, r_2, improves the capital account by more than the deterioration in the current account brought about by the simultaneous increase in income (to y_2). In terms of the balance of payments diagram (Figure 6.4(a)), even after the upward shift in the FF schedule, the interest rate is still too high for long-run equilibrium, as we can see at point H.

Again the solution lies in a change in the endogenous component of the money supply, which duly occurs through reserve accumulation, as foreigners take advantage of the high UK interest rate by buying pounds so as to hold British securities. In the process, the money stock swells, pushing the LM curve down to generate a long-run equilibrium at B in Figure 6.4(b), where the further increase in income and fall in the interest rate have worsened both current and capital account sufficiently to bring external payments back into balance (at J in Figure 6.4(a)).

The net outcome, then, is a balance of payments that shows a substantial deficit on current account (at D in Figure 6.4(c)) financed by capital inflows attracted by the relatively high domestic interest rate.

The more willing foreigners are to increase their lending to the UK, the less is the need for a rise in British interest rates, because the less spending by the domestic private sector needs crowding out. In the limit, with perfect capital mobility, foreigners can be persuaded to shoulder the burden of financing the whole of the additional spending at no perceptible increase in interest rates. With no crowding out, the effect is to increase income very substantially.[6]

The general conclusions in this case can be summarized as follows:

> **Proposition 6.4** In the M–F model of a fixed exchange rate, fiscal expansion causes the following changes, provided capital is not completely mobile:
>
> - in the short run, a rise in the interest rate and income and an overall surplus on the balance of payments (a net reserve gain)
> - in the long run, a further increase in income while the interest rate falls somewhat and the overall balance of payments surplus shrinks to zero, leaving a substantial current account deficit.

6.7 The monetary model and the Mundell–Fleming model compared

It is useful to compare the monetary model and the M–F model directly. The differences can be considered under the following three headings: price level, income, and expectations and interest rates.

6.7.1 Price level

In the monetary model, since the aggregate supply curve is vertical at all times, the price level moves with perfect flexibility to clear both money and goods markets. Then PPP ensures that the real exchange rate is preserved at its equilibrium level.

In the M–F model, the price level is simply an exogenously fixed index that can have no role to play in the domestic macroeconomy. Neither can it play any part in determining equilibrium in the open sector.

6.7.2 Income

The corollary of these contrasting assumptions about the supply side of the economy is two totally different views of the part played by income in the model.

In the monetary model, with full employment and perfectly functioning factor markets, changes in real income can only be exogenous events. Furthermore, consumption is implicitly taken to depend on interest rates rather than income. It follows that the only role left for income to play is in helping to determine the demand for real balances. As we saw, because exogenous increases in income swell the demand for money, they are associated with currency *appreciation*.

In contrast, income is one of the three endogenous variables in the M–F system, the others being the domestic interest rate and the exchange rate (if floating), otherwise the balance of payments. An (endogenous) increase in income is associated with three types of effect in this context. First, in so far as it raises the demand for money, it leads to a rise in the interest rate, other things being equal. Second, by feeding back on to consumption (the Keynesian multiplier effect), it boosts demand for goods and services. Third, and more particularly, it is associated with a worsening current account via the marginal propensity to import and, *ceteris paribus*, either reserve losses or currency *depreciation*.

6.7.3 Expectations and interest rates

Neither model provides an explicit role for expectations, although both have provided the framework for more complicated models that fully rectify this omission, as we shall see later on in the book.[7]

None the less, the flavour of the monetary model is *either* that expectations are exogenously given *or* that they depend in some more complicated fashion on the other variables (see Chapter 13). Furthermore, in the spirit of the classical tradition to which it belongs, the monetary approach assumes the real interest rate is determined purely in the savings market.[8] When combined with interest rate parity, these two facts imply that nominal interest rates cannot fluctuate freely to clear the money markets. That job is left to the price level. The domestic interest rate is effectively tied to (although usually not equal to) the foreign rate.

The Keynesian approach takes goods market equilibrium as dependent at least as much on income as on interest rates. The corollary is that, in a domestic context, the interest rate is free to help clear both money and goods markets. Viewed from the international perspective, the link with foreign interest rates is almost completely broken. In place of UIRP, we have something like:

$$r = r^* + \Delta s_t^e + \rho \tag{6.5}$$

Now if the required risk premium (the last term) rises with the quantity of domestic currency assets held, it follows that the scale of the capital inflow at any point will be an increasing function of the domestic interest rate, *for a given value of the expected rate of depreciation* (the second term on the right-hand side).

This is all very well, provided, first, that the expected rate of depreciation can actually be taken as given in the face of significant macroeconomic policy shifts and, second, that the required risk premium is determined independently of the other variables. On this last point, we shall have more to say in Chapter 14.

As far as expectations are concerned, it seems highly unlikely that the policy measures considered in this chapter would leave expectations unchanged.[9] Once it is allowed that expectations are very likely to depend on the government's policy stance, the logic behind the M–F conclusions begins to unravel.

Stocks and flows

The differing treatments given to interest rate determination in the two models are very much related to their contrasting approaches to defining equilibrium.

Following the classical tradition, equilibrium in the monetary model, in its floating rate version at least, is a steady state in the fullest sense: the stocks of both money and goods are willingly held, with no tendency for net flows in either direction. Once the economy has adjusted to a monetary expansion, for example, there is no reason why the new equilibrium should not persist forever, if left undisturbed.

Contrast this with the M–F analysis: the response to money supply expansion involves a depreciation-induced surplus on current account, which then finances the continuing net export of capital, in response to the new, lower level of domestic interest rates.

Now this cannot be an equilibrium in the full, static sense. A net capital flow into or out of a country is prima facie evidence that disequilibrium holdings are in the process of being adjusted and it is quite plausible that adjustment may be protracted. In fact, the international capital markets are never at rest.[10] But, however long the process may take, at some point it will be complete. Stocks of assets will have adjusted fully to the disturbance, with no further tendency for capital to move into or out of the country – and *this is the situation one would expect to find in full equilibrium.*

And this is not purely a theoretical nicety. If, for example, the capital inflow following on fiscal expansion under a floating exchange rate is only temporary, then the current account deficit that it finances can be only temporary. As the influx of funds dries up, the exchange rate must depreciate, other things being equal, thereby reducing the current account deficit, pushing interest rates up even further and reducing income. In the limit, there would be no change in income or the interest rate. There would simply be an appreciation of sufficient scale to crowd out the additional spending.[11]

As has already been mentioned in the introduction, the M–F analysis was highly influential precisely because of its conclusions about the relative efficacy of monetary and fiscal policy under fixed and floating rates. No comparable analysis is possible in the context of the monetary model, simply because it has nothing to say about the effect of changes in government spending. Why not?

One way of understanding this feature of the classical model is to go back to the goods market identity of flows of injections and leakages. Rewriting Equation 4.3, we have:

$$Savings \equiv I + G + B \tag{6.6}$$

When net government spending expands, there is a *ceteris paribus* rise in the volume of injections on the right-hand side of this identity. How is the equality maintained?

In the Keynesian view, the equality is preserved by some combination of a rise in income, which increases savings, and an increase in interest rates, which also raises savings somewhat but which, more importantly, deters investment ('crowding out'). The M–F analysis follows through the open economy implications of this mechanism.

By contrast, the classical view[12] is that an increase in the government's budget deficit will bring forth the requisite additional saving spontaneously. The reason is simply that economic agents realize that the extra spending will have to be paid for by future taxation, even if it is financed by borrowing at the moment. They will therefore wish to step up their current saving *at any given interest rate* so as to be able to pay the taxes when they fall due.

In fact, it can be shown that, provided taxation does not actually distort the savings decision,[13] responsible, non-myopic agents will be happy to buy the additional government debt issued to finance its extra spending *at the same price as before the change took place*. They will do so because the return they earn on the debt, properly measured,[14] will be just sufficient to cover the additional tax burden.

If we can rely on this mechanism of Ricardian equivalence (as it is called, after the great classical economist, David Ricardo), we need not distinguish between spending by the private and public sectors. The government is simply an agency created by a democratic state to act on behalf of its citizens – in borrowing as in everything else. The fact that a private citizen prefers to buy now and pay later does not automatically raise interest rates. Why should it do so when he channels the whole process (spending and borrowing) through the agency of the government?[15]

On these and similar grounds, one would expect an increase in *G* on the right-hand side of Equation 6.6 to be automatically associated with the increase in savings needed to finance it. In other words, the IS curve need not shift as a result of what is simply a change in the share of spending between public and private sectors.

In practice, there are certain to be a number of breaks in the circuit leading from the nation's budget to household budgets.

In the first place, households may simply be myopically unconcerned about the future tax burden being imposed on them. The facts are not easily accessible: government spending changes are made public only in the opaque form of official statistics, nationalized industries' accounts, white papers, and so on. In any case, it is one thing to absorb the fact that £1 of extra government spending today will have to be paid for at some point in the future by additional taxes whose present value is £1.[16] It is quite another to accept that I or even my children, if I have any, will have to pay those taxes. By the time the chickens come home to roost, I may no longer be inside the tax net: I may be dead, retired, emigrated or unemployed. Moreover, unless my coupon payments are exempt from income tax, buying government securities will yield less than I need to pay the tax bill, when it falls due.

For these reasons, the most likely outcome for an economy like that of the UK or the USA would seem to be some degree of crowding out greater than zero (as predicted by Ricardians) but smaller than is suggested in Keynesian models such as the one analysed in this chapter.

The question is ultimately an empirical one and one that, in spite of its importance, has yet to be answered satisfactorily.

6.8   Evidence

It is not of very great interest to test the M–F model in the form presented here, at least as far as the floating rate era is concerned – it seems pointless to try to explain the facts by starting from the assumption that prices are fixed. On the other hand, introducing price flexibility in one way or another changes the model quite drastically, as we shall see in Chapter 7.

None the less, the M–F approach lies at the heart of much of the market commentary in the media. For example, the simultaneous rise of both the dollar and US real interest rates to record levels in the first half of the 1980s led many commentators to point to the growing federal deficit as the likely culprit.

Unfortunately, whatever may be true in the criminal courts, in economics circumstantial evidence rarely points in a single direction. In the present case, real interest rates were at or around their peak levels throughout the industrialized world, in spite of the conservative budgetary stance of some of the countries involved. Moreover, the dollar's subsequent fall took place well in advance of any tangible sign that the US deficit could even be stabilized, let alone reduced.

Of course, the dollar's fall, when it finally took place, was immediately rationalized by some commentators as a market reaction to the Federal deficit.

It is easy to be facetious about these ad hoc explanations. However, it should be realized they *could* both be correct, and attempting to reconcile these two apparently contradictory positions takes us back to one of the central weaknesses of the M–F model.

The point has already been touched on in discussing the issue of capital mobility in the section on stocks and flows. Suppose that the USA was able to fund additional federal spending by borrowing from abroad (primarily Japan) in the early 1980s. In return, it offered a (very slightly) higher return. However, if the Japanese had fully adjusted their holdings of dollar securities by the mid-1980s, they would then stop exporting capital to the USA unless the risk premium rose still further, a development that failed to materialize, for some reason or other. Hence, the dollar had to fall. International money managers could hardly ignore the fact that where they had initially (in 1982) been lending to the world's largest creditor nation, by 1987, they were being asked to lend to the world's largest debtor – with no end in sight to the deterioration in the USA's external finances.

This retrospective rationalization (it certainly does not merit being called an explanation) illustrates the shortcomings of the M–F concentration on flows rather than stocks of capital. Of course, it also illustrates the need to beware of the spurious power of *ex post* rationalizations![17]

6.9 Conclusions

Forty years after it was developed, the analysis presented in this chapter looks naive, as well it might, in view of the upheavals that have taken place in currency markets in the intervening years. None the less, the model focuses on mechanisms that are almost certainly still at work in one guise or another today and in the process provides some useful insights.

Moreover, although this book is not concerned primarily with issues of policy design, it is worth noting that the questions raised by Mundell and Fleming with regard to the appropriate assignment of policy instruments still crop up from time to time. However, answering them satisfactorily involves analysing models that are vastly more complicated than the one given here.

Much of the more recent research derives directly or indirectly from the work of Mundell and Fleming, as we shall see. In Chapter 7, we shall examine a model that attempts to rectify two of the weaknesses of the M–F model: the constant price level and the static expectations. Chapter 8 extends the model further to provide an explicit specification of asset market equilibrium.

Summary

- The M–F model is set in the context of a flat aggregate supply curve (that is, a constant price level), the absence of PPP, less than perfect capital mobility and static expectations.

- With a floating exchange rate, equilibrium requires the domestic money and goods markets to clear, as in the IS–LM model, while in the open sector the sum of the deficits on current and capital accounts is zero. The latter condition ensures a balance of supply and demand in the currency market.

- With a floating exchange rate, expansionary monetary policy causes depreciation and a fall in interest rates, while fiscal expansion has the opposite effect.

- With a fixed exchange rate, expansionary monetary policy has the long-run effect of causing a fall in the reserves, while fiscal expansion produces a rise in income and the interest rate with a short-run reserve gain.

- The M–F model contrasts with the monetary model in a number of respects: its emphasis on the level of activity and interest rates rather than the price level, its concentration on flows of spending and capital movements rather than stocks of assets, and the central role it gives to the crowding-out mechanism.

Reading guide

Of the original work on which this chapter is based, the most accessible (technically and physically) is Mundell (1962) and Fleming (1962). If you can get hold of a copy, the book by Mundell (1968) is well worth reading, as it goes into some detail and provides proofs, generalizations, and so on.

amazon.co.uk®

Paid by:
Daniel Asher Brill
5 The Dene
WEMBLEY, Middx, HA9 7QT
United Kingdom, GB

Delivered to:
daniel brill
5 The Dene Wembely Middx HA9 7QT
London, Brent, HA9 7QT
United Kingdom, GB

Invoice/Receipt for

Your order of 19 February, 2009

Order ID 202-8093577-7977134

Invoice number DMD5tBR
20 February, 2009

Qty	Item	Description	Our Price (excl. VAT)	VAT Rate	Total Price (excl. VAT)
1	Exchange Rates and International Finance Copeland, Laurence 9780273710271		£40.49	0.00%	£40.49

Shipping Subtotal (excl. VAT) £2.75	Subtotal (excl. VAT) 0.00% £40.49	Order Total £43.24

Sale order paid by Switch Card: £43.24
Balance due: £0.00

You can always check the status of your orders from the "Your Account" link at the top of each page of our site.

This shipment completes your order.

Thinking of returning an item?

Our Returns Support Centre (www.amazon.co.uk/returns-support) will guide you through our Returns Policy and provide you with a printable personalised return label. Please have your order number ready (you can find it next to your order summary, above). This Returns Policy does not affect your statutory rights.

Thank you for shopping at Amazon.co.uk!

Amazon EU S.a.r.l; 5, rue Plaetis. L-2338 Luxembourg
VAT Number, GB 727255821

For an up-to-date assessment and further references, see Frenkel and Razin (1988).

On Ricardian equivalence, the most important modern reference is Barro (1974). For a textbook treatment, see Barro (1984), Chapter 15.

Web page: **www.pearsoned.co.uk/copeland.**

Notes

1. The reader would be well advised to acquire a firm grasp of the analysis in Chapter 4 before starting the present chapter.

2. Notice that the superscript d (for demand) used in Chapter 4 is unnecessary here, because aggregate demand is automatically identical to actual income and output.

3. The notation F_x means the partial derivative of the function F with respect to the argument x; that is, the effect of a minute increase in the variable x on the value of the function, holding all the other arguments constant.

    By convention, when there is only one argument in F, the derivative is written F'.

4. In the 1960s, this view of international capital markets seemed far more realistic than it does today. At the time, most countries other than the USA and Switzerland still imposed tight restrictions on movements of foreign exchange, the eurocurrency markets were tiny compared with their present size and there were few large portfolios owned outside the industrial world. In addition, the large financial institutions that nowadays operate as arbitrageurs were at that time regulated more closely and far less competitive.

5. That is, the balance for official financing or the net change in the foreign currency reserves (see Section 1.3, if necessary).

6. In fact, by an amount equal to the increase in government expenditure multiplied by the Keynesian income expenditure multiplier.

7. In Chapter 7, we examine what amounts to an M–F model modified to incorporate expectations. The same is done for the monetary model in Chapter 13.

8. In other words, the classical model assumes an IS curve that is flat at the interest rate that equates savings to investment (plus any other injections in the economy). Remember that in this view savings are not a function of current income.

9. Even if this were credible where a once-and-for-all policy change is concerned, the same could certainly not be true of any change that provoked expectations of further changes to come, for example the issue of domestic money to sterilize a reserve loss under fixed exchange rates.

10. Although why this should be so is not always clear. For a bank to adjust its holdings of, say, US Treasury Bills should take no more than a few hours or days at most. It is precisely these kinds of consideration that have led some researchers to look for explanations to the impact of 'news' on currency markets (see Chapter 13).

11. In terms of Figures 6.1–6.4 this would amount to saying that the BP and FF lines are ultimately vertical, since the external balance depends on only income and the exchange rate. Fiscal expansion would then shift the IS curve temporarily to the right, as in Figure 6.2. In the long run, however, the IS curve would be pushed by exchange rate appreciation all the way back to its original position.

12. Revived by Barro (1984).

13. For example, by taxing interest earned on savings.

14. That is, discounting appropriately both the flow of payments to the debt holder and that to the future taxation.

15. In addition, in a democracy, much of public sector spending ought in principle to be perceived as substituting directly, pound for pound, for private consumption (for example, government purchases of medicines, school meals, textbooks, and so forth).

16. It is the author's impression that the average member of the public is and always has been well aware of the truth that there is no such thing as a free lunch – and is certainly less inclined to forget the fact than some members of the economics profession.

17 For example, why should it have taken so long (two or three years) for Japanese investors to adjust their dollar holdings in the first place? And what stopped the relative return on dollar assets rising sufficiently to sustain the flow of funds into the USA in 1985 and beyond? Ironically, since this chapter was originally written, the positions of the USA and Japan have completely reversed, with Japan accumulating vast debts as a result of unprecedented fiscal expansion, while the USA runs fiscal surpluses that are rapidly reducing its debt. However, while the yen has been strong, so has the dollar, and Japanese interest rates have tended to fall (as has income) and so the M–F model can hardly be said to fit the facts of this episode either.

7 Sticky prices: the Dornbusch model

Introduction

As we have seen, the monetary model of the exchange rate is incapable of explaining the facts, not least because it relies on the assumption of purchasing power parity, but possibly also because it ignores the role played by expectations in determining international interest rate differentials. In particular, it appeared that exchange rate fluctuations were far more violent than could ever be explained by the comparatively sluggish movements we observe in relative money stocks and national incomes.

By the same token, the Mundell–Fleming model not only takes no account of expectations but also assumes a fixed price level, which limits its relevance to only the very shortest horizons.

The model to be outlined here, which was published by the late Professor Rudiger Dornbusch of the Massachusetts Institute of Technology in 1976, is a hybrid. In its short-run features, it fits into the established Keynesian tradition, with its emphasis on the stickiness of prices in product (and labour) markets. Simultaneously, however, it displays the long-run characteristics of the monetary model.

The originality of Dornbusch's work lies in his exploration of the consequences of the following observation: while product markets adjust only slowly, financial markets appear to adjust far more rapidly – almost instantaneously, in fact. The consequence of allowing for this feature of the real world turns out to be that financial markets have to *over*adjust to disturbances, in order to compensate for the stickiness of prices in goods markets. The reason is that, with goods prices initially fixed, a change in the *nominal* money stock, for example, amounts to a change in the *real* money stock. It follows that there has to be an instantaneous change in the demand for real balances if the money market is to clear and the change can be brought about only by an upward or downward movement in interest rates – especially if output is assumed fixed. In the short term, therefore, monetary policy changes have what is nowadays known as a 'liquidity effect'.

However, the deviation of domestic interest rates from world levels can be only temporary. Ultimately, as product prices begin their delayed response, the change in the real money stock starts to reverse itself and, with it, the whole process goes into reverse, driving interest rates, aggregate demand and the real exchange rate back towards their original values. The process ends with all the real magnitudes back where they started, as in the monetary model, and the nominal exchange rate at a new long-term level that reflects the proportionate change in the money supply.

The overshooting phenomenon is also likely to characterize the response to a real (rather than monetary) disturbance, for example the UK's emergence as an oil exporter in the late 1970s. Again, the exchange rate is likely to overadjust to the disturbance, with potentially damaging consequences for UK industry and employment.

Since the material to be covered in this chapter is somewhat more complex, the approach will be in two stages. In Section 7.1, we shall set out the Dornbusch model in informal terms, relying for the analysis on an extension of the diagrammatic framework introduced in Chapter 6. In Section 7.2, we examine the aftermath of a monetary expansion in the same context.

The subsequent section, however, marks a change of pace. A formal, but highly simplified version of the model is set out and used to re-examine the response to monetary policy and, in Section 7.4, to outline the likely reaction to a disturbance such as the discovery of North Sea oil.

7.1 Outline of the model

Two conventions will be followed.

■ We continue to focus on a single, 'small' economy, say the UK. By this, we mean that developments in Britain are assumed to have no perceptible effect on the economy of the rest of the world. In particular, we may take as given the price level, P^*, and the interest rate, r^*, obtaining in the outside world ('the USA').

■ The analysis will proceed from a 'standing start'. In other words, we assume there is initially no inflation and static exchange rates and we consider the impact of an increase in the *level* of the money supply on the *level* of the exchange rate and of goods prices.

The model has a similar general structure to that of the Chapter 6. In fact, we can start with the following assumption:

Assumption 7.1 Aggregate demand is determined by the standard open economy IS–LM mechanism.

Remember that this means that the position of the IS curve is determined by the volume of injections into the flow of income (for example, government expenditure) and by the competitiveness of UK output, as measured by the real exchange rate, $Q = SP^*/P$.

We depart from the Mundell–Fleming model in making two special assumptions, one regarding the determination of interest rates, and the other relating to aggregate supply.

7.1.1 Financial markets and expectations

We start by specifying the model of financial markets:

> **Assumption 7.2** Financial markets adjust instantaneously. In particular, investors are risk neutral, so that uncovered interest rate parity (UIRP) holds at all times.

As we saw in Chapter 3, this means that perfect capital mobility preserves a situation such that expected depreciation or appreciation is just great enough to offset any interest rate differential between London and New York. In other words:

$$r = r^* + \Delta s^e \tag{7.1}$$

where r is the UK interest rate, r^* is the (exogenously given) US interest rate and Δs^e is the expected rate of depreciation in the value of the pound sterling relative to the dollar.

The question now arises: how are expectations actually determined? Dornbusch provides a simple but elegant answer to this question.

Suppose there exists at any moment a (long-run) *equilibrium* exchange rate, Q, which is assumed to be determined at any moment by the level of the UK money stock, national income and interest rates, relative to those of the USA – in other words, by what we have so far called the monetary model. (As before, denote long-run equilibrium values of the variables by a bar.)

The difference is that here, in the Dornbusch model, the exchange rate is assumed to be at its equilibrium level only in the long run. In the short run, as we shall see, it will deviate from its equilibrium level, as a result of the sluggishness with which goods prices react to a disturbance.

Now Dornbusch argues that when the exchange rate is below its long-run equilibrium level, there will be a natural presumption that its future path will carry it upwards in the direction of equilibrium, rather than downwards and away from equilibrium, and vice versa when it is above equilibrium. Moreover, the exchange rate will be expected to converge more rapidly on its long-run level the further away it is at any moment – that is, the greater the distance it has left to cover.

| Box 7.1 | **How the Dornbusch expectations mechanism is derived** |

Equation 7.2 could have been derived by starting from the following assumption:

$$\frac{S^e - S}{S} = \left(\frac{\bar{S} - S}{S}\right)\Theta$$

The left-hand side is the expected depreciation, relative to the current level of the exchange rate. On the right, we have the gap between its equilibrium and actual levels, likewise in proportionate terms, raised to the power of Θ. So, when the rate is at its equilibrium level, the ratio on the right equals zero and hence no change is expected – the left-hand side is also zero.

Now take natural logs of both sides and note that, for two numbers, X and Y, which are reasonably close together, the following approximation applies:

$$\frac{X - Y}{X} \approx \ln X - \ln Y = x - y$$

and Equation 7.2 follows.

Formally, this expectations mechanism amounts to the following:

$$\Delta s^e = \theta(\bar{s} - s) \quad \theta > 0 \tag{7.2}$$

The right-hand side is simply the gap between the (natural) logarithm of the current *actual* exchange rate, s, and the logarithm of its current equilibrium value, G. (Note the lower-case s, to denote the log of the exchange rate, S). Remember that the difference of the logs is equivalent to the log of the ratio (see Box 7.1). The parameter θ is a coefficient reflecting the sensitivity of market expectations to the (proportionate) over- or undervaluation of the currency relative to equilibrium. The greater it is, the more rapidly the exchange rate is expected to depreciate, for any given degree of overvaluation. This relationship is illustrated in Figure 7.1.

Suppose, initially, we are in equilibrium at point A, with an exchange rate of $\bar{s}_0$, the UK interest rate equal to the US rate, r^*, and hence with the exchange rate expected to remain unchanged.

Now, imagine for some reason the domestic interest rate were suddenly to fall to r_1. By the UIRP condition, we know that could occur only if market participants became convinced that the pound would appreciate against the dollar over the coming months, so as to compensate for the lower explicit interest paid on sterling securities. Given Dornbusch's special assumptions about how market forecasts are made, it follows that the pound's value will have to be *below* its long-run level (s will be greater than its equilibrium level), so as to generate the expectation of a future sterling appreciation as it moves back towards equilibrium. Furthermore, the lower the UK interest rate relative to the US, the lower the pound's value will need to be in order to ensure that the future prospects are for it to appreciate sufficiently. We conclude that the system will need to settle in the short run at a point such as m in the diagram, where the exchange rate is s_1.

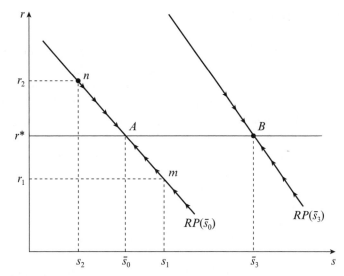

Figure 7.1 Short-run equilibrium in the securities market

Conversely, when the UK interest rate is relatively high, say r_2, the market must be anticipating a fall in the pound's external value, otherwise assets denominated in sterling will be irresistibly attractive relative to those in dollars. The short-run problem will be resolved at the point n, where the pound has appreciated (s fallen) to s_2, and the expectation is for a future fall to its equilibrium level, back at point A.

Clearly, the same argument applies to short-run divergences from any other long-run equilibrium, like the one at B, for example.

> We conclude that, for any equilibrium long-run exchange rate, such as $\bar{S}_0$ or $\bar{S}_3$, there is a line (labelled RP in the diagram) sloping downwards from left to right, which plots the feasible combinations of s and r consistent with short-run equilibrium. Along that line, the pound will be either appreciating (at points below the horizontal line through r^*) or depreciating at points above r^*.

Note that the gradient of the RP lines is equal to (minus) the value of the expectation adjustment parameter, θ.

> Notice also that uncovered interest rate parity holds at all points along the RP lines – the international financial markets are in (short-run) equilibrium at all times.

Summing up, the sub-model outlined in this section amounts simply to an implementation of uncovered interest rate parity, incorporating a specific expectations mechanism.

By contrast, the treatment of the goods market is very different, as we now see.

7.1.2 Goods market

Deviations from the equilibrium exchange rate result from the following assumption:

> **Assumption 7.3** The price level is sticky. In other words, the aggregate supply curve is horizontal in the immediate impact phase, increasingly steep in the adjustment phase and, ultimately, vertical in long-run equilibrium.

This scenario should be familiar from Section 4.2.3.

In the long run, the exchange rate is at its equilibrium level – in other words, its market-clearing real value, given UK and US price levels.

However, *in the short run*, the price level is fixed, due to the inherent rigidities that are so typical of markets for labour and goods: long-term contracts, lack of information in thousands of far-flung product markets, sluggishness in changing prices and wage rates, and so on. As a result, shocks that move the nominal exchange rate are associated with changes in the real exchange rate and hence with current account deficits or surpluses. With the passage of time, unless there are further disturbances, the economy moves back to its long-run real exchange rate, as a result of movements in both the nominal exchange rate and the price level.

From this point on, all we need to do is follow through the implications of these assumptions to understand how Dornbusch arrives at his conclusions. For this purpose, we shall make use of Figure 7.2.

Notice that Figure 7.2(a) illustrates the path taken by the exchange rate to satisfy UIRP, more or less repeating Figure 7.1. Figure 7.2(c) shows a version of the familiar

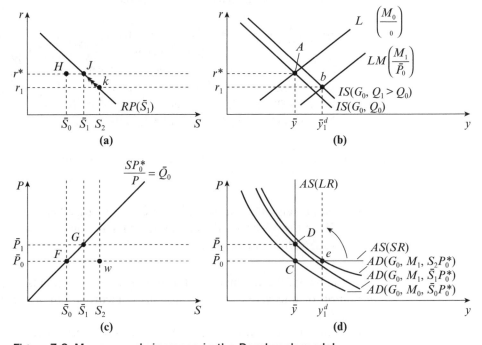

Figure 7.2 Money supply increase in the Dornbusch model

PPP diagram, plotted for a given value of the US price index, P^*. It is assumed that the UK current account clears at the real exchange rate $Q_0 = SP_0^*/P$. At combinations of P and S above the line, the pound's real value is higher than Q_0, so that the UK is uncompetitive, and hence runs a current account deficit, and vice versa below the line. UK trade is in balance only when the exchange rate/price level combination is such as to place the domestic economy exactly on the line.

Figure 7.2(b) contains the IS–LM diagram, showing the determination of aggregate demand, for given real money balances, while the aggregate demand curve for each nominal money stock is plotted in Figure 7.2(d), along with the long- and short-run aggregate supply curves.

7.1.3 Long-run equilibrium

By definition, long-run equilibrium is characterized by the following conditions:

- *Aggregate demand is equal to aggregate supply.* Hence, there is no upward or downward pressure on the price level.
- *UK and US interest rates are equal*, so that the exchange rate is static, with no expectation of either depreciation or appreciation.
- *The real exchange rate is at its long-run level.* It follows that there is neither a surplus nor a deficit in the current account of the balance of payments.

These conditions are satisfied at points A, C, F and H in Figure 7.2(b), (d), (c) and (a), respectively. With the initial equilibrium domestic price level, P_0, and the nominal money supply, M_0, the real money stock implies that the LM curve is the one that cuts the IS curve at the interest rate, r^*, and the aggregate demand, J. This in turn implies a zero interest rate differential with the USA and hence no expected depreciation or appreciation in the exchange rate (at H). It also means the goods market is in equilibrium, with national income and output at the long-run level of J (point C). Finally, as we can see from point F, the combination of a domestic price level of $\bar{P}_0$ and an exchange rate of $\bar{S}_0$ means that the UK current account is in balance.

We now consider the effect of a specific disturbance: an unanticipated money supply increase.

7.2 Monetary expansion

It will be recalled that monetary policy had no real effects in the monetary model. In the present case, this is no longer true, at least in the short run.

Suppose the UK economy's equilibrium is subjected to the following disturbance:

> The UK authorities increase the money supply from M_0 to M_1. For example, suppose they actually expand the money stock by a quarter. In other words, $M_1 = 1.25M_0$.

What will be the effect of the disturbance, in the short run and in the long run?

7.2.1 Long-run effect

Sometimes it is easier to understand the plot once we know the end of the story. At any rate, the way to handle the Dornbusch model is always to start by looking at the effect of a disturbance on its long-run properties, and then go back and look for the route the variables must have taken to get there.

The consequences for long-run equilibrium are straightforward. Start in Figure 7.2(d) and (b). The new long-run equilibrium must lie somewhere along the original, unchanged vertical supply curve, which means that aggregate demand will have to equal J. By contrast, the interest rate will have to end up at r^*, since long-run equilibrium requires that no further change in the exchange rate be expected. It follows that *both the IS and LM curves will have to end up in the same position as before the money supply increase.*

As far as the LM curve is concerned, this can be the case only if the real money stock is back at its pre-disturbance level, which obviously requires a 25% rise in the price level, since:

$$\frac{M_1}{\bar{P}_1} = \frac{1.25M_0}{1.25\bar{P}_0} = \frac{M_0}{\bar{P}_0}$$

In the absence of any change in fiscal policy, the position of the IS curve depends only on the real exchange rate, $Q = SP^*/P$. For the IS curve to be unchanged in long-run equilibrium therefore, the real exchange rate will need to have returned to its initial, pre-disturbance level.

The rise in the price level means the aggregate demand curve will need to shift upwards, in proportion to the increase in the money stock, so as to keep output unchanged at its long-run level, $\bar{y}$. The new equilibrium will therefore be at D.

Reading across from the new price level to Figure 7.2(c), it follows that we require the exchange rate to have depreciated (S to have risen) to $\bar{S}_1$, at point G, where there is again a zero balance on the UK current account.

Notice that, as in the simple monetary model, the new equilibrium involves a depreciation in strict proportion to the rise in the domestic price level and the money supply increase that brought it about. In other words, the sterling price of US dollars will have risen from $\bar{S}_0$ to $\bar{S}_1 = 1.25\bar{S}_0$, to offset the 25% inflation in the price of UK output, thereby keeping relative competitiveness constant.

As we have seen, with the *real* money stock back at its original level and the economy again in equilibrium at the point A in the IS–LM diagram (Figure 7.2(b)), the interest rate must also be at the US level, r^*. Thus, interest rate parity will obtain, as always, but with a zero expected change in the current exchange rate. In terms of Figure 7.2(a), the new equilibrium is at J instead of H.

7.2.2 Impact effect

Now that we have established where the change in the money supply is ultimately going to land us, it will be easier to work out the impact effect.

Start in Figure 7.2(b), where it can be seen that the LM curve has shifted down because, with the nominal money stock increased and the price level unchanged, the real money supply is now one and a quarter times as great as before the disturbance. The result has to be an immediate fall in interest rates.

Why does the interest rate fall?

The reason is that, with national income unchanged and the real money stock greater by a quarter, there would be an excess supply of money at the old interest rate, r^*. But remember, we are assuming financial markets clear at all times. So any incipient excess supply of money will be instantaneously choked off by a fall in the interest rate, offsetting the increase in the supply of real balances by a compensating increase in the demand. Thus, the lower interest rate is necessary to bring about the absorption of the new, temporarily higher real money stock.

The impact on the interest rate, sometimes known as the *liquidity effect*, is the key to understanding the Dornbusch model. We can see its implications in Figure 7.2(a), where the fall in the interest rate creates a differential in favour of New York. To prevent a flood of money out of London, there needs to be some compensating attraction for holders of sterling securities. In fact, the compensation is provided by an instantaneous depreciation in the exchange rate to a point at which the market views the pound as being so undervalued, relative to its new equilibrium level of Q_1, as to offer the prospect of appreciation sufficient to offset the lower interest rate on UK securities.

However, the fall in the interest rate is mitigated somewhat by an induced shift in the IS curve. Since the nominal exchange rate has fallen while the domestic price level stayed fixed, the competitiveness of the UK economy has improved, stimulating demand for its output and pushing the IS curve to the right. The net effect is to leave the economy in short-run equilibrium at point b, where aggregate demand has been boosted by both these effects and the interest rate has fallen to r_1.

At the same time, aggregate demand has risen to y_1 and, given our assumptions about supply conditions, this is also the real national income actually produced (at point e in Figure 7.2(d)).

With an interest rate of r_1, temporary equilibrium is at point k in Figure 7.2(a), on the RP line through the new, long-run equilibrium exchange rate, $\bar{S}_0$. (There was, of course, an RP line through the old equilibrium exchange rate, $\bar{S}_0$, but it has not been drawn, since it plays no part in the proceedings.) We assume that, as soon as the money supply is increased, the financial markets form their view as to where the exchange rate is going to end up, once the dust has settled. So it is with respect to this new long-run exchange rate that they judge what is going to happen to the rate over the near future. With the exchange rate at S_2, they reckon on balance that the pound is going to appreciate (S to fall) by just enough to compensate for the lower interest rate on sterling deposits – in other words, at the rate ($r^* - r_1$).

> This is the key to the whole mechanism. The immediate effect of the monetary expansion has been to cause the exchange rate to rise from its initial position at $\bar{S}_0$ to point S_2, beyond what we know will be its long-run resting place, at level $\bar{S}_1$ To get to its new long-run equilibrium position, at $\bar{S}_1$, it will need to fall. In other words, the impact effect is to make the pound overshoot its long-run devaluation, with a consequently exaggerated effect on UK competitiveness, driving the economy to a point such as w in Figure 7.2(c).

In numerical terms, the 25% increase in the money stock leads *ultimately* to a 25% *rise* in the UK price level and a 25% *fall* in the value of the pound, keeping the relative price of UK output on world markets constant. However, since the price level is fixed, the *instantaneous* effect on the value of the pound might be to cause it to fall by 40% say, giving a temporary boost to UK competitiveness of the same scale.

We can see from Figure 7.2(a) that the extent of the overshoot depends on two factors:

- *The interest sensitivity of the demand for money*, denoted by *l* in Equation 4.9.[1] The smaller it is, the steeper is the LM curve and the greater the fall in the interest rate resulting from any given increase in the real money stock.
- *The slope of the RP line*. The flatter it is, the more the exchange rate must overshoot its long-run equilibrium, for any change in the interest rate. Since, as already pointed out, the gradient of the *RP* line is (minus) the expectation adjustment parameter, θ, it follows that the more sluggish are market anticipations, the greater the degree of overshooting.

The intuitive explanation is that when θ is small, any given interest rate differential (and hence required rate of expected depreciation) must be balanced by a larger gap between the current and equilibrium levels of the exchange rate. In fact, if it were zero, then no differential would ever be possible because, however large the gap between *S* and its equilibrium value, it would generate no expected depreciation.

7.2.3 Adjustment process

So much for the impact effect of monetary expansion. What will happen in the weeks and months following the increase in the money supply?

Obviously, the excess demand for goods and services will tend to push up prices in the domestic economy, at a speed that will depend on the scale of the initial disequilibrium and on the rapidity with which the individual product (and labour) markets respond. In the process, we can think of the economy moving successively through a series of aggregate supply curves, each steeper than the last.

As prices rise, the excess demand is progressively eliminated in two ways. First, the UK's temporary competitive advantage is gradually eroded by the rise in domestic prices, so the demand for UK output is reduced – that is, the IS curve slips back towards its original position. Second, assuming no further monetary expansion, the real money supply is progressively reduced by the inflation, shifting the LM curve back to its pre-disturbance position. In the process, as the real money stock falls back, the interest rate rises to choke off the additional demand for money, at the same time helping to reduce the differential in favour of New York. As the domestic interest rate rises, the exchange rate appreciates up the $RP(\bar{S}_1)$ line, further eroding the UK's competitive advantage and hastening the return to equilibrium.

Presumably, if the Dornbusch model is a true picture of the working of a floating exchange rate, most economies are to be observed most of the time in the adjustment phase.[2] It is important to note, then, that in this model the adjustment phase following a monetary expansion is characterized by:

- a domestic currency whose value is *appreciating*, albeit at a diminishing rate
- a (decreasing) current account surplus
- (decelerating) price inflation
- (relatively) low, but rising, interest rates.

At first glance the association of an appreciating currency with rising interest rates corresponds with a pattern that is frequently observed. Exchange rate appreciation is often attributed to an accompanying rise in interest rates. However, it should be apparent that, in the Dornbusch model, rising UK interest rates cannot be said to *cause* the rise in the value of the pound. Rather, both phenomena result from the same cause: expansionary monetary policy and the concomitant, albeit temporary, undervaluation of sterling.

By the same token, the current account surplus accompanies, but does not cause, the appreciation. In fact, by the time the process of adjustment has worked itself out fully, the surplus has disappeared – but the value of the pound is at its highest level since the monetary expansion took place.

7.3 A formal explanation

The analysis so far has been only heuristic. Unfortunately, there is a limit to how far one can go with diagrams backed up by nothing more than intuition. In this section, we give a more formal presentation of one (simplified) version of the Dornbusch model and use it to derive some further results. In fact in Section 7.4, with only a slight modification to the same framework, we shall be able to draw some conclusions about the impact of oil on the UK economy.

First, we set down the equations, which should by now look broadly familiar – especially the first two, the UIRP condition and the exchange rate expectations mechanism introduced in Section 7.1, both of which are repeated here for convenience:

$r = r^* + \Delta s^e$	Uncovered interest rate parity	**(7.1)**
$\Delta s^e = \theta(\bar{s} - s)$	Expectations	**(7.2)**
$m - p = ky - lr$	Demand for money	**(7.3)**
$y^d = h(s - p) = h(q) \quad q \equiv s - p$	Demand for UK output	**(7.4)**
$\dot{p} = \pi(y^d - \bar{y}) \qquad \bar{y}$ constant	Demand adjustment	**(7.5)**

$$\dot{p} \equiv \frac{d \ln p}{dt}$$

With regard to the remaining equations, notice that we have stuck to the convention that m, p, s and y denote natural logarithms of the respective upper-case variables.[3] All the parameters are assumed positive.

Equation 7.3 is simply a log linear formulation of the demand for money. Since we are treating the money stock as given exogenously, the condition that $m^d = m^s$ is implicit: both demand and supply are written simply as m.

Equation 7.4 is a deliberately simplified aggregate demand schedule. To include a relationship between demand and other variables (income, the interest rate, and so on, as in Section 4.1.1) would complicate matters without adding any significant insight into what follows. As it stands, the equation captures the essential link between aggregate demand for domestic output and the (log of) the real exchange rate, which is $q = s - p$, if we scale the (constant) foreign price level, P^*, to unity.[4] The higher the real exchange rate, the more competitive are UK products and hence the greater the demand.

Equation 7.5 is a price adjustment equation, which says that the wider the gap between demand and capacity output, $\bar{y}$, the higher the rate of inflation, $\dot{p}$. Again, in order to simplify matters, income is taken as fixed exogenously at the full employment level.[5] If demand deviates from that level, the outcome is a protracted change in the level of prices in the economy.

The system can be reduced to two equations. Substituting from Equation 7.1 and Equation 7.2 to eliminate the domestic interest rate from the demand for money equation (Equation 7.3), we derive:

$$p = L - l\theta(s - \bar{s}) \tag{7.6}$$

where:

$$L \equiv m - k\bar{y} + lr^*$$

and, using Equation 7.4 to replace y^d in Equation 7.5:

$$\dot{p} = \pi[\mathrm{h}(s - p) - \bar{y}] \tag{7.7}$$

7.3.1 Long-run equilibrium

In long-run equilibrium, the following conditions apply:

- The rate of inflation is zero. In other words, we have $y^d = \bar{y}$. That means, denoting steady state values of the variables by a bar, we must have:

$$\bar{s} - \bar{p} \equiv \bar{q} = \frac{\bar{y}}{h} \tag{7.8}$$

from which we conclude that, in the long run, the only thing in the model that changes the real exchange rate is growth in capacity output. *Otherwise, any change in the nominal exchange rate is matched by a change in the price level.*

- The expected rate of depreciation is zero. The exchange rate is static and is not expected to change because it is at its equilibrium level. From Equation 7.6, this means we have:

$$\bar{p} = L \equiv m - k\bar{y} + lr^* \tag{7.9}$$

which simply says that the equilibrium price level is the ratio of the money stock to the level of demand when it is at its long-run level – that is, when the UK and US interest rates are equal.

Using Equation 7.9 in Equation 7.8, it follows that the nominal exchange rate settles at the level:

$$\bar{s} = (h^{-1} - k)\bar{y} + m + lr^* \tag{7.10}$$

Our conclusions from the informal model of Section 7.2 are vindicated by Equations 7.9 and 7.10. Plainly, a given percentage rise in the money stock pushes up the long-run values of both the nominal exchange rate and the price level in the same proportion (see Box 7.2), and hence leaves the real exchange rate untouched. In this respect, the properties of the monetary model are preserved in long-run equilibrium.

Box 7.2

Remember, m is the log of the money stock. Hence:

$$dm = d \ln M = \frac{dM}{M}$$

is the proportionate change or growth rate of M.

On the other hand, it can also be observed from Equation 7.8 that a rise in output ultimately results in a real depreciation. The reason is that an increase in capacity requires an improvement in competitiveness to stimulate demand and thereby absorb the extra supply. Although it causes a fall in the price of both goods and foreign currency, as it does in the monetary model and for the same reason, the appreciation is proportionately smaller than the reduction in the price level.

7.3.2 Disequilibrium

Now let us see how the model behaves out of equilibrium.

The standard practice is to rewrite the two basic equations (Equations 7.6 and 7.7) in terms of deviations from the steady-state values. To accomplish this, all we need do is note that Equation 7.7 implies, in equilibrium, that;

$$0 = \pi[h(\bar{s} - \bar{p} - \bar{y}] \tag{7.11}$$

Now subtract this from Equation 7.7 itself to give:

$$\dot{p} = \pi h(q - \bar{q}) \tag{7.12}$$

In other words, the rate of inflation is positive whenever the real exchange rate is above its equilibrium level, and vice versa below. So, for given values of the exogenous variables determining $\bar{q}$, the combinations of s and p consistent with zero inflation lie along a 45-degree line. See Figure 7.3, where the goods market equilibrium line has been drawn through the origin, on the harmless assumption that, by appropriate choice of units, we start with $s = p$.

Now apply the same treatment to the money market equation. Take Equation 7.9 from Equation 7.6 to give:

$$p - \bar{p} = l\theta(s - \bar{s}) \tag{7.13}$$

which shows the conditions necessary for *short-run* equilibrium in the money market. Once the values of $\bar{p}$ and $\bar{q}$ have been set, or rather reset by a change in one of the exogenous variables, the system adjusts in such a way as to preserve this relationship at all times. It follows that, even in the adjustment phase, the economy lies somewhere

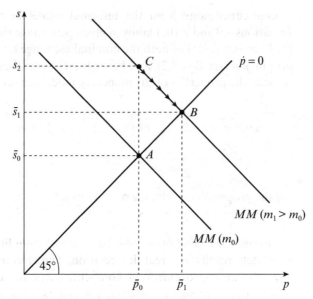

Figure 7.3 Dynamics of a money supply increase

along a downward-sloping line in (s, p) space, like the money market (MM) lines in Figure 7.3.

Notice that the MM lines have a gradient of (minus) $1/l\theta$. It follows that they are steeper, the less sensitive the demand for money to changes in the exchange rate relative to its equilibrium level. This sensitivity is the product of the interest semi-elasticity and the expectations adjustment parameter.

At a position such as A in Figure 7.3, the system is in short-run equilibrium, as always, because it is on the appropriate money market line, $MM(m_0)$. However, it is also in long-run equilibrium, because it is on the zero excess demand line ($\dot{p} = 0$).

7.3.3 Monetary expansion revisited

Now return to the example of an unanticipated money supply increase.

The ultimate outcome, we know, will be to raise both the exchange rate (from $\bar{s}_0$ to $\bar{s}_1$) and the price level (from $\bar{p}_0$ to $\bar{p}_1$). However, the stickiness of the price level precludes an immediate move from A to B.

To see what happens initially, notice first that the zero inflation line is unaffected by the disturbance, because goods market equilibrium depends only on the real exchange rate, and that is going to remain unchanged. By contrast, the money market clearing conditions certainly are affected. With a larger money stock, any given exchange rate is consistent with a proportionately higher price level, so that the MM schedule must shift outwards to $MM(m_1)$. (As can be confirmed by differentiating Equation 7.13 and setting $d\bar{s} = d\bar{p}$.)

Now from the fact that the economy must be on the relevant (that is, new) MM line at all times, but that the price level is initially fixed at its old level, $\bar{p}_0$, we conclude that the exchange rate must jump to s_2, carrying the system to point C on the downward-sloping arrowed path.

This confirms that, in this simple case, the nominal (and real) exchange rate overshoots in response to a monetary shock. The scale of the overshooting is dependent on the gradient of the money market line: the steeper the line, the greater the overshoot. Now it has been shown that the gradient of the MM line is inversely proportional to the product of the interest rate semi-elasticity of the demand for money and the expectation adjustment parameter. It follows that overshooting is greater when the overall expectation sensitivity of money demand is smaller. The reason is simple: the less sensitive the demand for real balances to depreciation, the more the exchange rate needs to depreciate in order to raise the demand to equality with the supply (see Box 7.3).

Given the important role played by this parameter, it should be pointed out that there is one value of the expectations coefficient, θ, that is consistent with perfect foresight; in fact, it is given by the positive solution of the equation:

$$\theta = -\pi h[1 + (l\theta)^{-1}]$$

While there is nothing particularly illuminating in computing this value, it is nonetheless interesting to note that the model as presented includes as a special case the situation where the market's rule of thumb is self-fulfilling, so that its anticipations always turn out to be correct in the short run as well as the long run.

Box 7.3 | **Proof that the exchange rate overshoots in the Dornbusch model**

The interested reader may confirm this result by differentiating Equation 7.6, noting that $dp = 0$ at the moment of impact and that $dm = d\bar{s}$, as we have seen, from which it follows that:

$$ds|_{dp=0} = [1 + (l\theta)^{-1}]dm$$

The term in the square bracket is obviously greater than unity.

Notice that, with the price level fixed, the depreciation at C in Figure 7.3 is real as well as nominal. The impact effect of a monetary expansion is a temporary improvement in the competitiveness of UK output.

From this point on, the economy adjusts by moving from C to B, with the exchange rate appreciating and inflation decelerating.

7.4 Oil and the UK economy

More complicated versions of the Dornbusch model have been used quite extensively to provide insights into the effect of North Sea oil on the UK economy (see reading guide). None of the models is able to take account of all the possible channels through which a disturbance of this nature could affect the international value of the pound. However, if we make a number of simplifying assumptions, we can arrive at some useful conclusions with only two slight modifications to the model set out in the previous section.

In the first place, no attempt will be made to distinguish between the effects of the oil price increase of 1979 and the build-up of production in the British sector of the North Sea that took place throughout the 1970s. Instead, we shall treat the total disturbance as though it were a sudden oil discovery. (Of course, it makes no difference from a macroeconomic point of view whether an increase in oil revenues is due to a rise in the number of barrels extracted or a rise in the price per barrel. For macroeconomic purposes, the 1979 oil price shock affected the UK in exactly the same way as a sudden discovery – provided that we ignore the impact on other countries, which ultimately must impinge on the British economy.)

Specifically, we make the following assumptions:

- The oil discovery is unexpected in advance. Revenues are untaxed.
- The extraction costs of oil are zero.
- The oil produced in the UK is sold at a price determined exogenously (on world markets). For simplicity, assume this price is constant.
- Oil carries negligible weight in both UK and world consumption baskets, and hence its contribution to the price index can be ignored. Likewise, its importance as an input to production is ignored.
- The UK authorities change neither fiscal nor monetary policy in response to the oil shock.

To see how we need to modify the basic equations, consider first the impact on aggregate demand for non-oil goods. What counts for consumption is the underlying change in the wealth of the UK household sector, as measured by the permanent income value of oil revenues.[6] We can therefore rewrite Equation 7.4 as follows:

$$y^d = h(s - p) + c\bar{V} \quad h, c > 0 \quad \text{Demand for UK non-oil output} \qquad \textbf{(7.4a)}$$

where the parameter c is the average propensity to consume, V is the value of oil revenues at any given moment and the bar denotes, in this case, a permanent income value.

By the same token, the *current* value of oil revenue seems more consistent with our transactions motive interpretation of the income term in the demand for money. That being so, we replace Equation 7.3 with:

$$m - p = k(y + V) - lr \quad k, l > 0 \quad \text{Demand for money} \qquad \textbf{(7.3a)}$$

which makes the demand for money at any moment dependent on national income at the time, inclusive of current revenue from oil, V.

These two modifications turn out to have somewhat different effects. To highlight the difference, we take them one at a time.

7.4.1 Wealth effect in the goods market

Undeterred by the artificiality of the assumption, let us temporarily set V to zero. In other words, suppose the oil discovery has no effect on transactions requirements.

If we now follow the same procedure as before in solving the system with Equation 7.4a in place of Equation 7.4, but with the other equations unchanged, we find that, as far as equilibrium is concerned:

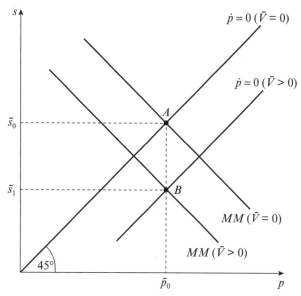

Figure 7.4 Effect of oil revenue on the goods market

- With the volume of non-oil production fixed, the real exchange rate must ultimately fall, so as to reduce the relative competitiveness of UK non-oil production. The appreciation crowds out enough foreign demand to make room for additional consumption by the newly enriched UK residents.

  In terms of Figure 7.4, this means the goods market equilibrium line ($\dot{p} = 0$) shifts outwards, associating a higher price level with any given nominal exchange rate.[7]

- On the other hand, the equilibrium price level is unchanged. The reason is obvious from the long-run demand for money (see Equation 7.9). Nothing has occurred to affect the money market, so the price level cannot move.

There are two immediate corollaries of this result. First, in the long run, the system must settle at B in Figure 7.4, and hence the new money market line must go through this point. Second, if no change is required in the price level in the long run, there can never be any disequilibrium. The initial disturbance never opens up any gap between the short- and long-run price levels. With only the nominal exchange rate needing to change so as to effect the reduction in competitiveness, there is nothing to prevent the entire adjustment taking place at once. We conclude that the price of foreign currency falls from s_0 to s_1 immediately and the economy moves smoothly and instantly to its new steady state.

7.4.2 Transactions effect in the money market

By contrast, we now switch to a scenario where the oil revenue has no permanent income value whatsoever and therefore has no effect on demand for output, but is simply a transient addition to the level of economic activity. In this case, we replace

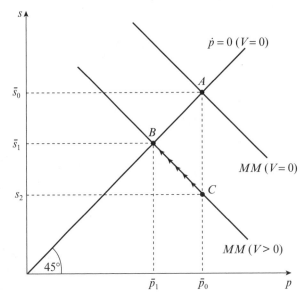

Figure 7.5 Effect of oil revenue on the money market

Equation 7.3 by Equation 7.3a, but stick to the remaining original equations, in particular Equation 7.4.

If we do so, we find:

- Because the product market is not affected by the original shock, the real exchange rate must remain unchanged, since it is the sole determinant of demand. The product market line ($\dot{p} = 0$) is therefore unmoved (Figure 7.5).

- On the other hand, the addition to the demand for real balances must result in a lower equilibrium price level.

At the same time, a lower price level can be consistent with a constant real exchange rate only if it is accompanied by appreciation. Thus, the new equilibrium is at B, where the real exchange rate is preserved by deflation and appreciation of equal proportions, keeping $s - p$ constant. This effect ought to be familiar: it is identical to a rise in income in the monetary model (Section 5.1.4).

In the short run, however, we again find overshooting. This is simply the reverse of the process that we saw with a monetary expansion. In the present case, increased demand for money with an unchanged supply means interest rates have to rise rather than fall. Higher interest rates are possible only if depreciation is anticipated, a condition that would apply only when the exchange rate is perceived by the currency market as overvalued – as it is when it has overshot as far as C in the diagram.

7.4.3 The general case

What the special cases confirm is that overshooting is inherently a money market response to the sticky price level. Changes that do not affect the money market cause no overshooting.

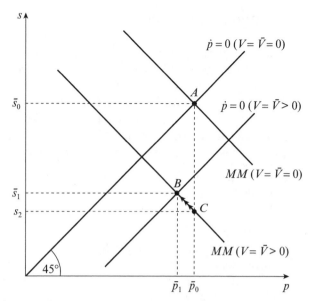

Figure 7.6 Effect of oil revenue on both money and goods market

Putting the two effects together, Figure 7.6 shows the outcome when oil revenue takes the form of a constant stream, so that $H = V$. Not surprisingly, we have over-shooting in the short run and real appreciation in the long run.

The impact effect is, as we saw, to raise interest rates so as to choke off the additional demand for money. Adjustment is then characterized by a depreciating currency and falling price level.

In summary, the depressing conclusion seems to be that the discovery and exploitation of oil are bad news in both the short and the long run. In particular, consider the implications for the current account. As always, assume the domestic country starts from a position of a zero deficit.

First, the long-run real appreciation must cause a fall in net exports of non-oil products, an example of the phenomenon sometimes called the Dutch disease.[8] This conclusion has an obvious interpretation.

Ultimately, the proposition involved is simply that, since in long-run equilibrium the current account must balance, an addition to net exports must be offset by an equal increase in net imports. In the present case, the large surplus on oil trade must have as its counterpart an equal deficit on non-oil items so as to keep the overall current account in balance. In that sense, *the oil surplus crowds out (net) exports of non-oil products and the real appreciation is the mechanism whereby the crowding out takes place.*

Worse is to come, however. As we have seen in Section 7.4.2, the impact effect involves a real exchange rate overshoot. It follows that, in the immediate aftermath of the disturbance, the current account is in deficit, *in spite of the oil 'bonus'*. The reason is that the competitiveness of non-oil production, as measured by the real exchange rate, has deteriorated beyond the point at which it can be covered by net oil exports.

7.4.4 Limitations and extensions

Perhaps fortunately, these gloomy conclusions are a long way from being the last word on the subject. To see why, the reader need only look back at the list of the assumptions we made when introducing oil into the model at the start of Section 7.4. All were additional to the limitations implicit in the original Dornbusch model. In many cases, relaxing these assumptions complicates matters very substantially, to a point well beyond what can be covered here. In other cases, the change is trivial. The results of some of these extensions can be summarized as follows:

■ The formal analysis in Sections 7.4.2 and 7.4.3 involved a simplification of the original Dornbusch model in so far as we ignored the dependence of aggregate demand on the interest rate. Allowing for this relationship makes no qualitative difference to the results.[9]

■ The conclusions are substantially mitigated if we allow for the fact that, in an open economy, the appropriate deflator relevant to money balances is a price index including an import component. This modification means that the exchange rate plays a part in equilibrating the money market even in the long run. It also means that undershooting rather than overshooting is a possible reaction to oil revenue, depending on whether the dominant impact of the disturbance is felt in the goods or money market.[10]

■ Incorporating a 'core' rate of inflation by adding a constant to the right-hand side of Equation 7.5 makes the model more realistic, especially when applied to the UK, but otherwise changes little. All it does is introduce a long-run equilibrium rate of depreciation and consequently a steady-state interest rate differential of the same scale.

■ Another possibility would be to replace the price adjustment equation with something like:

$$\dot{p} = \pi(y - \bar{y})$$

a relationship that will be familiar to many readers as a version of the famous Phillips curve. When output is at its long-run level,[11] the inflation rate is zero. Otherwise, if it is above (below) its capacity level, the price level is rising (falling). This change can have no effect on the long-run outcome, of course, but it too can be shown to open up the possibility of short-run undershooting.

■ In each of the cases analysed, the disturbance was assumed to arrive like a bolt from the blue: the money supply increase, for example, unleashed by the authorities on a completely unsuspecting market. It is easy to see that, if this were not the case, then we would get a different result, because currency speculators would buy or sell the currency (as they do, in reality) on the strength of their guesses as to future money supply changes.

In an important extension of the Dornbusch model, it was demonstrated that if a money supply increase is anticipated (for example, if it is announced in advance), then the effect on the exchange rate is somewhat moderated, with less overshooting and a longer adjustment period. Intuitively, the reason is that, from the moment the market becomes aware that the money supply is going to increase, it will change its judgement as to the long-run equilibrium. The result will be to start the whole process of adjustment immediately, thereby smoothing somewhat the impact of the money supply increase when it actually takes place. Of course, this presupposes that the market is correct in anticipating a money stock increase – in practice, it may often anticipate monetary expansion that fails to materialize, causing exchange rate movements that cannot be rationalized retrospectively.[12]

In the oil discovery case, the situation is even more complicated, because in reality what happened was that the true nature and scale of the shock emerged only gradually over a number of years during the 1970s. First came encouraging geological reports, then an enthusiastic response to the auction of drilling permits, then the first discoveries and, finally, assessment of the rate of flow from a succession of wells. Even then, after the major discoveries had been made, a number of questions remained open (and still do today): the technological feasibility of exploiting some of the finds, the life expectancy of existing wells, the likely rate at which exhausted resources would be replaced by new discoveries in the area and, most of all, the future (relative) price at which the oil could be sold.

Viewed from this angle, what actually took place was a process of slow resolution of uncertainty. Each new item of information will have caused the financial markets to react (in the Dornbusch world, to overreact) by buying or selling sterling securities, depending on whether the information involved an up- or downgrading of future North Sea production prospects. Furthermore, at each stage the exchange rate will have reflected probability assessments, rather than established certainties.

■ The analysis in this chapter takes the world economic environment as completely static. While this may be acceptable for many purposes, it is very unrealistic if the objective is to find the cause of the pound's appreciation in the early 1980s, at a time when the world economy was subjected to so many different types of shock, the effects of which, even taken individually, are often impossible to gauge. For example, if the owners of the new oil wealth (that is, OPEC governments and their citizens) had smaller relative demands for sterling than did the old wealth owners (the oil consumers), this fact might on its own reduce the value of the pound, other things being equal.

7.5 Empirical tests: the Frankel model

As it stands, the Dornbusch model is difficult to test. This is particularly true of its predictions about the dynamics of exchange rates. Most researchers have used an extension of the Dornbusch model developed by Jeffrey Frankel: the so-called real interest differential model.

The starting point is a small addition to the Dornbusch expectations mechanism. Instead of Equation 7.2, we have:

$$\Delta s^e = \theta(\bar{s} - s) + \Delta \tilde{p}^e \quad \theta > 0 \tag{7.14}$$

which asserts that when the exchange rate is at its equilibrium level, instead of being constant, it is expected to depreciate by the difference between the expected domestic and foreign inflation rates. (Remember, the tilde signifies the ratio of the domestic to the foreign variable.) This amounts to no more than a generalization of Equation 7.2 to accommodate long-run inflation: the deviation from equilibrium determines whether the currency's depreciation is thought likely to accelerate or decelerate.[13]

Exploiting UIRP to eliminate the expected depreciation from Equation 7.14, and solving for G, we have:

$$\bar{s} = s + \frac{1}{\theta}(\tilde{r} + \Delta \tilde{p}^e) \tag{7.15}$$

Finally, follow Dornbusch in assuming the monetary model only determines the *equilibrium*, not the *actual* exchange rate. Specifically, suppose we have:

$$\bar{s} = \tilde{m} - k\tilde{y} + l\Delta\tilde{p}^e \tag{7.16}$$

where, for simplicity, we take domestic and foreign demand for money parameters as equal. This formulation is familiar, apart from the last term. Frankel notes that, in the absence of PPP, real interest rates must diverge. It follows, therefore, that the inflation rate (differential) is reflected in long interest rate (differentials), but not necessarily in short rates.[14]

The equation most often tested by researchers comes simply from combining Equation 7.15 and Equation 7.16 to give:

$$s = \tilde{m} - k\tilde{y} - \theta^{-1}\tilde{r} + (\theta^{-1} + l)\Delta\tilde{p}^e \tag{7.17}$$

or, alternatively:

$$s = \tilde{m} - k\tilde{y} - \theta^{-1}(\tilde{r} - \Delta\tilde{p}^e) + l\Delta\tilde{p}^e \tag{7.18}$$

which shows more clearly the role played by the real interest rate differential.

Provided one can find a way of measuring inflation expectations, then Equations 7.17 or 7.18 are testable. Indeed, as an added bonus, they include the basic monetary model as a special case: if the exchange rate expectations elasticity, θ, is infinite, then the coefficient of real interest rates will be zero.

Frankel himself, proxying inflation expectations by long-run interest rates, found this hypothesis appeared to fit the facts for the DM/$ rate in the mid-1970s – explaining some 80% or 90% of the exchange rate variation over the period. However, almost all work since then suggests that equations such as these fail to track the major exchange rates, particularly in the 1980s (see reading guide). Furthermore, this remains the case even when alternative measures of inflation expectations are used.

7.6 Conclusions

The Dornbusch model appears at first glance to offer a potentially powerful explanation for the observed volatility of floating exchange rates, in particular the tendency for currencies to swing erratically from positions of apparent overvaluation to massive undervaluation and back again. The assumption that price levels are sticky is extremely credible and Dornbusch successfully demonstrates that a consequence could well be overreaction by the exchange rate to a disturbance. Furthermore, in the light of the evidence discussed in Chapter 2 that PPP does not hold in the short run, but possibly in the long run, the analysis here looks superficially plausible, since it generates the same conclusions as the monetary model in the long run, but allows for real effects in the short run.

The limitations discussed in Section 7.4.4 are real enough, however. By way of contrast, as was indicated there, the strength of the model is as a prototype for more complicated examples of the genre. Furthermore, the mechanism at its core can be shown to have wide applicability: similar dynamics are displayed whenever two related prices adjust at different speeds.

Nevertheless, the poor performance of the model and its derivatives in explaining the facts is undeniable and has acted as a spur to the development of other approaches to exchange rate modelling.

Summary

- Financial markets are assumed to clear instantaneously, with perfect capital mobility ensuring uncovered interest rate parity (UIRP) is maintained at all times.
- Market expectations are for the exchange rate to depreciate at a rate proportional to the gap between its current level and its long-run equilibrium value.
- In the goods market, the price level is sticky, adjusting over time at a rate proportional to the excess demand.
- The conclusions of the monetary model are preserved in long-run equilibrium.
- In the immediate term, since the price level is fixed, shocks that create excess supply (demand) in the money market have liquidity effects, requiring a fall (rise) in the interest rate to clear the domestic money market. The change can be reconciled with UIRP only if there is a simultaneous expectation of exchange rate appreciation (depreciation). Given the assumption about the way market expectations are formed, this in turn is possible only if the exchange rate jumps to a level beyond (in other words, overshooting) its long-run equilibrium.
- An extension of the Dornbusch model suggests that the discovery and exploitation of North Sea oil may have been associated with long-run real appreciation and short-run overshooting in the sterling exchange rate.
- The original Dornbusch model can be extended in a number of different directions to make it more realistic. However, these modifications result in models that sometimes exhibit under- rather than overshooting.
- One derivative of the Dornbusch model, developed by Frankel, has been extensively tested, with results that are generally disappointing. Apart from a short period in the 1970s, it fails either to track or to forecast the exchange rate adequately.

Reading guide

Readers are strongly recommended to progress from reading this stripped-down version of Dornbusch's model to tackling the original journal article in Dornbusch (1976a) or, for a slightly different presentation, Dornbusch (1976b). An excellent textbook discussion is to be found in Begg (1982).

The original article is only moderately technical, but the extensions are much more so. Subject to this caveat, the important landmarks in extending the model are Wilson (1979) on pre-announced policy changes and Buiter and Miller (1982).

On oil shocks, see Eastwood and Venables (1982) and Buiter and Purvis (1983). Copeland (1983) extends the Dornbusch analytical methods, so as to calculate the impact on the UK economy of a shock to public sector prices.

More recently, see the influential work by Meese and Rogoff (1983). Macdonald (1988) gives a summary of the tests and results achieved.

The model in Section 7.5 is from Frankel (1979). Froemmel, MacDonald and Menkhoff (2002) make an interesting attempt to breathe new life into the model with the benefit of more up-to-date econometrics.

Web page: **www.pearsoned.co.uk/copeland**.

Notes

1 In fact, in Dornbusch's paper, and in most modern work of this type, the demand for money is set in a log linear formulation so that the parameters correspond to elasticities.
2 Although, of course, they will often be in the process of adjusting to a number of earlier disturbances that, if not simultaneous, took place at intervals close enough for their adjustment phases to overlap.

   Of course, many of the disturbances will not have involved money supply increases; some may have been decreases, and still others may have been real rather than monetary disturbances.
3 Unfortunately, the convention that y is real and Y nominal income clashes with this. At any rate, here y is the log of real income and we shall simply avoid references to nominal income. Another caveat relates to the parameters in Equation 7.3, which obviously should not be the same in a log linear demand function as they were in the natural number version. However, we persist with the letters originally used in Chapter 4 (k, l, h, and so on) in order to economize on two scarce resources – symbols and memory (the reader's and the author's).

   Notice that the interest rates, r and r^*, are most certainly not logs.
4 Remember the log of one is zero. Alternatively, when $P^* = 1$, we have:

$$\log(SP^*/P) = \log(S/P) = s - p$$

5 In other words, it is determined along the lines described in Section 4.2.
6 For readers unfamiliar with the concept, permanent income can be visualized simply as the average over time of a variable flow, after appropriate discounting. Alternatively, it is the annuity that could be bought with the present value of the stream of oil revenues.
7 Although it is still a 45-degree line, the new goods market equilibrium locus is obviously associated with a lower value of $s - p$.
8 After the syndrome that is supposed to have afflicted the Netherlands, following the discovery of large reserves of natural gas.
9 The reader may easily verify that its main result is to make the goods market equilibrium line ($\dot{p} = 0$) steeper than the 45-degree line.
10 It should be pointed out that whether or not a model of the Dornbusch type exhibits under- or overshooting depends only on its structure. If it overshoots in reaction to one disturbance, it does so to exactly the same extent in response to another disturbance.
11 Usually known in the labour market literature as the 'natural' level, but nowadays given the more longwinded title of 'non-accelerating inflation rate output'.
12 More generally, what counts is not the absolute value of the change in an exogenous variable but rather the extent to which the change comes as 'news' to the market – that is, the extent to which it had not already been discounted in the market before announcement or implementation. The implication (that we should be looking only at disturbances viewed as 'surprises' or 'innovations', given pre-existing expectations) will be followed up in Chapter 13.

13 Frankel justifies this mechanism by demonstrating that, under certain circumstances, it is consistent with perfect foresight.

14 A view that has a long Keynesian pedigree is that short rates reflect monetary tightness (via the liquidity effect), while long rates are determined by trends in the (relatively sluggish) core inflation rate. According to this view monetary policy acts on the short end of the yield curve rather than on the general level of interest rates.

8 Portfolio balance and the current account

Introduction

In Chapter 7, we modified the monetary model to allow for the possibility that adjustment in the real sector may well take longer than in financial markets. The models to be analysed in this chapter rely on the same assumption. They differ from the Dornbusch model, however, in a number of important respects.

The point at which the divergence starts is the uncovered interest rate parity assumption. Portfolio balance theorists argue instead that risk aversion is the predominant motive in investors' choice between domestic and foreign currency securities and that financial markets will therefore be characterized by risk premiums large and pervasive enough to make UIRP inoperative.

Now the detailed implications of allowing for risk aversion involve the analysis of utility maximization under conditions of uncertainty and for that reason coverage of the whole subject has to be deferred to much later in the book (Chapter 15). However, it turns out that for once the economics profession's misfortune is good news for the textbook writer (and reader). In fact, portfolio balance models of the exchange rate make use only of the ultimate conclusions of risk premium analysis. No attempt has yet been made to integrate the two literatures, so that it is quite convenient to treat them separately in this way.

The only insight from the risk premium literature that is relevant here is that *investors will tend to diversify their holdings of risky assets, with portfolio shares that increase as the return on them rises relative to competing assets.* To put the matter differently, assets are no longer perfect substitutes, particularly if they are denominated in different currencies. Instead, they are, at least in part, complements within a diversified portfolio, so that the interest rate elasticity of the demand for securities will be far less than infinite.

Portfolio balance theorists therefore specify the model of the financial sector in much greater detail than the models considered so far. In doing so, they also integrate the process of wealth accumulation (saving) into the model, as the vital link between short-run equilibrium in the financial sector and long-run equilibrium in the rest of the economy. Now private sector saving can only take the form of accumulation of foreign currency assets via the capital account of the balance of payments and, under a floating exchange rate, the balance on capital account has to be the reflection of the current account surplus or deficit. It follows that a role has been found for the balance of payments – or at least a link between events in that sector and the exchange rate.

The outcome is a model that is very general indeed – to such an extent that it can be formulated to include all the other models in this book as special cases. As we shall see, it is perhaps best regarded as an integration of the Mundell–Fleming and Dornbusch models, sharing with the former the assumption of imperfect capital mobility and, with the latter, the assertion that product prices adjust slowly. It is also richer in its insights and in some respects more plausible than the models covered in the book so far. In particular, many economists and commentators (and possibly market participants) would find it difficult to accept a view of the exchange rate that did not allow some role for the balance of payments, even if only in the long run.

Unfortunately, however, the portfolio balance approach is also far more complex. The price of the complications is not only analytical difficulty. The result is also the introduction of variables that are almost impossible to measure (for example, wealth), a fact that makes the whole approach difficult to apply in practice and of little use for forecasting purposes.[1]

We start in Section 8.1 by describing in some detail the model of the financial sector. In Section 8.2, we analyse the short-run impact of three different types of disturbance, before going on to cover long-run equilibrium and the significance of the current account. The chapter closes with a brief consideration of the evidence and some conclusions.

8.1 Specification of asset markets

The portfolio balance model takes as its setting a small country, which in the present context means one whose assets are not held by foreign residents (unlike the UK, in reality). The opposite is certainly not taken to be the case. In other words, UK residents *are* assumed to hold foreign currency assets. In fact, the residents of the domestic country – we shall continue to call it the UK – hold three types of asset: the sterling money supply, M, the total stock of bonds issued by the British government, B, and a quantity, F, of dollar-denominated assets[2] issued by the federal government in Washington. The last is taken as fixed in the short run (but not in the long run) at the level $\$F$, which is equivalent to £FS. We assume that other forms of wealth can safely be ignored.[3]

Given this framework, UK nominal wealth (in pounds) at any moment will consist of:

$$W = \bar{M} + \bar{B} + SF \qquad (8.1)$$

where the bars denote the variables that are taken as exogenous.[4]

Consider the demand for each of the assets. What factors will determine the level of demand for the three assets?

To understand the answer given by portfolio balance theorists, it is necessary to place the demand for money and domestic and foreign bonds in the appropriate setting.

In the first place, the demand for each of the assets is taken as interdependent. In other words, rather than considering the demand for any single asset in isolation, we need to think of a decision process whereby an individual's stock of wealth is distributed between the available list of assets.[5] The problem for investors then is how to choose what *proportion* of their wealth (or net worth) they should hold in each possible form: money, domestic bonds or foreign bonds. Moreover, their objective in selecting a particular portfolio is taken to be the maximization of their future welfare, as measured by their utility.[6]

Notice the change in emphasis compared with the models examined hitherto, where individuals were viewed as preoccupied with financing a flow of transactions in goods and services.

Now the problem of how investors can maximize their utility in this type of context is complicated, because the return on some of the competing assets is uncertain, so that the investor's decision will typically involve trading off prospective returns against potential risk. The problem will be analysed in some detail in Chapter 14. For the moment, we rely on an intuitive justification of the model.

Consider an individual faced with a choice between (for the moment) only two assets, one riskless, A, and one risky, B. A offers a guaranteed return of r^A over the holding period. The return on B, however, is highly uncertain, but its most likely value is r^B.

Now, we know that if in general people are risk averse, as we assume in this chapter they are, they will require compensation for the uncertainty associated with asset B. They will not simply plunge all their wealth into asset B whenever the likely return r^B is greater than r^A. Instead, they will compare the two returns to see whether the gap between them is great enough to offer what they regard as adequate compensation for the risk associated with B.

But if the excess return $r^B - r^A$ is great enough to persuade an individual to take a chance on B, how great a proportion of his wealth should he risk? The answer is not obvious. What is clear, however, is that it would be foolhardy to respond to a tiny increase in r^B by suddenly plunging 100% for B. Common observation shows that people usually follow the old maxim: 'Don't put all your eggs in one basket'. In other words, they *diversify*. So, the most likely response, and one that can be shown to be consistent with rational behaviour, is for the individual to respond to each small increase in r^B by increasing his holding of B. There will be some level so low that he will choose to hold none at all. There will equally be some level so high that he will choose to convert his total portfolio to holding B. But as long as r^B remains within these bounds, he will hold a mix – that is, a *diversified portfolio* of both A and B.

Moreover, *the individual will usually hold a greater proportion of any asset the higher is the return it offers and the lower is the return on competing assets, other things being equal.* This will be the case because the higher the return, the greater the compensation for risk (if any).

The next point to notice is that, if the demand for one of the assets, say B, depends on *both* rates of return, r^A and r^B, so must the demand for the other asset, A. This must be true for two reasons. First, because the statement in italics obviously implies that the demands are symmetrical. Second, with the amount available for investment fixed, whatever proportion is invested in B – call it b – it follows that the proportion $1 - b$ must be held in the asset A.

Bearing these points in mind, and applying the same logic to our three-asset case mentioned at the beginning of this section, it follows that equilibrium in each market will be defined by these equations:

$$\bar{M}/W = m(r, \bar{r}^* + \Delta s^e) \quad m_1 < 0 \quad m_2 < 0 \tag{8.2}$$

$$\bar{B}/W = b(r, \bar{r}^* + \Delta s^e) \quad b_1 > 0 \quad b_2 < 0 \tag{8.3}$$

$$SF/W = f(r, \bar{r}^* + \Delta s^e) \quad f_1 < 0 \quad f_2 > 0 \tag{8.4}$$

In each case, the left-hand side represents the supply (relative to wealth) and the right-hand side the demand as a function of the two rates of return: the interest rate on domestic bonds, r, and the sterling value of the return on foreign securities, which is equal to the sum of the (exogenously given) foreign interest rate, r^*, and the rate of depreciation of the pound, Δs^e (see Box 8.1). Notice that in previous chapters, it was assumed these two rates of return were driven to equality by risk-neutral arbitrageurs. Here, of course, the risk premium drives a wedge between domestic and foreign interest rates, as it implicitly does in the Mundell–Fleming model.

Box 8.1 **Why we can ignore the price level in the asset demand function**

Some readers may feel uneasy about the absence of any reference to the price level in these equations, particularly in view of the necessity, stressed in Chapter 4, of treating the demand for money as the demand for a stock of purchasing power.

In fact, the problem does not arise here for two reasons. First, we assume the price level is constant in the short run. Second, even if we explicitly included the price index, P, it would cancel out on the left-hand side in each equation, because both numerator and denominator are nominal quantities. So we would have:

$$\frac{\bar{M}/P}{W/P} = \bar{M}/W$$

and so forth.

This argument is summarized in the signs given to the partial derivatives on the right-hand side of the equations, where we follow the standard notation for a function $g(x, y)$:

$$g_1 \equiv \frac{\partial g}{\partial x} \quad \text{and} \quad g_2 \equiv \frac{\partial g}{\partial y}$$

Thus, the demand for money decreases when either rate of return falls, while the demand for each type of bond is affected positively by increases in its 'own return'[7] and negatively by increases in the return on the other asset.

To understand the remainder of this section, it is essential to bear in mind that the variables in the portfolio balance model are of three types:

- *Endogenous*, even in the short run: the (spot) exchange rate, S, and the interest rate, r. Both react instantaneously, so that financial markets clear at all times.

- *Exogenous in the short run, endogenous in the long run*: total wealth, W, the stock of foreign securities, F, the UK price level, P, and the expected rate of depreciation, Δs^e, are all assumed 'sticky' – that is, slow to react to disturbances.

- *Exogenous in both short and long run*: the US variables (interest rate, r^* and price level, P^*), and the (UK) government policy variables: the stocks of money, $\bar{M}$, and gilt-edged securities (bonds), $\bar{B}$ are all marked with a bar.

These equations are very general indeed and, moreover, it is easy to see how the model can be generalized further in order to incorporate additional assets. However, the complications can easily get out of hand, since each additional asset involves not only one more equation but also an extra rate of return argument in each equation. Therein lie both the strength and the weakness of the model.

The first point to notice is that nothing is specified with regard to the form of the demand functions m, b and f, other than a number of restrictions on the partial derivatives. In each case, as can be seen in Equations 8.2–8.4, it is assumed that demand responds positively to changes in its *own* rate of return and negatively to returns on competing assets. Furthermore, the own-return effect is usually assumed greater, in absolute terms, than the cross-return effect:

$$b_1 + b_2 > 0 \quad and \quad f_1 + f_2 > 0$$

In the jargon, assets are 'gross substitutes'.

Finally in this regard, it should be noted that the definition of wealth in Equation 8.1 means that for a change in either rate of return, the sum of the impact effects on all three assets must be zero. In other words, we must have:

$$m_1 + b_1 + f_2 = 0 \quad and \quad m_2 + b_2 + f_2 = 0$$

In a world with a zero-risk premium, all four of the partial derivatives of the functions b and f would be infinite, reflecting the fact that since investors view domestic and foreign bonds as perfect substitutes, the slightest deviation from the (common) world rate of return would result in massive flight to or from the asset in question. This was why, in Chapter 7, we were able effectively to replace asset demand equations with a simple, (uncovered) interest rate parity condition.

In the present case, by contrast, a rise in the return on, say, UK bonds causes (British) investors to reallocate their portfolios instantaneously in favour of UK securities and at the expense of both the other assets. However, the shift in portfolio composition is marginal – which is not to say small necessarily, but certainly not infinite. In other words, instead of converting their total wealth into domestically issued bonds, as they would if they were risk neutral, they switch to holding a greater proportion in bonds and less in money and foreign assets. In other words, they remain appropriately diversified after the change.[8]

8.2 Short-run equilibrium

The standard way of analysing the model's short-run properties is with the aid of portfolio balance lines: MM, BB and FF for the money, bond and foreign asset markets, respectively (Figure 8.1). The curves show equilibrium combinations of S and r, given the initial level of the return on foreign assets, the value of total UK wealth and the stocks of money and bonds.[9]

To understand the diagram, consider the effect of an increase in the price of foreign exchange, S. The key here is that the fall in the value of the pound has two effects. By raising the sterling value of the given stock of dollar assets (with F given, the value of SF increases), it brings about an increase in the value of wealth, hence raising the demand for all assets, *other things being equal*.

As far as the money market is concerned, the increased wealth would lead to a rise in the demand for money. With the supply unchanged, equilibrium can only be preserved by a rise in one of the rates of return – and the return on dollar assets is assumed constant in the short run. Hence, a *rise* in UK interest rates is required to preserve equilibrium and the MM schedule slopes upwards, associating higher values of S and r.

In the market for UK gilt edged, the opposite is true: excess demand needs to be offset by *lower* interest rates – in other words, higher bond prices. It follows that the BB line slopes downwards.

Finally, the impact on the market for foreign assets of the increase in S takes two forms. The effect of the rise in total wealth, which tends to increase the demand, is

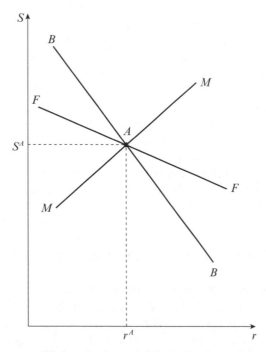

Figure 8.1 Short-run equilibrium in the portfolio balance model

more than offset by the increased sterling value of the supply. The *net* impact is to create incipient excess supply. This can be prevented by reducing the attractiveness of competing assets, which means given our assumptions, a *lower* domestic interest rate. Hence, the *FF* schedule is also downward-sloping.

Since we have assumed that the impact of a lower UK interest rate is likely to be greatest in the domestic bond market, the *BB* line will be steeper than the *FF* line, as can be seen in Figure 8.1.

The intersection of any two of the lines generates the equilibrium exchange rate–interest rate combination, (S^A, r^A). The third line must pass through the same point, A, by virtue of the adding-up condition: given fixed wealth, equilibrium in any two of the markets implies equilibrium in the third. This is obvious as soon as it is realized that total asset demand as well as supply must add up to wealth, simply because the only way to demand any asset is to offer another in exchange. So we could choose to ignore the bond market for example, since equilibrium in the other two markets would mean that Equations 8.2 and 8.4 were satisfied at the current exchange rate and interest rate, which would in turn mean that:

$$b \equiv 1 - m - f$$
$$= 1 - \bar{M}/W - SF/W = \bar{B}/W$$

The model as it stands allows us to ask a number of questions about the impact of changes in policy variables (the stocks of money and/or bonds), in the short-run exogenous variables (the quantity of domestic wealth or of foreign assets) or even in the behavioural relationships summarized by the functions m, b and f.[10] The answers are often complicated and not always unambiguous. For illustrative purposes, we shall confine our attention to the examples of an increase in the money supply and in the stock of foreign assets. There turns out to be an immediate complication to be sorted out before we can proceed.

So far, whenever expansionary monetary policy was considered in previous chapters, the question of *how* the money stock actually increased could safely be ignored. In the present context, however, this is no longer the case, since money supply changes have differing effects depending on whether they involve changes in the stock of bonds or foreign exchange. In other words, we have two alternative types of open market operation. The possibility of money creation as a result of deficit spending is ruled out at this point, because money created in this way would have to be treated as asset accumulation – that is, an increase in (nominal) wealth. Although this case is not analysed explicitly in this chapter, the reader ought to be able to work out the implications with the help of the three cases covered here. We shall take each possibility separately.

8.2.1 Case 1: money supply increase, domestic asset decrease

Suppose that the UK authorities buy up their own gilt edged with newly printed money, an *open market purchase* in the jargon of central banking. In this way, the government engineers an equal and opposite change in the stocks of money and bonds.

Consider the impact effect in domestic financial markets. Other things being equal, and assuming we start from a position of equilibrium where investors are content

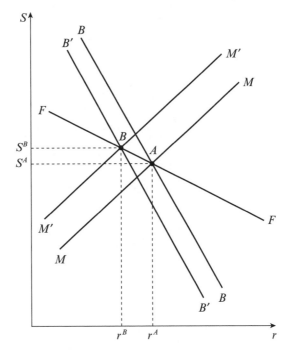

Figure 8.2 Open market purchase of domestic bonds

with their portfolio allocation, there has to be an immediate excess supply of money and excess demand for bonds.

The outcome must be that a large proportion of the new money goes to swell the demand for bonds, driving the interest rate down (and the price of bonds up). It can be shown that the net effect is to cause both money and bond market lines to shift to the left, as in Figure 8.2. The MM line moves further than the BB line. The reason is that the direct effect in the money market is greater than the impact on the bond market, because the latter is in part dissipated by a spillover effect on to the demand for foreign assets, which become more attractive when domestic interest rates fall. The increased demand for dollar-denominated securities explains the rise in the price of foreign exchange at the new equilibrium (point B in Figure 8.2).

We conclude that the money supply increase results in a short-run fall in the interest rate and a rise in the price of foreign currency. But notice: there is no reason to suppose that the depreciation will be anywhere near in proportion to the change in the money stock.

8.2.2 Case 2: money supply increase, foreign currency asset decrease

Alternatively, the UK authorities could buy dollar-denominated securities from British holders. (In practice, of course, it might be difficult to distinguish the nationality of the sellers. For our purposes it is essential that they are UK residents, otherwise the whole framework of asset market equations, wealth constraint, and so on breaks down.)

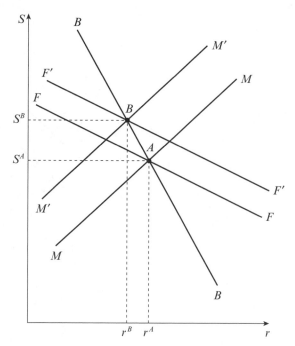

Figure 8.3 Open market purchase of foreign bonds

Obviously, the impact on the *MM* schedule would be the same as in the previous case. On the other hand, the decrease in *F* (the dollar value of the stock of foreign currency assets) creates an excess demand that can be offset only by an increase in the price, *S*, at which those securities translate into sterling. Hence, the equilibrium moves up the *BB* schedule, with a fall in *r* and a rise in *S*, as before (Figure 8.3).

The difference between this case and the previous one is quantitative rather than qualitative. Given the assumptions made here, it can be shown that open market operations in domestic securities have a greater effect on the UK interest rate and a smaller effect on the exchange rate than do purchases of dollar assets.

8.2.3 Wealth effects: an increase in the stock of foreign currency assets

Now consider a very different type of disturbance. Suppose there is an increase in the (dollar value of the) supply of foreign securities. This case differs in two important respects from those analysed so far.

First, we are concerned here with a net increase in wealth, rather than the exchange of one type of asset for another, as before. In other words, what is involved is *private sector asset accumulation (that is, saving) rather than public sector policy changes.*

Second, not only is an increase in foreign currency assets equivalent to saving, but it is also the *only* form saving can really take, given the structure of the model. Thus, saving is to be understood in the present context as a flow accumulation of dollar assets via a current account surplus.

In terms of the balance of payments (see Chapter 1), as long as the pound is float-ing freely, a UK capital account deficit (that is, the accumulation of claims on the USA) must be the counterpart of an equal surplus on the current account of Britain's balance of payments. Conversely, a UK current account deficit must be associated with the net import of capital, in other words dissaving in the form of a reduction in UK net dollar claims on the USA.

This is, in fact, the central feature of portfolio balance models. As in the Dornbusch model examined in Chapter 7, prices (and output) are assumed fixed in the short term, as a result of the relative sluggishness of goods and labour markets. Hence, short-run adjustment is confined to the financial markets, which may well settle on an exchange rate–interest rate combination incompatible with equilibrium in the goods market (that is, a zero current account balance), given the initial price index and level of national income. The result will be a continuing flow of capital across the exchanges, adding to or subtracting from the stock of claims on the rest of the world, and causing a perpetual shift in the financial markets.

It is a shift of this nature that is illustrated in Figure 8.4.

Take the *FF* schedule first. It must shift downwards, because the increased supply of dollar assets can be absorbed only if sterling appreciates (*S* falls), thereby neutral-izing the rise in the value of *F* through a fall in the price of dollars and keeping the product, *SF*, constant.

Furthermore, since there is no possibility of a change in the interest rate (there has been no change in the quantities of either of the domestic currency assets), the other two schedules must shift vertically downwards. The mechanism whereby this occurs will be as follows:

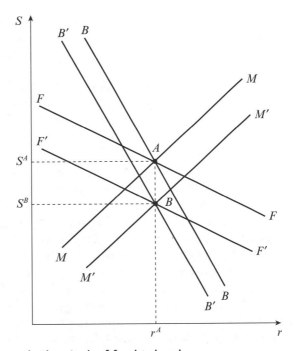

Figure 8.4 Increase in the stock of foreign bonds

As UK residents accumulate dollar securities, and they attempt to exchange them for domestic assets, in the process generating an excess supply of dollars and driving down their price, S. The induced excess demand for money would, in other circumstances, require a rise in the UK interest rate, while the excess demand for gilt edged would require the very opposite. In the event neither can occur and the system remains in disequilibrium until the change in the exchange rate has been sufficient to reduce the sterling value of foreign currency assets to their previous value.

The size of the required appreciation should by now be clear. If the interest rate is to remain constant, wealth must be unchanged once the short-run adjustment process is complete. Since the quantities of domestic securities are constant, that must mean the sterling value of dollar securities ends up back where it started. We must therefore have an appreciation in proportion to the increase in the quantity of dollar claims that initiated the whole process. In other words, the outcome has to be:

$$\frac{\Delta S}{S} = \frac{\Delta F}{F}$$

This conclusion about the short run is critical, because it provides the key to the whole adjustment process, as we now see when we move on to describe the long run.

8.3 Long-run and current account equilibrium

The model of equilibrium in financial markets takes a number of variables as given, as we have seen. The background against which the financial markets adjust is a real economy, where the values of the two key long-run variables, the price level, P,[11] and the volume of foreign currency assets, F, are determined. We shall continue to assume that expectations are unchanged.[12] The model of the real sector, of which there are a number of possible variations, will only be given in broad outline here.

The specification of the real sector can be thought of as simply an extension of the goods market model analysed in Chapter 7. Again, excess demand for goods is mainly a function of the real exchange rate, Q, which is simply the ratio S/P, given that the foreign price index is fixed. Other factors that impinge directly or indirectly on aggregate demand or supply are taken as exogenous 'shift factors'. Excess demand (supply) in domestic goods[13] markets results in net imports (exports), in order to maintain short-run equilibrium.

The volume of net exports is not quite the same thing as the current account surplus, however. Some portfolio balance theorists stress the importance to the current account of the balance of payments of investment income accruing to the domestic economy from UK holdings of dollar assets. A short-run increase (decrease) in the value of these holdings, if not reversed in the long run, will be associated with a rise (fall) in UK dollar interest income, $r*F$, and a consequent decrease (increase) in the surplus required on other current account items consistent with a zero balance. It follows that, in the long run, the higher F is, the less competitive the UK needs to be for the current account to balance and vice versa.

Any particular current account surplus (or deficit) will determine a rate of accumulation (or depletion) of the UK's dollar assets. It is this interaction between the real sector and the financial markets that ultimately returns the economy to long-run equilibrium.

As far as the price level is concerned, inflation is assumed to take place as a result of the gap between the current real money stock and the level consistent with equilibrium in the goods market – that is, with the long-run level of the real exchange rate.

Long-run equilibrium occurs when both the UK price level and the quantity of foreign securities in the domestic economy are such as to generate a zero balance on current (and therefore capital) account. When this position is reached, there is no further disequilibrium in UK product markets, so that the price level is constant and there is no net tendency to accumulate or decumulate wealth in the form of dollar securities.

8.3.1 Money supply increase in the long run

We shall consider the long-run impact of only one type of disturbance: a once-and-for-all permanent increase (of, say, 10%) in the UK money stock, accomplished by a central bank purchase of domestic bonds at time 0.

One might expect that the outcome would ultimately be the same as in the benchmark monetary model (Chapter 5): a 10% increase in the price level and in the price of foreign exchange, with all real variables back at their pre-disturbance equilibrium levels.

Now, in this context, the rise in the UK money stock, from whatever cause, raises the long-run equilibrium price level in proportion (that is, by 10%), so that the real money stock is unchanged. However, the pound depreciates by less than 10%, so that the *real* exchange rate, $Q = S/P$, ends up lower. In other words, the net effect is to reduce the competitiveness of UK production.

The reason is to be found in the adjustment process following the money supply increase.

Recall our conclusion in Section 8.2.1: the impact effect of an open market purchase would be to increase the price of foreign currency. Now, as in the Dornbusch model, with the price level still at its pre-disturbance level, the pound's depreciation must be real as well as nominal: the numerator of the ratio S/P increases at time 0, before the denominator can react.

Assuming that the UK was in long-run equilibrium before 0, the result has to be an incipient current account surplus, as the improved competitiveness shows up in increased net exports and hence *in a build-up of dollar claims on the USA*. Now we have seen in Section 8.2.3 that a rising stock of foreign currency assets implies exchange rate appreciation. It follows that adjustment to the shock must be characterized by sterling appreciation, tending to reverse the impact of the real devaluation.

Moreover, as time passes, prices begin to rise in the domestic economy, further eroding the competitive advantage provided by the devaluation. At some point, say at time t, the UK price index has risen by 10%, so that the real exchange rate is back where it started and the relative competitiveness of UK and US production is restored. At this point net exports from the UK are zero and the volume of dollar assets is constant.

Even though the stock of dollar claims on the USA has stopped growing at time t, it is still positive and therefore still generating a flow of investment income to the UK private sector. The fact that the UK's real exchange rate is back where it started no longer implies a zero current account balance. Instead, with zero net exports from the UK, it implies a current account surplus equal to the investment income on the net asset accumulation that took place over the period between 0 and t.

We conclude that the exchange rate needs to continue appreciating so as to carry the real exchange rate to a level higher than before the disturbance. The system will only be back in full long-run equilibrium when (at some time, T) the real appreciation relative to time 0 is sufficient to generate an excess of UK imports over exports equal to the value of the income accruing on the dollar assets accumulated over the period from 0 to t.

In other words, by the time the economy is back in long-run equilibrium at time T, its competitive position will have been eroded (compared with before the monetary shock) and it will be paying for net imports with capital service.

Furthermore, the *nominal* exchange rate will have undergone a sudden depreciation, at time 0, followed by a protracted appreciation until long-run equilibrium is restored at T. The appreciation will have taken the exchange rate part of the way back in the direction of its original, pre-disturbance value, although it will of course still ultimately be devalued. Thus, as in the Dornbusch model, *the slow adjustment of goods markets leads to the conclusion that the nominal exchange rate will overshoot its long-run equilibrium value in the immediate aftermath of a disturbance.*[14]

8.4 Evidence on portfolio balance models

The portfolio balance model generates a number of qualitative predictions that one might expect to see reflected in the data. Apart from overshooting and the appearance of PPP only as a long-run phenomenon, if at all (both of which were discussed in the last chapter) perhaps the most obvious implication concerns the role of the balance of payments.

If the portfolio balance model is correct, current account surpluses will be associated with appreciating and deficits with depreciating currencies. Notice that this is not a genuine relationship of cause and effect. The current account imbalance is itself a consequence of a disturbance, the adjustment process to which requires a long-run change in the volume of foreign currency assets in the economy.

Figures 8.5–8.10 show effective exchange rates and current account balances for six industrialized countries: the UK, the USA, West Germany, Japan, France and Switzerland. If there is any underlying relationship between the two variables, it is far from obvious. Take the USA for example. As can be seen from Figure 8.6, the dollar's great appreciation in the early 1980s continued for two years after the country's current account had gone into deficit. Again, the dollar's rise from the 1990s onwards has been set against a background of current account deficits on an unprecedented scale. For the UK, too, the link between the balance of payments and the currency is ambiguous at best. The surpluses produced by the start of oil production in the early 1980s were reflected in appreciation of the pound, but fluctuating deficits since then seem to bear little relationship to the exchange rate. The correlation for the other countries is no clearer. In general, the best that can be said is that any relationship that exists must be very weak. If anything, it is slightly easier to discern the competitiveness mechanism whereby a weak exchange rate causes the current account to improve.

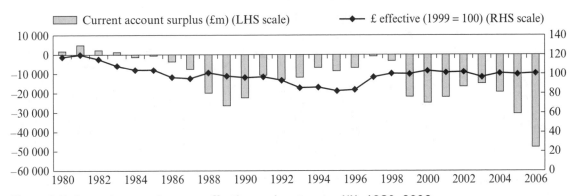

Figure 8.5 Current account versus effective exchange rate: UK, 1980–2006

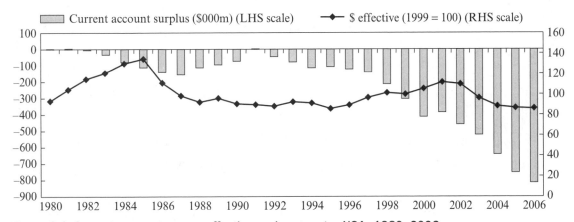

Figure 8.6 Current account versus effective exchange rate: USA, 1980–2006

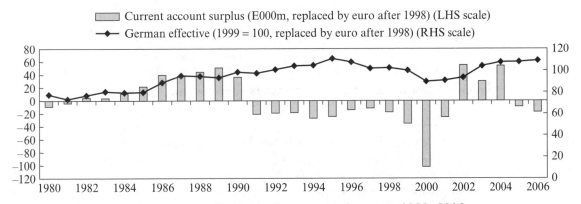

Figure 8.7 Current account versus effective exchange rate: Germany, 1980–2006

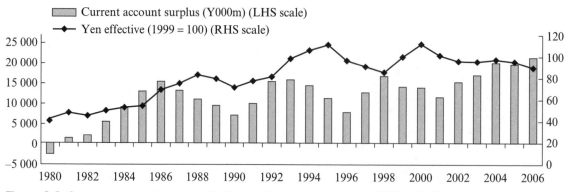

Figure 8.8 Current account versus effective exchange rate: Japan, 1980–2006

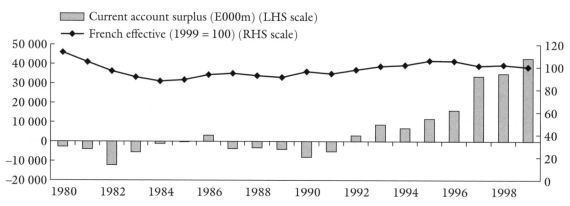

Figure 8.9 Current account versus effective exchange rate: France, 1980–99

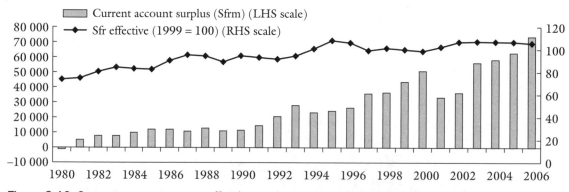

Figure 8.10 Current account versus effective exchange rate: Switzerland, 1980–2006

Now, of course, a casual 'eyeball test' like this can never be decisive. In the present case, however, it cannot be regarded as auguring well for more rigorous tests, for a number of reasons. First, since the data plotted in the graphs are annual averages, they are likely to be more favourable than higher-frequency data, which exhibit far greater volatility. Second, bilateral data would almost certainly contradict the model's predictions even more sharply.[15] Third, as has already been emphasized, if the portfolio balance model is to be believed, then the link between current account and exchange rate is not causal: the former is simply a by-product of changes in the latter. The natural interpretation is, then, that *the relationship ought to be more or less contemporaneous*. It follows that the apparently weak link cannot be explained away by delays in the chain from cause to effect.

As far as rigorous tests of the portfolio balance model are concerned, the published results are of two kinds. Some writers test the model directly, while others use portfolio balance equations in an attempt to answer the question of whether or not there is a risk premium and, if so, what determines it. The latter will be considered in Chapter 15.

The first problem that confronts researchers in this field is finding data. It is virtually impossible to find reliable data on holdings of assets denominated in the different currencies – at least at a frequency high enough to be of any use for research purposes. In some cases, researchers have taken an initial estimate and added each period's current account surplus adjusted for central bank purchases so as to arrive at an approximate series for domestic holdings of foreign assets. This method has a number of disadvantages: it ignores capital gains or losses, it effectively assumes all domestic assets are domestically owned and it also builds into the estimates the widely acknowledged inaccuracy of current account statistics.

The second problem is more fundamental. As has already been made clear, the portfolio balance approach relies on an analysis of the determination of the risk premium. As we shall see, this analysis implies stable asset demand functions only under fairly restrictive conditions, which are probably inconsistent, even in principle, with the context to which they are being applied here.[16] None the less, most researchers have attempted to fit equations that simply have the exchange rate on the left-hand side and the financial variables on the right.[17]

In addition, remember that in order to explain a *bilateral* exchange rate in what is in practice a *multilateral* world, we need to make use of six financial stock variables, even if we maintain the fiction that the UK's bonds are not held in the USA, and vice versa.

In view of these problems, it is perhaps not surprising that research results have been largely disappointing and certainly do not represent a significant improvement over simpler models. In the first place, it has proved largely impossible to fit equations in which all six financial stock variables (UK and US money stocks, UK and US holdings of domestic bonds, UK and US holdings of foreign currency bonds) make a significant contribution. The problem often necessitates eliminating more or less arbitrarily one or two of the variables at the cost of potentially distorting the estimates of the remaining variables. Even then, the typical shortcomings of fitted exchange rate equations were still present: poor fit, evidence of persistent autocorrelation (possibly indicating omitted variables), poor forecasting ability, and so forth.

Furthermore, this failure applies even to tests on data from the 1970s, a period when simpler exchange rate equations appeared to fit reasonably well. Results for the 1980s and 1990s look even less encouraging.

8.5   Conclusions

To travel hopefully, it is said, is better than to arrive. In this chapter, we have presented a model with a relatively sophisticated financial sector. Its analytical properties provide insights that are both interesting and plausible, not least with regard to the linkage between the balance of payments and the exchange rate.

Unfortunately, if the ultimate test of a theory's acceptability is its ability to explain the facts, then the portfolio balance model fails on at least two counts. First, because of lack of data, it is well-nigh impossible to test in its full-blown form. Second, in truncated form, it fails to fit the data – even for the early part of the floating rate era. It seems that successful implementation of the model must await the collection of more accurate data and probably also a tighter specification of the demand functions.

None the less, the portfolio balance model has been influential in shaping thinking about asset markets, not least because it is the most general model of exchange rates – by comparison, most other models can be regarded as special cases.

Summary

- Portfolio balance models concentrate not simply on the demand for money but on the demand for a menu of assets.

- The demand for each type of asset is seen in the context of a general portfolio allocation problem and, since it is the proportion of total wealth to be held in a particular form that is to be decided, the determining variables are rates of return on the whole spectrum of available assets. So the demand for any asset as a proportion of wealth will tend to rise when its own return rises and fall when the return on competing assets increases.

- We assume domestic residents hold only three types of asset: domestically issued money and bonds, and foreign currency bonds issued by a foreign government or central bank. As in the Dornbusch model, (goods) prices are taken as fixed in the short run.

- Under these conditions and assuming financial markets clear at all times, short-run equilibrium will be obtained when the exchange rate and (domestic) interest rate are at a level such that demand is equal to supply for any two of the three assets.

- Open market purchases of either domestic or foreign bonds will cause depreciation and a fall in the interest rate in the short run, the repercussion on the exchange rate being greater and on the interest rate smaller, in the case of operations in the market for foreign securities.

- Increases in the stock of foreign bonds can come about only as a result of current account surpluses. The short-run impact on financial markets is an appreciation, keeping the domestic currency value of foreign bonds constant.

- Long-run equilibrium is characterized by a zero balance on current account, as well as static prices, interest rates and exchange rate.

- The production sector adjusts to a disturbance as a result of changes in the real exchange rate. As the price level moves during the adjustment phase, it interacts with the (nominal) exchange rate to change the balance of aggregate demand and supply, hence generating a current account surplus or deficit that persists until the stock of foreign currency assets has reached a level consistent with long-run equilibrium.

- In practice, the portfolio balance model is difficult to apply and the approximations tested have not been very successful in explaining the facts.

Reading guide

The antecedent of the portfolio balance model is to be found in the general equilibrium monetary theory of Tobin (1969), which itself harks back to Metzler (1951).

The most prominent exponent of the portfolio balance approach is Branson – see particularly Branson (1983), Branson and Halttunen (1979) and Branson, Halttunen and Masson (1979). Frankel (1983b) is also worth reading for a taste of the problems involved in implementing this approach.

Branson and Henderson (1985) is a survey that will be of help to those readers who can cope with the analysis of wealth dynamics – the first half deals with the subject of this chapter, and the second half covers the material of Chapter 14.

Web page: **www.pearsoned.co.uk/copeland**.

Notes

1 In general, the models share most of the advantages and disadvantages of the closed economy macroeconomic models of Tobin and others, from which they largely derive (see reading guide).

2 Either short-term securities (for example, US Treasury Bills) or federal bonds near maturity. Both domestic securities, B, and foreign securities, F, have to be assets of maturity short enough for us to be able to ignore holders' capital gains or losses when the interest rate changes.

3 This simplification will be justified if other, mainly non-financial assets, are poor substitutes for financial assets, at least in the short run. If this is the case, then it means wealth owners (or, more likely, the institutions that act on their behalf) will select their portfolios of financial assets without paying any attention to their holdings of non-financial assets – surely not a grossly implausible assumption to make.

4 Note that the portfolio balance model cannot be formulated in terms of logs, because of the adding-up condition defining wealth, hence the reversion to upper-case S and so on in this chapter.

5 The portfolio selection process has to be thought of as taking place after (in the logical rather than chronological sense) the vital decisions about how much to spend and how much to save have already been made. In the accepted jargon, we assume that the separation theorem can be applied here.

6 Those with a background in microeconomics will recognize the concept of utility as the economist's (largely invisible) index of satisfaction. Note that, in the context of uncertainty, as here, it is only the *expected* value of utility that can be maximized, as we shall see in Chapter 15.

7 We assume money balances pay neither an explicit nor an 'own' return.

8 The question of what is meant by an appropriate level of diversification will be dealt with in Chapter 15.

9 The interested reader may prove any of the propositions in this section (the slopes of the schedules, the effect of changes in the exogenous variables, and so on) by the standard methods of comparative static analysis. In other words, simply differentiate each equation

totally, holding appropriate variables constant, and make use of the restrictions on the partial derivatives of the three functions.

Notice that one way of looking at the three portfolio balance schedules is as an open economy generalization of the LM curve (see Chapter 4).

10 The model is probably most useful for analysing the impact of monetary policy.

11 The foreign price level, taken as given and constant, can be set equal to 1.0 and ignored from now on.

12 Note that as far as the dynamics of adjustment are concerned, the assumption that expectations are either fixed or at least backward-looking is vital. As can be seen from several of the references at the end of the chapter, imposing rational expectations makes the adjustment process far more complicated to analyse and in any case is less compatible with the essentially Keynesian tone of the rest of the model.

Of course, the expectations mechanism makes no difference to our conclusions about long-run equilibrium.

13 We assume that all goods are traded, although the model can accommodate a non-traded goods sector – at the cost of increased complexity, as always.

14 The conclusions about the adjustment process are sensitive to the expectations mechanism assumed. However, overshooting seems likely in most cases.

15 Bilateral current account data are difficult to obtain and probably unreliable. In any case, in the real (n-country) world, it is not clear that the exchange rate between countries A and B ought even in theory to be unaffected by the current account balance between countries A and C – particularly in a world of increasingly well-defined currency blocs.

16 For those familiar with time-series jargon, we require stationarity of expected returns, a condition that is difficult to reconcile with a world of fluctuating interest rates.

17 Note that the rates of return are usually excluded, on the grounds that they can be substituted out, since they in turn depend on the asset stocks.

9 Currency substitution

Introduction

In Chapter 8, we allowed for the possibility that the demand for nominal assets may not be perfectly elastic with respect to expected depreciation, as the result of a non-zero-risk premium. At the same time, we persisted with the assumption first introduced in Chapter 7 that financial markets adjust more rapidly than goods markets.

In this chapter, both of these assumptions will be maintained while we investigate the implications of what is known as *currency substitution*.

Now, it should be said at the outset that the name is something of a misnomer, because in one respect what is involved hardly amounts to currency: we are concerned here exclusively with money as a store of value. In other words, we ignore the means of payment function of money and treat it instead simply as an asset that happens to carry a fixed, zero rate of interest.[1]

None the less, even defined in this restricted sense, the question of how currency substitution might affect exchange rates is potentially of considerable interest, not least because of its practical relevance. Among the factors that seem likely to make currency substitution more and more prevalent in the next few years are widespread deregulation of financial markets and further reduction of exchange controls in a number of countries, the continuing trend to international financial and commercial integration and the increasing sophistication in attitudes to money management.

The starting point for the analysis is to consider the situation of a (reasonably sophisticated) inhabitant of a country where holding foreign as well as domestic currency is both feasible and legal.[2] What will determine the proportions of the two currencies in the agent's portfolio of non-interest-bearing assets?

The answer depends in general on what other assets are available. Here, and in most of the literature, we assume there are only two assets involved in the choice: domestic and foreign money (pounds and dollars). It follows that the proportions in which the two currencies are held will depend exclusively on the rate of currency depreciation. The risk-averse wealth owner will respond to a higher rate of depreciation by raising the proportion of foreign money in his portfolio.[3]

It can be seen that what is involved is only a small modification to the portfolio balance model. Instead of domestic and foreign bonds as alternatives to money, the menu of assets is restricted here to the two currencies.

Now consider how the (dollar value of the) stock of foreign currency can change. If we continue to suppose that the home currency is *not* held by agents outside the domestic economy, as in the last chapter and, given that neither borrowing nor lending is allowed,[4] it follows there is only one way the stock of foreign exchange can increase: *via a current account surplus*. Once more we have the same broad structure as in the portfolio balance model, with instantaneous equilibrium in the financial sector and a flow excess demand or supply in the real sector changing the stock of foreign currency during the adjustment phase.

At the same time, we introduce a richer specification of the real sector, with two products: a traded good whose price is determined in world markets and a non-traded good whose price depends only on conditions in the local economy.[5] The result is that changes in the real exchange rate affect the value of wealth both through a real balance effect and over the longer term, through the impact of a change in the terms of trade on the current account of the balance of payments.

As the complete model is relatively complicated to analyse, even diagrammatically, the analysis in this chapter is in outline form only. More detailed analysis is available in a number of the references given in the reading guide at the end of the chapter.

The model generates a number of conclusions about the short- and long-run impact of changes in macroeconomic policy, only one of which is covered here. It is shown that the effect of accelerated monetary growth is to cause instantaneous exchange rate overshooting, with a consequent temporary boost to the competitiveness of the domestic economy, as in the Dornbusch model of Chapter 7.

The chapter starts with a description of the model, which is then used to examine the impact of a change in the rate of monetary growth. Section 9.2 gives a brief overview of the evidence on currency substitution.

9.1 The model

We start by listing the assumptions underlying the model, before going on to describe the working of the production and financial sectors. Finally, we look at the properties of the model in long-run and short-run equilibrium with the help of Figures 9.1 and 9.2.

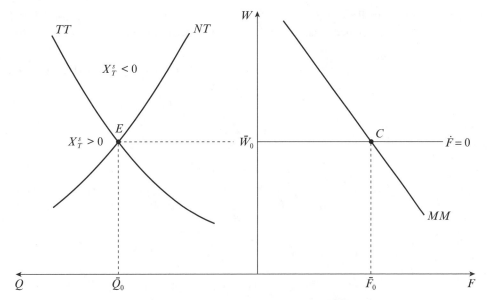

Figure 9.1 Long-run equilibrium in the currency substitution model

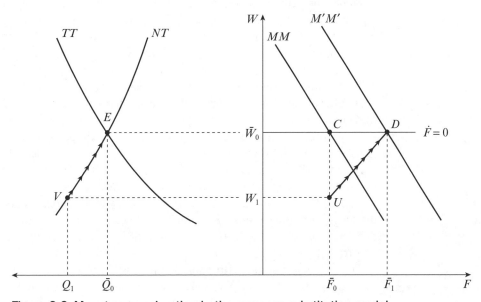

Figure 9.2 Monetary acceleration in the currency substitution model

9.1.1 Assumptions

- Two goods are produced in the domestic economy: a tradeable and a non-tradeable.
- The price of the non-tradeable, P_N, is determined in the domestic economy by the condition that *the market for non-traded goods clears at all times.*
- The (dollar) price of the tradeable is determined exogenously in the international economy. For simplicity, assume it is fixed at 1.0.[6] It follows that the sterling price of tradeables is simply S, the price of a dollar.

- Portfolio choice is restricted to only two assets: non-interest-bearing currency issued either by the domestic monetary authority ('pounds') or by a foreign government ('dollars').

- The value of financial assets held ('wealth' for short) is measured with respect to the *traded* good.[7] So, we have:

$$W = \frac{M}{S} + F$$
$$= m + F \qquad (9.1)$$

where, for convenience:[8] $m \equiv M/S$.

- Economic agents enjoy the benefit of perfect foresight, which means that their expected rate of exchange rate depreciation is equal to the actually occurring rate.[9]

9.1.2 Production sector

What will determine the volume of production in the two sectors of the domestic economy?

Under competitive conditions, productive resources will be attracted into a sector the higher the relative price of its output, other things being equal.[10] In the present case, with only two sectors, the relative price in question is obviously the ratio of the price of traded goods, S, to the price of non-traded goods, which we shall call P_N. In fact, the ratio S/P_N is almost the same thing as the real exchange rate, so we shall ignore the slight difference and denote it by Q, as we did when it was first introduced in Chapter 2.

It follows therefore that when the real exchange rate, Q, is high, the supply of traded goods will be *greater* and the supply of non-traded goods *lower*.

Now consider the demand by consumers in the domestic economy. The relative price will have the opposite effect on demand: when the price of traded goods is relatively high, demand will be relatively low, while consumption of non-traded goods will be comparatively strong, and vice versa.

Putting the two halves of the story together, when the real exchange rate is high, the supply of traded goods will be high and the demand low, so the *excess supply* (the difference between supply and demand) will be large. The opposite will be true of non-traded goods.

There is only one point to be added to this characterization of the way that the economy works. While we can sweep away all other influences in the catchall expression 'other things being equal', we have to recognize explicitly the role played by wealth. Plainly, the greater is wealth, the higher we would expect the demand for *both* products to be.

We can summarize the discussion so far in two equations, one for each sector. As far as non-traded goods are concerned, remembering that this market is assumed to be in equilibrium at all times, we have:

$$X_N^S = H(Q, W) = 0 \quad H_1 < 0, H_2 < 0 \qquad (9.2)$$

where X^S means the excess supply and the subscript N refers to the non-traded goods sector. The two inequalities on the right simply capture our convictions about the effect of the relative price of traded goods and wealth respectively on excess supply, H.

This relationship is plotted as the upward-sloping line labelled NT on the left-hand side of Figure 9.1, where, note, the vertical axis measures wealth and the horizontal axis plots the real exchange rate, Q. The slope of the line is explained easily in the light of what has already been said. At high levels of wealth, the demand for non-traded goods is relatively buoyant. Hence, equilibrium requires a large supply and therefore a high relative price or low real exchange rate. Conversely, when wealth is low, so is consumption. Therefore, excess supply can be prevented only by having a high relative price in the other sector – that is, a high value of Q.

> Notice that since the market for non-traded goods is assumed to clear at all times, the economy must always be somewhere on the NT line.

As far as traded goods are concerned, we assume equilibrium obtains only in the long run. In the short run, an excess supply amounts to a current account surplus whose counterpart must be the accumulation of foreign currency, written $\dot{F}$.[11] So, if we use the subscript for traded goods, we have:

$$X_T^S = J(Q, W) = \dot{F} \quad J_1 > 0, J_2 > 0, \tag{9.3}$$

Again, we can plot all the combinations consistent with market equilibrium. They will lie along a line like the one labelled TT in Figure 9.1. As before, high levels of wealth are associated with strong consumption, other things being equal, and must therefore be offset by a high relative price, Q, to damp down demand and stimulate supply, and vice versa at low levels of wealth.

> Since the traded goods market is not always in equilibrium, the economy is not always to be found on the TT line. Points on that line are associated with a zero balance on current account and therefore with static foreign currency balances – conditions that are satisfied only in long-run equilibrium.

What will happen when the economy is *not* on the TT line? Suppose for argument's sake that the economy were at a point above and to the right of the line. This would imply a level of wealth too great to be consistent with equilibrium, given the real exchange rate at the time. Clearly, this in turn must mean demand for traded goods in excess of supply, and hence a current account deficit, with consequently declining balances of foreign currency. Conversely, below and to the left of the TT line, the current account is in surplus, with rising stocks of foreign money.

Where the two curves cross, at E, the combination of the value of wealth and the level of the real exchange rate, $(\bar{Q}_0, \bar{W}_0)$ is the unique pair compatible with equilibrium in *both* product markets.

On the right-hand side of Figure 9.1, the horizontal line marked $\dot{F} = 0$ is at a height $\bar{W}_0$. It divides the space into two halves. Above the line, wealth is greater than its equilibrium level: hence there is a current account deficit and a consequent outflow of foreign exchange. Below it, the country is adding to its stock of foreign currency. Notice the line is flat because the volume of foreign currency balances at any point in time has no direct bearing on equilibrium in the market for traded goods.

9.1.3 Money markets

The specification of the relative demand for money – the currency substitution function – is the crux of the model. It can be expressed as follows: the ratio of real domestic balances to foreign currency, m/F, depends on the rate of change of the nominal exchange rate, $\dot{s}$:

$$m/F = L(\dot{s}) \quad L' < 0 \tag{9.4}$$

Note the critical importance of our assumption that economic agents' expectations about the future rate of depreciation can be identified with the actual rate, $\dot{s}$. In reality, the future is never known with certainty. However, this simplification allows us to use the actual rate in place of its expected value.

It will help in what is to come if we transform the relative demand for money relationship into its inverse. If the ratio m/F is a function, L, of $\dot{s}$, then the reverse must equally be true: $\dot{s}$ must depend on m/F. So we can write:

$$\dot{s} = l(m/F) \quad l' < 0 \tag{9.5}$$

where the function on the right-hand side is simply the inverse of the one in Equation 9.4. Notice the inequality at the end: market clearing requires a lower ratio of domestic money to foreign currency when the rate of depreciation rises. It follows that higher rates of depreciation are associated with lower values of m/F, and vice versa.

Another helpful change is to use the definition of wealth in Equation 9.1 to eliminate m on the right-hand side of Equation 9.5, giving:

$$\dot{s} = l\left(\frac{W - F}{F}\right) = l\left(\frac{W}{F} - 1\right) \tag{9.6}$$

Now consider the conditions necessary for wealth to be static. Plainly, since the change in wealth will be the sum of the change in its two components, it will be zero only if we have:

$$\dot{F} = -\dot{m} \tag{9.7}$$

that is, if the change in the volume of foreign and domestic currency balances offset one another. To see what this implies, remember that the variable m is the *nominal* quantity of domestic currency, M, deflated by the price of traded goods (alias the exchange rate), S.

Now the change in any ratio can always be written in terms of the difference between the growth rates of the numerator and of the denominator (see Box 9.1). In other words, the increase in real domestic currency balances is given by:

$$\dot{m} \equiv \frac{d}{dt}\left[\frac{M}{S}\right] = \frac{M}{S}(\mu - \dot{s}) \tag{9.8}$$

This simply says the real value of the domestic money supply increases by a multiple equal to the difference between the growth rate of the nominal money stock, μ, and the rate of currency depreciation, $\dot{s}$.

It remains only to substitute Equation 9.6 in Equation 9.8 to eliminate $\dot{s}$, and then use the resulting expression for $\dot{m}$ in Equation 9.7 to end up with:

$$\dot{F} = \frac{M}{S}\left[l\left(\frac{W}{F}-1\right)-\mu\right] \tag{9.9}$$

which is the desired relationship between $\dot{F}$, W and F consistent with a constant level of wealth.

For illustrative purposes, this relationship has been plotted as the downward-sloping line MM on the right-hand side of Figure 9.1, although it could possibly be upward-sloping.[12] It crosses the horizontal line at point C, where long-run equilibrium is obtained with static wealth – that is, a balanced current account and a foreign currency money stock of $\bar{F}_0$.

Box 9.1 **The meaning of log differentiation**

For those readers uncomfortable with log differentiation, consider as an example the change in a country's per capita income. Suppose it starts the year at £10 000 per annum. If national income grows by 10% during the year, while the population rises by 3%, the country's per capita income will change during the year by:

$$£10\ 000 \times (10\% - 3\%) = £700$$

that is, the change in the ratio of income to population = the ratio itself multiplied by the difference between the growth rate of income and the growth rate of population.

For those able to take the fast track:

$$\log(M/S) = \log M - \log S$$

so that:

$$d\log(M/S) = \frac{d(M/S)}{M/S} = d\log M - \log S = \frac{dM}{M} - \frac{dS}{S}$$

which gives Equation 9.8 once we multiply both sides by M/S and substitute:

$$m \equiv M/S \qquad \frac{dM}{M} \equiv \mu \qquad \frac{dS}{S} \equiv \dot{s}$$

9.1.4 Change in monetary policy

In this context, the effect of a change in the domestically printed money stock, M, is as in the benchmark monetary model: as long as it has no effect on expectations, a once-and-for-all increase in M causes a rise of the same proportion in the price of both goods, leaving the real money stock, wealth and foreign currency balances unchanged.

The question this model is meant to answer is rather the effect of a *rise in the rate of monetary growth*, μ. It is easy to see that starting from a position of long-run equilibrium at C, the change in monetary policy will have the effect of pushing the MM curve out to the right.[13] Since μ does not occur in either Equations 9.2 or 9.3, the change has no direct effect on either of the product markets, so that the TT and NT schedules remain where they were.

The new long-run equilibrium position is at D in Figure 9.2. At this point, wealth is constant and back at its pre-disturbance level, $\bar{W}_0$. Similarly, the real exchange rate is back where it started – if that combination of relative price and wealth cleared the product markets *before* the change, it ought to do so *after* it as well. The only change, once the dust has settled, is that the proportion of wealth accounted for by foreign currency increases at the expense of domestic money. The reason is obvious. In the steady state, the rate of monetary expansion equals the rate of currency depreciation. Hence, the monetary acceleration leads in long-run equilibrium to a higher opportunity cost of holding domestic money and therefore to a rise in the share of foreign relative to domestic currency in the total asset portfolio.

Figure 9.2 also illustrates the mechanism by which the increase in foreign currency holdings (from $\dot{F}_0$ to $\dot{F}_1$) takes place. The moment the acceleration is announced, the opportunity cost of holding domestic money is perceived to rise, with a consequent fall in the desired proportion m/F. However, the quantity of foreign currency balances cannot be changed in an instant. For the moment it must be regarded as fixed. It follows that the only immediate way in which the desired reduction in the ratio m/F can be achieved is via a fall in the numerator, $m = M/S$. Since the nominal stock is momentarily constant, S has to rise: the exchange rate must depreciate.

The outcome is not only a fall in the real value of domestic money but also a fall in wealth, from $\bar{W}_0$ to a temporarily lower level, W_1 at point U. With lower wealth, consumption falls. The fall in demand for non-traded goods must be offset by a lower relative price for the industry's output, so as to reduce the supply (remember that this sector clears at all times); hence the higher real exchange rate, Q_1, at point V on the left-hand side of the diagram.

The instantaneous rise in the real exchange rate, $Q = S/P_N$, implies that the rise in the numerator, S, is greater than the rise in the denominator, P_N. This means that, judged by a crude price index made up of some type of weighted average of S and P_N, the nominal exchange rate changes by *more* than the price level – in that sense, it *overshoots*.

The transition to the new long-run equilibrium (along a path like the one marked with arrows in the diagram) is characterized by a falling real exchange rate, so that the overshooting pattern is reversed, with the rate of depreciation less than the rate of inflation in the non-traded goods sector. Notice that, at V, the combination of a relatively high price of traded goods, Q_1, with low wealth, W_1, leads to a current account surplus. It follows that in the aftermath of the monetary acceleration and consequent depreciation, the domestic economy gains foreign exchange and, consequently, the level of wealth begins to recover from its initial fall.

It is now clear what we should expect to see in an economy passing through this adjustment phase (the phase in which economies are presumably to be found most of the time). In the wake of monetary acceleration, the economy will be characterized by:

■ currency depreciation at a slower rate than domestic inflation, hence an appreciating real exchange rate

■ a current account surplus, on a decreasing scale as adjustment proceeds

■ a consequent rise in foreign currency balances and wealth.

Notice that we observe the combination of *nominal* depreciation (albeit at a diminishing rate) with a current account surplus, in contrast with the predictions of the portfolio balance model. The basic reason is the currency substitution process itself: higher domestic inflation implies a long-run shift in desired asset proportions in favour of foreign currency, which can be satisfied only by a short-run payments surplus.

The central mechanism of the currency substitution model can be viewed as a hedging process. Given the constant, or at least exogenous, dollar price of traded goods, it follows that foreign currency represents a direct and riskless claim on a fixed consumption basket. In fact, one can go further and identify foreign currency with an (undated) forward purchase of traded goods. From this standpoint, economic agents respond to a rise in the rate of monetary expansion by increasing the inflation-hedge proportion of their portfolios, in the process locking in the price of their future imports. Of course, since the quantity of foreign currency in the country is fixed at the moment of the change, they cannot *in aggregate* achieve any increase in their dollar holdings. The only possible outcome is a rise in the price of foreign currency.[14]

9.2   Evidence on currency substitution

There are really two questions one would like to see answered with regard to currency substitution: is it significant in practice and, if so, is its effect captured by theoretical models such as the one analysed in this chapter?

There is one very serious problem that arises in trying to get to grips with the first question, and it is obvious as soon as we consider how a researcher might go about testing the hypothesis of currency substitution. In reality, all such tests are bound to involve fitting some form of open economy demand for money, with interest rates measuring the opportunity cost of holding money – more or less as in the monetary or portfolio balance models. So, in that sense, tests of these models were, indirectly, tests of currency substitution too.

As such, we encounter all the problems already mentioned with this approach, particularly with regard to the correct way to deal with expectations. In addition, however, we face the specific difficulty that it is never clear whether interest elasticities estimated in this fashion measure the degree of substitutability between domestic and foreign money, between money and bonds, or even between one or other currency and goods.

Subject to these very serious reservations, it has to be said that surprisingly little evidence to support direct currency substitution has been reported so far, even for economies that are obviously linked very closely (for example, Canada and the USA).[15] By and large, such evidence as has been produced seems to suggest that the cross-elasticities are small relative to the coefficients on the own rates and very often insignificantly different from zero.

As far as the second of the two questions listed at the beginning of this section is concerned, no answer has yet been attempted. In part, this reflects the nature of the currency substitution model. The literature should be viewed more as an investigation into the implications of a particular mechanism than as an attempt to actually build a complete model of exchange rate determination. As such, assumptions such as the absence of a bond market are made more for simplicity than for realism – and, of course, reintroducing them takes us straight back to the portfolio balance model. Similarly, the specification of the product market in terms of traded and non-traded goods has theoretical attractions as well as, more debatably, some measure of plausibility. Unfortunately, however, it is extremely difficult to apply operationally.

In a sense, then, answers to the empirical questions can really be found, by default, in tests of other more or less general models of the exchange rate, since they amount to asking the question: can currency substitution be ignored? So far, the answer seems to be yes, at least for the industrialized countries, although this question may need to be reopened, now that electronic money transfer is being made accessible to almost everyone, via the Internet. This is a point to which we shall return in Chapter 11.

9.3 Conclusions

In this chapter we have examined a model with, at its core, a demand for money mechanism that is *potentially* very important in any truly open economy. Furthermore, it is a mechanism that may well become more important if there is a continuation of current trends towards increased convertibility, deregulation, a greater degree of economic integration, and so forth.

However, the extent to which currency substitution actually affects exchange rates remains an empirical question.

Empirical issues apart, however, there are a number of theoretical drawbacks to the currency substitution analysis. Perhaps the most obvious is the absence of a transactions role for money. In one sense, this makes little difference. Simply introducing a means of payment function for domestic money explicitly seems unlikely to change the conclusions to any great extent.[16]

None the less, it would be of interest to know what happens if this function is in part usurped by foreign currency, as is likely to happen precisely in those circumstances where currency substitution becomes most prevalent, for example under hyperinflationary conditions or where economies are exceptionally open. This development has two possible aspects: first, a reduction in the demand for domestic money at a given level of economic activity and, second, the spread of foreign currency accounting.[17]

A related issue is the exclusion of foreign holdings of domestic currency. This restriction is not introduced merely for simplicity. It serves among other things to rule out the possibility of UK and US wealth owners exchanging pounds for dollars *directly*, independently of any immediate transactions requirements. If this were permitted – and it seems a plausible enough scenario for a country the size of the UK – it would sever the link between the stock of foreign currency and the current account, with consequences for the model that are far from obvious, although almost certainly critical.

Summary

- If economic agents in an open economy are free to hold foreign as well as domestic money, they will hold a mix of currencies – at the margin, substituting one that seems likely to depreciate rapidly for one that looks set to appreciate (the currency substitution mechanism).

- In an economy with a non-traded goods sector that clears at all times, long-run equilibrium obtains when the value of wealth and the real exchange rate are such as to clear the traded goods sector, thereby bringing the current account into balance and keeping the stock of foreign assets constant. Short-run equilibrium requires only that wealth and the real exchange rate clear the non-traded goods and monetary sectors, with a current account surplus or deficit changing the foreign money stock as the economy adjusts.

- Expansionary monetary policy in this context causes the real exchange rate to depreciate, raising domestic competitiveness and causing a short-run surplus in the current account. Over the adjustment phase, however, the stock of foreign currency rises, increasing wealth and replacing domestic money in portfolios. We conclude that rapid monetary growth leads to accumulation of foreign currency.

- The model is very difficult to test for a number of reasons – theoretical, technical and practical. Such results as have appeared in published work are inconclusive but by and large not very supportive of the currency substitution hypothesis.

Reading guide

There are a number of published papers incorporating a currency substitution mechanism, although not always as the centrepiece of the analysis.

The best known and most influential work has been the single-sector analysis of Kouri (1976, 1983) and, particularly, Calvo and Rodriguez (1977).

Perhaps the most worthwhile reading of all is the paper by Frenkel and Rodriguez (1982), since, in addition to the currency substitution model on which this chapter is based, it also sets out the conditions required for over- and undershooting. In particular, it shows the importance of the choice of inflation hedge. It turns out that if the alternative to domestic money is non-traded rather than traded goods, then the exchange rate would *under*shoot its long-run equilibrium.

Further investigation of the dynamics of this type of model is to be found in Dornbusch and Fischer (1980).

McKinnon (1982) is of interest not only for the data presented but also for the useful discussion of the relationship between capital mobility and currency substitution.

None of these includes any empirical work. For the results of some single-equation tests, see Hamburger (1977). Also of interest is Chrystal (1977), which takes the portfolio balance approach. Both, inevitably, look out of date, so that the relevance of their results to the present day is in some doubt.

Web page: **www.pearsoned.co.uk/copeland**.

Notes

1 In fact, none of the conclusions in this chapter would be changed if we allowed for a non-zero rate of interest on money balances, as long as the rate was constant.

    Notice that this is one of the weaknesses of the model. If (domestic or foreign) money is not used for transactions purposes, then there is no reason to hold it – it is dominated by riskless (domestic or foreign) bonds, which pay an explicit rate of interest. So the true alternative to sterling nominal assets is dollar nominal interest-bearing securities.

2 Conditions that narrow the field down considerably, more or less to the industrialized world in fact. Moreover, before 1979 neither the UK nor most of the European countries would have been included, at least as far as the household sector is concerned. Currency substitution was believed to be rife in the UK corporate sector during the fixed exchange rate era – disguised as what were known at the time as 'leads' and 'lags' – that is, delayed payments for exports and prepayments for imports whenever sterling devaluation seemed imminent.

    Currency substitution is probably most prevalent in hyperinflating countries where it is illegal and involves black market trading, overinvoicing of imports and underinvoicing of exports and possibly even non-economic crime, such as drug trading.

3 Notice that we have to insist on risk aversion. Otherwise, all exchange rates would have to remain fixed. At the slightest sign of possible weakness, a currency's value would collapse as investors attempted to dump their entire holdings.

4 That is, as we have said, there are no bonds in existence – or at least if there are, the stock is constant.

5 The distinction between traded and non-traded goods (or tradeables and non-tradeables) was discussed in Chapter 2, Section 2.2.

6 It is easy to reconstruct the model putting the foreign price level back in, if we want to analyse the effect of international inflation on the domestic economy.

7 It appears that the same results would apply if we defined wealth in terms of the non-traded good, as do Calvo and Rodriguez (1977), or even in terms of a price index.

    Note that in either case we are concerned with real wealth, rather than nominal wealth as in the portfolio balance model.

8 And at the expense of consistency with the convention used in earlier chapters that lower-case letters represent logarithms. The variables in this chapter are all in natural numbers.

9 The assumption of perfect foresight is the analogue under conditions of certainty of rational expectations (see Chapter 12). In the present context, it serves the purpose of allowing us to reach definite conclusions about how the system behaves out of equilibrium. Our conclusions would not be very different if we allowed expectations to be determined by the same mechanism as in Chapter 7.

10 This proposition is familiar from microeconomics: given production costs, the higher the price (and therefore marginal revenue), the greater the profit-maximizing output of the competitive firm and industry.

    For those unfamiliar with microeconomics, it amounts simply to stating that the higher relative prices are in an industry, the higher the real wage it will offer (thereby attracting labour from industries with low relative prices and hence low real wages) and the greater the profitability it will offer to investment (to the detriment of investment in low-price industries).

11 The notation $\dot{F}$ means dF/dt: the change in X over a very small interval of time.

12 The reason for the ambiguity about the slope of the MM line is as follows:

    As we move down the graph in the direction of decreasing W, the current account deficit is decreasing or the surplus is increasing, so that the left-hand side of the equation becomes greater.

    The ratio of wealth to foreign currency, W/F, has two kinds of effect on the right-hand side of Equation 9.9. First, since M/S outside the bracket is equivalent to $(W - F)$, a decrease in W and an increase in F diminishes the right-hand side. This on its own would suggest we need an upward-sloping line, associating increases in W with increases in F. On the other hand, the contents of the bracket on the right-hand side will increase only if $l(W/F)$ rises (that is, if the ratio W/F falls), which suggests a downward-sloping line.

13 Starting at C with the current account balance at zero (hence the right-hand side of Equation 9.7 is zero) a higher value of μ means the value of the function $l(W/F)$ needs to increase, which requires a lower value of W/F – therefore an increase in F at the current level of $W = \bar{W}_0$.

14 Readers familiar with the Cagan (closed economy) hyperinflation model and its derivatives may notice a similarity. In that model, monetary expansion leads people to substitute in favour of the inflation hedge: either consumer goods, in the original Cagan model, or capital goods, in the Mundell–Tobin–Johnson money-in-growth literature. In either case, the outcome is a long-run fall in holdings of real money balances relative to the inflation hedge, as a result of the more rapid fall in the value of money.

15 Furthermore, much of the published work looks increasingly out of date, because it relates either to the fixed exchange rate era or to the early or mid-1970s.

16 In fact, if foreign currency is not used as a means of payment domestically, it can never find a place in portfolios held by UK residents, since they would always prefer interest-bearing dollar assets.

17 Thus, prices were often quoted in foreign currency in the high-inflation economies of the 1980s (for example, Israel, Argentina), especially for 'big-ticket' items and, at the time of writing, both Deutschmarks and US dollars are widely used throughout the former Soviet bloc. The same is true of prices in Canada, due to the proximity of the USA.

10 General equilibrium models

Introduction

Until now, we have been concerned in this book with exchange rate models that were incomplete, in so far as they concentrated narrowly on equilibrium in the asset markets, either completely ignoring the real economy or dealing with it only in a highly simplified form. In particular, no attention was paid to the microeconomic choices facing agents in the economy: households, as consumers and suppliers of labour, and firms, as producers and investors. In the jargon of economic theory, we were dealing with *partial equilibrium* models. In this chapter, we set out to remedy the omission by considering the so-called Redux model, introduced by Obstfeld and Rogoff (1995). *General equilibrium* models start from a specification of the choice problem facing the two sets of agents in the economy, consumers seeking to maximize their utility and firms seeking to maximize their profits, and follow through the implications of their optimal choices for the endogenous variables of interest – in our case, the exchange rate primarily, but with occasional side glances at other important variables, such as interest rates and the current account of the balance of payments.[1]

There is one other important difference between this chapter and the rest of the book. Here, for the first time, we shall be dealing with a two-country model. The analysis in previous chapters took place in the setting of what is called a small country model – in reality, a type of two-country model in which the 'domestic' economy is tiny compared with the 'world' economy. In this asymmetric scenario, the small country (think, perhaps, of Singapore) interacted with a world economy so much larger in relative terms as to be completely unaffected by anything that happened in Singapore. In particular, we were able to rule out the possibility of any feedback from changes in Singapore to changes in the global economy and thence back to Singapore. For example, an increase in Singapore's money supply could safely be assumed to have no impact on the world's money supply, conveniently avoiding the need to consider the effect on global money markets, interest rates and income of domestic monetary policy. Likewise, a rise in Singapore's output could safely be taken to have no noticeable impact on global markets and on the world price level.

The relevance to the real world of this scenario is obviously limited. Although one can imagine a number of other countries that may to some extent fit the Singapore template, the list is not very long and seems to be getting shorter.[2] Perhaps the time has come to examine the consequences of abandoning this simplification.

If neither country A nor country B is small enough to be regarded as negligible, then we need to take explicit account of the fact that changes in A will unavoidably have repercussions on B, which in turn will have an impact on the outcome for A, which will feed back on B . . . and so forth. In other words, we need to undertake a simultaneous analysis to arrive at a simultaneous equilibrium solution. From now on, let us call the two countries 'Europe', the home country, which uses the euro, €, and 'the USA', which uses the US dollar, $.[3]

Now, without prejudging the analysis, readers familiar with general equilibrium analysis in a closed economy context will know that, as always, if we set out with perfect competition, no uncertainty and smoothly functioning product and asset markets, the standard results follow. Since prices move instantaneously to clear goods, labour and asset markets, we inevitably arrive at the conclusion that relative prices, the real wage, the real interest rate and the real exchange rate never change and, as far as nominal variables are concerned, the monetary model tells us all we need to know. The focus of the models in this chapter is on the consequences of deviations from this benchmark model and, in particular, from the perfect competition paradigm. Different forms of imperfection (especially price discrimination) result in different sorts of price level stickiness and hence different patterns of real exchange rate behaviour. Fluctuations in the real exchange rate, in turn, have implications for the current account of the balance of payments.

There is another important innovation in the models considered here. First, note that as long as the current account of a country's balance of payments is in disequilibrium, its net international asset position is changing: a deficit means it is increasing its international indebtedness, or reducing its stock of assets, and a surplus implies the opposite. Equally, we can view the change in its wealth as its national saving or dissaving, the extent to which the country increased or decreased its claims on the rest of the world.[4]

This relationship, which has played a more or less invisible part in the models considered so far in this book, is central to the Redux model, leading to a focus on the household choice between consumption and saving as the determinant of the current account balance and exchange rate. Moreover, since real balances appear in the Redux utility function, the consumption-saving choice is determined simultaneously with the demand for money.

With such an ambitious agenda, it will come as no surprise that the models analysed in this chapter are vastly richer and more complex than those covered so far in this book. In order to cope with this level of complexity, a number of simplifications will be introduced without compromising the underlying story. In order to keep the notation to a minimum, the following conventions are followed by default:

- all quantities are defined as *per capita* variables
- all unsubscripted variables are to be understood as dated t. Values at $t - 1$, $t + 1$, etc. are given explicit subscripts.

Although this chapter draws on a large literature including contributions by a number of different researchers, the most important by far are those of Obstfeld and Rogoff. The literature starts with their Redux model (see reading guide). It is analysed in some detail in Section 10.1, which sets out the basic equations and sketches the derivation of the main results (albeit with some of the more tedious steps relegated to the appendices). Then Section 10.2 discusses important extensions of the model, in particular the implications of *pricing to market* (PTM), while Section 10.3 provides a brief discussion of some of the problems involved in attempting to test this type of model.

10.1 The Redux model

10.1.1 Setting

In the Redux model, Obstfeld and Rogoff visualize a world consisting of a large number[5] of 'households', indexed by z, each of which plays a dual role in the economy. On the one hand, each z is a consumer unit, sharing a well-defined, identical utility function with every other household throughout the world. On the other hand, it operates simultaneously as a firm supplying a product, also called z, which is unique to the extent that the household has the monopoly power to choose a price/output $(p(z), y(z))$ combination for z so as to maximize its profit.[6] This world is divided into two 'countries': of the total N households in the world, the first N_1 are in Europe, where they use €, and the remainder are in the USA, where they use \$. For the sake of convenience, we can normalize the respective populations by dividing by N, so that we have:

$$\text{Population of the world} = N/N = 1$$

of which:

$$\text{population of Europe} = N_1/N = n$$
$$\text{population of USA} = (N - N_1)/N = 1 - n$$

Although they are specialized in production, households are eclectic consumers. Not only does the typical European household consume the output of its fellow citizens, but it is also free to consume goods or services produced by Americans (imports into Europe) and the same is, of course, true of households in the USA. It follows that we start off with four types of consumption: by Europeans of the output of their own population, by Europeans of American products, by Americans of each other's output and by Americans of European products.

Now Obstfeld and Rogoff postulate an infinite number of consumer–producers in each country, whereas we are assuming a fixed, albeit large, number of households. It turns out to make little difference however, because in either case we can go on to simplify matters even further. If we follow Obstfeld and Rogoff in assuming that the elasticity of demand is the same in all markets, then all European households will choose to produce the same output and sell it at the same price. Likewise, each American household will choose the same output level as every other household in the USA. This statement will be more obvious once the basic equations of the model have been set out. For the moment, we simply note that a common price elasticity of demand implies a common (local currency) marginal revenue. Since marginal costs will also turn out to be identical (because all consumers have the same marginal disutility of labour and hence the individual household labour supply curve is identical in Europe and the USA), it follows that every European (American) household optimally produces the same output and sells it at the same relative price as every other European (American) household. Of course, this should certainly *not* be interpreted as implying that Europeans choose to produce the same level of output as Americans. Instead, it reflects the fact that any difference in output between the two countries is due entirely to the exchange rate, which translates the common marginal physical products into differing revenue products.

Under these circumstances, we can safely cut to the chase and assume from the outset a two-good world, with each of the n European households producing an identical product, and each of the $(1 - n)$ Americans producing the same, distinct American product. Europeans consume a quantity c_E of home products at the price p_E and a quantity c_A of American-made products at the price p_A. Likewise, c_E^* represents America's imports from Europe and c_A^* is American consumption of its own output, with associated prices p_E^* and p_A^*. All four prices are denominated in the currency of the consumers, and so p_E and p_A are in €, while p_E^* and p_A^* are in $.

Notice this simplifying step is not inconsistent with the assumption that households are monopolists. In this (admittedly rather artificial) situation, each household is a monopoly firm, but since each faces an identical cost and revenue curve, each sets the same price for its output. Moreover, since they are all monopolists selling a differentiated product, they choose an output price that is above the marginal cost of production, so that the situation is suboptimal relative to competitive equilibrium.

10.1.2 Private sector

Given this framework, the first modelling problem is how to aggregate across the two types of good so as to derive macroeconomic relationships. Here, the Redux model is critically dependent on a particular functional form, the so-called *constant elasticity of substitution* form, or CES as it is known to those on familiar terms with its properties.[7] Start with the definition of consumption:

$$C = [nc_E^{\theta-1/\theta} + (1-n)c_A^{\theta-1/\theta}]^{\theta/\theta-1}$$

$$C^* = [n(c_E^*)^{\theta-1/\theta} + (1-n)(c_A^*)^{\theta-1/\theta}]^{\theta/\theta-1} \quad \theta > 1 \qquad \text{(10.1)(10.1')}$$

where $\theta > 1$ is the elasticity of substitution, the parameter measuring the proportionate change in consumption of z or z^* in response to a change in the relative price. It is demonstrated in Appendix 10.1 that, for consistency, we need to define the price index as:

$$P = [np_E^{1-\theta} + (1-n)p_A^{1-\theta}]^{1/1-\theta} \quad P^* = [n(p_E^*)^{1-\theta} + (1-n)(p_A^*)^{1-\theta}]^{1/1-\theta} \qquad \text{(10.2)}$$

Remember that both prices are measured in the currency of the country's consumers, so p_E and p_A are denominated in €, while p_E^* and p_A^* are \$ prices.

In this section, we assume that there are no barriers to trade so that the law of one price applies at all times and we can write:

$$p_E = Sp_E^* \quad \text{and} \quad p_A = Sp_A^* \qquad \text{(10.3)}$$

where, as usual, S is the domestic-currency price of foreign currency, i.e. the € price of \$1.00. Consequently, the price indices can be rewritten as:

$$P = [np_E^{1-\theta} + (1-n)(Sp_A^*)^{1-\theta}]^{1/1-\theta} \quad \text{and} \quad P^* = \left[n\left(\frac{P_E}{S}\right)^{1-\theta} + (1-n)(p_A^*)^{1-\theta} \right]^{1/1-\theta}$$

$$\text{(10.4)}$$

so that there are effectively only two relevant prices in the model: the price of European products, p_E, and the price of American products, p_A^*. Now a comparison of the two price indices and a line or two of algebra are sufficient to show that PPP holds:

$$P = SP^* \qquad \text{(10.5)}$$

which illustrates a key point made in Chapter 2: that PPP relies on two conditions. We require not only the law of one price, but also that the price index have identical weights in the two countries, which in the present context follows on from the assumption that the critical parameter, θ, has the same value in both countries. The importance of this parameter is clear if we derive the consumption demand for the two goods (see Appendix 10.2). For Europe:

$$c_E = \left[\frac{p_E}{P}\right]^{-\theta} C \quad \text{and} \quad c_A = \left(\frac{Sp_A^*}{P}\right)^{-\theta} C \qquad \text{(10.6)}$$

and for America:

$$c_E^* = \left[\frac{p_E}{SP^*}\right]^{-\theta} C^* \quad \text{and} \quad c_A^* = \left(\frac{p_A^*}{P^*}\right)^{-\theta} C^* \qquad \text{(10.6')}$$

which shows that θ is actually the (relative) price elasticity of (relative) demand. In other words, it is the answer to the following question: if there were a small change in the price of z relative to the price index, what would be the proportionate change in the demand for z as a proportion of the total consumption basket? Since $\theta > 1$, a 1% increase in the relative price of z causes the expenditure weight of z to fall by more than 1%.

Equations 10.6 and 10.6′ determine the typical household's allocation of its total consumption, C, C^*, between domestic and foreign products, given relative prices.[8] Notice that since the ratio in the square brackets is the same for each of the two goods across countries, it follows that Europeans and Americans have identical *relative* demand curves. In other words, both populations allocate their consumption basket in the same proportions between the two goods, so that:

$$\frac{c_E}{C} = \frac{c_E^*}{C^*} \quad \text{and} \quad \frac{c_E}{C} = \frac{c_E^*}{C^*}$$

The size of the European household's total consumption basket is the solution to the optimal choice problem it faces, which involves maximization of the following intertemporal CES utility function:

$$U_t = \sum_{s=t}^{\infty} \beta^{s-t} \left[\log C_s + \frac{\chi}{1-\varepsilon} \left(\frac{M_s}{P_s} \right)^{1-\varepsilon} - \frac{\kappa}{2} y_s^2 \right] \quad 0 < \beta < 1 \quad \varepsilon, \kappa, \chi > 0 \quad \textbf{(10.7)}$$

which makes utility for the typical European depend on all future values of the expression in the square bracket, from the present day (when $s = t$) onward to the infinite future. However, each future period is discounted at a geometrically increasing rate, so the current period has a weighting of 1.0 (since $s = t$, $\beta^{s-t} = \beta^0 = 1$), next period is weighted by $\beta^1 = \beta$, which is less than one, the next period by β^2, which is even smaller, and so on. The smaller is the parameter β, the more heavily future consumption is discounted relative to present consumption and the greater the household's time preference.

The square bracket contains the three elements of each future period's utility. The first component is the log of the household's total consumption, aggregated across the different goods by the formula in Equation 10.1. The second is a familiar feature of many modern macroeconomic models, where it is assumed that real money balances contribute directly to individual welfare by providing convenience, liquidity, security, and so forth. Finally, the third term represents the household as producer. The more output the European household supplies (i.e. the greater is y in any period s), the less leisure time it can enjoy, and hence the lower its welfare level.[9] Moreover, this effect is assumed to be proportional to the square of output, which implies a rising marginal disutility of labour, i.e. that households find additional hours of work more and more onerous as the number of hours per day or per week increase.

Notice that although Equation 10.7 is the maximand in the consumer–producer's decision process at time t, it involves no explicit expectations. Instead, it is assumed that the future is known with certainty, a point to which we shall return later.

Americans have the same tastes as Europeans, so they maximize an identical utility function:

$$U_t^* = \sum_{s=t}^{\infty} \beta^{s-t} \left[\log C_s^* + \frac{\chi}{1-\varepsilon} \left(\frac{M_s}{P_s} \right)^{1-e} - \frac{\kappa}{2} (y_s^*)^2 \right] \quad \textbf{(10.7′)}$$

where the final term involves US output in the period in question.

10.1.3 Asset markets and the household budget constraint

The specification of the international capital market is a critical feature of the Redux model. The only kind of capital transaction permitted is borrowing and lending, which involves the exchange of a one-period real discount bond in the setting of a fully integrated international loan market. In other words, at any time, t, the representative European (American) borrower issues a quantity $B(B^*)$ of the bonds, each of which promises (with no risk of default) to pay the lender one unit of consumption, $C_{t+1}(C^*_{t+1})$, at $t + 1$. The discount rate on these bonds is, by definition, the real interest rate, r,[10] which in an integrated international capital market must be the same in both countries.

Given real interest rates, nominal interest rates are determined by the Fisher equation (see Section 3.6.1):

$$1 + i = \frac{P_{t+1}}{P}(1 + r) \quad \text{and} \quad 1 + i^* = \frac{P_{t+1}}{P^*}(1 + r) \qquad \textbf{(10.8) (10.8')}$$

Bear in mind that the future price level is assumed to be known with certainty. As we saw in Chapter 3, by PPP, Equations 10.8 and 10.8′ imply UIRP:

$$1 + i = \frac{S_{t+1}}{S}(1 + i^*) \qquad \textbf{(10.9)}$$

Before going any further, it is worth clarifying the nature of the bonds in this model. First, note that private agents (i.e. household firms) are the only borrowers. In particular, governments do *not* issue debt. Second, household firms can consume more (less) than they produce by running down (accumulating) money balances or by borrowing (lending), i.e. selling (buying) bonds. Since Europeans all have the same tastes and therefore all make the same decisions, if one household chooses to borrow, so do they all and the same can be said of Americans. It immediately follows that B and B^* are the equivalent in the model of the per capita current account of the balance of payments. However, although the adding-up constraint applies at the global level (since there are only two countries), this does not mean that $B = -B^*$, because B and B^* are in per capita terms, and the number of households is not necessarily the same in Europe as in America. Instead, the adding-up constraint gives us:

$$nB + (1 - n)B^* = 0 \quad \text{or} \quad B^* = -\frac{n}{1-n}B \qquad \textbf{(10.10)}$$

It remains to specify the budget constraints facing households in each period. For Europe:

$$PB + M = (1 + r_{t-1})PB_{t-1} + M_{t-1} + p_E y - PC - PT \qquad \textbf{(10.11)}$$

As of period t, each European household has total nominal wealth equal to the sum of its money balances, M, plus the value of its bonds, PB, with the allocation between the two assets dependent on its own decisions. On the right-hand side of the budget constraint, but ignoring for a moment the first term, the sources of wealth at t are the volume of money carried over from the previous period, M_{t-1}, plus the proceeds from the (current) sale of output, $p_E y$, less consumption spending, PC, and the amount paid in (lump sum) taxes,[11] PT. As far as the first term on the right-hand side is concerned, $(1 + r_{t-1})$ is the payoff (in units of consumption) per bond purchased at $t - 1$. Hence $(1 + r_{t-1})B_{t-1}$ is the real consumption available from this source as a result of the household's thrift (or profligacy, if it is negative) in the previous period and multiplying it by P converts it into nominal terms at the time t price level.

The US budget constraint is as follows:

$$P^*B^* + M^* = (1 + r_{t-1})P^*B^*_{t-1} + M^*_{t-1} + p^*_A y^* - P^*C^* - P^*T^* \qquad (10.11')$$

The real interest rate is, of course, the same as for Europe, while all other variables are their American equivalents.

10.1.4 Government

The sub-model of the household sector is assumed to be paralleled in the government sector of each country, with the same demand elasticity, θ, in both countries, so that we have government consumption given by demand curves of the same form as Equations 10.6 and 10.6′:

$$g_E = \left[\frac{p_E}{P}\right]^{-\theta} G \quad \text{and} \quad g_A = \left(\frac{Sp^*_A}{P}\right)^{-\theta} G \qquad (10.12)$$

$$g^*_E = \left[\frac{p_E}{SP^*}\right]^{-\theta} G \quad \text{and} \quad g^*_A = \left[\frac{p^*_A}{P^*}\right]^{-\theta} G \qquad (10.12')$$

Note that g_E and g_A are total spending by the European government on domestic and foreign-produced goods respectively, normalized by European population; similarly for g^*_E and g^*_A. So these equations determine per capita spending on each good by the two governments as a proportion of total per capita government spending, G and G^*, with the proportions depending on relative prices. In other words, government spending is allocated to domestic output and imports in exactly the same way as private sector consumption.

Having government demand for each good determined in the same way as private sector demand, with exactly the same elasticity in the two countries – in fact, in all four sectors – serves to keep the model tractable (more or less!). However, the very idea of a price-elastic demand curve applied to government consumption may seem strange to some readers. The key point is, however, that only the relative share taken by home and foreign output is price-sensitive, while aggregate government spending, G and G^*, remains an exogenous variable, determined in the usual way by fiscal policy subject to the public sector budget constraint:

$$G = T + \frac{\Delta M}{P} \quad \text{and} \quad G^* = T^* + \frac{\Delta M^*}{P^*} \qquad (10.13)\ (10.13')$$

That is, since the two governments are assumed to do no conventional borrowing, their government expenditure can be financed from only two sources: tax revenue and *seignorage*. Notice that G and T are real per capita spending and tax, so the nominal value of *seignorage* $\Delta M = M - M_{t-1}$ needs to be deflated by the price index, P.

10.1.5 Solution of the model

The model specified in the last section is too complicated to solve by standard methods, and even Obstfeld and Rogoff offered only an approximate solution. We will be content with a simplified outline of their approximation. Some of the intervening steps are presented in Appendices 10.3 and 10.4.

Preliminary: aggregating demand

An essential preliminary is to formulate the market-clearing conditions in the markets for the two goods. This involves simply noting that, for the European product, there are four sources of demand: European and American consumers and their two governments, which have conveniently been assumed to have demand functions of the same basic form. Remembering that all of the variables C, C^*, G, G^* were specified in per capital form, it follows that we can write world consumption demand, C^W, and government spending, G^W, as:

$$C^W = nC + (1 - n)C^* \quad \text{and} \quad G^W = nG + (1 - n)G^* \qquad \textbf{(10.14)}$$

Adding Equations 10.6, 10.6′, 10.12 and 10.12′ allows us to formulate the world demand curves as:

$$y_E^d = \left[\frac{p_E}{P}\right]^{-\theta} (C^W + G^W) \quad \text{and} \quad y_A^d = \left[\frac{p_A^*}{P^*}\right]^{-\theta} (C^W + G^W) \qquad \textbf{(10.15) (10.15′)}$$

Equating the demand functions to supply of the two goods defines equilibrium in output markets.

Solution of the consumer's problem

Households in each country optimally choose levels of three variables, C and C^*, M and M^*, y and y^* to maximize the utility function in Equations 10.7 and 10.7′ subject to the budget constraints Equations 10.11 and 10.11′, resulting in the following first-order conditions or Euler equations.[12] First, from the consumption condition:[13]

$$C_{t+1} = \beta(1 + r)C \quad \text{and} \quad C_{t+1}^* = \beta(1 + r)C^* \qquad \textbf{(10.16) (10.16′)}$$

which is the standard intertemporal choice equilibrium condition familiar from models of optimal consumption. Its interpretation is perhaps best understood if we (temporarily) replace β by a new parameter:

$$\delta \equiv \frac{1 - \beta}{\beta} > 0$$

which has the same dimensionality as r and must be positive, since we have assumed $0 < \beta < 1$. The new parameter, δ, is known as the *rate of time preference* and it measures the premium placed by households on current consumption relative to future consumption. The greater is δ, the more impatient are consumers and the more present is preferred to future consumption.

We can now rewrite Equations 10.16 and 10.16′ as:

$$C_{t+1} = \frac{1+r}{1+\delta}C \quad \text{and} \quad C_{t+1}^* = \frac{1+r}{1+\delta}C^* \tag{10.17}$$

which says that equilibrium consumption is greater than it was in the previous period when $r > \delta$. In other words, consumption is allocated over time in a pattern that reflects a comparison between the individual's subjective premium on present consumption, δ, and the premium the market places on present consumption, r_t. Notice that this comparison involves a parameter of taste, which is assumed constant, and a variable, r_t, the real interest rate. When r rises, consumers substitute future for present consumption – in other words, the higher price penalty imposed by the market on instant gratification deters consumers and persuades them to wait. Note also that since tastes are assumed identical in Europe and the USA, and capital markets are integrated, so that there is a unique real interest rate, it follows that the rates of consumption growth are the same in the two countries.[14]

As far as money balances are concerned, the relevant condition is:

$$\frac{M}{P} = \left[\chi\frac{1+i}{i}C\right]^{1/\varepsilon} \quad \text{and} \quad \frac{M^*}{P^*} = \left[\chi\frac{1+i^*}{i^*}C^*\right]^{1/\varepsilon} \tag{10.18} \tag{10.18′}$$

a specification of the demand for money as a function, not of national income, but of consumption in each country. Notice that, as always, demand for real balances in each country is a decreasing function of the opportunity cost, given by the nominal interest rate, i or i^*. Finally, the optimal labour–leisure choice satisfies:

$$y^{\theta+1/\theta} = \left(\frac{\theta-1}{\theta\kappa}\right)\frac{(C^W+G^W)^{1/\theta}}{C} \quad \text{and} \quad (y^*)^{\theta+1/\theta} = \left(\frac{\theta-1}{\theta\kappa}\right)\frac{(C^W+G^W)^{1/\theta}}{C^*}$$

$$\tag{10.19} \tag{10.19′}$$

which simply equates the increase in utility from an extra unit of output with the cost in disutility of the effort required to produce it. Notice again that since all parameters are identical across the two countries, the only factor accounting for output differences between Europe and America is different consumption levels.[15]

Solution method

Unfortunately, the model does not have a closed form solution (i.e. one that provides simple relationships between the endogenous and exogenous variables), and so Obstfeld and Rogoff are forced to rely on an approximation involving three stages.

(1) We start by formulating an initial steady state at time 0. If we assume no government spending or taxation and, most importantly, no international debt hangover so that $B_0 = B_0^* = 0$, the model becomes symmetrical, in the sense that the solution values are the same for Europe and the USA. Under these circumstances, the model has a number of straightforward properties that can serve as a benchmark for what follows.

(2) Starting from the initial symmetric steady state at time 0, Obstfeld and Rogoff set out to answer questions of comparative dynamics such as: what happens to

the steady state when there is a change in one of the monetary or fiscal policy variables? In order to answer this question, they impose two further simplifying conditions. First, they assume the system goes from the initial symmetric steady state at 0 to its new post-shock steady state at time 2 after only a single intervening period of disequilibrium (at time 1), caused by the failure of prices to adjust immediately to the policy shock. Second, they cope with the non-linearities in the model by the technique of log linearization, a procedure that involves approximating the outcome of small disturbances in the neighbourhood of the initial equilibrium. Even then, there remains a crucial problem to be overcome before the nature of the new steady state can be deduced. It turns out that the solution depends on the cumulative change in the stock of international assets brought about by the balance of payments deficit during the intervening disequilibrium period. The reason for this feature is that any accumulation of assets (liabilities) will generate a steady-state inflow (outflow) of interest payments, which itself will have an impact on consumption patterns, and hence on relative prices in equilibrium. This dependence on the cumulative asset change, which is a defining characteristic of the Redux model, means that the solution for the new steady-state values of the endogenous variables is only provisional. Since the previous period's balance of payments disequilibrium will have caused a redistribution of wealth between the two countries, the new allocation will itself change the nature of the steady state that is eventually established. So the full solution for the post-shock steady state awaits the new value of each country's stock of assets. In the interim, we can only solve for the new equilibrium as a function of the change in the international allocation of assets in the intervening period.

(3) In the final stage, we backtrack to analyse the disequilibrium at time 1. Assuming prices are stuck at their initial time 0 values for one period, we are in a position to deduce the disequilibrium impact of a disturbance and to solve for the balance of payments surplus or deficit – that is, the net change in the international allocation of assets at time 1 carried over into the next period. This allows us not only to draw conclusions about the disequilibrium impact of a monetary disturbance but also to solve fully for the steady state at time 2, allowing for the changed international allocation of wealth.

We now follow through these three stages.

Initial steady state

In a steady state, by definition, all variables are either constant or growing at a rate that is sustainable in the long run. With no technological progress and no population growth, a steady state here must involve constant consumption levels, $C_{t+1} = C$. Looking back at Equation 10.17, this clearly means:

$$\bar{r} = \frac{1 - \beta}{\beta} \tag{10.20}$$

where, following the same convention as in Chapter 7, a bar over a variable denotes its long-run steady-state value.

If, in addition, we assume the initial (time 0) steady state is symmetrical in the sense already explained in the previous section, then imposing $M_0 = M_{-1}$ and $B_0 = B_0^*$ $= G_0 = G_0^* = T_0 = T_0^* = 0$ in Equations 10.11 and 10.11′ gives:

$$\bar{C}_0 = \frac{\bar{p}_{E,0}\bar{y}_0}{\bar{P}_0} \quad \text{and} \quad \bar{C}_0^* = \frac{\bar{p}_{A,0}^*\bar{y}_0}{\bar{P}_0} \tag{10.21} \tag{10.21′}$$

as the time 0 steady state values for consumption in each country.[16] But we can go much further in this very special case. We can only ever have $B = 0$ if the current account is in balance, so that consumption is equal to output – that is:

$$\bar{C}_0 = \bar{y}_0 \quad \text{and} \quad \bar{C}_0^* = \bar{y}_0^* \tag{10.22} \tag{10.22′}$$

which in turn must imply:

$$\bar{p}_{E,0} = \bar{P}_0 \quad \text{and} \quad \bar{p}_{A,0}^* = \bar{P}_0^* \tag{10.23} \tag{10.23′}$$

so that the relative prices in Equations 10.6, 10.6′, 10.15 and 10.15′ are all unity and:

$$\bar{c}_{E,0} = \bar{c}_{A,0} = \bar{C}_0 = \bar{c}_{E,0}^* = \bar{c}_{A,0}^* = \bar{C}_0^* = \bar{C}_0^W \tag{10.24}$$

In other words, consumption is allocated equally across imports and exports.[17] Looking back at Equations 10.18 and 10.18′, note that, with a static exchange rate, nominal and real interest rates must be equal – that is, $i_0 = i_0^* = \bar{r}$, so that the terms in the square brackets must be equal in the two countries. Using PPP, it follows that:

$$\bar{S}_0 = \frac{\bar{M}_0}{\bar{M}_0^*}$$

which is no more than the benchmark monetary model (Equation 5.7) applied to a case where both countries share the same level of income and the same income elasticity of the demand for money.

Finally, output in this symmetrical steady state must be, from Equation 10.19:

$$\bar{y}_0 = \bar{y}_0^* \left(\frac{\theta - 1}{\theta\kappa}\right)^{1/2} \tag{10.25}$$

This result is instructive because it can easily be shown that the socially optimal output is greater than this.[18] Equilibrium output is lower because monopolistic producers keep their output below its competitive level, since any additional effort would reduce the relative price of their output, benefiting consumers as a whole, but yielding a smaller welfare benefit to themselves (recall that the marginal disutility of labour is sharply diminishing, as was made clear when Equation 10.7 was introduced).

Log-linear approximation

The next stage in the process of solving for the properties of the Redux model involves a reformulation to make it possible to answer questions such as what would happen if, starting from the initial symmetric time 0 state, there were to be a disturbance such as a monetary or fiscal policy change? Mathematically, this involves rewriting the basic equations of the model in terms of log-linear approximations to changes in the variables around their time 0 levels. However, much of the working of the model can be seen from an analysis in terms of *relative* values of the variables, which is a lot simpler and more economical. Reverting to notation first introduced in Chapter 5, the log-linearized equations of the model are presented here in terms of relative changes in variables:

$$\tilde{x} \equiv \frac{\Delta x_t}{\tilde{x}_0} - \frac{\Delta x_t^*}{\tilde{x}_t^*} \equiv \hat{x} - \hat{x}^* \quad \text{where} \quad \Delta x_t \equiv x_t - X_{t-1}$$

A caret ('hat') over a variable, $\hat{x}_t$, indicates the change in x_t over a small interval of time from $t - 1$ to t relative to its initial steady-state value at time 0. In fact, the 'small interval' will be either from 0 to 2, when we are defining the new steady state, or from 0 to 1, when we are analysing the temporary disequilibrium between the two steady states. In most cases, we shall be dealing with the difference between 'hat' variables for Europe and the USA, indicated by a tilde over the top, $\tilde{x}$, to denote the size of a small change in any European variable, x, relative to its baseline steady state value, *minus* the change in its equivalent for the USA.[19]

Of course, there is only one exchange rate, so we shall be concerned with $\hat{S}$, the proportional devaluation of the €.

We make two important deviations from this convention. First, it is more convenient to normalize the two government spending variables by aggregate world consumption:

$$\tilde{g} \equiv \frac{\Delta G}{C_0^W} - \frac{\Delta G^*}{C_0^W} = \frac{G}{C_0^W} - \frac{G^*}{C_0^W}$$

where the second equality is simply a reminder that the change in government spending is from zero in the initial steady state to G, G^* respectively in the next period (i.e. $G - G_0 = G - 0 = G$ and the same for G^*). Second, we treat the balance of payments in the same way, normalizing relative to aggregate world consumption, but in passing, it is helpful to remember that we need only solve for the European variable:

$$\hat{b} \equiv \frac{B}{C_0^W} = \frac{\Delta B}{C_0^W}$$

since, from Equation 10.10, we can replace the US balance of payments by:

$$\hat{b}^* = -\left(\frac{n}{1-n}\right)\hat{b}$$

This simply follows from the fact that in a two-country world there is only a single current account to be determined: the European surplus is just the US deficit, appropriately scaled for the relative populations.

With this notation, the essence of the model set out in the last section can be expressed in the four equations L1–L4. The derivation is explained in Appendix 10.3.

$$\hat{S} = \hat{P} \qquad\qquad\qquad\qquad \text{PPP} \qquad\qquad\qquad\qquad \text{(L1)}$$

$$\tilde{y} = -\theta(\tilde{p} - \tilde{P}) \qquad\qquad\qquad \text{Demand} \qquad\qquad\qquad \text{(L2)}$$

$$\tilde{y} = -\frac{\theta}{1+\theta}\tilde{C} \qquad\qquad\qquad \text{(Labour) supply} \qquad\qquad \text{(L3)}$$

$$\tilde{M} - \tilde{P} = \frac{1}{\varepsilon}\tilde{C} - \frac{\beta}{(1-\beta)\varepsilon}(\tilde{P}_{t+1} - \tilde{P}) \quad \text{Demand for money} \qquad \text{(L4)}$$

L1 is straightforward and it is *not* an approximation. It simply says that PPP applies to steady-state changes: in the long run, the exchange rate depreciation reflects inflation differentials.

To understand the next two equations, note that if we think of the real price of each country's output as the ratio of p or p^* to the respective price index, P or P^*, then:[20]

$$\tilde{p} - \tilde{P} = (\hat{p}_E - \hat{p}_A) - (\hat{P} - \hat{P}^*) = (\hat{p}_E - \hat{P}) - (\hat{p}_A - \hat{P}^*)$$

represents the difference between the change in the real price of European and US output. So L2 and L3 together imply that higher European (relative to US) consumption is associated with a reduction in the output of European goods relative to the USA and a rise in their price. Note that the relative price elasticity of aggregate demand in L2 is $\theta > 1$, while the relative price elasticity of consumption is $(1 + \theta) > 2$.[21] This means that a 1% rise in the price of European exports while US prices remain unchanged is associated with a fall in demand for European output greater than 1% but a rise in the European standard of living of over 2%. Looked at from the American point of view, the rise in European prices causes consumers on both sides of the Atlantic to switch their spending towards American goods. The net outcome is that Europeans enjoy a double windfall. On the one hand, the improvement in the relative price of their output makes it possible for them to enjoy higher consumption at their previous level of effort. On the other hand, they are able to consume some of the windfall gain in the form of lower labour supply and the utility function (Equation 10.7) is quadratic in hours of work. Finally, L4 tells us that the change in the relative value of the stock of real money balances in Europe is related positively to the change in its aggregate consumption – the equivalent of the transactions demand effect – and related negatively to relative inflation over the next period, which simply reflects the interest differential between Europe and the USA via the Fisher effect (see Section 3.6).

New long-run equilibrium

We now need to use the log-linear approximation approach to address the following question: what would happen to the steady state if there were a change in one of the exogenous variables? In the new steady state, we must allow for the fact that the symmetry of time 0 will have been disturbed not only by a change in one of the policy variables but indirectly also because the stock of net wealth in the form of international bonds, B, will now be non-zero. To be more explicit, unless the adjustment to the policy disturbance is instantaneous, the intervening disequilibrium will have been characterized by a balance of payments deficit for one of the two countries and an associated transfer of wealth to the surplus country. The resulting asymmetry in the distribution of wealth is critical, since the Redux model gives a central role to a mechanism that usually appears only as an unnoticed extra in exchange rate models. When the post-disturbance steady state is reached, the values of the endogenous variables settle at new long-run levels reflecting the cumulative wealth transfer during the intervening period of disequilibrium.[22] Hence, we solve for the new steady state in terms of the exogenous variables and the wealth transfer, taking the latter as given. Its value will be determined in the next section, when we consider the adjustment process.

The solution involves seven equations in log-linear approximations to the proportional changes ('hat values') for seven endogenous variables: income, the relative price level and consumption for each country, and aggregate world consumption. The full solution is complicated, but if we again concentrate on relative values (Europe less the USA), the flavour of the results can be captured in two equations:[23]

$$\hat{\tilde{S}} = \tilde{M} + \left(\frac{1+\theta}{\theta\varepsilon} \right) \tilde{y} \qquad (10.26)$$

$$\tilde{y} = \frac{1}{2} \left[\tilde{g} - \frac{r\hat{b}}{1-n} \right] \qquad (10.27)$$

Note that $\tilde{y}$ denotes the difference between the equilibrium growth rate of European and US output and $\tilde{M}$ refers to relative money growth, while $\hat{b}$ is the change in Europe's net asset position as a proportion of total world consumption, comparing the initial steady state (when it was zero) with period 2, when it reaches the new steady state.

From Equations 10.26 and 10.27, we can draw the following conclusions:

■ The monetary neutrality of the benchmark monetary model is preserved, in so far as the long-run exchange rate change reflects movements in relative money stocks, *provided relative income is unchanged*. In fact, Equation 10.26 can equally be written:

$$\hat{\tilde{S}} = \tilde{M} - \frac{1}{\varepsilon} \hat{\tilde{C}} \qquad (10.28)$$

which illustrates the significance of consumption in the model. The long-run exchange rate dynamics differ from the monetary approach, because with consumption replacing income as the determinant of the transactions demand for money, the steady-state depreciation is greater or less than the change in relative money stocks to an extent that depends on the ultimate change in relative consumption and income.

■ If for any reason the distribution of wealth changes as between the two steady states, relative income certainly *does* change. Suppose the new steady state involves greater wealth for Europe and less for USA, i.e. $\tilde{b} > 0$. Then, from Equation 10.27, output is lower in Europe relative to USA. Why? The accumulated stock of bonds held by Europe (and owed by USA) generates a steady-state level of income, in the form of a flow of interest payments from the USA to Europe. Europeans respond to their higher long-run income by consuming more, while Americans consume less. But these statements about changes in consumption apply not only to the two consumer goods in the world economy but also to leisure time: Europeans react to their new wealth by working less, while Americans do the opposite, thereby reducing European production relative to American production. The reduction (increase) in supply of the European (American) good must be accompanied by a rise (fall) in its relative price.

■ We can now see why the relative income term occurs with a positive sign in Equation 10.26. Wealthier Europeans both consume more and produce less output for sale at a higher price, while Americans do the opposite. So the relative income term $\tilde{y} \equiv \hat{y} - \hat{y}^* < 0$ and the effect on the exchange rate through this mechanism alone must be negative. In other words, a 1% rise in the European money stock relative to the USA causes the € to depreciate against the $ by less than 1%, *if it is associated with a rise in Europe's net assets* (which, as we shall see, is in fact the case).

■ Overall balance of payments disequilibrium is, of course, inconsistent with the definition of a steady state. However, the new steady state is characterized by an underlying European current account deficit, which is just sufficient to offset the surplus on capital service represented by the interest inflow from USA to Europe, leaving the basic balance zero in both countries.

These are interim conclusions regarding the steady state. They describe a long-run equilibrium contingent on the change in the distribution of international assets, b. To arrive at any final conclusions, we now need to focus on what determines the change in b and, starting from the symmetric time 0 equilibrium, that will require an analysis of the short-run disequilibrium at time 0.

Sticky prices in the short run[24]

As usual, there is no distinction between long run and short run if we allow all variables to adjust instantaneously. Equations L1–L4 lead inexorably to a new steady-state equilibrium whenever there is a change in an exogenous variable.

Instead, we address a more interesting question: what happens to the exchange rate if prices are sticky? As we saw in Chapter 7, the answer given by Dornbusch in the context of a far simpler model was that the exchange rate would overshoot its long-run value in the immediate aftermath of a monetary shock. Is the same true here, in a model that incorporates sub-models of consumer behaviour and labour supply?

In order to analyse disequilibrium, we need to be specific about the sequence of price setting. In the Redux scenario, the price p_E is set by European producers in their own currency at time 0 and cannot be changed again until time 2 – in other words, it is fixed throughout period 1 at the level chosen in the previous period and cannot be changed to reflect the conditions prevailing in the interim. Symmetrically, we assume the same applies to the dollar prices set by US producers, p_A^*, so that the situation is as can be seen in Figure 10.1.

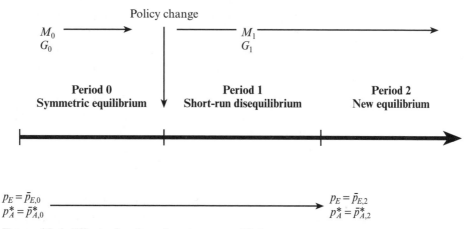

Figure 10.1 Effect of policy change on equilibrium

Why might prices remain fixed? Much has been written on this subject, without arriving at any clear conclusion. However, one of the less implausible explanations of the observed sluggishness of price changes in the real world is what were called *menu costs* in Chapter 2 – that is, the costs of deciding on new prices, publicizing the changes and informing existing and potential customers, and so forth.

Note that we still assume that PPP holds. The inflexibility affects only domestic currency prices. Any movement in the exchange rate is reflected immediately in the foreign currency price of domestic output, which, of course, raises the question: if American importers can change the dollar price of European products instantaneously in response to every whim of the currency market, why do European producers find it prohibitively costly to change their prices for the domestic market? We return to this point in Section 10.2.1.

Notice also that sticky prices are consistent with monopolistic behaviour, at least in the sense that producers are in any case selling at prices above marginal costs. In that respect, they can make suboptimal output/price decisions and still survive (i.e. continue to earn normal or supernormal profits). As far as market supply is concerned, the implication is that output becomes demand determined in the short run. Monopolistic household/firms in the model are locked in to time 0 prices and must supply whatever quantity is demanded at those prices. In other words, the disequilibrium at time 1 means that households are no longer supplying their optimal amount of labour. In terms of our equations, *the labour supply schedule L3 does not apply*.

As far as notation is concerned, time 1 disequilibrium values will be given the time 1 subscript, where necessary.

Effect of a monetary shock

We now ask the following question: what would be the short-run effect of a monetary disturbance? Specifically, suppose the European money supply increases from its initial time 0 level to a new, higher level, M_1 at time 1. Furthermore, assume the increase in the European money supply is permanent but *unanticipated*. Once it has occurred, no further change is expected in the European or US money stocks, from which it follows that we can rule out inflation in the steady state. Lastly, to keep the analysis simple, assume there is no simultaneous change in fiscal policy, so that government spending remains fixed at its initial value of zero. In terms of the time line given in the previous section, we set $G_1 = G_0 = 0$ and, of course, both this value and the new value of the money stock, M_1, carry over into the new steady state at time 2. In all three periods, equivalent US values are unchanged: $M_0^* = M_1^* = M_2^*$ and $G_0^* = G_1^* = G_2^* = 0$.

First, look back at the Euler equations (Equations 10.16 and 10.16′), which are the rules for optimal household consumption. Clearly, the ratio of Equation 10.16 to, Equation 10.16′ is just:

$$\frac{C_{t+1}}{C_{t+1}^*} = \frac{C}{C^*} \tag{10.29}$$

so that consumption grows at the same rate in both countries. Alternatively, Equation 10.29 tells us that the ratio of European to US consumption at time 1 will be the same as the ratio in the previous period. But since in the previous period, time 0, the system was assumed to have been in steady-state equilibrium, Equation 10.29 tells us the ratio will have been unchanged between times 0 and 1. In terms of log differences, this means:

$$\tilde{C}_1 = \tilde{C}_0 = \tilde{\tilde{C}} \tag{10.30}$$

which implies that relative consumption remains unchanged in disequilibrium.

A more important conclusion relates to the short-run impact of the monetary shock on the exchange rate. Combining equations L1 and L4, we get:

$$\tilde{M} - \hat{S}_1 = \frac{1}{\varepsilon}\tilde{C}_1 - \frac{\beta}{(1-\beta)\varepsilon}(\hat{S}_2 - \hat{S}_1) \tag{10.31}$$

But by period 2, the system is assumed to be back in equilibrium, so $\hat{S}_2 = \hat{\bar{S}}$ and we can solve Equation 10.31 for $\hat{S}_1$ to give:

$$\hat{S}_1 - \tilde{M} = \frac{1}{\varepsilon}\tilde{C}_1 - \frac{\beta}{(1-\beta)\varepsilon}(\hat{\bar{S}} - \hat{S}_1) \tag{10.32}$$

or:

$$\left[1 + \frac{\beta}{(1-\beta)\varepsilon}\right]\hat{S}_1 = \left\{\tilde{M} - \frac{1}{\varepsilon}\tilde{C}_1\right\} + \frac{\beta}{(1-\beta)\varepsilon}\hat{\bar{S}} \tag{10.33}$$

But using the fact that $\tilde{C}_1 = \tilde{\tilde{C}}$, as has just been shown, and looking back at Equation 10.28, we can see that the term in the curly bracket in this equation is $\hat{\bar{S}}$, so Equation 10.33 simplifies to:

$$\hat{S} = \hat{\bar{S}} \tag{10.34}$$

In other words, the post-shock exchange rate is the long-run equilibrium exchange rate. Unlike in the Dornbusch model, there is no overshooting here, even though prices are fixed in the short run. The exchange rate simply jumps immediately to its new steady state. Notice that this result follows essentially from the fact that relative consumption is constant and is expected to remain constant into the future. As we have seen, in the Redux model, consumption plays the role taken by real income in standard exchange rate models. Given that the money supply is also assumed constant and is expected to remain fixed at its new, higher level, constant relative consumption means that relative price levels must be unchanged. By PPP, this is possible only if the exchange rate is expected to remain constant at its new level. Since all variables will be at their steady-state levels next period (time 2), the exchange rate must already be there at time 1.

10.1.6 Graphic analysis

The nature of the equilibrium is illustrated in Figure 10.2, which plots the proportionate exchange rate change, $\hat{S}$, against relative consumption, $\tilde{C}$, on the horizontal axis. The downward-sloping *MM* line is simply Equation 10.28 after substituting $\tilde{C}_1 = \tilde{\tilde{C}}$ from Equation 10.30 and exploiting the fact that the short- and long-run exchange rate are the same (as established in the last section):

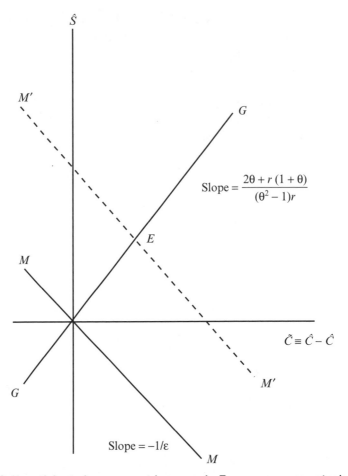

Figure 10.2 Unanticipated permanent increase in European money stock

$$\hat{S} = \tilde{M} - \frac{1}{\varepsilon}\tilde{C} \qquad\qquad (10.35)$$

which represents the necessary conditions for short-run money market equilibrium. It is downward-sloping because, as we have seen, an increase in European consumption plays the same role here as an increase in real income in the simple monetary model (see Chapter 5), raising the demand for money, requiring a fall in European prices and an appreciation of the €.

The line labelled *GG* is more complicated to derive, but by using the aggregate demand relationship L2[25] and equations for the balance of payments, we arrive at the following:

$$\hat{S} = \frac{2\theta + r(1+\theta)}{(\theta^2 - 1)r}\tilde{C} \qquad\qquad (10.36)$$

Since $\theta > 1$, this is an upward-sloping line. The positive relationship is explained by the fact that higher European consumption requires higher European output relative to the USA. With prices fixed in the short run, the Americans will buy more European output only if its $ price is lower, i.e. if the € depreciates.

Unlike the other figures in this book, Figure 10.2 makes no distinction between the long and short run. The reason is that, as we saw in Equations 10.30 and 10.35, both consumption and the exchange rate jump to their long-run steady-state values at time 1. So starting from the time 0 equilibrium at the origin, a sudden increase in the European money stock will shift the MM line vertically upwards by the extent of the increase. The new short- and long-run equilibrium will be at the intersection of the dotted $M'M'$ line and the original GG line.

Notice the effect is to cause a currency depreciation *less* than proportional to the increase in the money stock. This conclusion was hinted at earlier, where it was demonstrated that the steady state would be associated with a proportionate change in the exchange rate, provided relative income remained unaffected. But relative income *is* affected. Since the additional supply of euros is immediately associated with exchange rate depreciation, the fact that prices are unchanged in exporters' own currencies gives Europe a short-run competitive advantage. It follows that European income and output increase in the short run. But not all the additional income is spent and, to the extent that some of it is saved,[26] the outcome is a current account surplus.

The implication is that in the new steady state at time 2, Europeans will enjoy a higher level of wealth, in the form of claims against Americans accumulated in period 1 through their balance of payments surplus. However, being wealthier, Europeans will choose to work less, produce fewer goods and sell them at a higher price than in the time 0 steady state, when they had no assets. Notice the result is that the terms of trade reverse themselves. In the short run, there is a disequilibrium deterioration, as devaluation of the € with fixed prices makes Europe's exports cheaper and imports from America dearer. In the new steady state, however, the reduction in Europe's output is accompanied by a higher price for its output, and vice versa for the USA.

In the new equilibrium, as we can see at point E in the diagram and as has already been established, European consumption is greater, which implies a higher demand for money. It follows that some of the new money is absorbed by an increase in the transactions demand for real money balances, leaving the remainder as excess supply to be eliminated instantly by currency depreciation. In the light of what has been said about the gradient of the GG line, we conclude that the exchange rate effect will be smaller the higher is the relative price elasticity of supply, θ. By the same token, if the supply elasticity approaches its minimum value $\theta \rightarrow 1$, then the GG line is near vertical and the outcome tends to the benchmark result of a one-for-one depreciation.

Notice that this conclusion is a direct contradiction of the Dornbusch model. Redux predicts that, with sticky prices, exchange rate volatility will be *lower* than with flexible prices, not higher.

There is another noteworthy aspect of the Redux model's non-neutrality, which is perhaps not obvious as long as we concentrate exclusively on changes in Europe relative to the USA. The short-run effect of an unanticipated monetary expansion is, as has been explained already, a real depreciation in the value of the € and consequent increase in Europe's share of world output. But the increased output has a welfare cost, in the form of less leisure and more effort. Conversely, for Americans, the opposite is true. In both cases, if we restrict attention to the *expenditure-switching* effects of the change in the real exchange rate – that is, the diversion of demand towards European goods at the expense of American goods – it can be shown that the net change in welfare as measured by the utility function Equation 10.7 is zero. What remains is an increase in global welfare caused by higher world consumption following the rise in the stock of real money balances. Moreover, this increase in welfare is shared equally between Europe and the USA.

A warning is in order, however. Obstfeld and Rogoff make no claims to having discovered the ultimate global free lunch, because their conclusion relies on two critical features of the model. First, it requires that the money supply increase be completely *unanticipated*.[27] Second, and most importantly, it flows from the assumption that producers are monopolists, producing less than the social optimum in the initial equilibrium, so that a demand-determined increase in output moves them closer to the competitive equilibrium.

10.2   Extensions of Redux

The Redux model provides a new framework for exchange rate theorizing, but in its original basic form its relevance is limited by the simplifications required to keep the model tractable. For example, the assumption that prices are fixed for one period is open to question. The labour market is barely modelled and accumulation is permitted only in the form of foreign currency loans, so there is no role for private capital markets or for public sector debt, since the government never borrows. Most obviously, Redux ignores uncertainty and the problems it poses for economic agents.

Most of these shortcomings have been addressed in one way or another by researchers in the decade since Obstfeld and Rogoff's original work.

10.2.1   Pricing to market

The basic Redux model relies on the law of one price, which amounts to assuming PPP, given equal weights in the price indices. However, as we have seen in Chapter 2, the evidence shows that even if PPP holds in the long run, it most certainly does not fit the facts in the short run. Moreover, as has already been pointed out, the sticky price Redux model involves a rather strange price-setting mechanism. For example, in the immediate aftermath of a European money stock change, producers in Europe are assumed to be unable to change their prices, constrained as they are by the menu costs of informing their domestic customers, resetting quoted prices in €, and so on. Yet their exports are sold by importers in the USA who face no such constraints, changing the dollar-denominated prices at which they sell European products with every ripple in the exchange rate. Neither can we explain this asymmetry by superior pricing efficiency (i.e. lower menu costs) in the USA, because exactly the same applies to American prices, which are sticky in the short run for products sold in the home market but adjusted instantaneously to reflect exchange rate changes for products exported to Europe.

Instead, a number of researchers have investigated the implications of replacing the Redux assumption that all export prices respond immediately in strict proportion to exchange rate changes with one that allows for a more varied response. A number of published papers have investigated the implications of *pricing to market* (see Section 2.6.4), by assuming either zero short-run pass-through (*local currency pricing*) or a degree of pass-through that varies across household firms. The most important conclusions of this literature (see reading guide) are as follows:

- In the first instance, incomplete pass-through reduces the expenditure-switching effect of exchange rate changes. Obviously, if the impact of exchange rate movements on prices is muted, then the scope for the price mechanism to work is reduced.

- If the expenditure-switching mechanism is weakened, any given disturbance to equilibrium requires a larger exchange rate response than in the Redux model. PTM therefore implies greater exchange rate volatility and probably a degree of overshooting. The original Dornbusch insight that sticky prices force the exchange rate to overadjust is therefore reinstated in a general equilibrium setting.

- A country with a depreciating currency also has a depreciating real exchange rate. In general, the more prevalent the PTM mechanism, the greater the correlation between real and nominal exchange rates in the short run – an attractive feature of these models, in so far as it is consistent with one of the stylized facts about PPP deviations, as we saw in Chapter 2.

- The ability to use monetary policy to influence real exchange rates leaves scope for governments to pursue *beggar-my-neighbour* economic policies. In other words, by engineering a depreciation of their own currency, they are able to gain a short-run competitive edge in world markets, but the advantage is *not* associated with an increase in their share of world trade and output. Instead, the outcome of a devaluation of the €, for example, with fixed dollar prices for European exports must be an increase in the profitability of the European corporate sector, other things being equal. But, symmetrically, if American exporters keep their prices fixed in a terms, they must become less profitable. The net outcome is an increase in European income at the expense of the USA. This marks a significant departure from the original Redux conclusion that monetary policy generates an increase in welfare shared equally between the two countries. By contrast, the PTM model appears at first blush to be a recipe for competitive devaluation. However, two things should be noted in this regard. First, since PTM can only be a short-run phenomenon, it follows that, in order to preserve its exporters' enhanced profit margins, a country would have to bring about a continuous devaluation, so that a new steady state were never reached. This is of course impossible, not least because markets would quickly realize what was going on and react accordingly, with the consequences for interest rates and the money market explored elsewhere in this book. Sustained depreciation would, in any case, destroy the rationale for PTM itself.

- As far as the long run is concerned, the model allows a country to retain the benefits of devaluation, but only in the form of a steady-state increase in income from foreign assets. The terms of trade effects are reversed, compared with the short run, with export prices falling to PPP levels. More importantly, in so far as foreign income rises, it must be associated in the long run with a current account deficit. This may make competitive devaluation an attractive option for a rational democratic government, if one can be found, but for the moment populist mercantilism seems as dominant as ever.[28]

10.2.2 Other extensions

A number of other extensions of the Redux model have been explored in the published literature. There is no room here to do more than mention some of the variants. (References can be found in the reading guide.)

■ The consequences of allowing for the existence of a range of non-tradeable goods (or services) have been investigated in a number of papers (including the appendix of the original Obstfeld and Rogoff (1995) paper). The greater the proportion of the household's consumption basket that is unaffected by changes in the terms of trade, the more the impact of any shock must be absorbed by the tradeables sector and hence the more the exchange rate must move, other things being equal. Unsurprisingly, the outcome could well be overshooting. More recently, Obstfeld and Rogoff have argued that the tradeable/non-tradeable dichotomy is potentially misleading. Instead, they appear to believe that most of the puzzling features of exchange rate behaviour can ultimately be explained by the existence of significant transport costs. A number of experiments with the *iceberg* model of transport costs (see Section 2.6.3) lend some support to this view.

■ The original Redux model involves no uncertainty. The fundamental relationships in the model are non-stochastic. Consistent with this scenario, agents are assumed to be blessed with perfect foresight, which means that wherever agents' expectations affect their decisions, they are able to forecast the future with perfect accuracy. So, for example, in the Fisher equations (Equations 10.8 and 10.8′), nominal interest rates are the sum of real rates plus the actual inflation rate over the next period, from t to $t + 1$, which is, of course, never known in advance.

The question of how agents behave when faced with uncertainty will be the subject of Part III of this book. In advance of that, it should be noted that there are two dimensions to the introduction of uncertainty. First, when the future is clouded by the possibility of random shocks, agents have to base their decisions on their forecasts of the relevant variables, rather than on the unknown future values (see Chapter 12). Second, unless they are indifferent to the risk that their forecasts may be wrong, agents will require compensation for risk bearing, which will distort the equilibrium outcome relative to the solution in the absence of uncertainty (see Chapter 14).

Neither issue is addressed in the original version of the Redux model, a shortcoming of which Obstfeld and Rogoff were well aware but that was unavoidable in a first attempt at exploring the general equilibrium approach. In the past few years, they and others have attempted to remedy the omission. This is an ongoing research agenda, but it seems clear that the conclusions will be critically dependent on the details of the way uncertainty is introduced. In particular, the conclusions will depend on how much information agents are allowed to use as inputs to their decisionmaking and on the assumed probability distributions of the stochastic shocks generating the uncertainty in the model.[29]

There are broadly two sorts of approach to testing the type of model outlined in this chapter.

The direct econometric approach is at present almost impossible, since it would involve estimating either the basic equations describing the behaviour of households, firms and government or the equations defining the model solution.[30]

The indirect approach might appear more promising, since, as we have seen, the models generate a number of clear qualitative conclusions, mostly with respect to the correlations between prices and exchange rates and the relative amplitude of fluctuations in them, but also regarding the effect of policy changes on the current account and the exchange rate. This type of evidence has to be viewed with some scepticism, however, for two reasons. First, the observed pattern of correlations could be consistent with a number of different models – some already existing in the literature and others yet to be formulated. Second, the formulation of the Redux model and its successors was in part motivated by the failure of its predecessors to explain precisely these facts. Indeed, in a previous collaboration with Meese (1983), Rogoff had been involved in the most influential published demonstration of their failure (see the discussion of evidence in Chapters 5 and 7 of this book). On the one hand, this is all to the good, since it seems pointless to develop a model that patently fails to explain even the established facts. On the other hand, it is hard to accept as supporting evidence facts that were both known and targeted from the outset. To some extent, as time passes and more data become available, this problem will be alleviated, but for the present it is a serious obstacle to arriving at a conclusion on the validity of the models. The problem here, known to econometricians as *data snooping*, is particularly acute in this case compared with the other models covered in this book, for two reasons. First, earlier open economy macromodels of the kind covered in previous chapters predate the establishment of an accepted body of facts regarding exchange rates and prices and so are, to some extent, immune from this criticism. Second, most (although not all) of the research in later chapters will be seen to rely on high-frequency data, so that new datasets are always available for testing. Macromodels such as Redux and its successors rely on evidence from low-frequency time series – data on GDP, trade balances, aggregate consumption, and so on, which are published only on a quarterly basis, at best.[31]

In view of these problems, almost all researchers have taken an indirect approach, looking at evidence that can cast light on the predictions of the model with respect to prices, exchange rates and current account balances. As far as prices and exchange rates are concerned, much of the relevant results relate to the nature of deviations from PPP and/or the law of one price. As such, they have already been discussed at some length in Chapter 2. Not surprisingly, the evidence that exchange rates are more volatile than prices, and indeed than all the other fundamental variables that are believed to drive them, is broadly consistent with the PTM model. In particular, there is clear evidence that monetary disturbances can affect real exchange rates and possibly to an extent consistent with those generated by experiments with calibrated PTM models.[32] Other approaches have involved looking at relative consumption growth rates, the correlation between the openness of an economy and the volatility of its real exchange rate.

While the bulk of the evidence is consistent with the predictions of one or more of the Redux family of models (mostly its PTM variant), it remains impossible to arrive at any firm conclusion on the basis of these rather weak tests that really serve only to refine the stylized facts in this area. What is required is a direct test of the models. But a moment's consideration is enough to expose the daunting problems that would be involved in this undertaking. For example, the elasticity of substitution between domestic and foreign output θ is clearly one of the key parameters. It is hard enough to estimate this parameter for a single country. But we then face the problem that it is assumed to have the same value in the 'other' country – or, in an empirical application, maybe in *all* other countries. Without this restriction, the model becomes vastly more complicated and may exhibit quite different behaviour, with predictions dependent on the relative size of the two (or more) values of θ. By the same token, while it may be acceptable as a simplifying restriction in theoretical work, one has to question whether it can serve as a basis on which to confront real-world data.

10.4 Conclusions

The Redux model has revitalized research on exchange rate determination in a number of respects. However, it opens up a long research agenda, which is still in its infancy. Although the implications of a variety of different pricing processes – export currency pricing, local currency pricing, tradeables and non-tradeables – have been investigated, it is still unclear how far the results are sensitive to the more basic assumptions needed to keep the model tractable.

For example, imposing identical tastes in the two countries may be essential for a closed form solution, but it is not necessarily an innocuous assumption.[33]

Likewise, specifying that the public sector allocates its spending to domestic and foreign output in the same proportions as consumers is unrealistic, if only because in reality the bulk of government consumption takes the form of non-tradeable services. The idea that it responds to relative prices in the same way as private sector spending is convenient, but unrealistic.

Another problem arising out of the model's complexity relates to the solution method, which as we have seen relies on a log-linear approximation starting from an initial symmetric steady state. In particular, it starts from a zero current account balance, and then proceeds to analyse how disturbances create an imbalance that has implications for the new steady state with a re-allocation of international assets and consequent change in relative income and consumption. In general, therefore, different net asset positions are associated with different steady-state equilibria, which appears to create a circularity. The choice of the initial zero net asset steady state is, in this sense, arbitrary.

As far as its relevance is concerned, there are a number of shortcomings. On the one hand, it is plainly not a model of short-term day-to-day exchange rate movements. On the other hand, with sticky prices, no physical capital and only local perturbations, it cannot relate to the long run either. Yet, if we consider the medium-term scenario today (March 2004), the dominant feature in the currency markets is the behaviour not of private agents but rather of national monetary authorities, in particular those of the USA, on the one hand, and the major Asian economies, China and Japan, on the other. It is their propensities to borrow and lend respectively which appear to be driving the key $-¥ and indirectly $-€ exchange rates. Now, even if one were happy to concede that these governments were simply reflecting the tastes of their own consumers, the basic Redux model cannot capture the impact of intervention on their base money stocks. Some, but not all of these shortcomings have been addressed in subsequent work.

Summary

- The Redux model takes a general equilibrium approach. In other words, it models a simultaneous equilibrium in all the main sectors of the economy explicitly, not just in a single market. It is also set in a two-country world.

- The basic model postulates two countries populated by household–consumers who also operate as suppliers of differentiated goods/services, which they produce using nothing but their own labour and sell, in equilibrium, at a profit-maximizing price greater than their marginal costs.

- Given a consistent CES formulation for the index of aggregate consumption and an associated utility function making welfare dependent not only on consumption but also on real money balances and on labour supplied by the household, with identical parameters in each country, it follows that domestic and foreign residents allocate their spending to their own output and imports respectively in similar proportions.

- The only capital transaction in the model takes the form of sales by the private sector of an internationally acceptable one-period real bond, with the proceeds used to fund current account deficits and the surplus country accumulating assets.

- In an initial symmetric equilibrium, with zero current account balances and no government spending, output will be below its competitive level, so that expansionary monetary policy actually improves global output and consumption causing an increase in welfare in both countries.

- Both the long- and short-run effects of expansionary monetary policy depend critically on the current account.

- If all prices are sticky and remain fixed at their initial level in domestic currency terms (but with 100% pass-through on exports) for one period after the money supply increase, the exchange rate jumps immediately to its long-run depreciation level, making domestic output more competitive and generating a current account surplus and associated build-up of claims on the foreign country.

- In the new long-run steady state, prices will have risen and equilibrium will be established at higher levels of output in both countries. However, output will have risen more in the foreign country, associated with a current account surplus at the expense of the domestic economy, whose deficit will be offset by the flow of income from the claims it accumulated during the intervening disequilibrium.

- A more realistic assumption would be that instead of complete pass-through, we actually have zero pass-through of exchange rate changes to export prices in the short run. The implication is that the expenditure switching mechanism is inoperative in the period of disequilibrium following a money supply increase, so that the exchange rate has to overshoot (for most parameter values).

■ Recent and ongoing work on extensions of the Redux model has dealt with issues such as the effects of uncertainty and more complex price-setting processes. But empirical research remains inconclusive on the question of how well the model fits the facts.

Reading guide

Basic Redux dates from Obstfeld and Rogoff (1995b), which contains a model of traded and non-traded goods in its appendix. The same authors, together or individually, have extended the model and surveyed the flourishing literature. Obstfeld (2001) and Obstfeld and Rogoff (1998, 2000b), in particular, take the analysis further in the direction of dealing with uncertainty. Much of the work on the implications of local currency pricing and related issues is due to a series of papers by Betts and Devereux (1996, 2000). There are a number of excellent surveys of this literature and the related question of the nature of PPP deviations. See especially Obstfeld (2002) and Lane (2001).

Web page: **www.pearsoned.co.uk/copeland**.

Notes

1 Since the whole point of this literature is the attempt to provide exchange rate theory and open economy macroeconomics with a firm basis in microeconomics, readers who are not familiar with the rudiments of price theory may face a struggle to understand the material in this chapter.

2 For a start, only industrialized countries are eligible, since most poor countries are not really open economies. Moreover, a number of otherwise eligible small countries have joined the eurozone or are about to do so (e.g. Austria, Czech Republic, Finland).

3 I ignore the fact that some of Europe is currently outside the eurozone. It should be clear that we are assuming that there are only two countries in the world. This is not entirely unrealistic. After all, at the time of writing (October 2003), the USA and Europe together account for about 60% of world trade. In fact, if we think in terms of the dollar zone rather than just the USA (as we should for many purposes) and, in particular, if we include China as a major component of the dollar bloc, then the percentage rises to well over 75%.

4 Recall from Chapter 1 that the equality of the current account of the balance of payments and aggregate saving in the economy is a national income identity, and not a behavioural relationship potentially open to question.

5 In fact, they assume an infinite number of households, which forces them to resort to integral calculus. However, the essentials of the model can be presented without this degree of generality.

6 Readers who have difficulty visualizing the scenario might find it helpful to think of an economy consisting exclusively of self-employed service providers, with each plumber, lawyer, dentist, schoolteacher, business consultant, etc. offering a service that is different in terms of quality, specialism or convenience from that offered by any other.

7 For those who are not, microeconomic textbooks are the obvious starting point, although readers will most likely find an explanation in terms of the CES production function, which is where it first made its appearance in the economics literature.

8 In the original version of the model, with an infinite number of producer households, each individual economic unit enjoyed a monopoly in the production of its own, unique good, z, while at the same time it was assumed to take the relative prices of all other goods as given. In short, it was a monopoly supplier of its own output, but a perfectly competitive consumer in every other market.

9 We write y, y^* respectively for European and US output. Country subscripts are unnecessary, since it is clear that each country's output is of its own goods.

10 That is, the real interest rate is the value of r that makes the bond's market price equal to $1/(1 + r)$, the present value of its real payoff to the bondholder.

11 T is in real per capita terms a fixed quantity taken by the government from each household without reference to its level of consumption or income.

12 Strictly speaking, we need a number of other conditions to be satisfied, including a so-called transversality condition, which simply requires that the prospective present value of future financial asset creation does not grow without limit. There is no apparent reason to think this condition will be violated.

13 In fact, the budget constraints should first be rewritten with $p_{\dot{E}}$ and $p_{\dot{A}}^*$ eliminated, using Equations 10.15 and 10.15′ respectively. Then households are assumed to take world demand $C^W + G^W$ as given.

14 In fact, provided δ is small, Equation 10.17 implies that consumption grows in both countries at a rate approximately equal to $r - \delta$. Of course, when $r = \delta$ consumption is constant over time.

15 In fact, $\dfrac{y}{y^*} = \left(\dfrac{C}{C^*}\right)^{\theta/\theta+1}$.

16 Note that the variables in Equation 10.21 are marked with bars to denote steady-state values and 0 subscripts to make it clear that they apply only in the initial *symmetrical* steady state. By contrast, the value of r in Equation 10.20 applies in *all* steady states, symmetrical or otherwise, and so there is no need for a subscript.

17 Some readers may be wondering at this point how each of the components of total world consumption can be the same as the total itself. Recall first that all of these variables are in per capita terms, so C^W is always defined as a weighted average of C and C^*. Since the weights n, $(1 - n)$ sum to one, whenever $C = C^*$, they will both be equal to C^W. The same applies (in logarithmic terms) to the components of each country's consumption basket, as can be established by setting $c_{\dot{E}} = c_{\dot{A}}$ in Equation 10.1.

18 Setting output equal to consumption and choosing y to maximize the utility of output, net of the disutility of producing it, leads to the conclusion that optimal output is $\kappa^{-1/2}$, whereas the solution in Equation 10.25 is smaller by $(\theta\kappa)^{-1/2}$.

19 We continue to suppress the subscript on $\hat{x}$, t being understood, including a subscript only when it relates to $t - 1$. We could also dispense with bars over the variables, but they are retained as a reminder that we are dealing here with steady-state values, a distinction that will be crucial in the next section.

20 Notice that we need no subscript on $\tilde{p} \equiv \hat{p}_{\dot{E}} - \hat{p}_{\dot{A}}$, since it is now unambiguously the relative price change.

21 Since L2 and L3 together imply $\tilde{C} = (1 + \theta)(\tilde{p} - \tilde{P})$.

22 In fact, we are assuming that the disequilibrium lasts for only a single period, but in principle the statement applies to the accumulated deficit or surplus over however long it takes to reach the new steady state.

23 Equation 10.26 is derived straightforwardly by using L3 in L4 and setting the inflation rate to zero for steady-state equilibrium.

24 See Appendix 10.4 for the solution of the sticky price model.

25 Reminder: we cannot use L3, since it does not apply in disequilibrium.

26 In the jargon of intertemporal choice, the utility function implies that household behaviour is characterized by consumption smoothing in the face of temporary income fluctuations. In other words, since they prefer a smooth to a jagged consumption path, households allocate some part of any unexpected increase in income to saving, so that they are able, symmetrically, to consume their assets (dissave) whenever their income falls. The outcome of their inclination to save for a rainy day is that income fluctuates by more than consumption.

27 Readers who see themselves as future central bank governors should note that if market expectations are rational (see Chapter 11), then unanticipated monetary policy would require them to decide money supply changes randomly. This would involve tossing a coin or spinning a roulette wheel or using a random number generator, and then accepting the outcome without hesitation, even though half the time it would dictate a *reduction* in the money stock.

28 For example, at the time of writing, European countries and even more so the USA are greatly exercised about the loss of their share of world markets to China and their consequent trade deficit, resulting, supposedly, from the undervaluation of the Chinese currency, the RMB. Yet little of the rhetoric is directed at export profit margins. If the PTM model is to be believed, however, a Chinese revaluation would leave the trade deficit unchanged in the short run and

would simply serve to reduce the profitability of Chinese exporters. It would certainly leave China in possession of a far greater share of the world's international reserves and, in the long run, with the income they generate.

29 Since the basic Redux model is set up so as to be (relatively) easily formulated in logs, there are obvious attractions in introducing jointly log normally distributed shocks. However, this potentially creates other problems, not least because it rules out fat tails by assumption.

30 Econometricians call the former the structural equations and the latter the reduced form.

31 The problem is not just that data are available only quarterly and even then subject to revision years after the event. Even worse, there are frequent 'regime changes' to cloud the picture further. One need only consider the case of the continental European countries, which have seen two major fixed exchange rate regimes and now a currency union (or two, if the unification of Germany is counted.)

32 Calibrations are experiments in which a model's parameters are given what are regarded as plausible values and a simulation is then carried out to generate predictions of the result of a variety of exogenous shocks.

33 Of course, it can always be argued that differences in the parameters of the two utility functions are only second-order effects. But this hardly deals with the problem in the present context. After all, the effect of current account surpluses on the accumulation of foreign assets and thence on interest income in subsequent periods has most often been dismissed as a second-order effect. Yet, as we have seen, it plays a central role in the basic Redux model.

Appendix 10.1

Derivation of price index (Equation 10.2)

The price index has to be the minimum sum of money I sufficient to buy 1 unit of C as defined by Equation 10.1, so it solves the problem of choosing $c(z)$ to satisfy:

$$\text{min } I = \int_0^1 p(z)c(z)dz \tag{10.37}$$

subject to:

$$\int_0^1 c(z)^{\theta-1/\theta}dz = 1 \tag{10.38}$$

where the setting is the same as in the original Obstfeld and Rogoff paper, i.e. a continuum of households (and therefore of differentiated goods or services) indexed by z filling the [0, 1] interval. Here, $c(z)$ denotes consumption of the output of household z, which is priced at $p(z)$ and $p(z)c(z)$ is therefore expenditure on item z, so that the integral on the right-hand side of Equation 10.37 is simply the total cost of the consumption basket. Then, Equation 10.38 serves simply to set the unit of consumption to unity, given the aggregation formula chosen here. Then, solving the problem:

$$L = \int_0^1 p(z)c(z)dz - \lambda \left[\int_0^1 c(z)^{\theta-1/\theta} dz - 1 \right] \tag{10.39}$$

gives first-order conditions:

$$p(z)I = \lambda \frac{\theta-1}{\theta} c(z)^{-1/\theta} \quad p(z^*)I = \lambda \frac{\theta-1}{\theta} c(z^*)^{-1/\theta} \tag{10.40}$$

for all z, $z*$, giving (from the ratio):

$$\frac{p(z)}{p(z^*)} = \left[\frac{c(z^*)}{c(z)}\right]^{1/\theta} \tag{10.41}$$

Assume only two goods, z, $z*$. Then, setting $C = 1$ in (10.1) gives:

$$nc(z)^{\theta-1/\theta} + (1-n)c(z^*)^{\theta-1/\theta} = \frac{nc(z)}{c(z)^{1/\theta}} + \frac{(1-n)c(z^*)}{c(z^*)^{1/\theta}} = 1 \tag{10.42}$$

Multiplying by $p(z)$ and substituting $I - (1-n)p(z^*)c(z^*)$ for $np(z)c(z)$ gives:

$$\frac{I - (1-n)p(z^*)c(z^*)}{c(z)^{1/\theta}} + \frac{(1-n)p(z)c(z^*)}{c(z^*)^{1/\theta}} = p(z) \tag{10.43}$$

so:

$$I - (1-n)p(z^*)c(z^*) + (1-n)p(z)c(z^*)\frac{c(z)^{1/\theta}}{c(z^*)^{1/\theta}} = -p(z)c(z)^{1/\theta} \tag{10.44}$$

Using Equation 10.41:

$$I - (1-n)p(z^*)c(z^*) + (1-n)p(z)c(z^*)\frac{p(z^*)}{p(z)} = p(z)c(z)^{1/\theta} \tag{10.45}$$

or:

$$I = p(z)c(z)^{1/\theta} \quad \text{or} \quad I^{\theta} = p(z)^{\theta}c(z) \tag{10.46}$$

Using Equation 10.41 in I gives:

$$I = np(z)c(z) + (1-n)p(z^*)c(z)\left[\frac{p(z)}{p(z^*)}\right]^{\theta} \tag{10.47}$$

$$= np(z)c(z) + (1-n)c(z)p(z)^{\theta}p(z^*)^{1-\theta} \tag{10.48}$$

giving:

$$\frac{I}{np(z)c(z)} = 1 + \frac{1-n}{n}p(z)^{\theta-1}p(z^*)^{1-\theta} \tag{10.49}$$

Multiplying by $np(z)^{1-\theta}$ gives:

$$\frac{np(z)^{1-\theta}I}{np(z)c(z)} = \frac{I}{p(z)^{\theta}c(z)} = np(z)^{1-\theta} + (1-n)p(z^*)^{1-\theta} \tag{10.50}$$

and, by Equation 10.46:

$$\frac{I}{I^{\theta}} = I^{1-\theta} = np(z)^{1-\theta} + (1-n)p(z^*)^{1-\theta} \tag{10.51}$$

so:

$$I = [np(z)^{1-\theta} + (1-n)p(z^*)^{1-\theta}]^{1/1-\theta} \tag{10.52}$$

Proved

Appendix 10.2

Derivation of household demand (Equations 10.6 and 10.6′)

In Equation 10.46, set $I = P$, use PPP, and recall that we have imposed $C = 1$, then rearrange.

Proved

Appendix 10.3

Log linearization of model solution (Equations L1–L4)

For each country, aggregate the government and household budget constraints, Equations 10.11, 10.11′, 10.12 and 10.12′, respectively, and use Equation 10.10 to eliminate B_t^* and B_{t-1}^* to give:

$$C_t = (1 + r_{t-1})B_{t-1} - B_t + \frac{P_{E,t}y_t}{P_t} - G_t \tag{10.53}$$

and:

$$C_t^* = -(1 + r_{t-1})\frac{n}{1-n}B_{t-1} + \frac{n}{1-n}B_t \frac{p_{A,t}^* y_t^*}{P_t^*} - G_t^* \tag{10.54}$$

which gives a world budget constraint by taking Equation 10.53 multiplied by n plus Equation 10.54 multiplied by $(1 - n)$ to give:

$$C_t^w = n\left[\frac{p_{E,t}y_t}{P_t}\right] + (1-n)\left[\frac{p_{A,t}^* y_t^*}{P_t^*}\right] - G_t^W \tag{10.55}$$

which can be log linearized about the steady state (dividing by C_t^W and using $C_0^W = y_0 = y_0^*, P_0 = p_0, P_0^* = p_0^*$):

$$\hat{C}_t^w = n[\hat{p}_{E,t} + \hat{y}_t - \hat{P}_t] + (1 - n)[\hat{p}_{A,t}^* + \hat{y}_t^* - \hat{P}_t^*] - \hat{g}_t^w \tag{10.56}$$

and from PPP:

$$\hat{S}_t = \hat{P}_t - \hat{P}_t^* \equiv \tilde{P} \tag{10.57}$$

which is Equation L1 from earlier in this chapter.

Then, giving the same treatment to (4):

$$dP_t = \frac{1}{1-\theta}[np_{E,t}^{1-\theta} + (1-n)(Sp_{A,t}^*)^{1-\theta}]^{[1/(1-\theta)]-1}$$

$$\times [n(1-\theta)]P_{E,t}^{-\theta}dp_{E,t} + (1-n)(1-\theta)(Sp_{A,t}^*)^{-\theta}(S_t dp_{A,t}^* + p_{A,t}^* dS_t)] \tag{10.58}$$

from which it follows that:

$$\frac{dP_t}{\bar{P}_0} \equiv \hat{P}_t = \frac{[np_{E,t}^{1-\theta}dp_{E,t} + (1-n)(Sp_{A,t}^*)^{-\theta}(S_t dp_{A,t}^* + p_{A,t}^* dS_t)]}{[np_{E,t}^{1-\theta} + (1-n)(Sp_{A,t}^*)^{1-\theta}]} \tag{10.59}$$

Making use of the fact that at time 0 the law of one price holds, so $P_{E,0} = \bar{S}_0 P_{A,0}^*$, the denominator above is just equal to:

$$\bar{P}_{E,0}^{1-\theta} = (\bar{S}_0 \bar{P}_{A,0}^*)^{1-\theta} \tag{10.60}$$

It follows that we can write:

$$\hat{P}_t = \frac{[n\bar{p}_{E,0}^{-\theta} dp_{E,t} + (1-n)\bar{p}_{E,0}^{-\theta}(\bar{S}_0 dp_{A,t}^* + \bar{P}_{A,0}^* dS_t)]}{\bar{p}_{E,0}^{1-\theta}}$$

$$= \frac{[ndp_{E,t} + (1-n)(\bar{S}_0 dp_{A,t}^* + p_{A,t}^* dS_t)]}{P_{E,0}}$$

$$= n\frac{dp_{E,t}}{P_{E,0}} + (1-n)\frac{\bar{S}_0 \bar{p}_{A,0}^* dp_{A,t}^*}{P_{E,0} \bar{P}_{A,0}^*} + (1-n)\frac{\bar{S}_0 \bar{p}_{A,0}^* dS_t}{P_{E,0} \bar{S}_0}$$

$$= n\hat{p}_{E,t} + (1-n)(\hat{p}_{A,t}^* + \hat{S}_t) \tag{10.61}$$

and the same for $>_t^*$ giving:

$$\hat{P}_t^* = n(\hat{p}_{E,t} - \hat{S}_t) + (1-n)\hat{p}_{A,t}^* \tag{10.62}$$

The world demand functions (Equations 10.15 and 10.15′) yield:

$$\hat{y}_t = \theta(\hat{P}_t - \hat{p}_{E,t}) + \hat{C}_t^W + \hat{g}_t^W \tag{10.63}$$

$$\hat{y}_t^* = \theta(\hat{P}_t^* - \hat{p}_{A,t}^*) + \hat{C}_t^W + \hat{g}_t^W \tag{10.64}$$

Subtracting the second from the first of these equations gives L2.

The labour market equilibrium conditions (Equations 10.19 and 10.19′) give us:

$$(1+\theta)\hat{y}_t = -\theta\hat{C}_t + \hat{C}_t^W + \hat{g}_t^W \tag{10.65}$$

$$(1+\theta)\hat{y}_t^* = -\theta\hat{C}_t^* + \hat{C}_t^W + \hat{g}_t^W \tag{10.66}$$

Again, subtracting the second from the first of these equations gives L3.

Using Equation 10.20 in the consumption equilibrium conditions (Equations 10.16 and 10.16′):

$$\hat{C}_{t+1} = \hat{C}_t + (1-\beta)\hat{r}_t \tag{10.67}$$

$$\hat{C}_{t+1}^* = \hat{C}_t^* + (1-\beta)\hat{r}_t \tag{10.68}$$

Finally, the demand for money equations (Equations 10.18 and 10.18′) become, using Equations 10.8 and 10.8′:

$$\hat{M}_t - \hat{P}_t = \frac{1}{\varepsilon}\left[\hat{C}_t - \beta\left(\hat{r}_t + \frac{\hat{P}_{t+1} - \hat{P}_t}{1-\beta}\right)\right] \tag{10.69}$$

$$\hat{M}_t^* - \hat{P}_t^* = \frac{1}{\varepsilon}\left[\hat{C}_t^* - \beta\left(\hat{r}_t + \frac{\hat{P}_{A,t}^* - \hat{P}_t^*}{1-\beta}\right)\right] \tag{10.70}$$

the difference of which yields L4.

Sticky prices

In the short run, prices are fixed, i.e. $\hat{P}_{E,t} = \hat{p}_{A,t}^* = 0$, so Equations 10.61 and 10.62 give:

$$\hat{P}_t = (1 - n)\hat{S}_t \tag{10.71}$$

$$\hat{P}_t^* = -n\hat{S}_t \tag{10.72}$$

and using these equations in Equations 10.63 and 10.64 and taking the difference gives:

$$\tilde{y}_t = \theta\hat{S}_t \tag{10.73}$$

(which could equally have been derived from L1 and L2). The other equation needed is the solution for the short-term impact on the current account. Going back to Equations 10.53 and 10.54 and recalling that, viewed from time period 1, $B_{t-1} = B_0 = 0$, we get:

$$B_t = \frac{P_{E,t}y_t}{P_t} - C_t - G_t \tag{10.74}$$

which means that:

$$dB_t = \frac{P_{E,t}y_t}{P_t}(\hat{y}_t - \hat{P}_t) - dC_t - dG_t \tag{10.75}$$

but also that in the initial symmetric equilibrium at $t = 0$:

$$\frac{\bar{P}_{E,0}\bar{y}_0}{\bar{P}_0} = \bar{C}_0 \tag{10.76}$$

so that, in terms of deviations from the time 0 steady state, Equation 10.75 can be written:

$$dB_t = \bar{C}_0(\hat{y}_t - \hat{P}_t) - dC_t - dG_t \tag{10.77}$$

Then dividing through by $\bar{C}_0 = \bar{C}_0^W L_0 = L_0^W$ (by Equation 10.24) gives:

$$\hat{b} = \hat{y}_t - \hat{P}_t - \hat{C}_t - \hat{g}_t \tag{10.78}$$

(remembering that $\hat{b} \equiv dB_t/C_0^\omega$ and $\hat{g}_t \equiv dG_t/C_0^\omega$). Finally, using Equation 10.71:

$$\hat{b} = \hat{y}_t - (1 - n)\hat{S}_t - \hat{C}_t - \hat{g}_t \tag{10.79}$$

Similarly, for the USA:

$$\hat{b}^* = \hat{y}_t^* + n\hat{S}_t - \hat{C}_t^* - \hat{g}_t^* \tag{10.80}$$

11 Optimum currency areas and monetary union

Introduction

Throughout most of this book, we have taking for granted that each currency is un-ambiguously and irrevocably identified with one particular country, in spite of the fact that, as has been pointed out before, there are many examples of countries in which foreign currencies are used widely, whether officially or unofficially. Chapter 9 focused explicitly on the issue of currency substitution – that is, a situation in which the asso-ciation between currencies and countries becomes blurred. In this chapter, we move on to address the question of whether there is such a thing as an *optimal* currency area.

The question has to be answered in two stages. We first need to deal with a set of preliminary questions of a positive nature.[1] What economic difference does it make whether countries or regions share a common currency? What, if any, are the real effects? To what extent do countries entering a currency union sacrifice their eco-nomic independence? Then we can attempt to provide an answer to the normative question: what is the optimal scope of a single currency?

Fortunately, we have already answered most of the positive questions in earlier chapters, and so much of the analysis will be simply an application of previous models.

In what follows, it will help if we have some examples of currency union in mind. For this purpose, we shall focus for the most part on the case of the European Monetary Union (EMU), which has the virtue of being topical, already widely researched and involving issues that are largely familiar. But it should be clear that we could have picked any region as a potential candidate for currency union.

More importantly, the reader should be aware that the arguments for and against monetary integration can always be turned on their head and related instead to the question of monetary *dis*integration. In that sense, this chapter is equally concerned with the following question: what are the implications for a region or country of starting to issue its own money?[2] Would Scotland, Wales or California be better off issuing its own currency? Or London or New York? Would the UK or the USA be left any worse off if those regions opted for independent currencies?

As it happens, California *does* issue its own money. Dollar bills printed there carry the inscription 'Issued by the Federal Reserve Bank of California, San Francisco', and the same is true of all the Fed's 12 regional branches across the USA. Scottish banknotes, too, carry the name of the private commercial banks that have issued them.

Nonetheless, neither Scotland nor California[3] can be said to have its own currency at present. The reason is not simply that, in both cases, the notes issued are printed under licence to the respective central banks. Rather, it is that, having subcontracted the job of printing banknotes to its agents, each central bank then treats the currency issued as indistinguishable from those that it prints itself. In particular, it stands ready to exchange any or all regionally printed notes for those issued centrally. It follows that an individual who feels inclined can exchange any number of Californian dollar bills for the same number of dollars issued by the New York (or Philadelphia or St Louis) Federal Reserve, and Scottish and English banknotes are similarly interchangeable.

At this point, it should be clear that what we are talking about is simply a special case of a fixed exchange rate. These are examples of currencies that are physically distinguishable but are governed by an exchange rate regime with two essential features that can be regarded as being the defining characteristics of a single currency system:

> A **single currency zone** (or **monetary union**) is one where the accepted means of payment consists either of a single, homogeneous currency or of two or more currencies linked by an exchange rate that is fixed (at one for one) irrevocably.

It is worth noting those properties that have *not* been included. There is no reason, at least in principle, why a monetary union cannot embrace a proliferation of currency issuers, printing notes or coins as different from one another as are today the banknotes of any two members of the United Nations.[4] Neither is there any mention of political or geographical requirements. There are plenty of cases of currencies being used and even officially accepted over areas that are non-contiguous, politically diverse or even currently at war with each other. Panama, for example, has used the US dollar in place of a national currency for many years.

However, the most important word in the definition given here is the last. What really distinguishes a monetary union from a fixed exchange rate regime is more than just the fact that the exchange rate is fixed at *one for one*. That is merely an arithmetic convenience. Rather, it is the fact that the exchange rate is fixed irrevocably and irreversibly and, moreover, is universally *believed* to be so. It is easy to see why this feature is so critical. Suppose it were thought possible that at some future date the Californian dollar was going to be revalued against, say, the New York dollar. Plainly, the result would be an immediate deviation from the current one-for-one

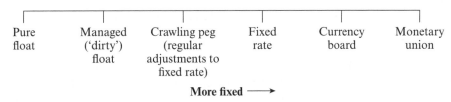

Figure 11.1 Exchange rate regimes

exchange rate, as holders of New York dollars rushed to swap their money for Californian dollars. Moreover, lenders and borrowers would soon start to specify in their contracts the currency in which repayment was to be made. In short, the situation would be unstable and the New York dollar would cease to exist, as the whole stock found its way back to the vaults of the Federal Reserve. In this respect, it helps if a currency is homogeneous. Because there is no way of distinguishing between one dollar bill and the next, there is no way they could ever differ in value. Where the fiction of a separate currency is maintained, the mechanism for creating a separate currency is already in place and therefore the threat or promise may still be felt to exist.[5]

Monetary union can be viewed as the extension of a fixed exchange rate regime to a point where the possibility of parity changes is ruled out completely (Figure 11.1). The distinction is an important one, as EMS members discovered to their cost. As long as countries or regions preserve separately issued currencies, the market will always take the view that they have preserved the potential escape route of exchange rate changes in order to make use of it when fixity proves too painful.

Before proceeding to the analysis, there is one other aspect of the question that ought to be acknowledged. Obviously, there is a sense in which a country's currency is perceived widely as a vital part of its national sovereignty. Like its postage stamps, its national airline or even its own armed forces, a country's currency is felt to be a vital part of its identity, one of the essential insignia of statehood. Why this should be the case is not entirely obvious, except as a particular example of the general rule that from the moment any activity becomes state-sponsored rather than private, it is liable to become the focus of a degree of nationalistic fervour. What is true of sport is certainly true of currencies. Anyone who doubts the fact need only consider the haste with which most of the new states of Eastern Europe declared their intention to issue their own national money when the Soviet empire ended.[6]

However, these issues are appropriate to textbooks on economic psychology and politics, not economics. The question of sovereignty will be viewed here exclusively from the economic angle.

None the less, it should be said that the subject matter of this chapter is linked more closely to political value judgements than the material in the rest of the book. At a number of points, we will find the train of the economic argument running into the buffers of political issues. In order to avoid trespassing into these areas, therefore, we shall have to come to an abrupt halt at several points in the discussion as we reach the boundaries of economics. The reader should not feel frustrated by this coyness. In dealing with a topic of this nature, the job of the economist can never be any more than to follow through the implications of the policy options under consideration. Perhaps the most important outcome of the analysis will be to delineate clearly the points at which the economic arguments end and political concerns take over.[7]

In Section 11.1, we shall consider the benefits of monetary union, in terms of reduced transaction costs and the elimination of exchange rate uncertainty. In Section 11.2, we turn to a consideration of the factors determining the costs of integration: the degree of labour mobility and the openness of the economy. Section 11.3 addresses an assortment of other issues: the impact of currency union on government monetary and fiscal policy choices, the transition costs of integration and the relationship (or lack of) between common markets for goods and common currencies. Section 11.4 deals with a possible alternative to monetary union, the currency board system. Conclusions are in Section 11.5.

11.1 Benefits of monetary union

The benefits of monetary union are all microeconomic in nature.[8]

In a sense, the case for monetary union is a negative one, since the supposed benefits stem from eliminating the costs of maintaining multiple currencies. Essentially, the argument is that the existence of multiple currencies imposes costs on individual economic agents or on society as a whole. These costs, which reduce overall welfare both directly and indirectly, via their inhibiting effect on trade and investment, can be grouped under two broad headings, depending on whether they arise out of the conditions of economic life under certainty (mainly transaction costs of one type or another) or out of the intrinsic uncertainty of floating or potentially variable fixed exchange rates.

It is straightforward to enumerate the costs imposed by the existence of multiple currencies. However, in evaluating the potential savings from their elimination by a monetary union, it is important to bear the following points in mind:

■ Not all the costs of foreign currency transactions could be saved by the use of a common currency. For example, some foreign currency loans are simply hedging exchange rate risk. Alternatively, firms often borrow in foreign markets because they find it the cheapest source of finance. Only in the former case is there a potential saving from monetary union. In the latter case, there would be scope for saving only if the reason for the difference in borrowing costs was attributable to exchange rate risk. Very often, however, the reasons have little to do with exchange rates. For example, a multinational company may find it cheapest to raise funds on its home capital market, simply because it is better known there and therefore attracts a higher credit rating.

■ Some of the apparent costs of foreign trade are simply rents extracted by banks, currency dealers and other intermediaries, exploiting the economies of scale open to them from the volume of transactions they handle on a regular basis. To some extent, there are genuine resource costs that could be avoided by monetary union. But the rents in excess of true marginal (social) cost would only be redistributed to other sectors of the economy, a change that may or may not be considered desirable depending on one's outlook. In other cases, costs may be not so much illusory as zero sum, so that one country's cost is another's benefit. Again, monetary union results in no overall benefit but simply a reallocation of income from pre-union winners to losers.

- Even where monetary union seems likely to yield cost savings, there may often be other, less radical ways to achieve the same results, as we shall see.

11.1.1 Foreign exchange transaction costs

We are all familiar with some of the costs of converting from one currency to another. As we saw in Section 1.1.3, large-scale currency conversions involve a bid–ask spread. On the one hand, this spread is probably quite small relative to the size of the individual transaction and hence of negligible importance in terms of its impact on behaviour. On the other hand, given the staggering volume of foreign currency transactions compared even with the world economy as a whole, the aggregate resource cost could be quite substantial. For example, if total currency transactions in the London market add up to around $600bn on an average business day and the typical spread is about 0.05%, then the implied cost is $300m, or well over $60bn per year – a very large amount by any standards.[9]

However, from the point of view of a single country, for example the UK, the potential resource saving from EMU is probably far smaller than this. For one thing, as the City of London's public relations machine cheerfully reminds us at every opportunity, a large proportion of the currency traded there is on behalf of foreign principals and, hence, far from being a resource cost to the UK, represents service exports by the British financial sector. Moreover, even where the costs are borne by UK residents, the potential savings from EMU are not applicable to the considerable proportion of transactions with countries outside Europe.

Of the remaining trade volume, the bulk almost certainly involves little or no true transaction cost to the economy. In the first place, the $600bn figure is gross – that is, counting offsetting trades. Many trades are netted out and, hence, are either not charged the spread or at any rate involve a genuine marginal cost that is only a tiny fraction of the quoted spread. Moreover, even where costs apply, economies of scale are likely to mean that the spread is far greater than the marginal cost that could be saved by a common currency.

The bottom line is that savings in transaction costs are likely to be somewhere between one-quarter and one-half of 1% of EU income.[10] Although this may not seem a very large sum, it would be enough to justify the change to a single currency – if we could be sure the costs of integration were negligible.

11.1.2 Costs of uncertainty

The argument most often used to justify monetary union is that exchange rate uncertainty is inherently damaging to the volume of real flows of trade and investment. The proposition is superficially persuasive. There can be little doubt that businessmen prefer certainty to uncertainty, other things being equal. This means that, faced with investment or trade opportunities, entrepreneurs are likely to be less enthusiastic where the decision involves the risk of currency fluctuations.

However, on closer examination, the issue is nowhere near as clearcut as it might appear at first glance. Consider an example from pre-EMU Europe. Suppose a British multinational was considering building an aircraft assembly plant in Germany. At the time, the pound/Deutschmark exchange rate was apparently floating freely. Therefore, in so far as the costs of the project are primarily denominated in Deutschmarks, and moreover spread out over a number of years, the sterling cost is uncertain, as is the exchange rate at which the cashflows from operating the plant will be converted into pounds.

But clearly the contribution of currency volatility to the risk of the project is likely to be very much overstated by, say, the variance or standard deviation of the exchange rate. In the first place, the UK company if it is truly multinational may well have Deutschmark-denominated assets with which it can finance the project. Failing that, it has the alternative of funding the investment by borrowing in Germany, a policy that amounts to hedging its prospective Deutschmark asset by a liability in the same currency. As we saw in Section 3.3, this is equivalent to a forward purchase of Deutschmarks, with the useful difference that it offers more flexibility over both contract size and maturity dates. Similarly, the cashflows from the sale of the product (aircraft) can be hedged by forward sales of Deutschmarks against pounds.

Moreover, the ultimate risk to the company associated with the investment and the ensuing cashflows is measured by their impact on its *net position* (sometimes called *net exposure*) in Deutschmarks in any period, not by their gross foreign currency value. Most cross-border transactions of this type will be netted out in the balance sheets of large multinational companies. Thus, if the company in our example has previously been a seller of aircraft to Germany, then the Deutschmark-denominated proceeds of the sale, although risky taken in isolation, obviously help to offset the foreign currency risk of the company's investment.[11]

This is far from being the end of the story, however. To make matters simple, suppose the British firm in our example has no other business in Deutschmarks, so that we can consider the proposed investment project in isolation. Under these circumstances, it is obviously true that if the Deutschmark falls by, say, 10% after the investment is made, then the sterling value of the company's German asset will also fall by 10%, *other things being equal*. But, as is so often the case in economics, other things are unlikely to remain equal because, in so far as the exchange rate is not expected to change any further in the interim, the competitiveness of production at the new assembly plant has been enhanced. The increase in prospective cashflows will to some degree offset the fall in asset values resulting directly from the Deutschmark depreciation and might even reverse it.

In general, then, it is easy to overstate the true costs of exchange rate uncertainty, at least as far as the typical multinational corporation is concerned.[12] Smaller companies have to rely on the ability of financial intermediaries to match positions in different countries, charging fees that are reduced to the level of the transaction costs referred to in the last section. What is left is the residual risk that has to be carried either by the individual company or by the forward market.[13]

As far as the latter is concerned, it is often said that covering foreign exchange transactions is costly. The statement is completely misguided. As we saw in Chapter 3, forward cover is likely to involve a cost in the form of a risk premium. However, most of the published research suggests that the premium is probably quite small (see

Chapter 15). None the less, the situation involves a number of subtleties that have been a source of confusion in many commentaries. Take an example.

Suppose at some point the situation with regard to the £/DM exchange rate is as follows:

Spot rate: DM1 = £0.40

30-day forward rate: DM1 = £0.404

Expected 30-day ahead spot rate: DM1 = £0.403

Comparing the spot and forward rates, it is plain that the Deutschmark stands at a forward premium to the pound of (0.404/0.40) − 1 = 0.01 or 1%. However, there is no reason to regard this figure as giving an indication of the potential saving from uniting the UK and German currencies. For one thing, the pound's discount is the Deutschmark's premium. When, as here, sterling holders have to pay more than the spot rate for 30-day German currency, Deutschmark holders pay less than the spot rate. Monetary union might save money for UK importers, but every penny saved would be at the expense of UK exporters – or their German counterparts.

Moreover, most of the forward premium has nothing at all to do with risk as such. In the example given above, three-quarters of the forward premium (that is, 0.75%) reflects the market's (albeit unobservable) expectations. This component of the premium is hardly to be regarded as a cost, because if the market's expectations are fulfilled, then it will be just sufficient to compensate Deutschmark borrowers and sterling lenders for movements in the exchange rate during the month.[14] To put the matter another way, the 0.75% premium is compensation for the fact that payment will ultimately be made with depreciated pounds. It is only the residual 0.25% that is a genuine cost of insuring against exchange rate fluctuations and even this cost is symmetrical – a cost to Deutschmark buyers but a gain to Deutschmark sellers.

11.1.3 International unit of account

Economists view money as having a number of important functions, of which one of the most important is as a *unit of account*. In this respect, it fulfils an essential information-bearing role, shortcutting what would otherwise be the cumbersome mechanism of barter. Without a stable unit of account, the drafting of long-term contracts would be impossibly complex. However, when this analysis is applied to cases such as EMU, there turns out to be somewhat less to the argument than meets the eye, as we shall see.

To understand the point, suppose I am looking through a mail-order catalogue in the UK. Now in the absence of anything qualifying as money (that is, in a world of barter), the catalogue would have to be very thick indeed if it were to serve the purpose of telling me the true price of anything more than a handful of goods. The reason is that the price of each good would have to be quoted in terms of all other goods. So, for example, instead of a money price of £10 for a compact disc, the catalogue would have to quote a long series of *relative prices*: 20 large white loaves of bread, two tickets for the cinema (specifying the cinema and the film), 0.75 days of tuition on a first degree arts course (specifying the university, etc.), and so on.

Put like this, it should be clear why it is absolutely essential to agree on a substance – commodity, paper, metal, or whatever – to nominate as a unit of account.[15] Having done so, the information problem becomes manageable. Once I get used to pounds sterling, I know immediately what is meant by a cost of £10 in terms of all the goods and services I buy regularly and, equally important, I have a fairly precise idea of its cost in terms of leisure – that is, how many hours I have to work in order to pay for it.[16]

Obviously, the advantage of any form of money resides in its very uniqueness as a common standard of account. Hence, some proponents of currency union go on to argue that a common currency for Europe, for example, is a substantial informational improvement on the 22 national currencies it replaces.

The argument is possibly correct, up to a point. But in the first place, its force really relates to the advantages of fixed compared to floating exchange rates. After all, the 22 currencies add a mere 21 prices – the 21 exchange rates against the pound – to the tens or hundreds of thousands of sterling prices with which a UK resident must cope. This is hardly a significant additional burden. Second, the argument relies for its superficial attraction on a number of conditions that are not really satisfied. Perhaps most importantly, it is not obvious that a single currency is optimal when relative prices differ between regions, as they do in Europe.

To be explicit, ask yourself how much better off the average European would be, in terms of informational requirements, if all prices were quoted in euros. Would a Londoner really benefit if supermarket prices were quoted in the same currency in Madrid as in London? Very little, one suspects. Indeed, the most likely reaction to a changeover would be total apathy. The reason Spanish prices are of little interest to UK residents has little to do with whether they are quoted in pesetas or euros or pounds, but far more with the obvious fact that there are very few practical ways for a Londoner to take advantage of any bargains in Madrid, and vice versa. Moreover, that is nearly as true for tradeables as for non-tradeables.

Take a more controversial example. It is well known that, when converted at current exchange rates, prices of many motor vehicles appear to be as much as 25% more expensive in the UK than in Belgium. Anyone seeking to establish whether the price differential is real or only apparent must examine carefully the makers' claim that the specification of UK vehicles is higher than in continental Europe, as well as the additional cost of shipping cars across the English Channel, converting them to meet UK specification where necessary, and so on. Having estimated the costs of converting the vehicles to a common specification and added the charges for transportation, insurance, and so on, those costs have then to be translated into a common currency.

It should be clear that, in all these tiresome computations, the role played by uncertainty about the number of Belgian francs or euros per pound is negligible. The complications all arise from the failure of the European single market, which has nothing whatsoever to do with the existence of multiple currencies, as we shall see (Section 11.3.5). In general, the reader may look back at the discussion in Chapter 2 to see that few of the reasons given there for the failure of PPP have anything to do with exchange rate uncertainty.

Of course, it is just about conceivable that at some future date products may have become standardized across the European market to such a degree that currency considerations really do stand out as the most serious remaining obstacle to integration.

Other than in this unlikely (and unattractive) scenario,[17] however, the benefits from a shared unit of account seem likely to be extremely slim.

11.2   Costs of monetary union

Two points need to be clear at the outset regarding the costs of monetary union.

First, they are largely *macroeconomic* in nature. There are no obvious microeconomic disadvantages.

Second, they are not concerned primarily with the nature of the macroeconomic equilibrium under currency union and disunion, but with differences in the patterns of *adjustment to disequilibrium* following a disturbance in the foreign sector. In other words, although there is little reason to suppose the ultimate outcome of a disturbance is affected by whether countries share a common currency, there is every reason to expect the adjustment mechanism to vary considerably, with important consequences for output and employment over what could be a very protracted period. The reason why the equilibrium outcome is unchanged by currency union is easily stated. As has already been pointed out, currency union is to all intents and purposes the same as a permanently fixed exchange rate as regards its comparative static properties. It is only when we come to examine the implications for adjustment that the differences become apparent.

To understand what is involved, take the monetary model as the starting point. As usual, we take as our benchmark a pure float with perfectly flexible prices and we contrast the effect of a disturbance in this simple case (Section 5.1) with the effect in the fixed exchange rate case (Section 5.2).

The type of disturbance to consider for our purposes is a shock to the domestic country's price level relative to the foreign price level. Suppose, for example, the foreign price level falls suddenly by 10%, while the domestic price level is initially unchanged. We saw in Chapter 5 that the final result is the same in both cases: competitiveness is restored, with real income, output and the real exchange rate back where they started. The difference is that, whereas under a floating exchange rate regime the domestic currency depreciates so as to restore competitiveness (Section 5.1.5), with a fixed exchange rate the process involves a fall in the domestic money stock and price level.

Take the fixed exchange rate case first. As we saw in Section 5.2.3, in the aftermath of a relative price shock, equilibrium is restored through reserve changes impacting on the domestic money market. In this case, the home country loses reserves as a result of the deterioration in its competitive position, until the fall in its money stock reduces its price level to match the 10% fall in foreign prices.

Now, it is a sad fact of macroeconomic life that falling price levels tend to be accompanied by considerable economic pain, in the form of unemployment, bankruptcies and misery. The critical question is this: *is the process more painful when the option of devaluation is ruled out because the home country and the foreign country are bound up in a currency union?* If it is, then it would obviously be desirable from the macroeconomic point of view to preserve that option (if not actually to allow the exchange rate to float freely). If, however, the adjustment mechanism is no more sluggish when the exchange rate is fixed irrevocably, then the microeconomic benefits of union are available at little or no macroeconomic cost.

11.2.1 Labour market

The consensus among economists is that the labour market is the critical factor in determining how smoothly adjustment proceeds.

Consider the impact of the initial disturbance on wage levels in the domestic economy. The fall in foreign prices means that, at pre-existing money wages, domestic production has become uncompetitive because real wages are now higher than before by an amount of up to 10%. Roughly speaking, if internationally traded goods prices account for, say, 40% of the cost of living, then real wages will have risen by 4% (that is, 40% of 10%), with a consequent loss of competitiveness, other things being equal. As long as this situation persists, there will be downward pressure on the level of economic activity, with accompanying increases in unemployment, the level of bankruptcies, and so forth.

The question is this: to what extent, if any, would devaluation make the return to equilibrium speedier and less painful?

With the exchange rate fixed, as the domestic economy loses reserves, the excess demand for money exerts downward pressure on product prices and may also push up interest rates (Chapter 6). If prices fall faster than money wages, then it follows that real wages increase, resulting in unemployment. In fact, if the price level falls by the full 10% while money wages are unchanged, real wages increase by 10%, and the level of employment bears the brunt of adjustment to the disturbance. Unless both money wages and prices fall at the same rate, and more or less immediately, there must be temporary unemployment.

By contrast, if the domestic currency depreciates, whether under a free float or a once-and-for-all devaluation, the domestic price of traded goods rises by 10%, reducing real wages pro rata and preserving labour market equilibrium – provided money wages remain unchanged in the face of the fall in their purchasing power, a point to which we shall return later.

Importance of labour mobility (Mundell)

At this point, it would appear that floating exchange rates are unambiguously superior to fixity, because they allow a near-painless reduction in real wages, through a devaluation-induced inflation of the domestic price level. Does that mean that every country should have its own currency with a freely floating exchange rate? Why stop there? After all, everyone agrees that unemployment is undesirable. Why not have currency zones smaller than countries? Then California could reduce or even eliminate its unemployment by devaluing its currency and reducing real wages in the state relative to the rest of the USA, as well as the rest of the world. Or go further: in US cities where unemployment is high as a result of the post-Cold War cuts in defence spending, a devaluation would provide a useful boost to the local economy; the same applies to the small towns in northern England still suffering from the impact of pit closures. It looks as though there are arguments in favour of ever-smaller currency zones.

There is in fact an obvious limit, however, as is clear from the last example. As Mundell pointed out many years ago, the argument for flexible exchange rates presented here presupposes that labour is immobile.

By contrast, suppose labour is mobile internationally or interregionally. Then it is easy to see that, even with a fixed exchange rate, equilibrium can be restored without transitional unemployment. Instead, workers who cannot find jobs in the domestic economy will move abroad (or to the next town or region), where they will be absorbed into employment because, at the lower prices and wages, production is relatively profitable. As the domestic economy loses labour, its marginal product rises, until higher real wages are validated. Thus, labour mobility obviates the need for exchange rate flexibility, by making it possible to preserve full employment, more or less, without devaluation.

Now international labour mobility is unusual in anything but the very long run. By and large, people only leave their own country to emigrate, drawn by what they see as vastly better prospects stretching into the indefinite future. But within a small country or group of countries (for example, Benelux) or a single region, they may well be ready to move in response to temporary differences in labour market conditions.

For these reasons, Mundell concluded that the optimal zone for a single currency was determined by the area within which labour was willing and able to move freely. In practical terms, this would appear to mean very small currency zones indeed, far smaller than most (although not all) of the countries in the industrialized world. For example, it probably means a separate currency for California or, better still, for the southwest USA. Likewise, on these grounds Scotland needs an independent currency,[18] as do the other regions of the UK, a point that was made clear in 1998 and 1999 when the Bank of England repeatedly raised interest rates to choke off incipient inflation in the southeast, while the rest of the country still had excess capacity (and, in some cases, high unemployment). By the same token, West and East Germany are probably better off having a common currency, and it may be that the Benelux countries could also be integrated.

In general, considerations of labour mobility militate in favour of smaller currency zones. Moreover, on these grounds there ought to be more currencies in Europe than in the USA if, as is normally assumed, the degree of population mobility is lower in Europe. It is also worth noting that anything serving to reduce labour mobility (for example, language differences, generous unemployment benefits, non-portable pensions) will also tend to make the optimal currency area smaller.[19]

In fact, evidence suggests that wages fall very little in the states of the USA in response to unfavourable demand shocks. Virtually the whole burden of adjustment falls on labour migration between states, so that it is estimated to take about six years for regional unemployment rates to return to the national average in the aftermath of a disturbance. From this point of view, it would appear that even the USA is a candidate for monetary disintegration.

Importance of openness (McKinnon)

We appear to have arrived at the conclusion that, from a macroeconomic point of view at any rate, the optimum currency area is very small, at least relative to present-day nation states. It turns out, however, that the requirements of labour market adjustment can equally be taken as justification for a movement in the opposite direction altogether.

The issue turns on the mechanism whereby devaluation serves to reduce real wages. Recall that in the aftermath of a devaluation it was assumed that money wages remained unchanged, in spite of the rise in prices, allowing the real wage to fall – hence, the desirability of a flexible exchange rate in the absence of labour mobility.

Notice that what is involved is a kind of sleight of hand, a monetary confidence trick whereby devaluation and the consequent rise in prices bring about a fall in real wages, *because labour suppliers fail to notice or respond to the inflation by raising* their money wage *demands*. To the extent that wage earners *do* respond, no reduction in real wages takes place and hence depreciation is ineffective. The Mundell case for flexibility therefore requires an inert labour force.[20]

How likely is such passivity on the part of the labour force? Obviously, it very much depends on the circumstances: how competitive the labour market is, how far wages are fixed by long-term contract, and so forth. But, as McKinnon argued in reply to Mundell, other things being equal (that is, given the other features of the labour market), that there will be one overriding factor determining how far workers passively accept a fall in their real wage as a result of devaluation: the degree of openness of the economy.

To see the force of the argument, consider the following question: how far do real wages fall when the exchange rate depreciates by, say, 10%? The answer obviously depends on the impact of the devaluation on the cost of living.

At one extreme, in a very small economy, almost all consumption is likely to consist of imports or import-competing goods – that is, tradeables. The effect of a 10% devaluation is therefore likely to be a near-10% rise in the cost of living index. It seems highly improbable that workers would accept this without attempting to claw back some of the drop in their standard of living by pressing for higher money wages.

By contrast, in a large economy, where imports may well be only a negligible proportion of the typical consumption basket, the impact of even a 10% devaluation will be small. For example, if imports carry only a 5% weight in the consumption price index, then the direct effect will be only 1/2% (that is, 10% of 5%). Hence, McKinnon argues, in large economies, devaluation is unlikely to provoke a significant response on the part of wage earners.

In general, therefore, McKinnon puts forward the case for very large currency areas. The larger the zone, the more closed the economy of the region it covers; hence, the smaller the weight of traded goods in the consumption baskets of its workforce and the easier it will be to sneak a reduction in the real wage without workers realizing or bothering to respond.

It looks as though labour market considerations suggest a trade-off between labour mobility, which suggests smaller currency areas, and openness, which indicates choosing larger areas.

11.3 Other considerations

11.3.1 Government behaviour: common currency versus fixed exchange rate

The macroeconomic arguments about the efficacy of devaluation as a tool for preventing unemployment really relate to the debate over the relative attractions of floating versus fixed exchange rates, rather than to the pros and cons of currency union. The reader may well wonder whether there are likely to be any macroeconomic implications specific to currency union. According to Mundell, one difference is to be found in the probable response of governments under the two types of arrangement, which, he argues, is likely to be different under a common currency than under a multiple currency system with fixed exchange rates.

His argument is as follows. Suppose there is a sudden decrease in the demand for the output of country (or region) A, to the advantage of country or region B. If the two zones are linked by a fixed exchange rate, then the natural reaction will be for A's monetary authority to tighten credit so as to reduce the money stock, thereby raising interest rates and strengthening the balance of payments. These measures will inevitably have the effect of reducing demand even further in B, leading to multiple deflation.

Notice that the problem arises out of a basic asymmetry of fixed exchange rate systems. The burden of adjustment falls mainly on the country or region whose currency is in excess supply, which is forced to deflate, while there is no comparable pressure to reflate on members of the system whose currencies are in excess demand.

By contrast, Mundell argues, if A and B form part of a common currency area, the authorities will be preoccupied with preventing unemployment in A. Hence they will tend, in response to the same initial demand shift, to loosen monetary conditions, in the process giving a boost to inflation in both A and B.

Mundell concluded, therefore, that although fixed exchange rate systems suffer from an inherent deflationary bias, common currency zones have a built-in inflationary bias.

A similar argument has often been put in balance of payments terms. Fixed exchange rate systems, whatever their written rules, invariably impose an unofficial burden of adjustment on deficit rather than surplus countries. By the same token, within any single country there is pressure to equalize levels of employment and output at the level of the most fortunate region – in other words, to increase demand in the deficit regions.

The argument is not entirely convincing, however. Take, for example, the Bretton Woods system (Section 1.5.1). In most cases, it did appear to throw the burden of adjustment on to the deficit country, while surplus countries felt immune to pressure to reflate their economies. However, the one glaring exception to this de facto rule was the USA itself, which was able to run unlimited deficits, thereby swamping any possible deflationary bias in a tide of newly printed dollars. In a sense, the Bretton Woods system involved enforced transfers to the USA from each member country in proportion to its dollar reserves, by a mechanism that is the international analogue of what is called *seignorage* in the context of the domestic economy.

By contrast, the ERM fulfilled Mundell's prophecy. In the early 1990s, Germany generated domestic inflation within the new currency union so as to sustain the level of demand in its eastern provinces. At the same time, it attempted to preserve the external purchasing power of the Deutschmark by a tight credit policy, thereby imposing deflation on its ERM partners.[21]

Unfortunately, as the last example makes clear, Mundell's argument is difficult to verify, because the issue is inseparable in practice from questions of sovereignty, as currencies have so far invariably been associated with independent countries. Putting the matter crudely, the government of a surplus country in a fixed exchange rate system usually feels free to pressure deficit countries to deflate, secure in the knowledge that it will not have to face voters embittered by higher levels of unemployment, interest rates, bankruptcies and recession. By way of contrast, the pressure on a government to inflate so as to reduce unemployment within one of its own regions obviously arises out of political necessity rather than from the fact that the regions share a common currency. Whether the same pressure would be felt within a system such as EMU is doubtful.[22]

In any case, since neither an inflationary nor a deflationary bias can be considered a desirable outcome, it is hard to see how this factor can decisively affect the choice between the two systems. If anything, it would be preferable to have a system that was neutral rather than one with an inherent bias.

In practice, the inflationary bias within individual countries tends to be mitigated somewhat by the existence of so-called fiscal stabilizers. For example, suppose the demand for Scotland's output declines, its unemployment rises, its income falls and its balance of payments with the rest of the UK deteriorates. The result is that tax revenues from Scotland fall, as Scots earn lower incomes and spend less, in the process reducing both their direct and indirect tax bills.[23] In addition, there will usually be an immediate inflow of government transfer payments, in a variety of forms: more unemployment benefits, higher means-tested welfare payments, and so forth. The net effect amounts to an automatic (that is, unlegislated) fiscal stimulus to offset, at least partially, the deflationary effect of the original demand fall. Under these circumstances, the perceived need for government intervention to boost demand in the stricken region is reduced, as indeed is the urgency of a real devaluation, at least in the short run.

It follows that, from this point of view, a common currency is likely to be tolerable where significant fiscal stabilizers are in place, as in the UK and, in particular, in federal systems such as the USA and Germany. The same is certainly *not* true of the EU, where fiscal transfers are negligible in scale and almost never automatic. Europeans still pay taxes to their national governments, not to Brussels. Hence, there is no spontaneous fiscal subsidy to the UK when its balance of payments with the rest of the EU deteriorates,[24] although in the long term poorer countries do enjoy some slight (and politically contentious) subsidies through the EU Regional Fund and a number of other programmes.

11.3.2 Fiscal sovereignty and the treasury[25]

The need for fiscal stabilization is only one of the arguments that have motivated the demands from a number of sources for the imposition of constraints on national fiscal policy and its ultimate subordination to a centralized European budgetary process.[26] Whether or not surrendering national fiscal autonomy in this way is judged to be desirable depends on one's political perspective and is therefore not our concern here. All that can be said is that the desirability or otherwise of a common currency cannot nowadays be considered independently from the issue of fiscal sovereignty.

Apart from the question of fiscal stabilizers, it might appear that fiscal policy independence and currency union are unrelated issues and, indeed, *in principle*, there is no connection between the two. None the less, in the European case at least, fiscal policy has been drawn fully into the sphere of supranational political economy.

Again, the reason has little or nothing to do with macro- or microeconomics. To understand what is at stake, consider the analogy with local government budgeting within a country such as the UK. Broadly speaking, local authorities face a budget constraint that is almost the same as that facing the central government, with one exception (see Section 4.1.2). Both levels of government can finance their expenditure either by raising tax revenues or by borrowing. The only difference is that de facto the central government is not only able to borrow in the normal way (that is, by issuing short- or long-term debt) but also can fund its activity by printing IOUs, which are treated as money by the rest of the economy.

We have already mentioned in the last section the fact that this power generates revenue for the central government from seigniorage. What has not been pointed out so far is that this power to print money has another dimension. Take the case of the UK. As long as the British government restricts itself to borrowing in sterling-denominated forms, it need never – indeed, can never – default on its debt. For example, its gilt-edged stock promises to pay the holder nothing more than a certain number of pounds every six months (the 'coupon') and £100 at maturity. Her Majesty's government will never run out of pounds as long as it controls the Bank of England's printing presses. In other words, its obligations to repay its sterling debts can always be covered by printing pounds and its only obligation to holders of pounds is to redeem banknotes with more banknotes.

Notice that the same is certainly not true of the British government's borrowing in foreign currency. The UK Treasury cannot repay debts denominated in dollars or yen by printing those currencies. That right belongs exclusively to the Federal Reserve and Bank of Japan, respectively.[27]

By contrast, a local authority in Britain could well default, if allowed to do so by central government. If it is either unable or unwilling to pay for its spending by local taxation, then it must borrow and, ultimately, it makes no difference whether it borrows sterling or foreign currency. In either case, it incurs debts that are not denominated in terms of its own IOUs and therefore cannot be repaid from its own printing presses. In this sense, *all local authority borrowing is denominated in a foreign currency* – that is, a currency that is 'foreign' or externally printed from the point of view of the local government in question.

The dilemma is obvious. Again, *in principle* this simply puts the local authority on a par with private institutions such as firms, households, and so forth. But this presupposes that the central government would be willing ultimately to allow the local authority to default or even be driven into bankruptcy, if ever it were unable to pay its debts. By and large, central government is very unhappy indeed about this possibility and tries to avoid it at all cost. In order to do so, it is forced to place direct or indirect constraints on the spending decisions of local government,[28] so as to pre-empt as far as possible a situation where it is forced to choose between being compelled to finance a local authority's borrowing, on the one hand, and allowing it to default on its debts, on the other. This unenviable choice would, of course, be made more difficult by the fact that it would almost certainly involve conflict between local and central governments of different political complexions.[29]

Now, since EMU will reduce national governments to the status of local authorities, with no power to issue their own money, either they must be permitted to default on their debts or they must be constrained. Otherwise, the new integrated monetary authority, the European Central Bank, will ultimately be forced to monetize any and every budget deficit that a national government is unable or unwilling to fund by borrowing, effectively surrendering control over the supply of the common currency. Surrendering the prospect of a member country becoming insolvent is presumably too awful to contemplate, at least for the major European governments, which are less than wholeheartedly committed to market disciplines in other, less sensitive areas of economic life. The only remaining alternative is the imposition of permanent constraints on the fiscal policies of national governments, which then become essentially instruments of the central government, restricted to determining the allocation of expenditures and the tax burden (that is, the microeconomics of fiscal policy), with no direct control over the key macroeconomic variable, the budget balance.[30]

This is a dilemma that ought to have been resolved before currency union took place. In fact, an attempt was made to do this in the Stability Pact (officially, the Stability and Growth Pact), drawn up at the end of 1996, argued over for some months and, subsequently, ignored. However, it is hard to believe that anyone takes this treaty seriously, with its scale of increasing fines for overspending governments,[31] its wide-open escape clauses and its pious commitments to growth. Note that if (or more likely *when*) this problem arises, it is likely to generate far more bitterness than any conflict between a national and local government, because in addition to any current political differences the protagonists are very likely to see the conflict in terms of historic intra-European rivalries.

It is not possible to assess the costs and benefits of this abrogation of fiscal policy by national governments. What can be said is that there are at least two aspects to be considered. In the first place, countries face a cost in so far as they may be forced to relinquish the right to operate a countercyclical fiscal policy. Keynesians especially would argue that the cost of this constraint could be higher unemployment and lower output. But even if (as seems probable) countercyclical fiscal policy is impossible, it is still the case that budget deficits tend automatically to balloon in recessions, as tax revenues fall and welfare and unemployment benefits rise. In order to ensure that the budget deficit stays within the 3% limit in recessions, countries will have to keep their deficits a long way below this level on average over the business cycle, or possibly even to run surpluses on average.

In the second place, as far as the benefits are concerned, if the constraints are binding, the imposition of fiscal rectitude from above may well reduce the borrowing costs for previously profligate member governments, especially if the European Central Bank is a guarantor of their debts. However, governments with a long-established record of conservative budgeting will have little to gain and may well lose. Indeed, an anomalous situation may well arise whereby the conservative countries end up being forced into less responsible fiscal policies.

To see why, consider the situation of a country such as Switzerland, which is expected to join the new union at some stage. Suppose the rules of the currency union permit budget deficits that are higher than Switzerland is running before entry, by whatever measure is adopted (probably in relation to GNP). Under the circumstances, it appears that Switzerland would have little to gain by keeping its borrowing below the maximum permitted. As long as its common currency debt is credibly guaranteed by the European Central Bank that issues it, Swiss government debt would carry no default risk (but then neither would the debt of any other member country) and hence it would pay the same interest rate on its borrowings whether its deficit was bumping up against the ceiling level or only one-quarter as high. Morover, the less it borrowed, the more it would be subsidizing the more profligate governments. There would be no rewards to persuade any country to borrow less than the maximum permissible level. On the contrary, the fact that a thrifty government (especially of a large country) was directly reducing the borrowing costs for less conservative neighbours would act as a strong disincentive to saving.

We conclude that the fiscal constraints will need to be set at a lower level than otherwise (that is, than the pre-entry average or maximum of the member countries) in recognition of the fact that the maximum levels are likely in practice to become the norm. This in turn implies a greater degree of stringency for the majority of member countries.

11.3.3 Monetary sovereignty and the central bank

In practice, the type of monetary policy found in a currency union is likely to depend far more on the character and political complexion of the central bank than anything else. Thus, the recent hyperinflation in Russia had far more to do with the internal politics of its government sector than with the fact that the rouble is used over so many regions with such diverse and divergent economies.

Let us return to the example of Europe. We saw in Chapter 5 that a fixed exchange rate regime is consistent with an independent monetary policy only in the very short run. In practice, this meant that ERM member countries found themselves forced to accept Bundesbank monetary discipline as the cost of remaining in the system.[32]

Now there are two ways of interpreting this fact.

On the one hand, ERM members by and large had far less convincing records of monetary discipline than Germany. By making a public commitment to accept the monetary discipline imposed by the Bundesbank, they hoped to be able to achieve relatively rapid credibility as low-inflation countries. They tried, as it were, to hitch a ride to their desired destination of credibility as low-inflation countries on the Bundesbank's coattails. Without ERM membership, they would have been forced to tolerate far higher interest rates to compensate for the risk indicated by their pre-ERM history of relative laxity in monetary policy. Moreover, they would have had to sustain these high interest rates for as long as it took to convince markets that they really had changed their priorities and were now truly committed to permanently lower inflation. According to this view of events, while it survived, the ERM allowed the UK, France and Italy to reduce their inflation at lower cost (in terms of lost output, high interest rates, unemployment, and so on) than would have been possible outside the system. Of course, with the demise of the ERM this interpretation looks somewhat implausible.

On the other hand, the freedom to purchase short-term benefit at whatever cost in inflation might be regarded by some people as worth preserving. In so far as a country's inflation is the freely chosen outcome of democratic choice, it is hard to see how it can be renounced without some meaningful loss of freedom.[33]

The issue becomes acute only if there is actually a divergence between member countries' preferences in this regard. Of course, the very fact that Germany had so different an inflation history from the other major economies is prima facie evidence of just such a divergence in tastes prior to entry into the system. Was ERM entry ever likely *on its own* to trigger a change in tastes? Or was it expected somehow to make the transition from high- to low-inflation country less painful than otherwise by sig-nalling unambiguously to financial markets a change that had already taken place?

Alas, we shall never know whether ERM entry was actually accompanied by the requisite convergence of tastes, because the system was undermined by an unforeseen calamity rather similar to the one that destroyed Bretton Woods. It will be recalled that a sudden increase in spending by the USA on fighting its wars against Com-munism in Vietnam and poverty at home ultimately proved fatal to the world's fixed exchange rate system in the early 1970s (Section 1.5.2). In a bizarre parallel, the effort to raise East German living standards to West German levels dealt a mortal blow to the ERM. This was the outcome in spite of the fact that the reaction of the monetary authority in the centre countries was completely different in the two cases. While the Federal Reserve accommodated US government spending in the late 1960s by printing dollars and generating worldwide inflation, the Bundesbank preserved its independence in the 1990s by refusing to accommodate an avalanche of fiscal spending it had never endorsed in the first place.

The resulting high real interest rates effectively forced the other ERM members to devote their savings to funding the rebuilding of East Germany. Thus, whereas US overspending in the 1960s was paid for by an inflation tax on Bretton Woods member countries, the ERM meant that German overspending in the 1990s was financed by forced loans from its satellite countries. If given the choice, the other European countries might have preferred the inflation tax to the forced lending, or possibly neither. As it was, the UK and Italy eventually found the price too high and left the ERM, followed soon afterwards by a crisis that finally put an end to the fixed exchange rate system in all but name (see Section 16.2.2).

How have matters changed with the advent of European monetary unification?

On the one hand, the new supranational monetary authority seems admirably independent of political pressure – at least, so far – and has used its independence to retain tight control of the euro money stock. Almost all observers (including the author) anticipated a protracted tug-of-war in the early years of EMU over the appropriate monetary stance, with the ECB host nation Germany using its influence on the side of tight money, alongside Austria and the Netherlands, while France and the so-called ClubMed countries pressed for relaxation.

In the event, the line-up has been almost the opposite, in defiance of Germany's long post-war record of conservatism in economic policy. According to conventional eurowisdom, high German unemployment requires more expansive monetary policy, a view that may yet prevail (as it already has done in the fiscal policy sphere), not-withstanding the more or less universal agreement that Germany's real problem is with the working of its labour markets and its crippling level of social wages. Added to the long-term problem of looming fiscal deficits and the prospect that they will eventually be monetized, it is small wonder that the euro initially fell heavily against the other major currencies after its launch (Figure 11.2), only recovering against the dollar as a result of the US monetary expansion following 9/11. In fact, against the other major currencies it has only recovered its post-launch losses, which suggests it still inspires little confidence, benefiting only from the extreme weakness of the dollar. Indeed, it is a testimony to the lack of confidence in the euro that, at the time of writing, five years after its inception, there are still few signs that the new currency might supplant the dollar as the world's major reserve currency (as was widely

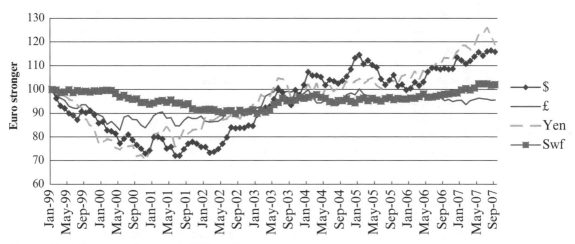

Figure 11.2 The euro (January 1999 = 100)

predicted by euro enthusiasts). Moreover, this is in spite of the exceptionally auspicious circumstances created by the weak dollar policy being pursued by the current US administration.

11.3.4 Costs of transition

For the most part, this chapter has concentrated on the advantages and disadvantages of two possible scenarios: a number of regions with and without a common currency respectively. Little has been said about the transitional costs of moving from one scenario to the other. To some extent, this was because the costs of arriving at a common currency are difficult to assess and would seem to depend on the specific circumstances in the region or regions involved.

At the macroeconomic level, there are, *in principle*, no transition costs. In practice, however, just as some people might think a happy marriage requires the courting couple to start the process of compromise while they are still courting (or cohabiting), those who formulated the original plans for EMU in the early 1990s laid great emphasis on the need for an agreed timetable of economic convergence to precede monetary union. The process was embodied in the so-called *convergence criteria* set out in Table 11.1, which laid down the conditions that candidates would need to satisfy before being admitted to the union in January 1999. The conditions were intended to guarantee inflation and interest rate convergence (for reasons that were never entirely clear) and some degree of fiscal rectitude (for the very clear reasons given in Section 11.3.2).

The costs of satisfying the convergence criteria are impossible to quantify. In so far as they required governments to renounce to a large extent their discretion in setting both monetary and fiscal policy, they actually imposed very tight constraints on national macroeconomic management.[34] In the event, only Luxemburg and Ireland satisfied the fiscal convergence criteria when EMU started, although all the aspiring countries were admitted, with the sole exception of Greece.

Table 11.1 EMU convergence criteria

Fiscal policy		
1	Budget deficit	<3% of GDP
2	Government debt	<60% of GDP
Monetary policy		
3	Inflation (RPI)	<1.5% above the three best-performing countries
4	Long-term interest rates	<2% above the three best-performing countries

As far as microeconomic costs are concerned, there is an important (if obvious) point to be made that serves to emphasize the extent to which the contentious aspects of monetary union are inevitably political rather than economic. The point relates to the cost of changing over to a new currency.[35]

Consider the options facing an economic agent when a new currency is introduced. Where the individual has a choice between using a national currency and adopting a new common currency, the relative attractiveness of the two alternatives will depend on how many other people have already made the switch. Everybody waits for everybody else. Nobody wants to be a pioneer, the lone user of a new standard that is incompatible with everyone else, and with no guarantee, moreover, that the others will ever make the switch. Equally, nobody wants to be left stranded on the old standard. It is a dilemma familiar to all of us from many similar situations where new standards are being introduced.[36]

There is no easy solution to this problem, which is precisely why, under the arrangements for EMU, economic agents were not allowed any such choice. The new currency was simply imposed, while national currencies were simultaneously abolished to become so-called 'legacy currencies'.

Now there were undeniably costs involved in actually switching over from the old to the new common currency: resetting millions of prices and relabelling millions of goods, recomputing wages, presumably rewriting many contracts, and so on and so forth. These costs were unavoidable, with one obvious and important exception: *they could have been reduced to a minimum by adopting as a common currency a national money already in circulation*. The reason is simply that, in this way, the switching costs would be nil for at least one nation in the new union.

For example, had the Deutschmark been chosen as the common currency instead of the euro for Europe, at least the Germans would have been saved the costs of switching over to a new money, while the costs of the other member countries would have been no greater.[37] The fact that this solution was never actually proposed is testimony to the predominance of politics over economics, which is characteristic of most aspects of the plans for EMU.[38]

11.3.5 Common currency and common market

Before leaving this topic, there is one important confusion that needs to be clarified. It arises because many of the arguments used to support the idea of currency union in Europe have in reality little or nothing to do with the subject. In many cases, the supposed benefits are actually the outcome of integrating markets for goods and services and sometimes also of allowing free movements of capital across national borders.

Now there are some situations where it is natural to think of currency union in the context of a single market. There is, however, no *necessary* connection. A single market without currency union is quite possible to visualize, and indeed is perfectly feasible, and although the reverse seems improbable, it is not inconceivable either.

Take the case of the USA. On the one hand, the USA is a more or less completely integrated market[39] with a single currency. On the other hand, in the recently founded North American Free Trade Association, it shows no sign of wanting currency unification with Canada and Mexico. Moreover, the fact that wages and prices still vary somewhat between the different US states would appear to suggest that inter-regional price differentials usually stem from transport and other transaction costs, geographical and climatic variation and, most importantly for Europe, cultural hetero-geneity. If this is the case, there would appear to be little prospect of any immediate narrowing of intra-European prices, even after currency union.

In fact, it has been pointed out by Krugman (see reading guide) that in one import-ant respect currency union is actually less attractive in the context of an established single market. Recall McKinnon's argument that a currency union is justified where the individual economies are very open and hence where exchange rate changes would have a large impact on consumption baskets and, consequently, on wages. On this view, if economies are very open, the option of being able to respond to dis-turbances by devaluing is not very useful.

However, thanks to the single market, European economies are likely to become progressively more specialized, as production concentrates in the lowest cost loca-tions. Inevitably, the result will be a greater vulnerability to shocks. For example, when (if ever) a truly free market in coal is established, whichever country ends up with the lion's share of European production will have an economy that is highly sensitive to fluctuations in world energy markets. Thus, although it may be true that currency union involves few sacrifices in coping with a *given* level of shocks, future disturbances are likely to be increasingly severe for individual European countries as they become more and more specialized and hence more and more dependent on a small number of industries. In these circumstances, they may well regret the sacrifice of their own currencies.

One further comment should be made regarding the political economy of inter-national trade. From time to time in the 1990s, there appeared to be a serious danger of trade war in the industrialized world. To a great extent, the battle lines are drawn up, in three groupings that have been gradually coalescing over a number of years: Europe, North America and the Far East. The almost interminable skirmishing over the World Trade Organization (WTO) agreement exposed the divisions very clearly. The fact that the negotiations ended reasonably successfully is not entirely reassuring in this regard.

Now the construction of the EU has undoubtedly played a major part in splitting the industrialized world into three blocs. Although there is no *economic* reason why currency union should hasten the slide towards a trade war, there is every reason to fear that it may well do so in terms of the political economy of international trade.

11.4 **Currency boards**

11.4.1 Basic principle

A halfway house between fixed rate regimes and complete monetary integration that became increasingly popular during the 1990s is the currency board system. In its simplest form, this involves nothing more than a fixed exchange rate regime with the volume of domestic credit set *by law* at zero. In other words, the (base) money supply equation (Equation 4.10) becomes just:

$$FX + DC = MB \equiv FX$$

The idea is straightforward enough: if every unit of local currency is backed by the equivalent quantity of foreign exchange in the central bank's vaults, then the exchange rate is speculation proof, since, if required to do so, the authorities could afford to buy back the whole domestic money stock. In principle, therefore, the fixed exchange rate is supported by a copper-bottomed guarantee.

As we shall see, most of the currency board systems in the world today are somewhat more complex than this, but the basic principle remains the same. What are its advantages and disadvantages?

First, one obvious drawback to the system is that it is little more than camouflage for a foreign currency regime. Setting up a currency board system based on the dollar,[40] for example, amounts to moving over to a proxy-dollar regime. Instead of disguised dollarization, why not go the whole way and simply use dollars?

Inevitably, the answer relates for the most part to issues of national pride, perceived (as distinct from actual) economic sovereignty and so forth. It is not surprising that the currency board system originally developed as a way of dealing with the money supply control problem in British and French colonies. The colonial power could then supply the reserve currency while exercising direct and more or less immediate control over the money stock of a colony thousands of miles away, without having to concern itself with the state of local money markets, which would often be very thin and unsophisticated. More recently, currency board mechanisms have been adopted as (ostensibly, at least) transitional arrangements, notably by countries emerging from the Soviet Union and hoping to win international credibility either as a prelude to full monetary sovereignty or conversely to incorporation into EMU.[41]

11.4.2 Currency board mechanisms

The detailed working of currency board systems varies somewhat from country to country, but the basic mechanism is as follows. Suppose a country wishes to fix its exchange rate at the level $1.00 = K$ units of domestic currency. Instead of a central bank as normally understood, it has an institution whose sole remit is to hold on to and manage the country's dollar reserves and to use these reserves to preserve the fixed exchange rate. In particular, the currency board is *not* allowed to print money, except in return for foreign currency. It is expressly forbidden from making loans to fund government spending.

Now, suppose an exporter receives a payment of $1m from a foreign importer, deposits the money in a local commercial bank[42] and is credited with K million units of local currency. The commercial bank in turn deposits the $1m with the currency board, in exchange for the equivalent in domestic money. What happens next depends on the bank's cash ratio, which in a pure currency board system would be 100% but is actually lower in some systems. If we assume that the cash ratio is in fact 100%, the commercial bank now has additional deposits and matching reserves of precisely K million units of local currency. The latter are liabilities of the currency board, but they are matched by assets that have risen by $1m.

Clearly, this system keeps the money supply equal to the domestic currency value of the reserves. What would happen if for any reason speculators became convinced the currency would be devalued, because they expected the currency board regime to be terminated? However much domestic currency they presented to the currency board for conversion, there would always be sufficient dollars to meet the demand. Ultimately, speculators could, at least in principle, convert the whole domestic money stock into dollars, at which point the reserves would be exhausted, but all private holdings of domestic currency would also be zero. The assumption is, of course, that, since even under these extreme circumstances speculators could all be satisfied at the fixed exchange rate, they would never have any reason to mount an attack in the first place.

In practice, most currency board systems are less rigid than this. For example, a number of the Caribbean currency boards permit their dollar reserves to fall as low as 60% of their monetary base, while at the other extreme the regime in Hong Kong prevents the ratio falling below 105%. In fact, in 1997 its dollar reserves were over four times as great as its monetary base. Most regimes allow fractional reserve banking, so that the monetary base is determined in the way described, but the money stock is a multiple of the reserves, since commercial banks are permitted to lend in excess of the cash in their tills.

> **Question** *Work through the consequences of a foreign currency inflow into a currency board regime where commercial banks are allowed to lend as much as they like, subject to maintaining a cash reserve of 10%.*

11.4.3 Gold Standard

One particular variant of the currency board system deserving of special mention is the Gold Standard, since it was the predominant international monetary mechanism of the pre-World War I economy. Under the classic Gold Standard, countries fixed the price of an ounce[43] of gold in terms of their own currency. Then their high-powered money stock was simply given by the formula:

$$MB_t = K_g G_t$$

where K_g is the fixed price of gold, G_t is the quantity of gold in the vaults of the central bank at time t and MB_t is the monetary base at the same time. As long as international payments were made in gold, the monetary base would rise when the country had a current account surplus, and hence gained gold, and contract when they had a deficit and a consequent outflow of gold. In practice, flexibility was introduced by allowing fluctuation margins in the gold price, with so-called gold shipment points above and below the central price creating what amounted to a target zone (see Chapter 17).

The way the Gold Standard actually worked in the pre-World War I industrialized countries is still subject to some debate among economic historians. However, what is certainly true is that its breakdown in the 1920s occurred because countries were unwilling to allow their money stocks to contract in proportion to the fall in their gold reserves. Thus, as with all fixed exchange rate systems, the fact that they are made by politicians and can be unmade by politicians leaves them at the mercy of speculators who keep one eye on the country's political scene, a point to which we shall return in Chapter 18.

11.5 Conclusions

The reader may feel that what has been presented here represents a somewhat jaundiced view of the costs and benefits of monetary union. However, this is not necessarily the correct interpretation of the arguments presented in this chapter.

Instead, the position taken here has been that, at least as far as Europe is concerned, the *economic* arguments deployed in support of monetary union are in most cases overstated, in some cases misguided and in others unconfirmed by the evidence produced to date. That broad conclusion should not detract from any purely *political* arguments for or against currency unions, although this is not a subject on which judgement can be passed here.

None the less, it is difficult to escape the feeling that EMU is an idea whose time is past. Rather than a genuine step forward, it is more like an imposed solution, which technology makes it easy to bypass, to yesterday's problems, which technology has already solved. Thus, on the one hand, it avoids the burden of computation, which is trivial nowadays, avoids the costs of conversion, which are minimal, and provides a common accounting standard, which is easily achieved even with multiple currencies. And, on the other hand, it eliminates the need to deal with exchange rate volatility, at a time when derivatives markets are creating more and more instruments to handle currency exposure and when the currency markets anyway look less of a source of instability than stock and bond markets and it seeks to impose a single currency over a group of advanced economies in which currency substitution may well make the task impossible. In the same way that traditional marriage patterns have broken down (or so we are told), to be replaced by serial monogamy or sometimes by polygamy or polyandry, the relationship between citizens and their national currency will dissolve, giving way to a series of temporary loyalties to currencies with momentary attractions or possibly to multiple-currency portfolios held in order to diversify risk and minimize transaction costs.

The most likely result is that, at the very best, the political objectives of EMU will fail to be achieved, simply because the monetary future of Europe will be largely the same as it would have been in the absence of EMU. Of course, at worst, the result will be no less than catastrophic.

Summary

- A monetary union is simply a special case of a fixed exchange rate system, where the exchange rate is fixed irrevocably at one for one. It follows that the advantages and disadvantages of currency unions are for the most part those of fixed exchange rate systems.

- A monetary union holds out the prospect of lower transaction costs in international trade and investment, but the scope for savings seems likely to be small.

- Firms involved in international trade and investment would gain from the elimination of exchange rate uncertainty. But it is in any case only their *net* exposure that is relevant and this will often be relatively small for multinational corporations. Moreover, there are a number different ways in which currency exposure can be hedged at low or in some cases negligible cost.

- In principle, the larger the area covered by a common currency, the lower the cost of gathering price information. The theoretical benefits, however, are likely to be rather limited in practice, at least in the European context.

- The costs of currency union depend on the behaviour of national labour markets, but two contradictory arguments need to be considered:

  - Extending currency zones over areas within which labour is mobile is costless. However, where labour markets are separate for reasons of distance, immigration controls, travel costs, and so on, exchange rate flexibility is helpful in returning real wages to their equilibrium level in the aftermath of a shock. It follows that common currencies should apply only over areas *small* enough to be characterized by labour mobility.

  - On the other hand, devaluation can only reduce real wages as a result of a form of money illusion, and the illusion is likely to be preserved most easily where the cost of living increase following devaluation is smallest – in other words, in relatively closed economies. Hence, on these grounds, currency zones ought ideally to be *large* enough to behave like closed economies.

- One of the few meaningful differences between common currencies and fixed exchange rates is in terms of the political economy of international policymaking. Because fixed exchange rate systems tend to impose the burden of adjustment on deficit countries, they probably suffer an inbuilt deflationary bias, while common currency zones may well suffer from an inflationary bias.

- It is hard to see how a currency union between a number of countries can avoid imposing constraints on the fiscal policies of the different ('local') authorities unless it is willing to contemplate a national government becoming insolvent.

- The question of sovereignty cannot be avoided in determining the complexion of monetary policy within a currency union. If national monetary policy reflects national tastes, it remains an open question how these tastes can or should be aggregated to determine a supranational monetary policy.

- There is no necessary connection between currency union and a common ('single') market. Currency union would be possible without integration of commodity markets, and the opposite is not only theoretically possible but a commonplace occurrence.

Reading guide

The seminal contributions are Mundell (1961) and McKinnon (1963), although see also their very important precursors in Meade (1955) and Friedman (1953).

For a useful collection of readings on the topics covered in this chapter, see the *Greek Economic Review*, 1993, and in particular the contributions by Krugman, Frenkel and Goldstein, and Christou and Dellas. This volume also contains the paper by Dowd and Greenaway, which makes a number of important observations about currency union in the context of a model of network externalities. The evidence on labour mobility within the USA mentioned in Section 11.2.1 was collected by Blanchard and Katz (1992) and quoted in Krugman and colleagues' article in the above-mentioned *Greek Economic Review*. As far as transaction costs are concerned, Hau, Killeen and Moore (2002) find that bid–ask spreads have apparently widened since EMU (see Note 1).

Feldstein (1992) covers many of the points raised here.

Currency board arrangements are summarized in two IMF publications, Baliño and Enoch (1997) and Ghosh, Gulde and Wolf (1998).

The web page of Nouriel Roubini (http://pages.stern.nyu.edu/~nroubini/Emu/Emu.htm) contains useful articles, discussion of EMU and links to other related pages.

Web page: **www.pearsoned.co.uk/copeland**.

Notes

1 Positive analysis attempts to explain why the economy is the way it is, whereas normative analysis seeks to prescribe how government or corporate policies, laws, institutional arrangements, and so on ought to be framed for the economy to operate in a desirable fashion.

2 Monetary disintegration is actually far more topical than monetary integration. After all, EMU is the only formal example of monetary union to be taken seriously since World War II, whereas almost every ex-colony has issued a new currency on gaining its independence and the components of the old Soviet empire are doing the same. In general, monetary disintegration has been far more common than monetary integration.

3 Examples such as these are not frivolous. On grounds of size alone, California is a very serious candidate for monetary independence. After all, its economy is larger than that of Canada or indeed any European country except Germany. Even Scotland has a slightly larger population than Denmark, whose monetary independence was taken for granted before EMU.

4 Not only do Scottish banknotes differ from one another, depending on the particular commercial bank issuing them, but there is even a £1 note, in spite of the fact that in England the £1 note has long since been phased out in favour of a small nickel coin. In some situations, this feature limits substitutability. For example, there are few if any machines that will accept both notes and coins of the same denomination.

5 This is more or less what happened with the Irish punt, which had been unofficially interchangeable with the UK pound for many years, before its being floated as an independent currency on 13 March 1979. On the other hand, the very fact that Scottish and Californian banknotes are universally accepted throughout the UK and the USA respectively can be taken as evidence that almost nobody takes seriously the possibility that they might one day be independent currencies. In fact, Scottish monetary status is very similar to a currency board (see Section 11.4.2).

6 Their flight from the rouble was understandable in the light of near-hyperinflation in Russia. But since dollars and Deutschmarks were already circulating widely throughout the old Soviet Union, the temporary solution of relying on foreign money would have been a perfectly reasonable option. One would have expected issuing their own currency to rank far lower in the list of priorities for governments faced with an array of more pressing economic and social problems.

7 The author has tried to remain neutral in this chapter as elsewhere in the book, although his views may well be apparent if only because, alongside the most frequently aired arguments, we also give space to aspects of the question that are discussed only rarely by British economists.

8 This is not to deny that a variety of supposed macroeconomic advantages have been adduced to support the case for currency union. For example, it could be argued that, under fixed exchange rates, currencies perceived as depreciation-prone may need to be protected by high interest rates for long periods, presumably until the national monetary authority in question has earned enough credibility. In this respect, a national currency could be viewed as a liability, imposing higher interest rates than would otherwise be necessary on the domestic economy.

Even if one takes this argument at face value, however, it has the drawback of being symmetrical: if low-credibility countries (such as the UK, Italy and France in the ERM) carry the burden of excessively high interest rates, then high-credibility countries (such as Germany and Holland) enjoy the benefit of relatively low interest rates.

More to the point, the argument appears to rest on the assumption that currencies are divided into devaluation or revaluation candidates on a more or less arbitrary basis or, at the very least, that there is no close connection between a country's monetary policy and its credibility. If there is any rationality in the way the market assesses the reputation of the respective national monetary authorities, then the credibility of a supranational currency (and hence the accompanying level of interest rates) will depend on the respective national shares in the postunion monetary decisionmaking process (see Section 11.3.2).

9 In the event, some researchers report that spreads on currency transactions in the euro are actually somewhat wider than they were on the old Deutschmark, in spite of higher volumes and, presumably, greater liquidity.

10 The estimates, which may well be overoptimistic, are those published by the EU itself. They assess potential savings as being somewhat greater for the smaller countries and those with less sophisticated financial markets. Moreover, technological advance in money transfer mechanisms in the past decade or so will almost certainly have reduced the true figure below the one given here.

11 Readers familiar with modern portfolio theory will recognize the fundamental proposition involved here. In general, the riskiness of an investment can never be judged in isolation. What determines an investment's contribution to the total risk borne by a company is the covariance of its return with the return on the rest of the company's activities. In so far as the two returns are dependent on a single common factor (for example, the pound/euro exchange rate), there will be some covariance between them. The covariance will be positive if both returns tend to rise when the pound strengthens, and negative if one return rises in situations where the other falls. Unless the covariance is so great as to create 100% correlation between the new risk and the pre-existing risks, the investment still increases the degree of diversification of the company's activities, reducing the overall risk. Indeed, if the covariance is actually negative, then it is a case of swings and roundabouts, with good news on one front offset to some extent by bad news on the other. Under these circumstances, the new investment provides a degree of hedging for the rest of the company's business.

12 These are some of the reasons why, in practice, it is often a very complicated exercise indeed to estimate the impact of exchange rate fluctuations on a company. The situation is complicated further by the fact that the answer depends very much on the currency in which the multinational chooses to do its accounting. Shareholders of US-based multinationals, for example, are normally assumed to prefer to see the accounts in dollars, and so management is preoccupied with currency exposure relative to the dollar. In general, in a world with increasingly integrated equity markets, the presumption that shareholders are exclusively concerned with values measured in their home currency is somewhat dubious. It is probably even less relevant in Europe, where the major Dutch-based multinationals, for example, have millions of shareholders outside the eurozone and, indeed, outside Europe (and where, in any case, two of the very biggest have operated as Anglo-Dutch companies, with accounts in two currencies and shares quoted in more than two).

13 In reality, there is nowadays a whole range of different derivative instruments that can be used for hedging currency risk, for example futures, options, swaps and others. For an explanation of how they work, see the relevant chapter of any up-to-date finance textbook.

14 In terms of domestic macroeconomics, there is no reason to suppose real (that is, inflation-corrected) interest rates will diverge between UK and Germany. The reason is that, under CIRP, nominal interest rates will differ only by the forward premium, which, in turn, is accounted for mostly by the expected depreciation of the currency and, if PPP holds, the latter reflects relative inflation rates.

15 It should also be clear why people organized in barter rings in the UK and the USA are deluding themselves if they think they are somehow behaving more efficiently than those of us in the monetary economy. Even allowing for high transaction charges in banks, they are unlikely to be saving anywhere near enough to cover the inconvenience of barter. However, if barter enables them to avoid or evade direct or indirect tax, then it could be worthwhile for the individuals involved, although not, of course, for society as a whole.

16 Suppose there are N goods in the economy. It turns out that, with barter, $N(N-1)/2$ (relative) prices need to be given in the catalogue, whereas nominating one of the N goods as money reduces the number of (money) prices required to only $N-1$. So even if the number of different goods and services traded in the UK is only 10 000 (an extremely conservative estimate), monetary exchange is more efficient by a factor of 5000.

17 Standardization is unlikely to be successful beyond a certain point simply because pressure from the authorities is in large part offset by the continuing market tendency towards product differentiation. Moreover, it is hard to see why product diversity should be less attractive to politicians and civil servants than it is to consumers.

18 Notice that the presence of hundreds of thousands of Scots or people of Scottish descent in England, North America, Australia, and so on is evidence not of labour mobility but rather of the exact opposite. For the most part, Scots in London have not moved south in response to temporary employment opportunities resulting from the sluggish response of wages to random demand shocks, any more than have the Scots now living in Australia. Instead, in so far as they have been drawn by economic factors, they relate to very long-term growth prospects that have little or nothing to do with exchange rate regimes or indeed with macroeconomics altogether.

19 Unemployment benefits should, of course, be interpreted broadly to include all the benefits available to those not working, including other welfare provisions, benefits in kind, and such like. Experience in the USA shows that where labour mobility exists, the unemployed have a tendency, not surprisingly, to gravitate to wherever the benefits are most generous.

20 Notice that it cannot be argued that workers are simply unable to retrieve the situation. After all, unless labour market participants suffer from some form of what economists call money illusion, one would expect agreements between employers and the labour force to relate implicitly or explicitly to real rather than nominal wages. Hence, what was an equilibrium real wage before devaluation will still be the equilibrium afterwards, unless there has been some other change affecting the relative bargaining strengths of the two sides of the labour market.

21 Notice that the scope for Bundesbank seigniorage under the ERM was presumably much smaller than was available to the USA under Bretton Woods, simply because ERM members had a more or less free choice as to which reserve currencies to hold. By the same token, it is impossible to know how much of the increase in the Deutschmark money stock during the late 1980s and early 1990s was actually circulating as currency in the ex-Soviet bloc countries.

22 One example to illustrate the point is the Republic of Ireland, which until 13 March 1979 was in a de facto currency union with the UK, since it kept the exchange rate of the Irish punt fixed at par with the pound sterling. Yet, of course, no British government felt under any compulsion to reflate in the UK so as to reduce unemployment in Ireland (even supposing reflation would have helped in that regard – a highly dubious proposition).

As far as EMU is concerned, it very much depends, of course, on whether any significant degree of democratic accountability is introduced into the formulation of European macroeconomic policy.

23 Direct taxes are those paid on personal and corporate incomes, while indirect taxes are imposed on expenditures, which in the UK means mainly value-added tax and customs and excise duties.

24 At the risk of labouring the point, it must be emphasized that just because the UK's balance of payments would be more or less unobservable within a currency union, it certainly does not follow that it would be unimportant. Going back to the example of Scotland, a regional balance of payments deficit indicates a net outflow of wealth to the rest of the world. The fact that the

region is not faced with the immediate problem of how to preserve the external purchasing power of its currency is of little comfort if it faces instead a loss of output, employment and wealth.

25 To some extent, this section has been overtaken by events since it was written in early 2002. In particular, I only expected the Stability Pact to be tested seriously in the medium or long term. I certainly never expected it to be exposed as a sham at its first testing. The last year has proved me wrong on both counts and, in practice, it is now consigned to the dustbin of EU history. I have left the section unchanged because it is important for readers to understand the motivation for the treaty and the problems it was intended to solve, which the eurozone is now left to face.

26 In principle, at least, this type of concern is completely independent of arguments about the desirability or otherwise of 'coordinating' (that is, unifying) the detail of fiscal policies, as it affects tax rates, subsidies, payments to and receipts from social security, and so forth, although, of course, the two arguments are likely to be mutually reinforcing in practice.

27 This is precisely why so many countries, mainly in Latin America and Africa, have been forced to default on their debts in the past 20 years, in spite of the insistence of one prominent, if confused, commercial banker in the 1970s that 'National governments don't go bankrupt'.

The reader may well wonder what would be the case in a country with an independent central bank. It all depends what one means by 'independence'. One might think an independent central bank could refuse to print money to redeem a government's (domestic currency) debts. However, this scenario is hard to imagine in practice, at least in any western country. None the less, it must be admitted that the argument here has become very slightly less clearcut following the crisis of autumn 1998, when the Russian government actually defaulted on its rouble debts. Alas, it is too late for Italy or Belgium to go down this route, even if they felt inclined, since their debts have now been translated into euros.

28 The way these limits actually operate is extremely complicated and not relevant to the issues involved here. Note that half or more of local authority spending in the UK is, in any case, funded directly or indirectly by central government. The bulk of the subsidy is in the form of a grant computed according to a formula that is both complicated and little publicized, a fact that, if anything, makes it even harder for the central government simply to turn its back on an insolvent local authority.

Whether the EU will draw any lessons from this sort of situation (and similar problems in other European countries) remains to be seen.

29 As in the case of the City of Liverpool's insolvency in the early 1980s. A similar scenario when New York City was in financial difficulties prompted the notorious headline in one local newspaper: 'RON [Reagan] TO CITY: DROP DEAD'.

30 Notice that even the microeconomic control may ultimately be reduced to near zero (see Note 26).

31 The idea of fines to punish countries with excessive budget deficits, treating them like offending motorists, is a masterpiece of black humour. After all, the reason motorists pay their parking fines is not because they feel any deep sense of guilt but because they know they may lose their car, their salary and ultimately even their liberty if they fail to pay. Fines imposed under the terms of the Stability Pact would be particularly onerous, since they would be adding to the fiscal burden on a high-deficit country, so the question of sanctions to enforce fines is clearly relevant. Unfortunately, the Pact is silent on this subject, either to hide the fact that no sanctions exist or in recognition of the fact that they are too redolent of the 1920s and 1930s to be mentioned in polite society. After all, the outstanding European precedent for international debt collection methods was France's reoccupation of the Rhineland in 1923 (which, in any case, failed to extract the fine).

32 That is to say, their interest rates followed German rates up or down, while in most cases (especially the UK, France and Italy) remaining above German levels.

33 Anyone who doubts that this is the case ought to ask themselves the following question: why are Germany and Switzerland so zealous in their pursuit of low inflation, while the UK and to a lesser extent the USA are so much laxer? The answer surely relates ultimately to the priorities of voters in the different countries, embodied not only in their directly expressed preferences regarding inflation rates but also in the institutional framework they erect. Thus, apart from obvious differences in the extent to which governments exert political control over monetary policy, one notable distinction is in the fact that both the USA and the UK have tax regimes that encourage people to invest in inflation. In the USA, tax relief is granted on consumer

borrowing, but interest income on lending is, for the most part, taxable. In the UK, tax and other incentives have been used over the years to persuade Britons to invest in real estate, thereby giving them a significant stake in inflation.

34 Most of the European electorate seemed to be under the impression that the fiscal conditions had been included in the convergence criteria purely as a temporary transitional measure. In spite of the Stability Pact, politicians did everything they could to keep the electorate blissfully unaware of the need for permanent fiscal constraints on member governments, the Italian government even going as far as to introduce a special one-off 'convergence tax'. Of course, a cynic would say that, since the Stability Pact is probably even less likely to be enforced than were the convergence criteria, it is hardly worth the trouble of informing voters. In any case, the EMU project has never relied on popular support to any noticeable degree.

35 See the reference to Dowd and Greenaway in the reading guide.

36 Among instructive examples of this type of situation are the changeover to unleaded petrol (or catalytic converters in the USA), the conversion of PC users to MS-DOS and more recently to Windows (and the attempts to wean them off those standards), the effort to persuade people to communicate through email, and so on. The *ne plus ultra* of standardization projects must be Esperanto, which has made little headway after over a century of efforts by its enthusiasts, in spite of the fact that the balance of argument must be vastly more favourable to the notion of a common language than to a common currency. Of course, while the notion of a government imposing a common language is regarded as undemocratic, coercion is, for some reason, viewed as acceptable in the case of money.

37 It should be clear that the argument about the choice of currency to minimize transition costs has nothing to do with the question of who ultimately controls the money supply. Thus, although the Deutschmark would be optimal in terms of switching costs, it does not follow that post-unification monetary policy ought to be any different from what is desirable for a new currency.

38 The analogy of a common language for Europe is instructive (see Note 36). Thus, it would be wasteful to adopt Esperanto, for the same reason that a new European currency would be wasteful. The obvious, most economical choice of a *lingua franca* would be English, which is precisely why nobody is contemplating a common language for Europe.

39 Notice that it is not a completely unified market in terms of goods and services. For example, the export of banking services between the states of the Union is limited by the Glass–Steagall Act, which restricts the extent to which banks can set up branches outside their home territory. Moreover, if harmonization of indirect tax rates (as envisaged in the Delors Plan for Europe) and of social security benefits (as in the Social Chapter of the Maastricht Treaty) are to be regarded as essential for a single market, then the USA is a highly fragmented market, with little or no apparent tendency towards integration. Of course, by any sensible criteria, for example the degree of convergence of prices and wages across the country, the percentage of interstate relative to international trade and so on, the USA is undeniably a single market, far more so than Europe.

40 Most use either the dollar or the euro as their reserve currency.

41 The most notable current example is Argentina, which adopted a currency board system in 1991 to convince the markets that it had given up its inflationary habits. By way of contrast, the Hong Kong dollar has been managed by a currency board ever since 1983, even though it has no record of monetary irresponsibility. The ultimate failure of Argentina's currency board system and its consequent default on its large foreign currency debts have in any case cast doubt on this type of halfway house solution. Notice that a currency board system is a compromise between currency sovereignty and monetary union ('dollarization') in the same sense that a fixed exchange rate system is halfway between floating and monetary union. Both compromises rely on the credibility of the government's commitment to the system and, as such, are liable to become unstable the moment that credibility comes into question (as it did in Argentina).

42 The regime may forbid private companies or individuals from holding foreign currency. Alternatively, the exporter may deposit the funds because of the need to pay workers, suppliers, etc. in local currency or because local banks pay attractive interest rates on foreign currency deposits. Of course, if the exporter (and most other people) hold on to foreign currency receipts, the economy ultimately becomes completely dollarized.

43 One ounce is just over 31 grams.

PART III

A world of uncertainty

So far, we have only acknowledged the existence of uncertainty so as to sweep it aside and avoid having to deal with it explicitly. In this part, we confront the issues it raises, starting in Chapter 12 with the introduction of the concepts of rational expectations, market efficiency and unbiasedness. In this context, it is shown that the spot exchange rate can be thought of as containing three components: (1) the forward rate, reflecting market anticipations; (2) other, unobservable random components, resulting from 'news' about the fundamentals; and (3) a risk premium. Chapters 12, 13 and 15 deal with components 1–3, respectively. While the subject matter of the first two chapters overlaps somewhat, Chapter 15 is very different, since it analyses the determination of the equilibrium risk premium using the microeconomics of choice under uncertainty. Chapter 14 also takes a microeconomic approach, but it concentrates on an analysis of how the structure of currency markets affects the way news is embodied in exchange rates in the short run. Chapter 16 examines the mathematics of non-linear systems so as to explain another possible cause of exchange rate volatility, one that is only now being investigated by researchers.

12 Market efficiency and rational expectations

Introduction

The idea of market efficiency is one we have already encountered in Chapter 3. Recall that an efficient market was defined there as one in which prices fully reflect all available information. In this chapter, we go into the subject in greater depth and, in particular, see how market efficiency relates to the concepts of rational expectations and unbiasedness.

Although market efficiency made its first appearance in the finance literature in the early 1970s, the basic idea should be familiar. At some time or other, we have all been given a 'hot tip' on a horse, a share or, nowadays, perhaps even a collectible antique, *objet d'art* or painting. In order to profit from the tipster's information, it has to be true that the quoted odds on the horse, for example, fail to reflect its true prospects ('it can't lose', 'it's a dead cert', and so on). In the case of the share tipster, if we are to make money, we need to know more than simply that company X is going to make large profits. We also need to be sure that those profits are under-estimated by the stock market and hence not fully reflected ('undiscounted') in its current price. Similarly, before investing in a painting, we need to be convinced not simply that it is good but that its true worth has yet to be fully appreciated by the rest of the art world.[1]

The obvious question to ask before acting on a tip is: can we really believe the market has failed to take account of the true prospects for the horse, share or painting, as the case may be? If our tipster has access to information that is not publicly available, then we may be inclined to believe him, on the grounds that the horse's odds or the price of the share is unlikely to reflect inside information, almost by definition.[2] However, if our tipster has no privileged access to information, then we are unlikely to be impressed, unless there is some obvious reason why the rest of the market should be so sluggish in the first place.

In a sense, market efficiency is simply a special case of a fundamental principle of economics, one we have already encountered a number of times in this book. In essence, it is the application of the 'no free lunch' argument to the field of information, because in so far as the market price fails to incorporate publicly available information, there must exist unexploited profit opportunities.

Our concern in this chapter is with the consequences of market efficiency for the relationship between spot and forward exchange rates. In the first section, as an essential preliminary to the material in this part of the book, we explain what is meant by an expected value. (Readers who are familiar with elementary statistics can safely skip this section.) This concept is central both to the rational expectations hypothesis, which is the subject of Section 12.2, and to the idea of market efficiency, covered in the next section. We go on to look at two special cases of market efficiency: unbiasedness and the random walk model, in Sections 12.4 and 12.5 respectively.

When we turn to look at the facts, we find that there are some very severe difficulties to be overcome in arriving at any kind of test of the theories outlined in this chapter. These problems are described in Section 12.6. Some of them are apparent simply from an eyeball scan of the data, as is shown in the next section. However, more rigorous methods have been applied by the many researchers in this field and their work is briefly surveyed in Section 12.8. The chapter ends, as usual, with some conclusions, a summary and a reading guide.

12.1 Mathematical expected value

As a preliminary to the exposition in this section, we introduce a concept taken directly from the theory of statistics.[3]

> The (**mathematical**)[4] **expectation** or **expected value** of a (random) variable, X, written $E(X)$, is the weighted average of all possible outcomes, where the weight on any outcome is equal to its probability.

Since this concept is an important building block for what follows in this and succeeding chapters, it is worth looking at a very simple example. Imagine a lottery, in which 300 tickets are sold, half of which (that is, 150) will win no prize at all. Of the remaining 150 tickets, half will win a prize of £1 and half the top prize of £5. To demonstrate what is meant by a mathematical expectation, the expected value of a ticket in the lottery has been calculated (Table 12.1).

Table 12.1 How to calculate an expected value

1 Outcome of ticket purchase: prize value	2 Probability of outcome	3 Product $(1) \times (2)$	4 Error $(1) - E(X)$	5 Product $(4) \times (2)$
£0	0.50	£0.00	−£1.50	−£0.750
£1	0.25	£0.25	−£0.50	−£0.125
£5	0.25	£1.25	+£3.50	+£0.875
Expected value of ticket: $E(X)$		£1.50	Expected value of error: $E[X - E(X)]$	£0.000

Now consider the value of a lottery ticket to a potential purchaser. In the first column, we have listed all three of the possible outcomes resulting from the purchase of a single ticket and in the second column the probability of each outcome's actually occurring. In Column 3, we put the product of the value of the outcome to the ticket holder (that is, the prize) and the probability of its occurring. In Column 3, therefore, we have a zero whenever we are dealing with an outcome valued at zero, as in the first row, or whenever we are dealing with an outcome with zero probability. Of course, there are an infinite number of outcomes with a zero probability weighting (that is, impossible events), all of which can safely be ignored since they contribute nothing to the total at the bottom of Column 3. By the same token, we must include all outcomes that are associated with both a positive probability and a non-zero prize value.

Notice that the probability weights in Column 2 add up to one, since we have taken account of all possible outcomes of the lottery. In that sense, the expected value of £1.50, calculated by totalling Column 3, is a weighted average.[5]

Since we could in principle compute the expected value for any prospect, however complicated, it should be clear that the expected value has considerable superficial attractiveness as the best single number to use in comparing alternative risky propositions. More importantly, it corresponds to what we might intuitively feel to be the best guess of a person's likely winnings, in the sense that, if we took a random sample of ten ticket holders, the chances are they would win an average prize of £1.50 each.

Notice the paradoxical situation: the average prize is the 'most likely outcome' for the average taken over a random sample or for an individual's average winnings if the lottery is repeated a number of times. Yet, at the same time, we can be absolutely certain that not a single ticket will actually end up winning £1.50.[6] A more intelligent guess for a single individual would be to take the most frequently occurring outcome or modal value, as it is called, which, in this case, is a zero prize.

There is another sense in which the expected value provides the best forecast. In Column 4, we see the errors that would be made by someone using the expected value of £1.50 as a forecast of the payoff to holding a ticket. Thus, if the outcome turned out to be a zero prize, the error made would be −£1.50; if it turned out to be £1.00, the error would be only −£0.50; and in the event that the ticket won the big prize, the error would be + £3.50. Column 5 weights these errors by the probability of their occurrence, 0.5, 0.25 and 0.25 respectively, to arrive at their weighted average – in other words, the expected value of the error. As can be seen, the expected error is zero, with overestimates exactly offsetting underestimates.

This calculation illustrates a very important property of expected values. What we have found is that even in cases where the outcome is never equal to (or anywhere near equal to) the expected value, *a forecast based on it will still be correct on average*. Even though I know a lottery ticket picked at random will not win £1.50, that remains my best guess. Since, by definition of a mathematical expectation, the best forecast of the error is that it will be zero, there are no grounds for adjusting it either up or down.

Unfortunately, most decisions involving uncertainty are a lot more complicated than our hypothetical lottery. This is the case not only because we typically have to deal with far more complicated prospects, with a greater number of possible outcomes and consequently more difficult computations. Most important of all, it is really only in games of chance that we can be sure of the probabilities that are attached to the outcomes – which is precisely why examples such as these figure so largely in textbook expositions of probability theory. In real-world situations, for example when we are forced to take a view about the future value of the exchange rate, there is no equivalent of the rulebook to tell us how many tickets have been sold and how many prizes are on offer. In this respect, we have to deal with a genuine forecasting problem, rather than a purely arithmetic exercise like the one in this worked example.

In practice, what we have to do is to make use of whatever relevant information is available, so as to arrive at an assessment of the probability of each possible outcome for the future exchange rate. From that point onward, the computation of the expected value is straightforward, as we have seen. What information will be used in arriving at an estimate of the probabilities? That will depend on the circumstances, but in principle any information that is relevant could be of use. We shall have much more to say on this question later. For the moment, we introduce an important extension of the concept of expected value:

> The **conditional (mathematical) expectation** of a variable, X_t, written $E(X_t/I_{t-j})$ is the expected value computed with the aid of a particular set of facts, I_{t-j}, known as the **conditioning information set**.

The definition might appear to the reader too vague to be of practical application. After all what does it mean to say 'computed *with the aid of . . . facts*'? In fact, provided the conditioning set contains only quantifiable information, the problem is more apparent than real, since statistics and econometrics have established well-researched techniques for deriving an estimate of the expected value of a variable from the observed values of a set of conditioning variables.

12.2 Rational expectations[7]

We are now in a position to introduce the concept of rationality in expectations.

Consider a hypothetical agent in the foreign currency market.[8] Until now, we have taken for granted that all such individuals hold some view or other of what is likely to be the value of the spot exchange rate in the future, and we have called that view 'the representative investor's expectation' or 'the market expectation'. From now on, since there is a possibility of confusion, let us refer to this as the investor's *subjective expectation*. It is subjective in the sense that it is inside the investor's head, unobservable and unquantifiable, other than by asking the agents directly.[9]

In particular, a subjective expectation need bear no specific, clearly defined relationship to the facts – which is not to say that it is formed without any reference whatsoever to the facts, but simply that the relationship between a *subjective* expectation and the *objective* data is purely arbitrary. That is precisely why, so far, nothing has been said about how the investor arrives at his subjective forecast. It might be by pure intuition, by a more visceral gut reaction, or by consulting charts showing past movements in exchange rates or other variables. It might be with the aid of astrology or it could be by frequenting the same pubs and restaurants as the foreign currency traders and listening to their gossip. A subjective expectation is simply one held by the individual in question – in other words, *one that is not necessarily the same as the conditional expected value of the variable in question*.

Now suppose it happened to be the case that the two *were* the same. Suppose that an investor did hold a subjective expectation that happened to be the same as the (objective) conditional mathematical expectation. Furthermore, suppose the same state of affairs applied to the market as a whole or, at least, to a majority of market participants. As we shall see, a number of important conclusions would follow from that fact with regard to the relationship between spot and forward exchange rates. For the moment, we introduce the following definition to refer to situations such as this:

> An economic agent is said to hold a **(fully) rational expectation** with respect to a variable if his subjective expectation is the same as the variable's (mathematical) expected value, conditional on an information set containing all publicly available information. The **rational expectations (RE) hypothesis** states that the market's (subjective) expectations are in fact the same as the expected value, conditional on the set of all available information.

Put more loosely, an investor whose expectations are rational does the best that he (or anyone else) could do in forecasting the future exchange rate. A point worth noting, however, is that for an expectation to be rational, it does not need to have actually been derived by performing any particular set of calculations, neither of the kind in the lottery example considered earlier nor of any other kind. It might have been calculated in a way that we feel is completely subjective, or even by methods viewed by many as downright irrational, such as astrology, Chartism, or whatever. As long as the outcome is a number that coincides with the objective conditional expectation, it is rational in the economist's sense of the term. Putting the matter differently, we could say that experienced traders, whose livelihoods depend on their ability to keep ahead of the market, behave *as if* they computed expected values.[10]

Now, if we recall the properties of the mathematical expectation, we can see what is implied by the RE assumption. If investors are rational in forming their expectations, they will often be wrong; in fact, they may be wrong all the time (as in the lottery example), but however large their errors, *on average* they will be correct. In this respect, their behaviour is consistent with the traditional view of rational economic man. The rewards to being correct are large – potentially unlimited (at least in principle). It would therefore be irrational to employ any forecasting method that could be improved. Any forecasting process that generates systematic errors – that is, errors that exhibit a non-random pattern, however complicated – can be improved by a method that exploits the pattern in the errors. It would therefore be irrational of agents not to squeeze this remaining element of forecastability out of the data.

Consider the implications for an observer, an economist, say, watching the behaviour of rational investors. If he can build a model, however complicated, that forecasts more accurately than the subjective expectations of the agents in the market, then by definition their expectations cannot be rational. If, however, their expectations are truly rational, they will be identical with those emerging from the best model that the economist can build, putting all the available information to the best possible use. In this respect, RE can be viewed as a consistency requirement: if the economist believes in a particular model of the economy (or of a part of it), he must believe that agents form expectations consistent with its prediction.[11]

Before going any further, it would be as well to write the RE hypothesis formally. Up to this point, we have used S^e to denote the spot exchange rate that agents expect to see prevailing one period hence (say, at time $t + 1$, assuming that the current period is time t). Under RE, that subjective market expectation will be the same as the mathematical expectation of the next period's spot rate, conditional on a particular information set, the one containing all publicly available information. In terms of the notation introduced along with the definition in the last section, this conditional expectation is $E(S_{t+1}|I_t)$, where I_t is the set of all data in the public domain at time t. Since we will often have cause to refer to expectations conditional on this broad set of publicly available information at some period or other, we shall use the abbreviation E_t. So, $E_t S_{t+1}$ means the expected value of the period $t + 1$ spot rate, conditional on information available to the market at t. Similarly, $E_{t-j} S_{t+k}$ means the expectation of the period $t + k$ exchange rates, based on information dated $t - j$ or earlier.[12]

Using this notation, RE implies that market expectations can be written:

$$S_t^e = E(s_{t+1}|I_t) \equiv E_t s_{t+1} \tag{12.1}$$

where the lower-case s means the natural logarithm of the exchange rate.

It is normal to specify the RE hypothesis in terms of logarithms so as to avoid a problem in translating from pounds per dollar to dollars per pound. Obviously, it would be desirable to have a situation where, if the market anticipated an exchange rate of £1 = \$2.00 at some point in the future, it also expected to see at the same date that \$1 = £0.50. Since the sterling price of dollars, S, is the reciprocal of the dollar price of sterling, $1/S$, this amounts to requiring that the market's (subjective) expectation of S is the reciprocal of its (subjective) expectation of $1/S$ – in other words, that:

$$S^e = 1 \bigg/ \left(\frac{1}{S}\right)^e$$

or, alternatively, that:

$$\frac{1}{S^e} = \left(\frac{1}{S}\right)^e$$

Unfortunately, however, it is a feature of the mathematical expected value that it does *not*, in general, satisfy this criterion. In other words by and large:[13]

$$\frac{1}{E(X)} \neq E\left(\frac{1}{X}\right)$$

The advantage of specifying Equation 12.1 in log terms is that, since the log of S is simply the negative of the log of $(1/S)$, we have $-(\log S) = E(-\log S)$ or, in the shorthand introduced earlier in the book: $-E(s) = E(-s)$, and the problem is solved.

Note that Equation 12.1 formalizes the RE assumption about the market's (period t) expectation of the period $t + 1$ exchange rate. Ask yourself the question: under RE, what will have determined the exchange rate the market expected at $t - 1$ for the current period, t? Plainly, at $t - 1$, the information set available consisted only of I_{t-1}, hence:

$$s_{t-1}^e = E(s_t | I_{t-1}) \equiv E_{t-1} S_t \qquad (12.1')$$

and so on.

Before going on to consider the implications for market efficiency, it will be helpful to introduce one more definition. Since the cost of collecting and processing information (measured in terms of effort, time or money) can be prohibitive, even when the information is in principle accessible, there may well be circumstances where rational individuals base their expectations on only a subset of the available data. In a sense, this is what we mean by 'a rule of thumb': trading a measure of accuracy, which may not always be needed, for convenience and speed, which certainly are needed, particularly in guiding day-to-day, hour-to-hour trading decisions.

One possible simplification would be for agents to limit themselves to looking at the past history of the series being forecast. For example, they might form their forecasts of the future exchange rate by deriving the best possible prediction, based solely on the history of the exchange rate over the more or less recent past. In other words, faced at time t with the problem of predicting the future exchange rate, S_{t+1}, they might simplify the task by limiting the conditioning information set to the series of past exchange rates: $S_t, S_{t-1}, S_{t-2}, S_{t-3} \ldots$[14] We introduce the following definition:[15]

An economic agent will be said to hold **weakly rational expectations** with respect to a variable if his subjective expectation is the same as the variable's (mathematical) expected value, conditional on an information set containing only the past history of the variable being forecast. Formally, weak rationality implies subjective expectations of the variable, X_t, are given by:

$$X_t^e = E(X_t | X_{t-1}, X_{t-2}, X_{t-3}, X_{t-4}, \ldots)$$

Notice that a weakly rational expectation can never be a better forecast than a fully rational one and will usually be a poorer one. From now on, rational expectations will always be assumed to be *fully rational* – that is, conditioned on all publicly available information – unless we explicitly state otherwise.

12.3 Market efficiency

Having dealt with market expectations, we now refocus attention on the way the currency market operates. Suppose the forward and spot markets are characterized by the following conditions:

■ presence of a number of investors with ample funds available for arbitrage operations when opportunities present themselves

■ absence of barriers to movement of funds (no exchange controls)

■ negligible transaction costs.

Now consider the following scenario. Imagine a British investor who thinks that the spot price of dollars in terms of sterling is going to be 10% higher in 12 months than it is today. Will he be able to profit from his hunch?

Plainly, if he is willing to back his judgement, and transaction costs are negligible, then he may be able to profit by buying dollars (selling pounds) forward, then selling the dollars spot at the end of 12 months. If he proves right, his profit will be 10%, less any transaction costs, *less the premium paid for forward dollars*.

However, if the same view is shared by the rest of the market, or at least by investors with access to sufficient funds, the situation cannot persist. In the absence of any impediment, the forward dollar will be bid up until the premium is high enough to deter any further speculation.

At what point will the forward premium be sufficiently high to deter speculators? It is tempting to argue that speculation will continue until the forward exchange rate has reached a point at which it is just equal to the consensus view of the future spot rate at the relevant horizon. That would be going too far, however. At some point, investors will feel that although they can still see the likelihood of a profit from speculation, *the probable reward is no longer great enough to compensate for the risk of being wrong*. In other words, speculation will cease (equilibrium will be reached) at the point where the gap between the forward rate and the market's expectation of the future spot rate is just equal to the required risk premium.

Now if we assume the market's expectations are rational, we can write this equilibrium as follows:

$$f_t^{t+1} = E_t s_{t+1} + \rho_t$$
$$= u_{t+1} + \rho_t \tag{12.2}$$

where the left-hand side is the (log of the) forward price of dollars at time t for delivery one period later (at $t + 1$), and ρ_t is the market's risk premium. Equation 12.2 represents an efficient market equilibrium[16] because the forward rate reflects both the publicly available information summarized in the rational expectation, $E_t s_{t+1}$, and the market's attitude to risk, as embodied in the risk premium.

To see the implications, rewrite Equation 12.2 by subtracting s_{t+1} from both sides, to give:

$$f_t^{t+1} - S_{t+1} = [E_t S_{t+1}] + \rho_t \qquad (12.3)$$
$$= u_{t+1} + \rho_t$$

The crucial term is u_{t+1}. It has been substituted for the expression in the square brackets on the right-hand side, which is simply the percentage gap between what the market expected the exchange rate to be at $t + 1$ and the actual outcome. Now since, by assumption, the market's expectation is rational, that error will have very special properties, as we have seen. Specifically, it will be strictly random, showing no discernible pattern – with a mean value of zero and correlated with neither contemporaneous nor past spot or forward rates. In particular, u_{t+1} viewed in isolation will show no systematic pattern of variation over time.[17] The reason for this is that under RE, as we have seen, the expectational error must itself be unpredictable, otherwise potentially profitable information remains unexploited.

Equation 12.3 summarizes the efficient market hypothesis as stating that the gap between the forward rate and the spot rate actually ruling when the forward contract matures (the left-hand side) is the sum of two components: a completely random expectational error and a risk premium. The latter could be positive or negative, constant or variable, large or small relative to the expectation error – in the absence of any knowledge about investors' attitudes to risk, we are in no position to judge.

Finally, notice that Equation 12.3 implies:

$$S_{t+1} = \rho_t + f_t^{t+1} - u_{t+1} \qquad (12.4)$$

or alternatively, shifting the process back one period:

$$S_t = -\rho_t + f_{t-1}^t - u_t \qquad (12.4')$$

which implies that the spot rate can be viewed as the sum of three components: the previous period's forward rate, plus the risk premium ruling in the market at the time, plus an unpredictable, expectational error. This general relationship is the subject of the remainder of the present chapter. The next two chapters will focus on the factors determining the unpredicted component, u_t, and the risk premium, ρ_t.

In terms of estimation, which we shall consider at greater length in Section 12.4, notice that unless we are willing to make some assumptions about how the risk premium is determined, Equation 12.4 does not allow us to relate the spot rate time series to the series of forward rates observed one period earlier. However, if we are happy to impose some kind of tractable structure on the risk premium (for example, that it is constant over time, that it fluctuates randomly about its mean value, or whatever), then we can proceed to test whether the spot rate and forward rate are related in the way predicted by the efficient market hypothesis.

Finally, notice that it is quite possible to imagine a situation where the market price reflects only the restricted information set used in forming weakly rational expectations. In this case, the expected values in Equations 12.2 and 12.3 would be conditioned only on the past history of the exchange rate, rather than on the universe of publicly available information.

> A **weakly efficient market** is one where the market price reflects the information in its own past history. There are, therefore, no unexploited opportunities to profit by making use of the price series alone.

Notice that, in a weakly efficient market, there will normally remain opportunities to make a profit by exploiting information *additional* to the past history of the market price.

12.4   Unbiasedness

In Section 12.2 we saw what was involved in assuming that expectations were formed rationally. In the next section, we made additional assumptions about the way the currency market functions so as to allow us to follow through the implications of the efficient market hypothesis. In the present section, we take the process one stage further. In addition to the assumptions embodied in forward market efficiency, let us make the simplest possible assumption about investors' attitudes to risk: *suppose they are risk-neutral.*

We saw in Section 3.1.3 that risk neutrality meant, by definition, that market agents required no risk premium to persuade them to undertake risky transactions. In the present instance, that means they are willing to speculate on their judgement as to the future spot rate for no reward – or at least, up to the point where the reward is negligible. In other words, they will push the forward rate to the point where it is equal to the rationally expected future spot rate, so that ρ_{t-1} in Equation 12.4′ is reduced to zero.

At that point, we will have:

$$S_t = f_{t-1}^t - u_t \tag{12.5}$$

That is, the spot rate is simply the forward rate that was set in the previous period, plus or minus a random error. We shall refer to this restricted form of forward market efficiency as the unbiasedness hypothesis.[18] Formally:

> **Unbiasedness** will be said to obtain when the forward market is efficient and investors are risk-neutral, so that the forward rate is equal to the (mathematical) expectation of the spot rate at the time the contract matures.

Notice that Equation 12.5 can be rewritten in terms of the rate of depreciation, by taking s_{t-1} from both sides to give:

$$S_t - S_{t-1} = (f_{t-1}^t - S_{t-1}) - u_t \tag{12.5′}$$

which says that the actual rate of change in the exchange rate is equal to the one anticipated in advance, as reflected in the previous period's forward premium or discount (in parentheses on the right-hand side), plus or minus a random error.

Consider the implication for exchange rate forecasting. If Equation 12.5 is a true description of the way that currency markets operate, then the forward rate we observe at any time is actually an optimal forecast of the next period's spot rate, in the sense that it will be proved wrong only to the extent of a random error. As we have seen, that means it cannot be improved on by any other forecast using publicly available data. In fact, since there is little in the way of inside information[19] in currency markets, we can say categorically that unbiasedness implies that the forward rate cannot be bettered as a forecast.

12.5   The random walk model

As already noted, the concept of an efficient market was developed in the finance literature, where it was applied for the most part to the operation of stock markets. The theory was developed to explain an apparent regularity in share prices observed by statisticians examining time-series patterns in stock markets. What the statisticians found was that stock prices seemed to follow a pattern known as a random walk. Ever since then, the notion of a random walk and an efficient market have been associated in many people's minds, though there is in fact no necessary connection, as will be demonstrated later.

First, the definition:

> A time series, X_t, is said to follow a (pure) **random walk** if the change in X_t from one period to the next is purely random.

That is, if we have:

$$X_t = X_{t-1} = u_t \tag{12.6}$$

or alternatively:

$$X_t - X_{t-1} = \Delta X_t = u_t \tag{12.6'}$$

where u_t is *completely random*, displaying no pattern over time.

Slightly more generally:

> A time series, X_t, is said to follow a **random walk with drift**, d, if the change in X_t from one period to the next is equal to the drift factor, d, plus a purely random component.

That is, if we have:

$$X_t = X_{t-1} + d + u_t \tag{12.7}$$

or alternatively:

$$X_t - X_{t-1} = \Delta X_t = d + u_t \tag{12.7'}$$

where u_t is completely random, displaying no pattern over time.

Now, as far as exchange rates are concerned, it is easy to show that:

■ The random walk model is perfectly compatible with RE, efficiency and unbiasedness.

■ Having said that, there is nothing in RE, efficiency or unbiasedness that *requires* the spot rate to follow a random walk.

Take RE first. If the spot rate follows a random walk with drift:

$$S_t = S_{t-1} + d + u_t \tag{12.8}$$

then, taking expectations in Equation 12.8 conditional on the information set at $t - 1$, we have:

$$E_{t-1}s_t = E_{t-1}s_{t-1} + E_{t-1}d + E_{t-1}u_1 \qquad (12.9)$$
$$= S_{t-1} + d$$

because s_{t-1} is presumed known at time $t - 1$, and so is the (constant) drift factor, d, and because the expected value of the next period's random error, u_t, is always zero. Hence, with a random walk, the RE forecast of the next period's spot rate is simply the currently observed rate plus or minus the drift factor, if any. In the absence of drift, an agent's best guess is that the next period's rate will be the same as the current rate. In fact, the reader will find that it is quite straightforward to demonstrate[20] that, at time $t - 1$, s_{t-1} is the RE forecast of the spot rate in *all* future periods, in the absence of any drift.

In terms of the *change* in the spot rate, the pure random walk model implies that agents with rational expectations forecast neither depreciation nor appreciation over the next period.

On the other hand, suppose that the spot rate does *not* follow a random walk. Take, for example, the following process:

$$s_t = \alpha s_{t-1} + \beta s_{t-2} + \gamma Z_t + \delta Z_{t-1} + u_1 \qquad (12.10)$$

where Z is some other variable (for example, the relative money stock). Since past values of both s and Z are assumed known at $t - 1$, we have as the RE forecast of the next period's spot rate:

$$E_{t-1}s_t = \alpha s_{t-1} + \beta s_{t-2} + \beta s_{t-2} + \gamma E_{t-1}Z_t + \delta Z_{t-1} \qquad (12.11)$$

which, although more complicated than a random walk, is no less acceptable.

It is now easy to see that both efficiency and unbiasedness of the forward market are potentially consistent with *any* of these processes: the random walk (Equation 12.8), the example of a more general process (Equation 12.10) or indeed any other process. Looking back at our formal definition of forward market efficiency in Equation 12.2 it is obvious that, for a random walk, we will have simply:

$$f_t^{t+1} = S_t + \rho_t \qquad (12.12)$$

In other words, the forward rate ruling at t for delivery at $t + 1$ will be equal to the spot rate in the market at t plus the risk premium. Under unbiasedness (in other words, with risk neutrality) the forward rate fixed at any period will be simply that period's spot rate, so that the forward premium will always be zero.

On the other hand, with the spot rate generated by Equation 12.10, efficiency implies that the forward rate is given by Equation 12.11 plus any risk premium.

It has been demonstrated that a random walk is neither necessary nor sufficient for forward market efficiency. None the less, it is worth giving an intuitive explanation of why a random walk is not a necessary implication of the 'no free lunch' condition. It might seem, at first glance, that any process other than a random walk leaves open the opportunity for profit. Certainly, it is true that the expected return from holding the currency over a single period, which is the same as the change in the (log of the) spot rate, will be zero only if the spot rate follows a random walk. In virtually all other cases, the return will be predictably non-zero. How can this fact be reconciled with efficiency?

The crucial point to understand is that as long as any predictable component in the spot rate depreciation is fully embodied in the forward rate, as it will be in an efficient market, the opportunity for profit is illusory. Suppose that the spot rate is actually generated as in Equation 12.10, so that the expected spot is given by Equation 12.11. Subtract the latter from the former to give:

$$S_t - E_{t-1}s_t = \gamma(Z_t - E_{t-1}Z_t) + u_t \qquad (12.13)$$

as the profit made by a speculator paying the rationally expected spot rate at $t - 1$ and selling on the spot in the next period. Now although this profit is likely to be non-zero in any particular instance, it is *on average zero*, as can be seen by taking expectations conditional on $t - 1$ information in Equation 12.13, and remembering that, under RE, the error made in forecasting Z_t will itself be random.

Alternatively, if for simplicity we assume risk neutrality, then the left-hand side of Equation 12.13 is the return to signing a forward contract at $t - 1$ to buy foreign currency in the next period at the RE rate (that is, $E_{t-1}s_t$), and, on delivery at t, selling the currency spot.

A numerical example will show that the point amounts simply to a generalization of our conclusions in Chapter 3 regarding interest rate parity to take account of uncertainty.

Suppose that rational economic agents expect the exchange rate of the pound to depreciate by 5% over the next month, on the basis of their knowledge of the past history of the pound (if at all relevant), the past history of other relevant variables, if any (for example, Z, in Equation 12.11) and, if necessary, their (equally rational) forecasts of future values of Z. If the forward rate is an unbiased index of the expected future spot rate, the pound will stand at a 5% discount so that a speculator will, on average, gain nothing by buying dollars forward in order to sell spot next period. Neither will speculating on the spot be profitable. Recall the conditions of interest rate parity: with the pound expected to depreciate by 5%, the interest rate on dollars must be 5% lower than on sterling. Hence, the gross 5% return from holding dollars for one month will be just equal to the opportunity cost in interest forgone. So much will be true whatever the underlying process driving the spot rate.

12.6 Testing for efficiency: some basic problems

We now move on to the problem of assessing the evidence on efficiency and the related concepts introduced in this chapter. In view of what has already been said, the reader should not be surprised to learn that, in practice, there are a number of very serious obstacles to be overcome before we can arrive at satisfactory answers to questions: Are the currency markets actually efficient? Is the forward rate an unbiased forecast of the future spot rate? Are expectations rational? And so on.

Notice first that RE *on its own* is not a testable hypothesis. Looking back to the formulation in Equation 12.1 it is obvious that even if we had access to data on subjective expectations, from surveys of market sentiment for example, we would still need to specify a model of the exchange rate itself, from which to derive the objective, conditional expectation. We would then face the problem that, in so far as market expectations differed from the predictions of the model, the divergence could be attributed *either* to irrationality *or* to a misspecified 'objective' model. In other words, since we have no way of knowing the true model of the exchange rate, it is impossible to say whether the market's expectations are derived from the right model, while ours are from the wrong one, or vice versa. This dilemma should be familiar from Section 3.4, where it was referred to as the joint hypothesis problem.

Fortunately, however, there is a way round the problem, provided that we have direct evidence on subjective market expectations, and it involves a stratagem that is frequently of use in applying RE models empirically. Consider the implication of writing s_{t+1} in place of $E_t s_{t+1}$ on the right-hand side of Equation 12.1. In view of what we know to be the property of the mathematical expected value, this substitution would introduce a random error into the equation. In fact, we can always follow this strategy since, by definition, for *any* variable, X:

$$E_t X_{t+1} \equiv X_{t+1} + W_{t+1} \qquad (12.14)$$

where w_t has a mean of zero and is serially uncorrelated. For convenience, we shall henceforth refer to this device as an *RE substitution*.

We shall defer consideration of the results of testing RE directly by this method until Section 12.8.

As far as efficiency is concerned, there are also very serious difficulties encountered when testing an equation as general as Equation 12.4. Intuitively, the problem can be seen from the fact that as long as we place no restrictions on the risk premium (which is, of course, not directly observable), there will always be some path or other that it might have been presumed, after the fact, to have taken in order to preserve the relationship – that is, to be consistent with a random error term, u_t. A practical test of efficiency, then, requires that some additional assumption be made about the behaviour of the risk premium, the obvious one being that it is constant, though more complicated time-series models have been tried.[21]

12.7 Spot and forward rates: background facts

In looking at the background to efficiency studies, we shall concentrate on the exchange rate between the pound and dollar since January 1971. The reader may rest assured that the salient features of the relationship between the spot and forward rates are shared by all the major currencies.

Start with Figure 12.1, which plots the spot rate against the lagged one-month[22] forward rate. Unbiasedness requires, as we have seen, that the spot rate on, say, 15 February 1984 is *on average* equal to the one-month forward rate that ruled in the market on 15 January 1984. The graph superimposes those two observations (spot for February, forward for January, and so on) so as to provide an eyeball test of unbiasedness.

At first glance, Figure 12.1 may look encouraging. Certainly, the forward rate does appear to track the spot rate very closely. However, the match is more apparent than real. Look first at the turning points of the two graphs. In virtually every case, it is the spot rate that leads the change of direction, up or down. Only at the

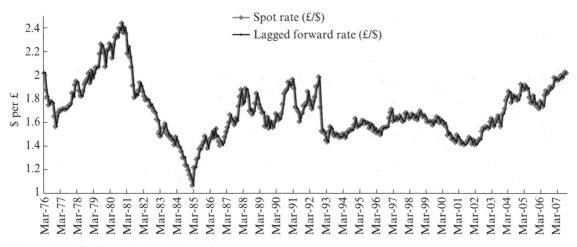

Figure 12.1 Spot and lagged forward rate

next observation does the (*lagged*) forward rate follow. In other words, February's change of direction was completely missed by January's forward rate and is only reflected in February's forward rate. The interpretation has to be that when market sentiment changes, it results in a change of direction in both spot and forward rates simultaneously. For example, a sudden wave of bullishness about the pound pushes up both the spot price of sterling and its price for 30-day delivery, so that *the predominant influences on the forward rate are exactly the same set of factors that determine the spot rate.*

This suggests that spot rates may be linked more closely to contemporaneous than to lagged forward rates. In fact, this conjecture turns out to be absolutely correct – to such an extent that a graph of the spot exchange rate against the contemporaneous forward rate would show the two lines so close together as to be completely indistinguishable. In statistical terms, the correlation coefficient between the spot and unlagged forward rate is 0.9998,[23] compared with 0.9730 for the lagged forward rate.

Figure 12.2, which plots the relationship between the change in the spot rate and the previous period's forward premium, confirms the impression that forward rates simply mimic spot rates after the fact, with little or no predictive content. Notice first how small the premium or discount is compared with the amplitude of the subsequent changes in the spot rate. Furthermore, the premium is not only invariably smaller in absolute terms but also far less volatile. Not surprisingly, it seems that the volatility of spot exchange rates, which has been mentioned so many times already in this book, has for the most part been unanticipated. Statistically, the forward premium has a standard deviation less than one-fifth that of the actual outcome it ought to predict. Moreover, the correlation between the two series is virtually nil.[24]

At this point the reader might well pause and consider the following question: under what type of circumstances would it be *rational* for the market to set the forward rate equal to the concurrent spot rate? For what type of (spot rate) process is the observed value at *t* the best forecast one can make of the future rate?

The answer, as we have already seen in Section 12.5, is the random walk model. Now, it is probably not true that spot rates follow a pure random walk. But the

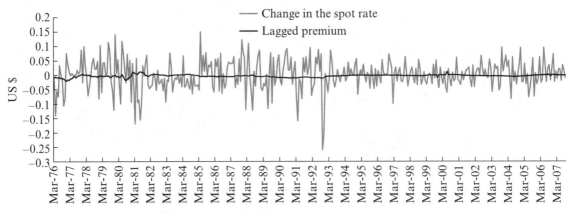

Figure 12.2 Spot rate and the lagged forward premium

approximation is close enough for a forecast based on a random walk to be quite hard to beat.[25] For the data period in the graphs, the forward rate forecasts better than the previous period's spot – in other words, the forward premium or discount is a better prediction than no change at all – but the improvement is tiny.[26]

12.8 Results

To summarize the facts, it appears that the forward rate contains little of use in the way of a *forecast* of the future spot rate but instead is dominated by the trend in the spot rate at the time it is set. Does this finding in itself contradict the unbiasedness hypothesis?

Looking back at Section 12.4 it plainly does not. Nothing in Equation 12.5 or Equation 12.5′ requires the forward rate to be a *good* predictor of the future spot rate. All that is required for unbiasedness is that the forward rate be an *unbiased* predictor – in other words, one that is not systematically wrong.[27] In terms of Equation 12.5′ we have established, as background information, that u_t is both large and highly volatile relative to the lagged premium. But the question that is relevant to unbiasedness is whether u_t is random (that is, unpredictable) or not.

This question was the starting point for most of the early research and the results are now well established. Although the first studies seemed broadly to support unbiasedness, most recent work has pointed to the opposite conclusion. This may be due partly to the more sophisticated and powerful tests applied by later researchers.[28] However, it may also indicate that currency markets have become more inefficient in the past decade or so, contrary to what one might reasonably have expected in view of the continued removal of controls on international capital movements, the enormous improvements in the technology of money transfer, and the consequent fall in the cost of transactions.

Specifically, most of the early work involved fitting equations of the following form:

$$s_t = a + b f_{t-1}^t + v_t \tag{12.15}$$

by ordinary least squares regression.[29] Looking back at Equation 12.5 it is clear that unbiasedness implies that the fitted equation ought to have the following properties:

(1) estimate of the intercept, a, insignificantly different from zero

(2) estimate of the slope coefficient, b, insignificantly different from unity

(3) v_t serially uncorrelated.[30]

Tests on data from the 1920s seem broadly supportive. Results for the post-1972 floating rate era seem much less so, particularly when more powerful testing methods are deployed, with some currencies appearing not to satisfy properties 1 and 2[31] and others not satisfying property 3.[32] Far worse, however, is the fact that many researchers report finding a negative slope coefficient in tests of the equation:

$$\Delta s_t = a + b(f_{t-1}^t - s_t) + v_t \tag{12.16}$$

If $b = 1$ in Equation 12.15, then Equation 12.16 is the same equation with s_{t-1} deducted from both sides, stating formally that the forward premium at $t - 1$ is an unbiased forecast of the exchange rate depreciation over the future period. It would be bad enough to find that empirical estimates of b were significantly less than one, and even worse to end up with results that left it insignificantly greater than zero. But the common conclusion that b is actually negative is a major puzzle for the economics profession, and one to which we shall return in Chapter 15.

Notice that the evidence from fitting equations such as Equation 12.15 is not only relevant to the question of unbiasedness. As noted in Section 12.2, efficiency implies an equation such as Equation 12.15, *if the risk premium is constant*. Under these circumstances, we should only expect to find properties 2 and 3 satisfied. In fact, the evidence reported by recent research provides little or no support even for this hypothesis.

Among the other approaches to empirical testing have been:

- a battery of tests on the properties of the forecasting errors (u_t in Equation 12.5)
- similar tests on the errors from Equation 12.5′
- tests of Equation 12.15, allowing for a non-constant intercept – in other words, allowing for a varying risk premium
- tests on the interest rate differential. Recall that under uncovered interest rate parity, the interest rate differential is equal to the expected rate of depreciation. If we can assume RE, then we have:

$$E_t s_{t+1} = S_t = r_t - r_t^* \tag{12.16}$$

Now an RE substitution in Equation 12.16, replacing the expected exchange rate by the *actual* exchange rate, should introduce only a random error, so we can write:

$$s_{t+1} - s_t = r_t - r_t^* + u_t \tag{12.17}$$

The question then is whether or not, in regressions of the change in the exchange rate on the interest rate differential, we find, first, a regression coefficient not significantly different from unity and, second, a truly random error term.

The enormous volume of published (and unpublished) research is in many cases highly technical, since it often involves the solution of some very awkward statistical problems.[33] None the less, at this stage a consensus view seems to have emerged – and it is clearly *against* unbiasedness and, by and large, against the constant risk premium version of efficiency. In other words, in terms of Equation 12.15, even allowing for a non-zero intercept is insufficient to rescue the model.

This conclusion is reinforced by the results of direct tests of the no-unexploited-profit condition. If the foreign exchange market is efficient, then it should be impossible to find a trading rule to beat the market. The best strategy ought to be simply buy and hold, since this involves the minimum of transaction costs. A typical system of the kind traditionally used by some traders can be defined as follows:

> An *x%* **filter rule** allows the would-be speculator to profit from a trend by buying a currency whenever the exchange rate rises by *x%* from a trough and selling it short[34] whenever it falls by *x%* from a peak.

This definition of a filter rule, while broadly accepted, is somewhat incomplete. First, it needs to be modified in order to take account of transaction costs, since they are likely to be sizeable, at least in comparison with the naive, buy-and-hold alternative. Second, the returns to the filter rule need to be adjusted for interest costs in order to preserve comparability with the naive strategy.

Even allowing for these costs, however, the results for the most part show that a number of filter rules turned out profitable over the floating rate period. More surprising still is the fact that these trading rules appear to make money even in an *ex ante* sense: filter rules that were found to have been profitable in one period seem to have remained profitable for years after the original results were published![35]

However, looking beyond this more or less unanimous negative conclusion, the consensus evaporates.

There are, as we have seen in Section 12.6, two possible explanations for the failure of the efficiency hypothesis: either the market is efficient, but with a non-constant risk premium, or expectations are irrational; or both. This particular issue is currently still unsettled. A number of studies have been published purporting to show that, once allowance is made for fluctuations in the risk premium, efficiency is preserved, at least for some of the major currencies.

By way of contrast, consider attempting to test RE directly, using survey data. To see how that could be achieved, introduce an RE substitution on the right-hand side of Equation 12.1 to give the following:

$$S_t^e = S_{t+1} + v_{t+1} \tag{12.18}$$

That is, under RE, market expectations will be fulfilled, plus or minus a random error. In other words, if we carry out a survey of market participants' forecasts of the future exchange rate, they should turn out to be correct *on average*.

It might seem a simple matter to carry out the exercise of sampling the market participants' views and comparing them with the actual outcome. In practice, it has proved difficult to accomplish until quite recently. In the first place, for a number of reasons (probably including cost) the requirements of research had to await those of the practitioners, who have only in the past few years organized an ongoing survey of market sentiment in London and New York. There are therefore relatively few data at the moment, although this problem will become progressively less important as the survey data accumulate.

More intractable are the problems of actually interpreting survey findings so as to derive a single number that measures, on a particular date, the market's expectation of the exchange rate expected for a future date. For example, what is to be done about the fact that, while we have assumed that the market is unanimous in its view of the future, surveys tend in reality to find a wide divergence of expectations? The usual solution has been to take the median response as the 'market expectation', but this is obviously far from satisfactory, particularly if the degree of unanimity varies over the sample period. Furthermore, since in a postal survey there is no way of pinpointing with complete accuracy the date at which the expectation is formed, it is difficult to be sure that any apparent bias is not due to misdating.

In spite of these and a host of other problems, a number of attempts have been made to extract information about market expectations from survey data, with mixed results. Again, early work seemed consistent with rationality. However, the most thorough study to date, by Frankel and Froot (1987),[36] concluded that:

- Apparent irrationality was indicated by the persistent bias found in respondents' expectations, particularly in the mid-1980s.

- Since expectations bias tended to be associated with forward premium bias, it could not be explained by a risk premium. In any case, the gap tended to be far too large (an average of 7%) to be explained away in this fashion.

- The nature of the bias appears to have varied over different episodes in the recent history of the currency markets.

However, note that the same authors, notwithstanding their own findings, conclude:

> There is nothing in our results to suggest that it is easy to make money speculating in the foreign exchange markets.

12.9 Conclusions

What can we conclude about the forward market? Are the facts consistent with RE and/or efficiency and/or unbiasedness? It should be clear from Section 12.8 that unbiasedness looks, at least at this point in time, a completely untenable proposition. As far as rationality and efficiency are concerned, the jury may still be out, but the case for the prosecution certainly looks very strong and it seems more and more likely that the verdict will ultimately go against either or both of the hypotheses.

The theoretical implication is clear: there is money to be made in the forward market. However, the reader would be well advised to sit tight and finish the book rather than rush out to make his fortune as an amateur currency trader.

The recurring problem in financial markets is that opportunities always seem to open up *ex post* – with the benefit of hindsight – never *ex ante*. It is possible to identify discernible patterns in time series of exchange rate movements but, once isolated, the patterns seem not to be repeated. If the future cannot be reliably assumed to follow the patterns established in the past, then any forecast will be built on shifting sand.

None the less, this writer cannot help but finish an assessment of the research results with a sense of bewilderment at the apparent inefficiencies uncovered: the trading rules that seem to deliver clear profit, the expectational bias and, most amazing of all, the increasing evidence of irrational expectations.[37] To uncover such anomalies in labour or goods markets would hardly be surprising. But, as has been mentioned several times before, currency markets are dominated by the large-scale traders: commercial banks investment banks and treasury departments of multinational corporations. They have instant access to massive databanks, and they have at their fingertips the technology with which to analyse the information. The rewards for being right are enormous, but the penalties for being wrong are as great.[38] Can it really be the case that this type of market is *systematically and predictably* wrong – time after time? It is difficult to credit and even more difficult to imagine why this should be so.

Summary

- The (mathematical) expectation or expected value is a type of average result and it is computed by taking the probability weighted sum of all the possible outcomes of an uncertain event. The expected value, conditional on a particular information set, is the mathematical expectation calculated using that information. The expected value of deviations from the mathematical expectation is itself zero.

- The rational expectations hypothesis is the theory that the market consensus forecast of the future value of a variable is identical to its (mathematical) expectation, conditional on all publicly available information. If expectations are formed rationally the market will still make wrong forecasts, but its errors will be random.

- The forward market can be said to be efficient if the forward rate ruling at any time is equal to the rational expectation of the future spot rate when the contract matures, plus the risk premium that speculators require in order to compensate them for the additional risk they bear.

- If investors are risk-neutral, the risk premium will be zero. In this special case it follows that efficiency requires the forward rate be an unbiased forecast of the future spot rate – the so-called unbiasedness hypothesis.

- The so-called random walk model of the spot rate is not inconsistent with RE and efficiency. Having said that, it is not required by either RE or efficiency.

- Even a casual examination of the facts reveals that the forward rate is without doubt a very poor forecast of the future spot rate. In general, the forward premium drastically underestimates the amplitude of subsequent spot rate fluctuations. Furthermore, it appears to be dragged along with the concurrent spot rate, showing no tendency whatsoever to foreshadow future changes of direction.

- Published research results indicate fairly conclusively – at least for the moment – that the forward rate is not an unbiased predictor of the future spot rate. Furthermore, the results are not encouraging for the more general hypothesis of market efficiency. There is substantial, albeit not overwhelming, evidence of unexploited profit opportunities in the currency markets. Moreover, the deviations from efficiency that have been uncovered seem difficult to square with any simple pattern of risk premium variation. Research using survey data appears to indicate that the explanation may lie in irrational expectations.

Reading guide

See Minford and Peel (2003) for a textbook treatment of RE in general. The classic reference on RE is Muth (1961) and, on efficiency, Fama (1970).

Surveys of empirical work on forward market efficiency date very rapidly indeed. A simple one is to be found in Froot and Thaler (1990). Among the graduate-level textbooks that cover this topic are Sarno and Taylor (2002).

Among the most influential articles in the literature have been: Frenkel (1976), Frankel (1980), Hansen and Hodrick (1980) and Baillie, Lippens and McMahon (1983), the last two focusing on the technical issues, and Frankel and Froot (1987), which uses survey data. See also Bansal (1997) and Baillie and Bollerslev (2000).

Web page: **www.pearsoned.co.uk/copeland**.

Notes

1   We are, of course, considering the painting purely as an investment, abstracting from any non-pecuniary value that it may give to its owner.

2   It is, however, not completely impossible for the market price to incorporate inside information. For example, in the equity market, once it becomes clear to market participants, or at least to a sufficient number of them, that a particular individual habitually trades on the basis of inside information, they can benefit from a free ride by mimicking his trading pattern. In the process, they may cause the market price to behave exactly as though the inside information were publicly available. Arguments scuh as these have led some people to argue that insider trading ought to be legalized.

3   For more details, see any textbook on mathematical statistics or probability.

4   Where there is no possibility of confusion, it is normal to refer simply to the 'expectation' or 'expected value' of a variable, with the *mathematical* expectation understood.

5   The reader may check for himself that if the probabilities of the three outcomes had been equal (that is, one-third each), the expected value calculated in Column 3 would have turned out to be exactly the same as the (unweighted) average, or arithmetic mean – in other words, (£0 + £1 + £5)/3 equals £2. We could, in this special case, safely ignore the probability weighting.

   Some readers might find it helpful to think of the mathematical expectation as analogous to a centre of gravity for the distribution of the outcomes.

6   Of course, most of us have encountered this paradox before in the case of social statistics. For example, the average number of children per household or the average number of cars per person is never a whole number.

7   The reader would be well advised to look back at Section 3.4 before proceeding.

   Note that, for the most part, we ignore transaction costs throughout this and succeeding chapters. In practice, they are a negligible factor in currency markets and, in any case, allowing for them would change our conclusions only minimally and in straightforward ways.

   It should be understood, however, that these remarks refer exclusively to the cost of actually dealing (brokerage commissions and so on). They certainly do *not* apply to the costs of collecting and processing information, which may well be very substantial and whose existence may well have very important effects, some of which are considered in the text.

8   We restrict attention to the currency markets at this point. In fact, the rational expectations hypothesis was developed in the context of (closed economy) macroeconomics and has been applied to markets as diverse as those for financial instruments, labour, capital goods, consumer goods, shares, insurance, and no doubt many others.

9   For example, by survey methods. For some years, a number of economists in the USA have gone straight to the horse's mouth in researching market expectations.

10 Those familiar with elementary microeconomics will recognize the force of the 'as if' caveat. Consumers, for example, are assumed to maximize satisfaction without even knowing the meaning of the term 'marginal rate of substitution', let alone computing it and consciously equating

it to the price ratio. Likewise, firms are supposed to maximize profits without, in most cases, consciously setting marginal cost equal to marginal revenue. The assumption is that whatever considerations guide their decisionmaking, they behave, on average, as if they follow the operating principles necessary to result in a profit-maximizing output choice.

If all this seems far-fetched, given the enormous difficulties in actually calculating the RE value of the future exchange rate, consider the following analogies from outside economics. If we wished to model the behaviour of a car driver, calculating whether or not he has time to overtake in traffic, we would have to build a horrendously complicated mathematical model of speeds of convergence, rates of acceleration, and so on. We would then assume that the driver behaved as if he solved the problem instantaneously when deciding whether or not to overtake. Similarly, programming a snooker-playing robot to apply the correct force to the cue so as to play even the simplest shot would involve some very involved mathematics indeed.

In each case, what we call a person's judgement, intuition or experience results in a shortcut to the solution of an apparently complex mathematical problem.

11 For this reason, it might have been better if the theory had been called the consistent expectations hypothesis.

Note the paradox. The applied economist expends vast amounts of time, computer power and such brainpower as he can muster in an effort to arrive at the true model, while laymen operating in the market know the model and its predictions all along or, at least, behave as if they do. In this respect, the RE hyphothesis turns traditional approaches to economic modelling on their heads. Instead of models that assume an omniscient economist observing blinkered agents, we now have (almost) omniscient agents being observed by ignorant economists. Surely such humility is unparalleled in any other profession?

12 We assume that information is never lost. In other words, the market's knowledge never decreases as time passes. New information arrives and is added to the information set, without anything ever being forgotten – at least, not if it is relevant to the expectation. It follows that the information set at any time includes all previously available information, plus whatever 'latest news' arrives during the period. So comparing $E_{t-5}S_{t+1}$ and $E_{t-4}S_{t+1}$ for example, if the two differ at all, the latter will be the more accurate forecast, as a result of new information arriving during the period $t - 5$. If no new information that bears on the exchange rate for $t + 1$ arrives during that period, then the two forecasts will be identical, since $I_{t-4} = I_{t-5}$. What can never arise is a situation where the later expectation is less accurate than an earlier one.

13 This characteristic of expected values is known as Jensen's inequality.

14 We assume here and throughout the book that the values of all variables subscripted t are actually known at time t.

15 This definition is not in standard usage. It is introduced largely for consistency with the widely used concept of weak form efficiency, which will be introduced in Section 13.3.

16 Strictly speaking, the interpretation of efficiency given here corresponds to what Fama (1970) calls semi-strong form efficiency. Strong form efficiency applies when the market price reflects *all* information, whether publicly available or not. Since inside information is not usually regarded as important in currency markets, we ignore this distinction here.

17 In the jargon of statistics, the time series u_t will be pure white noise – that is, with a (theoretical) zero autocorrelation function and zero cross-correlations with, in other words, other variables whose values are known at time t.

18 Although this usage is by no means universal. A number of writers identify Equation 12.5 with efficiency, which seems over-restrictive, while Bilson (1981) calls this condition speculative efficiency.

19 It could be argued that knowledge of day-to-day central bank intervention policy constitutes inside information. Even so, it is hard to imagine this knowledge actually giving central banks a forecasting edge over the market.

20 By repeated substitution, writing each future period's spot rate as the previous period's rate plus a random error.

21 Ideally, the assumptions would themselves be derived from a model of the determination of the risk premium (see Chapter 15).

22 Strictly, the 30-day forward rate. We shall ignore this complication in the text, although the graphs plot properly synchronized series.

23 Meaning that over 99% of the variation in the spot rate was associated with a move in the forward rate. Interestingly, although the dataset has been extended for successive editions of this book, these correlation coefficients have changed by less than 0.01% as the end date has stretched from 1988 to 2007.

24 In fact, the correlation coefficient is negative, although not statistically significant.

25 In fact, in two well-known papers, Meese and Rogoff (1983) showed that this naive model outperformed all other models on a number of different criteria.

26 In terms of one of the standard criteria for assessing forecast accuracy, mean squared error (the square root of the mean of the squared prediction errors), the forward premium improves on the random walk model by less than one-half of 1%.

27 To paraphrase Churchill on democracy, all we require is for the forward rate to be the worst predictor of the future spot rate . . . apart from all the others.

28 Early work used single-equation regression, for the most part, while a majority of the studies appearing in recent years have involved estimating multivariate time-series models of one kind or another.

29 For an explanation of regression techniques, see any textbook of statistics or econometrics.

30 That is, uncorrelated with its own past and hence containing no further information. In any case, the hypothesis tests on the coefficients a and b are invalid unless v_t satisfies this condition.

31 For technical reasons, most researchers test the joint hypothesis: $a = 0$ and $b = 1$.

32 Interestingly, the currencies that tend to fail the tests seem to vary from researcher to researcher, a fact that may indicate data inconsistencies.

33 The literature concentrates, for the most part, on refining tests of different versions of the basic equation. Among the refinements are multivariate tests (that is, taking account of possible linkages between the spot rate for currency A and the forward rate for B, and so forth), tests with overlapping contract periods, spectral analysis, a number of non-linear tests, and so on.

34 An investor is said to be 'long', or have a long position in a currency (or other asset), when he has more assets than liabilities denominated in the currency (or asset). Conversely, he is short when his assets in the currency are less than his liabilities. 'Going short' or simply 'shorting' a currency, then, means borrowing in the currency so as to incur debts that will be devalued if the currency subsequently depreciates. A short position is therefore one that generates a profit if the currency's value falls, and vice versa if it rises.

35 At least, according to Dooley and Shafer (1983), who used 1%, 3% and 5% filter rules. On the one hand, this could be taken as evidence that foreign exchange traders are missing out on the profits they could make by reading the academic literature. On the other hand, of course, it could be that traders are busy actually applying more successful trading rules than those found by academics – and are unwilling to share their secrets with the rest of us. Notice that even if this is the case, it still begs the question of why the opportunities unearthed by Dooley and Shafer and others are left unexploited.

36 For the US dollar against the pound, Deutschmark, Swiss and French francs, and yen.

37 Evidence of irrationality has been reported by Taylor (1988) in survey data on forecasts made by professional investment managers with respect to inflation and stock market indices.

38 For example, according to *The Economist* on 28 May 1988, one US bank made profits of $338m from foreign exchange trading in the final quarter of 1987 alone. It lost $19m in the same department over the next three months.

Of course, on the one hand, the profit switchback is an indication of the rewards to good forecasting. On the other hand, the profits earned are also prima facie evidence of *ex ante* market inefficiency.

13 The 'news' model and exchange rate volatility

Introduction

Chapter 11 focused on the relationship between the spot exchange rate and the previous period's forward rate. In this chapter and the next attention is switched to the factors which account for the gap between the two. Look back at Equation 11.4′: in words, this says that the spot rate at time t can be written as the sum of the forward rate and risk premium set in the previous period, *plus a random error*.[1] We will be concerned in this chapter with the latter. As will be seen, the error arises from the mistakes made by economic agents in forecasting the future spot rate errors, which, if we can assume rationality, must be attributable to newly arrived information – 'news',[2] for short.

Now at a superficial level, identifying news might appear simple, in conceptual terms at least, if not in practice. We can all conceive of news items that are bound to be relevant to the exchange rate: announcements of economic statistics, political changes, new international monetary arrangements, and so on. But, apart from the (often insurmountable) problem of how to quantify the news, there remains the difficulty of actually isolating the element of surprise. This is critical because, taking a simple example, it is not the *gross* estimate of the UK trade deficit that has an impact on the pound's exchange rate. Rather, it is the extent to which the announced trade balance is greater or less than anticipated by the market before the fact. This, in turn, means that in order to arrive at a measure of the underlying *net* 'news' component in any 'gross' information, we need first to have an estimate of the market's *ex ante* expectations with regard to the variable in question.

The outline of this chapter is as follows. We introduce the concept of 'news' in Section 13.1 by analysing an ultra-simple model. The next section examines a more complicated example: the monetary model with interest rate parity imposed, an unresolved issue from Chapter 5. In Section 13.3, we look at some of the problems involved in making the 'news' approach operational and Section 13.4 gives a brief summary of the main findings of empirical research in this field. The final section focuses in more detail on some of the possible explanations offered for the volatility of exchange rates, which is so difficult to reconcile with the 'news' approach – or, indeed, with any of the other models we have examined in this book.

Before going any further, it is worth drawing the reader's attention to one point about the material in the present chapter. As will become clear, the 'news' model is, by its very nature, less of a self-contained theory of exchange rate determination than an approach to estimating a variety of (possibly competing) theories. Because this is the case, it is almost impossible to separate the analysis of the underlying model from the implications for empirical testing, so that the present chapter inevitably involves somewhat more detailed discussion of the technical (and especially econometric) issues than the other chapters in this book.

13.1 The 'news' model: a simple example

We start by examining an ultra-simple model in order to illustrate the 'news' approach, as well as some of the problems associated with it. The simplest and most general example of a news model would take the following form. Suppose the (log of the) spot exchange rate is given by the relationship:

$$s_t = \gamma z_t \tag{13.1}$$

where γ is a slope coefficient and z_t is the variable or variables[3] determining the exchange rate. We shall call z_t the 'fundamentals' or 'fundamental variables'.[4]

Now, assuming RE, agents will form their expectations of next period's spot rate using Equation 13.1, specifically, at time $t-1$ they will use the available information in the set I_{t-1} so as to form the conditional expectation of s_t, which, given Equation 13.1, means:

$$E_{t-1}s_t = \gamma E_{t-1}z_t \tag{13.2}$$

In other words, *forming a (rational) expectation of the exchange rate involves, as a prerequisite, forecasting the fundamentals*. In terms of the forecast errors we obviously have, subtracting Equation 13.2 from Equation 13.1:

$$s_t E_{t-1}s_t = \gamma(z_t - E_{t-1}z_t) \tag{13.3}$$

The left-hand side of this equation is the unexpected component of the spot exchange rate. The term in the brackets on the right is the 'news': the surprise component of the fundamental variables in z_t. So Equation 13.3 tells us that the relationship between the unexpected exchange rate and the 'news' about the fundamental variables that drive it is identical to the one between the *level* of the exchange rate and the *level* of the fundamentals.

Notice that the RE assumption is critical in two respects. First, because it amounts to assuming that economic agents know the true structural model linking the endogenous variable s_t to the fundamentals, it allows us to conclude that the same structure will link expectations of those variables. So if, as in the case considered here, the spot rate is simply a multiple, γ, of the fundamental variable or variables in z_t, the *expected* spot rate will likewise be the same multiple of z_t.

Second, RE allows us to deduce that the 'news' will be that part of the fundamental variable which is not only unforeseen but also *unforeseeable* – at least using the dataset I_{t-1}. This is a very important point. The term in brackets in Equation 13.3 is the deviation of the actual outcome of the fundamental variable (or variables) from its (or their) mathematical expected value. As we saw in Chapter 6 these deviations are random, in the sense that they have an average value of zero and display no systematic pattern over time. Any non-random component that remained would represent a potentially predictable element unexploited by market agents using the information available at the time.

Note that under *pure* RE (as distinct from weak rationality) the information set, I_{t-1}, includes all publicly available information. Under weak rationality it is simply the past history of each of the fundamental variables. We shall return to this point later.

In addition to demonstrating the philosophy of the 'news' approach, and in particular the central role of RE, this ultra-simple model illustrates two further points.

First, as already mentioned, Equation 13.3 bears a straightforward relationship to the efficient market model of the previous chapter, as can be seen by using Equation 11.2 to rewrite it as:

$$s_t E_{t-1} s_t = \gamma(z_t - E_{t-1} z_t)$$
$$= f_{t-1}^t - \rho_{t-1} + \gamma(z_t - E_{t-1} z_t) \tag{13.4}$$

where, it will be recalled, the first two terms on the right-hand side are the forward rate set at time $t-1$ for currency to be delivered at t and the risk premium respectively. Now, Equation 13.4 is simply the general version of the efficiency model with the expectational error (u_t in Equation 11.4' for example) written out explicitly in terms of 'news' regarding the fundamentals. In fact, it is in this setting that most researchers have preferred to deal with the 'news' model, for purposes of empirical testing at least. However, it should be emphasized that it is quite possible to formulate a 'news' model without any reference to forward market efficiency, as indeed has been done most simply at the start of this section. The only really essential building block is RE, and it is by this assumption that the 'news' approach stands or falls.

On the other hand, the simple model illustrates the sense in which the 'news' approach is just that and no more – hardly a model at all, more a methodology or an approach to modelling. To see that this is the case, notice that nothing has so far been said about the contents of z_t. Nor is this accidental. The 'news' approach is essentially agnostic about the fundamentals of exchange rate determination, with the choice being based on the particular researcher's theoretical predilections or on purely ad hoc criteria, occasionally on market lore or sometimes simply on practical considerations of data availability.

Whatever kinds of consideration guide the choice of fundamental variables, there is one inescapable feature of real-world foreign exchange markets that is ignored in this ultra-simple model: the central importance of the prospective capital gain or loss from holding a currency. It is now time to rectify this omission and, in the process, tie up a loose end from one of the earlier chapters of this book.

13.2 The monetary model revisited

The reader may recall that one issue left unresolved in the analysis of the monetary model in Section 5.3 concerned the impact of interest rates. The problem arose because although there could be no doubt about the sign of their effect on the exchange rate, it seemed implausible to treat interest rates as exogenous in view of what had already been said about uncovered interest rate parity (UIRP) in Chapter 3. We now return to the model so as to deal with this question.

Let us reformulate the problem. Recall that in the monetary model the exchange rate depends on three variables: relative money stocks, income and interest rates. If we again write the relationship in logs, we have:

$$S_t = \tilde{m}_t - c\tilde{y}_t + b\tilde{r}_t \qquad (13.5)$$

where c and b are positive parameters, $\tilde{m}$ and $\tilde{y}$ refer to (the logs of) relative money stocks and income respectively (that is, the difference between the logs), and $\tilde{r}$ is the interest differential.

Now UIRP will not hold in the form that we encountered it in Chapter 3 unless we persist in assuming risk neutrality, as we did there. Allowing for risk aversion, however, means replacing UIRP (as in Equation 3.4) by:

$$\tilde{r}_t \equiv r_t - r_t^* = \Delta s_t^e + \rho_t \qquad (13.6)$$

where ρ_t is the premium required by speculators who switch from one currency to another in order to profit by expected, but uncertain, exchange rate fluctuations. The reader may verify by using the CIRP condition (in which there is, of course, no risk premium) that Equation 13.6 is consistent with the formulation of forward market efficiency in Equation 11.2 – the risk premium is one and the same, ρ_t, for both transactions.

Now if we use Equation 13.6 to eliminate the interest differential from Equation 13.5, we have:

$$\begin{aligned} S_t &= \tilde{m}_t - c\tilde{y}_t + b\Delta s_t^e + b\rho_t \\ &= \gamma z_t + b\Delta s_t^e \end{aligned} \qquad (13.7)$$

where z_t has been written as shorthand to summarize the impact of fundamentals other than the interest rate (see Box 13.1).

Although our starting point in this section was the monetary model, this exchange rate equation is a very general example of the genre. Its only specific assumption (apart from linearity in the fundamentals) is that expectations are rational and that anticipated capital gains or losses influence the current spot rate – hardly a controversial proposition one would imagine. Although the obvious candidates for inclusion as fundamentals are the variables figuring in the monetary model, there is no reason to insist on this. Simply by respecifying the list of fundamentals in z_t, the same framework could accommodate any other exogenous variables.

Box 13.1

Fundamentals in a 'news' model

We define:

$$\gamma z_t \equiv \tilde{m}_t - c\tilde{y}_t + b\rho_t$$

or for readers who are familiar with vector notation:

$$\gamma z_t \equiv \begin{bmatrix} 1 & -c & b \end{bmatrix} \begin{bmatrix} \tilde{m}_t \\ \tilde{y}_t \\ \rho_t \end{bmatrix}$$

What Equation 13.7 says is that the spot rate at any time depends not only on the current level of a number of fundamental variables *but also on the expected capital gain or loss from holding the currency* – which is simply (the negative of) its own rate of increase. The greater is $b\Delta s_t^e$, in other words, the more the pound is expected to depreciate against the dollar, the greater the capital loss to sterling holders, and hence the lower will be the pound's international value (that is, the higher the sterling price of dollars), other things being equal.

The mathematical complexities of the model (most of which will be bypassed here) all stem from this 'bootstrap' feature: *the more the exchange rate is expected to appreciate over the coming period, the higher will be its level today.* Its current level depends on its (expected) rate of change. This is a familiar feature of asset markets: other things being equal (that is, for given values of the fundamentals), asset prices are high when they are expected to go even higher and thereby yield capital gains to current holders.

It will now be demonstrated that, under RE, Equation 13.7 implies that the current level of the exchange rate depends on the market's view of the whole pattern of future movements in the fundamentals.

Start by noting the following:

$$\Delta s_t^e \equiv s_{t+1}^e - s_t \tag{13.8}$$

which serves simply to define the expected depreciation as the (log of the) spot rate anticipated for next period, $t + 1$, less the rate actually observed at the present moment (period t).

Assuming RE, we can write Equation 13.8 as:

$$\Delta s_t^e = E_t s_{t+1} - s_t \tag{13.9}$$

where the exchange rate level anticipated for $t + 1$ is conditioned on the information available at t.

If we now substitute Equation 13.9 in Equation 13.7, we have:

$$s_t = \gamma z_t + b(E_t s_{t+1} - s_t) \tag{13.10}$$

which can be simplified by collecting terms involving s_t to give:

$$s_t = \gamma(1 + b)^{-1}z_t + b(1 + b)^{-1}E_t s_{t+1}$$
$$= \gamma(1 + b)^{-1}z_t + \beta E_t s_{t+1} \qquad \textbf{(13.11)}$$

where, for convenience, we have introduced the definition:

$$\beta \equiv b(1 + b)^{-1}$$

This parameter, β, plays an important part in what follows. Notice that since the coefficient b must be presumed positive – the value of a currency must be *higher* the greater the prospective capital gain – it follows that β must lie between zero and plus one.

Now, if Equation 13.11 tells us how s_t is determined as a function of z_t and $E_t s_{t+1}$, ask yourself this question: what will determine next period's exchange rate, s_{t+1}? The answer is, plainly:

$$s_{t+1} = \gamma(1 + b)^{-1}z_{t+1} + \beta E_{t+1}s_{t+2} \qquad \textbf{(13.12)}$$

Notice the capital gain term at the end: the exchange rate next period (that is, at time $t + 1$) will depend on the level that it is expected to reach at $t + 2$, on the basis of the information available *then*, at $t + 1$.

However, what cropped up in Equation 13.11 was not s_{t+1} but its expected value at t, $E_t s_{t+1}$, so in order to make progress, take the expectation in Equation 13.12 conditional on the information set, I_t, to give:

$$E_t s_{t+1} = \gamma(1 + b)^{-1}E_t z_{t+1} + \beta E_t(E_{t+1}s_{t+2})$$
$$= \gamma(1 + b)^{-1}E_t z_{t+1} + \beta E_t s_{t+2} \qquad \textbf{(13.12')}$$

The last line requires explanation. First, note that the information set, I_t, must contain fewer data than the next period's information set, I_{t+1} (see note 12 of Chapter 12), the difference being 'news' about the fundamentals. It follows that the last term on the first line of Equation 13.12' is: the level of s_t the market expects now (at t) will be a rational expectation of s_{t+2} when the new information emerging at $t + 1$ has become available. But, at time t, the market cannot know what will appear a rational expectation of s_{t+2} at time $t + 1$, because that depends, as has been said, on information not yet available. It follows that the best guess the market can make about the level expected for $t + 2$ on the basis of $t + 1$ data is precisely the level that currently appears rational, as of t (see Box 13.2).

Box 13.2 | **The law of iterated expectation**

More formally, since:

$$I_t \subseteq I_{t+1} \subseteq I_{t+2} \subseteq \dots$$

and so on, it follows that:

$$E\{E(s_{t+2}|I_{t+1})|I_t\} \ E(s_{t+2}|I_t) = E_t s_{t+2}$$

Now if we use the second line of Equation 13.12' to replace $E_t s_{t+1}$ in Equation 13.11, we have:

$$s_t = \gamma(1+b)^{-1}(z_t + \beta E_t z_{t+1}) + \beta^2 E_t s_{t+2} \tag{13.13}$$

which expresses the current exchange rate in terms of the current fundamentals, the expected value of next period's fundamentals and the expected exchange rate two periods hence.

The obvious next step is to repeat the process, in order to eliminate $E_t s_{t+2}$. Write out the expression for s_{t+2} in terms of z_{t+2} and $E_{t+2} s_{t+3}$, take expectations conditional on the information set I_t, and use the result in Equation 13.13 to give s_t as a function of z_t, $E_t z_{t+1}$, $E_t z_{t+2}$ and $E_t s_{t+3}$. Then repeat the process to eliminate $E_t s_{t+3}$ . . . and so on.

The result, as can be verified with a little patience and some rough paper, is that we can write the exchange rate after N substitutions as follows:

$$s_t = \gamma(1+b)^{-1}(z_t + \beta E_t z_{t+1} + \beta^2 E_t z_{t+2} + \beta^3 E_t z_{t+3} + \ldots + \beta^N E_t z_{t+N}) + \beta^{N+1} E_t s_{t+N+1} \tag{13.14}$$

This looks awfully messy at first glance. However, it can be simplified by noting, first, that since β is a fraction between zero and one, it will get smaller and smaller as it is raised to a higher and higher power. For a large number of substitutions (that is, large N), it follows that β^{N+1} will be so small as to be negligible, so that we can safely ignore the final term of the equation. Next, remembering that $\beta^0 = 1$, we can rewrite Equation 13.14 as follows:

$$s_t = \gamma(1+b)^{-1}\left(z_t + \sum_{k=1}^{N} \beta^k E_t z_{t+k}\right)$$

$$= \gamma(1+b)^{-1}\sum_{k=0}^{N} \beta^k E_t z_{t+k} \tag{13.15}$$

Consider the interpretation of the equations. At the outset, Equation 13.10 told us that the level of the exchange rate at time t was determined by two factors: the level of the fundamentals at t and the expected capital gain or loss accruing to an investor who held the currency over the period from t to $t + 1$. The latter will be equal to the difference between the exchange rate expected for next period, $E_t s_{t+1}$, and its known current level. The question is then: what determines the exchange rate expected for $t + 1$? Under RE, the answer is clear. It is the value that the fundamentals are expected to take next period and the prospective capital gain from $t + 1$ to $t + 2$, which is equal to $(E_t s_{t+2} - E_t s_{t+1})$. The latter depends on the expected level of the fundamentals at $t + 2$ and the capital gain over $t + 2$ to $t + 3$ . . . and so on.

The conclusion is Equation 13.15. It tells us that the value of the exchange rate at any point is determined by market perceptions of the entire future path of the fundamentals, starting with z_t and up to z_{t+N}.

In principle, N should be infinite, because we could go on substituting for the expected future spot rate forever more. However, if we look more closely at Equation 13.15 (comparing it, if necessary, with Equation 13.14), we see that the summation term is in fact a weighted total of future expected fundamentals, where the weights on successive periods take the following pattern:

$$
\begin{array}{cccccc}
t & t+1 & t+2 & t+3 & \ldots & t+N \\
\beta^0 & \beta^1 & \beta^2 & \beta^3 & \ldots & \beta^N
\end{array}
$$

This series of weights diminishes as we go further and further into the future. In fact, it is a geometric series, with each term equal to β times the preceding one. So the weights will diminish faster the smaller β is.

The practical implication of this weighting scheme is that the importance of expected future values beyond three or four periods is very small. For example, if the capital gains elasticity, b, were 0.9 (remember it is in any case smaller than one), the series of weights would go:

$$
\begin{array}{ccccccc}
t & t+1 & t+2 & t+3 & t+4 & t+5 & t+6 & \ldots \\
1.000 & 0.474 & 0.224 & 0.106 & 0.050 & 0.024 & 0.011 & \ldots
\end{array}
$$

so that only six periods out, the weighting has fallen to barely 1%. For a smaller value of b, the weights diminish even more rapidly, falling below 1% after only three periods when b is 0.25, and after two periods when b is 0.1.

We can sum up our conclusions so far as follows. If the current level of the exchange rate depends on the prospective capital gain or loss, then it follows, assuming RE, that its level can be viewed as depending on the whole of the future path that the fundamentals are expected to take, with the weight attached to succeeding future periods diminishing as the period becomes more distant.

In mathematical terms, what we have accomplished, in this laborious fashion, is to solve a *difference equation*. Viewed from this standpoint, Equation 13.15 sets out conditions relating s_t and the future expected path of z_t, such that the difference equation (Equation 13.11) is satisfied at all times. The interested (or incredulous) reader can satisfy himself that this is the case by rewriting Equation 13.15 for $E_t s_{t+1}$ and using the result in Equation 13.11 to give Equation 13.15 again.[5]

For our purposes, it is convenient to write the model in a different form from Equation 13.15. To see how this can be achieved, look back at Equation 13.14 and ask yourself: what will be the value of $E_{t-1}s_t$? The answer is obviously:[6]

$$
\begin{aligned}
E_{t-1}s_t &= \gamma(1+b)^{-1}(E_{t-1}z_t + \beta E_{t-1}z_{t+1} + \beta^2 E_{t-1}z_{t+2} + \beta^3 E_{t-1}z_{t+3} + \ldots \\
&\quad + \beta^N E_{t-1}z_{t+N}) + \beta^{N+1}E_t s_{t+N+1}
\end{aligned}
$$

$$
= \gamma(1+b)^{-1}\sum_{k=0}^{N}\beta^k E_{t-1}z_{t+k} \tag{13.16}
$$

Now simply subtract Equation 13.16 from Equation 13.15 to give:

$$
s_t - E_{t-1}s_t = \gamma(1+b)^{-1}\sum_{k=0}^{N}\beta^k (E_t z_{t+k} - E_{t-1}z_{t+k}) \tag{13.17}
$$

This serves to emphasize the sense in which the 'news' model is really only a way of rewriting a generalized asset model, with RE imposed. The left-hand side of Equation 13.17 is that part of the current (time t) exchange rate that was unanticipated in the previous period (at $t-1$) – in other words, the exchange rate 'news' or surprise. The right-hand side is $\gamma(1+b)^{-1}$ multiplied by the weighted sum of the 'news' about future fundamentals. The surprise for period $t + k$ is the difference between the value of z_{t+k} that is expected at t and the value that was anticipated last period, at $t - 1$. The summation therefore represents a weighted total of the extent to which expectations about the future are revised in the current period in the light of new information made public between $t - 1$ and t. If, having heard the 'news', the market has no reason to revise its forecast of z_{t+k}, then $E_t z_{t+k} - E_{t-1} z_{t+k}$ will be zero and will have no impact on the exchange rate.

It must be stressed that, however large or small the surprises are in any period, each term $E_t z_{t+k} - E_{t-1} z_{t+k}$ is purely random – for each and every period, $t + k$, and *for any or all fundamentals*. The reason is that a systematic pattern in the 'news' would imply, by that very fact, that it was not a complete surprise. Expectation revisions that display a pattern over time could be predicted in advance.

It is worth dwelling for a moment on this point, because it illustrates both the empirical content of the 'news' approach and another important aspect of RE.

To put matters in a personal context, suppose I hold a particular expectation with regard to a variable of importance to me – for example, my earnings in the year 2010. For simplicity, assume that I update my expectation with regard to that year each 31 December, so as to incorporate the new information that I have received in the 12 months since the last update. Now suppose I notice, as the years pass, that for every 1% I *up*grade my expectation of 2010 earnings by in one year, I end up *down*grading my forecast by 5% the next year. What would be a rational response to this discovery?

Clearly, I cannot let matters rest if I am to preserve a reputation for rationality. Suppose that on 31 December 2005 I decide that in the light of the good news received during the year I ought to raise my forecast of 2010 earnings by 7%. As things stand, I do so in the confident expectation that next year, on 31 December 2006, my 2005 forecast for 2010 will seem to have been outrageously overoptimistic – and will therefore be downgraded again by 35%. This plainly contradicts rationality. If I *know* I will hold a different expectation in the next period, I must adopt it *now* – or forego any claim to being a rational agent.

There may well be a simple explanation of why I find a repeated pattern in the way that I revise my earnings forecasts. Every time my employer grants a pay rise of 1%, it is reversed in the next year by a 5% fall, both of which I am naively extrapolating to arrive at my forecast for 2010. Obviously, I can improve my forecasting technique by taking this pattern into account, so as to replace my naive extrapolation process with a forecasting model that embodies the predictable component in my employer's behaviour.

In this simple example, an outside observer seeing the stable, systematic pattern to my expectation revisions would conclude (*correctly*) that I was irrational, because I was failing to make full use of all the information available to me. In the same way, as observers of the currency markets, we likewise would expect to find no consistent pattern to the revisions in traders' forecasts.

To see the relationship between Equation 13.17 and the forward rate models examined in Chapter 11, take $E_{t-1} s_t$ over to the right-hand side to give:

$$s_t = E_{t-1} s_t + \gamma (1+b)^{-1} \sum_{k=0}^{N} \beta^k (E_t z_{t+k} - E_{t-1} z_{t+k}) \tag{13.18}$$

At this point it is worth glancing back at Section 12.3 on the forward market efficiency condition. It is clear from looking at Equation 12.3, for example, that the 'news' term in Equation 13.18 can be identified with the random error, u_t, which was included but left unexplained throughout the last chapter. In fact, if we assume that the forward market is efficient we can rewrite Equation 12.4′ as:

$$s_t = -\rho_{t-1} + f_{t-1}^t + \gamma(1+b)^{-1}\sum_{k=0}^{N}\beta^k(E_t z_{t+k} - E_{t-1}z_{t+k}) \qquad \textbf{(13.19)}$$

which says that the spot rate can be thought of as made up of three components: the previous period's forward rate plus the risk premium set when currently maturing forward contracts were signed, plus the impact of 'news' about current and all future values of the fundamental variables, the importance of the latter being less the further into the future they are dated.

Recall the background facts presented in Section 12.7. They indicated that, whatever else might be true, one thing could be said with absolute confidence: the forward rate is a very poor forecast of the future spot rate. If we set aside for the moment the possibility that the risk premium is highly variable, the conclusions we have reached in this section suggest that the explanation for the poor forecasting performance of the forward rate is to be found in the predominance of 'news'. If, month after month, major items of 'news' arrive, forcing agents in the market to make substantial revisions in their assessment of future fundamentals, the result will be that movements in the spot rate will overwhelmingly reflect these surprises. Any movements in the spot rate that are predictable in advance, as reflected in the forward premium, will be completely swamped by the impact of new information arriving like a bolt from the blue.

This explanation of the facts looks, at first sight, convincing. How well does it stand up to more rigorous testing? It is to this question that we now turn.

13.3 Testing the 'news'

Consider the simple model (Equation 13.3). In order to test how well it fits the facts, we need to be able to answer three questions: first, how do we measure market expectations of the exchange rate itself? Second, which are the fundamental variables? Third, how do we measure market expectations of their level?

As far as the first question is concerned, most researchers have taken the line of least resistance and used the forward rate as a proxy for the expected spot rate. Looking back at Equation 13.4 it is obvious that this solution is far from ideal, since it simply involves replacing one unobservable variable with an observable, the forward rate, and another unobservable, the risk premium. Now if we can safely assume that the risk premium is zero, or constant at least, then this substitution will not bias the results. If the risk premium is variable, however, then it will almost certainly distort the conclusions.

On the second question, researchers have picked candidate variables on a more or less atheoretical basis. Most have recognized the claim of the basic monetary variables and a number of others have been tried, notably current account balances. There are many 'news' variables, or at least strong candidates, that have never been employed, usually because they are inherently difficult to quantify: for example, information bearing on the likelihood of a change of government (opinion polls and so on), 'news' affecting a possible future move to a fixed exchange rate regime (for example, the UK joining the European Monetary System), and so on.

The issue which has received most attention has been the measurement of expectations with respect to the fundamentals. A number of different approaches have been taken.

13.3.1 Univariate time series

Much of the early work involved modelling each fundamental variable as a univariate time series. This obviously amounts to assuming weak RE: market expectations are conditioned only on the past history of the variable in question, so that the innovations in each of the fundamentals are simply that part that could not be predicted by looking at the pattern of fluctuations in the variable in question, taken in isolation. So, for example, this approach would involve extracting an estimate of the future money stock, $E_t m_{t+1}$, from a linear[7] combination of m_t, m_{t-1}, m_{t-2}, and so on; that is:[8]

$$m_t = a_0 + a_1 m_{t-1} + a_2 m_{t-2} + \ldots + a_p m_{t-p} + v_t$$

Then the 'news' is simply the residual from the estimating equation, v_t. Unless one believes that market expectations are only weakly rational, this approach is unsatisfactory, although it does have the attraction of simplicity.

13.3.2 Multivariate time series and vector autoregression

From a theoretical point of view, conditioning each 'news' variable on a broader information set is obviously preferable. Whether market agents are supposed to arrive at their RE predictions by formal forecasting procedures, by crude rules of thumb or more likely by intuitive gut feelings, there is certainly no reason to suppose that they close their eyes to *all* information other than the past history of the variable in question.

To take this point a little further, consider a market forecast of the future money stock in the context of the RE version of the monetary model covered in Section 13.2. One approach would be to estimate $E_{t-1} m_t$ using a special array of variables selected by the researcher as relevant: say, the government's budget deficit past and present, the rate of inflation, the growth rate of the economy, and so forth. In fact, this arbitrary approach to the specification of the sub-model was the one taken in some of the early work on 'news' models.

Remember it is not only the money stock surprise that figures in the basic model: we also have to deal with an income variable. Now there is nothing to prevent our following the same arbitrary approach to forecasting income. But, at the very least, it would make sense to include the money stock among the conditioning variables, on the grounds that orthodox closed economy macroeconomic theory suggests that it plays a central role in determining the level of activity, and the evidence by and large supports this view. Furthermore, it would be grossly inconsistent to exclude the money stock on the grounds that it is absent from the market's information set, or that agents pay no attention to it, *since it appears as one of the other fundamentals.* In that sense, its inclusion is not completely arbitrary.

In fact, taking this approach to its logical conclusion would suggest the following procedure. Suppose we have m variables in the set of fundamentals. Call the first z^1, the second z^2, and so on, so that z_{t-3}^4, for example, denotes the value of the fourth fundamental variable three periods ago. Then generate a forecast of z_t^1 by using past values of z^1, in combination with past values of all the other fundamentals, z^2 to z^m. Similarly, condition a prediction of z_t^2 on past values of z^2 itself as well as on the history of the other fundamentals. In general, the jth fundamental is modelled as:

$$z_t^j = f(z_{t-1}^1, z_{t-2}^1 \dots z_{t-L}^1, z_{t-1}^2, z_{t-2}^2 \dots z_{t-L}^2 \dots z_{t-1}^m \dots z_{t-L}^m)$$

where L is the maximum lag (the 'memory length') judged relevant on the basis of the standard tests used in time-series statistics.[9] Again, the 'news' about z^j is simply the residual error from this equation.

This type of very general, unstructured model is known as a vector autoregression (VAR). The VAR has the theoretical advantage that neither is it arbitrary in the selection of variables for the information set and nor does it impose an arbitrary structure on the sub-model. In addition, it has two practical advantages: first, it obviates the need to build a sophisticated (and possibly incorrect) sub-model of the fundamentals and second, it can also be shown to have some desirable econometric properties.[10]

13.3.3 Survey data

As we saw in Chapter 11, a number of researchers have made use of data taken from direct surveys of market participants or of the economists who advise them. In the present context, survey data has two advantages to offset against the shortcomings discussed in Section 12.8. First, if we have survey data on market expectations of the fundamentals, we can avoid having to build a sub-model altogether. Second, if our data allow us to measure market forecasts of the exchange rate directly, we have no need to use the forward rate in our main model – a very considerable advantage, given the problems we have already mentioned in using the forward rate.

13.3.4 Announcement/event studies

To be useful, survey data need to be easily translatable into a statement about forecasts for a specific horizon. In the case of discontinuous variables – such as the money stock or national income, which only have observable, measurable values on announcement dates – survey expectations can be directly compared with outcomes only if they are viewed as relating to a specific announcement.

A number of studies have been published attempting to relate movements in the exchange rate to the 'news' content of money supply announcements.[11] The work has the characteristics of an event study: data are examined over a very short time scale surrounding announcements, often hourly.

Notice that although this work can provide potentially important evidence on the impact of individual packages of news, it is not really a test of the standard 'news' model. First, this is true because announcements tend to wrap up several news items in the same package. For example, the figure for the UK narrow money supply is released at the same time as that for broad money, as are the data on the volume of bank advances. Likewise, a number of different price index announcements are made simultaneously. It therefore becomes impossible to isolate the effect of any single element in the package. Second, the other approaches all relate to the impact of 'news' aggregated over the whole of the time period involved, whereas the announcement approach attempts to disaggregate the impact of 'news' by concentrating on very short periods of at most a few hours, so as to be sure of isolating the impact of a single 'news' package. Third, and most importantly, using directly observed expectations involves no assumption of RE. It is quite possible to imagine a scenario where money supply announcements are associated consistently and closely with exchange rate fluctuations, but where the 'news' content of the announcements is the residual from a non-rational forecasting process. In other words, the results could be consistent with a non-rational 'news' model.

13.3.5 Financial variables

One possible way to sidestep some of the problems involved in modelling the fundamentals would be to look at other financial variables that may embody the same information as the spot exchange rate, albeit within a different structure. The only work along these lines published so far uses a share price index as a proxy for expected future national income.

On the one hand, there are some considerable potential advantages in using financial variables. First, they share with the major currencies the intrinsically forward-looking characteristics of continuously traded assets: prices are continuous, instantaneously reflecting (or so one might hope) daily or hourly changes in market perceptions about the level of all the relevant variables, whether they are immeasurable (for instance, political factors or market confidence) or more straightforward macroeconomic variables. Second, since the same agents are often active in both markets, there seems reason to suppose what is true of perceptions in one will equally hold good in the other market.[12]

On the other hand, a major difficulty with this approach is that if it is to avoid being completely arbitrary, then it requires a model relating the stock price index or other financial variable to the fundamentals. Share prices *ought* in principle to be discounted (probably risk-adjusted) sums of expected future cashflows. If the latter are related directly to expectations with regard to levels of economic activity, then stock market indices embody useful 'news'.

Before going on to a very brief survey of the type of results that have been published in the 'news' literature, return for a moment to the general model analysed in Section 13.2. Recall that the bottom line of the analysis was an equation relating the exchange rate not simply to news about the immediate prospects for the fundamentals but to the extent to which new information led agents to revise their expectations for *all* future periods. How should this complication affect our estimation methods?

In the event, the answer is: not a great deal. It turns out that for any *linear* time-series model of the fundamentals, whether multivariate or univariate (in other words, whether we opt for the methodology in items 1 or 2 of this section), future revisions will simply be multiples of the news for the most recent period, albeit somewhat complicated multiples in most cases. Given that the revision for period $t + k$ will in any case appear with a weight of β^k, it will be virtually impossible to unscramble the time-series weights from the values of β and γ in the coefficients of future 'news'. It is hardly surprising, then, that researchers have regarded the problem as being of second-order importance and have concentrated only on looking for a relationship between the exchange rate and concurrent surprises.

13.4 Results

The objective of the 'news' approach is to explain the unexpected component of exchange rate movements. In view of the volatility of this variable, this is a very tall order indeed, as can be seen from a glance at Figure 12.1 – a point that must be borne in mind when assessing the results of testing the 'news' approach.

The first published results appeared in 1981 and the verdict seems to be that the approach is a qualified success. On the one hand, most researchers have found that some 'news' variables contribute significantly to explaining (unanticipated) exchange rate movements. On the other hand, not only is it difficult to identify the fundamentals, and thence to isolate their surprise components, but also it is apparent that the 'news' approach does little to answer the question it was originally advanced to resolve: why are exchange rates so volatile?

The conclusions emerging from the published literature can be summarized as follows:

- By and large, 'news' variables make a significant contribution to explaining exchange rate fluctuations. The percentage of exchange rate variation explained by surprises in the fundamentals depends on whether we look at weekly, monthly or quarterly data, on our choice of currency and of data period, and on other factors, for example how the 'news' is extracted from the fundamentals. However, a fair assessment of the evidence so far, in this author's opinion at least, would be to say that 'news' variables explain somewhere between 5% and 20% of monthly variation in the major currencies.

- The conclusions do not seem to be very sensitive to the way the 'news' is extracted from the fundamentals. In spite of the theoretical advantages of multivariate (and especially VAR) methods over univariate modelling, the increased sophistication has yet to yield any noticeable improvement in the results.

- The variable that most consistently yields significant results is certainly the interest rate differential, though there is some doubt as to the direction of the effect, with possibly a positive coefficient in the 1970s (reflecting unexpected inflation?) and negative in the 1980s. Money supply variables give more erratic results, often appearing insignificant and frequently wrongly signed – at least for consistency with the monetary model.[13] Income variables are problematic in the extreme, almost invariably fitting very poorly. Neither does the problem appear to be relieved by the use of stock market price indices as a proxy for expected future levels of economic activity.

- Some researchers quote results suggesting that lagged 'news' terms have a significant part to play. If this is not simply due to lack of synchronization between the date attached to the 'news' variables in question and their true publication date, then it could be an indication of irrationality or, less plausibly, slow portfolio adjustment by currency traders. In some cases, it could result from exchange controls.

- Some of the most robust results emerge from studies of announcement effects. For example, a near-unanimous finding (at least for the USA and the UK) is that unexpectedly rapid monetary expansion is associated with exchange rate *appreciation*. Furthermore, this result has in some cases been supported by proper 'news' studies (that is, using explicit models of the fundamentals). The explanation seems to be that where the authorities are seen as firmly committed to non-accommodating money supply policies, unexpectedly high monetary growth generates anticipation of policy countermeasures, the effect of which will be to cause an appreciation of the domestic currency. This view, known as the *policy anticipation hypothesis*, is consistent with evidence from a large number of studies of the announcement effect in a closed economy context, most of which looked at exchange rate effects only in passing, if at all.

- The unsatisfactory results, particularly the residual autocorrelation reported in some econometric studies, may possibly be due to some extent to the fact that most researchers use the lagged forward rate as their proxy for the expected spot rate. As noted already, this will make little difference to their results as long as the forward market is efficient and the risk premium is more or less constant. However, this procedure will almost certainly distort the results if, as the evidence would appear to suggest (see Section 11.8), either the forward market is inefficient or the risk premium is highly volatile.

  As an alternative to the lagged forward rate, this author has used s_{t-1}, the lagged spot rate itself. The justification is simple. If the spot rate follows a path that is close to a random walk, as we saw in Section 12.7, then the best possible forecast (the rational expectation) of s_t is just s_{t-1}. And, indeed, this device does improve the fit of the equation quite noticeably.

- All of the published work suffers from one shortcoming. No combination of 'news' variables has yet come anywhere near explaining the *volatility* of exchange rates. Now this particular failing is not unique to work with 'news'. As we have already seen in previous chapters, it characterizes *all* attempts at exchange rate modelling so far. None the less, the fact is a little more disappointing in the present case, precisely because the 'news' approach was originally advocated as an explanation (and rationalization) of the turbulence of currency markets.

  Striking evidence that new information cannot be the whole story comes from comparisons of volatility when currency markets are closed with volatility when they are open.[14] One researcher found the variance of the return on yen (per dollar) was three times as great when the exchange was open as when it was shut. Now, if 'news' arrives in a more or less steady stream over the week, this ratio cannot be rationalized as a reaction to perceived changes in the fundamentals.

If informational surprises cannot explain volatility, we must examine what explanatory alternatives remain.

Volatility tests, bubbles and the peso problem

One explanation for volatility that has received a considerable amount of attention in recent years is the possibility that currency markets may be characterized by temporary, *rational bubbles*.[15]

At an intuitive level, bubbles are easy to understand, reflecting the familiar phenomenon of a self-reinforcing movement in the price away from its equilibrium level. Since time immemorial, laymen have observed that in this type of situation 'everyone thinks that the price is too high but no one expects it to fall yet.' And, indeed, it is hard to find any other explanation for some of the most spectacular price surges (or collapses) – even long after the event.

Viewed with the benefit of hindsight, it has usually been taken for granted that the most notorious price bubbles in history resulted from investor irrationality: 'market psychology', 'mass hysteria' and so forth. Although this type of explanation certainly cannot be ruled out, recent work has shown that bubbles can be reconciled with rational market behaviour. Remember that once a bubble has started, it becomes the reality with which the investor has to live. However loudly the economist may appeal to exchange rate fundamentals and the notional equilibrium they imply – it will all be irrelevant to the trader actually in the market as long as the bubble persists, *even if the trader is perfectly rational.*

Take an example. Many people (including the majority of economists, traders, bankers and politicians) believed that the US dollar was vastly overvalued on any reasonable criterion during the mid-1980s.[16] Yet, in the face of this consensus, the high exchange rate was maintained for two years or more. Why? It is difficult to say with any confidence, but what is certainly true is that it was *not* obviously rational at the time to sell dollars, even if one shared the view that the dollar was overvalued. On the contrary, it made sense to hold dollars – as long as one believed that the bubble would last and as long as one was adequately compensated for the perceived risk that the bubble might burst.

Now consider for a moment the implication of this. How can I be adequately compensated for the risk of holding a currency that, as a rational agent, fully aware of the market fundamentals, I *know* is overvalued? Obviously, the risk can be offset by the prospect of capital gain. But this leads us to the conclusion that, at any point in the history of a bubble, the more overvalued the currency, and the greater the probability the bubble will burst, the more rapidly it must rise so as to compensate for the increased risk.[17]

This picture of life inside a price bubble has probably been familiar to practitioners ever since the first caveman–speculator stored food so as to gamble on an exceptionally hard winter ahead.[18] However, as the reader will by now have become aware, economists take comfort from being able to replicate the wisdom of the ages in mathematical models. In the case of the rational bubble, the comfort comes from noting that Equation 13.15, the market fundamentals solution to the RE model of Section 13.2, is *not* unique, as was pointed out at the time. Consider the following:

$$s_t = \gamma(1+b)^{-1} \sum_{k=0}^{N} \beta^k E_t z_{t+k} + B_t \qquad \text{(13.20)}$$

which simply adds on to the market fundamentals solution in Equation 13.15 a term B_t – the price bubble at time t. Now, as long as B_t has the property that:

$$E_t B_{t+1} = \beta^{-1} B_t \qquad (13.21)$$

which is a condition satisfied by a number of commonly encountered economic series, it can be shown that Equation 13.21 satisfies the original difference equation (Equation 13.11) every bit as well as the pure market fundamentals solution does.[19]

The bubble term, B_t, can be defined as simply the extent of the deviation from the market fundamental equilibrium. Unfortunately, the theory has, as yet, nothing to say about *how* or *why* a bubble develops. There are two ways of looking at the role it plays. First, it is sufficient that agents perceive the bubble factor to be important for it actually to be important – if it figures in their subjective model, then it will find its way into the objective model driving the exchange rate. Second, we could be said to be dealing with a variable that is unobservable to economists but observable to market agents.[20]

At any point in time, there must be some perceived probability that the bubble will burst next period. If it does burst, then the exchange rate will return to the level dictated by the fundamentals. Otherwise, its movements will continue to reflect the behaviour of the bubble.

The simplest model would take the following form. Suppose the probability that the bubble, B_t, will last another period is Π and the probability it will burst is $(1 - \Pi)$. We then have the following possible outcomes for the next period, $t + 1$:

$$B_{t+1} = (\beta\Pi)^{-1} B_t \quad \text{with probability } \Pi$$
$$= 0 \qquad\qquad \text{with probability } (1 - \Pi)$$

The reader can easily verify that this is consistent with the restriction in Equation 13.21.

In this simple case, as long as the bubble persists, the exchange rate will appreciate sufficiently enough in order to compensate a risk neutral currency holder for the possibility of loss when the bubble bursts. What this means is that in addition to any rise justified by changes in the fundamentals, there will need to be an explosive bubble superimposed, because the greater the current divergence from equilibrium, the further the currency has left to fall, and hence the greater the prospective capital gain needs to be if the process is to be sustained.

Notice that this is more a detailed description of the phenomenon than an explanation. The literature has, as yet, little to say about what causes bubbles to start or end.[21] On the basis of casual observation, it seems that some bubbles (or apparent bubbles) are triggered by movements in the fundamentals, actual or perceived. Others seem to be spontaneous. In this respect, the theory offers little enlightenment since it treats the bubble as simply a fact of life, exogenous not only to the behaviour of the market but also to the fundamentals themselves. Indeed, as we can see from Equation 13.20, as long as the bubble persists, it will cause the exchange rate to move, even when the fundamentals are unchanged.[22]

How will the presence of bubbles show up in the data? Obviously, the effect will be to weaken the overall link between the exchange rate and the fundamentals, even supposing that one can identify them. In terms of RE models, it can be shown that ignoring the bubble term in standard econometric work may well produce results that apparently contradict rationality – intuitively because a persistent positive bubble will generate a series of underpredictions in forecasts based on the fundamentals, and vice versa for negative bubbles.

Work on bubbles is still proceeding, and it is as yet difficult to say how far the facts are consistent with the theory, though some direct tests have been published. By and large, the evidence on some recent episodes (for example, the overvaluation of the dollar in the mid-1980s) is consistent with rational bubbles, though it could also be explained, as always, by investor irrationality.

The presence of bubbles could possibly account for the failure of 'news' models to explain the variability of exchange rates. Indirect support for the view that bubbles have been at work in currency markets in recent years is provided by formal comparisons of the variability of the exchange rate, on the one hand, and the fundamentals, on the other, *excess volatility or variance bounds tests*, as they are called.

To understand how these tests are formulated, compare the following equation with Equation 13.15:

$$s_t^* = \gamma(1+b)^{-1} \sum_{k=0}^{N} \beta^k z_{t+k} \tag{13.15'}$$

The right-hand side is simply Equation 13.15, with *actual* values of z_{t+k} replacing *expected* values. In other words, s_t^* is the level at which the exchange rate would settle if the market participants had perfect foresight. Since they cannot know the future, and have to rely on expectations, the actual exchange rate is given by:

$$s_t = E_t s_t^* \tag{13.22}$$

which is simply a tidy way of rewriting Equation 13.15, using our newly introduced definition of the perfect foresight exchange rate.

Now the only reason why the perfect foresight value of the exchange rate, s_t^*, differs from its expected value, s_t, is because of 'news' about future fundamentals. Since, under RE, 'news' items are all random, their total impact, as measured by the weighted sum on the right-hand side of Equation 13.15, must equally be random. It follows that we can write:

$$\begin{aligned} s_t^* &= E_t s_t^* + u_t \\ &= s_t + u_t \end{aligned} \tag{13.23}$$

where, as we saw in Chapter 12, u_t not only has an average value of zero but also is uncorrelated with the expected value itself. It other words, if we take the variances (see Box 13.3) of the right- and left-hand sides of Equation 13.23, we derive:

$$var(s_t^*) = var(s_t) + var(u_t) \tag{13.24}$$

since we know that the covariance between s_t and u_t must be zero. As variances are always positive, this implies the following inequality test:

$$var(s_t^*) \geq var(s_t) \tag{13.25}$$

which states that, under RE, the variance of the actual exchange rate must be no greater than the variance of the fundamentals that drive it.

| Box 13.3 | Variance and covariance of random variables |

The variance of a random variable, X, is a measure of its dispersion, computed by taking the average of the squared deviations from its mean value. In general, for two random variables, X and Y, if we define:

$$Z = aX + bY$$

then it follows that:

$$var(Z) = a^2var(X) + b^2var(Y) + 2ab.cov(XY)$$

where $cov(XY)$ denotes the covariance of X and Y, defined as the average of the product of the deviations of X and Y from their respective means. Obviously, if $cov(XY)$ is zero, we can conclude that:

$$var(Z) = a^2var(X) + b^2var(Y)$$

For details, see any elementary statistics textbook.

Notice that this test is very general, in so far as it places no restriction on the variables to be included among the market fundamentals. In other words, it is not purely a test of the RE monetary model.

For technical reasons, many researchers test slightly modified versions of Equation 13.23. In any case, the result is a near-unanimous conclusion: *exchange rate volatility is excessive relative to the volatility of the fundamentals*. In other words, the right-hand side of Equation 13.25 is unambiguously greater than the left.

To put this conclusion in perspective, it is worth pointing out that variance bounds tests were originally used in research on stock market prices and dividends, with similar results: share price volatility is too great to be consistent with the degree of variation in dividends.

Notice the crucial distinction between tests in these two cases. In the case of stock prices, we can identify the fundamentals with some confidence. Under these circumstances, inequality tests not only are more informative but also can legitimately be interpreted as tests of stock market efficiency.

In the case of the exchange rate, we can have far less confidence in our choice of fundamental variables. It follows that these tests can only throw light on the question of how far the facts are consistent with the view that exchange rates are (1) driven by a particular set of fundamentals and (2) not subject to bubbles. They are not very illuminating on the more general question of spot market efficiency.

There are a number of possible explanations of the apparent excess volatility of the major exchange rates: currency markets are irrational, or there are significant (rational) bubbles or important and highly volatile fundamental variables have been omitted. The latter explanation seems improbable, at least in so far as it relates to economic variables. The only variables that fluctuate anywhere near enough to overturn the main findings are financial series, such as stock market prices, which are themselves excessively volatile, as has already been mentioned.[23]

However, at least one other conceivable explanation has been offered: the so-called *peso problem*.[24] This relates to the inherent difficulties that arise in sampling economic events, which are by their very nature once-and-for-all experiments, incapable of ever being replicated. To see what is involved, take a topical example.

Suppose in late 1999 currency markets perceive the UK authorities to be likely at some stage to give in to the mounting pressure to join the eurozone.[25] And suppose the market believes that accession, if and when it occurs, will be at the rate of £1.00 = €1.50.

Clearly, the event will be influencing expectations at the present moment. It may be the case, for example, that the probability of accession within the next year is regarded as tiny – say, only 0.01, or one in 100 – but the probability rises to 10% for accession within two years, 40% within three years, and so on.

This means that today's spot rate of £1.00 = €1.56 is lower than it otherwise would be because of the probability, however small, that sterling will be devalued to the accession level of £1.00 = €1.50 during the holding period of the currency trader. Moreover, this effect will be felt in the forward market too, where the premium or discount will be less favourable to the pound than seems warranted on the basis of the *observable* fundamentals alone.

As can be readily seen, the result will be that models based on RE will apparently fail. In the current scenario, the otherwise 'correct' model (that is, the one that appeared to fit the facts *before* the prospect of EMS membership appeared on the horizon) will seem to overestimate the value of the pound. There are two ways of looking at the reason why the relationship between the fundamentals and the exchange rate will seem to have broken down.

The first would be to say that there is a variable omitted from the list of market fundamentals: the probability of a once-and-for-all discrete change in the currency regime. The omission is not simply an oversight. We are dealing with a variable that is inherently difficult to measure – but that certainly does *not* mean that it is unimportant. Indeed, it may be the case that many of the apparent departures from rationality are in reality due to unexpected shifts in unobservable or immeasurable variables.

The second is that the peso problem is also a sampling problem. In principle, just as we should expect to find approximately 50 heads in 100 tosses of a coin, so we should expect to find one example of an event like EMU accession in a 100-year sample if, as we suppose, the probability of its occurring is really 0.01. However, if our sample period is only 50 years, then our sampling frequency may be zero, leading us, mistakenly, to discount the event altogether as impossible. Indeed, the event may *never* occur. But that fact alone does not mean that it was irrational to take the possibility into account – any more than we can say a man who survives a game of Russian roulette was irrational to make out his will before playing.

Note that there are similarities between the peso problem and the phenomenon of rational bubbles. Both, it must be emphasized, are entirely consistent with rational behaviour displayed by individual market participants. The difference is that whereas bubbles represent a divergence from the equilibrium associated with the market fundamentals, the peso problem arises out of the small probability of a large, discrete shift in the value of one or more of the fundamental variables themselves.

As a consequence, it follows that the interpretation of variance bounds tests is or, rather, could be different in the case of the peso problem from what it would be in the presence of bubbles. As we saw, the common finding that the volatility of exchange rates is greater than that of the fundamentals could well be indicative of the presence of price bubbles. However, if over some part of our data period there were a widespread feeling that a major shift in the fundamentals could not be ruled out, then it will follow that our estimate of the variance of the fundamentals will be an underestimate of the market's (rational) perception of the variance at the time.

This possibility may well invalidate our conclusion altogether: the fact that the variance bounds are breached could be a result of neither irrationality nor bubbles but simply of the failure to take account of a significant event to which the market allocated a non-zero probability, even if it never subsequently materialized.

The peso problem is a particularly intractable obstacle to research, at least where standard econometric methods are concerned. The most hopeful approach would seem to be direct measurement of market expectations, although the relevant data have only recently become available and, as was mentioned in Chapter 12, survey data present researchers with a new set of methodological problems. Alternatively, there is one other way in which we could directly observe the market's assessment of exchange rate volatility: by extracting implied variances from traded options data.

13.6 Conclusions

In a sense, the conclusions reached in this chapter have been negative: the 'news' approach can explain some of the variation in exchange rates but is ultimately defeated by their sheer volatility. The impression that the task is hopeless is reinforced by direct comparisons of the variance of exchange rates with the variance of the elements that are supposed to explain it.

Moreover, these conclusions will almost certainly be supported by research using the most recent data, when they are published. Currency markets, along with other financial markets, seem to have become more volatile throughout the 1980s. In fact, the trend appears to be accelerating, at least since the cataclysmic events of October 1987.

Appropriately, then, Chapter 14 will deal with a different aspect of exchange rate volatility: the risk premium and its implications.

Summary

- The 'news' approach involves relating unexpected movements in the exchange rate to revisions in the market's rational forecast of the fundamental variables. In a simple RE model this relationship will be the same as the one between the level of the exchange rate and the level of the fundamentals.

- In general, the value of a currency will depend crucially on the prospective capital gains or losses (that is, the expected rate of appreciation or depreciation) that the market expects to see accruing to holders.

- When the value of a currency depends on its expected rate of change as well as on the market fundamentals, its behaviour will follow a difference equation, the solution of which relates the current level of the exchange rate to a weighted sum of current and expected future values of the fundamental variables. The weights will decline geometrically as we go forward in time, starting with a weight of unity on the current value of the fundametals. Furthermore, the identical relationship will hold between the unexpected component of the exchange rate and the innovations (or 'news') in the fundamentals – the formulation known as the 'news' approach.

- There are a number of problems to be overcome in making the 'news' model operational, notably the problem of how to estimate the 'news' variables themselves. Most published work has used univariate or multivariate time series or econometric methods in order to model the fundamentals, taking the residuals as estimates of the 'news'.

- The results of implementing the 'news' approach are mixed. On the positive side, the equations tend to fit reasonably well, frequently explaining a non-negligible proportion of the substantial degree of exchange rate fluctuation left undiscounted by the forward premium. On the negative side, the volatility of (unanticipated) exchange rate movements remains largely unexplained by the 'news'.

- Under RE, it ought to be the case that the variance of the observed spot rate is no greater than that of the fundamentals determine it. Most tests suggest that the opposite is the case. In other words, the volatility of the exchange rate is greater than can be rationalized by reference to the market fundamentals.

- One possible explanation of the observed volatility could be rational price bubbles, which are said to occur when a gap opens up between the level of the spot rate and its equilibrium value, as determined by the fundamentals. Another explanation could be that agents attached a (possibly small) probability to the chance of a discrete, step change in the fundamentals, in which case the apparent, measured variance taken from the data may be an underestimate of the variance as actually perceived by rational traders (the 'peso problem').

Reading guide

The paper that started the 'news' literature was Frenkel (1981), though the approach was derived in some respects from one already well established in closed economy macroeconomics (for example, Barro 1977). Both papers are relatively non-technical. Other influential papers have been by Edwards (1983) and Hartley (1983).

An up-to-date (but fairly technical) survey is to be found in MacDonald and Taylor (1989), which gives a particularly good treatment of the subject matter of Section 13.5. For a discussion of some of the outstanding issues in this area, particularly the estimation problems, see Copeland (1989) and references therein.

The peso problem was first discussed by Krasker (1980). Most of the original work on variance bounds focused on stock markets (for example, Grossman and Shiller, 1981), although researchers have tended to develop specialized versions of the tests to deal with exchange rates (for example, Meese and Singleton, 1983). For dissenting views on volatility see West (1987) on the Deutschmark/dollar rate and Honohan and Peruga (1986), who claim the bounds are breached only if PPP is imposed.

Both bubbles and the peso problem are discussed briefly and in non-technical fashion by Dornbusch (1982). Two important early papers on the theory of bubbles (and the related question of collapsing fixed rate regimes) are to be found in Chapters 10 and 11 of Wachtel (1982), written by Flood and Garber and Blanchard and Watson. More recently, see Diba and Grossman (1988).

As far as empirical work is concerned Evans (1986) is of interest, claiming to find a bubble in the returns to sterling holders in the early 1980s. Meese (1986) is accessible only to readers with a background in time-series econometrics. For a historical perspective on bubbles in financial markets, see Kindleberger (1978).

Web page: **www.pearsoned.co.uk/copeland**.

Notes

1 The fact that u_t in Equation 12.4′ appears with a negative sign can be ignored, of course, since the positive sign that it was given in Equation 12.3 was purely arbitrary in any case.

2 Also often called 'surprises' and 'innovations'.

3 Realistically, z_t will be a vector of values of the fundamental variables at t, possibly with a 1 as the first element, and γ a coefficient vector, so that Equation 13.1 relates the exchange rate to a constant plus a linear combination of a number of fundamentals.

4 The expression comes from stock exchange jargon, where it has a long pedigree.

5 As we shall see in Section 13.5, this solution is not unique.

6 Making use of the fact that $E_{t-1}(E_t z_t) = E_{t-1} z_t$ (see Box 13.2).

7 Almost all published work has involved linear time series, although non-linear models would appear a promising avenue for future exploration.

8 The example given here is known as pth order autoregressive. Along the same lines it is possible to include among the regressors on the right-hand side lagged values of the residual: v_{t-1}, $v_{t-2}, \ldots v_{t-q}$, making the model autoregressive (of order p)-moving average (of order q), or ARMA(p, q) for short. Although the statistical properties are changed somewhat by this extension, its implications for RE are identical.

9 It should be noted that, in principle at least, this modelling procedure needs to be repeated for each exchange rate observation in the dataset. In other words, if we are trying to explain monthly exchange rate movements starting, say, in January 1980, then our 'news' variables for the first month will need to have been conditioned on data from the 1970s. For obvious reasons, market anticipations cannot have been predicated on information dated later than January 1980. By the same token, by February more information will have arrived and there is no reason why market agents could not have updated their forecasting model. Hence, a new VAR with newly estimated parameters ought to be fitted, and so on, throughout the data period.

Although this updating approach is undoubtedly correct, it is not only tedious, even with the latest computer technology, but it also appears to yield results that are little if any improvement on a VAR estimated once over the entire period. A cynic might say that this is because the relationships between the variables are in any case so weak. More positively, if there really is a stable relationship between the (current) fundamentals and their past values – if they are 'stationary', in the jargon of time-series analysis – then the distinction will not matter.

10 See reading guide for references.

11 This approach was actually pioneered by researchers looking at the relationship between interest rates and the money stock in the context of domestic macroeconomic policy.

12 Although market commentary often produces, at first sight, convincing evidence of inconsistent behaviour in the two markets – for example, the episodes in spring 1988 when the pound's international value rose on the perception in currency markets that UK fiscal, and presumably monetary policy, was tight, while share prices fell in London, apparently on fears that monetary policy was far too permissive.

13 It has already been noted that the 'news' approach is consistent with many possible models of the exchange rate. The monetary model was selected in Section 13.2 as a convenient example only. If, instead of tying ourselves down to a particular model relating the exchange rate to the fundamentals, we take a more agnostic view, then we have no reason, a priori, to expect the signs on the 'news' variables to be positive or negative.

14 The contrast is between the extent to which rates vary over the business day and the variance overnight – that is, between closing rates in the evening and the opening rate on the following day (or the next Monday, for a weekend). Thus, if 'news' arrives evenly over 24 hours and the exchange is open, say, for 12 hours, then one would expect to find the variance of the overnight change equal to that of the opening-to-closing change.

15 Also known as 'bootstraps', 'sunspots' and 'will o' the wisp' equilibria. Note that this is another case where research on exchange rates has accompanied research on other financial assets, particularly share prices.

16 See Section 2.5.

17 In other words, the critical question facing the investor in this type of situation is not the direction of the next major price movement, but its timing. As this author found out to his cost in 1985, even when you are right in judging a currency to be mispriced, you can still lose money if it continues to be mispriced for longer than you expected.

18 History records a number of spectacular events that were regarded as bubbles either at the time or fairly soon after they burst, for example the Dutch Tulip Bubble, the Mississippi Bubble, the South Sea Bubble and, more debatably, the bull markets that preceded the Wall Street crashes of 1929 and 1987 and the ongoing (at the time of writing) boom in Internet stocks.

In some cases, the bubbles were initiated by fraudsters who successfully duped irrational, or at least ill-informed, traders. However, that fact does not rule out the possibility that at some point a rational bubble mechanism may well have been at work in the market.

19 To prove that this is true, follow the same procedure as the one outlined for Equation 13.15, making use of Equation 13.21 en route.

Note that the analysis of bubbles exploits the well-known property of difference equations that they permit an infinite number of solutions, each being the sum of a general and a particular component.

20 This is not quite as implausible as it sounds, if only because there are many factors affecting exchange rates which are not included in economists' datasets because they are inherently difficult to quantify, for example political factors.

21 Although in the example given here, it can be shown the bubble will have an expected duration of $(1 - \Pi)^{-1}$.

22 There is no reason, in principle, why we could not respecify the simple model given here to make the probabilities depend on the market fundamentals; however, not only does this complicate the analysis, but also it is completely arbitrary.

There are a number of other possible extensions to the model which would make it more realistic, inevitably at the cost of some considerable complication. For example, allowing for the fact that investors may be risk-averse will exacerbate the explosive behaviour of the exchange rate, because an additional capital gain will be required to compensate currency holders, over and above the capital gain needed under risk neutrality. Also, the market might well perceive the chance of a crash to depend on the length of time the bubble has already run. Since the greater the probability of a crash, the more rapidly the exchange rate must increase, this modification makes the model even more explosive.

23 An unexplored question is how far rational or irrational bubbles in one market are associated with bubbles in another.

24 The term was coined by a researcher who took as his classic case the behaviour of the Mexican peso, which, although notionally on a fixed exchange rate, traded consistently at a forward discount to the US dollar in the mid-1970s, in anticipation of a devaluation that duly materialized in 1976.

25 Officially, the UK will accede to membership when a number of (fairly vague) tests of the British economy's readiness have been satisfied. The first edition of this book used the example of UK accession to the ERM to explain the peso problem. The fact that EMU membership serves as an equally good example speaks volumes about the wearyingly repetitious nature of British policy dilemmas.

14 Microstructure models

Introduction

So far in this book, we have been concerned exclusively with the question: what determines the exchange rate? Moreover, the focus was invariably on the equilibrium exchange rate, by default, with deviations from equilibrium assumed to be temporary and self-correcting. For the most part, the analysis involved aggregate variables, the stock-in-trade of international macroeconomics.

Instead, in this chapter, we look to microeconomics for an explanation of how currency markets work at the day-to-day minute-to-minute level, starting in the first section with an overview of market microstructure in as much detail as is needed to understand what follows. We then go on to deal with a question that has not so far been confronted directly in this book. Instead of asking what determines the exchange rate, we consider the question: *how* does the exchange rate get from one equilibrium to another?

This approach, which has been developed in the past few years, rests on the contention that exchange rate determination models of the type considered elsewhere in this book are potentially misleading for two reasons:

■ The assumption made at the start of the book in Section 1.2 and maintained ever since, that excess demand is eliminated instantaneously by exchange rate movement, involves a dangerous simplification. In fact, the response to demand changes is complex and can only be understood by a detailed analysis of the structure of currency markets, and in particular of the way agents react to the flows of information relating to fundamentals. In other words, the path taken by the exchange rate on its way to its ultimate equilibrium will depend on the fine detail of how markets function, a subject that is usually summarized as *market microstructure*.

■ Much research in this area goes further than this, asserting that the second-order effects of temporary disequilibrium on the real economy may themselves have an impact on the nature of the equilibrium at which the exchange rate finally rests, once the dust has settled.

In order to tackle these questions, we start by examining the structure of the currency markets in more detail than in any of the previous chapters in this book, in order to provide a context for analysing the pricing process – that is, the mechanism by which the market reacts to news about fundamentals so as to move the exchange rate from its old to its new post-shock equilibrium.

The emphasis on the dissemination of information across the market is typical of the microeconomic approach – again, in contrast to the theories covered in the rest of the book, which all explicitly assume homogeneous information. Instead, the microeconomic approach explicitly recognizes that not all news arrives by an out-of-the-blue announcement on TV, Internet or RSS feeds. Some of it probably filters into the market via informal, less public channels to privileged individuals who are then able to trade from an advantageous position with counterparties who are still in the dark. In the second half of this chapter, we examine the implications of this state of affairs for agents who make a living by supplying liquidity in the form of firm quotes at which they stand ready to buy and sell currency for forward delivery. Optimal behaviour by these so-called marketmakers turns out to imply an apparently perverse relationship between the forward premium and the expected change in the exchange rate.

14.1 Order flow analysis

There is a voluminous literature on all aspects of financial market microstructure, but the fact that most of it relates to stock markets creates a problem, because currencies are traded in a very different environment from stocks and shares. On the one hand, in each financial centre, shares are traded in an organized market with its own rules, customs, trading mechanisms and institutional arrangements, including opening hours. In fact, until the advent of computerized trading, all dealing took place in a single physical location ('the trading floor'), which defined the heart of the trading district. In contrast, currencies are exchanged in all sorts of places at all sorts of times. In quantitative terms, the bulk of trading takes place directly or indirectly between the currency-dealing departments of large financial institutions, mostly located in the major financial capitals – London, New York, Tokyo and Frankfurt – but smaller-scale deals go on all the time in local banks, retail bureaux de change and wherever individuals meet to exchange one currency for another. However, in this chapter we ignore everything except large-scale trading in major centres on the grounds that it is vastly more important in quantitative terms and that in any case the net demand by retail traders is ultimately reflected in the major financial centres.

Even with this relatively narrow focus, the structure of currency markets is complex. Moreover, for the past two decades, currency markets have been in a continual state of flux as telephone trading has been superseded by a sequence of ever-more sophisticated computerized trading systems. For that reason, we will consider only the broad outline of market structure.

14.1.1 The structure of currency markets

The microstructural literature starts from the observation that the key agents in the currency markets can be divided into three broad classes:

- *Customers* ('the non-bank public') are the original source of the demand for foreign exchange. In fact, they are the economic agents who figure in all the other chapters of this book: exporters and importers, international investors, tourists, speculators and arbitrageurs. Their demand is often expressed through retail ('high-street') banks, which aggregate transactions to exploit economies of scale or through the treasury departments of multinational corporations. Customers' motivation, however, is assumed here to be exactly the same as elsewhere in the book. The difference is that the microstructural approach starts from the observation that these agents are unable to buy and sell foreign currency directly between themselves. Instead, we make the more realistic assumption that they have to buy their foreign exchange from specialists, who form a second class of agents in the model.

- *Dealers* are agents who do nothing but trade foreign currency. They will usually be departments of major financial institutions ('money-centre banks'[1]). Dealers undertake two types of transaction: first, they supply currency to their customers from the non-bank public; second, they deal with each other in so-called interdealer trade. Sometimes, interdealer business is done directly on the phone or, more likely nowadays, through customized computer dealing systems. Frequently, however, the deals are indirect, done through an intermediary from the third class of agents.

- *Brokers* are agents whose speciality is matching buyers and sellers for each currency pair. Again, they may be independent firms or simply departments or subsidiaries of international banks, but with the difference that they specialize in matching buyers and sellers of a particular currency pair. By specializing, they aim to offer more competitive prices, but above all, they offer a degree of anonymity to the dealers on either side of the trade.

To give an idea of the scale of these market segments, it is estimated that about a third of volume is dealer–customer, while the remainder is split approximately equally between dealer–dealer and dealer–broker trades.

For customers, the transaction costs of buying foreign exchange, which we have for the most part ignored so far in this book, are a cost of doing business. For dealers and brokers, on the other hand, they are the source of the profits that motivate their activity, so they can no longer be ignored. The market structure is mapped in Figure 14.1, where it can be seen that the key players are the dealers, whose decision determines the size of the two related submarkets in the bottom half of the diagram. We can imagine the following idealized sequence of events.

In the first stage, at the start of the day as it were, customers contact dealers in order to buy or sell foreign exchange. Dealers profit by the gap between the prices at which they buy and sell to their clients. The market is, in the jargon, *quote-driven*. In other words, dealers post prices at which they are willing to buy foreign currency (*bid* prices) and at which they are prepared to sell (*ask* prices), with the gap between the two being the spread. Note that each dealer quotes a bid and ask ('makes a market') for each currency traded in advance of making contact with its clients. Quotes are said to drive the market, in the sense that dealers attract business by posting competitive prices: high bid prices to attract agents who have currency to sell, and low ask prices to attract buyers.

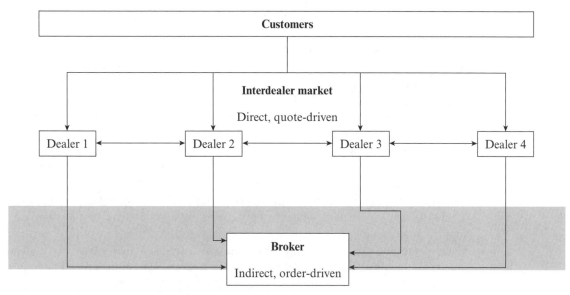

Figjure 14.1 Structure of the currency market

Having bought and sold large quantities of foreign exchange in their transactions with the non-bank public, dealers are likely to be left holding net non-zero positions in the different currencies,[2] which they can offload in either of two ways. One possibility is to deal between themselves in the interdealer market. Alternatively, they may have recourse to an intermediary, a currency broker who generates a profit by matching the orders of dealers who wish to buy with those who wish to sell. To appreciate what is involved here, it is important to understand the difference between the way business is conducted in these two markets.

14.1.2 Quote-driven versus order-driven trade

Direct trade between dealers proceeds very much as it does between dealers and the non-bank public. In what is physically and logically a decentralized market, trades are based on the quoted bid and ask prices posted by dealers.[3] On the other hand, they may opt to deal through a broker in the indirect market who will accept two kinds of order: a *limit order*, i.e. an offer to buy (sell) at a maximum (minimum) price, or a *market order*, which is an order to deal at the best available current price ('at best'), whatever that may turn out to be. Limit orders have the attraction of offering the dealer some degree of control over the price paid or received: a buy order for dollars with yen with a limit of 122 means that the dealer is willing to pay any price up to 122 per dollar – but no more – and likewise a 120 sell order would offer dollars at a price of, at least, 120. If the dollar starts the day at 119, but is strengthening against the yen during the morning, then a buy order with a 122 limit guarantees that the buyer will end up paying no more than 122 and may manage to acquire the dollars for less. On the other hand, if the order is placed too late, and the upward swing in the dollar has already taken it past 122, then the order will remain unfilled. Conversely, if the dollar starts out at 123 and falls from that point onward, then the trade will take place as soon as the exchange rate reaches the 122 buy limit. Note that if the fall continues beyond 122, then the limit order will have resulted in the buyer overpaying relative to the price he would have paid if he had waiteduntil later.

There are three points to note here. First, the direct market offers not only price certainty but also liquidity: each dealer offers a firm commitment to trade at the bid and ask that it is currently quoting, so that with modern technology trades can be completed instantaneously. By contrast, a limit order in the indirect market may take time, if it ever takes place at all – it is simply an offer to deal that may never be accepted. If certainty is required, the broker offers immediate liquidity but with no price guarantee – a market order will be filled more or less instantaneously, but in a fast-moving market or, alternatively, in a relatively thin market for a minor currency, the price actually achieved could be quite a long way from the one anticipated when the order was placed. Second, limit orders are, in an important sense, the true indicators of effective demand, since they are the expression of each agent's underlying supply and demand curves for the currency. Aggregation is therefore critical, because it will determine the 'equilibrium' prices at which trades actually take place. (The inverted commas are in recognition of the fact that equilibrium here means simply a balance between buy and sell orders placed with this particular broker, which may of course be unrepresentative of supply and demand in the market as a whole. Moreover, even at market level, there is at this stage no presumption of any equilibrium in the sense that we have used the word in earlier chapters.)

The traditional way to aggregate orders is via what is known as the broker's *book*, so called because before the age of computers it did involve a large ledger in which all limit orders would be entered. Dealers seeking to deal 'at the market' would then be quoted the cheapest current offer and bid prices (the broker's 'best' prices) from the order book. This process is now completely computerized, but the principle remains the same none the less. In this way, we can be sure that any purchase is made at the lowest of all the ask prices and that sales, likewise, take place only at the maximum of the range of bids.[4]

Notice the importance of the broker's quotation. It is the *internal spread*, i.e. the best available buying and selling prices from the limit orders on his book. Clearly, without this degree of transparency, there could be overlapping limit orders. For example, if a broker had on his book an existing unmatched limit order to buy dollars at 120, then an offer coming in to sell at 119 or better would leave the price indeterminate, since the two could be matched anywhere between 119 and 120, which is clearly unsatisfactory. Instead, the 120 either is dominated by a more attractive buy order on the book, for example a buy with a limit of 120.25, or, if it is the best on the book, it is quoted to dealers as one side of the internal spread. In either case, a dollar seller who might have been willing to accept a price as low as 119 is able simply to 'hit' the buy limit at 120 or 120.25, as the case may be.

Transparency is also very important from another point of view. Since the direct market is fragmented, in the sense that deals are conducted bilaterally between an individual customer and a dealer, the volume and nature of transactions remain hidden from other market participants.[5] By contrast, the modern screen-based indirect market offers a measure of transparency. Participants pay a subscription to one of the service providers such as Reuters or EBS to gain access to screens that report the best available buy and sell limit orders for the different currencies. They can either hit one of the limit orders displayed on the screen (which amounts to executing a market order) or post one of their own. However, since the anonymity of traders is preserved, the system retains a significant element of anonymity.

To sum up, there is a critical distinction to be made between the role played by dealers acting as marketmakers and brokers. The former actively makes a market by operating as principal on his own account, sometimes accumulating a sizeable net position (though probably aiming for a zero overnight position). The broker, by contrast, simply matches buy and sell orders according to a predetermined rule implemented in the program code of the computer that nowadays lies at the heart of every brokerage business. Although the broker normally takes no risks, the market-maker's business is to carry risk in return for appropriate compensation. One aspect of that risk will be considered later in Section 14.3.

14.2 Order flow

This albeit stylized representation of the market allows us to make a distinction that is fundamental in this type of approach to the analysis of the way markets work. In all the transactions described above, there has been an implicit asymmetry. One side of each deal was clearly viewed as the active party, and the other as passive. Thus, the dealer posting quotes in the hope they will be hit by non-bank customers or other dealers is plainly a passive trader, as is the trader placing a limit order with a broker, because in both cases the right to choose whether or not to deal has been surrendered. On the other hand, anyone approaching a dealer or broker for quoted bid and ask prices obviously retains the right not to trade and so plays an active role in the business.

This distinction is crucial. The microstructure approach rests critically on the assertion that although every trade must involve a buyer and a seller, one side must be regarded as active and the other as passive. The distinction between active and passive traders is crucial to this whole literature because, without it, there would be no way of defining the variable that lies at its heart. Once we accept this distinction, we can divide all trades over any period into those initiated by buyers (the volume of buy orders) and those where sellers were the active party (total sell orders). More-over, *the two will not necessarily be equal – neither in terms of number of trades nor in terms of volume of currency*. In fact, the fundamental concept in this literature is the difference between the two.

> Order flow is the **signed** difference between purchases and sales of a currency by the active parties to transactions – that is, with purchases counting as positive and sales as negative.

Note that, on the one hand, the unsigned total of all transactions is a number normally called simply 'volume' and as such is not believed by microstructuralists to convey any useful information about the balance of supply and demand. On the other hand, if we fail to distinguish between active and passive traders, then the signed total of purchases plus sales is identically zero, which is equally uninformative.

In fact, if any readers were wondering how order flow differs from excess demand, this point goes to the heart of the distinction. Since there will always be passive traders willing to absorb any imbalance between buyers and sellers provided they receive adequate compensation in the form of an acceptable dealing price, excess demand will always be zero, for all the reasons given at the very start of this book. But the volume of transactions initiated by buyers and sellers will not necessarily be equal, and the difference between the two conveys information useful to currency dealers – and, if microtheorists are correct, to exchange rate economists too.

Moreover, there is another important aspect to the distinction between the concept of order flow and demand as normally understood. Whereas demand and supply are notional answers to a hypothetical question 'How much would agents buy or sell if the price were . . . ?', order flow relates to actual transactions. As such, it has the attraction of being empirically operational.[6]

At the heart of the microstructure approach is the following assertion:

> Order flow is an indicator of market sentiment.

In other words, the balance of active buy and sell orders reflects a type of consensus view of what is going to happen to the exchange rate.[7]

At this point, it is worth pausing to ask the question: why does this variable have no role to play in mainstream exchange rate economics (or, in fact, in the rest of financial economics)?

This question, which may well have been worrying readers with experience of the currency markets from the very start of this book, can be answered on a number of different levels. First, economic theory concentrates for the most part on the analysis of equilibrium, static or dynamic, with relatively little attention given to the transition between equilibria. In the context of the stock-flow distinction, most exchange rate theory is concerned with equilibrium defined as a situation where the supply of money or of a broader menu of securities is equal to the demand, so that portfolios are in balance and investors are content with their current holdings of all assets. In that respect, equilibrium analysis not only rules out a role for order flow but also ultimately eliminates the need for any transactions at all, with markets gliding instantaneously from one equilibrium to the next whenever any of the exogenous variables changes.[8]

The issue is related closely to the question of how news is disseminated in financial markets. Through most of this book, we have assumed that information is at all times spread uniformly across the market, which means, if agents behave rationally, that they all make the same deductions and arrive at the same beliefs. There is therefore no informational motive for trade.[9] Perhaps the implicit scenario is best understood in terms of an event such as one of the regular macroeconomic announcements – the monthly price index data, for example. In this sort of situation, the information is anticipated and announced simultaneously in a number of media, all of which are monitored continuously by traders in the market and can therefore be regarded as a synchronized addition to the information set of all participants in a single instant.

But it is obvious that not all relevant information reaches the market by this route. Instead, there is a continuous flow of news percolating through to traders by a variety of different channels. A broker may start to get a flow of business from a central bank intervening to manage its exchange rate[10] or simply adjusting the share of each currency in its reserves,[11] or from the government of an oil sheikhdom exchanging dollars for euros to pay for upgrading its fleet of luxury European cars. A dealer may find the supply of pounds unexpectedly low one day as a spell of unusually sunny weather dissuades British tourists from holidaying abroad . . . or the opposite, more likely.

Notice that regardless of whether the events are publicly observable, such as the weather in UK, or as private as portfolio rebalancing (which has to be kept secret at least until it is completed), it remains the case that the associated order flow carries valuable information. This is true because even if we are well informed about the events that cause dealing activity to increase, as might be the case with the weather in Britain, the best we are likely to be able to do is to anticipate the direction of the impact on the exchange rate. As far as its scale and timing are concerned, we can do little more than guess. Of course, the dealers and brokers who are on the receiving end of any wave of buying or selling are aware of little more than a change in order flow (or, more precisely, a deviation of order flow from its expected level) without in most cases having any way of knowing which event is the ultimate cause. They may hazard a guess about the reason for the change in order flow, but identifying its cause is not ultimately their concern.

Given the market structure set out in the previous section and the trading mechanisms set out in some detail here, how does an individual dealer's private information find its way into the market?

14.2.1 Fear of arbitrage, common knowledge and the hot potato

Suppose a dealer finds at some point that he is facing an order level in yen/US dollars that is higher than expected; in other words, an excess of orders to buy yen over orders to sell, to an extent that he had not anticipated.[12] The immediate outcome is that he now has a lower inventory of yen and higher inventory of dollars than he would normally wish to hold. How should he react?

The reader might assume that a dealer would typically respond in this situation by raising his asking price (and presumably his bid price too). Whether this assumption is justified or not, however, will depend on the nature of the news. If it has just been announced that the growth rate of Japanese GDP was unexpectedly high in the most recent quarter, then it may well make sense for the dealer to raise both his selling and buying prices for yen, because he can be reasonably confident that other dealers will be doing the same. To that extent, the increased order flow simply reflects the common knowledge content of the public news.

On the other hand, if there is no obvious new public information – no 'news' – then the dealer dare not risk posting prices that deviate from the rest of the market, for fear of suffering ruinous losses from arbitrage. This is true even though the dealer's rational expectation of the true underlying demand for yen has increased relative to what it was before he encountered the wave of buy orders. But the expected demand has increased by far less than the additional order flow because the probability that he is the only one to have experienced the extra order flow is non-zero – in most cases, approaching certainty. If he raises his yen bid price while all the other dealers keep theirs constant, he will rapidly find large quantities of yen dumped in his lap, while his dollars are snapped up at a bargain price.[13] The expected payoff to adjusting his prices to reflect the additional order flow will therefore be nowhere near enough to compensate him for the loss if the increased order flow turns out to be idiosyncratic, and certainly not enough to provide the necessary risk premium if, in addition, he is risk-averse. We conclude that he will raise his quote by very little, if at all, and certainly not enough to bring his inventory level back to normal.

So if we are to rule out adjusting his quoted prices, how should the dealer respond? Continuing to sell yen and buy dollars is impossible, because even if holding the excess supply of dollars could be tolerated, at some point the dealer's inventory of yen will be exhausted.[14] The only remaining course of action is to sell the dollars on to another dealer in exchange for yen, who then in turn will feel the same increased order flow and, faced with exactly the same decision, will react similarly. The result is that the demand embodied in additional order flow will be passed from dealer to dealer like a hot potato, generating a total volume of trade many times greater than the original increase in order flow that initiated the process.

This scenario has two implications for empirical work. First, it opens up the possibility of explaining the apparently excessive volume of trade in currency markets, which, as already mentioned at several points in this book, seems to be out of all proportion to the size of the changes in any conceivable menu of fundamentals. However, starting from the recognition that the flow of information means that the markets are buffeted by continual waves of buying from the non-financial sector, the volume of trade we actually observe could, according to the order flow model, consist largely of hot potato trades between dealers reacting to shocks associated with relatively trivial items of news.

Second, the hot potato mechanism has implications for the informativeness of trade. If in practice most trade in currency markets is motivated by nothing more than interdealer risk-sharing, then it follows that we can learn little by observing trade other than about how that particular market segment reacts to news. In particular, we can learn very little about what actually causes the exchange rate to move.

14.2.2 The pricing process

What sort of pricing process is implied by the order flow model?

Recall Equation 13.18:

$$s_t = E_{t-1}s_t + \gamma(1+b)^{-1} \sum_{k=0}^{N} \beta^k (E_t z_{t+k} - E_{t-1}z_{t+k}) \qquad (13.18)$$

which expresses the exchange rate at time t as the sum of the rate that was expected at $t-1$ and the appropriately weighted sum of the revisions made in the current period to the market's expectation of the level of all future fundamentals – that is, the impact of news received during period t.

Essentially, the order-flow approach amounts to the assertion that, even if this equation is correct in theory, in practice the fundamental variables included in z_t can rarely be expected to explain more than a small proportion of exchange rate movements, for one or more of the reasons already mentioned. The news that actually moves exchange rates, according to this view, often involves variables that cannot be captured by z_t, either because they are intrinsically unquantifiable, like statements by finance ministers or central bank governors, or because they are secret, like most central bank trading.[15] However, since everything that impinges on the exchange rate must at some point be expressed in the form of currency dealing, we can monitor the flow of news by measuring order flow, which reflects everything in z_t and much more besides.

Now consider the sequence of events following a news event. Depending on whether the news becomes known to all traders or to only a handful, the outcome is demand to buy or sell the currency by some or all agents in the market who have revised their expectations in response to the information. This in turn means some dealers experience an unexpected volume of buy or sell orders, triggering the hot potato sequence of events. At each stage, quoted prices change only by a small amount, but each tiny movement brings the exchange rate closer to the value implied by the new level of expectations regarding the fundamentals. The process thus converges on the exchange rate in Equation 13.18 by a series of tiny steps, generating a large volume of trade on the way.

Notice the potential importance of how widely the news is disseminated. At one extreme, after a public announcement to the whole market, the hot potato process might be expected to converge more rapidly, since the only reason to fear arbitrage would be due to divergences of opinion over the interpretation of news. On the other hand, when only a single trader changes his views, either because he is the sole recipient of the information or because he interprets public news differently, then convergence would presumably be a lot slower.

Section 14.3 sets out an explicit model of market behaviour when information is sometimes made available only to a subset of traders. First, however, we consider the empirical evidence on order flow.

14.2.3 Empirical studies of order flow

From the outset, order flow analysis is an inherently empirically oriented approach to exchange rates. As such, it has to be judged above all by how successful it is in explaining the observed facts. The past few years have seen a flood of papers using order flow data with apparent success in a number of different empirical applications. A complete survey is impossible here,[16] but we can at least provide an overview of the sorts of question that have been addressed so far.

Questions and answers

How great is the direct relationship between order flow and the exchange rate? In other words, what is the price impact of trades in the currency market? Direct estimates of the effect of order flow on exchange rates have been published by a number of authors. For example, Evans and Lyons using data for a four-month period in 1996 estimated that when $1 billion of Deutschmarks are bought, the value of the currency rises by just over one-half of 1%, other things being equal. However, the actual size of the response is not in itself very interesting, especially as it is unclear whether parameters derived from such a short period can be applied more generally.

Does order flow predict exchange rate movements? This is the most obvious question to ask. More precisely, we are concerned with the question: does order flow beat the standard macroeconomic variables in explaining and/or forecasting exchange rates? Since we have seen that, in the short run at least, relative money stock, national income, and so forth, explain very little, the two questions are more or less identical. However, consider the following equation:

$$\Delta s_{t+1} = \gamma_1 \Delta(r_t - r_t^*) + \gamma_2 O_t + u_t \tag{14.1}$$

where O_t denotes order flow at time t. If order flow has nothing to add to our understanding of the way exchange rates move, then the coefficient γ_2 will be insignificantly different from zero. In fact, a number of researchers have found it highly significant, usually contributing more than the interest rate differential, which is often reduced to insignificance by the introduction of order flow into the equation.

The consensus view on this point is therefore a resounding: yes. In fact, Evans and Lyons (2007) have claimed that nearly two-thirds of the actual depreciation over a typical trading day can be accounted for by order flow, compared with virtually zero attributable to macroeconomic variables, a result that appears to be robust (at least in qualitative terms) across different currencies and different sample periods.[17]

It is important to emphasize that the fact that order flow plays an empirically independent role in equations such as Equation 14.1 does not necessarily mean it has some kind of economic significance. As has already been made clear, it could simply be a proxy for unobservable components of z_t fundamentals – either unquantifiable news or future values of quantifiable fundamentals. In other words, order flow may be simply the fundamentals observed at an earlier stage, a possibility that motivates another research question.

Is order flow related to news about fundamentals? There is evidence consistent with the hypothesis that what have previously been called announcement effects are actually the net outcome of the churning process generated by traders as they 'debate' the implications of the news for exchange rates. The argument, of course, is conducted by traders voting with their orders for what they believe is the appropriate level of the exchange rate in the aftermath of a news release. In operational terms, this view implies that order flow ought to be correlated with real-time announcements regarding obviously relevant fundamental variables. Indeed, this is exactly what has been found to be the case by a number of researchers examining the pattern of order flow response to wire service news items.

Is order flow related to the fundamentals? Many, probably most, changes in the fundamentals are unannounced. Take national income, for example. Even if all changes are reflected accurately in quarterly GDP growth announcements, then it does not follow that the growth is totally unanticipated, as has been repeatedly stressed in the past few chapters. In the intervening months, much of the change will have been anticipated either as a result of news about indirectly relevant variables or, more often, through private information (e.g. about unexpectedly high or low sales at a major retailer), which is then incorporated into the exchange rate via order flow.

There are a number of practical problems in trying to provide a rigorous empirical answer to this question, not least the fact that most fundamental variables are observed at such low frequency (monthly, or quarterly in the case of national income and balance of payments data) that correlation with real-time order flow becomes tenuous, especially as the statistics stored in historical databases are often the last of a whole series of revised estimates published over succeeding quarters or even years.

None the less, one or two authors have been able to report significant correlations for the USA and other countries.

Interpretation problems

Empirical research in this area has had to confront three issues, and all three need to be borne in mind when interpreting results of econometric work.

Consider the following equation:

$$\Delta s_{t+1} = \gamma_2 O_t + u_t \tag{14.2}$$

which would be the simplest, most obvious test of the order flow model. In implementing the model, we face the problem that, since O_t is a flow, and not a stock, it is defined only in terms of an elapsed time. The other flow variables that figure in this book – national income, balance of payments components, and so on – are available only at monthly or quarterly frequency. In the case of real-time order flow, it is a matter of choice whether we aggregate as net buys per hour or per day or per month. But clearly, both the size and the interpretation of the coefficient γ_2 will vary, depending on the frequency of the time aggregation.

The direction of causality may well be debatable in estimates of an equation such as Equation 14.2, especially when the aggregation is over very short periods. There are many possible reasons why very short-run exchange rate fluctuations may feed back on to demand. For example, traders who fear that they are at a disadvantage in collecting or processing information may regard the exchange rate change itself as news and then react accordingly. Or, since each time a currency appreciates, the value of all assets denominated in that currency rise in value, other things being equal, exchange rate movements may trigger a rebalancing of internationally diversified portfolios, setting off a ripple of second-, third- and fourth-round order flows, which could be as large as or even larger than the one that started off the process.

These potential feedbacks can be allowed for in a number of different ways. Perhaps the most convincing is to estimate the two-dimensional vector autoregression made from Equation 14.2 by appending an equation with O_t on the left-hand side and augmenting both equations with lagged values of the two variables. Estimates of this type of system yield explicit estimates of the feedback mechanism, if any exists. In fact, research along these lines concludes that, even allowing for feedback effects, order-flow imbalance still moves exchange rates.

In an equation such as Equation 14.1, the interpretation of γ_1 and γ_2 is far from straightforward. To see why, recall that the hot potato process is a stylization of the sequence of events that leads from an unannounced disturbance in a fundamental at time 0, for example the level of economic activity, to a change in the exchange rate. The elapsed time from 0 to the point at which the market might be adjusted fully to the shock and the exchange rate is at its new level might be, say, three hours. At some point, however, perhaps long after the ripples from the original disturbance have died away, the change that set the process going becomes part of the public information set. In other words, the new GDP figures are announced, incorporating the disturbance. This might be as much as a month or more later. If this sort of time frame is typical, then the implication is that, at a frequency higher than monthly, the exchange rate will appear to bear virtually no relationship to national income but will be closely linked to order flow. On the other hand, at a lower frequency, the opposite will apply, because the effect of order flow will have been completely impounded in the published income data. In practice, of course, with many different types of news arriving at more or less random intervals across observation periods, the situation will be far less clearcut. None the less, it remains the case that to a great extent γ_1 and γ_2 are measuring the same thing, with the former eclipsing the latter as the frequency is reduced.

14.3   Microstructural analysis

Order flow analysis is only one strand of the microstructural approach. It has been discussed in some detail in this chapter because it has generated a large empirically oriented literature with claims to a relatively high degree of success in explaining exchange rate movements. However, inspired by work on stock markets, micro-economic analysis has been applied in a number of other ways to the currency market. Attempting to survey this literature would not be very helpful,[18] and so instead we will concentrate on one particularly interesting (and relatively simple) example, a paper by three US-based researchers, Burnside, Eichenbaum and Rebelo (2007), which uses a microeconomic approach to explain the anomaly of the perverse relationship between forward premia and the subsequent depreciation. Recall from Section 12.8 that, assuming risk neutrality, the coefficient of the forward premium in regressions such as Equation 12.16 ought to be 1.0, whereas in practice estimates invariably turn out to be far below unity, and very often negative. We start in the next section with an informal overview of the model, leaving the details to follow afterwards.

14.3.1   Basic mechanism

The model considered here starts from the observation that, in reality, markets are not populated by thousands of identical investors. It is impossible for them all to have the same information at their fingertips, because they cannot all have access to the same data or the same hardware and software, and nor do they all have the same level of expertise to analyse the situation or the same number of years of experience. Some are plainly better-informed than others or simply better able to interpret the data than the mass of ordinary investors. In order to make operational this recognition of reality, replace the default assumption of homogeneous information that has been maintained elsewhere in this book with the following:

> A proportion α of investors are informed – that is, aware of news ('private information') that is hidden from the remaining $(1 - \alpha)$ of uninformed investors, who know only what is publicly announced.

Note that we have only two classes of investor trading in the market, divided on the basis of the information sets that they are able to use in forming their expectations. Nothing is said about the source of the informed investors' advantage – whether through their position as insiders to the market (e.g. major foreign currency traders) or to important institutions (e.g. governments or central banks) or simply through their long experience or sophistication. Moreover, we assume that all informed investors have the same information and interpret it similarly. In fact, both classes of trader are homogeneous.

Given these assumptions, we need to think of the exchange rate process in terms of three components, as follows:[19]

$$\Delta s_{t+1} = \phi_t + \varepsilon_{t+1} + \eta_{t+1} \tag{14.3}$$

where each has a different information status. The first component on the right-hand side of this equation is ϕ_t, which summarizes the information available in the public domain in period t. In other words, it captures the predictable component of the exchange rate, or what we have so far called 'the expected rate of depreciation'. We know both from casual observation and from the mountains of evidence produced by academic researchers that this element accounts for a negligible proportion of the actual outcome. The next element, ε_{t+1} captures the hidden or secret news that is outside the public information set available to the market as a whole. In the present context, however, it is to some extent anticipated by a subset of the market ('informed' traders).[20] More precisely, the market segment we call informed receives a signal hinting at the value of ε_{t+1}. The details of this signal process will be made clear later.

The only part of the process that comes as a complete surprise to all agents in the market is η_{t+1}, which is the usual zero-mean innovation process. Neither class of investors has any information relevant to forecasting this component.

Now consider the implication for the forward rate. Clearly, the uninformed proportion of the market, $(1 - \alpha)$, expects the future depreciation to be:

$$\Delta \hat{s}_{t+1} = \phi_t \tag{14.4}$$

whereas the informed traders, with the benefit of the signal they receive, are able to make the forecast:

$$\Delta \hat{s}_{t+1} = \phi_t + \hat{\varepsilon}_{t+1} \tag{14.5}$$

which, unless their signal is worthless, will clearly be more accurate on average than Equation 14.4.

Both sets of investors are assumed to be confident that they can profit by taking a long position in the forward foreign currency whenever their forecast is positive and a short position whenever it is negative.

Now, in this model, traders are assumed never to trade directly with each other, nor through brokers. Instead, all deals in the forward[21] currency market are invariably made via market makers, who are taken to be uninformed agents but who none the less have to quote ask (bid) rates at which they are willing to sell (buy) currency. In terms of Figure 14.1, these market makers can be thought of as dealers doing business with the public, but in a setting without brokers to provide an alternative trading channel.

In quoting rates for buying and selling forward foreign currency, the problem faced by market makers is that they are unable to distinguish between informed and uninformed traders. Since the cost of doing business is exogenous, and approximately a constant proportion of each deal, we may as well treat it as zero. Given risk neutrality, we know from previous chapters that, if there were no informed investors, then market makers would simply quote a premium equal to the expected future exchange rate. But in the presence of informed traders, this would be suicidal. If they quote a premium equal to the depreciation predicted on the basis of public information alone, which is all they know, they run the risk of being systematically 'hit' by informed investors buying at the ask when their signal tells them ε_{t+1} is positive and selling at the quoted bid when they think it is negative. By following this myopic price-setting policy, marketmakers would end up guaranteeing informed investors a systematic long-term profit at their own expense, a situation that would clearly be unsustainable over anything more than the short term. They can only survive and generate a normal level of profit if they can find a way indirectly to filter out the informed from the mass of uninformed trades.

To understand how they protect themselves, imagine the decision facing a marketmaker in a situation when, for the sake of example, the publicly available information is pointing to a rise in the price of foreign currency – in other words, when $\phi_t > 0$. In this scenario, it is reasonable to expect the majority of (uninformed) traders to be concentrating on the quoted ask rate at which they can buy currency forward.

What about informed traders? They will follow the crowd if their private news source agrees with the public information – in other words, if they have reason to suppose that $\varepsilon_{t+1} > 0$. But if, on the other hand, they tend to think that $\varepsilon_{t+1} < 0$, then they will be concerned with the bid rate at which they can sell foreign currency.

It follows that when the public news indicates buying foreign currency, sellers will be predominantly informed traders who (on average, correctly) expect its value to fall. Marketmakers will therefore set the price at which they buy foreign currency forward lower than the exchange rate expected on the basis of the public information alone, because they will suspect that those traders who swim against the tide by selling when the public information suggests buying are actually better placed to know what is going to happen next period.

Conversely, when $\phi_t < 0$ and all the indications are that the price of foreign currency is going to fall, buyers will arouse the suspicion that they know something that the rest of the market does not, and so again the ask rate will need to be higher than otherwise to protect the market maker from being taken to the cleaners by informed traders.

In summary, when the information in the public domain is positive for the future price of foreign currency (i.e. $\phi_t > 0$) bid rates will be lower than the expected future price indicated by public information. On the other hand, when the information in the public domain is negative (i.e. $\phi_t < 0$), ask rates will be higher than the expected future price indicated by public information.

If informed traders are only a small proportion of the market and if private information predicts a far greater proportion of exchange rate movements than public, in other words if insiders are at a very substantial advantage relative to the bulk of uninformed traders, then it can be shown that this price distortion can be sufficient to make the relationship between the forward premium and the expected depreciation negative, in other words to make estimates of the coefficient b in Equation 12.16 negative.

This has been a very casual explanation of how the model works. We now consider a more formal derivation, starting as always by setting out the assumptions.

14.3.2 Model assumptions

- All agents are risk-neutral. This is purely for the sake of simplicity. Recall the implication: agents are concerned exclusively with the expected value of payoffs.
- All deals with marketmakers involve a fixed order size.[22]
- Marketmakers compete in an environment with no barriers to entry, so that on average they earn only normal (i.e. zero) profits.[23]
- The exchange rate process is given by Equation 14.3.
- At any time t, some of the information relevant to forecasting the level of the exchange rate at $t + 1$ is in the public domain and therefore freely available to all agents in the market, and in particular to traders and marketmakers. This information, denoted ϕ_t, only ever takes two values: $\phi_t = \phi > 0$ with probability $1/2$ and $\phi_t = -\phi < 0$ with probability $1/2$. In other words, as far as the future value of the foreign currency is concerned, the news is as often positive as it is negative.
- When the public news is positive, in other words when $\phi_t = \phi$, uninformed traders buy the currency forward, and when $\phi = -\phi$, they sell the currency.[24]
- The future value of the currency is also affected by hidden information summarized by a variable ε_{t+1}, which likewise can take the value $\varepsilon > 0$ with probability $1/2$ and $-\varepsilon < 0$ with probability $1/2$. Although ε_{t+1} is not directly observed by any agent, a small proportion, α, of the traders in the market receive a signal at time t hinting at its likely value. To keep matters simple, the signal, which we denote ξ_t, can take either of the same two values, ε or $-\varepsilon$. The catch, however, is that ξ_t will not always be correct. Sometimes it will take the value ε when the true value of ε_{t+1} is in fact $-\varepsilon$. It is assumed to be correct only with probability $1/2 \leq q \leq 1$. This assumption allows us to calibrate the extent of the informed traders' advantage. If q is only just above $1/2$, then informed traders have only a very slight edge over other traders and marketmakers. When $q = 1$, their advantage is at its maximum.[25] Note that this simple formulation of the private news process, with ε and $-\varepsilon$ being equal values, has the convenient property that the standard deviation of the process ε_{t+1} is just ε.[26]
- When informed traders receive a positive signal, $\xi_t = \varepsilon$, they buy the currency forward and when it is negative they sell. (Note that they are assumed to speculate in the forward market, never the spot market.)
- All three elements of the exchange rate process are mutually and serially uncorrelated.

14.3.3 Marketmaker's problem

As already explained, the model focuses on the problem facing the marketmaker whose behaviour ultimately generates the forward premium anomaly. The problem he faces is a classic example of the phenomenon known to economists as *adverse selection*, because unless he takes precautions and adjusts the price that he quotes accordingly, he will find that he is unintentionally dealing disproportionately with informed traders. He will, in other words, be inadvertently selecting counterparties to his own disadvantage, picking informed buyers when the public information indicates it is best to sell and the opposite whenever it seems best to buy.

The solution to the problem involves a very simple case of Bayesian learning, so called because it relies crucially on Bayes theorem,[27] which shows how the marginal probability of an event, A, is related to the conditional probability of A given another event, B:

$$P(A|B) = \frac{P(B|A)P(A)}{P(B)}$$

Consider the decision the marketmaker faces in setting the forward ask rate, f_t^A at which he stands ready to deliver foreign currency next period. The analysis hinges on the value of ϕ, so assume initially that the public news is bullish, i.e. $\phi_t = \phi > 0$.

The marketmaker's profit from a forward sale will be equal to the difference between the ask rate he sets and the actual exchange rate realized at time $t + 1$, s_{t+1}. On average, we know this profit will be zero, so the forward rate will be fixed at a level equal to the expected future spot rate. However, the latter is not simply the unconditional expectation. The marketmaker is offering a quote to prospective buyers. The expectation on which it is based ought to reflect the two relevant pieces of information he possesses: first, that the public news is positive, and second, that the counterparty is seeking to buy the currency. In other words, the relevant expectation is conditional on these two facts. Hence, from Equation 14.3, we can state the zero-profit condition as follows:

$$f_t^A = \phi + E(\varepsilon_{t+1}|buy, \phi) \tag{14.6}$$

since the conditional expectation of η_{t+1} is the same as its unconditional expectation (i.e. zero), $\phi_t = \phi$ by assumption, and where the final term in Equation 14.6 means the expected value of ε_{t+1} given that a buy order has turned up and the public news is positive.

So the marketmaker bases his decision on a forecast of the exchange rate that reflects both the public news, on the one hand, and on the other hand, the expected value of the hidden component taking account of the fact that he is dealing with a buyer in a scenario when the public news is positive. The latter is clearly a less significant fact than it would be if the outlook for the currency were negative, in which case the arrival of a buyer would be a strong indication that the counterparty was informed.

In order to evaluate the conditional expectation in Equation 14.6, recall the definition of an expected value as the probability-weighted sum of the possible outcomes. The random variable, ε_{t+1}, can take only two possible values, ε and $-\varepsilon$, and so we can write:

$$E(\varepsilon_{t+1}|buy, \phi) = \Pr(\varepsilon_{t+1} = \varepsilon|buy, \phi)(\varepsilon) + \Pr(\varepsilon_{t+1} = -\varepsilon|buy, \phi)(-\varepsilon) \tag{14.7}$$

Now applying Bayes' law to the first conditional probability on the right-hand side, we get:[28]

$$\Pr(\varepsilon_{t+1} = \varepsilon|buy, \phi) = \frac{\Pr(buy|\varepsilon_{t+1} = \varepsilon, \phi)\Pr(\varepsilon_{t+1} = \varepsilon)}{\Pr(buy|\phi)} \tag{14.8}$$

Starting with the two terms in the numerator, the unconditional probability is simply $1/2$, by assumption, while the conditional probability can be evaluated in stages as follows:

- A buy order may originate from an informed or an uninformed trader.
- An uninformed trader will buy with probability one when the public news is positive, which is the case here. Since uninformed traders are a proportion $1 - \alpha$ of the market, the probability of receiving a buy order from one of them is just $1 - \alpha$ multiplied by one.
- As far as informed traders are concerned, they will buy only if they get a private signal, ξ, which is positive. When, as here, $\varepsilon_{t+1} = \varepsilon$, this event is the arrival of a correct signal, which occurs with probability q. Since they are a proportion α of the market, the probability of a buy order originating from an informed trader is αq.

In total, therefore, the probability of a buy order when both public and private news are positive is:

$$\Pr(buy|\varepsilon_{t+1} = \varepsilon, \phi) = 1 - \alpha + \alpha q \qquad (14.9)$$

The denominator of Equation 14.8 is the probability of a buy order when $\phi > 0$, irrespective of whether the private information is good or bad. In other words, it is the sum of the probabilities of a buy order in the two possible states, $\varepsilon_{t+1} = \varepsilon$ and $\varepsilon_{t+1} = -\varepsilon$, which is:

$$\Pr(buy|\phi) = \Pr(buy|\varepsilon_{t+1} = \varepsilon, \phi)\,\Pr(\varepsilon_{t+1} = \varepsilon) + \Pr(buy|\varepsilon_{t+1} = -\varepsilon, \phi)\,\Pr(\varepsilon_{t+1} = -\varepsilon)$$
$$(14.10)$$

The first term on the right-hand side is the probability in Equation 14.9 multiplied by $1/2$, and the second can easily be computed by logic similar to that used to derive Equation 14.9. Buy orders from uninformed traders come with frequency $(1 - \alpha)$ when $\phi_t = \phi$. On the other hand, with the hidden information unfavourable, informed traders will buy only if they receive the misleading signal, $\xi_t = \varepsilon$, which happens with probability $(1 - q)$. Remembering that informed traders account for a proportion α of all traders, it follows that:

$$\Pr(buy|\varepsilon_{t+1} = -\varepsilon, \phi) = 1 - \alpha + \alpha(1 - q) \qquad (14.11)$$

which, along with Equation 14.9, we can now use in Equation 14.10 to give:

$$\Pr(buy|\phi) = (1 - \alpha + \alpha q)\left(\frac{1}{2}\right) + [1 - \alpha + \alpha(1 - q)]\left(\frac{1}{2}\right) = 1 - \frac{\alpha}{2} \qquad (14.12)$$

Looking back at Equation 14.8, we can write:

$$\Pr(\varepsilon_{t+1} = \varepsilon|buy, \phi) = \frac{(1 - \alpha + \alpha q)\left(\dfrac{1}{2}\right)}{1 - \dfrac{\alpha}{2}} = \frac{1 - \alpha(1 - q)}{2 - \alpha} \qquad (14.13)$$

Now notice that since the only alternative to good hidden information is bad hidden information, it follows that:

$$\Pr(\varepsilon_{t+1} = -\varepsilon|buy, \phi) = 1 - \Pr(\varepsilon_{t+1} = \varepsilon|buy, \phi) = \frac{1 - \alpha q}{2 - \alpha} \qquad (14.14)$$

Recall that q is the probability that informed investors get a correct signal. As long as $q > \frac{1}{2}$, informed investors have an advantage. The higher is q, the greater is the advantage they enjoy. In other words, q is one aspect of what we mean in the context of this model by 'informed'. If q were just $\frac{1}{2}$, then there would be no point in distinguishing the two classes of trader, since the informed would in this situation be getting a signal that was as likely to be wrong as right.

From Equation 14.13, we see that in the good public news scenario, marketmakers are more inclined to guess that the hidden information is positive when they are approached by a buyer if q is large – that is, if they know that the informed traders are highly likely to have received the correct signal. For the same reason, Equation 14.14 is decreasing in q, because the probability of bad hidden information is low if q is large, since in those circumstances informed traders are unlikely to be buyers.

We are almost there. We can now return to Equation 14.7, and using Equations 14.13 and 14.14 gives:

$$E(\varepsilon_{t+1}|buy, \phi) = \frac{1-\alpha(1-q)}{2-\alpha}(\varepsilon) + \frac{1-\alpha q}{2-\alpha}(-\varepsilon) = \frac{\alpha}{2-\alpha}(2q-1)\varepsilon \qquad (14.15)$$

Notice that when there are no informed investors, so $\alpha = 0$, or when the informed investors have no advantage ($q = \frac{1}{2}$), Equation 14.15 is zero, which is the unconditional expectation of ε_{t+1}. In other words, in this situation, marketmakers can learn nothing from the fact that they are dealing with a buyer – on the other hand, they also face no adverse selection threat.

Finally, going back to the ask forward rate in Equation 14.6 and using this result, we get:

$$f_t^A = \phi + \frac{\alpha}{2-\alpha}(2q-1)\varepsilon \qquad (14.16)$$

so the forward rate quote to buyers is greater the higher the proportion of informed investors in the market, the more accurate their information and the more volatile is the hidden news component of exchange rate movements.

14.3.4 The solution

By the same logic, it is possible to solve for the remaining three forward rates: the ask rate when the public news is bad and the bid rate when the public news is good and bad respectively. For convenience, all four quotes are presented in the table below.

	$f(\phi_t = \phi)$	$f(\phi_t = -\phi)$
Ask rate premium	$\phi + \dfrac{\alpha}{2-\alpha}(2q-1)\varepsilon$	$-\phi + (2q-1)\varepsilon$
Bid rate premium	$\phi - (2q-1)\varepsilon$	$-\phi - \dfrac{\alpha}{2-\alpha}(2q-1)\varepsilon$

The solution for both bid and ask rates is illustrated in graphic form in Figure 14.2, with the quoted forward rate on the vertical and ϕ_t on the horizontal axis. For any

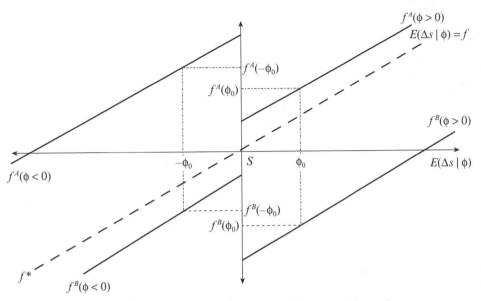

Figure 14.2 Determination of the forward premium/discount (general)

given value of ε, the forward rate increases one for one with ϕ, or decreases one for one with $-\phi$, which explains why all the lines in Figure 14.2 are at 45 degrees to the horizontal. Clearly, the lines for positive ϕ, labelled $f^A(\phi)$ and $f^B(\phi)$, start from points lower down the vertical axis than $f^A(-\phi)$ and $f^B(-\phi)$. To see why this is the case, note that since α is less than one (probably far less than one), the fraction $\dfrac{\alpha}{2-\alpha}$ is also less than one, and moreover $(2q-1)$ cannot be negative because q has to be greater than $1/2$. It follows that when ϕ_t is very near zero,[29] i.e. close to the vertical axis, the ask rate for $-\phi$ is greater than for ϕ. The same is true for the bid rate, but below the horizontal axis: for very small values of ϕ_t, the bid premium is more negative for ϕ than for $-\phi$.

The implication is that when ϕ is positive, say ϕ_0, the premium can be lower than it is at $-\phi_0$, as in Figure 14.2, where $f^A(\phi_0) < f^A(-\phi_0)$. In other words, the premium can be a decreasing function of the publicly perceived expected rate of change of the exchange rate. Equally, however, it is clear that for high values of ϕ, the standard pattern prevails, with higher values being associated with higher levels of the premium.

What is the critical value of ϕ, say ϕ^*, at which $f^A(\phi^*) = f^A(-\phi^*)$? The answer is given in Figure 14.3, where it is obvious that at any value of ϕ between ϕ^* and 0, both bid and ask rates are higher when $\phi_t = -\phi$ than when $\phi_t = +\phi$. More formally, taking the two solutions for the ask rate given above and setting them equal gives:

$$\phi^* + \frac{\alpha}{2-\alpha}(2q-1)\varepsilon = -\phi^* + (2q-1)\varepsilon \qquad (14.17)$$

from which we derive the value:

$$\phi^* = \frac{1-\alpha}{2-\alpha}(2q-1)\varepsilon \qquad (14.18)$$

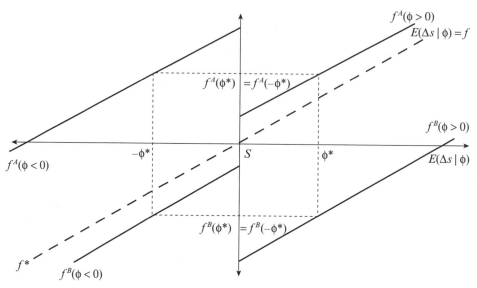

Figure 14.3 Determination of the forward premium/discount $f^A(\phi^*) = f^A(-\phi^*)$

As long as $\phi < \phi^*$, the relationship between the forward premium and the exchange rate movement forecast by the publicly available information sources is perversely negative.[30]

How likely is it that this condition will be fulfilled? The authors of this research do a series of computations based on what they regard as plausible values of the parameters and conclude that ϕ is highly likely to be in the perverse zone. Take the components of Equation 14.18 one at a time:

- It should be clear that ϕ itself is probably very small. So much is clear from the evidence summarized in earlier chapters, all pointing to the conclusion that the published data, which is all that is available to the researcher, is of little use in forecasting the future path of the exchange rate. Other things being equal, this makes it more likely that $\phi < \phi^*$. The exception to this generalization is to be found in high-inflation cases. As has already been mentioned elsewhere in this book, the basic parity relationships – PPP, UIRP, the Fisher equation – tend to fit best where inflation is highest. In other words, the publicly available information is useful in these situations, because it predicts quite a large proportion of the actual change in the exchange rate. With a relatively large value of ϕ, the adverse selection problem is small, since informed traders do not have a very great advantage – there is simply less left to predict using private information.

- The higher is α, the smaller is ϕ^*, and therefore the less likely it is that we will find a perverse relationship between the forward premium and the expected exchange rate change.

- The higher is q, the greater the adverse selection risk, and hence the greater is ϕ^*. In one limiting case, when $q = \frac{1}{2}$, informed investors receive a worthless signal about the value of ε_{t+1}, and so the marketmaker needs to take no precautions. In this case, the forward premium is simply ϕ, whether measured at the bid or the ask rate or at the mid-market rate, which is the average of the two. At the other extreme, when $q = 1$, informed traders know ε_{t+1} with complete certainty. If, in addition, $\alpha = 1$, then all agents except the marketmaker are fully informed, and so adverse selection is total, in the sense that a buy (sell) order indicates unambiguously that ε_{t+1} is positive (negative).

14.3.5 Comments

This model of marketmaker behaviour has been covered in some detail because it shows how microeconomics can generate useful insights into the way exchange rates are determined, in the short run at least, starting from simple assumptions which can mostly be generalized without changing the conclusions very greatly.[31]

There is, however, one major limitation that needs to be noted, and it can perhaps best be summarized in the question: do we really believe in currency market insiders? In stock markets, there are self-evidently individuals who have access to inside information, and the fact that they do sometimes trade on that knowledge has been proven in court in the USA, the UK and other countries from time to time. Indeed, there are grounds for believing that this may be only the tip of the proverbial iceberg. But is there anyone with comparable knowledge in currency markets?

To be specific, if for example I overhear a conversation that indicates that a major pharmaceutical company has developed a new wonder drug, then I am clearly in possession of information relevant to the value of the firm's shares, i.e. fundamental information. What is the comparably fundamental information in the case of exchange rates? Macroeconomic news is guarded quite carefully to prevent it leaking out before its public announcement. Moreover, we know from all the evidence accumulated over the floating exchange rate era that this sort of data – money stock, GDP growth rates, and so on – is of little use in forecasting the exchange rate anyway.

A conceivable scenario is one where insiders have access, legally or illegally, to news on which they can trade in the very short run, for example access to money supply figures a few hours or more likely minutes or seconds before they are announced, or advance warning of large currency deals about to go through the exchanges.[32] Opportunities such as these open up only very briefly. The implication in either case is that the scenario is inherently short-term in the extreme.

The most plausible interpretation is, as already mentioned at the start of this section, that this model zeroes in on the mechanism at work at each stage of the sequence of deals in succeeding stages of hot potato trading. But in this framework, note how limited is the nature of the private information involved. The only thing a buyer (seller) knows is that his position in the currency in question is suboptimally low (high) as a result of recent trades. He has no idea whether this is a situation unique to him, due simply to random variation in trade, or whether it is typical, reflecting the market impact of news. The sum total of his informational advantage can be summed up as being able to attach a small probability to the possibility that demand has increased or decreased.

As far as the model's usefulness is concerned, this is, in one sense, no drawback. After all, short-term behaviour is interesting in itself, and it is possible that the mechanism set out here does indeed play a part in explaining the apparently perverse relationship between exchange rate movements and the forward premium. But it has to be the case that there is a lot more to the paradox than simply marketmakers protecting themselves against adverse selection. For example, at the time of writing this chapter (summer 2007), the yield on 90-day Treasury Bills is around $4^1/_2\%$ in the USA and slightly over $^1/_2\%$ in Japan, an interest differential that has been fairly constant for several years. (Recall that since CIRP holds to within a fraction of 1%, this means that the dollar has been at a discount and the yen at a premium of around 4%.) Instead of depreciating during those years, however, the dollar has actually appreciated by 7% or 8% – which is precisely the forward premium paradox writ large. Clearly, there is something else going on here than simply marketmakers protecting themselves against informed traders.

In fact, the flood of borrowing in low-interest countries (mainly Japan) and lending in high-interest countries (primarily the USA, but also the UK, Australia and New Zealand), known as the *Asian carry trade*, contradicts almost all aspects of the model here. For example, throughout the past few years, most of the known fundamentals (money stocks, relative inflation rates, and so on[33]) have pointed to yen appreciation. In terms of the model, we had ϕ_t strongly positive – and yet investors sold yen in large quantities in order to buy assets in high-interest countries. Moreover, evidence suggests that the main sellers were Japanese householders, using the proceeds to buy dollar securities. Since it is hard to imagine that the redoubtable Mrs Watanabe had private information unavailable to major banks and hedge funds, it must be concluded that the model, interesting as it is, cannot cope with the real challenge of explaining longer-run anomalies.

14.4 Conclusions

What can the microstructural approach teach us? It is certainly an important advance in our understanding, though its results have, perhaps not surprisingly, been a little oversold by its key proponents. In particular, the evidence that order flow can make a significant contribution to explanations and forecasts of exchange rate movements is important, but the overwhelmingly positive results of direct comparisons with the type of exchange rate determination models covered in the rest of this book need to be kept in perspective.

Perhaps one can reasonably make an analogy here with political polling. Opinion poll forecasts of election results are often wildly inaccurate (though none the less far more accurate than exchange rate forecasts). Yet experience shows that exit polls, which catch a small sample of voters leaving the election booths and ask them the straightforward question 'How did you vote?', are very accurate indeed at predicting the election outcome about to be announced some hours later. Like exit polls, order flow-based forecasts use ex-post information, so their superior performance is not entirely surprising.

As far as the model of marketmaker behaviour is concerned, it provides an interesting insight into the way forward premia are determined in the very short run, and may be a substantial contribution to explaining the puzzle found in empirical work in this area. But it cannot be anywhere near the full story, so we have to conclude that the puzzle remains largely unsolved.

Another question that has been deferred until now is this: are the models covered in this chapter consistent with rational expectations? The answer is plainly in the affirmative, provided we allow for heterogeneous information. In other words, the microeconomic approach can be interpreted[34] as consistent with the assumption that agents make the best possible use of their available information sets, but it starts from the observation that different agents inevitably have different information sets – at least in the short term. Indeed, there is a sense in which this approach is almost self-evidently true. Only news that is carried by the major wire services – Reuters, Bloomberg, and so on – can be assumed to be instantaneously and universally disseminated to the markets. Any other news has to be regarded as at least partially private when initially generated. Moreover, the implications for equilibrium exchange rates of even the most public news items – money stock data, price indices, interest rate changes – are unclear. In so far as the implications of news take the form of order flow impacting on only a subset of the dealer community, information heterogeneity is unavoidable. From this starting point onward, the order flow analysis assumes rational behaviour on the part of all market participants. The outcome, however, is a price that reflects the gradual dissemination of news, asymptoting towards the efficient market equilibrium as information spreads from dealer to dealer.

In fact, one way of looking at the order flow literature is as an attempt to provide an empirical response to the famous challenge posed by Grossman and Stiglitz (1980), who argued that market efficiency would ultimately be impossible, since it ruled out any reward to those who gather and process information. If information is costly to collect and process, then nobody would bother to do so unless there were some return in excess of what was available to the rest of the market. Prices therefore would need at some point to be away from their fully efficient level, so as to offer a reward to agents who incur the costs of doing the research.

At one level, the order flow model solves this problem by postulating that nobody takes on the research task. Instead, the invisible hand of the market disseminates the order flow generated by news. Dealers may in the process benefit in the form of a higher volume of business, but no agent feels the need to relate the increase in order flow to news about any particular fundamental. In fact, the private component of news remains private. What is revealed is simply increased net demand and a consequent rise in the value of one currency against another. Nobody except the exchange rate economist is concerned with the fundamentals.

This interpretation may appear to contradict the model of marketmaker behaviour in the last section, but the two can be reconciled by recalling that ϕ_t is explicitly assumed to be small, and probably near zero. If we identify the signal, ξ_t, with the inventory blip resulting from the unexpectedly high or low level of demand for the currency at the previous stage, then it is plausible that the dealer in question could have a significant trading advantage over dealers further up the chain.

In this chapter, we have been dealing with the most important function of markets. In general, markets are essentially information-processing machines that make it possible for human beings acting as buyers and sellers to solve a data aggregation problem that would defeat even the largest computer. It is as if traders were voters whose preferences could be expressed only via their trades with each other. At the end, the price – in this case, the exchange rate – emerges as a consensus of the views of market participants, weighted appropriately by their relative financial voting power.

Summary

- Dealers operate as marketmakers quoting firm bid and ask prices at which they are willing to buy and sell currency to customers from outside the financial sector and to other similar agents in the interdealer market.

- Dealers often find it more attractive to deal with a broker who can offer the advantages of limit trading and also anonymity.

- Order flow is the difference between initiated purchases and sales of a currency, with purchases counting as positive and sales negative.

- When faced with unexpectedly high or low demand for a currency, dealers dare not blindly change their prices, for fear of being 'picked off' by other dealers looking for arbitrage opportunities. They can only respond to the fact that their inventories are no longer optimal by trading away the excess with other dealers, who then face the same problem and will respond similarly. The result is a sequence of trades across the dealer community, as the additional currency is passed around like a hot potato.

- If some market participants have access to private information, uninformed market makers face an adverse selection problem in setting their quoted forward rates.

- They will quote rates that offer a margin of protection to cover their informational disadvantage in dealing with informed traders, which will be greater the more informed traders are in the market and the more accurate their information.

- The resulting deviation of the forward premium from the depreciation predicted by public information can be sufficient to explain the perverse relationship between them often reported by researchers.

Reading guide

Rime (2003) gives an account of how the foreign exchange market operates, though the technology driving it is continually changing, so it may already be out of date in some of the detail.

The best starting point on order flow is Lyons (2001). A more up-to-date survey can be found in Vitale (2004). Frömmel, Mende and Menkhoff (2007) make an interesting attempt to take the order flow analysis a stage further.

For useful overviews, see Evans (2006) and Evans and Lyons (2006).

The model covered in the second half of the chapter is by Burnside, Eichenbaum and Rebelo (2007). There are, however, many other models of currency market microstructure. One of the most influential in recent years is Bacchetta and van Wincoop (2006). Sarno and Taylor (2001) survey the microstructure literature, though selectively, as the title implies. For an up-to-date starting point, see the papers introduced by Sager and Taylor (2006).

On the question of what constitutes news in the currency markets, see Dominguez and Panthaki (2006). On fundamentals and order flow, see Andersen *et al.* (2003).

Web page: **www.pearsoned.co.uk/copeland**.

Notes

1 That is, banks that act as wholesalers, conducting transactions in the money and foreign currency markets on behalf of retail banks or on behalf of their own retail branches.

2 Even if the aggregated demand to buy, say, euros with dollars was equal to the amount supplied by euro sellers, it does not follow that each individual dealer will have faced zero excess demand for euros, let alone for all the other currencies traded in the market.

3 Nowadays, of course, the process is electronic, with specialized systems such as Reuters Dealing 2000–1, which provide both online quotes and instant messaging on a single screen.

4 Note that the oldest order will not necessarily be the first to be filled unless it is also the best (i.e. lowest ask or highest bid). In fact, the oldest might have been on the book longest precisely because it is so uncompetitive that it will never be filled. For that reason, orders often carry a 'good till . . .' tag, i.e. a time limit for fulfilment (typically end of the day).

5 In some financial markets (e.g. the London stock exchange) there is a regulatory requirement to make information on all trades publicly available more or less immediately. Since there is no organized spot currency market, there can be no regulatory body with the power to enforce transparency.

6 In fact, at any moment, the book of unfilled limit orders represents points below the current price on the demand curve and above the current price on the supply curve.

7 The word 'sentiment' is used here for want of a better word to convey the vagueness of general market belief. What is involved is obviously not itself an expectation, but it is presumably related to expectations in some way, though it is unclear how or over what forecast horizon.

8 This is not to say that economists are blind to the possibility – in fact, the likelihood – that markets are often in disequilibrium. But until recently most economic models were of equilibrium states, with more or less *ad hoc* disequilibrium adjustment mechanisms tacked on as required (typically, when confronting the theory with the data). Explicitly analysing disequilibrium and following through its consequences results in models of considerable complexity and often involves abstruse mathematics, which is why so little attention is given to them in this book.

9 Of course, this does not rule out other motives, such as liquidity trades, but since these are not information-driven, they cannot tell us anything about market sentiment.

10 Central bank purchases and sales of foreign exchange are usually announced some time after the event. Even where the monetary authority is known to be pursuing a policy of intervening, the actual timing and scale of operations are never clear at the time.

11 Central banks may see their job as requiring them, at least to some extent, actively to manage their reserve portfolio, which means buying and selling currencies to achieve an optimal mix (however defined), rather than passively accepting whatever allocation results from their intervention operations.

12 Note that we are not assuming that the expected volume of buy and sell orders are necessarily equal.

13 He will also be sending out a signal that he has dollars to offload, which is not something he will want to reveal to the market.

14 Most foreign currency dealers clear their positions overnight in any case. Lyons (2001) quotes his own study of a single dealer trading in the $/DM market (the most important exchange rate at the time) on behalf of a major bank as showing that the half-life of non-zero balances was as little as 10 minutes, even though the volume traded amounted to as much as $1 billion per day.

15 Remember that the events mentioned here may still be fundamental, especially if they have a bearing on the future path of money stocks or income. An event that is impossible to quantify may none the less have an impact on quantifiable variables, or at least on expectations regarding quantifiable variables. Some researchers in this area might add so-called liquidity requirements to the list of determinants, but in the absence of a model, it is not clear whether they are actually fundamental.

16 See the reading guide at the end of the chapter for survey papers.

17 It is worth remembering that, given the enormous volume of real-time transaction data generated every day, sample periods in this sort of work tend to be short – sometimes as little as a single week. The good news is that this minimizes the impact of data-mining, since researchers rarely

need to reuse the same dataset (though they sometimes do so, in order to avoid having to rework a new block of raw data). The bad news is that it can sometimes leave one wondering whether the results reported might have been sample-specific.

18 Especially for readers without the requisite background in graduate-level microeconomics, including game theory and general equilibrium analysis.

19 The authors actually specify the model in terms of (discrete) proportional growth rates – that is, $(S_{t+1} - S_t)/S_t$, etc. For simplicity's sake, it is rewritten here in terms of log differences throughout, which is approximately the same.

20 The subscript on this component is a little arbitrary. The authors use $t + 1$ on the grounds that, unlike ϕ_t, it is not known with certainty until the exchange rate depreciation has actually occurred.

21 In this section, all currency deals are for (one period) forward delivery.

22 The point of this assumption is that risk neutrality on its own would imply an investment in the prospect with the highest expected payoff equal to the whole of an agent's resources, which in a perfect capital market would be infinite. On the other hand, allowing for risk aversion would make the order size finite but would involve a submodel of marketmaker choice under uncertainty. The assumption that orders are fixed in size avoids these unnecessary complications.

23 In elementary microeconomics, costs are defined to include a normal level of profit. Hence, by definition, competition ensures that total costs equal total revenue, and zero (excess) profit.

24 Again, this assumption avoids the problem of modelling traders' choice under uncertainty.

25 Even in this polar case, however, they have no 'money machine'. They make a profit over time on average, but any individual trade may make a loss if the residual error, η_{t+1}, is large and opposite in sign to ε_{t+1}.

26 This follows straightforwardly from the fact that, since the mean of ε is zero, its variance is clearly just:

$$E(\varepsilon_{t+1}^2) = (0.5)(\varepsilon)^2 + (0.5)(-\varepsilon)^2 = \varepsilon^2.$$

27 See any basic statistics and probability textbook for an explanation of this very important theorem.

28 Treating $\varepsilon_{t+1} = \varepsilon$ as the event A and *buy* as the event B, and conditioning all the events on $\phi_t = \phi$. Note that since ε and ϕ are assumed to be independent, $\Pr(\varepsilon_{t+1} = \varepsilon | \phi)$ is just the same as $\Pr(\varepsilon_{t+1} = \varepsilon)$.

29 Strictly speaking, the forward rate is undefined in this model when $\phi = 0$, and so this should be interpreted as applying when ϕ_t is negligibly small.

30 Burnside *et al.* (2007) provide a formal proof that $plim(\beta) < 0$ where β is the estimated slope coefficient in the regression of the exchange rate change on the forward premium (i.e. b in Equation 12.16) and *plim* denotes the asymptotic probability limit.

31 For example, the authors also present a version of their model in which uninformed investors do not always buy a currency that looks as though it will appreciate on the basis of public news. Instead, they buy (sell) a currency expected to appreciate (depreciate) with some probability greater than $^1/_2$. This complicates the equations somewhat, without substantially changing the conclusions.

32 The authors try to pre-empt these questions by offering the alternative interpretation that informed traders are simply better at processing the publicly available data. But this again strains credibility somewhat. While humility requires us to accept that the academic community may conceivably have failed where others succeeded, we are also being asked to believe that the same is true of all but a few of the financial institutions that operate in the currency markets. As far as large deals are concerned, note that traders tend to break up large trades into smaller lots precisely so as to minimize the price impact.

33 Some commentators have argued that in PPP terms, the dollar was (and still is) undervalued relative to the yen. This may be true in terms of consumer prices, but it is far less obvious where traded goods prices are concerned. In any case, it ignores the fact that, with prices in Japan actually falling or constant, the extent of any possible undervaluation of the dollar was diminishing all the time, and yet the interest rate differential has tended to increase over the past two years.

34 As has been pointed out, the possibility that instead of (or in addition to) having more information, some investors make better use of information than others is also consistent with these models.

15 The risk premium

Introduction

We have referred to the risk premium associated with international speculation on numerous occasions throughout this book, without making any attempt to say what factors determine its size. It is now time to rectify this omission.

Unfortunately, the subject not only is a difficult one but also involves different analytical tools from those used in the rest of the book. In particular, it relies on microeconomics – the theory of constrained choice – as well as on mathematical statistics. To make the material in this chapter as accessible as possible, many complicating issues will be sidestepped. For the most part, the simplifications introduced have little effect on the central question of what determines the scale of the compensation required by a risk-averse economic agent to persuade him to speculate.

The chapter takes the following form. We start in the first section by listing a number of basic assumptions that allow us to focus on the issue at hand, without getting sidetracked into consideration of extraneous questions. Then, in Section 15.2, a simplified model is analysed using the indifference curve techniques familiar from basic microeconomics. The next section, which some readers may choose to omit, goes on to analyse formally a model that, though not much more complicated, is a lot more general. Finally, as usual, the chapter closes with a brief review of the evidence on the risk premium, followed by some conclusions.

Before continuing, there are a number of preliminaries that the reader is advised to undertake.

- If necessary, check the definitions of risk aversion, risk neutrality, the risk premium and so on, introduced initially in Section 3.1.3.

- Where necessary, readers should refresh their understanding of what is meant by an *expected value* (Section 11.1) and a *variance* (Box 12.3 of Chapter 12). The concept of *covariance* also plays an important part in Section 15.3. A brief definition will be given there to refresh the reader's memory. Explanations of all three concepts can be found in any elementary statistics textbook. (Note that the *standard deviation* is defined simply as the positive square root of the variance.)

- Readers with no previous acquaintance with indifference curve analysis will find Section 15.2 heavy-going. Unless, as an alternative, they can take the material in Section 15.3 in their stride, they would be best to read the chapter on indifference curves in an introductory economics textbook before proceeding.

- Section 15.3 takes the theory of expected utility for granted. The reading guide provides references for those who wish to investigate these foundations further. However, an understanding of expected utility theory is certainly not required in order to cope with the material in this chapter.

15.1 Assumptions

The analysis in this chapter will focus on a representative economic agent ('the speculator'), whose environment is characterized by the following assumptions.[1]

- There is a perfect capital market, with no transaction costs of any kind, and in particular no margin requirements for forward purchases or sales.[2]

- Only two periods are relevant to the decision: 'the present' (period 0) and 'the future' (period 1).

- The speculator seeks to maximize the expected value of his utility, which depends only on the amount of consumption he can enjoy in period 1, C_1. Marginal utility diminishes as consumption increases, a condition equivalent to assuming risk aversion. For simplicity we assume that no consumption takes place in period 0.

- There is no inflation.

- Other than a given quantity of wealth, W_0 (a fixed 'endowment'), the resources available for consumption in the future can be increased only by the device of speculation in forward contracts. (In other words, the possibility of buying other assets in period 0 is ruled out by assumption.)

   Every pound spent on buying dollars forward costs (that is, reduces consumable resources by) £F_0, which is the current price of a dollar for delivery in period 1. On the other hand, it will increase consumption by £S_1, the spot price of dollars in period 1, when the currency is delivered and is available for exchange back into sterling on the spot market.

   Net, therefore, for each pound of forward dollars purchased, future consumption benefits (or suffers) to the tune of £$(S_1 - F_0)$. If the investor spends £A on forward purchases, then future consumption will be increased (or diminished) by £$(S_1 - F_0)A$. It follows that the total amount available for consumption will be:

$$C_1 = (S_1 - F_0)A + W_0 \qquad (15.1)$$

Obviously, unless A is *zero*, C_1 will be uncertain as of period 0. Forward purchases of dollars will *increase* future consumption if the price of dollars *rises*, but will *decrease* consumption if the opposite occurs.

These assumptions will be maintained throughout the next two sections. We shall examine briefly the consequences of relaxing each of them in Section 15.3.5.

15.2 A simple model of the risk premium: mean–variance analysis

One way of representing the problem facing the currency speculator is by using the indifference curve framework familiar from the analysis of household utility maximization. In order to use that analysis, we shall have to make an additional assumption, though it will be dropped in the next section.

Specifically, let us suppose that the agent in the forward market bases his decision-making solely on two parameters: the expected value of his future consumption and the risk associated with it, *as measured by its standard deviation*.

15.2.1 The indifference map

First, consider the objects of choice. In elementary microeconomics, the household's tastes are defined with respect to combinations ('baskets') of two goods, both of which are inherently desirable, so that more of either good is always preferable, other things being equal (that is, provided no sacrifice of the other good is required). Given that both goods are desirable, it follows that indifference curves tracing out all combinations of the two goods that yield any particular level of satisfaction will be *downward-sloping*, reflecting the fact that sacrifices of one good need to be compensated by increments of the other if a constant level of utility is to be maintained.

In the present case, the objects of choice on the two axes consist of one desirable characteristic, expected consumption, written *in this section only* as μ,[3] and one undesirable characteristic, risk – as measured by the standard deviation of consumption, written σ_C.[4] What will the indifference curves look like?

Consider a point on the vertical axis in Figure 15.1, like μ^0. It represents a position of no risk (no forward contracts), with a guaranteed future consumption level of μ^0. In order to draw the indifference curve through this point, we need to locate combinations of the two characteristics μ and σ_C that yield the same level of satisfaction as the certain consumption level μ^0.

Obviously, since any move away from the vertical axis involves taking on risk, the speculator will not voluntarily do so unless he is compensated – this is what is meant by risk aversion. Compensation can only take the form of higher expected consumption in the future. If the additional future expected consumption is great enough, he

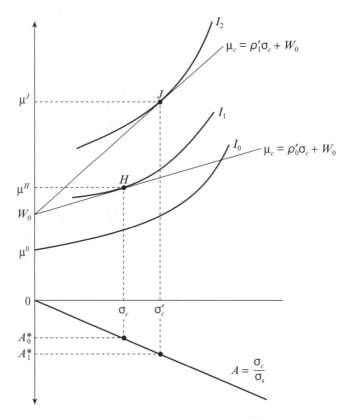

Figure 15.1 Speculator's equilibrium in the simple model

will willingly take on risk. The process can continue: he can be persuaded to take on even more risk by the carrot of greater expected consumption. Therefore, any combinations of μ and σ_c that yield the same utility as μ^0 must lie above and to the right of μ^0.

We conclude that the indifference curves will slope *upwards* from left to right, associating *greater risk* with higher *expected values* as compensation. Furthermore, the greater the degree of risk aversion, the steeper the curves, because the greater is the compensation needed to persuade the investor to accept risk.

In addition, by an argument analogous to the one used to guarantee the convexity of indifference curves in the elementary model of household demand, it is reasonable to assume in the present case that the indifference curves will get steeper, as the compensation required per unit of risk increases with the quantity of risk already undertaken. In other words, the indifference curves will be convex from beneath, as in Figure 15.1.

Plainly, we could have used any point on the vertical axis as our starting point for drawing an indifference curve. It follows that the higher up is the indifference curve, the greater the level of utility associated with the combinations on it. Thus, combinations along the curve labelled I_2 are preferable to those on I_1, which in turn are preferable to those on I_0, and so on. The speculator's objective is obviously to reach the highest possible indifference curve.

15.2.2 The constraint: the speculative opportunity line

The constraint on the investor is derived from Equation 15.1, which showed how consumption is related to the chosen value of A, given initial wealth, W_0, the forward rate, F_0, and the outcome for the spot rate, S_1.

First, consider what is implied for the *expected* value of consumption:

$$EC_1 \equiv \mu_C = (ES_1 - F_0)A + W_0 \tag{15.2}$$

because of course both the forward rate and the initial level of wealth are known as of time 0 – only the future spot rate is uncertain (see Box 15.1).

Box 15.1   Strictly, Equation 15.2 should read:

$$E_0 C_1 \equiv \mu_C = (E_0 S_1 - F_0)A + W_0$$

The subscripts on the expectations operator are suppressed throughout this chapter, however, since they always date from the first period.

Now we need to calculate the standard deviation of consumption. The variance of consumption, σ_C^2, is simply the expected value of the squared deviation from the mean (or expected value itself):

$$\begin{aligned}
\sigma_C^2 &= E[(C_1 - \mu_C)^2] \\
&= E\{[A(S_1 - ES_1)]^2\} \\
&= A^2 E[S_1 - ES_1]^2 \\
&= A^2 \sigma_S^2
\end{aligned} \tag{15.3}$$

where σ_S^2 is the variance of the spot rate.[5] Since the standard deviation is simply the (positive) square root of the variance, this means:

$$A = \pm \frac{\sigma_C}{\sigma_S} \tag{15.4}$$

A will be positive only when the premium is positive. If the premium is negative, that is $(ES_1 - F_0) < 0$, then a positive value of A would imply a *lower* expected value of consumption than W_0, for a position involving risk. For a risk-averse agent, this is out of the question. It follows that A must take the same sign as the premium, and for the purposes of the exposition here it will be assumed that both are positive.

Now if we substitute for A from Equation 15.4 into Equation 15.2, we find:

$$\mu_C = \frac{\sigma_C}{\sigma_S}|ES_1 - F_0| + W_0$$

$$= \rho' \sigma_C + W_0 \tag{15.5}$$

where:

$$\rho' \equiv \frac{|ES_1 - F_0|}{\sigma_S}$$

is the risk premium normalized by the standard deviation of the spot rate.

Equation 15.5 plays the same part in the speculator's problem as the budget constraint does in the household's demand decision. It shows the trade-off between the risk and expected consumption on offer in the market, at the current level of the (normalized) risk premium.

Starting from the vertical axis of Figure 15.1, with expected consumption of W_0 achievable without speculation and hence at no risk, then increased consumption can be obtained at the rate of ρ' multiplied by each additional unit of standard deviation. Speculation therefore moves the risk–return combination up a straight line with gradient ρ' and intercept W_0, like those through points H and J in Figure 15.1.

15.2.3 Equilibrium

With a risk premium of ρ_0', the utility-maximizing combination is the familiar tangency solution at H. At this point, the speculative opportunity line touches the highest possible indifference curve, so that the (normalized) market risk premium is equal to the agent's subjective marginal exchange rate between risk and expected consumption. The optimal position in forward contracts, A_0^*, can be read off in the bottom quadrant, where the straight line plots the relationship given by Equation 15.4.

Since the speculative opportunity line has gradient ρ', an increase in the normalized risk premium (from, say, ρ_0' to ρ_1') – whether originating in a fall in F_0 or σ_S, or rise in ES_1 – causes it to pivot upwards about the intercept W_0. Figure 15.1 shows what must be assumed to be the most likely outcome: an increase in the number of forward contracts held, from A_0^* to A_1^*.

The conclusion cannot be unambiguous, however, because a rise in ρ' makes the speculator better off, in so far as he is given the opportunity of enjoying more attractive combinations of expected consumption and risk. In response to this windfall gain, he may, depending on his tastes as reflected in the gradient of his indifference curves, react by settling at a point above and to the left of his original equilibrium at H. In other words, he might decide to take the benefit of the improvement in the market opportunities in the form of only a slim increase in his expected consumption and a major reduction in his risk exposure.

If the typical speculator had tastes like these, then the forward market would be completely unstable. It must be assumed, therefore, that the typical agent in the forward market will tend to increase his exposure when the risk premium rises (as illustrated in Figure 15.1 at the point J) – though possibly not by very much.[6]

15.3 A general model of the risk premium

The model outlined in the previous section was simplified by the special assumption that tastes were defined with respect to only two parameters of the distribution of future consumption: mean and standard deviation. Although this simplification made it possible to conduct the analysis using the well-known diagrammatic apparatus of indifference curves, it had the disadvantage of being very restrictive, in ways that will be made clear later in this section.

What we shall do now is outline a model that is general enough to require only the assumptions already listed in Section 15.1. In order to do so, however, we shall need to rely on algebra rather than diagrams.

15.3.1 The speculator's decision problem

The critical decision the speculator faces is how many pounds, A, to commit to forward purchases so as to maximize his expected utility. Formally, he must solve the following problem:

$$\max_{A} \quad E[U(C_1)]$$

subject to the constraint that the total available for consumption in period 1 is as given in Equation 15.1, repeated here for convenience:

$$C_1 = (S_1 - F_0)A + W_0 \tag{15.1}$$

Notice that this is *not* the same thing as saying our speculator tries to maximize expected consumption. The solution to the problem of how to maximize expected consumption is both easy and absurd: if the risk premium $ES_1 - F_0$ is positive (negative), buy (sell) an infinite number of forward contracts, making the expected value of consumption infinite. Only for a risk-neutral agent is expected utility maximization equivalent to maximizing expected consumption – which is precisely why we conclude that, if the *typical* individual in the currency markets is risk-neutral, the risk premium will be arbitraged down to zero.

If the typical agent is risk-averse, however, increased risk will carry a utility penalty, so that there will be a subjective trade-off between risk and the expected return to speculation, as we saw in Section 15.2.[7]

15.3.2 The solution

In order to find the maximum, we need only differentiate the utility function with respect to A, which yields:

$$\frac{\partial E[U(C_1)]}{\partial A} = E\left\{ \frac{\partial U}{\partial C_1} \frac{\partial C_1}{\partial A} \right\}$$
$$= E\{U'(C_1) \cdot (S_1 - F_0)\}$$
$$= E\{U'(C_1) \cdot S_1\} - F_0 E[U'(C_1)] \tag{15.6}$$

The first line comes from recognizing that the variation in expected utility arises out of the changes in C_1 induced by changes in A. Writing out the two partial derivatives explicitly (the next line), the final line follows, as long as we remember that F_0 is known, non-stochastic.

Now, for the utility-maximizing value of A – call it A^* – the derivative in Equation 15.6 must equal zero,[8] which means we must have:

$$F_0 E[U'(C_1)] = E\{U'(C_1) \cdot S_1\} \tag{15.7}$$

This is one way of presenting the solution. The left-hand side can be interpreted as the (marginal) opportunity cost (in terms of expected utility) per pound speculated in the forward market: the price of a forward dollar multiplied by the expected marginal utility of consumption. The right-hand side is the expected marginal benefit in utility terms. The solution thus fits into the familiar pattern of constrained choice, equating the marginal benefit to the marginal cost, appropriately redefined to accommodate uncertainty.

A more useful way of presenting the conclusion can be found. Start by rewriting Equation 15.7 in terms of the forward rate:

$$F_0 = \frac{E\{U'(C_1) \cdot S_1\}}{E[U'(C_1)]} \tag{15.8}$$

Now one way of presenting the definition of the covariance[9] of two random variables, X and Y, is as follows:

$$cov(X, Y) = E(XY) - (EX)(EY)$$

which in turn means that:

$$E(XY) = cov(X, Y) + (EX)(EY)$$

Using this relationship in the numerator on the right-hand side of Equation 15.8, we derive:

$$F_0 = \frac{E[U'(C_1)]ES_1}{E[U'(C_1)]} + \frac{cov[U'(C_1), S_1]}{E[U'(C_1)]}$$

$$= ES_1 + \frac{cov[U'(C_1), S_1]}{E[U'(C_1)]} \tag{15.9}$$

so that the ratio on the right is the risk premium.

In this form, the conclusion states that each agent will take a forward position such that the market risk premium is equal to the ratio of the covariance between his marginal utility and the spot rate to his expected marginal utility. As a group, speculators will drive the forward rate to a level that reflects the appropriately weighted aggregate covariance.

In equilibrium, with net demand for forward contracts equal to the supply, the market risk premium will reflect this covariance term. Intuitively, the explanation for this result is one that will look familiar to readers who have had a previous encounter with modern finance theory.

It is a commonplace of portfolio analysis that the risk associated with any particular investment can never be judged in isolation. Instead, it needs to be assessed in terms of the extent to which it increases or decreases the riskiness of the individual's position as a whole. Now, it is easy to see that, at the margin, the contribution of any asset (call it the nth) to the overall riskiness of a portfolio of assets is measured by the covariance of its return with those of the other $n - 1$. For example, in the simplest case where the initial portfolio contains only one security, buying another asset whose return mimics the first, being high in circumstances when the first is high and low on exactly the same occasions, only serves to scale up the risk. On the other hand, adding instead a second security that pays a good return in precisely the situations where the first loses money is an investment that reduces the overall risk of the portfolio, *even though the new security is risky when viewed in isolation.*

In the present case, holding forward contracts is a risky business in so far as the contracts tend to pay off in just those scenarios when marginal utility is high and lose money when marginal utility is low. This is because, given our assumption of risk aversion, marginal utility increases less from initially high levels than it does from low levels. Hence, the covariance term will be negative and the forward rate less than the expected future spot so as to compensate for the additional risk undertaken.

Notice that Equation 15.9 confirms the fact that there are two very special conditions under which the risk premium will be zero: first, when S_1 is not subject to uncertainty – in the jargon, when S_1 is non-stochastic – in which case, its covariance with any variable is identically zero; and second, when the speculator is risk neutral so that although S_1 varies, the marginal utility, $U'(C_1)$, is constant.

15.3.3 The simple model revisited: mean–variance assumptions

This conclusion has the advantage of being general in so far as it places no restrictions whatsoever on the form of the utility function. But, as is often the case with very general formulations, it is awkward both to interpret and to apply for purposes of empirical research. For that reason, we now examine a special case, virtually the same as the one covered in Section 15.2.

Suppose the utility function of the typical agent takes the following form:

$$U(C_1) = \alpha\mu_c - \frac{\gamma}{2}\sigma_c^2 \quad \alpha, \gamma > 0 \tag{15.10}$$

It must be emphasized that this formulation, known as a *quadratic utility function*, is very specialized[10] and in fact has a number of implausible features.[11]

On the other hand, it also has a number of very convenient properties. First, notice that it is compatible with the simple model of Section 15.2, because it allows us to draw indifference curves in terms of the expected value of consumption and its standard deviation.[12] Since both of its parameters are assumed positive and constant, it implies that utility increases with expected consumption and decreases with the variance.

Second, follow through the same procedure as in the last subsection. Maximizing $U(C_1)$ with respect to A will be found to yield the following conclusion:

$$F_0 = ES_1 - \frac{\gamma}{\alpha}A\sigma_s^2 \tag{15.11}$$

which says that the size of the risk premium depends on the variance of the exchange rate, the attitude to risk bearing (as measured by γ), and the size of the net forward position, A.

An alternative route to a similar conclusion involves placing restrictions on the distribution of the future exchange rate instead of on the utility function. Thus, if the distribution is approximately normal,[13] it can be shown (see Appendix 15.1) that our conclusion from the general model Equation 15.9 can be rewritten as:

$$F_0 = ES_1 - \Theta \frac{A}{C_1} \sigma_s^2 \qquad\qquad (15.12)$$

where:

$$\Theta \equiv -C_1 \frac{E[U''(C_1)]}{E[U'(C_1)]}$$

is a parameter known as the *coefficient of relative risk aversion*. It is often assumed constant on the grounds that people's attitudes to risk are likely to be fairly stable, provided that we measure risk relative to the individual's initial level of wealth or consumption.

As we shall see, this is the formulation that has been used most often in empirical work. Notice that *both* quadratic utility *and* normality lead to a formulation of the demand in terms of mean and variance alone. They are alternative justifications for what is called, in the jargon of portfolio theory, the *mean–variance approach*.

15.3.4 The risk premium and portfolio balance models

Much of the literature on the risk premium carries a slightly different orientation from the one in the models covered in this chapter. To see how they are related, notice first that what we have called future consumption, C_1, could equally well have been described as future *wealth*, W_1 for consistency. The speculator's problem would then have amounted to one of maximizing the expected utility of future wealth, given present wealth, W_0.

Looking back at Equation 15.12, this interpretation leads naturally to regarding the term A/C_1 as the proportion of wealth allocated to foreign assets. In fact, most of the literature treats the determination of the risk premium as a portfolio allocation problem.

Now portfolio balance models were covered at some length in Chapter 8. It is easy to see the relationship between the risk premium analysis and the asset demand equations used there – and, by the same token, the currency substitution model in Chapter 9. All we need do is to solve Equation 15.12 for the desired holding of foreign assets relative to what we now identify as wealth, to give:

$$\frac{A^*}{C_1} \equiv \frac{A^*}{W_1} = \frac{1}{\Theta \sigma_s^2}(ES_1 - F_0) \qquad\qquad (15.13)$$

In the bracket on the right-hand side we now have the risk premium, the expected return on the asset in question. So, under the restrictive conditions specified here, we have arrived at a formulation of the demand functions in Chapter 8 (Equations 8.2–8.4).

One further generalization is required in order to cover the portfolio balance approach. We need to be able to cope with more than two assets (or currencies and so on). The solution is quite complicated and will not be given here. As one might expect, it turns out to involve replacing the variance of the (single) exchange rate with the multi-currency variance–covariance matrix (see the reading guide for details).

15.3.5 Other possible extensions

The framework for all the models considered so far in this chapter has been the highly simplified environment defined by the assumptions listed in Section 15.1. Since the published literature usually deals with a far more general setting, it is worth briefly scanning the results of relaxing some of these assumptions.

First, extending the analysis to allow consumption in period 0 as well as period 1 makes no difference whatsoever to our conclusions, simply because there is nothing in the speculator's decision that can have any impact on current consumption.

Second, allowing the agent to borrow or lend in domestic or foreign currency – buy or sell sterling or dollar bonds – leaves the risk premium unchanged. All it does is to generate the additional conclusion that, in equilibrium, the gap between the current forward and spot rates has to equal the concurrent interest differential between the UK and the USA – the familiar covered interest rate parity condition.

As far as inflation is concerned, simply allowing for the fact that the price index may change between periods 0 and 1 leaves our conclusions unaffected, if the future price level (say, P_1) is assumed to be predictable with certainty. However, if, more realistically, we allow for the fact that P_1 itself will be a source of uncertainty, it has been shown that the risk premium becomes:

$$\frac{cov\left\{\left[\frac{U'(C_1)}{P_1}\right], S_1\right\}}{E\left[\frac{U'(C_1)}{P_1}\right]}$$

Under these more general conditions, it can be seen that the risk premium will be zero *only* if the future exchange rate is known with certainty (in which case, its covariance is zero, as already pointed out). On the other hand, it is no longer true that risk neutrality on its own implies a zero risk premium. The reason is that even if the marginal utility is invariant, the covariance term will still be non-zero if there is any covariance between (the reciprocal of) P_1 and S_1.

There is one final point concealed by the simplifying assumptions made in Section 15.1. Effectively, it has been assumed that the price index relevant to the speculator's consumption is not only constant but denominated entirely in domestic currency.

To see the implication of this, consider, for example, the effect of an expected sterling appreciation. When consumption is exclusively domestically produced goods priced in pounds, the *only* way that the agent can benefit from the event is by selling dollars (that is, buying sterling) forward. On the other hand, if we were to allow for the fact that the relevant consumption price index ought to contain a component reflecting the value of imports priced in dollars, then the sterling appreciation would be seen to bring direct benefit, in the form of the higher real purchasing power of existing wealth, W_0.

In this case, ought the rational agent to enter the forward market? Intuitively, the answer should be: not to the same extent as in the case where consumption is exclusively sterling-denominated. In fact, it can be shown that, in this more general context, the appropriate definition of the speculator's exposure to risk is the extent to which a currency's portfolio share exceeds its contribution to his cost of living.

15.4 The evidence on the risk premium

There are at least three questions about the risk premium to which one would ideally like an answer:

- Is there in fact a (non-zero) risk premium?
- If so, is it variable?
- If variable, is it sufficiently large and/or volatile enough to explain a substantial proportion of the fluctuations observed in floating exchange rates in recent years?

Section 11.8 covered much of the relevant background – particularly the problems faced by researchers in this area.

From the point of view of the material in this chapter, there would appear to be three possible approaches to answering the questions.

One possibility is via what were called efficiency tests in Chapters 11 and 12: using an RE substitution to replace the expected spot rate, and then simply examining the forward rate forecast error for signs of systematic bias. In recent years, tests such as these have almost invariably produced evidence of systematic bias. As has already been pointed out, however, the weakness of this test is that although the results are consistent with the presence of a risk premium, they could also be explained in a number of other ways, such as non-rational expectations, for example. Even if other explanations could be ruled out, it would still be true that, for technical reasons, it is extremely difficult to distinguish between a random statistical error and a non-constant risk premium.

More convincing evidence has emerged in recent years from work exploiting survey data, where expectations are measured directly from the reponses of market participants themselves. Here, as we saw in Chapter 11, the evidence suggests a substantial and variable forward rate bias, though there are reasons for supposing that it cannot be identified easily with the risk premium.

There have been a number of attempts to attack the problem directly. Essentially, these involve testing equations such as Equation 15.13 – in other words, portfolio balance equations with explicit formulations of the asset demand functions. This approach has the drawback that it relies on the mean–variance approach, with its well-known (and, some would say, implausible) restrictions.[14]

None the less, the most prominent exponent of this approach, Jeffrey Frankel, has generated some extremely interesting results. He summarizes them as follows:

> . . . a time-varying risk premium does not seem a promising explanation for any empirical findings of . . . conditional bias in the prediction errors made by the forward rate. (Frankel, 1986, p.72)

which is a conclusion based on a number of studies of different currencies.

What is particularly interesting is the reason he gives for the statement: the estimates he derives of the risk premium are simply too *small* to contribute significantly to explaining the very substantial bias in forward rate predictions. In fact, according to his estimates, a 1% increase in the supply of dollar assets relative to world wealth would raise the risk premium by only 0.02% per annum. Or, in other words, the risk premium would rise by 1% if the share of dollar assets in the world portfolio rose by no less than 50%.

In the end, these conclusions are so unambiguous as to cast doubt on their validity, as Frankel himself has recognized:

> . . . the suspicion may arise that . . . mean–variance optimization is steering us wrong . . . The hitherto persuasive argument against perfect substitutability has been that it requires . . . highly implausible assumptions. But we now see that conventional estimates of risk-aversion and return variances imply a degree of substitutability so high that for some purposes it might as well be infinite. (Frankel, 1986, p.72)

which is precisely why so much of the material in this book uses the working assumption of risk neutrality. The zero risk premium/perfect substitutability hypothesis is, for the moment, accepted by default.

15.5 Conclusions

In this chapter, we have shown how the risk premium is determined both in general and in the context of a set of highly specialized assumptions (the mean–variance model). In both cases, it depends on the parameters of the probability distribution of the future exchange rate, on attitudes to risk and on the quantity of assets in existence.

Since all three are extremely difficult to measure, it is perhaps hardly surprising that most of the evidence collected has been indirect, usually from efficiency tests. Much of it appeared to hint at the existence of a relatively large and highly variable risk premium. More recently, direct tests using the mean–variance framework appear to have cast doubt on that possibility, as do the results of tests using survey data.

Where does that leave us? It is quite conceivable that the mean–variance model, with all its well-known shortcomings, is the wrong one to use for direct testing, though it is hard to see an alternative that is both plausible and capable of being implemented, given the current state of the econometrician's art and the limitations of the data.

Otherwise, we are left with two alternative explanations, both uncomfortable in the extreme: *either* expectations are not rational *or* the spot and/or forward markets fail to operate properly, presumably due to some invisible trade barrier or concealed transaction cost.

Summary

- The context of the simple two-period model is perfect capital markets, no inflation and utility functions that depend only on the expected return and variance of return to currency speculation.

- In this setting, the optimum speculative portfolio can be derived in the standard choice-theoretic manner – that is, analogous to the consumer's equilibrium that underlies the household demand curve. The result implies that the speculator chooses a portfolio such that the market risk premium is equal to the gradient of his indifference curves. If substitution effects dominate income effects, then he will take on more risk when the risk premium rises.

- In a more general model, where the investor's utility function is almost unrestricted, it is shown that the risk premium is given by the ratio of the covariance between marginal utility and the spot rate to the expected marginal utility itself. This result can be generalized further in a number of directions, for example to deal with more than two periods, inflation uncertainty, traded and non-traded goods components in the price index, and so on.

- The portfolio balance equations of Chapter 8 can be derived from the risk premium model, interpreted appropriately.

- The empirical results on the risk premium are ambiguous, to say the least, though it has to be said that this is a particularly difficult research area because of the paucity of data and the importance of unobservable parameters relating to attitudes to risk, probability distributions and investors' expectations.

Reading guide

For the background on the analysis of choice under uncertainty, there are many excellent text-book treatments. Basic microeconomics texts such as Varian (2005) and Katz and Rosen (1998) are a good starting point.

For an introduction to the elementary statistical concepts used here, see a statistics textbook such as Mood and Graybill (1963) or Wonnacott and Wonnacott (1977).

The classic references on mean–variance in general are the works of Tobin (1958) and Markowitz (1959), though the material is nowadays covered in every textbook on financial theory, for example Sharpe (1985) or Copeland and Weston (1983). An influential application to exchange rates is that of Dornbusch (1983).

What has been called here the general model is based on Frenkel and Razin (1980). For an exhaustive (and highly mathematical) analysis of the possibilities, see Section 3 of Branson and Henderson (1985).

As far as empirical work is concerned, most of the references in Chapters 8 and 11 are relevant. However, for mean variance tests, see Frankel (1982; 1983a,b; 1986). Other notable (though highly technical) contributions are Hansen and Hodrick (1983) and Hodrick and Srivastava (1986).

Web page: **www.pearsoned.co.uk/copeland**.

Notes

1 These assumptions, though restrictive, for the most part serve only to simplify the analysis. Most can be relaxed without weakening the conclusions very significantly (see Section 15.3.5).

2 In principle, a forward transaction requires no advance commitment of funds. In practice, however, margin calls are often required by brokers from would-be buyers of forward contracts.

3 The Greek letter μ ('mu') is often used to denote the mean of a random variable. Here, it replaces $E(C_1)$, which is difficult to use in a diagram.

4 This notation is logical, given that the standard deviation is the square root of the variance, which is by convention denoted σ^2. Note the subscript C, to allow us to distinguish between the standard deviation of consumption and the standard deviation of the future spot exchange rate, σ_s, on which, among other things, it depends.

5 The second line of Equation 15.3 is computed simply by subtracting Equation 15.2 from Equation 15.1.

6 In other words, in terms of the textbook model of choice, we assume the substitution effect dominates the windfall-gain (or income) effect.

7   The point being made here is familiar from the literature on risk bearing in general (see the reading guide for references).

8   Strictly, a maximum requires not only that the first derivative be zero but also that the second derivative be negative. The latter condition is simply the risk-aversion assumption in Section 15.1.

9   The covariance of two random variables, X and Y, is given by:

$$cov(X, Y) = E[(X - EX)(Y - EY)]$$

In other words, the expectation of the product of the deviations from their respective mean values. As the name implies, the covariance is a measure of the extent to which two variables tend to move in unison. If both tend to be above (or below) their expected values at the same time, then their covariance will be positive. However, if one tends to be relatively high when the other is low, then the covariance will be negative.

Notice that the variance is a special case of the covariance – the variance of X is the covariance of X with itself. As such, it is always positive.

10 The interested reader may expand the general utility function in a Taylor series about its expected value, thereby verifying that it involves all moments of the distribution of outcomes and not just the second. Imposing a quadratic utility function therefore amounts to assuming either that all higher moments of the distribution are zero (for example the normal distribution) or that all higher derivatives of the utility function itself are zero. It can also be seen from the same exercise that the coefficient γ is equivalent to (minus) the second derivative of the utility function.

11 Not least the fact that we need to impose the restriction:

$$C_1 \leq \frac{\alpha}{\gamma}$$

otherwise marginal utility becomes negative.

12 Note that since Equation 15.10 gives utility in terms of the variance rather than the standard deviation, the indifference curves drawn with respect to the standard deviation have a non-constant gradient.

13 For the definition of the normal distribution and a list of properties, see the references at the end of the chapter. For the moment, note that the normal distribution is for practical purposes the only distribution that is characterized completely by its mean and variance.

It should be pointed out that the future exchange rate cannot be distributed normally for a number of fairly obvious reasons, but it may approximate normality in the neighbourhood of equilibrium. Alternatively, proportionate changes in the exchange rate may be more or less distributed normally.

14 Of which there are many, both theoretical and practical. Not all, by any means, were mentioned in Section 15.3.3. Mean–variance theory has a (relatively) long and chequered history in the theory of finance, and even to some extent in the world of practical stock market analysis. In both cases disenchantment has been apparent for some years.

Many of the objections are technical. Perhaps the most serious, and convincing, is the charge that the observed distribution of returns is non-stationary, an objection that would seem to apply with even greater force to exchange rates than to share prices.

Appendix 15.1

Derivation of Equation 15.12

This appendix demonstrates how Equation 15.12 is derived from Equation 15.9.

The proof relies on a useful theorem proved by Rubinstein (1976), which states that if two variables, x and y, are bivariate normal, then provided the first derivative of the function $g(y)$ exists, if follows that:

$$cov[x, g(y)] = E[g'(y)] \cdot cov(x, y)$$

In order to use this theorem to evaluate the numerator of the expression for the risk premium in Equation 15.9, note that if we assume S_1 is normally distributed, then the same must apply to C_1, which is simply a linear transformation of S_1. We can therefore proceed to write:

$$
\begin{aligned}
cov[U'(C_1),\, S_1] &= E[U''(C_1)]\, cov(C_1,\, S_1) \\
&= E[U''(C_1)]\, cov\{[(S_1 - F_0)A + W_0],\, S_1\} \\
&= E[U''(C_1)]A\sigma_s^2
\end{aligned}
$$

Substituting this in Equation 15.9, we have:

$$
\begin{aligned}
F_0 &= ES_1 + \frac{E[U''(C_1)]}{E[U'(C_1)]}\, A\sigma_s^2 \\[2mm]
&= ES_1 + C_1 \frac{E[U''(C_1)]}{E[U'(C_1)]}\, \frac{A}{C_1}\, \sigma_s^2 \\[2mm]
&= ES_1 - \Theta \frac{A}{C_1}\, \sigma_s^2
\end{aligned}
$$

16 A certain uncertainty: non-linearity, cycles and chaos

Introduction

Uncertainty and unpredictability are unavoidable issues in any analysis of financial markets, and they have been continuing themes of this book so far. In general, we have taken for granted that the two are inseparable features of systems characterized by volatility. In making this connection, we were doing no more than following standard practice not only of economists but also of mathematicians, physicists, meteorologists, psychologists – in fact, of all those who use mathematics to model the relationship between variables over time. However, it has become clear relatively recently, following the work of a number of pure and applied mathematicians (see reading guide), that even processes involving no uncertainty may sometimes be unpredictable, even in principle.

This chapter will attempt to explain the apparent paradox, as it relates to financial markets, and, in particular, to exchange rates. To achieve this, we shall cover (albeit informally) the basic results using, for the most part, graphical methods only. In the process, we start by introducing a number of essential concepts that can be used to elucidate the source and nature of the unpredictability and its implications for empirical research and for policy.

It should be made clear at the outset that, since the mathematical developments covered in this chapter are relatively recent, and their introduction into economics even more so, some of the results are still provisional. Moreover, the significance of the topic as a whole for economics and finance is as yet undemonstrated, although it seems at this stage likely to prove important (at least in the view of this author).

However, it should also be plain that the material covered here involves some very advanced mathematics, much of it unfamiliar even to academic economists. For that reason, the treatment can only be sketchy, emphasizing as always the intuition behind the results and omitting a number of mathematically important concepts where they are not absolutely essential to an understanding of the argument.[1] To readers already in possession of the requisite degree of mathematical sophistication, the exposition may seem like *Hamlet* without the prince or, indeed, Ophelia and the king and queen. Anyone in the fortunate position of having the mathematical tools and the time to spare is urged to follow up the references in the reading guide. Other readers should be aware that if the story looks simple as told in this chapter, the unabridged version is very complicated indeed.

16.1 Deterministic versus stochastic models

So far, in Part III of this book, we have been dealing with models that take explicit account of the irresoluble uncertainty associated with exchange rate behaviour. This uncertainty was conveniently summarized by the zero-mean residual error term, denoted u_t in Chapter 12. These *stochastic models*, as they are sometimes called, involve uncertainty in a very fundamental sense, and it is important for what follows to make it clear why this is the case.

Take as an example one of the models given in Section 12.5, Equation 12.10:

$$s_t = \alpha s_{t-1} + \beta s_{t-2} + \gamma Z_t + \delta Z_{t-1} + u_t$$

Now, the crucial point to understand is the following. In order to forecast s_t at time $t - 1$ *with complete accuracy*, we would need to have perfect knowledge of:

- the values of the parameters α, β, γ and δ
- the values of the predetermined variables s_{t-1}, s_{t-2} and Z_{t-1} and the current value of Z_t
- the value of the random variable u_t.

The first two types of element are, in principle at least, knowable at time $t - 1$. If Equation 12.10 had no random variable in it, then this knowledge would be sufficient to forecast s_t with complete accuracy. For that reason, models that contain no random terms are often called *deterministic* – that is, predetermined and, hence, predictable in advance. Subject to the qualifications to be made in the remaining sections of this chapter, any inaccuracy in forecasting a deterministic model can originate only in computational errors.

However, in the presence of the random or *stochastic* component u_t, the future is unpredictable. Even in principle, the value of u_t is unknowable in advance of the time t – otherwise, it would not be a truly random innovation or 'news', as it was called in Chapter 13.[2] As should be clear from previous chapters, the best that can be achieved is the forecast represented by the conditional mathematical expectation (Equation 12.11):

$$E_{t-1}S_t = \alpha s_{t-1} + \beta s_{t-2} + \gamma Z_t + \delta Z_{t-1}$$

which, as we saw, will rarely be an accurate forecast, at least in the types of situation encountered in financial markets. The inaccuracy in this forecast is precisely the stochastic component, u_t, so that the greater its variance, the larger the variance of our optimal forecast error.

The point is worth stressing. Since the error in an optimal (or rational) forecast is simply the random component itself, it will mimic the properties of u_t. Whatever the statistical properties of u_t, for example normality or non-normality, serial dependence or independence, constant or non-constant variance, those properties will be mirrored in the error from a forecast based on Equation 12.11. The prediction error in forecasting a statistical model is a random variable and can therefore be described in *statistical terms*.

The distinction between deterministic, hence forecastable, and stochastic, unforecastable models was accepted more or less without question until very recently in economics, as well as in most natural and social sciences. It has deliberately been laboured somewhat here, because an understanding of the dichotomy is essential to an appreciation of the importance of what follows. As we shall see, research has shown that a third type of model can be formulated. The most significant feature of these new models for our purposes is that although they involve no random component and are therefore deterministic, they are even in principle unforecastable and, in practice, can only be approximately forecast over a very short horizon.

16.2   A simple non-linear model

To explain the mechanism involved, we shall employ an ultra-simple model. It must be stressed that it is being introduced purely as an example for expository purposes. There is no intention to suggest that it actually describes how exchange rates are determined. Rather, it is chosen purely as an easily manipulated example of the class of model that may give rise to the type of outcome we intend to describe.

Our starting point is to assume that the (log of the) exchange rate changes according to more or less the same mechanism used in Section 7.1 to describe the way currency speculators form their expectations:

$$\Delta s_t = \theta(\bar{s} - s_{t-1}) \tag{16.1}$$

That is to say, the change in the log price of foreign currency, Δs_t, is proportional to the previous period's gap between the actual exchange rate, s_{t-1}, and its long-run equilibrium level, $\bar{s}$. The latter is taken as given exogenously (by relative money stocks, output capacity and so forth) and, for present purposes, may be regarded as constant. Note that this mechanism is meant to describe the way the *actual* and not the *expected* exchange rate moves. (It was pointed out in Section 7.3.3 that under certain circumstances, the exchange rate would indeed follow this type of path in the context of the Dornbusch model.[3])

Now consider the term θ. As we saw in Section 7.1, it is an indicator of the speed of adjustment of the actual exchange rate to deviations from its equilibrium level: the larger the gap, the more rapid the adjustment. It was assumed to be positive; otherwise, adjustment would be *away* from equilibrium, rather than towards it. Moreover, it was implicitly assumed to be smaller than one, so as to guarantee an uncomplicated path to the new equilibrium. However, this restriction is one we now relax. Instead, we examine the possible implications of a more complicated mechanism.

Suppose that one of the processes whereby the exchange rate adjusts is as follows. When exporters (who are, we assume, paid in foreign currency) feel optimistic about the prospects for the domestic currency, they convert their receipts as early as possible. On the other hand, when they are gloomy about the home currency, they delay conversion and instead hold on to foreign currency deposits. Under these circumstances, the greater the volume of export receipts, the more funds available to support speculation in this way and therefore the greater the value of θ, other things being equal.

Now, given the level of domestic and foreign prices as well as the other relevant factors, exports are likely to be an increasing function of the price of the foreign currency, s_t. As a result, we conclude that θ itself may well be an increasing function of s_t. If the relationship is linear, we can write simply:

$$\theta = \alpha s_t \quad \alpha > 0 \tag{16.2}$$

When the domestic currency is relatively cheap (s_t high), exports are buoyant and there is more scope for speculation against it when it is overvalued or in favour of it when it is undervalued. Hence, it adjusts more rapidly.

Combining Equations 16.1 and 16.2, we conclude that the exchange rate moves as follows:

$$\Delta s_{t+1} = \alpha s_t(\bar{s} - s_t) \tag{16.3}$$

which says that the exchange rate moves towards equilibrium at a rate that is greater the higher its initial level. Alternatively, we can rewrite Equation 16.3 as:

$$s_{t+1} = (1 + \alpha\bar{s})s_t - \alpha s_t^2 \tag{16.4}$$

A useful simplification follows from taking advantage of the fact that since the equilibrium exchange rate has been taken as given, we may as well specify a convenient value for it. So, by the use of an appropriate scaling factor, we can set:

$$\bar{s} = -\left(\frac{1-\alpha}{\alpha}\right) \tag{16.5}$$

which allows us to reformulate Equation 16.4 simply as:

$$s_{t+1} = \alpha s_t - \alpha s_t^2 = \alpha s_t(1 - s_t) \tag{16.6}$$

or, for convenience:

$$s_{t+1} = f(s_t) \tag{16.7}$$

Now, this is a deceptively simple equation. In fact, f is a function of the type known to mathematicians as the *logistic*, although it amounts to no more than a particular type of quadratic in s_t. None the less, it turns out that this innocuous-looking equation can generate a bewildering variety of different types of path, depending on the value of α, which is known as the *tuning parameter*. In particular, values of α approaching 4 can be shown to result in time paths characterized as *chaotic*. However, as we examine the implications of successively higher values of α, many interesting and potentially important phenomena are encountered, long before we reach the point where chaos reigns.

16.3 **Time path of the exchange rate**

In order to examine the exchange rate behaviour implied by Equation 16.6, we first demonstrate the use of a simple diagrammatic apparatus to analyse non-linear dynamics. It then becomes possible to study the time paths implied by different values of α.

16.3.1 Phase portrait

If the notion of equilibrium is to have any meaning in the system described by Equation 16.6, then plainly it must correspond to a position such that, having arrived, s_t stays there indefinitely, unless it is disturbed again. In that sense, it must be what mathematicians call a *fixed point*.

Consider drawing a diagram with values of s_t along the horizontal axis and s_{t+1}, on the vertical. Any point in the diagram would therefore represent a combination of s_t and s_{t+1}. Where would the fixed points lie? Obviously, if any fixed points exist, they would lie along a 45-degree line through the origin, since it is the locus of all points equidistant from the axes – that is, all points at which $s_t = s_{t+1}$.

Now, given some positive value of α, if we plot the values of s_{t+1} corresponding to s_t – that is, the function $f(s_t)$ – we generate a parabola, which is no more than the graph of a quadratic equation familiar from elementary algebra. Each point on the graph is an answer to the question: if s takes the value on the horizontal axis in one period, then what value will it take in the next period? This line is known as the *phase curve* of the logistic function and the diagram is its *phase portrait*.

Before examining the general features of this parabola, it would pay to follow through its implications for the dynamic path.

Start the system off with s_t at an arbitrary value, say s_t^0 (see Figure 16.1, which is drawn for a value of $\alpha = 1.5$). As we can see from the point A on the phase curve of $f(s_t)$, starting from this initial value, the value of the variable next period will be s_{t+1}^0, because this is implied by the equation:

$$s_{t+1}^0 = \alpha s_t^0 (1 - s_t^0) \tag{16.8}$$

However, if it is s_{t+1}^0 in the second period, it starts the next two-period phase at that same value. Moreover, that value can be found at the point B' on the 45-degree line (points labelled with a prime are on the 45-degree line); that is, $s_t^1 = s_{t+1}^0$ Again, starting the next phase at s_t^1, the exchange rate will clearly rise to s_{t+1}^1 in the subsequent period. Repeating the same logic as before, it will enter the next phase at the point corresponding to E', where $s_t^2 = s_{t+1}^1$, and so on.

The usefulness of the 45-degree line is apparent. The path of s_t is traced out by the steps marked with arrows in the diagram, generating the points $A, D, F, H \ldots$ corresponding to the sequence of values: $s_t^0, s_t^1, s_t^2 \ldots$ The significance of this is that we now have a device for deriving the path of the exchange rate given only the phase diagram.[4]

Table 16.1 traces out the sequence of values taken by s_t over the first 25 periods, starting from levels of 0.5 and 0.25 respectively. Thus, to six decimal places, the exchange rate settles down to its long-run level of $1/3$ by the nineteenth period in the

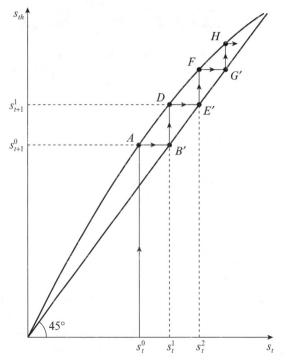

Figure 16.1 Smooth convergence (α = 1.5)

first case and by the eighteenth period starting from 0.25. Notice that the step size diminishes exponentially.

One obvious conclusion follows immediately. If, at any value s_t^*, the phase curve crosses the 45-degree line, the path degenerates from that point onward, because each phase starts at s_t^* and results in the same point in the next period. Formally, under those circumstances we would have: $f(s_t^*) = s_t^*$ and hence s_t remains fixed forever at the level s_t^*.

Armed with this convenient analytical tool, we can trace out the successive values taken by s_t starting from any initial value on the horizontal axis. We shall see that there is a variety of different types of path that the exchange rate can follow, depending on the shape of the phase portrait. In fact, the critical feature of the graph turns out to be its curvature. The greater the curvature, the richer the array of possibilities. Moreover, the degree of curvature depends on the value of the so-called tuning parameter, α.

The following properties will turn out to be crucial:[5]

Property 16.1: since the gradient of the phase curve is $\alpha(1 - 2s_t)$, it is upward-sloping (positive) as long as s_t is less than $^1/_2$ and downward-sloping whenever s_t is greater than $^1/_2$.

Property 16.2: the gradient is zero when s_t is $^1/_2$. In other words, the phase curve peaks at this point. Moreover, at its maximum, s_{t+1} is just $\alpha/4$, which means that the height of the curve increases with α and reaches 1.0 when α is just 4.0.

Table 16.1 Stable convergence: two examples

t	s_t	Step size	s_t	Step size
0	0.5		0.25	
1	0.375000	0.125	0.281250	0.03125
2	0.351563	0.023438	0.303223	0.021973
3	0.341949	0.009613	0.316918	0.013695
4	0.337530	0.004419	0.324721	0.007803
5	0.335405	0.002125	0.328916	0.004195
6	0.334363	0.001042	0.331095	0.002179
7	0.333847	0.000516	0.332207	0.001111
8	0.333590	0.000257	0.332768	0.000561
9	0.333461	0.000128	0.333050	0.000282
10	0.333397	6.4E–05	0.333192	0.000141
11	0.333365	3.2E–05	0.333262	7.1E–05
12	0.333349	1.6E–05	0.333298	3.5E–05
13	0.333341	8E–06	0.333316	1.8E–05
14	0.333337	4E–06	0.333324	8.9E–06
15	0.333335	2E–06	0.333329	4.4E–06
16	0.333334	1E–06	0.333331	2.2E–06
17	0.333334	5E–07	0.333332	1.1E–06
18	0.333334	2.5E–07	0.333333	5.5E–07
19	0.333333	1.2E–07	0.333333	2.8E–07
20	0.333333	6.2E–08	0.333333	1.4E–07
21	0.333333	3.1E–08	0.333333	6.9E–08
22	0.333333	1.6E–08	0.333333	3.5E–08
23	0.333333	7.8E–09	0.333333	1.7E–08
24	0.333333	3.9E–09	0.333333	8.7E–09
25	0.333333	2E–09	0.333333	4.3E–09

Notes: $A\text{E} - B$ means A divided by 10 to the power of B.

t = time period.

Initial values: $s = 0.5$ and $s = 0.25$.

Notice two immediate implications. When α is less than 2.0, s_{t+1} can never be greater than $\alpha/4 = \frac{1}{2}$. Hence, if s_t starts out less than $\frac{1}{2}$ (that is, to the left of the peak), then it will remain there.

Property 16.3:[6] whatever the gradient, the fixed points where $s_t = s_{t+1}$ are at $s_t = 0$ and $s_t = (\alpha - 1)/\alpha$.

Property 16.4: the phase curve cuts the horizontal axis at the two points, zero and one. In other words, the positive values of s_t are restricted to the range between zero and one.[7]

Property 16.5: if s_t were ever to escape from the range from zero to one, then it would become negative. Moreover, once having become negative, the exchange rate never again becomes positive and, in fact, goes on diminishing without limit. In the jargon of mathematics, it tends to minus infinity.[8]

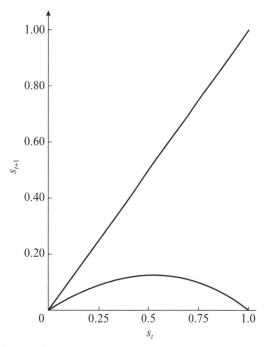

Figure 16.2(a) Phase portrait ($\alpha = 0.5$)

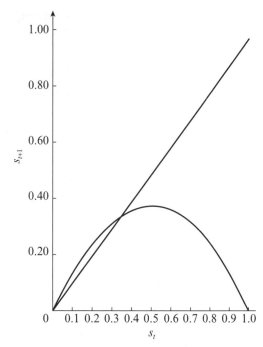

Figure 16.2(b) Phase portrait ($\alpha = 1.5$)

Plainly, the system's behaviour depends critically on the value of the tuning parameter. We take the different possibilities one by one, following the graphs in Figures 16.2(a) to (f). In each case, the first 50 points on the time paths are displayed in Table 16.2[9] so that the interested reader can refer to the data given there for confirmation of the pattern shown in the graphs.

16.3.2 Case 1: $0 < \alpha < 1$

When α is between 0 and 1, the phase curve lies below the 45-degree line at all points (Figure 16.2(a)). The explanation can be found by looking at the data used to plot the phase curve. As can be seen from Table 16.2, when α is in this range (in the case shown here, α is 0.5), the exchange rate collapses to the fixed point at zero. Moreover, the other fixed point is negative, as can be seen from Property 16.3. More improbable still, the negative fixed point is unreachable because, by Property 16.5, the exchange rate would tend to minus infinity, once having dropped below zero. The two facts taken together mean that this scenario can be safely ruled out as a possible description of reality.

16.3.3 Case 2: $1 < \alpha < 2$

The case when α lies between 1.0 and 2.0 is somewhat uninteresting. In fact we have already more or less covered it: Figure 16.1 is simply a close-up of Figure 16.2(b).

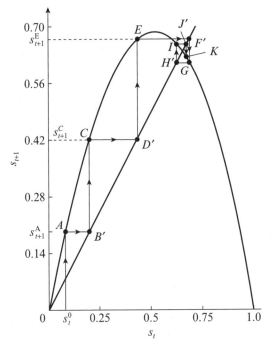

Figure 16.2(c) Phase portrait ($\alpha = 2.75$)

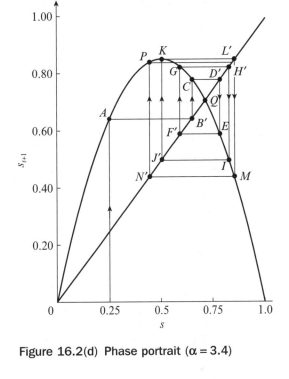

Figure 16.2(d) Phase portrait ($\alpha = 3.4$)

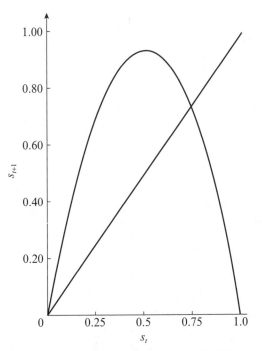

Figure 16.2(e) Phase portrait ($\alpha = 3.75$)

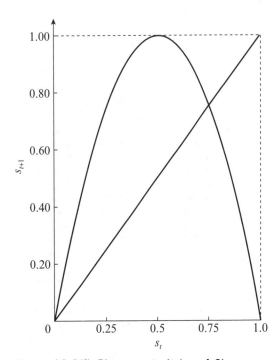

Figure 16.2(f) Phase portrait ($\alpha = 4.0$)

Table 16.2 Time paths for different values of α

t	0.5	1.5	2.75	α = . . . 3.4	3.47	3.75	3.99
0	0.25	0.25	0.25	0.25	0.25	0.25	0.25
1	0.093750	0.281250	0.515625	0.637500	0.650625	0.703125	0.748125
2	0.042480	0.303223	0.686829	0.785719	0.788773	0.782776	0.751852
3	0.020338	0.316918	0.591511	0.572440	0.578137	0.637642	0.744417
4	0.009962	0.324721	0.664471	0.832158	0.846314	0.866455	0.759138
5	0.004931	0.328916	0.613111	0.474881	0.451331	0.433914	0.729562
6	0.002454	0.331095	0.652316	0.847855	0.859281	0.921123	0.787233
7	0.001224	0.332207	0.623699	0.438590	0.419584	0.272459	0.668314
8	0.000611	0.332768	0.645421	0.837178	0.845060	0.743344	0.884465
9	0.000305	0.333050	0.629345	0.463457	0.454339	0.715439	0.407725
10	0.000153	0.333192	0.641492	0.845460	0.860265	0.763448	0.963527
11	0.000076	0.333262	0.632445	0.444236	0.417125	0.677231	0.140221
12	0.000038	0.333298	0.639260	0.839427	0.843667	0.819709	0.481030
13	0.000019	0.333316	0.634168	0.458283	0.457669	0.554198	0.996064
14	0.000010	0.333324	0.637997	0.844083	0.861282	0.926485	0.015642
15	0.000005	0.333329	0.635131	0.447463	0.414579	0.255415	0.061436
16	0.000002	0.333331	0.637284	0.840616	0.842181	0.713168	0.230071
17	0.000001	0.333332	0.635671	0.455535	0.461206	0.767097	0.706781
18	0.000001	0.333333	0.636882	0.843278	0.862278	0.669971	0.826894
19	0.000000	0.333333	0.635974	0.449345	0.412079	0.829162	0.571130
20	0.000000	0.333333	0.636655	0.841276	0.840677	0.531198	0.977313
21	0.000000	0.333333	0.636145	0.454005	0.464770	0.933850	0.088468
22	0.000000	0.333333	0.636528	0.842807	0.863193	0.231653	0.321761
23	0.000000	0.333333	0.636241	0.450443	0.409775	0.667461	0.870741
24	0.000000	0.333333	0.636456	0.841650	0.839252	0.832338	0.449080
25	0.000000	0.333333	0.636294	0.453136	0.468131	0.523319	0.987155
26	0.000000	0.333333	0.636416	0.842533	0.863976	0.935461	0.050595
27	0.000000	0.333333	0.636325	0.451082	0.407800	0.226402	0.191659
28	0.000000	0.333333	0.636393	0.841864	0.838002	0.656790	0.618154
29	0.000000	0.333333	0.636342	0.452638	0.471068	0.845313	0.941798
30	0.000000	0.333333	0.636380	0.842373	0.864595	0.490345	0.218708
31	0.000000	0.333333	0.636351	0.451454	0.406234	0.937150	0.681791
32	0.000000	0.333333	0.636373	0.841987	0.836991	0.220873	0.865638
33	0.000000	0.333333	0.636357	0.452353	0.473436	0.645331	0.464072
34	0.000000	0.333333	0.636369	0.842281	0.865051	0.858296	0.992350
35	0.000000	0.333333	0.636360	0.451668	0.405079	0.456089	0.030291
36	0.000000	0.333333	0.636367	0.842058	0.836235	0.930269	0.117201
37	0.000000	0.333333	0.636361	0.452188	0.475202	0.243256	0.412824
38	0.000000	0.333333	0.636365	0.842228	0.865366	0.690310	0.967177
39	0.000000	0.333333	0.636362	0.451793	0.404281	0.801683	0.126665
40	0.000000	0.333333	0.636365	0.842099	0.835708	0.596202	0.441378
41	0.000000	0.333333	0.636363	0.452093	0.476432	0.902795	0.983788
42	0.000000	0.333333	0.636364	0.842197	0.865573	0.329086	0.063637
43	0.000000	0.333333	0.636363	0.451865	0.403758	0.827957	0.237754
44	0.000000	0.333333	0.636364	0.842122	0.835359	0.534165	0.723097
45	0.000000	0.333333	0.636363	0.452038	0.477245	0.933123	0.798909
46	0.000000	0.333333	0.636364	0.842179	0.865703	0.234018	0.641007
47	0.000000	0.333333	0.636364	0.451906	0.403426	0.672200	0.918167
48	0.000000	0.333333	0.636364	0.842136	0.835137	0.826301	0.299794
49	0.000000	0.333333	0.636364	0.452006	0.477761	0.538228	0.837571
50	0.000000	0.333333	0.636364	0.842169	0.865784	0.932020	0.542823

Since the non-zero fixed point is below $^1/_2$ (in fact, at $^1/_3$), the 45-degree line cuts the phase curve to the left of the peak and the exchange rate converges smoothly in gradually diminishing steps. In the jargon of mathematics, convergence is said to be *monotonic*: that is to say, it is always moving towards equilibrium, with no detours or doubling back on itself, as can be seen from the third column of Table 16.2.

It is important for what follows to step back a moment from the dynamics of the phase portrait to examine the explanation for this outcome in terms of our basic model of the exchange rate. Equation 16.3 can be rewritten as follows:

$$s_{t+1} = (\alpha s_t)\bar{s} + (1 - \alpha s_t)s_t \qquad (16.9)$$

This says that next period's level of the exchange rate is a weighted average of its long-run equilibrium level, $\bar{s}$, and its current actual level, s_t, with the weights being αs_t and $(1 - \alpha s_t)$ respectively.

Notice that the term αs_t is nothing other than our more complicated version of θ, in the non-linear form that we introduced in this chapter.

Now as long as α is between 1.0 and 2.0, this crucial term can be no greater than $2s_t$. Hence, when s_t is to the left of the peak (that is, less than $^1/_2$), αs_t must be less than 1.0, and therefore the weights in Equation 16.9 must both lie between 0 and 1.0.

From here, the explanation is straightforward. Starting from below equilibrium, an increase in the current exchange rate will move the next period's value closer to equilibrium, by raising its weighting αs_t and reducing the weighting on its present level, $1 - \alpha s_t$. The smooth convergence to the fixed point follows accordingly.

In fact, in this case, the dynamics of the exchange rate are more or less identical to those of the linear model analysed in Section 7.3. Just as in the linear case, the greater the gap $\bar{s} - s_t$, the more rapid the increase in s_t and the higher its level in the next period. Starting at any given distance below equilibrium, it closes a proportion of the gap each period, as the fall in the value of the domestic currency induces a greater volume of exports, hence more speculation by exporters delaying repatriation of their receipts.

The important point is in the balance of these two effects. On the one hand, what we could call the linear effect inside the parentheses in Equation 16.3 gradually reduces the rate of depreciation, Δs_{t+1} in subsequent periods, as the gap between the exchange rate's current level and its equilibrium diminishes. On the other hand, the non-linear effect continues to provide acceleration, as successive increases in s_t raise the value of the variable adjustment coefficient αs_t. As long as α is less than 2.0, however, the first effect predominates and the net outcome is deceleration as equilibrium is approached.

This unexciting conclusion has been laboured because it turns out to be the key to understanding the richness of the possible outcomes in the more complicated (and interesting) cases to be analysed in subsequent sections.

16.3.4 Case 3: $2 < \alpha < 3$

The story gets monotonically more interesting as α passes the value of 2.0. In terms of the phase portrait, when α is exactly 2.0, the hump is high enough to cut the 45-degree line at its peak, so that the long-run equilibrium exchange rate is just $^1/_2$. At any value of α higher than this, the fixed point is beyond the hump, at an exchange rate greater than $^1/_2$. Although the numbers in Table 16.2 start at 0.25, a lower starting point has been chosen here, simply to make the graphics clearer.

Suppose $\alpha = 2.75$ (Figure 16.2(c)). Starting at an arbitrary value of the exchange rate, s_t^0, the path proceeds as before towards equilibrium via the points A, B', C and D', to E, where something not seen in the previous examples occurs. When the exchange rate reaches the level at E (that is, when $s_{t+1} = s_{t+1}^E$), it starts the next two-period phase at a value that generates an overshoot to F' and hence G. Following the path on to H', I, J', K . . . , the pattern is clearly cyclical. This process, often called a *cobweb*, takes the exchange rate beyond its equilibrium level (at G), then back below it in the next period (at I), then beyond it again (point K), and so on.

As is clear from Figure 16.2(c), the cyclic fluctuations continue forever, with each phase taking the exchange rate back and forth around its fixed point. The important point, however, is that at each stage the exchange rate moves closer to equilibrium. In other words, the *cycle is stable*, with the swings becoming less wild as period succeeds period. In time-series terms, each succeeding peak in the two-period cycle is lower and each trough higher than its predecessor. Figure 16.3(a) plots the sequence of points in this stable cobweb against the time periods, showing clearly how the cycle converges on its long-run level, which in this case is:

$$\frac{\alpha - 1}{\alpha} = \frac{2.75 - 1.0}{2.75} = 0.64$$

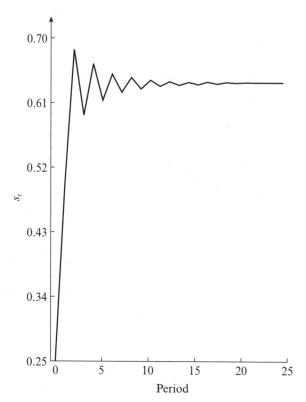

Figure 16.3(a) Path of exchange rate ($\alpha = 2.75$)

The explanation for this outcome is to be found, as before, in the value of αs_t. At low levels of the exchange rate, as at points such as A and C in Figure 16.2(c), this term is less than 1.0. Hence, convergence proceeds gradually towards equilibrium, as in the previous case.

However, since the fixed point is at a value of s_t greater than $^1/_2$, at some stage αs_t must exceed 1.0. If α is only slightly above 2.0, this situation will occur only when s_t is very close to $^1/_2$ – that is, just before the peak of the phase curve. The greater is α, the lower the value at which the cycle begins. For $\alpha = 2.75$, as in Figure 16.2(c), the condition is fulfilled when s_t passes 0.36 (at E).[10]

The implication of having αs_t greater than 1.0 is that the weights in Equation 16.3 are greater than 1.0 on the equilibrium and *negative* on the current exchange rate. That in turn means that the next period's exchange rate is dragged down below its current level, but not by enough to reverse its ultimate convergence. In other words, the (albeit artificial) speculative mechanism assumed in our model makes for a progression towards equilibrium proceeding by two steps forward and one step back.

As before, the nature of the process is illustrated (for a value of α of 2.75) in Table 16.2, where it can be seen that the sequence in this case goes: 0.25, 0.52, 0.69, 0.59, 0.66, 0.61, 0.65, 0.62, 0.65, 0.63, 0.64 . . . so that, by the end of ten periods, it has already settled down to a range of fluctuation of only 0.01. By the time the 50 periods shown in the table have elapsed, it has reached its steady state – at least, as close as the sixth decimal place can show. This path is shown as the time series in Figure 16.3(a).

16.3.5   Case 4: $3 < \alpha < 3.68$

The really interesting situations arise for values of α greater than 3.0. Consider Figure 16.2(d), drawn for an α value of 3.4. The sequence of points generated at successive stages of the process starts as though it is again following a cobweb: A, B', C, D', E . . . But then F' implies a lower level of s_{t+1} than at B', and so the cycle is now diverging. At the next point, G, s_{t+1} is above its level at the same phase of the previous cycle (at C).

Although we have not drawn more than two cycles, the impression of instability could be confirmed by following the process on for a few more iterations. As can be seen from the time series for this value of α (Figure 16.3(b) and the appropriate column of Table 16.2), the initial stages consist of a number of cycles of increasing amplitude. Surprisingly, however, the instability is only temporary, in the sense that, at some point, the amplitude settles down and we see that the system is ultimately characterized by a regular two-period cycle, tending neither to explode to infinity nor to implode on the fixed point (Q in the phase diagram). Thus, although the fixed point is never reached (other than fortuitously), and would in any case be unsustainable even if the exchange rate were ever to arrive there,[11] the long-run behaviour of the exchange rate follows a highly stable pattern. Once the pattern has been established, it is sustained indefinitely, in the absence of any further disturbance.

In the present case, as we can see from Figure 16.3(b), a perfect two-period cycle with absolutely constant peaks (equal to 0.84) and troughs (at 0.45) ensues after period 24. In the jargon of non-linear dynamics, the exchange rate path is said to

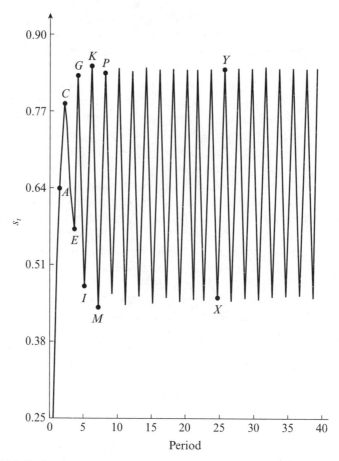

Figure 16.3(b) Path of exchange rate ($\alpha = 3.4$)

have periodicity of two, because it is characterized by the feature that the same values recur every second period, so that we find:

$$s_t = s_{t+2} = s_{t+4} = \ldots$$

and

$$s_{t+1} = s_{t+3} = s_{t+5} = \ldots$$

This unrealistically neat pattern turns out to be only the first of the possibilities, however. As the value of the tuning parameter is raised, the cycle increases in amplitude. But at a value of α of just under 3.45, the two-period cycle becomes unstable. Instead of fluctuating between only two values, the exchange rate begins to follow a pattern of switching between four values, s_t, s_{t+1}, s_{t+2}, s_{t+3}, with $s_t = s_{t+4}$, $s_{t+1} = s_{t+5}$, $s_{t+2} = s_{t+6}$, $s_{t+3} = s_{t+7}$, the next cycle beginning again with $s_{t+4} = s_{t+8}$, and so on ad infinitum. This four-period cycle is illustrated in Figure 16.3(c), where the points A, B, C and D form one complete cycle consisting of a high peak (at A), followed by a low trough (B), then a lower peak (C) and finally a higher trough (at D), and back to the original level at the start of the next cycle (E).

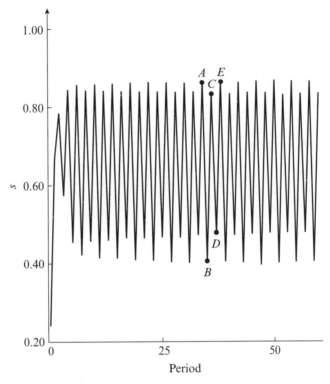

Figure 16.3(c) Path of exchange rate ($\alpha = 3.47$)

The story does not end there, however. The process of sudden change from a stable cyclic pattern to one with a period twice as long is known as *bifurcation* and it occurs repeatedly as the value of α is increased, with successive 8-period, 16-period, 32-period cycles establishing themselves over an increasingly narrow range of values of the tuning parameter. It is important to note that although at each bifurcation a cycle of period n appears and replaces the old cycle of period $n/2$, never the less the old cycle is, in a sense, still present. All that happens is that the lower period cycle becomes unstable from the bifurcation point onward. In principle, therefore, it could still make an appearance, although the probability of its occurring is negligible.[12]

The *period-doubling* pattern, or *cascade* as it is sometimes known, can therefore be thought of as a play, with a cast list made up of all possible periodicities. As the play progresses (α increases), all the characters ultimately make an entry on stage, albeit mostly in bit parts, and in strict order of appearance. As each new periodicity steps out into the limelight, the previous one steps back into the shadows stage left or right. *But it is still present, even if it is not currently playing a part in the proceedings.*

This fact has important implications in the present case, because it turns out that, in the approximate range $3.45 < \alpha < 3.68$, cycles of every period assert themselves in a predictable order, starting with all the even-number periods and finishing with odd-period cycles.[13] Eventually, by the time a cycle of period 3 is established at about $\alpha = 3.68$, all other periodicities have made their appearance and the stage is full. We are ready for the finale.

16.3.6 Case 5: 3.68 < α < 4

The process reaches its climax when α passes a value of about 3.68, at which point the three-period cycle ceases to be stable. From here on, the number of possibilities becomes almost endless. It is only from this point on that the type of behaviour known as *chaos* may (or may not) be observed.[14]

To appreciate some of the subtleties and pitfalls in this area, we need to introduce some additional mathematical concepts (as usual, in deliberately informal definitions):

> An **aperiodic path** is one characterized by no regular cycle or pattern. Alternatively, it has a period of infinity. That is to say, it would only repeat itself after an infinite number of periods have elapsed so that the path never revisits any point that it has visited previously.

It can be seen that this amounts simply to the absence of periodicity.

Much of the mathematics literature in this area is concerned with notions of measure and measurability. For this purpose, we use the following definition:

> The **measure**[15] of an interval is equal to its length, where single points are given a length of zero.

This follows straightforwardly on the idea familiar from elementary geometry that a single point has zero length. It follows that two or more points, as long as they are isolated, also have zero length. By extension, even where we have an infinite number of isolated points, the length in this sense is still zero. We can therefore have an interval or, more generally, a set with an infinite number of points in it, but none the less with measure zero.

To appreciate the relevance of this approach, consider the following experiment. Imagine a set of measure zero – that is, containing a large number of discrete points. For example, it might be a map of the world, with the points defined by the intersections of the lines of latitude and longitude thoughtfully drawn by the publishers at, say, 100 intervals. Now suppose I were to stick a pin in the map somewhere at random. Plainly, the probability of my landing on one of the intersection points is very small. But even if I did actually appear to the naked eye to have landed precisely on the point where the 30-degree east line of longitude crosses the 50-degree north line of latitude, it is very likely that examination under a magnifying glass would show my pinhole to be both too big and too off-centre to coincide precisely with the 'true' point 30° *E* 50° *N*. In the unlikely event that I was absolutely spot on under the magnifying glass, a look through a microscope would always show that I was in fact slightly off-centre to one side or the other.

In other words, the probability of my pin landing on any of the finite number of grid references marked on the atlas is zero. The obvious next step might seem to be to draw a finer grid. But a moment's consideration will bring the reader to the realization that the same argument applies again. The finer the grid, the more points there are on the map. None the less, the probability of landing exactly on one of them is zero.

In the limit (that is, as the grid is made infinitely dense), the probability of landing on any of the points is therefore zero.

In the same way, *any property of our series that applies only to a set of measure zero will never actually be observed.* Specifically, any feature that applies only to paths starting out from a set of measure zero cannot be expected ever to be seen in practice.

Armed with these concepts, we now return to the analysis of the logistic function. Once the three-period cycle has appeared, all other cycles have become unstable. In other words, they apply only over a set of initial points whose measure is zero. From this point onward, a number of possibilities appear.

First, consider Figure 16.2(e), the phase diagram drawn for $\alpha = 3.75$. Other than the fact that the hump has become even larger, there is no obvious qualitative change in the phase curve compared with lower values of the tuning parameter. But when we come to generate the exchange rate path in the usual way, we find a sequence of points meandering around the whole region from 0 to 1, with no apparent pattern.

In time-series terms, Figure 16.3(d) is typical in its eccentricity. For this value of α, it shows the first 100 periods starting with $s_0 = 0.25$. At a casual glance, it may seem to follow a somewhat erratic two-period cycle. But closer inspection shows that any pattern is illusory, with relatively high peaks separated sometimes by one lower peak and sometimes by two or three lower peaks. Moreover, even the high peaks are uneven. There are also two sequences of five or six low-volatility periods.

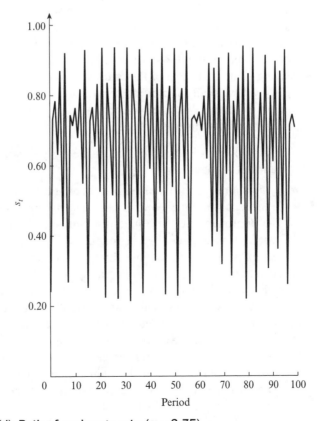

Figure 16.3(d) Path of exchange rate ($\alpha = 3.75$)

It is also quite easy to see how patterns might seem to be present even when they are not. From about periods 12–55, the series in Figure 16.3(d) might well appear to the observer to follow a reasonably regular (albeit high-amplitude) cycle. Then suddenly it settles down for two or three periods, before regaining its former volatility over the subsequent periods. This type of behaviour seems fairly typical of chaotic processes.

16.4 Chaos

The explanation given so far of how chaotic processes arise was inevitably over-simplified, so as to remain within the limits of what could be explained with graphic methods alone. In the process, many of the more complicated aspects of non-linear equations were sidestepped or ignored altogether.

In this section, we deal with some of these issues, albeit at a superficial level. Before doing so, however, it is worth repeating that the logistic function in Equation 16.6 is only one example of the class of functions that can result in chaotic behaviour for some values of the basic parameters. A quadratic was chosen for its simplicity and for the fact that it has been analysed more thoroughly than any other type of non-linear function. But there is an almost limitless number of different possible functional forms that could give rise to chaotic behaviour over some range of parameter values. In particular, there is a far richer variety of dynamic possibilities in multi-variate equation systems, which some writers claim are more relevant to economics than univariate models such as the logistic and tent maps.[16] These possibilities are not explored here, although they figure largely in the published literature (see the reading guide at the end of the chapter).

Instead, we shall concentrate here on an understanding of what is meant by chaos and on dispelling a number of common misapprehensions about its properties. The following points must be stressed:

- A chaotic process need not be particularly volatile. It can in fact display long periods of quiescence.

- By definition, an essential feature of chaotic processes is that they display sensitive dependence on initial conditions. What this means is illustrated in Figure 16.3(e). The unbroken line there plots the outcome for periods 200–250 with $\alpha = 3.75$, starting from an initial value for the exchange rate of 0.25 (as in Figures 16.3(a) to (d)), while the dotted line shows exactly the same computation, with the sole difference that it assumes a starting value of the exchange rate of 0.249. As can be seen, not only is each series more or less indistinguishable from a completely random variable, but there is also virtually no relationship between the two lines, in spite of the fact that they were both generated by exactly the same function.

It should be made absolutely clear what is so surprising about this outcome. In the first place, the fact that the graph shows the situation after 200 periods have elapsed should be seen in the right context. It certainly does not mean that the phenomenon can be dismissed as unimportant because 200 years is a long time. After all, there is no obvious translation of mathematical periods into calendar time. In financial markets, the appropriate modelling period may be as short as a

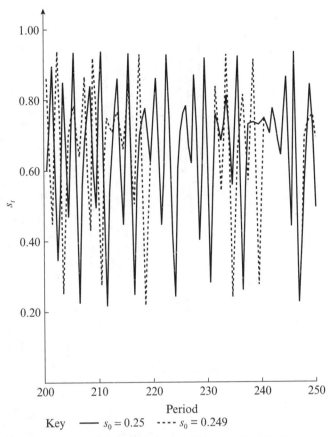

Figure 16.3(e) Path of exchange rate ($\alpha = 3.75$) ($t = 201$–250)

single trading day or even an hour or minute. Certainly, a 200-period horizon may be far from irrelevant for practical purposes.[17]

More importantly, however, the reader should realize that one would normally (that is, for non-chaotic series) expect to find one of the following three scenarios: the two series should get closer together as time passes (corresponding, roughly speaking, to stability); they should diverge to an ever-increasing degree (instability); or the difference between them should fluctuate regularly (periodic or cyclic behaviour). What is surprising is the fact that the difference between the two chaotic series in Figure 16.3(e) shows no sign of diminishing, of growing or of following any regular pattern. Quite simply, the similarity between the two seems to be temporary, with the two series sometimes being almost identical (for example, from $t = 219$ to $t = 230$) and at other times following paths that seem to bear virtually no relationship to each other.

What is so disturbing about chaotic functions is that their sensitivity is infinite, in the sense that even the smallest variation in their initial conditions results in a process that is totally transformed. Figure 16.3(f) gives another example of this effect. It graphs the time series for $\alpha = 3.99$ from $t = 101$ to $t = 200$, for processes that started at $t = 0$ from $s_0 = 0.25$ (the solid line) and from a value smaller by only

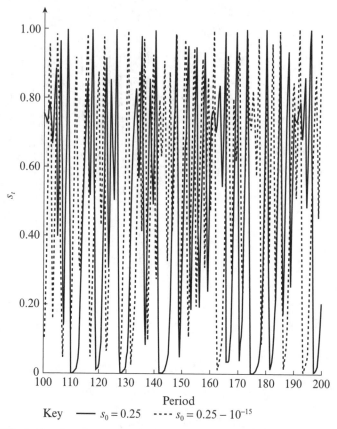

Figure 16.3(f) Path of exchange rate ($\alpha = 3.75$) ($t = 101–200$)

10^{-15} (the broken line). As can be seen, the two lines are sometimes close enough to be indistinguishable, but most of the time they bear little similarity to one another.

- This phenomenon is sometimes known as the *butterfly effect*. The expression derives from meteorology, where it was first investigated. It implies that even the minuscule effect on initial weather conditions of a butterfly's wings fluttering in one part of the world might be sufficient to trigger a causal chain leading ultimately to a hurricane on the other side of the world.

  For our purposes, perhaps its most important implication is for forecasting. Every forecast has to have a point of departure, a starting value from which to make projections into the future. If a series is non-chaotic, then we can forecast with the confidence that, at the very least, we know the current value of the variable in question. By contrast, when the function is chaotic, this confidence is likely to be misplaced, simply because, however accurately we know the current value, it will never be accurate enough to prevent possibly unlimited divergence between the forecast and actual values as time passes.

  Moreover, this danger would still exist even if the process generating the variable, the 'true' model, could be identified with 100% precision – which it never can be, of course.

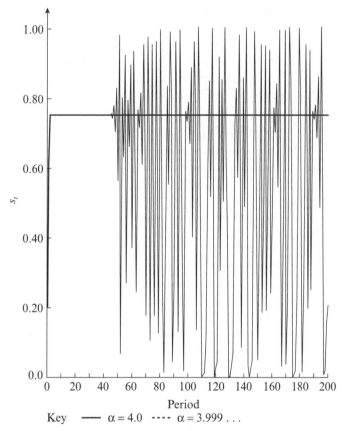

Figure 16.3(g) Path of exchange rate ($\alpha = 4.0$ vs $\alpha = 4.0-10^{-12}$)

- This is not the only aspect to sensitive dependence. Chaotic functions are also sensitive to their parameter values. Figure 16.3(g) gives a simple (and extreme) example, comparing the behaviour of the logistic function with values of the tuning parameter, α, that differ by only 10^{-12}, but starting from the same initial value, $s_0 = 0.25$. It can be seen that even the tiniest error in estimating parameter values can be every bit as damaging as inaccuracies in the initial values. This is important because in the case of a variable such as the exchange rate, errors in estimating model parameters are absolutely unavoidable.

- One possible conclusion is that forecasting is feasible only, if at all, at very short horizons. This was (and remains) the position taken by meteorologists in response to their discovery of the butterfly effect. At the risk of being defeatist, it amounts to taking a pragmatic view of the scope for forecasting: the prediction horizon is simply as long as proves practicable. Forecasts are updated as often as is necessary to preserve a specified minimal level of accuracy, without which they are completely useless.

- It has been stressed that tracking errors in chaotic systems, whether due to small variations in the initial conditions or in the parameter values, persist indefinitely. In that sense, there is no convergence between the series. But, by the same token, there is no tendency to increased divergence either, at least in the sense that a chaotic function remains within certain bounds. This boundedness is a crucial feature of chaos. In the present case, it means that the exchange rate visits all points in the [0, 1] interval if we wait long enough. In other words, all values between 0 and 1 crop up eventually but of course never recur.

This point needs emphasizing because it implies, among other things, that chaos need not necessarily be associated with excessive volatility and certainly does not imply a tendency towards extreme values or an exceptionally broad range of fluctuation.[18]

■ We saw that chaos can be viewed as the culmination of a sequence of changes in the cyclic behaviour of a non-linear function. In a sense, therefore, the concept of chaos is related closely to the notion of periodicity. As we saw, a one-period process repeats itself every (one) period, a two-period process is repeated every second period, and an N-period process every N periods. It is natural, therefore, to say that a process that never repeats itself has infinite period, or no period at all (hence aperiodic).

This perspective may not come naturally to readers accustomed to thinking in terms of mainstream economics and econometrics. After all, we know that economic variables almost never display an unambiguous regular cyclical pattern. In what sense is chaos any different? And, in any case, we tend to think of cycles as being the exception rather than the rule in economics. By and large, we do not expect to find a very marked periodicity (or 'seasonality') in financial variables, not least because any obvious pattern may well imply the persistence of unexploited profit opportunities. However, far more is at stake here.

In the first place, remember that we are dealing in this chapter with a deterministic model. It is one thing to say that stable patterns in the data are hidden by random disturbances, which is essentially the position taken by applied economists in normal empirical research. It is a different thing altogether to suggest that there may be no underlying regularities even in the simple 'true' model.

Second, the concept of periodicity needs to be interpreted very broadly. It covers far more than seasonality. Essentially, by periodicity we mean to encompass any discernible pattern. An n-period cycle is a pattern that is replicated every n periods. The pattern can be as complicated as it is possible to imagine. For example, if n is 27, then it could involve a value of 1.23 multiplied by the cycle average at the fourteenth period of the cycle, 0.45 multiplied by at the fifteenth period, 0.21 times at the sixteenth, and so on. As long as the next 27 periods display the same pattern, the periodicity is maintained.

In this sense, *periodicity amounts to the same thing as forecastability. An aperiodic series cannot be forecast.*[19] Putting the matter another way, a random series can be visualized as one with infinite periodicity.

For high values of n, and when the period in question is relatively long (that is, when we are looking at relatively low-frequency data – say, monthly or annual), then the periodicity may be too long for us to observe in practice. For example, in the unlikely event that there is actually a 300-year cycle in the exchange rate, then it will obviously be many years (indeed, centuries) before we shall be able to observe it. For practical purposes, therefore, it may make very little difference whether a series is strictly aperiodic or simply characterized by very long periodicity.[20]

Conversely, in financial markets, a day or even an hour could be viewed as a long time in terms of the underlying behaviour patterns driving the variables. In this context, an apparently long-period cycle may be quite short in terms of observations – for example, $n = 300$ when dealing in minutes.

16.5 Evidence

The problems involved in testing for chaotic behaviour or, more generally, for non-linearity in exchange rates are many and too complicated to be explained in any detail here. Not the least of the problems (and one that has barely been addressed in the published literature) is the possibility that reality may be best described by a model that is *both* non-linear (chaotic or non-chaotic) *and* stochastic.

The next section attempts to give an intuitive outline of the major difficulties facing researchers in this area and of the solutions that have been proposed.

16.5.1 Testing problems

Faced with a block of exchange rate data, how can signs of chaotic behaviour be identified?

The starting point for testing has to be the question of linearity or non-linearity. After all, chaos is an essentially non-linear phenomenon. If a time series is linear, then it cannot be chaotic. As has been shown, chaos occurs as a consequence of what might be called extreme non-linearity. Research in this area starts, therefore, from a search for evidence of non-linearity.

Now, in a sense, this work has entailed a fundamental change – a paradigm shift, as it is sometimes called – in attitudes to empirical work on financial markets. With few exceptions, previous research (including the work summarized in earlier chapters of this book) had concentrated exclusively on a search for linear relationships, usually not even allowing for the possibility of non-linearity.[21] Attention was explicitly or implicitly restricted to linear models.

For example, the whole emphasis in testing had previously been on finding *correlation* between variables: correlation between explanatory variables and the dependent variable, with success defined in terms of an absence of correlation in the residual error. However, a zero correlation coefficient between two random variables, X and Y, is evidence only that there is no *linear* relationship between them. A non-linear relationship can be present even if the correlation coefficient is zero.

What kinds of test can one use to isolate evidence of non-linear relationships between variables or, indeed, between current and past values of the same variable? As always, we avoid the technicalities, which are amply explained elsewhere (see reading guide), concentrating instead on the intuition underlying the tests deployed.

Notice that in many cases the search for non-linearities is applied to the residuals from a linear model. This practice either reflects the fact that the 'true' model is presumed linear by default (that is, in the absence of convincing evidence of non-linearity) or sometimes that it is simply easier to extract any linear relationship at the outset.[22]

The tests can be divided into three broad classes:

- The simplest tests are straightforward extensions of those applied to linear models. For example, correlation-based tests on a set of residuals $[u_t u_{t-1} \ldots u_{t-N}]$ can be replaced by tests on the set of squared residuals $[u_t^2 u_{t-1}^2 \ldots u_{t-N}^2]$ The problem here, of course, is that the test will only isolate a quadratic relationship. For example, if the residuals in question are actually linked by a cubic relationship, then this fact is unlikely to be revealed by a test on the squared residuals.

- To remedy this defect, tests that make no assumptions about the nature of any non-linearity are required. The most commonly used tests of this general type are a class based on the notion of *correlation dimension*. The idea here is illustrated in Figures 16.4 and 16.5, which show a scatter of points s_t, s_{t+1} for two (imaginary) time series of exchange rates suspected of concealing a linear or non-linear pattern. Clearly, the series in Figure 16.4 shows little sign of any regularity. By contrast, Figure 16.5 looks highly promising.[23] What sort of test might reveal the pattern in Figure 16.5, while discounting any regularity in Figure 16.4?

In Figure 16.4, the observations are scattered in haphazard fashion around the space. Consider drawing a square of a given size, say 1 cm by 1 cm, somewhere in

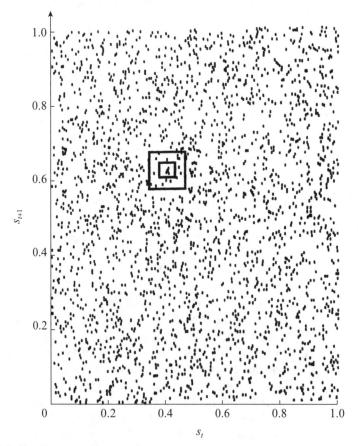

Figure 16.4 Random numbers: noise

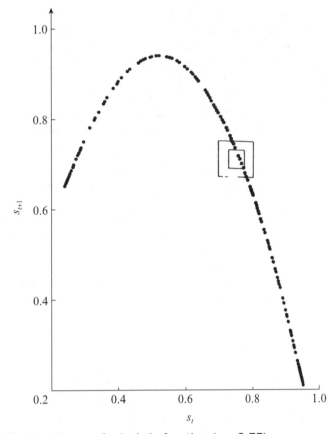

Figure 16.5 Scatter diagram for logistic function ($\alpha = 3.75$)

the space (the inner of the two boxes). As can be seen, in the present case there are only four points in the box.

Now draw a square with sides that are double the length – that is, 2 cm by 2 cm. Of course, doubling the length of the sides increases the area by a factor of four. But what happens to the number of points inside the box? Since in Figure 16.4 the points are spread evenly over the space, the number of points in the square also increases by about the same factor, from 4 to 16 or 17.

By contrast, performing the same exercise on the data in Figure 16.5 produces a very different outcome. As the lengths of the square's sides are doubled, the number of points increases by far less than four times. In fact, it goes from four to around eight or nine (one of the points is on the edge of the box) – slightly more than double. The extent to which the number of points increases as the square is expanded is an indicator of how far the series deviates from a random spread. Moreover, where a non-linear relationship does exist, it can also provide some hints as to the form of non-linearity.

A number of test statistics have been developed based on generalizations of this sort of measure, although there are still a number of difficulties in applying them. The most obvious problems relate first to the distributional characteristics of the tests, particularly in view of the shortage of data points in research on exchange rates. This may seem strange to readers with a background in economics. After all, macroeconomists are accustomed to empirical research on annual or quarterly datasets, for example GNP or the balance of payments, where 200 or 250 observations are the norm. By comparison, 2000 or 3000 daily exchange rates might seem more than adequate.[24]

However, there are grounds for believing that investigating the kind of behaviour covered in this chapter requires far larger datasets than this. Some researchers have used datasets made up of 30 000 or 40 000 minute-by-minute observations, and a number of studies have been published using over a million data points.

■ As has already been seen, chaotic series are forecastable, but only at short horizons. Because of their sensitivity to the initial conditions, forecasting errors rapidly accumulate to the point where the forecast becomes useless.

This fact suggests that tests for chaos could be based on forecastability. The problem is, of course, that the forecast used in the test could hardly presuppose any particular non-linear model. The standard techniques in the applied economist's toolbox – econometrics and time-series analysis – are ruled out in advance. However, researchers in the natural sciences are accustomed to using non-parametric methods in this kind of context, and these techniques form the basis for a number of different tests.

One frequently followed approach involves using these forecasting methods to arrive at measures of the extent to which adjacent values of the variable diverge as time passes – in other words, direct tests of sensitivity to initial conditions. These tests are based on the concept of the *Lyapunov exponent*,[25] an indicator of the speed with which adjacent points diverge. Even more than the other testing approaches, this type of work requires large datasets (an absolute minimum of 10 000 observations, in the view of some researchers) and commensurate computing power.

16.5.2 Results

Investigating non-linearity in financial markets is still in its infancy. However, at this stage a number of reasonably sound conclusions seem to have emerged. Before listing them, however, the reader should be aware of near-simultaneous developments in econometrics.

It should be pointed out that the advent of non-linear testing of the type described in the previous section coincided with an important development in mainstream time-series econometrics. As has been pointed out already in this book, the evidence suggests clearly that the volatility of exchange rates varies between periods of extreme turbulence and periods of relative calm. In other words, volatility tends to cluster, with days or weeks of high variance movements succeeding each other. Researchers in the 1980s responded to this finding by suspending the assumption of an independent identically distributed (IID) error term. In its place, they incorporated an error term with a variance that followed an explicit time-series process. The so-called autoregressive conditional heteroscedasticity or ARCH models and its variants[26] seem to fit the facts quite well in most financial markets, including currency markets, in the sense that they improve the accuracy of the standard models.

Against this background, non-linear research in financial markets has broadly attempted to address the questions in the following sequence:

- Is the original dataset (the rates of return) IID? In other words, is there evidence of linear or non-linear dependence? By and large, the evidence from correlation dimension and related tests seems to point to the existence of some underlying non-linear structure, although its nature is still in some doubt.

- If the data are characterized by non-linear dependence, is the system chaotic? This question is extremely difficult to answer. However, the few published results of forecastability tests show little sign of chaos.

- Some studies appear to indicate that residuals from appropriately specified GARCH models show little sign of any remaining non-linear dependence.[27] This would seem to suggest that GARCH models may be an adequate representation of exchange rate time series.

We await further developments on both the methodological and application fronts. In particular, there is likely to be a large volume of research emerging in the next few years deploying a battery of more advanced tests and applying them to data observed at very high frequencies (minute by minute and more).

In the meantime, it should be realized that it is to some extent a matter of choice as to whether we think of a series as a stochastic or a deterministic process. In practice, there are several reasons why both may be possible. In the first place, as has already been pointed out, if the 'true' deterministic process is of high dimension, then it may be simpler to conceive of it as random. Second, it seems improbable that a financial series could ever be completely deterministic. Third, there is a reasonably straightforward way of treating outcomes of chaotic processes as if they were random variables. It may well be that agents in financial markets form expectations as though they are operating in a truly stochastic environment. In that sense, a stochastic model may well be consistent with their beliefs.

16.6 Conclusions

How should one interpret these results? To put them into context, one needs to back-track to the questions discussed at the beginning of the chapter.

Ultimately, one cannot avoid asking what is meant by randomness. If, like Einstein, you do not believe in true randomness – in other words, if you conceive of the error term in a stochastic equation as simply a portmanteau intended to hold all the unobserved or immeasurable variables that cannot be explicitly included elsewhere – then, *other things being equal*, you will always prefer a deterministic model to a stochastic model. From this standpoint, a stochastic model is simply a temporary fix, intended to do a job until a permanent (that is, deterministic) solution can be found. As such, it may work better than the best available deterministic model for the moment. But, as always, that judgement is purely temporary, pending further research to take us closer to a situation where residual error terms can be suppressed.

If the empirical results so far suggest that stochastic models provide a marginally better representation of exchange rate time series than deterministic models, readers who take the Einstein line may remain unimpressed. They may demand that stochastic models substantially outperform deterministic in order to justify their inferior theoretical basis.

By the same token, many people will find inherently implausible the idea of a deterministic model of a financial variable. From this viewpoint, randomness must be intrinsic to a price set in a market populated by human beings who are prone to moods and to illness, who react unpredictably, who are liable to spill their coffee just at the moment when important news appears on their trading screen and so on. People who take this view will be unimpressed by models that purport to explain everything, leaving no room for randomness.

There are a number of reasons why this school will carry the day for a long time to come, at least in the sense that we shall invariably have to allow for a stochastic component, even where it is superimposed on chaos. One obvious point is that even if we believe that all events can in theory be modelled (even the moment a trader spills his coffee), it is out of the question in practice to build such a universal model and will remain so for the foreseeable future. A second reason for randomness is that, for all sorts of technical reasons (not least, the limits on the size of available datasets and on the computing power to analyse them), it is at present impossible to test for chaotic processes of dimension beyond about 10 or 12. Thus, by default, the choice facing researchers lies between low-dimension chaos and a stochastic model.

Finally, it should be said that even if we were capable of detecting the 'true' model generating the apparently random behaviour of financial variables, then the likelihood is that it would involve an extremely complicated mathematical structure. Under these circumstances, we might well end up preferring a stochastic model as a more manageable representation of reality.

Whatever answer one gives to the philosophical question of whether or not irreducible randomness exists, it has to be recognized that, empirically at least, there is a major practical difference between modelling a currency market and the types of model developed by the physicists who pioneered chaos theory.

The dilemma for economists is as follows: on the one hand, it is every bit as important for us to know whether markets are chaotic or not and, if they are chaotic, to find the equation that describes their motion. After all, if financial markets are indeed characterized by sensitive dependence on initial conditions, then the scope for butterfly effects is potentially unlimited. Moreover, the policy implications of chaos could be momentous.[28]

On the other hand, even if one believes in an ultimately deterministic truth, then it is a Holy Grail that, in the case of currency markets, is unlikely ever to be achievable. However sophisticated and all-embracing our model, it seems that we are always going to require a random term to cover myriad accidents and coincidences that characterize any financial market: the trader whose computer screen malfunctions or who presses the wrong key, the actual or threatened political upheaval following a scandal involving a finance minister, and so forth. Not least, we need to model a market full of traders making decisions with the help of computer models of chaotic financial markets.

Summary

■ An exchange rate model involving a non-linear iterative deterministic process can be analysed with the aid of a phase diagram, relating the value of the variable in any period to its level in the previous portrait.

■ In the case of the simple model selected as an example, the phase portrait and the resulting behaviour depend on the value of the critical tuning parameter, which, in a sense, measures the degree of non-linearity (that is, the deviation from linearity) of the model.

■ Depending on the value of the critical parameter, the exchange rate may follow a path that is characterized by monotonic convergence to equilibrium, or by either stable or unstable periodic oscillations around the equilibrium.

■ For some values of the tuning parameter associated with extreme non-linearity, the system exhibits what is known as chaotic behaviour. That is to say, it follows a path that is ostensibly random.

■ Chaotic behaviour is defined by extreme sensitivity to initial conditions, so that the smallest inaccuracy in defining a starting point results in a forecast that bears less and less resemblance to the actual outcome as time passes.

■ Empirical testing for non-linear dependence and more specifically for chaos in economic data is still in its infancy. The results so far are mixed. However, a number of researchers have detected some degree of complexity, especially in high-frequency financial data. In general, one would have to conclude that the question of the relevance of chaos to financial markets remains an open question.

Reading guide

As regards the material in this chapter, it should be clear that references vary enormously in the level of mathematical sophistication required of the reader. In most cases, topology is the main barrier to entry. The majority of the readings on chaos theory are from the maths/physics/general science literature, although economics is fast catching up.

In general terms, the best casual reading on the subjects is Stewart (1990), which gives plenty of background material on the major researchers in the field. Gleick (1987) is even more casual and has been a bestseller.

The most readable non-technical introductions to the material covered in this chapter are May (1976) and Baumol and Benhabib (1989), the latter written from the perspectives of economics. Two useful textbooks are by Peitgen, Jurgens and Saupe (1992), which is non-technical but gives especially good coverage of fractal geometry, and Devaney (1989), which is more formal. Azariadis (1993) contains some excellent chapters on linear and non-linear dynamics and covers a number of interesting applications in financial economics and general macroeconomics.

There are a number of useful collections of readings. Cvitanovic (1989) is a good buy for those wanting quick access to the seminal papers (mainly from the physics literature), especially those on bifurcation theory, universality, and so forth. For specifically economics readings, see Anderson, Arrow and Pines (1988) and Barnett, Geweke and Shell (1989).

The literature on non-linearity and chaos in exchange rates is still in its infancy. The best starting point, however, is Brock, Hsieh and LeBaron (1991), which devotes a chapter each to stock markets and exchange rates. Hsieh (1993) looks for non-linearities in currency futures prices.

Web page: **www.pearsoned.co.uk/copeland**.

Notes

1 Among the notable absentees (all covered at length in the references given in the reading guide) are the various types of bifurcation, fractals and attractors, universality, and the different measures of complexity found in the literature. Moreover, all topological concepts are studiously avoided here.

2 In Chapter 13, we examined the view that this randomness originates in news about what were called the fundamentals. For our purposes in the present chapter, it makes no difference whether this explanation of the random component is correct or not. All that matters is to understand that a truly random component makes a model unforecastable.

   Readers who believe that every event has a cause will want to insist that u_t must in any case reflect the influence of some other variables, whether or not we choose to label them 'fundamentals'. After all, in Einstein's famous words: 'God does not play dice.' However, as long as the omitted variables summarized in u_t are unknowable, we can regard it as having been generated by the throw of a celestial die and in the process avoid straying on to the wilder shores of epistemology.

3 For reasons of simplicity, we ignore expectations in this chapter. In fact, as we shall see, even defining rational expectations in this context is a serious problem.

4 Moreover, the method is completely general, in the sense that it would work just as well with almost any other equation.

5 Both these points can be confirmed by differentiating $f(s_t)$ to give:

$$\frac{ds_{t+1}}{ds_t} = \alpha(1 + 2s_t)$$

which is obviously positive (negative) whenever s_t is less (greater) than $^1/_2$ and zero when s_t is exactly $^1/_2$.

6 As can be seen by solving the equation:

$$s_{t+1} = s_t = \alpha s_t(1 - s_t)$$

to give the solutions:

$$s_t = 0 \quad \text{and} \quad s_t = \frac{\alpha - 1}{\alpha}$$

7 Although if α is greater than 4, the exchange rate can temporarily escape from these bounds. This possibility is ignored here.

8 As the reader may verify by following the same graphical procedure as was used in Figure 16.1.
   It should be remembered, incidentally, that in so far as we are modelling the log of the exchange rate, rather than a natural number, negative values are not impossible.

9 Notice that the time paths in Table 16.2 all start from the initial value $s_0 = 0.25$, although we shall discuss a number of other possibilities in the coming sections. However, the graphs are only approximately scaled, and so disparities between the values in the table and the phase portraits may occur as the iterations proceed.

10 It should be clear that point E is the departure point for the cycle only for the particular path starting from the arbitrarily chosen initial value in Figure 16.2(c) (approximately 0.08), because it is the first time the exchange rate passes the 0.36 level. For another starting value, it might take fewer or more iterations. Of course, starting from an exchange rate greater than 0.36, the cyclic behaviour would start at once.

11 Readers interested in the mathematics should note that, in general terms (that is, for broader classes of functions than the logistic), the borderline between stability and instability of the fixed point is determined by the gradient of the phase curve in the region in question. If it is greater than 1.0 (in absolute terms), then the fixed point is unstable. Since at the fixed point the gradient is $(2 - \alpha)$, in the case of the logistic function, it is unstable for values of α greater than 3.0.

12 In fact, zero in the limit.

13 The order of appearance of the different periodicities was set out very precisely by a Russian mathematician named Sarkovskii, as follows:

$$2^0 < 2^1 < 2^2 < 2^3 < 2^4 \ldots < \ldots <$$
$$\ldots < \ldots < \ldots$$
$$\ldots 2^N.9 < 2^N.7 < 2^N.5 < 2^N.3$$
$$\ldots < \ldots < \ldots$$
$$\ldots < \ldots < \ldots$$
$$\ldots < \ldots < 2^2.9 < 2^2.7 < 2^2.5 < 2^2.3$$
$$\ldots < \ldots < 2^1.9 < 2^1.7 < 2^1.5 < 2^1.3$$
$$\ldots < \ldots < 2^0.9 < 2^0.7 < 2^0.5 < 2^0.3$$

For mathematicians, the exciting aspect of this series is that it is not peculiar to the logistic function. Its applicability is much broader. In fact, it is one of a number of so-called universal features of non-linear functions.

For our purposes, two major implications are worthy of note. First, an infinite cast of cycles with even periods makes its appearance before the first odd cycle. Second, the last cycle to appear on stage has a period of $2^0.3$ – that is, just 3. Hence, by the time a three-period cycle arises, all other periodicities have already appeared.

14 What follows in this section is an attempt to provide the reader with an intuitive understanding of what is meant by chaos (or complexity, as it is sometimes known) and of its implications. The mathematical literature contains a number of different formal definitions of chaos, emphasizing varying aspects of the phenomenon: sensitive dependence, mixing and so on. For an example, see Devaney (1989).

15 Slightly more strictly, the Lebesgue measure. There are a number of other concepts of measure used in the literature that amount to more or less the same thing in the present context.

16 For any variable x_t, the so-called tent map (for example, Devaney (1989)) takes a form like:

$$x_{t+1} = \begin{cases} 2x_t & 0 \le x_t \le \dfrac{1}{2} \\ 2 - 2x_t & \dfrac{1}{2} \le x_t \le 1 \end{cases}$$

It also generates a chaotic time-series process and in some respects is even easier to study than the logistic.

17 As it happens, this particular time slice (periods 201–250) was chosen purely for practical purposes: the two graphs deviated enough to show up reasonably well in print, given the limitations of the software and hardware being used. For those interested in simply replicating these and similar graphs, all that is required is a reasonably powerful PC and one of the more sophisticated spreadsheet programs. The graphs given here were originally generated running QUATTRO-Pro under Windows on a PC with a 50MHz 80486 processor. Readers wishing to explore more sophisticated models can choose between a number of specialist maths packages available nowadays for PCs and workstations.

18 As we have seen, for all values of α less than 1.0 or greater than 4.0, the value of s_t 'escapes' to $-\infty$.

19 The problem here for applied economists (such as the author) is that we are accustomed to thinking of forecasting in multivariate terms, in the context of econometric models for example, with univariate forecasting as a special (and restrictive) case. However, given the processes for the exogenous variables, linear models that are complete are reducible to univariate processes, which can then be used for forecasting, at least in principle.

Note that the theory of multivariate non-linear processes is much more complicated and in any case not yet fully understood, and hence the concentration here on univariate models.

20 Notice that there is a sense in which computer random number generators can never be truly random, precisely because they must always have some periodicity, albeit an extremely long one.

21 Except for very simple forms of non-linearity, for example, log linearity and, more recently, models of variance autocorrelation, so-called ARCH processes.

22 There seems to be no consensus in the literature about the advisability (or otherwise) of fitting linear time series before testing for non-linearity.

23 In fact, Figure 16.4 consists of the output from a random number generator, whereas Figure 16.5 plots 200 iterations of the logistic with a tuning parameter of 3.75.

24 Almost all research on exchange rates before chaos (that is, almost all the work covered in earlier chapters) involved daily data, at best, and, for the most part, monthly, weekly or quarterly data.

25 See reading guide for explanations of this measure of sensitivity.

26 ARCH models spawned a whole family of offspring, all known by acronyms: GARCH, EGARCH, IGARCH, and others. Interested readers can find out more by consulting any up-to-date econometrics textbook.

27 See especially the papers by Hsieh mentioned in the reading guide.

28 It is not at all obvious that they point towards the need for any form of intervention by the authorities, least of all fixed exchange rates, as is sometimes assumed. After all, if the instability originates in the underlying net demand for a currency, then fixing the exchange rate may prove impossible altogether. Moreover, the effect of any intervention that simply changes the 'initial values' for the demand will be unpredictable over anything longer than the very short term. The question of how to stabilize chaotic systems is yet to be answered, but it would appear that, at the very least, successful intervention would need to alter the parameters of the underlying system. Given the difficulties involved in simply identifying a chaotic system, this is a formidable task indeed and far beyond the competence of present-day statisticians.

PART IV

Fixed exchange rates

There can be very few countries that have not run a fixed exchange rate regime at some period in their history. Yet, so far in this book, we have had relatively little to say on the subject, except in Chapters 5 and 6, where fixed exchange rates were treated as though they had no implications for the economy or the financial markets beyond the direct effect of changes in the foreign currency reserves. The next two chapters take a more realistic view of the situation.

In Chapter 17, we take explicit account of the fact that fixed exchange rates usually involve imposing some form of target zone and this arrangement has dynamic implications that are not immediately obvious. Then, in Chapter 18, we consider the crises that, sooner or later, afflict fixed exchange rate regimes, often fatally.

17 Target zones

Introduction

So far in this book we have dealt only with polar cases, as if there were only two possible types of exchange rate regime, fixed or floating. In practice, of course, most floating exchange rates are managed, at least to some extent, and most fixed rate systems allow some measure of flexibility. In fact, for reasons that will become clear later, so-called fixed rate systems usually permit a currency to float between upper and lower bounds.

This chapter analyses the working of what is known as a target zone system. Recall from Chapter 5 that, with a completely fixed exchange rate, the money supply is outside a small country's control. One of the key questions we shall seek to answer concerns how far the introduction of a measure of flexibility into an otherwise rigid exchange rate system can actually restore a country's monetary independence. We need to start by defining target zones, and then proceed to an informal analysis of their effect in Section 17.2. This will lead to an explanation of what is known as smooth pasting, a phenomenon that is familiar from the literature on how options

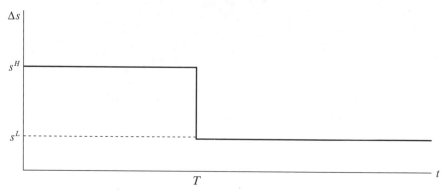

Figure 17.1 An arbitrage opportunity

are priced. For this reason, Section 17.3 on smooth pasting is followed by an alternative view of target zones, which is aimed mainly at readers familiar with the basics of option pricing (Section 17.4). As far as policy is concerned, the controversial aspect of target zones is whether or not they allow for a so-called honeymoon effect, as is explained in Section 17.6. As always, we attempt to confront the theory with the facts and, as usual, the theory comes off worse, for reasons explained in Section 17.7. The final two sections present extensions of the model intended to make it more realistic in its assumptions and more consistent with the facts.

Before proceeding, however, there is a preliminary piece of analysis that will be extremely helpful in understanding the rest of this chapter and the next. Consider the exchange rate path shown in Figure 17.1. For the moment, we need not relate it to any particular model. It simply shows the level of the (log of the) exchange rate constant at the level s^H until the time period T, at which point something happens (an 'event'), causing an appreciation of the domestic currency (fall in the price of foreign exchange) to a new lower level, s^L.

Now, obviously, in this scenario an investor with perfect foresight could borrow foreign currency at the instant before T, call it T^-, *and use the proceeds to buy the domestic currency, to make a profit of $s^H - s^L$ per unit of currency borrowed.* If there are no limits on borrowing – that is, if the capital market is perfectly competitive – then this profit can be increased indefinitely by borrowing an infinite amount.[1] This therefore is clearly not a plausible scenario, since it implies one-way traffic in the currency market at time T^-.

The critical point of course is that in reality nobody has perfect foresight. What if there is uncertainty? Plainly, our conclusion is unchanged if the exchange rate path in Figure 17.1 is only the *conditional expectation* of a random variable, because if investors are risk neutral, they will by definition accept the chance to speculate when the prospective mean return is positive. If investors are risk-averse, then the argument still stands. The reason we can say this is because, as the holding period for the speculation gets shorter in the limit – that is, as we think of the interval from T^- to T and from T to T^+ collapsing – the associated risk also reduces, so that ultimately speculation becomes arbitrage.

We conclude that *discontinuities in the path of the expected exchange rate are impossible.* To be consistent with the absence of arbitrage opportunities, the exchange rate must be expected to follow a smooth path.

Notice that this is not to rule out the possibility of sudden jumps in the level of the actual exchange rate. These are clearly not only possible but also very much a feature of the real world. All we are saying is that jagged paths reflect unexpected rather than expected movements in the time series.

Now that we have established this point, consider the fundamentals whose behaviour drives the exchange rate. Chapter 13 focused on unexpected changes in these fundamental variables, which were called 'news'. But it is by no means the case that all changes in the fundamentals are unexpected. There are frequently movements in fundamental variables that are widely or even universally anticipated. For example, there are regular seasonal changes in some of the relevant variables, such as the fall in the level of economic activity over the Christmas and New Year holidays. An election result may well mean an overnight change in people's expectations with respect to the future rate of monetary expansion, and so on.

If all these variables are genuinely fundamental to exchange rate determination, how can fully anticipated, discrete changes in their levels be consistent with a smooth continuous path for the financial variable whose level they determine?

The answer varies from case to case, but in this chapter and the next we shall be concerned with two specific scenarios, both originally analysed by Paul Krugman. In the target zone model, the anticipated discrete change is a currency market intervention by the authorities to preserve a fixed exchange rate regime, with the usual consequences for the money stock. In the crisis model, the change is an endogenous monetary contraction brought about by a flight from the domestic currency. Both models have to reconcile these predictable monetary changes with a smooth exchange rate path, and a central feature of our exposition will involve explaining how this is achieved. In the target zone model, the paradox is resolved by making the exchange rate a non-linear function of the fundamentals, with a gradient of zero at the point where intervention occurs, while in the crisis model the monetary contraction (i.e. the crisis) is moved forward in time to a point when it can have no immediate impact on the exchange rate.

17.1   What is a target zone?

The model of a fixed exchange rate regime was first introduced in Section 5.2. But the type of fixity envisaged there was deliberately oversimplified. In this chapter, we analyse a more realistic scenario, because completely fixed exchange rate regimes are rare in practice, for reasons that will be apparent after a moment's consideration.

Perhaps the best way to understand the point is by analogy with the thermostat inside a domestic air-conditioning system. By setting the dial on our air conditioning to 25 °C, we establish a target temperature, instructing the system to keep as close as possible to that level at all times. It is then left to the thermostat to switch the heating on when the house temperature falls too far below the target level and to start cooling whenever it gets too hot. But in order to maintain this degree of control, the thermostat has to be preprogrammed (usually by the manufacturer) to set the fluctuation limits for the temperature, otherwise it cannot know the definition of 'too cold' or 'too hot'. It might, for example, be set to switch the heating on when the temperature falls to 0.5 °C below the target (i.e. 24.5 °C, in our case) and start the cooling phase whenever the temperature rises to 0.5 °C above the target (i.e. 25.5 °C). In other words, the thermostat establishes a target zone of 1 °C (0.5 °C on each side) around the central, target temperature set by the user. Notice that as long as the temperature lies *inside* the target zone, neither heating nor cooling is required, and so the system is inoperative. It comes into action only to nudge the temperature up when it falls to the lower bound (the floor) and to nudge it down at the upper limit (the ceiling).

Since the target itself is simply a single number, it is difficult to see how else a control system could work other than along these general lines.[2] By the same token, it would be difficult to run a fixed exchange rate regime that did not permit some movement on either side of the target (or *par* or *central*) rate. Under the Bretton Woods system, for example, countries permitted their exchange rates to fluctuate by 1% on either side of their par values and for most of the 1980s the French franc was restricted to a band of 2.25% around its central Deutschmark parity under the terms of the ERM (see Chapter 1). This type of arrangement means that the monetary authorities are under no obligation to intervene in the currency market (although they may decide that it is desirable to do so) unless and until the exchange rate reaches its upper or lower bound. When the exchange rate does threaten to exceed one or other of these limits, the monetary authority is committed to taking the necessary steps to stop the rate breaching its bounds, by increasing the money stock at the lower bound (i.e. when the currency is too strong) or reducing it at the upper bound (when it is too weak).

17.2 Effect of target zones

In Chapter 5, we ignored the existence of these fluctuation bands, so as to keep the analysis of fixed exchange rates as straightforward as possible. However, in this chapter we address the question: *how do target zones affect matters?* In what follows, we restrict attention to a symmetrical target zone – that is, with limits of x% both above and below the central rate.[3]

To start with, think of the problem in this way: when a target zone is in force, the exchange rate is allowed to float freely in between the barriers set by the upper and lower bounds. We appear to be dealing simply with a limited float, so it might seem that we can immediately provide an intuitive answer to the question in just a few words: in the interior of the target zone, the exchange rate will reflect the fundamentals, but it will bump along the ceiling or floor if it ever reaches them. In graphical terms, if we plot the exchange rate on the vertical axis against the fundamentals on the horizontal, this amounts to asserting that the exchange rate will move up and down the path plotted as a solid line in Figure 17.2.

This is the obvious solution but, as so often happens in economics, the most obvious solution is not the correct one. To see why Figure 17.2 cannot be correct, consider what it implies in terms of the simple but general model used in Chapter 12. Rewrite Equation 12.7 as follows:

$$s_t = k_t + b\Delta s_t^e \quad b > 0 \tag{17.1}$$

which replaces the second term, γz_t, by k_t. Recall that z_t was introduced as a portmanteau term to summarize all the factors that determine the net demand for the currency, excluding only the expected change in the exchange rate itself, Δs^e. In the monetary model, for example, these factors (the so-called fundamentals) would be the domestic and foreign money stocks and the domestic and foreign levels of national income. The parameter γ from Equation 12.7 has been suppressed, since it will have no part to play in the analysis in this chapter. In other words, we can safely scale the variables so that the coefficient of k_t is one.

For the sake of clarity, we state our assumptions formally as follows:

Assumption 17.1 Random fundamentals Those components of k_t that are outside the control of the monetary authority change randomly. In other words, they are subject to zero-mean shocks or innovations, so that at any given moment they are equally likely to increase or decrease. Specifically, we assume the disturbances to k_t are distributed normally,[4] so that the probability of a positive shock of $x\%$ is the same as the probability of a negative shock of $x\%$ and moreover is smaller the greater is x.

Assumption 17.2 No intramarginal interventions The monetary authority operates in the way we have already described to change the exogenous component of the fundamentals (i.e. the money supply) only at the last moment, when the exchange rate is already at its upper or lower limit. It never intervenes as long as the exchange rate is inside the target zone.

Assumption 17.3 Credibility The target zone is credible. In other words, the currency markets believe that the authorities have both the will and the reserves needed to keep the exchange rate inside the limits of the target zone.

Assumption 17.4 Symmetry The target zone is symmetrical about the central rate – that is, the scope for upward movement is the same as the scope for downward movement.

Taken together, the first two assumptions imply that at any point in the interior of the target zone, the expected future value of the fundamentals, k_t, is simply k_t itself, because we can be sure that the money stock will remain unchanged (by A17.2), and the remaining factors are as likely to go up as down (by A17.1). In more formal terms, we are assuming that k_t is a random walk[5] as long as the exchange rate is not actually at the boundary of the target zone:

$$k_t = k_{t-1} + \varepsilon_t \quad \text{for} \quad \underline{s} < s_t < \bar{s} \tag{17.2}$$

where ε_t is a zero-mean error term or innovation. At the upper intervention point, $\bar{s}$, instead of Equation 17.2, the fundamental is given by:

$$k_t = \begin{cases} k_{t-1} + \varepsilon_t & \text{for} \quad \varepsilon_t < 0 \\ k_{t-1} & \text{for} \quad \varepsilon_t > 0 \end{cases} \quad \text{whenever } s_t = \bar{s} \tag{17.3}$$

In other words, the authorities reduce the money stock by just enough to offset any positive shock to the fundamental but of course do nothing if the shock is negative, since in that case there is no danger of the exchange rate barrier being breached. Symmetrically, at the lower bound:

$$k_t = \begin{cases} k_{t-1} + \varepsilon_t & \text{for} \quad \varepsilon_t < 0 \\ k_{t-1} & \text{for} \quad \varepsilon_t > 0 \end{cases} \quad \text{whenever } s_t = \underline{s} \qquad (17.4)$$

Notice what this specification implies with respect to expectations. In the middle of the band, it follows from Equation 17.2 that:

$$E_{t-1}k_t = k_{t-1} \qquad (17.5)$$

as usual for a random walk. But Equation 17.3 implies that at the upper boundary:

$$E_{t-1}k_t < k_{t-1} \qquad (17.6)$$

because the fundamental has no 'upside potential' from this point, but has the same scope for a downward movement as in the interior of the band. Symmetrically, at the lower boundary, from Equation 17.4:

$$E_{t-1}k_t > k_{t-1} \qquad (17.7)$$

Now return to the diagram. The implication of the 45-degree line through the origin and of points A and B in Figure 17.2 is clear. Since at all points on the line we have $s_t = k_t$, we must have $\Delta s^e = 0$, by Equation 17.1. In other words, the fundamentals are not expected to change, and so neither is the exchange rate.

This conclusion would be fine if it were not for the barriers set by the target zone. But consider the situation at a point like B, on the 45-degree line near the upper limit of the target zone. What would be the effect of a small change in the random component of the fundamentals starting from here?

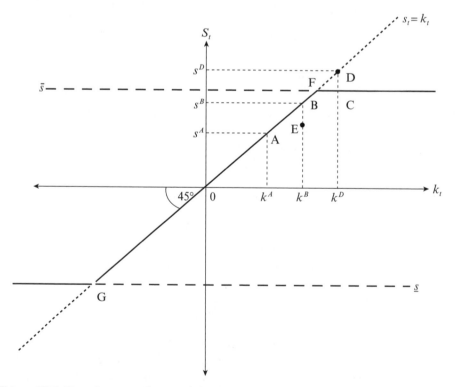

Figure 17.2 Target zones: the way it isn't

If the change is negative, then taking the fundamental down from k^B to k^A, it would reduce the price of foreign exchange, so that the new exchange rate would be something like s^A, further down the 45-degree line at A.

But what would happen if, instead, the fundamentals were to *increase*, in the same proportion, to the new level of k^D? In the absence of barriers, we know from Chapter 5 that the price of foreign currency would have to rise by the same proportion, so that the new exchange rate would be s^D. But the point D is above the ceiling, and so the monetary authorities would be forced to intervene as soon as the upper bound was reached. They would have to use the reserves to buy the currency at the upper bound, thereby reducing the money stock and offsetting the spontaneous rise in the random component of the fundamentals, so that the exchange rate ended up at a point on the ceiling like C.

Now if we go back to the starting point at B, we can see a clear contradiction. Recall that A17.1 implies that an increase and a decrease in the random fundamental are equally likely outcomes. It follows that, from B, the probability that the system will jump to A is the same as the probability that it will go to C. But this means that *the expected change in the exchange rate cannot be zero*.

The truth of this proposition will be demonstrated by the extended example given in the next section, but for the moment suppose that the probability of landing at A next period is exactly $1/2$. As has already been explained, if there is the same probability of an equal *rise* in k_t (i.e. a rise that would take the exchange rate to point D if the authorities permitted it to happen), then it follows that the system will be at point C next period with the same probability, $1/2$.

This implies that the expected level of the exchange rate next period[6] is:

$$\frac{1}{2}s^A + \frac{1}{2}\bar{s}$$

which is obviously less than s^B. It follows that the expected depreciation next period is not zero but it is negative – that is, an appreciation is expected since $\Delta s^e < 0$. Market commentators would say that, at B, the 'downside risk' of holding the domestic currency is less than the 'upside potential'.

Note that this is entirely consistent with the observation made earlier that the expected change in the fundamental is negative at the upper edge of the zone. By way of contrast, it is plainly inconsistent with the property that $s_t = k_t$, embodied in the 45-degree line. In fact, the point consistent with zero expected change in the exchange rate when the future outcomes are s^A and $\bar{s}$ with equal probability is somewhere like point E.

Having found the weakness in Figure 17.2, we can now see the outline of the solution. If point B is ruled out in favour of a point like E, then the same applies with greater or lesser force to all other points on the 45-degree line above the central rate. Thus, our first conclusion is: *the exchange rate has to follow a path that keeps it below the 45-degree line at all points in the top half of the target zone*. However distant it may be, the prospect that the money stock will ultimately be cut in order to preserve the target zone means that the exchange rate must always lie below the level implied by the current level of the fundamentals. From Equation 17.1, this in turn means that the expected rate of depreciation must be negative – that is to say, the market must anticipate an appreciation of the domestic currency. The expected appreciation increases the demand, other things being equal, thereby validating a lower value of s than would otherwise be justified by the current level of the fundamentals.

Now, by A17.1, the further we are from G, the smaller is the probability of s reaching the ceiling next period and triggering intervention by the central bank. It follows that the mechanism just described is weaker at lower values of s, so that the distance of the exchange rate from the 45-degree line gets smaller as we go back down towards the central rate. At points not far above the origin, the prospect of intervention being needed is relatively distant, so that the exchange rate behaves almost as if it were floating freely.

At the origin, the relatively small probability of the domestic currency having to be supported by reserve sales (money stock decrease) is equal to and just balanced by the probability of it having to be restrained by reserve purchases (i.e. monetary expansion). The expected depreciation is therefore zero, so that this is the only point at which the actual exchange rate coincides with the level dictated by the fundamentals alone. In other words, only at the central rate do the barriers have no effect on the actual exchange rate.

Now consider levels of the exchange rate below the central rate. Repeating the analysis given above will demonstrate that our conclusions are reversed (as will also be shown in the worked example that follows this section). The actual exchange rate will always be above the rate warranted by the fundamentals alone, so that there will be a positive expected depreciation, as the market takes account of the possibility that the exchange rate might reach s, triggering an immediate increase in the money stock. The closer the rate gets to the lower bound, the greater the probability that the money stock will need to be increased in order to preserve the target zone, hence the more the exchange rate path is bent upwards relative to the 45-degree line.

To recap, then, we have reached the conclusion that the actual exchange rate will fluctuate in response to random movements in the exogenous component of the fundamentals in such a fashion as to be continually below its pure float level in the top half of the zone and above its pure float level in the bottom half. This means, in particular, that the exchange rate path will never go into the corners at points like F and G in Figure 17.2.

17.3 Smooth pasting

These conditions are all satisfied by a path like the S curve in Figure 17.3. It lies below the dashed 45-degree line in the top half of the figure and above it in the bottom half. As the exchange rate approaches the floor or ceiling, it touches down smoothly, like an aeroplane making a perfect landing, so that the bounds become tangential to the S curve at its extremities. This feature is known as *smooth pasting*.

To understand why this is implied by the model, consider what would happen if there were no smooth pasting. The argument is broadly the same as the one from which we deduced that the exchange rate path would be flatter than a 45-degree line. Figure 17.4 illustrates the situation at the ceiling, when the exchange rate path is allowed to cross the upper bound. As before, suppose that k^A and k^C are the equally likely outcomes for next period when the (random) fundamental starts at k^B. Then, clearly, once we take account of the intervention that will occur if the next random

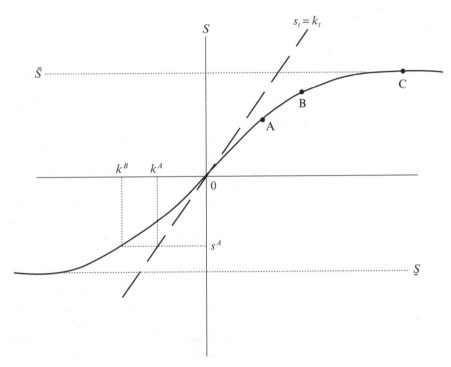

Figure 17.3 Target zone – the S curve

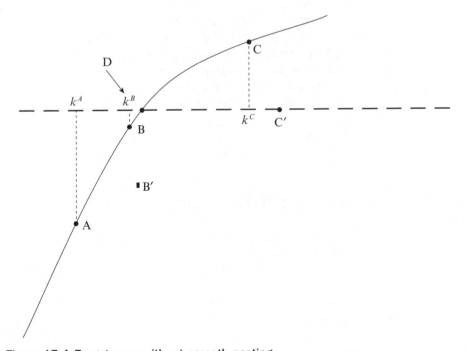

Figure 17.4 Target zone without smooth pasting

shock is positive, we can see that the situation is impossible. In the event of a positive shock, the system will go to somewhere like C′, not C. Hence, B itself could not have been an equilibrium, since whatever was the net expected depreciation at that point, it ignored the monetary contraction that was going to occur in the event of a positive shock. Expectations at B were therefore too pessimistic about the future value of the domestic currency. Instead, they should have been more bullish, which itself would have boosted demand for the currency and validated a higher exchange rate (lower value of s) at a point like B′.

Since the same argument would apply wherever the path crossed the upper or lower bound, we can conclude that it never does so. Hence, *smooth pasting is the only solution consistent with market rationality.*

Notice that this argument for smooth pasting is essentially the same as the one used in the previous section to rule out the possibility of corners in the exchange rate path, which is exactly what we would have if the solution ran through points A and B to D and thence to C′ after intervention to reduce the money stock. This sort of outcome could be possible only if agents were myopic about the prospects for intervention.

To put the matter another way, smooth pasting is the result of requiring the exchange rate to follow a continuous path, so as to eliminate possible arbitrage opportunities. At the limits of the target zone, the fundamental becomes predictable, in the sense that it no longer has a zero expectation, so that if the exchange rate were dependent on the fundamental, the rate of depreciation would also have a predictable bias. For example, at the upper boundary there would be no danger of a further depreciation (remember Assumption 17.3!), so speculators could look forward to non-negative returns with complete certainty. Such a one-way bet is impossible.

The paradox is resolved by having the exchange rate tiptoe up to the boundary, getting asymptotically ever closer to the line, and in the process making the functional relationship represented by the S curve ever flatter – in other words, making the exchange rate less and less sensitive to changes in the fundamental. By the time we reach the boundary, the S curve is completely flat, so that the fundamental has become irrelevant. The possibility of the one-way bet scenario has been anticipated for so long that, by the time it arrives, its effect is nil. Like traders who have spent months adjusting their spending patterns in anticipation of a bonus, its arrival comes as an anticlimax.

We conclude that the exchange rate moves up and down a curve like the unbroken line in Figure 17.3 (a formal proof is given in Appendix 17.1).

17.4 An option interpretation

The analysis of smooth pasting may look familiar to readers with a background in option-pricing theory. For their benefit, it is worth reinterpreting the analysis in terms of foreign currency option contracts, with holders of the domestic and foreign currencies as the respective counterparties.

Consider first the situation at a point close to the upper bound. Assume that the lower bound is far enough away to be unimportant when the exchange rate is so close to $\bar{s}$. In this situation, buyers of the domestic currency know that if they wish at some time in the future to switch back into the foreign currency, then they will be able to do so at a maximum price of $\bar{s}$. In buying the domestic currency, they are therefore simultaneously buying *a call on foreign exchange with an exercise price of $\bar{s}$.* Equivalently, they are buying the domestic currency plus a put allowing them to sell it for at least $1/G$ units of foreign currency.

Under either interpretation, they will have been willing to overpay for their domestic currency to the extent of the value of the embedded option. Hence, the overvaluation of the domestic currency relative to its fundamental value reflects the premium on the implicit option packaged with the spot currency.

If purchasers of the domestic currency have a long position in an option, then symmetrically, the monetary authorities must have taken short positions. They are counterparties to the option purchases, since they have sold a call on foreign exchange (a put on domestic currency) to the domestic currency buyers. In return for writing the options, they receive the premium in the form of a reduced price for foreign exchange, approximately equal to the distance between the S curve and the 45-degree line.

Obviously, the value of this option is greater the nearer the exchange rate is to the upper bound, hence the increasing gap between the S curve and the 45-degree line. Conversely, as we move down the figure, at lower levels of s the option is further away from the money, and therefore less valuable, and so the gap diminishes.

In addition, the closer we get to the lower bound, the greater is the value of the option offered by the floor value of s, $\underline{s}$. This option is the reverse of the option at the upper bound, so the long and short sides of the implicit option transaction are reversed. Here, the option consists of a guaranteed price offered to domestic currency holders – that is, a call on the domestic currency at the strike price of $\underline{s}$. Hence, they willingly overpay for foreign exchange, in recognition of the put option packaged with it.

Notice that at the central rate, the two option positions have equal value, so that the net position is zero and the exchange rate is at the level implied by the fundamentals.

17.4.1 A simple example[7]

To understand the mechanism at work in this target zone model, we shall consider an ultra-simple example. We shall introduce an unfamiliar representation of a familiar process for the fundamental, on which we can base a benchmark model for analysing the target zone mechanism.

The benchmark model

Start with the process followed by the random fundamental in the absence of any action by the authorities. Assume:

Assumption 17.5 The random component of the fundamentals changes in each period according to the following simple rule: either it goes up to 150% of its level in the previous period (which we write as $k_{t+1} = uk_t$, with $u = 1.5$) or it goes down to only 66.67% (2/3) of its previous level, in which case $k_{t+1} = dk_t$, with $d = 0.66$. All other outcomes can be ruled out. Let the probability of the 50% rise be 0.4, so that the probability of the 1/3 fall must be 0.6. In short, the process can be summarized as:[8]

$$k_{t+1} = \begin{cases} uk_t = 1.5k_t, & w.p.\,0.4 \\ dk_t = 0.66k_t, & w.p.\,0.6 \end{cases}$$

The assumption that a random variable can take only two possible values might seem very restrictive. In fact, it turns out that, appropriately interpreted, a so-called *binomial process* provides a reasonably realistic model of a range of financial variables. Likewise, although these numbers may look implausibly large, this is not necessarily a serious problem since nothing has been said about the length of each period.[9]

Suppose the fundamental starts at the 100 level at $t = 0$. The sort of process implied by these assumptions is illustrated in Table 17.1, which takes the form known as a *binomial tree*. Ignoring for the moment the lower of the two numbers at each branching point ('node'), the fundamental either goes up to 150 or goes down to 66.67 at the end of the first period, i.e. at $t = 1$. In the first case, it may rise to 225 or fall back to 100 at $t = 2$. By the same token, if it falls to 66.67 in the first period, then it can only take the values 100 or 44.44 at $t = 2$.

Notice that, given our assumptions, the outcome of a fall followed by a rise is the same as a rise followed by a fall, because $udk_t = duk_t$. The tree is said to be *recombining*.

Table 17.1 follows the process through for only seven periods, at the end of which the fundamental may take any of seven values ranging from a minimum of 8.78 to a maximum of 1139.06.[10]

Given this process for the fundamental, we can now compute the value it implies for the exchange rate. In order to do so, however, we need to introduce an additional working assumption:

> **Assumption 17.6** At the end of the final period, the exchange rate is equal to the fundamental.

As can be seen from Equation 17.1, this implies that the exchange rate is expected to remain static in subsequent periods. This assumption is less restrictive than might appear at first glance. If we find it difficult to believe that the expected rate of depreciation could be zero only seven periods from today, then we need only extend the tree to 8, 9, 10 . . . periods. A17.6 amounts to no more than the assertion that a steady state exists at some horizon, however far in the future.

Now we can proceed to compute the value that the exchange rate must take at each node of the tree, starting, as always in this type of model, at the final period $t = 7$, where our answers are given trivially by A17.6 as 1139.06, 506.25, 225.00 . . . etc.

Consider the situation at the next-to-last stage (period 5). Starting at the maximum value of the fundamental, 759.38, the computation follows Equation 17.1:

$$s_t = k_t + b\Delta s_t^e$$
$$= 759.38 + \{0.75 \times [(0.4 \times 1139.06) + (0.6 \times 506.25) - 759.38]\}$$
$$= 759.38$$

The first term in the outside bracket is the assumed value of the parameter b (unrealistically high, but for illustrative purposes only), which multiplies the expression in the square bracket, the expected rate of depreciation. This is simply the expected exchange rate next period (0.4 times its value in the up state, 1139.06, *plus* 0.6 times its value in the down state, 506.25) less its current value, 759.38.

In similar fashion, we can fill in the values at the other period 6 nodes of the tree, to get 337.50, 150.00, 66.67, 29.63 and 13.17. Next, we use the results just computed for s_t in the six possible states at $t = 5$ to derive the values for period 4 and so on

Table 17.1 No barriers

Period →	0	1	2	3	4	5	6
							1139.06
u = 1.5							*1139.06*
d = 0.66666						759.38	
q = 0.4						*759.38*	
b = 0.75					506.25		506.25
Implied r = 0.00%					*506.25*		*506.25*
				337.50		337.50	
				337.50		*337.50*	
			225.00		225.00		225.00
			225.00		*225.00*		*225.00*
		150.00		150.00		150.00	
		150.00		*150.00*		*150.00*	
k(0) =	100.00		100.00		100.00		100.00
S(0) =	*100.00*		*100.00*		*100.00*		*100.00*
		66.67		66.67		66.67	
		66.67		*66.67*		*66.67*	
			44.44		44.44		44.44
			44.44		*44.44*		*44.44*
				29.63		29.63	
				29.63		*29.63*	
					19.75		19.75
					19.75		*19.75*
						13.17	
						13.17	
							8.78
							8.78

recursively until we arrive at the value of 100.00 as the level of the exchange rate implied by the assumed fundamental process.

Should we be surprised by this outcome? Certainly not. The exchange rate is at exactly the level justified by a fundamental factor that has an expected rate of change of zero in each period. (Check: 0.4 *times* one-half *plus* 0.6 *times minus* one-third.) Hence, although the fundamental cannot possibly remain unchanged next period, its expected value is still: no change.

By now, it should be clear that the fundamental process we are describing is a form of random walk, with properties similar to the process introduced in Section 11.5, at least if we imagine extending our binomial tree for an infinite number of periods.

Effect of a barrier

Now consider how the process set out here changes when a barrier is introduced.

We can simplify the problem without sacrificing anything if we concentrate on the effect of a single barrier rather than on a target zone. We choose arbitrarily to analyse the consequences of imposing an upper bound on the benchmark exchange rate process. So, from now on, *assume the exchange rate cannot go above 760.* In the downward direction, it remains unconstrained, and so we need be concerned only with what happens as we approach the upper bound. In fact, we can go further and simply concentrate on the case where the random fundamental repeatedly increases, taking the exchange rate up to the barrier by the quickest route.

Before we can make any progress, however, we need to be explicit about the decision rule followed by the authorities in the neighbourhood of the upper limit. So assume:

> **Assumption 17.7** The authorities intervene whenever allowing the fundamentals to evolve freely (i.e. according to the benchmark process in Table 17.1) would result in the exchange rate breaching its limit. Moreover, when they do intervene, their action is calculated to have the effect of reducing the fundamentals by just enough to bring the exchange rate back down to its limit of 760.[11]

Tables 17.2 to 17.8 show the evolution of the fundamental and the exchange rate through six periods under this new scenario. (We omit the bottom half of the tree, since it remains the same as in Table 17.1 throughout.)

In the first period, which we label $t = 0$, an agent looking forward six periods sees only a single scenario in which the authorities have to act to prevent the exchange rate breaching its limit of 760. This is, of course, the branch involving an unbroken sequence of up movements, leading ultimately at $t = 6$ to a level of the fundamental (and hence, by A17.6, of the exchange rate) of 1139.06. Given the assumptions made here, the authorities would react to this eventuality by reducing the fundamental to precisely 760.

Table 17.2 Barrier at 760
Start at $t = 0$

Period →	0	1	2	3	4	5	6
							760.00
$u = 1.5$							**760.00**
$d = 0.6667$						759.38	
$q = 0.4$						*694.39*	
$b = 0.75$					506.25		506.25
Implied r = 0.00%					*495.11*		**506.25**
				337.50		337.50	
				335.59		*337.50*	
			225.00		225.00		225.00
			224.67		*225.00*		**225.00**
		150.00		150.00		150.00	
		149.94		*150.00*		*150.00*	
$k(0) =$	100.00		100.00		100.00		100.00
S(0) =	*99.99*		*100.00*		*100.00*		**100.00**

Table 17.3 Barrier at 760
Start at $t = 1$

u = 1.5
d = 0.66666
q = 0.4
b = 0.75
Implied r = 0.00%

Period →	0	1	2	3	4	5	6
							760.00
							760.00
						760.28	
						760.00	
					759.38		
					760.00		
				506.25		506.25	
				495.11		*506.25*	
			337.50		337.50		337.50
			335.59		*337.50*		*337.50*
		225.00		225.00		225.00	
		224.67		*225.00*		*225.00*	
k(0) =	150.00		150.00		150.00		150.00
S(0) =	*149.94*		*150.00*		*150.00*		*150.00*

Table 17.4 Barrier at 760
Start at $t = 2$

u = 1.5
d = 0.6667
q = 0.4
b = 0.75
Implied r = 0.00%

Period →	2	3	4	5	6	7	8
							760.00
							760.00
						760.00	
						760.00	
					789.52		760.00
					760.00		*760.00*
				759.38		759.38	
				691.53		*694.39*	
			506.25		506.25		506.25
			494.13		*495.11*		*506.25*
		337.50		337.50		337.50	
		335.34		*335.59*		*337.50*	
k(0) =	225.00		225.00		225.00		225.00
S(0) =	*224.61*		*224.67*		*225.00*		*225.00*

The fact that the exchange rate bumps up against the barrier in this state, however, affects expectations in earlier periods. If we move back to period 5, consider the situation on the highest branch of the tree, when the fundamental is 759.38 (notice that we have no need to examine any of the other nodes, as they involve no change from the benchmark case in Table 17.1). The exchange rate cannot be 759.38 in the

Table 17.5 Barrier at 760
Start at _t_ = 3

Period →	3	4	5	6	7	8	9
_u = 1.5_							760.00 / _760.00_
_d = 0.6666_						760.00 / _760.00_	
_q = 0.4_					760.00 / _760.00_		760.00 / _760.00_
_b = 0.75_				789.52 / _760.00_		760.28 / _760.00_	
Implied r = 0.00%			759.38 / _691.53_		759.38 / _694.39_		759.38 / _759.38_
		506.25 / _494.13_		506.25 / _495.11_		506.25 / _506.25_	
_k(0) =_ / _S(0) =_		337.50 / _335.34_	337.50 / _335.59_		337.50 / _337.50_		337.50 / _337.50_

Table 17.6 Barrier at 760
Start at _t_ = 4

Period →	4	5	6	7	8	9	10
_u = 1.5_							760.00 / _760.00_
_d = 0.6666_						760.00 / _760.00_	
_q = 0.4_					760.00 / _760.00_		760.00 / _760.00_
_b = 0.75_				760.00 / _760.00_		760.00 / _760.00_	
Implied r = 0.00%			790.81 / _760.00_		789.52 / _760.00_		760.00 / _760.00_
		759.38 / _691.28_		759.38 / _691.53_		759.38 / _694.39_	
_k(0) =_ / _S(0) =_		506.25 / _494.02_		506.25 / _494.13_		506.25 / _495.11_	506.25 / _506.25_

present case, because the two possible future states are 760.00 (instead of 1139.06) and 506.25, as before. So the expected future exchange rate must be lower than in the unconstrained model, and hence the rate of depreciation must be lower and therefore the current exchange rate will also be lower. Repeating the computation in the previous section with 760.00 in place of 1139.06 gives the new level of the exchange rate in this scenario as 694.39.

Table 17.7 Barrier at 760
Start at *t* = 5

Period →	5	6	7	8	9	10	11
u = 1.5							760.00 *760.00*
d = 0.6666						760.00 *760.00*	
q = 0.4					760.00 *760.00*		760.00 *760.00*
b = 0.75				760.00 *760.00*		760.00 *760.00*	
Implied r = 0.00%			760.00 *760.00*		760.00 *760.00*		760.00 *760.00*
		790.81 *760.00*		789.52 *760.00*		760.28 *760.00*	
k(0) =	759.38		759.38		759.38		759.38
S(0) =	*691.28*		*691.53*		*694.39*		*759.38*

Table 17.8 Barrier at 760
Start at *t* = 6

Period →	6	7	8	9	10	11	12
u = 1.5							760.00 *760.00*
d = 0.6666						760.00 *760.00*	
q = 0.4					760.00 *760.00*		760.00 *760.00*
b = 0.75				760.00 *760.00*		760.00 *760.00*	
Implied r = 0.00%			760.00 *760.00*		760.00 *760.00*		760.00 *760.00*
		790.52 *760.00*		779.63 *760.00*		760.00 *760.00*	
k(0) =	759.81		759.81		790.81		760.00
S(0) =	*714.23*		*714.41*		*716.39*		*760.00*

Of course, this fact in turn leads to a lower level of the exchange rate than before at *t* = 4, *t* = 3, *t* = 2, *t* = 1 and ultimately to the conclusion that the current *t* = 0 exchange rate has to be slightly less than 100.00–99.99 in fact.

Notice what has happened. We have arrived at a lower *current* level of the exchange rate as a result of the prospect of a possible future intervention to reduce the fundamental. It is important to note that the intervention is not only six periods away in the future but also far from certain. In fact, the probability of it occurring is only 0.4^{12} or a mere 0.004, and so it is not surprising that the impact on the current price is small.

Now move forward one period and suppose that the fundamental goes up to 150.00. Starting from this higher level, a sequence of up moves would bring the process up to the barrier one period sooner, so that it is now constrained in the last two states on the uppermost branch in Table 17.3. The exchange rate sequence reaches 694.39 by $t = 5$, from which point a 50% increase must take it beyond the upper limit. So the authorities must reduce the fundamental to 760.28, which, given the two possible $t = 7$ states (760.00 and 759.38 respectively), results in a $t = 6$ exchange rate of exactly 760.[13]

Again, the effect of the barrier is felt in each preceding period and this time, of course, the effect is slightly greater, so that the current price is 149.94. The gap between the level of the fundamental and the level of the exchange rate is still small, but it is none the less greater than it was in the previous period.

Tables 17.4 to 17.8 repeat these computations with successively larger current starting values of the fundamental following along the uppermost branch of the tree in the benchmark case. As can clearly be seen, as the process approaches the barrier, the number of scenarios in which intervention is required increases, and hence the expected future exchange rate is reduced progressively. Consequently, the gap between the actual level of the exchange rate and its fundamental level grows.

The successive values of the exchange rate are plotted (in smoothed form) as the curve in Figure 17.5, with the upper limit of 760 along the top edge of the figure.

Although a crude example such as this cannot replicate very accurately the results of the original Krugman model, two of the results justified in the earlier parts of this chapter are clear from the graph. First, the exchange rate is consistently below the level of the fundamental. Second, the gap increases as the limit is approached.

17.5 A honeymoon for policymakers?

What does this analysis imply for exchange rate policy?

Recall the conclusions reached in Part II of this book regarding the scope for monetary policy in a small open economy. Monetary expansion simply flooded out via the current account deficit in a fixed exchange rate regime, while with a floating exchange rate it resulted in a pro rata depreciation.

In comparison with the limiting case of a fixed rate regime with no fluctuation margins, the S curve appears to offer some room for manoeuvre. The critical point here is that the exchange rate path is flatter than the 45-degree line associated with a pure float. The implication is that inside the target zone, when the exchange rate is weak (i.e. above its central rate), it is still not as weak as it would be under a pure float. Symmetrically, when it is too strong, it is none the less weaker than the fundamentals would imply. Hence, the target zone seems to be an inherently stabilizing factor. It not only prevents the exchange rate straying beyond the bounds set by the system *but also has a stabilizing effect in the interior of the zone, where it dampens the currency market's response to shocks in the fundamentals – the so-called 'honeymoon effect'*. The very fact that the authorities are committed to intervening at the upper and lower bounds makes the exchange rate less sensitive than it would be in the absence of the target zone.

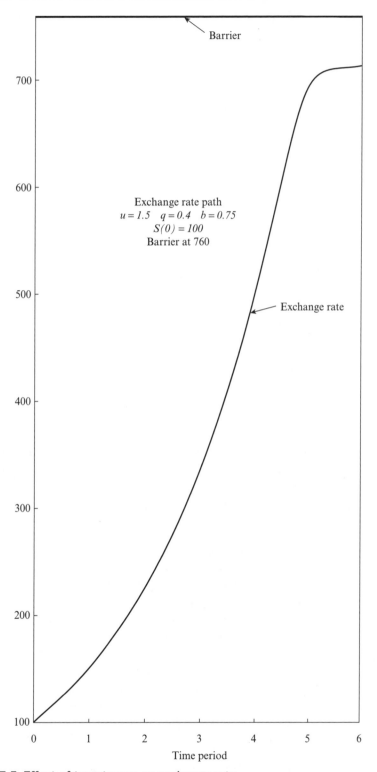

Figure 17.5 Effect of target zone on exchange rate

To appreciate the force of this conclusion, contrast the explicit and credible target zone we have analysed in the previous four sections with an informal (i.e. unannounced) target zone, achieved by a managed float. Suppose the authorities wish to stop the value of the exchange rate falling below the level marked s^A in Figure 17.3.

The secretly managed floating rate will move up and down the 45-degree line as innovations in the fundamentals ('news') impact on the demand for the currency, forcing the authorities to intervene by expanding the domestic money stock as soon as the fundamentals reach the level marked k^A. By contrast, with a publicly announced target zone in force, the exchange rate would reach s^A only when the fundamentals fell as far as k^B – which will happen less frequently, if ever. The fact that exchange rate bounds have been set, therefore, exercises an influence over the exchange rate long before it reaches those bounds.

This conclusion is more startling than it might look at first glance. Recall A17.2: no intramarginal intervention. So the reduced volatility inside the target zone is not caused by the activity of the monetary authority. Instead, it results purely from their credible *commitment* to intervene rather than from any actual intervention. Although the fundamental fluctuates continually, action is required only occasionally, since volatility is damped down most of the time simply by the promise (or threat) of intervention.

From a macroeconomic policy standpoint, this conclusion is attractive, since it seems to imply that as long as the fundamentals do not stray too far from the level associated with the central parity, exchange rate management is unnecessary. It suggests in fact that in the interior of the band, policy can be directed at objectives other than the exchange rate, freeing policymakers from an important (and often binding) constraint.

Is this an exception to the rule that economic life offers no free lunches? We appear to have found a way of reducing exchange rate volatility by doing nothing more than offering a policy commitment, a promise that may never need to be fulfilled.

In fact, this lunch is not free; it is simply paid for through another channel. In a target zone, financial market volatility is transferred from the exchange rate to the interest rate. To see that this is the case, consider what would happen to interest rates without intervention. Under our assumptions, the fundamental is expected to remain constant, since all changes are zero-mean random events. It follows, therefore, that the expected depreciation is always zero under a pure float, so that interest rate parity implies the interest rate differential is zero, at least if investors are risk neutral.

By contrast, consider a target zone that allows 2.25% fluctuation on either side of the central parity, as was the case with most of the currencies in the ERM. Under UIRP, the difference between the interest rate on otherwise identical one-year deposits in domestic and foreign currencies can be as great as the total width of the band, i.e. 4.5%, at least if the exchange rate starts the year at the edge of the band. This may not seem much, but we need to remember that the exchange rate has the same scope for fluctuation at any horizon, however short. The return on a 30-day deposit has to accommodate exactly the same range of possibilities: up to 4.5% exchange rate fluctuation. Hence, a one-month deposit may have to offer an interest differential of $12 \times 4.5\% = 54\%$. This has been presented by some authors as providing an extra degree of freedom for macroeconomic policymaking, which, in a sense, is true. However, the freedom to set interest rates that differ from those in the rest of the world is a two-edged sword, as France and some other ERM member countries discovered, when they were forced to raise their interest rates to 80% and more in the face of speculative pressure during crisis periods.[14]

17.6 Beauty and the beast: the target zone model meets the facts

The elegance of this analysis, which can best be appreciated from Krugman's original paper (see the reading guide), is irresistible. Unfortunately, yet again it turns out that a beautiful model cannot survive a confrontation with ugly reality.

We have already had a hint of a reality problem in the numerical examples in Section 17.5. In those examples, the numbers had to be completely unrealistic in order to generate any perceptible honeymoon effect: changes in the fundamental of 50% or (minus) 33% per period, and a value of the expectations elasticity, b, of 0.75 are far too high to be plausible. Unfortunately, however, more realistic parameter values result in a minuscule honeymoon effect. Moreover, allowing for a horizon longer than the six periods in our examples would reduce the effect even further.

More rigorous analysis has confirmed the suspicion that in a realistic setting, the honeymoon effect would be so small as to be negligible (see the reading guide) and certainly too small to have any practical implications for exchange rate policy. It is therefore unsurprising that the model fails to fit the facts. To see why, consider its implications for the frequency distribution[15] of the exchange rate within the target zone.

Start in the middle of the zone. Here, the exchange rate is equally likely to jump up as down. Moreover, starting from any value in the central region, we can think of the next period's value as a normally distributed random variable, with small changes having relatively high probabilities and larger changes having much smaller probabilities. The probability of the exchange rate encountering the upper or lower barrier is so small as to be negligible. The effect of a change in the fundamental on the exchange rate is therefore almost one for one, as in the case of a pure float.

By contrast, consider what happens in the neighbourhood of the barriers. For example, as the exchange rate nears the upper intervention point, its volatility is reduced for two reasons. First, because increases in the fundamental will (if large enough) trigger intervention, the scope for upward movement is clearly reduced. Second, however, the knowledge that intervention will occur, if necessary, actually stabilizes the exchange rate, by reducing the expected depreciation or indeed creating a bias in favour of appreciation. It follows that as it approaches the upper bound, the exchange rate will tend to stick somewhat, falling pro rata when the change in the fundamental is negative but rising far less than in proportion when the fundamental increases.

In general, it follows that the exchange rate will tend to spend longer at the edges of the band than in the interior. Once at the edge, it will tend to stick in the region as shocks to the fundamental have a damped effect on the exchange rate itself. The implication for the frequency distribution is clear and easily testable: *the exchange rate should more often be observed at the edges of the zone than inside it.*

Sadly, this prediction is not consistent with the facts. The reverse is actually the case, as can be seen from Figure 17.6, which is a bar chart showing the frequency with which the French franc/Deutschmark exchange rate fell 0.05%, 0.1%, 0.15% . . .

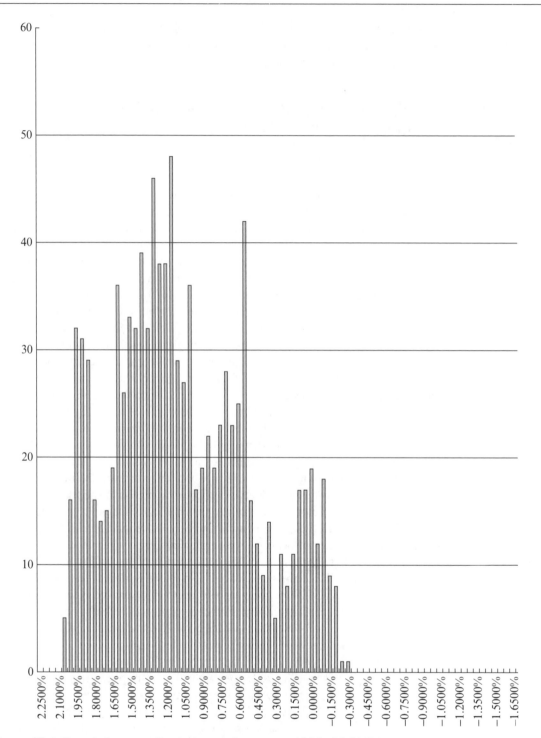

Figure 17.6 French franc per Deutschmark frequency, 1988–91 (daily)

2.25% above and similarly below[16] its central ERM rate between 1988 and 1991. Instead of the predicted U-shape, we have the exact opposite: the exchange rate spends a far greater proportion of the time in the interior of the band than at the edges. Results for other currencies would look similar.

The inescapable conclusion is that since the model as it stands is inconsistent with the facts, one or more of its assumptions needs to be removed or replaced. Both A17.2 (no intramarginal intervention) and A17.3 (perfect credibility) could be criticized as being unrealistic, and the effect of eliminating each has been investigated in the published literature.

17.7 Intramarginal interventions: leaning against the wind

In reality, a central bank, or whichever institution is given the responsibility of managing the currency, would be unwise simply to wait until the exchange rate is bumping up against its limit before acting. On the contrary, the very fact of reaching the limit is usually interpreted as signalling a severe crisis, a situation that the authorities would be very keen to avoid. It is not surprising, then, that in practice most target zones involve a considerable degree of intramarginal intervention. To put the matter another way, more often than not what we actually see is a target zone imposed on a managed float, not on a free float.[17]

Suppose that instead of the intervention rule given by Equations 17.2, 17.3 and 17.4, monetary policy is set (and publicly known to be set) so as to make the fundamental *mean reverting*. In other words, suppose the monetary authority tries to keep the fundamental in the region of some central, long-run level, by changing the money stock in proportion to how far it currently stands from that level. In practical terms, this amounts to the central bank's buying the domestic currency whenever it tends to weaken and selling whenever it is strong – hence the expression *leaning into the wind*.

To make matters explicit, if the target level of the fundamental is set to zero (which is simply a matter of appropriate scaling), then within the band the authorities follow the rule:

$$\Delta k_t = -\alpha k_{t-1} + \varepsilon_t \quad \text{for} \quad \underline{s} < s_t < \bar{s} \quad 0 < \alpha < 1 \tag{17.8}$$

which says that the change in k between $t-1$ and t would be zero whenever the previous period's fundamental is spot on its target level of zero (i.e. whenever $k_{t-1} = 0$). Otherwise, it is reduced (increased) by a proportion α of any positive (negative) deviation from its zero target. The logic of this assumption is that although they intend to keep the fundamental as close to its target level as possible, the authorities feel unable to react to random shocks drastically enough to restore the situation in a single period. Instead, they restore a proportion, α. The greater (smaller) this parameter, the more rapidly (slowly) the fundamental returns to zero.

Notice that Equation 17.8 implies:

$$k_t = (1 - \alpha)k_{t-1} + \varepsilon_t \tag{17.9}$$

At the borders of the zone, however, we assume that the rule becomes:

$$k_t = \begin{cases} (1 - \alpha)k_{t-1} + \varepsilon_t & \text{for} \quad \varepsilon_t < 0 \\ k_{t-1} & \text{for} \quad \varepsilon_t > 0 \end{cases} \quad \text{whenever} \ s_t = \bar{s} \tag{17.10}$$

at the upper boundary, and similarly:

$$k_t = \begin{cases} (1-\alpha)k_{t-1} + \varepsilon_t & \text{for} \quad \varepsilon_t > 0 \\ k_{t-1} & \text{for} \quad \varepsilon_t < 0 \end{cases} \quad \text{whenever } s_t = \underline{s} \qquad (17.11)$$

That is, the gradualism of the authorities gives way to more drastic measures at the limits of the zone, where adverse shocks to the fundamental have to be completely neutralized if the regime is to be preserved.

The result of this policy rule is illustrated in Figure 17.7. As before, the 45-degree line shows the benchmark outcome of a free float. The line labelled MM shows what would happen to the exchange rate in the absence of a target zone, but with the authorities operating a policy of leaning into the wind – that is, MM shows the effect of applying the policy rule (Equation 17.9), without Equations 17.10 and 17.11. As is intuitively obvious, the mean-reverting fundamental generates a honeymoon effect even without any bounds on the exchange rate's movements. The reason is straightforward: whenever the exchange rate is weak (above its central parity), then the fundamental is expected to fall, as the authorities contract the money stock and this expectation itself causes the currency to strengthen.[18]

Now take account of the imposition of the target zone. It turns out to have very little consequence, as can be seen from the curve labelled TT in Figure 17.7, which is very close to the managed float line MM, with only very slight curvature at the

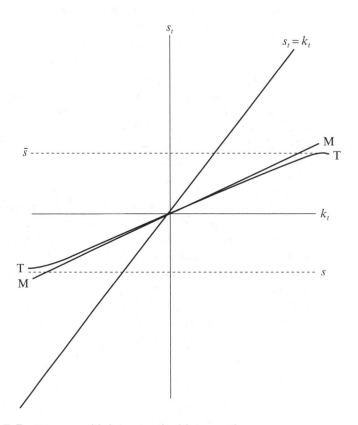

Figure 17.7 Target zone with intramarginal intervention

boundaries. The explanation here is again straightforward. Inside the zone, the honeymoon effect operates as before. The difference between this scenario and the Krugman model of a target zone imposed on a pure float is that the prospect of intervention at the boundaries is simply much less important here, since the probability of it ever being required is so much smaller when the authorities react intramarginally. It is only as the exchange rate nears one of the barriers that the effect of the potential intervention is felt. As long as the exchange rate is well inside the band, the contribution of the barrier intervention to the expected rate of appreciation or depreciation is negligible, because it is so unlikely to occur, given that the authorities can be relied on to act long before the situation gets so desperate.

The corollary of this conclusion is that the broader the fluctuation band, the less important the barriers become and the more the outcome resembles the straightforward managed float without barriers that would result from a mean-reverting monetary policy rule.

This model, it turns out, fits the facts much better than the basic Krugman model. Published empirical work suggests that the relationship between the exchange rate and the fundamentals is almost linear within the target zone, with barely perceptible curvature at the edges of the band.

The implication of this model's relative success is plain. If almost all the benefits of a honeymoon effect are achievable simply by leaning against the wind, then it seems hardly worthwhile going to the trouble of imposing a target zone, with all that this entails in terms of institutional arrangements, international commitments and investment of political and financial credibility.

17.8 Credibility and realignment prospects

The other glaring departure from realism in the models discussed so far is in the general area of credibility. As exchange rates approach the limits of a target zone, markets do *not* typically base their expectations on a blind faith in the will and commitment of the authorities to do what is necessary and adjust monetary policy in the required direction. On the contrary, the closer the edge of the band, the more they are inclined to question whether the central bank is willing and able to defend the target zone, or whether it will not in the end decide to give up the struggle. Two researchers, Bertola and Caballero (1992), showed that the implications of incorporating these factors into the target zone model can be sufficient to make it consistent with the facts. It is possible here to give only a broad outline of the general framework of their model, as its detailed workings are complex and many of their results were in any case presented only for calibrated versions of their model.

Suppose that, as in the original Krugman model, intervention takes place only at the boundaries of the zone. Intramarginal monetary policy is dormant, and so the motion of the fundamentals inside the zone is described by a random walk as in Equation 17.2 and by Equations 17.3 and 17.4 at the upper and lower bounds.

Although we continue to assume that the zone is symmetrical (i.e. A17.4 still stands) in this section, we need to introduce two new symbols. First, label the central parity c_t so as to allow for the fact that it will not normally be zero in the scenario we are currently dealing with and will be subject to change ('realignments') under circumstances to be outlined shortly. Next, define B as the maximum permitted fluctuation in the exchange rate under the target zone – that is, the distance from the central parity to the edge of the band. Given our assumption of symmetry, this is of course simply equal to $\frac{1}{2}(\bar{s} - \underline{s})$, but the use of B will be less cumbersome. So, with this notation, the initial target zone is from $c_t B$ to $c_t + B$.

Now consider what happens at t if the exchange rate reaches, say, the top edge of the zone. Intervention is called for, but we assume that it may take one of two possible forms. With probability p, the authorities decide not to defend the parity but instead to re-establish the target zone around a new central rate of $c_t + 2B$. In other words, the range of the new zone is defined by:

$$\underline{s} = c_t + B \quad \text{and} \quad \bar{s} = c_t + 3B$$

so that it adjoins the current band. However, with probability $1 - p$, the authorities choose not to realign the central rate but instead act to reduce the money stock, not simply by enough to prevent it breaking out of the zone but sufficiently to return it to the current central rate, c_t.

In this model, expectations can be decomposed into two components. As before, we need to consider the expected rate of depreciation within the band – that is, the expected rate of change of the exchange rate, conditional on the absence of a realignment. But, in addition, we need to take account of the expected rate of realignment at any moment, which plays the role of an additional fundamental in the model. Indeed, its presence is the key to understanding how the model seeks to explain the facts. For example, if this model is correct, then ignoring the existence of this factor explains the apparent failure of standard tests of UIRP on data from target zones (notably the EMS). In analytical terms, the decomposition of expectations turns out to be the key to analysing the model.

Consider the application of the no-arbitrage condition in the present context. For the reasons discussed in the introduction to this chapter, we cannot allow a situation in which the exchange rate is expected to change by a discrete amount when intervention is imminent. This means that at the point where the exchange rate reaches the barrier, its expected change must be zero. More formally, we require that:

$$p(c_t + 2B) + (1 - p)c_t = \bar{s} = c_t + B \tag{17.12}$$

where the left-hand side of the equation weights the future exchange rate in the event of a devaluation to a new central rate of $(c_t + 2B)$ by its associated probability, p, and the current, unchanged central rate by $(1 - p)$, the probability that the current zone is defended (remember that if they decide to defend the parity, then the authorities are assumed to intervene sufficiently to push the exchange rate all the way back down to the central rate).

In general, the conclusions of this model are complex and very much dependent on the parameter values, especially the value of the realignment probability, p. As long as this probability is less than $\frac{1}{2}$, the familiar S curve is preserved, but it gets flatter for higher values of p. At the critical value $p = \frac{1}{2}$, the S curve is flattened so much that it coincides with the 45-degree line – hence, a free float.

The most interesting cases, however, are when $p > \frac{1}{2}$. Here, the Krugman model conclusions are reversed: the exchange rate path is everywhere steeper than the 45-degree line. Moreover, instead of becoming flat at the margins, the exchange rate curve becomes vertical, which implies complete instability. Most importantly, the model generates a frequency distribution that is far closer to the facts, at least in so far as it predicts that the exchange rate will be in the central region of the band for most of the time, with few observations at the extremes near the bounds. The reason for this conclusion is that inside the band, the model predicts a stable, relatively placid scenario, with realignment only a distant possibility and hence very little currency market reaction to disturbances in the fundamentals. By the same token, at the margins, expectations are dominated by the prospect of a devaluation or revaluation, the more so if p is high. This means that we are likely to observe the exchange rate lingering for quite long periods in the interior of the zone, but passing rapidly through the extreme regions, whether as a result of remedial action by the central bank or alternatively as a consequence of the establishment of a new central parity. In either case, the model predicts the inverted U-shaped distribution of outcomes actually seen in fixed exchange rate regimes.

17.9   Conclusions

In one respect, the story of this chapter has been similar to so many others in this book. Once again, an elegant theory appears to generate predictions that are flatly contradicted by the data. This time, however, modifications that, in any case, bring the assumptions closer to reality also serve to make it consistent with the facts.[19]

It is appropriate that the final model considered in this chapter focused attention on the issue of credibility, because its importance in fixed exchange rate regimes of any kind is too overwhelming to be ignored. What Bertola and Caballero (1992) ignore[20] is that only with a crawling peg regime (which is what they really model) does the target zone shift seamlessly and painlessly from one central parity to another. Where there is no provision for a crawling peg, fixed rate regimes change only when they are forced to do so. In reality, most changes are brought about by crisis. The next chapter deals with the question of why crises occur in the currency markets and how they evolve.

Summary

- Target zones are ranges within which fixed exchange rates are allowed to fluctuate. When they are in force, however, and provided they are credible, they have a more complicated effect than might be expected. In particular, they do not make the exchange rate behave as if it were floating freely inside the zone.

- Under the assumptions of Krugman's well-known model, the exchange rate is less volatile (i.e. reacts less to changes in the fundamentals) than under a pure float in the interior of the zone. This extra stability is known as the honeymoon effect.

- In addition, the honeymoon effect is greater the closer the exchange rate gets to its boundaries, so that in the limit it is totally unaffected by the fundamentals when it actually reaches its floor or ceiling. In other words, it approaches the bounds from almost the horizontal, touching them tangentially, a property known as smooth pasting.

■ The holders of the domestic and foreign currency can be viewed as having undertaken reciprocal options trades. The fact that the target zone places an upper bound on the price of foreign currency means that domestic (foreign) currency holders have bought (sold) a call on foreign currency with an exercise price equal to the upper bound. The premium is paid (received) in the form of the inflated price paid for the domestic currency, via the honeymoon effect.

■ The Krugman model predicts that the exchange rate will be at or near its limits most of the time. The facts about target zone regimes suggest the exact opposite: exchange rates tend to be in or around their central parity for most of the time.

■ One possible explanation of this anomaly may be that central banks are wary of waiting until the last minute to intervene, instead preferring to offset fluctuations in the fundamentals as and when they occur, by leaning into the wind – that is, intervening to neutralize at least partially any changes in the value of the currency long before they drive the exchange rate to its bounds. However, once we allow for this type of policy, the advantage of actually having a target zone vanishes almost completely, in so far as the honeymoon effect is tiny and the exchange rate behaves more or less as it would under a managed float.

■ The markets are well aware that, at any given moment, there is some non-zero probability that the authorities will decide to move the central parity and re-establish the target zone around a new parity. With this innovation, market expectations incorporate not simply the anticipated rate of depreciation *within* the target zone but also the possibility of a devaluation or revaluation to a new level. Although the detailed conclusions depend on the probability of a new target zone being chosen, in general the results are potentially consistent with the facts about fixed exchange rate regimes.

Reading guide

An excellent background text is Section 8.5 of Obstfeld and Rogoff (1996), although readers should perhaps be warned that they cover the subject matter of this chapter and the next in reverse order from the one chosen here – that is, they tackle crises and speculative attacks in their Section 8.4.2, before target zones. The classic Krugman (1991) paper is a relatively easy read, although the mathematics involves a controlled diffusion process, which makes the details of the analysis difficult. Bertola and Caballero (1992) developed the model of realignments covered in the final section of this chapter, having first shown how and why the original Krugman model cannot explain the facts. An intuitive exposition of all three models is to be found in Svensson (1992), which also contains a number of references to important papers on the subject. For evidence that the honeymoon effect is extremely small, see Iannizzotto and Taylor (1999).

The route to understanding Section 17.4 is through the vast options literature. Although I know of no text that covers the application to target zones explicitly, there are many excellent general treatments of the binomial option pricing model, for example Chance (1998) and Hull (1998). The original model dates back to Cox, Ross and Rubinstein (1979).

Finally, for those readers who want to master the mathematics of continuous time stochastic processes, which features in most of the important papers in this area, the best starting point is Dixit (1993).

Web page: **www.pearsoned.co.uk/copeland**.

Notes

1 Notice that the *rate of return* on the transaction is infinite in any case. Not only is there no investment required upfront to generate a positive return, but also the profit is made, in principle at least, over an instant of time, so that measured on any discrete time basis (e.g. annually) it is equivalent to an infinite rate.

2 Mathematically speaking, in any case, a number or single point in a graph is infinitely small, so that there is a sense in which it would be impossible ever to be sure that the temperature was exactly right, let alone keep it there indefinitely. The problem is not quite as unambiguous in the case of exchange rates, since there is in principle nothing to stop a central bank declaring its readiness to buy or sell currency at the exact fixed rate, just as described in Chapter 5. In practice, however, a target zone is usually a more attractive option, for a number of reasons, one of which will be explained in the next section.

3 This is the usual case in practice, though there is no reason in principle why target zones have to be symmetrical.

4 The normal (or Gaussian) distribution is the symmetrical bell-shaped curve that is assumed to describe, for example, the probability distribution of people's height about the population mean. Further details can be found in any (randomly selected) statistics textbook.

5 In theory, the fact that any country's reserves are finite is not a problem here, as long as there is bilateral cooperation in maintaining the target zone, because the reserves of the strong currency country can always be used to support the weaker currency. For example, a dollar/euro target zone could be maintained by the US Federal Reserve agreeing to provide dollars (printing them, if necessary) whenever the euro needed support, while the European Central Bank promised to reciprocate by supplying euros to prop up the dollar if it fell to its floor. However, as we saw during the 1992 sterling crisis in the ERM, that presupposes the credibility of bilateral cooperation, which may also be finite.

6 See Section 12.1 for an explanation of mathematical expectations.

7 Since the example set out in this section is based on the binomial option pricing model (see the reading guide for references), it will look especially familiar to readers with some knowledge of the basics of derivative pricing. However, it is intended to be intelligible to all readers, whatever their background.

8 Note that we have chosen the letters u for up and d for down. The d should *not* be taken as indicating an infinitely small change, as in differential calculus.

9 Option pricing buffs will notice that the values of u, d and p have been chosen to be consistent with a zero-interest rate differential, which means we can ignore interest rates in what follows.

10 All computations in the table have been presented after rounding to two decimal places. The computations were actually generated in Excel™ to a far higher level of accuracy.

11 This assumption is an attempt to approximate two features of Krugman's model, which are otherwise difficult to replicate in the present setting: specifically, his use of continuous time mathematics and, in that context, his assumption that intervention only ever occurs at 'the very last moment' – that is, an infinitely small distance before the barrier is reached. So, for the purposes of the example in this section, we replace A17.2 by the assumption that the authorities restrict themselves to bringing the exchange rate back within the barrier. In other words, we explicitly rule out the possibility that they may make a more drastic cut so as to bring the exchange rate to a level safely below the limit.

12 If necessary, refer back to Chapter 12, especially Equation 12.6.

13 The figure 760.28 was computed by solving Equation 17.1 for the value of k, which sets s equal to 760. In other words, it is the value $k* = (1 + b)(760) - bs^e$.

14 Strictly speaking, of course, these high rates were not consistent with the model described here, because they resulted from the breakdown of credibility, contravening A17.3. However, the point still stands: if high interest rates are painful when credibility is challenged, then they could hardly be less painful when it is unchallenged.

15 The frequency distribution of a random variable is simply the graph of the number of times each possible value is observed in a particular sample.

16 The frequency drops to zero at –0.45% and remains at zero for all values to the right in Figure 17.6, and so nothing is lost by ending the axis at –1.65%.

17 According to Delgado and Dumas (1991), about 85% of intervention in the EMS was intramarginal.

18 Note the implicit policy anticipation hypothesis (see Section 13.4).

19 Some readers may think it obvious that more realistic assumptions should lead to a model that better fits the facts or indeed generates improved forecasts. In practice, this is not necessarily the case: models with assumptions known to be unrealistic may fit the data well, while more superficially plausible models contribute very little to explaining the data.

20 Deliberately, of course, because the model is complex enough without introducing further complications.

Appendix 17.1

Formal derivation of the model

In this chapter, the target zone model was set out in a simplified form in discrete time and with uncertainty represented by only two alternative outcomes. This appendix presents a more formal version of the Krugman target zone model, making use of a continuous time stochastic model that allows for uncertainty in a far more general way.

Start with the equation determining the (log of the) exchange rate itself. In place of Equation 17.1, we write:

$$s \equiv \phi(h) = h + \beta \frac{Eds}{dt} \tag{17.13}$$

which says that at any time, t (we suppress the time subscripts where there is no danger of confusion), the variable s is a function, $\phi(h)$ of the fundamental, h. Moreover, the function is simply h plus a component that reflects the speculative demand for the currency, a positive coefficient $\beta > 0$ times the instantaneous expected rate of depreciation. The term Eds can be thought of as the expected change over the next infinitesimal interval from t to t^+, a period of length dt.

Notice that the function $\phi(h)$ summarizes the relationship that is the subject of the chapter. In this appendix, we are investigating that function in order to check the conclusions we derived more casually in the body of the chapter regarding its shape.

We assume that in the interior of the zone, the fundamental is driven by a diffusion process – that is, a stochastic differential equation of the following form:

$$dh = \lambda dt + \sigma d\omega \tag{17.14}$$

which simply says the change in the fundamental over any tiny interval is the sum of an expected component, λ, and a random component with a standard deviation of σ. (The final term is a *Wiener process*, which is a sequence of normally distributed shocks.) It should be clear that Equation 17.14 is the continuous time analogue of a random walk with a drift of λ per period and a normally distributed error term.

In order to make progress, we utilize the most important theorem in stochastic calculus, *Ito's lemma*, that allows us to write the diffusion process for ds, given that the fundamental evolves according to the rule set out in Equation 17.14. Doing so leads us to the conclusion that the exchange rate process will be:

$$ds = [\phi'(h)E(dh) + {}^1\!/_2\phi''(h)\sigma^2]dt + \phi'(h)\sigma d\omega \qquad (17.15)$$

where:

$$\phi'(h) \equiv \frac{\partial\phi}{\partial h} \quad \text{and} \quad \phi''(h) \equiv \frac{\partial^2\phi}{\partial h^2}$$

Notice that, as promised, this equation has the same general structure as Equation 17.14 – that is to say, it is also a diffusion process, with a drift term in the square bracket and a residual shock involving the same Wiener process, $d\omega$. For our purposes here, what matters is the expected change in the exchange rate, given by the term in the square brackets.

Consider the situation just before a boundary of the target zone is reached. First, note that the variance of the random fundamental must be approaching zero. Second, as already explained, the expected change in the fundamental $E(dh)$ will be non-zero. It follows that we can have a zero expected change in the exchange rate only if the coefficient of $E(dh)$ in Equation 17.15 is also zero. So we need to have $\phi(h)$, the gradient of the $\phi'(h)$ function with respect to the h axis, zero. In other words, the curve representing the exchange rate as a function of the fundamental must be flat at the boundaries of the zone, which is exactly what we have with smooth pasting.

18 Crises and credibility

Introduction

This chapter is again concerned with fixed exchange rate regimes. This time, however, we are concerned not with how they work but with how they fail to work and, indeed, how they break down.

Countries rarely abandon an exchange rate peg voluntarily. More often than not, fixed exchange rate regimes collapse when the foreign currency reserves are exhausted or at least so depleted in such a short space of time that the government[1] decides to throw in the towel while it still has enough reserves left to allow it to intervene at some future date, for example in the run up to a forthcoming election. The end is typically a painful, bloody affair, with the air of crisis in the currency market spreading to the rest of the country's economic and sometimes political life. Rather than the steady draining away of the reserves that we might expect to see when a monetary policy is overexpansive, the end usually comes as the result of a sudden collapse, as speculators anticipate the ultimate breakdown of the regime. Their reaction is critical. The crisis is triggered by their rush to convert their money balances into foreign currency, while the central bank still has reserves left to offer them. The resulting raid devastates the reserves and leads to more or less inevitable abandonment of the exchange rate peg.

Why do these cataclysmic events occur? Why does the end come with a bang rather than a whimper?

As we saw in Section 5.2, a country that expands its money stock more rapidly than is consistent with the fundamentals (the foreign rate of monetary expansion and relative growth rates) will run a balance of payments deficit and the associated loss of reserves cannot be sustained indefinitely.[2] This fact need not necessarily imply a crisis, however. Why can we not rely on the reserves to decline smoothly to zero? Still more puzzling, even if in practice it is often easy to see why a currency is under pressure, the question that remains to be answered is: what determines the timing of the collapse? Why does it happen six months or a year or sometimes even longer after the balance of payments first goes into deficit and long after it has become apparent that a currency is overvalued relative to the equilibrium level implied by the fundamentals?

On the other hand, storms in the currency markets seem sometimes to appear out of a clear blue sky. In a number of cases in recent years, exchange rates have had to be devalued in the face of overwhelming selling, in spite of the fact that the fundamentals for the currency in question looked perfectly sound. Can we explain this – preferably without recourse to pop psychology?

In this chapter, we shall start by examining in some detail a model dating from the late 1970s that seeks to explain crises by the behaviour of currency traders who speculate against the fixed exchange rate in order to profit from an anticipated devaluation. The paradoxical result of their actions is a reserve crisis, but no step devaluation. Although the model is illuminating in a number of respects, it raises new questions, some of which are addressed in the second- and third-generation models discussed in the second half of this chapter. This chapter first appeared in the third edition of this book (August 1999), when the convulsions that accompanied the end of the European exchange rate mechanism (ERM) in 1992–93 and the more recent upheavals in Asia and Latin America had provided both the incentive for research on crises and the evidence on which to focus. The fifth edition is being prepared against the background of a looming crisis in world credit markets and a protracted fall in the value of the dollar, whilst in the intervening period we have witnessed a stock market slump associated with the end of the dot.com boom, exacerbated a year or so later by the repercussions of 9/11. The subject of crises is therefore very much alive. Although this chapter concentrates on the narrow issue of how fixed exchange rate systems collapse, the research agenda in this area, which is long and far from complete, overlaps at a number of points with broader questions relating to the nature of financial market crises.

18.1 First-generation model[3]

We start with a simple model of crises that has been influential ever since it was developed in 1979. It is simple in so far as it concentrates exclusively on the money market and is set in a world with no uncertainty, which means that agents carry no risk and have perfect foresight.[4] None the less, we shall see that the model gives useful insights, especially into how the timing of a currency collapse is determined.

18.1.1 Monetary model of a fixed exchange rate (again)

Our point of departure is the basic flexible price monetary model of a floating exchange rate introduced in Chapter 5, but it will be convenient to take the particular formulation used in Equation 13.5 as our starting point:

$$\hat{s}_t = \tilde{m}_t - c\tilde{y}_t + b\tilde{r}_t \tag{18.1}$$

where, it will be recalled, $\tilde{m}$ and $\tilde{y}$ were the logs of the money stock and real income relative to the foreign country and $\tilde{r}$ was the interest differential. Notice that we are assuming PPP holds. The exchange rate here has been written with a caret over the top to allow us to distinguish between two values. Equation 18.1 defines the *shadow exchange rate*, $\hat{s}_t$, as the exchange rate that would be established if there were no intervention in the currency markets, for a given level of the basic fundamentals. In other words, although the exchange rate is assumed fixed by the authorities at the level, $\bar{s}$, it would float freely to $\hat{s}_t$ if the authorities allowed it to do so, or rather if they were forced to do so by a speculative attack that exhausted the reserves.

If we reintroduce UIRP, we can replace the domestic interest rate by the sum of the foreign interest rate, r^*, and the expected rate of depreciation, to give:

$$\hat{s}_t = \tilde{m}_t - c\tilde{y}_t + br_t^* + b\Delta s_t^e \qquad (18.2)$$

which will look familiar to anyone who has read the earlier chapters. For convenience, we shall write it in the more compact form:

$$\hat{s}_t = m_t + k_t + b\Delta s_t^e \qquad (18.3)$$

where we have made the substitution:

$$k_t \equiv -m_t^* - c\tilde{y}_t + br_t^*$$

where k_t is the *basic fundamental*, as in the previous chapter, which collects in a single term all the variables we are treating in this chapter as given. Alternatively, if we denote the *total fundamental* by K_t, Equation 18.3 can be written:

$$\hat{s}_t = m_t + k_t + b\Delta s_t^e$$
$$= k_t + b\Delta s_t^e \qquad (18.4)$$

which is essentially the same as Equation 13.7. Unlike in Chapter 17, we assume here that the basic fundamental, k_t, is constant, which means that the total fundamental can change only as a result of monetary expansion. Notice also that if a fixed exchange rate regime is perfectly credible, then the expected depreciation is zero. A non-zero value of Δs^e in these circumstances reflects an anticipated breakdown.

18.1.2 Money stock

Now suppose we are in a regime where the exchange rate is fixed at the level $\bar{s}$. From Chapters 4 and 5, we recall that as an identity derived from the balance sheet of the central bank, the money stock must be given by:

$$M_t = R_t + C_t \qquad (18.5)$$

where the notation has been simplified by writing R in place of FX for the foreign currency reserves available to defend the fixed exchange rate, and C in place of DC to denote the stock of domestic credit – that is, the domestically generated component of the money stock.

We are concerned here with the following question: *what happens when the domestic authorities pursue a monetary policy that is inconsistent with the fixed exchange rate? In other words, what is the outcome when the policy variable C is allowed to grow too rapidly?*

The first task is simply to define a sustainable rate of credit expansion, given the (log of the) level chosen for the fixed exchange rate, $\bar{s}$. If the regime is totally credible, so that the expected depreciation is zero, then the solution here is obvious. From Equation 18.3, we must have:

$$m_t = \bar{s} - k_t \tag{18.6}$$

so that, *given* the level of the basic fundamental, k, at any moment – and we are assuming, quite realistically, that the authorities can do nothing to affect its level – the money stock must remain constant. This conclusion simply restates the results from Chapter 5.

Since the money stock must remain fixed, any increase in domestic credit will flow out through the balance of payments in the form of a reduction in the reserves. Formally, the change in the money supply at any point is given by:

$$\dot{M}_t = \dot{R}_t + \dot{C}_t \tag{18.7}$$

If domestic credit is allowed to grow at the rate μ per year – that is, if we have:

$$\frac{\dot{C}_t}{C_t} = \mu \tag{18.8}$$

then Equation 18.7 implies we can have a constant money stock only if:

$$\dot{M}_t = \dot{R}_t + C_t \mu = 0 \tag{18.9}$$

or, in other words, if the central bank loses reserves at the rate:

$$\dot{R}_t = -C_t \mu \tag{18.10}$$

By allowing domestic credit to grow faster than the zero rate implied by the fundamentals, we have set the scene for a collapse, because this situation is clearly unsustainable. Sooner or later, the country's reserves will be exhausted and it will be forced to devalue. But when? How long will it take before the fixed exchange rate regime finally collapses?

18.1.3 Post-collapse exchange rate

To answer the question, we need to make explicit our assumptions about what happens after a collapse. We rule out here the possibility that one fixed exchange rate is replaced by another, as sometimes happens in practice. Instead, we assume:

> **Assumption 18.1 A post-collapse float** When a fixed exchange rate regime collapses, it is replaced by a pure float.

Now we can compute the post-collapse value of the shadow exchange rate, $\hat{s}_{T^+}$, because that is, by definition, the rate that will prevail as soon as the authorities stop intervening to prop up the currency.

Suppose the collapse comes at the instant T. Then we seek the value of the shadow exchange rate at the instant after the collapse, which we shall call T^+. *But first, looking back at Equation 18.4, we face the usual problem of what to do about expectations. For the moment, let us assume speculators have perfect foresight, so Equation 18.4 becomes:*

$$\hat{s}_{T^\cdot} = m_{T^\cdot} + k_{T^\cdot} + b\dot{\hat{s}}_{T^\cdot}. \tag{18.11}$$

Now, if we bear in mind the situation after the collapse – with the reserves exhausted, the money supply must consist exclusively of a stock of domestic securities growing at the constant rate μ – it is obvious that the exchange rate itself must also be depreciating at a constant rate. Under these circumstances, we can compute the value of $\dot{\hat{s}}$ by differentiating Equation 18.11 to give:

$$\dot{\hat{s}}_{T^\cdot} = \dot{m}_{T^\cdot} = \mu \tag{18.12}$$

since we are assuming that k is constant and the second derivative of $\hat{s}$ must be zero. Subject to one important assumption, which will be discussed later, the previous two equations lead to the conclusion that:

$$\hat{s}_{T^\cdot} = m_{T^\cdot} + k_{T^\cdot} + b\mu \tag{18.13}$$

which says no more than the value of the domestic currency will be lower (price of foreign currency higher) the greater are the levels of the money stock and the basic fundamentals and the higher is the rate of money creation, because this determines the (expected and actual) rate of depreciation.

No surprises here, then. The post-collapse regime is simply a dynamic version of the monetary model of a floating rate, familiar from Chapter 5. However, from here we can go on to compute the collapse time by making use of the key insight of this literature, as we now see.

18.1.4 How the collapse occurs

The collapse mechanism hinges on the difference between the expected rate of depreciation before and after the crisis. Before the collapse, the market expects no change in the exchange rate. After the event, as we have seen, it expects a positive rate of depreciation equal to the growth in the total fundamental, which is just μ. A higher opportunity cost means the post-crisis demand for money must be lower than pre-crisis, which implies that the crisis has to reduce the volume of real balances if money market equilibrium is to be maintained. How can this be achieved? Two possibilities are suggested: either a fall in the nominal money stock or a rise in the price level.

In fact, it turns out that only a fall in the money supply can do the trick. The second possibility, a rise in the price level, can be ruled out because it would offer speculators an arbitrage opportunity. To see why, remember first that given the foreign price level, PPP implies that the domestic price level can rise only if the price of foreign currency rises. So the sudden discrete one-off rise in the domestic price level required to reduce the value of real balances could be achieved only by a step depreciation of the same proportion. *But, to have the desired effect on the real money supply, the depreciation would need to be fully anticipated.*

The consequences are not difficult to imagine. A step increase in the price of foreign currency would give a trader the opportunity to make potentially unlimited capital gains by simply borrowing domestic money at the last moment before the collapse and exchanging it for foreign currency. However small the depreciation, the *rate* of return available to an arbitrageur would be effectively infinite because it could be earned over the infinitesimally short period surrounding the moment of the collapse. As a whole, since all traders are fully informed, the demand for foreign exchange would become infinite the moment before T, at T^-, *so with the central bank committed to supplying the required foreign currency in order to defend the exchange rate peg, the reserves would be exhausted instantaneously.*

> **Questions** *Would the same logic apply if speculators were risk-averse?*
>
> *Would the same logic apply if, instead of having perfect foresight, speculators simply believed there to be some non-zero probability of collapse?*

In other words, the crisis would occur whenever traders decided to make their move to buy up the stock of reserves in the central bank vaults. The timing of this event is therefore crucial. The obvious presumption that a crisis occurs when the reserves are exhausted cannot be correct here. The crisis cannot possibly be delayed until the reserves have run out, for the simple reason that, given the transparency we have assumed, any individual agent would have an incentive to exchange domestic currency for foreign currency the instant *before* the reserves ran out, rather than wait until the vaults were empty. After all, once the reserves have been spent on buying up the excess supply of domestic currency, the party is over – there are no more free lunches available for speculators. Any individual trader would want to make a pre-emptive move before the final collapse, and if this logic applies to a single trader it applies to them all, so the crisis must come the instant before the reserves run out.

But if the crisis is now due an instant sooner, at T^-, the same logic applies: each trader will foresee a collapse at T^- and attempt to beat the rush by buying foreign currency an instant before everyone else. The market will therefore bring forward the crisis to the instant before T^-.

This inconsistency will apply whichever date we choose for the collapse, with one exception. *The only date that is not subject to this circularity is the unique moment when the shadow exchange rate is equal to the fixed rate, because then, and only then, a collapse can occur without resulting in a step change in the exchange rate.* At that moment, it is temporarily true that abandoning the fixed rate regime results in no instantaneous appreciation or depreciation, because the new floating rate is the same as the old fixed rate, $\bar{s}$.

If the collapse were delayed until the shadow price of foreign currency had risen above the fixed rate, traders would anticipate depreciation and we would face the circularity problem discussed above. Conversely, if the crisis came sooner, the shadow price would still be below the fixed rate, so that a post-crisis float could be expected to result in immediate *appreciation* of the domestic currency. Each trader would therefore believe a profit could be made by borrowing foreign currency and converting to domestic money to lend in the home country for repayment after the crisis. This clearly involves a contradiction.

Figure 18.1 tells the complete story graphically. In the top figure, the supply of money is plotted. To the left of T, the money stock is constant at the level M_0, although its composition is changing as the exponentially rising volume of domestic credit is matched by the haemorrhage of reserves through the balance of payments

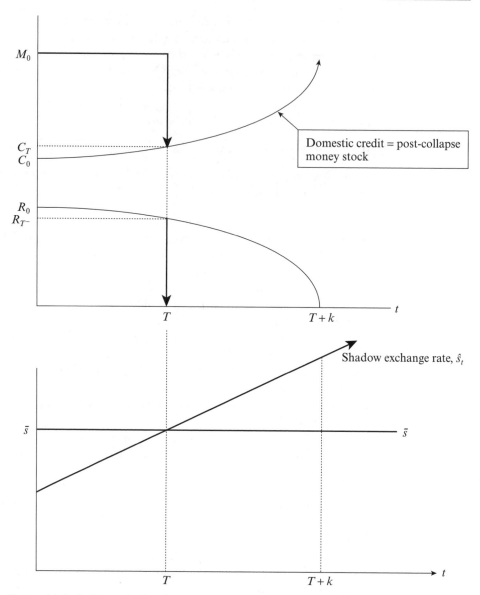

Figure 18.1 Collapse in the first-generation model

deficit. Under a floating exchange rate, the behaviour of the authorities would inevitably result in an ongoing fall in the value of the home currency, which means the shadow exchange rate $\hat{s}_t$ is on a steadily rising path, as we can see in the bottom half of Figure 18.1.

Note, however, that throughout the pre-crisis period the shadow exchange rate is below the actual, fixed rate, so that if the central bank stopped intervening, the result would be an immediate appreciation. This may seem paradoxical. After all, how can the exchange rate be undervalued (compared with its shadow value) if there is a balance of payments deficit? The answer is that if all the reserves were in the hands of private holders, the money stock would be lower than M_0 and therefore the equilibrium exchange rate would be lower (i.e. the value of the domestic currency would be higher). Since it seems reasonable to assume turkeys never vote for Christmas, we can rule out a speculative attack on the currency before T: it would have to result in a step appreciation, inflicting capital *losses* rather than gains on any speculators who had borrowed domestically to buy foreign exchange.

On the other hand, at any time beyond T, the result of a breakdown in the fixed exchange rate would be a discrete one-off depreciation. This is true in particular of time $T + k$, the point at which the reserves would be exhausted if no crisis occurred before then. As we saw, speculators will compete to capture the capital gains available to holders of foreign exchange by buying reserves from the central bank before they would otherwise be exhausted.

At T, they unanimously decide to convert their money balances to foreign currency, with the result that the reserves fall in an instant from R_{T-} to zero and hence the money stock contracts by R_{T-}. At its new level, C_T, the money stock is just great enough to validate a post-crash floating rate that is unchanged at the fixed rate level, $\bar{s}$.

18.1.5 Timing of the collapse

Armed with this crucial insight into the crisis mechanism, we are now in a position to answer the question about timing: *the crisis will occur when the shadow exchange rate is the same as the fixed rate.*

To see when this point is reached, note first that Equation 18.8 implies that the volume of domestic credit at any time t is:

$$C_t + C_0 + \mu t \tag{18.14}$$

where C_0 is its level before it started growing. Now remembering that, after the crisis, the whole money stock is domestic credit, we can use this result in Equation 18.13, and equate the shadow post-collapse exchange rate to the fixed rate to get:

$$\hat{s}_{T^+} = C_T + k_{T^+} + b\mu$$
$$= C_0 + \mu T + k_{T^+} + b\mu = \bar{s} \tag{18.15}$$

which can be solved for T:

$$T = \frac{\bar{s} - C_0 - k_{T^+} - b\mu}{\mu} = \frac{R_0 - b\mu}{\mu} \tag{18.16}$$

This conclusion can be given an intuitively plausible interpretation. Take each factor one by one. The collapse comes sooner the higher is the rate of domestic monetary expansion, because this hastens the crisis directly and indirectly, through its effect on expectations. Likewise, the basic fundamentals – the foreign money stock, relative income, the foreign interest rate – have the anticipated effect. That is to say: changes that tend to weaken the domestic currency bring the inevitable collapse forward and the reverse is true of changes that strengthen the currency. On the other hand, not surprisingly, the higher the exchange rate is pegged in the first place, the longer the crisis is postponed. As can be seen from the second equality, the matter can be put even more simply: the higher are the reserves at the outset, the longer the crisis is delayed. But the greater the speculative elasticity of the demand for money, the sooner the crisis occurs.

18.1.6 Collapsing bubble

The post-collapse shadow exchange rate was computed by surreptitiously inserting an additional assumption, as was hinted at the time. In the casual way Equation 18.11 was solved, the possibility of a bubble in the shadow exchange rate was ignored. What would happen if we allowed for this possibility?

Mathematically speaking, the reasoning is more or less the same as the argument in Section 13.5, where it was demonstrated that a bubble could occur in the solution to Equation 13.15, which is essentially a discrete-time version of Equation 18.11.

Incorporating a bubble, B_T, into the equation for the post-collapse exchange rate and solving as before for the crisis date, T, we get:

$$T = \frac{\bar{s} - C_0 - k_{T^+} - b\mu - B_T}{\mu} \qquad (18.17)$$

so that a positive bubble will further shorten the life of the regime. In itself, this is unsurprising. After all, a bubble in the shadow exchange rate makes it higher than would be justified by the fundamentals alone, thereby increasing the pressure on the fixed rate, other things being equal. The remarkable aspect of the bubble result here, however, is that it implies an immediate reserve crisis is possible *in the absence of any other cause*. Specifically, it means that a crisis could occur even with zero or negative monetary growth. As soon as the value of the bubble, B_T, is great enough to make the numerator of Equation 18.17 zero (or negative), a speculative attack can occur however favourable the level of the other variables.

> **Questions** *How would these conclusions change if we allowed the basic fundamental, k_t, to grow at the rate k?*
>
> *Could it ever be possible to devise a system that was invulnerable to attack by speculators?*

18.1.7 Shortcomings of the first-generation model

Before the advent of the model we have just analysed, economists could offer no formal description of speculative attacks in the currency markets and certainly no explanation of their timing, so the analysis it provides represents a significant advance. At the same time, the model has two theoretical weaknesses, in addition to a number of empirical shortcomings, which were clearly exposed during the fixed exchange rate crises of the twentieth century:

- Consider the behaviour of interest rates in the model. Alternatively, given CIRP, consider the implications for the forward market. Since the ultimate collapse causes no change in the exchange rate, the expected depreciation is zero at all times up to T and hence the interest rate differential and forward premium are also zero. The model is internally consistent, of course, but it strains credulity to imagine that the market would not discount the domestic currency even in the face of a clearly unsustainable monetary policy. Moreover, for the most part the facts justify incredulity. In the majority of cases, speculative attacks are mounted on currencies that are already weak, as evidenced by a forward market discount. Classic examples would include the devaluation of the pound in 1967 and the demise of the dollar at the end of the Bretton Woods system in 1971. In other words, although the timing and ferocity of speculative attacks may be nearly impossible to predict, there is often no problem in explaining *why* a currency was attacked.

■ The model is set in a world where all agents are completely rational (or indeed endowed with perfect foresight), with one glaring exception: the government itself. It embarks on a policy of ongoing monetary expansion that, since it will ultimately exhaust the reserves, must eventually destroy the fixed exchange rate system, which it presumably supports and wishes to see survive. Why? Perhaps we can visualize a situation in which, although the financial markets are rational, voters as a whole are gullible, so that seigniorage can be used to win an election, while foreign speculators can be blamed for the subsequent crisis, especially if T, the delay until the collapse, is long relative to the electoral cycle.

18.2 Second-generation crisis models

Now, of course, it is always possible to make additional side-assumptions about hidden agendas, electoral cycles and so on – it would be a naive economist who ignored these facts of life. But incorporating these factors into the analysis is not a trivial exercise. In the first place, most of these effects are possible only if the private sector (or at least the electorate) is either irrational or ill informed compared with the government. Second, as soon as any behavioural sub-model of the monetary authority is introduced, it becomes a subject for speculators' anticipations. In this way, we arrive at a more realistic world where the markets attempt to second-guess the government's strength of will in defending the exchange rate peg, while at the same time government policy is at least partly endogenous, since it is no longer set with complete disregard of the implications for market sentiment.

The new generation of models evolved largely as a response to the two-stage crisis that wrecked the ERM in 1991 and 1992. These cataclysmic events appeared to raise an important question that the existing literature could not answer: could speculators successfully destroy a fixed exchange rate regime that was *not* being undermined by irresponsible monetary policy? Not only were the main victims of the ERM crises (the UK, Spain and, especially, France) said to have sound fundamentals at the time,[5] but they also enjoyed the benefit of an explicit guarantee from the Bundesbank, which meant that, at least in principle, they could draw on infinite reserves of Deutschmarks to protect their bilateral exchange rate.

The question being addressed was, of course, very much at the heart of the wider debate about the nature of global capital markets that raged throughout the 1990s in Europe and more recently in the Far East in the aftermath of the Asian crises. Related questions were and still are being posed: are capital movements benevolent or, at least, a necessary evil? Or are capital controls of some description a *sine qua non* for stability as well as national sovereignty? And so on, to the furthest reaches of more or less veiled xenophobia.

These questions go a long way beyond the limits of exchange rate economics, and they are mentioned simply to set the technical details in context as well as to forewarn readers who set out to read more of the literature in this field that they should expect to encounter heat as well as light. There is more at stake here than simply algebra.

Economists, however, have a way of translating even the most incendiary issues into technicalities. In the present case, what is discussed in the academic literature is the possibility of *multiple equilibria*. Can a fixed exchange rate model have more than one solution? In particular, can we formalize a scenario in which either of two outcomes is possible: a crisis and a non-crisis equilibrium? If so, perhaps it can be argued that the outcome is entirely in the hands of the speculators. As we shall see, this is an interpretation that must be treated with some caution.

Previewing the content of this section, the possible ambiguity arises because these models visualize a world in which a community of speculators on one side and a government on the other come face to face in the currency market, each side trying to second-guess the other.[6] Speculators are concerned with assessing the pressures on the government – economic, political, social – and its likely reaction to them. Will monetary policy have to become more accommodating in response to squeals of pain from the labour market, the banking system or the corporate sector? Will short-term electoral considerations predominate? Or, on the contrary, will concern for long-term credibility be sufficient to make the government deaf to special pleading from whatever quarter?

At the same time, of course, the government for its part is assessing the likely effect of its actions on market sentiment. This creates a feedback loop. The market weighs up the government's assessment of market sentiment. At the same time, the government's actions are taken with one eye on the impact they will have on attitudes in the market. This circularity lies at the heart of the second-generation analysis, and from the resulting equilibrium or equilibria we hope to learn what factors determine whether or not a fixed exchange rate regime will survive unscathed or whether it will be attacked by speculators.[7]

18.2.1 A simplified model

Analytically speaking, the central feature of second-generation models is a government *loss function*. This is simply a formula summarizing the trade-offs facing the government, translating any combination of good and bad news into a single number that can serve as an index of the discomfort represented by that particular outcome.[8] The government's decision problem is then to find the course of action that will reduce the loss to the minimum. Essentially, the loss function for the class of models examined here visualizes a government facing three types of concern.

First, it would ideally like to be in a different state, in macroeconomic terms, than it currently is. Usually, this means that it would like to run the economy with a higher level of aggregate demand. So, for example, the government may wish it could devalue so as to reduce unemployment,[9] to reduce the current account deficit, to make its manufacturing sector more competitive[10] or to capture the capital gain from an overnight reduction in the value of its foreign debts. Since each of these outcomes would ultimately involve a more expansionary monetary policy, and hence a depreciation of the domestic currency, we can summarize the government's aspirations in a single number, which we shall call the *desired* exchange rate, $s*$, *the exchange rate the government would choose if it had not made a commitment to the fixed rate.*[11]

Second, set against the attractions of a devaluation, there is a cost that would have to be borne if the fixed rate peg were abandoned. It might be a high cost, because the country has defended the fixed rate for a long time and is now reluctant to dissipate the reputation that it has built up so painfully over many years. On the other hand, it may be high for the opposite reason: because the country has repeatedly devalued in the past and runs the risk of never again being able to sustain a fixed rate precisely because it has so poor a track record. Moreover, surrendering to speculators may mean that it will have to pay high borrowing rates for years to come, as international investors demand compensation both for expected devaluation and for the associated risk.[12] Whichever scenario applies, the creation of a fixed exchange rate regime must always involve some investment of political capital, whether domestic or international, most often both. We summarize all these factors in the abandonment cost, $I(\Delta s)$. It summarizes the effect of devaluation on the benefit the country is able to derive from trading on its past record.

Third, the government faces the reality that the exchange rate peg will be more costly to defend when devaluation is expected than when it is not. The simplest expression of this is likely to be in interest rates. Even if we cannot rely on UIRP as an exact relationship at all times, especially with a fixed exchange rate, none the less it will be true that the prospect of a possible devaluation will cause investors to demand compensation in the form of higher lending rates, other things being equal.[13]

These concerns are summarized in the following loss function:

$$L = [\psi(s* - s) + \eta \Delta s^e]^2 + I(\Delta s) \quad \psi, \eta > 0 \qquad \textbf{(18.18)}$$

The square bracket collects the two components of the ongoing loss suffered by the government in defending the peg. The term $(s* - s)$, which we can safely assume to be positive, is the extent to which the currency is overvalued relative to the level that the government would like, if its hands were free, and ψ times this gap is a measure of the loss associated with the overvaluation.

As has already been explained, expected depreciation also inflicts a loss via higher interest rates – hence the parameter η is positive, reflecting the pain associated with defending the peg in the face of sceptical currency markets.

Notice that these 'resistance cost' items are squared in their contribution to the loss function.[14] In other words, the costs of defending the parity rise more than in proportion to the degree of overvaluation and the expected depreciation.

By way of contrast, the value of the stock of credibility that the country has built up by defending the current exchange rate in previous periods is indicated by the final term on the right-hand side of Equation 18.17. For simplicity, we assume the function $I(\Delta s)$ can take only two possible values:

$$I(\Delta s_t) = \begin{cases} 0 & \text{for} \quad \Delta s_t = 0 \\ Q & \text{for} \quad \Delta s_t > 0 \end{cases} \qquad \textbf{(18.19)}$$

That is, the credibility cost, $I(\Delta s_t)$, is a fixed lump sum, Q, if a devaluation occurs in any period t, or zero otherwise.

In this setting, the government faces a choice each period. One option is to devalue to the exchange rate level that it would ideally like, s^*, in the process incurring credibility costs of Q. If it chooses this option, then it is assumed to have no further reason to want to change its exchange rate, and so from then onwards the expected rate of depreciation would be zero. It follows that the devaluation option makes the square bracket in Equation 18.17 zero, since it involves setting $s^* = s$ and $\Delta s^e = 0$. The cost of devaluation is therefore simply Q.

Suppose as before that we start from a position where the exchange rate is pegged at the level $\bar{s}$, and consider the range of possible scenarios for the next period, concentrating on the market's expectations, and in particular on the conditions required if those expectations are to be fulfilled.

Case 1: the government is expected to resist the pressure to devalue, so that, with $\Delta s^e = 0$, the loss from defending the peg is:

$$L_1 = [\psi(s^* - \bar{s})]^2 \tag{18.20}$$

The L_1 function is plotted against s^* as the flatter of the parabolas in Figure 18.2. The cost of this course of action will be compared with the cost of the alternative of devaluing, which is just Q. In this case, therefore, the government will choose to defend the peg, as the market expects it to do, if:

$$L_1 < Q \tag{18.21}$$

This condition is satisfied for all values of s^* between A and D in Figure 18.2.

Case 2: the government is expected to surrender and allow the rate to depreciate to its desired level, s^*. In this case, defending the parity is more costly, precisely because of the market expectations to the contrary. The loss function for the defence strategy becomes:

$$L_2 = [\psi(s^* - \bar{s}) + \eta(s^* - \bar{s})]^2$$
$$= [(\psi + \eta)(s^* - \bar{s})]^2 \tag{18.22}$$

which is the inner parabola in Figure 18.2. The term $(s^* - \bar{s})$ is both the expected depreciation and a measure of how far the fixed exchange rate currently is from its desired level. The market's expectations will prove wrong in this case unless the country finds it worthwhile to devalue, which it will do only if:

$$L_2 > Q \tag{18.23}$$

which is a condition satisfied at all values of s^* lower than B or greater than C in the graph. In other words, the government will be more likely to devalue, as expected, if its ideal exchange rate level is a long way from the fixed rate, since in that scenario the cost in terms of lost output, high unemployment, and so on, is large relative to the sacrifice of credibility associated with abandonment.

Putting the two cases together, we find that market expectations will be vindicated if both Equations 18.21 and 18.23 apply, i.e. if:

$$L_1 < Q < L_2 \tag{18.24}$$

As long as the situation satisfies this condition – in other words, as long as the respective parameters, including s^*, result in a loss function with this property – the

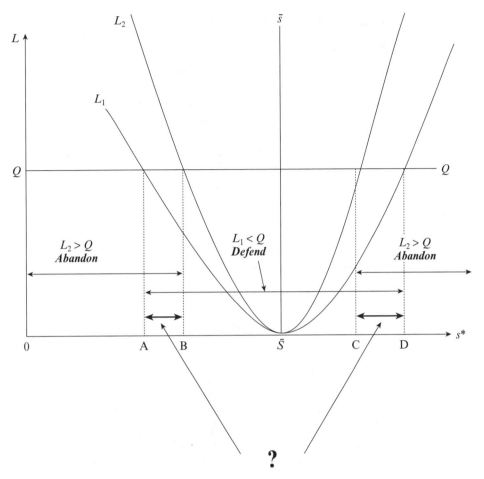

Figure 18.2 The second-generation model

government will find it optimal to validate the market's expectations, whether they involve defending the peg or allowing it to collapse. In fact, if we define equilibrium in the most natural way in this context, as applying whenever the market's expectations are fulfilled, we clearly have a case here of *multiple equilibria*.

We have now arrived at the heart of the academic debate in this area. For the most part, it is the question of multiple equilibria that has divided researchers. Without the ambiguity introduced by multiple equilibria, second-generation models do little more than fill in the details omitted by the first generation, explaining how or why the markets become convinced that an exchange rate peg cannot survive. So we need to ask: is the existence of multiple equilibria more or less *guaranteed* by the theory? Or is it simply that the conditions are *likely* to be satisfied in most real-world cases? Or indeed can their existence be ruled out as *highly improbable* in practice? Is there any evidence of multiple equilibria in recent episodes, especially in the well-documented crises of recent years in Europe and the Far East?

Obviously, the question is of far more than merely academic interest. In the case shown in Figure 18.2, the implication is that, given the values of the critical parameters, ψ and η, which determine the shape of L_1 and L_2, a country whose desired exchange rate s^* falls in either of the critical zones between A and B or between C and D could find it easy or completely impossible to defend a fixed exchange rate regime, depending entirely on whether its situation corresponds to Case 1 or Case 2 – in other words, depending entirely on whether the market *expects* it to devalue or not.

This conclusion is distinctly uncomfortable: in the critical regions, a speculative attack would be self-fulfilling. It would succeed simply because it was expected to succeed, *without any reference to the fundamentals*. It is a conclusion moreover that might well be seen by some people as a theoretical underpinning for any or all of the measures developed over the years to allow governments to suppress international capital movements. After all, it seems to lay the blame for currency crises squarely at the door of the speculators for having the 'wrong' expectations. Is this the philosopher's stone so long sought by those who have railed over the years against hot money movements, foreign speculators, international capital, and so on without actually being able to find any scientific underpinning for their accusations?[15]

Certainly, that is how it has been greeted by some researchers. However, even if we accept the model on its own terms, there are a number of points to be made:

- The smaller the gap between the desired exchange rate and the fixed parity, the easier it will be to defend, or, in terms of Figure 18.2, the more likely it is that the economy is in the segment BC, where a defence is successful. This is simply to say that if the difference between the country's actual position and the position it would like to occupy is perceived to be small, then it will have less difficulty convincing speculators of its determination to put up serious resistance to an attack.

- Clearly, the higher is Q, the cost of abandonment, the more likely it is that Equation 18.21 holds good, and so a government that is seen as having a sizeable political investment in the exchange rate peg will find it easier to defend, other things being equal. On the other hand, Equation 18.23 is less likely to be satisfied, and so abandonment is less attractive in this case too. The net effect, then, is to make defence more likely (and hence more likely to succeed), but at the same time, for large gaps between the desired and actual exchange rate, it increases the width of the multiple equilibria zone. In other words, raising Q has the effect of broadening the defence segment BC in Figure 18.2, while also making the crisis segments AB and CD longer.

The second-generation model is often interpreted as providing some kind of theoretical basis for an indictment of the role played by speculators. However, stepping back from the technicalities, it is clear that the ambiguity represented by multiple equilibria in this model is due neither to market failure nor to the behaviour of speculators, although they are usually cast in the role of villains. Rather, the ambiguity arises out of the initial context. From the outset, we assume a government that finds itself in a specific type of disequilibrium: it has saddled itself (or been saddled by a previous government) with an exchange rate that is not optimal, given its own stated or unstated objectives with respect to unemployment, the balance of payments or the level of economic activity. Clearly, this scenario is inconsistent with equilibrium in the broader context of a government that makes optimal choices, in the same way as other agents.

However, having locked itself into a suboptimal fixed exchange rate, it faces the temptation to break out by devaluing. What is the role played by currency speculators here? In fact, it could be argued that they play a highly beneficial part, by extricating the government from the hole into which it has stumbled, thanks to its commitment to an overvalued exchange rate. Presumably, the longer the regime is preserved, the more the desired exchange rate diverges, and hence the greater the pain of living with the fixed exchange rate, even if it can be defended effortlessly. In this situation, it is quite easy to visualize a speculative attack coming as a blessing. This was more or less what happened when the UK was forced out of the ERM, as we shall now see.

18.2.2 ERM crisis, 1992–93

Since the breakdown of the ERM in 1992–93 provided the impetus for much of the work on second-generation models, it is not surprising that the sequence of events during that episode appears to fit the template quite closely, at least at first glance. There are many detailed accounts of the events of that period (see the reading guide), but for present purposes the following are the salient points:

■ The UK had entered the ERM from what looked at the time like a position of strength. Although some felt that the level of £1.00 = DM2.95 was too high, sterling had been well above the DM3.00 level for much of the period March 1988 to September 1989. Moreover, its monetary policy was tight throughout the years 1990–92.

■ The end of the ERM was either a two-act tragedy played as farce or the opposite, depending on one's viewpoint. In the first act, in autumn 1992, Britain, Italy and Spain left the stage. The UK's departure[16] came at the end of one of the most dramatic days in British financial history, during which interest rates were raised twice (by 2% and 3%) and finally reduced again by 3% – more action than the money markets in some countries see in an average year. The second act, in the summer of 1993, came as something of an anticlimax and saw the effective end of the system, as the French franc was subjected to devastating attacks by speculators, although a wideband version of the ERM was actually preserved and survived until the inception of monetary union at the start of 1999.

■ The first act was dominated, at least as far as the audience was concerned, by the towering performance of George Soros as villain of the piece. Having established a short sterling position of $15 bn, he is reported to have made a profit of nearly $1 bn when the pound was forced to leave the system and promptly fell in value by more than 10% in the space of a few days.

■ The background against which the drama was played out involved extremely high rates of unemployment and clear evidence of deep recession throughout Europe, including the UK. In continental Europe, the level of unemployment was exacerbated by labour market inflexibility.

■ German actors were heavily involved in setting the scene for the drama. Superimposed on the Europe-wide recession were the effects of German reunification, the costs of which had raised real interest rates across Europe, as the increased investment demand interacted with a roughly constant pool of savings.

■ German actors also played a critical role in the climax to the first act. As has already been pointed out, a bilateral peg is, *in theory*, invulnerable to attack if it can count on unlimited reciprocal support. In other words, the sterling/Deutschmark peg would have been impossible to break had the Bundesbank been willing to buy unlimited quantities of sterling during the crisis. Of course, this would have meant surrendering control of the German money supply to market forces. This is simply another example of the central conclusion of Section 5.2: a fixed exchange rate is inconsistent with independent monetary policy as much for a strong as for a weak currency country. In the event, faced with the choice between preserving its own credibility and that of the European Union, the Bundesbank chose the former – a decision that had presumably been foreseen by the markets (or at least by George Soros).

■ The crisis came almost out of the blue. The money markets showed no sign of panic until the month before the breakup, when interest differentials started to widen. Up to that point, few commentators had voiced any doubts about the survival of the system.

■ Previous ERM crises had been countered by high interest rate policies, albeit with varying degrees of success. For example, in the early 1980s France had attempted to reduce pressure on the franc by raising overnight interest rates as high as 80%. The UK proved unwilling to see interest rates rise by more than 3% or 4%, for a number of reasons. First, as has already been mentioned, the 1992 crisis came at a time of deep recession, and so the prospect of further damping down demand was distinctly unattractive. Second, the British economy is probably more sensitive than other European countries to interest rates. Certainly, British public opinion reacts quickly to mortgage rate changes,[17] a factor that may well have diluted the government's willingness to raise interest rates.[18] Moreover, the commitment to ERM was not only weaker in the UK than in other European countries but also different in nature. Whereas, on the continent, the ERM enjoyed near-unanimous support on more or less theological grounds, the case made by its supporters in the UK was based on pragmatic arguments – especially on the promise that it was said to hold out of *lower* interest rates. Having entered ERM in search of lower interest rates, it was always going to be difficult for the British government to raise them to unprecedented levels, a point that was not lost on the speculators.

■ The aftermath of the crisis was beneficial for all three countries that left the ERM in 1992, most especially for the UK, which, since its departure, has enjoyed relatively rapid growth, sharply falling unemployment and high levels of investment. There have been two particularly surprising aspects of the UK's economic performance since 1992. First, the sterling exchange rate, which floated rapidly down to a devaluation of some 20%, has since risen and more or less stabilized around the £1.00 = DM2.90 level (although it has been even more stable against the dollar). Still more surprising is the fact that the initial post-ERM devaluation brought no perceptible inflation, for reasons that are not yet entirely clear. Instead, the demand reflation kickstarted a period of steady growth and falling unemployment that continues to this day.

■ One other puzzling feature of the post-crisis years is that even though they were left free to fluctuate by up to 15% from their (unchanged) central parities, the French, Belgian and Danish currencies remained close to their pre-crisis target zone levels for the remainder of the decade until the introduction of the euro.

These are the bare facts about the ERM crisis. What are their implications for second-generation crisis models? Certainly, the general context of the crisis appears to illustrate the inadequacy of the first-generation models. The fundamentals were not obviously inconsistent with fixed exchange rates for any of the countries under attack. France, in particular, pursued its *franc fort* policy with unwavering rigour throughout the period, and yet it was attacked just the same.

Was the ERM doomed from the outset? Or was it struck down in its prime by George Soros and his friends?

There is no clearcut answer in the literature. Indeed, the controversy continues to this day. None the less, there are certain facts that have to be borne in mind, since they set constraints on how far it is possible to go in the direction of embracing the second-generation position that perfectly sound currencies are potentially victims of speculators.

First, note the countries that were *not* attacked, Germany in particular. In spite of the fact that it faced a massive fiscal burden in rebuilding its eastern Länder in the short term and possibly an even greater problem in the long term with its unfunded pension commitments, that its labour markets were notoriously sclerotic (as evidenced by its high rate of unemployment) with little prospect of reform in the foreseeable future, none the less Germany's currency was never a prey to speculators. On the contrary, it was always the strength of the Deutschmark that was seen as the problem. Why? At one level, the answer is obvious: because of the credibility accumulated by the Bundesbank over the previous 40 years.

But in terms of the model, this amounts to no more than saying that however high s^* might be relative to the current fixed rate, $\bar{s}$ – however much the German government might long to see the Deutschmark devalued – as far as the Bundesbank was concerned, Q was more or less infinite. Moreover, if this was really how the markets saw the situation in advance of the crisis, their view was vindicated by events, especially by the Bundesbank's ultimate refusal to support the pound.

If this version of events is correct, however, then the apparatus of the second-generation model is largely redundant. Any relatively straightforward generalization of the first-generation model to allow for uncertainty, imperfect foresight and possibly non-constant monetary growth rates would have been sufficient to explain the speculative pressure for revaluation of the Deutschmark.

As far as the aftermath is concerned, the very fact that the departing countries prospered after their departure could be taken at first glance as evidence that the market correctly spotted a large (and probably growing) gap $(s^* - \bar{s})$ that would ultimately sap their willingness to defend the fixed rate. But the problem with this interpretation is that within a year or two of its ignominious departure, the pound had floated back to near its ERM level, which is difficult to explain in the absence of any obvious reason for why the UK's desired long-term exchange rate level should have appreciated pro rata.

One final point relates to the evidence that the crisis was unanticipated by the financial markets. This fact seems to be capable of interpretation as support for either model. On the one hand, it could be taken to indicate that perhaps the cavalier treatment of market expectations in first-generation models is not a very serious shortcoming after all. Alternatively, the fact that as little as one month before their destruction the EMS exchange rates were viewed as perfectly viable by the markets themselves has been seen by some people as proof that the fundamentals were sound, not only at the time but also in prospect, which is what would have concerned currency traders when setting interest rates.

18.3 Third-generation models

Although there were a number of questions that second-generation models seemed incapable of answering, the need for a third generation became apparent only later in the 1990s, with the Mexican Tequila crisis, as it was called, of 1994 and even more obviously with the turmoil in Asia that started in mid-1997.

The Asian crisis in particular has already inspired an enormous literature, which is not surprising since it was certainly the gravest to face the world economy since the 1930s. Perhaps its most worrying feature was that it was far broader in scope than previous crises – Latin America in the 1980s, the EMS breakdown, the Wall Street crash of October 1987 – spreading across almost all the asset markets in the affected countries, which included virtually every capitalist economy in the region.

The vast majority of the published papers do little more than survey and attempt to impose some shape on the mass of statistics that tell the story of how the crisis evolved and, especially, on how it spread from sector to sector and from country to country. In this section, we shall examine the facts first, which will allow readers to understand why the existing models are inadequate while at the same time showing some of the difficulties facing model builders. A caveat is necessary, however. What follows was written in late 1999 on the assumption that the crisis in Asia was over and that recovery was by then well under way. This assumption turned out to be justified, as none of the Asian crisis countries has since relapsed, and most have enjoyed robust growth in the intervening period. However, the need for caution is clear if the reader asks himself the following question at the end of each point listed below: how far has the situation changed in country x since the crisis began? In many cases, the answer will turn out to be: not very much.[19] *If* the causes of the turmoil have been identified correctly in the first place (a big if), then it looks therefore as though the preconditions for renewed collapse are still present.

18.3.1 Asian crisis, 1997–99

Tables 18.1 to 18.3 provide summary statistics on four of the crisis economies: Indonesia, Thailand, (South) Korea and Malaysia.[20]

The salient features of the crisis are these:

- Until 1997, the crisis economies were regarded by the majority of commentators as the most successful in the world, with unparalleled growth rates, low inflation rates (at least by developing country standards), highly competitive export sectors and current accounts either in surplus or modest deficit.[21] Moreover, they seemed to be immune from the usual developing country plagues of swollen public sectors and unsustainable budget deficits.[22] The public sector's relative parsimony was matched by private sector savings ratios of 30–35% of GDP – extremely high by western standards.

Table 18.1 Background data on Indonesia, Thailand, Korea and Malaysia

Indonesia					
	1975–94	*1995*	*1996*	*1997*	*1998*
Real GDP growth rate	6.4	8.2	8.0	4.7	−13.7
Inflation rate	11.0	9.4	7.9	6.6	60.7
Saving[1]	24.1	N/A	42.2	44.3	48.1
Investment[1,2]	27.9	31.9	30.7	31.37	14.0
Government deficit/surplus[1]	0.39[3]	2.22	1.44	1.40	N/A
Foreign debt[1]	22.4	30.1	23.9	72.1	N/A
Domestic credit growth	40.5	21.7	22.7	25.7	53.7
Growth in net foreign assets	7.5[4]	19.4	40.6	7.1	43.7
Current account surplus[1]	−2.3	−3.25	−3.40	−3.42	3.31

Thailand					
	1975–94	*1995*	*1996*	*1997*	*1998*
Real GDP growth rate	7.9	8.8	5.5	−0.4	−8.0
Inflation rate	5.9	5.8	5.9	5.6	8.1
Saving[1]	25.3	34.3	33.1	31.8	N/A
Investment[1,2]	29.2	41.8	40.8	35.6	26.7
Government deficit/surplus[1]	−2.6	3.2	0.9	−0.3	−2.8
Foreign debt[1]	5.3	2.9	2.8	5.5	5.4
Domestic credit growth	18.8	23.0	14.0	34.5	−13.0
Growth in net foreign assets[4]	119	−10 779	101.7	85.7	919.8
Current account balance[1]	−5.0	−8.1	−8.1	−3.0	11.3

Korea					
	1975–94	*1995*	*1996*	*1997*	*1998*
Real GDP growth rate	8.1	8.9	7.1	5.5	−5.5
Inflation rate	10.1	4.5	4.9	4.4	7.5
Domestic saving[1]	30.7	34.7	32.6	33.3	47.0
Investment[1]	31.2	36.6	36.9	35.0	29.4
Government deficit/surplus[1]	−0.1	0.5	0.03	−0.01	−2.9
Foreign debt[1]	7.2	1.5	1.3	3.6	N/A
Domestic credit growth	17.1	14.6	19.4	23.2	11.6
Growth in net foreign assets[4]	32.1	9.4	−12.1	−9.3	34.5
Current account balance[1]	−1.3	−1.87	−5.0	−3.3	N/A

Table 18.1 (*cont'd*)

	Malaysia				
	1975–94	*1995*	*1996*	*1997*	*1998*
Real GDP growth rate	6.9	9.4	8.6	7.7	−6.8
Inflation rate	3.7	3.4	3.5	2.7	5.3
Saving[1]	26.7	33.5	36.7	37.0	N/A
Investment[1,2]	30.9	43.0	34.9	34.3	19.4
Government deficit/surplus[1]	−6.0	0.9	0.7	2.3	−1.8
Foreign debt[1]	18.8	6.1	4.1	4.6	5.2
Domestic credit growth	13.1	29.5	31.2	29.3	−2.7
Growth in net foreign assets	24.7	−6.0	−9.2	−49.3	58.3
Current account balance[1]	−2.3	−9.8	−4.7	−6.8	N/A
External debt service[5]	N/A	6.0	5.1	N/A	N/A

1 As percentage of GDP.
2 Gross fixed capital formation.
3 1990–94 only.
4 1983–94 only.
5 Percentage of goods and services exports.

Table 18.2 Asian share prices before and after the crisis

Country	Sector	*1993*	*1994*	*1995*	*1996*	*1997*	*1998*	*1999*[23]
		End year (1995 = 100)						
Korea	Overall	98	116	100	74	43	64	109
	Property	107	138	100	69	25	32	41
Indonesia	Overall	115	91	100	124	78	77	110
	Property	N/A	N/A	100[24]	144	72	27	40
Thailand	Overall	131	106	100	65	29	28	34
	Property	238	126	100	55	10	6	7

Table 18.3 Asian exchange rates before and after the crisis

Country	*1992*	*1993*	*1994*	*1995*	*1996*	*1997*	*1998*	*1999*
	End of year per $US[25]							
Korea	788.4	808.1	788.5	774.0	844.6	1691	1203	1135
Indonesia	2064	2103	2198	2294	2362	4374	7849	6988
Malaysia	2.62	2.69	2.55	2.54	2.53	3.89	3.80	3.80
Thailand	25.5	25.5	25.1	25.2	25.7	48.1	36.5	37.7

- The two largest economies in the region, China and Japan, were not involved directly in the crisis, but the serious long-term problems they faced before the crisis were, of course, exacerbated by the collapse of demand in neighbouring countries. One puzzling feature of the broad picture is that the problems faced by Japan stretched back at least to the late 1980s and yet bore many of the hallmarks of the 1997 crises in its neighbours. Its banks had been made insolvent by bad debts associated with loans to conglomerates, which had in many cases over-invested in productive capacity, and to property firms, which had driven real estate prices to spectacularly high levels by the start of the 1990s. The banking system's profligacy was made possible by an extremely high level of household savings and by a distorted and uncompetitive domestic financial market that channelled those savings into banks and related intermediaries in spite of low (sometimes negative) rates of return. Whether this system could have continued indefinitely or not is unclear, but certainly the small degree of competition introduced into Japan's financial markets in the 1990s seems to have made the situation unstable. The result has been a sharp and continuing deceleration in economic growth, turning into a recession in recent years, and a decline in stock market prices that is quite spectacular when viewed against the backdrop of the greatest bull market in history in every major western economy. As a rough approximation, it could be said that the behaviour of the Japanese economy in the 1990s (and to date) has been like a slow motion version of the crisis in Thailand, Indonesia or Korea – which, of course, makes it even more puzzling that in one case we witness slow decline, while similar symptoms bring about collapse in so many other cases. The stagnation in Japan's domestic economy was mirrored in its exchange rate, with the yen being weak in the 1990s, but not collapsing, and indeed strengthening by the end of the decade.

- By contrast, China was insulated from financial collapse, thanks to the limited scale of its free market sector and, in particular, to the fact that its currency is not fully convertible. However, the crisis inevitably aggravated its pre-existing problems – a large, unproductive nationalized sector, a banking system never forced to apply rational business criteria in lending, and a private sector saddled with carrying the burden of the state-owned industries and hence made uncompetitive by international standards. Where, before the crisis in neighbouring countries, China had enjoyed robust growth and an export boom against a background of high and accelerating inflation, the crisis caused its growth rate to decelerate sharply, and the inflation to turn in the space of two or three years to deflation.

- Most commentators fix the start of the crisis at 2 July 1997, when Thailand devalued its currency, the baht, against the dollar, to which previously it had been pegged. The more or less immediate consequence was a serious crisis in its banking sector, since Thai banks had for some time been borrowing in low-interest money markets abroad (especially Japan), mostly in order to finance local currency loans to property developers.[26] In the subsequent credit squeeze as banks simultaneously sought to repair their balance sheets, many developers became insolvent and property prices dropped sharply. The consequence for the exchange rate was catastrophic, with the baht more or less halving in value against the dollar.

- The crisis spread throughout the second half of 1997 and most of 1998, the pattern varying somewhat from country to country. Thus, in Korea, the major problem centred not so much on real estate as on the *chaebol*, the country's gigantic industrial and financial conglomerates, which had overborrowed, overinvested (at home and abroad) and overemployed for many years, secure in their confidence that the economy would be managed so as to protect their interests. In Indonesia, the poorest of the crisis economies and scene of the most spectacular collapse, the financial markets witnessed more or less complete panic, with the value of the rupiah falling to only 15% of its pre-crisis value in the space of six months, the stock market index dropping to barely 10% of its pre-crisis value[27] and the insolvency of virtually its whole banking sector, the last problem exacerbated by years of what is tactfully known as 'connected lending'.[28]

■ Even more than in the ERM breakdown, the role played by international investors – especially hedge funds[29] – has been controversial. The only thing that can be said with any confidence is that the crisis countries were a magnet for western investment funds before the crisis and have been shunned in the years since it started. In crude terms, the crisis countries had net inflows of private capital that rose by a factor of three between 1990 and 1996 to over $70 bn, but a net outflow of $11 bn in 1997. Most of the turnaround could be attributed to net bank lending, which fell from $41 bn in 1996 to –$32 bn (i.e. an outflow) in 1997. This fact, however, does nothing to prove that capital flows played any significant part in *causing* the problems – they may simply have been reacting to events, possibly playing a part in, but not initiating, the vicious cycle of collapse.

■ The wisdom of the IMF's strategy was also fiercely debated, by economists as much as by politicians, and the question is far from settled even now. The crisis seems to have caught the IMF by surprise (as it did most observers). In the previous decade or so, the IMF had dealt with some success with a number of economies in Latin America and, in the process, had developed tried and trusted formulas for the conditions that it imposed on borrowers: take measures to balance the government budget by cutting fiscal expenditure, privatize loss-making public sector enterprises, deregulate industry and finance, and so forth. However, although the problems faced by the Asian economies overlapped in some respects with those in Latin America, they also differed radically in other respects. In broad terms, the most obvious common feature was misallocation of resources in both regions.[30] By way of contrast, although the Latin American countries have suffered for decades past from inflation, capital flight, low levels of foreign currency reserves and an inadequate flow of domestic saving, none of these problems had afflicted the Asian countries to any serious extent. As a (very rough) approximation, it could be said that Latin American problems were clearly macroeconomic as well as microeconomic, with the former usually triggering the actual collapse. By contrast, Asian problems were largely microeconomic, involving distortions in specific financial markets, with difficulties at the macroeconomic level appearing only at the last minute as a result of the upheavals in the financial sector.

18.3.2 Modelling issues

Against this background, there is as yet no identifiable consensus model, not even a convergence of opinion on which of the many possible questions arising out of these events are truly central. Among the many questions that might be addressed by a useful model, one might look for some insight into these: were currency crises inevitably linked with crises in other sectors? In particular, was it merely fortuitous that there were simultaneous crises in domestic banking and other asset markets, especially real estate, as observed in most of the Southeast Asian countries in 1997–98? If so, were they the result or possibly the cause of the currency crisis?

Given the geographical spread of the crisis, a central question relates to the issue of contagion. Did the problems spread from country A to country B because investors (especially in the west) perceived A and B as sharing similar features, as do many of the Asian economies? Or rather did the problems spread across the region by a more direct route? In other words, did the fall in the level of economic activity in country A as the crisis gathered strength there lead to a fall in its demand for imports from B and possibly also a reduction in its demand for assets in B (especially real estate and financial securities)?

In a contribution from 1997 (and hence more influenced by the Mexican collapse than the Asian crisis), Dooley[31] concentrated on the moral hazard problem created when governments with limited reserves none the less offer guarantees to bank depositors. In the process, he demonstrated that this commitment will have the initial effect of inflating private sector borrowing from abroad but will ultimately result in speculative attack as the situation becomes unsustainable.

Essentially, the mechanism he cites as the cause of all the problems is the insurance offered by the government to those who create certain classes of asset (usually bank deposits), providing them with the incentive to expand the supply far beyond its pre-insurance equilibrium level. Specifically, the mechanism involves banks operating under the umbrella of deposit guarantees (explicit or implicit) expanding their operations by making ever-riskier loans without adequate interest rate compensation. As long as depositors have faith in the insurance scheme, the mechanism is stable.

What determines whether they have faith or not? Plainly, the key question is what resources the government can summon to meet a call on the insurance scheme. In the general case, if the insured assets are denominated in domestic currency (e.g. ordinary bank deposits), then the government has, at least in principle, unlimited resources at its disposal. It can either meet the shortfall out of existing fiscal resources, or if, as is likely, this is impossible, then it can simply print sufficient money to ensure the solvency of the deposit insurance scheme.[32] This, of course, raises the difficulty that maintenance of the insurance scheme may involve a monetary policy inconsistent with the fixed exchange rate regime. In other words, one answer to the question posed at the start of Section 18.1.7 about why a government might pursue a monetary policy inconsistent with a fixed exchange rate may be: *because it is forced to do so by its commitment to deposit insurance*. In other words, we arrive again at conflicting policy objectives as the root cause of all the problems.

In practice, in the Asian crisis (especially in the case of Thailand), the insurance mechanism was undermined even more comprehensively, since, as already mentioned, the banks raised increasing volumes of deposits in foreign currency and used the proceeds to fund lending to local borrowers denominated in domestic currency. This meant that the country's foreign exchange reserves were effectively mortgaged twice: once to support the exchange rate and once more to insure the commercial banking system's foreign currency deposits. The effect is to impose a floor on the reserves at the level needed to insure deposits. As soon as the reserves fall below the implied floor, deposit insurance loses credibility and large-scale withdrawals begin.

More recent work has focused on the fragility of economies where land and commercial property serve as the only acceptable collateral for borrowing. In these circumstances, it seems to be the case that even a small fall in the value of property can have a magnified effect on the economy, as the enforced credit contraction ripples through the financial and real sectors, cumulatively reducing the level of activity and generating an outcome with many of the hallmarks of the crises in Thailand, Indonesia and Korea. However, this appears to suggest that the crisis economies were vulnerable because of the inability of their financial sectors to produce a broad enough range of assets to provide alternatives to real estate as collateral.

Although it is far too soon to say whether the evidence supports this view, it seems only plausible up to a point. In Thailand, for example, the problem could have been avoided by the simple device of making loans to local borrowers in dollars rather than baht.[33] After all, in a small open economy, a substantial proportion of lending would be (or should be) to exporters, for whom it would create no net currency exposure.[34]

18.4 Conclusions

Perhaps it is appropriate that a chapter on crises ends with the conclusion that the literature on this subject is itself in crisis. We started with a neat model that concentrated narrowly on the interaction between the currency and the domestic money markets in order to explain how a fixed exchange rate collapses. When this proved inadequate to explain the demise of the ERM, the analysis had to be broadened to incorporate a sub-model of government decisionmaking, which inevitably made the results far less clearcut. None the less, in spite of its broader sweep, this model in turn seemed to be no help in explaining the Asian crisis, for which a third-generation model is currently being developed, without the benefit of any consensus on the question of which are the critical mechanisms in propagating the collapse.

It is difficult to be optimistic about future progress in this area, when one remembers what is required. For the benefit of practitioners, whether in the private or public sector, it is next to useless simply to be told that the preconditions for some sort of crisis exist. To be of use, the analysis must offer some way of computing *when* the collapse will come. This was the promise held out by the original Krugman first-generation model, with a level of confidence that seems unlikely to be generated by any of the succeeding models.[35]

Summary

- Fixed exchange rate regimes break down when the monetary authority has either run out of reserves or, at least, can clearly foresee the point at which they will be exhausted. Breakdown is often the culmination of a crisis in which speculators attempt to capture the capital gains available from borrowing the domestic currency, which they think is about to be devalued and lending the foreign currency.

- *First-generation models* address two questions: why do crises occur and what determines their timing? Starting from the scenario of a government following a policy of monetary expansion inconsistent with the long-run maintenance of a fixed exchange rate, they proceed to assume that the post-collapse regime will be a pure float. Under these circumstances, they show first that the fixed rate regime will end as a result of an attack by speculators that will come *before* the reserves are exhausted, since they would otherwise be turning their backs on a riskless capital gain. They also show, however, that the timing of the attack will be such as to ensure that the potential capital gains are competed away, because the fixed rate collapses at precisely the point when it can make a smooth transition to floating.

- *Second-generation models* take as their starting point the failure of the first generation to explain the facts, especially the events surrounding the collapse of the ERM, when even countries with conservative monetary policies were subjected to speculative attacks. In essence, second-generation models take the analysis one stage further back: not only does actual monetary policy need to be consistent with the fixed exchange rate, but so too does *prospective* monetary policy. They therefore attempt to model the market's perception of future policy, focusing in particular on any potential conflict between the maintenance of the fixed exchange rate regime and other politically desirable objectives, especially those related directly or indirectly to the level of economic activity. Since the cost of defending the fixed rate is assumed to be higher the greater is the perceived potential for conflicts of this kind, the models generate the conclusion that, at least for some range of parameters, *multiple equilibria* are possible, with collapse occurring if it is expected and none otherwise.

- *Third-generation models* again arise out of the inadequacies of their predecessors. The Asian crisis was far broader in scope than any other, certainly since the 1930s. Since it was not confined to the currency markets, a more general model seemed (and seems) desirable. But there is as yet little agreement on what features the third-generation model should contain or even on the questions it should address.

Reading guide

The classic papers on what are called here first generation models are Krugman (1979) and Flood and Garber (1984). There is also a good textbook treatment in Section 8.4.2 of Obstfeld and Rogoff (1996). None of these readings is very difficult to follow.

By contrast, second-generation models are mostly far more challenging, since they invariably rely on game theory, with the government as one of the players and the speculators as the other. Perhaps the best starting point is Obstfeld and Rogoff (1995a) for the background to these models, and then Krugman (1996), which contrasts first- and second-generation models and on which much of this chapter is based. Obstfeld (1996) is one of the simplest examples of the genre, but it still incorporates all the salient features.

The history of the events surrounding the ERM crisis can be found in a number of places, notably the publications of the central banks involved, e.g. the *Bank of England Quarterly Bulletin*.

The Asian crisis is much described, in words and figures, but very little analysed, at least in a modelling sense. A superb source for data, discussion, polemics and some academic papers is the Asia Crisis Page of Professor Nouriel Roubini at www.rgemonitor.com/633. Dooley (1997) relies on diagrams to explain its logic. For a model of cumulative collapse via a fall in the value of collateral, see Edison, Luangaram and Miller (1998). Loisel and Martin (1999) present a game-theoretical analysis of the contagion effect and the associated questions relating to the likely effectiveness or otherwise of cooperation between different countries in a crisis region.

Web page: **www.pearsoned.co.uk/copeland**.

Notes

1　Which we assume for clarity controls the central bank. In other words, in setting out the *theoretical* arguments, we make no distinction between the government, the central bank and the agencies responsible for managing the reserves and printing the money stock, although one can easily point to cases past and present where these four roles have been separated – and indeed separating these functions is precisely the point of setting a currency board (see Section 11.4). Of course, in discussing the evidence, it is sometimes impossible to ignore these distinctions.

2　At least, not without a bilateral agreement with the reserve currency country. But see also note 5 in Chapter 17.

3　The classification is due to Krugman (1996).

4　It also follows that there is no distinction between arbitrageurs and speculators in this model. We shall refer to speculators in each case, in deference to common usage, but also as a reminder that the model's analysis can be generalized to cover uncertainty, albeit at the cost of quite a lot more complexity.

5　Although this has been disputed (see the reading guide).

6　It will not surprise the reader to learn that some of these models are set in a game-theoretical framework (see reading guide). We are able to avoid these complexities here, thanks to the simple exposition of a prototype second-generation model given by Krugman (1996).

7　It has been shown that even first-generation models can result in multiple equilibria.

8　The units in which the loss function is denominated are of no concern.

9　As was pointed out in Chapter 11, this will work only if unemployment has been caused by nominal wage rigidity, which can be bypassed by devaluation. However, nothing in the loss function itself presupposes that the government is rational – it is at least as likely as any private sector agent to be an adherent of the DIY model outlined in Chapter 1.

10　Governments always worry most about manufacturing and rarely about services.

11　Again, 'the government' is to be interpreted loosely. For example, the commitment to a fixed rate might have been given by a previous government.

12　That is, to take account of the mean and standard deviation of the rate of devaluation (see Chapter 15).

13　Notice that this is not quite the same point as was made in the previous paragraph. One way of explaining the matter is to say that the lack of credibility causes high interest rates via UIRP. If we ask *why* country A has higher credibility than country B in spite of the fact that A's monetary policy is more expansionary than B's, the answer may well lie in the fact that B has dissipated its stock of credibility by previous devaluations.

14　A quadratic loss function is often used in choice models, largely because it is the simplest departure from linearity (which would be impossible for reasons familiar from basic microeconomics).

15　One of the most depressing aspects of currency crises is how they unleash the latent xenophobia normally confined only to the most disreputable quarters. Thus, British prime minister Harold Wilson attacked the 'gnomes of Zurich', French crises are invariably attributed to Anglo-Saxons, and so forth. One thing is certain: there could never be a global currency – there would be no foreigners left to blame for financial crises.

16　On 16 September 1992, a day that was immediately dubbed Black Wednesday but that came later to be known as White Wednesday.

17　Most British households own homes purchased with mortgages, few of which (in 1992) were fixed interest.

18　Among the many delightful ironies in this affair is that, according to many political researchers, one of the major factors explaining the ultimate defeat of the Conservative government in the

1997 general election was the electorate's loss of confidence in its ability to manage the economy, as evidenced in the 1992 crisis. Would the Conservatives have retained that confidence had they been willing to let interest rates double or triple in order to protect sterling? It must be doubtful, although the fact that the electorate proved so ungrateful for the robust recovery that followed sterling's departure could be taken as an indication that, symmetrically, they might have rewarded a stout defence, even if it entailed quite severe hardship.

19 In fact, in Indonesia they appear to have worsened, for political reasons.

20 The crisis affected all the countries in the region, to some extent at least. These four were the most obvious victims. With the exception of Japan (and possibly China), most of the others seemed to suffer largely as a side-effect of the problems in these four.

21 It is interesting to note that one of the few observers to remain unimpressed with the Asian Tigers was Paul Krugman, who publicly questioned the so-called Asian miracle in a series of polemical pieces in the early 1990s.

22 It should be noted that all four countries satisfied the Maastricht convergence criteria (see Section 10.3.4) better than most of the EMU member countries, an object lesson in how misleading these arbitrary stability indicators can be, especially when the government indulges in creative national accounting, as has been the case in both Asia and Europe for some years past.

23 At 10 September 1999.

24 At 31 January 1996.

25 Source: Tables 18.1, 18.2 and 18.3 – data from Datastream International.

26 It has been said in their defence that the Thai banks believed this money machine to be riskless, on the grounds that their government was committed to defending the fixed exchange rate link to the dollar. If so, it makes one wonder how they were able to explain the interest differential. The most probable explanation is that they felt able to take for granted that in the event of devaluation, the Thai government would take responsibility for their currency exposure, an assumption that proved largely correct. This and similar situations in other countries has sparked a debate among academics and policymakers on the relative dangers of, on the one hand, *moral hazard* – that is, the inducement to private agents to take risks when the government stands ready to cover any losses – and on the other hand, the damage inflicted by bank collapses.

27 In dollar terms (the figures in Table 18.2 are local currency indices).

28 That is, connected to the bank's owners (which often meant the country's ruling elite), whether by other business ties, family links, friendship or, in some cases, golf.

29 Contrary to what is implied by the name, these are funds that set out to maximize the return on the capital deposited with them by their investors (mostly wealthy individuals), essentially by making high-risk investments wherever they can find them.

30 Usually via nationalized industries in Latin America and via (often informal) government intervention in private sector decisionmaking in Asia.

31 Dooley himself classes his model as first-generation, which it is in analytical terms. But in spirit, its concentration on moral hazard in financial intermediation is very much third-generation.

32 These problems are by no means restricted to developing countries. For example, the same dilemma faced the US authorities in dealing with the Federal Savings and Loan Insurance Corporation debacle in the 1980s and, in France, the rescue of Crédit Lyonnais involved similar problems on a smaller scale. In western countries, so far at least, the problems have never been allowed to reach a level where they could seriously undermine monetary policy, although they can (and sometimes do) cause it to deviate temporarily from its chosen path. For an example, one need look no further than the cut in US interest rates in August 1998 in response to the insolvency of the Long-Term Capital Management hedge fund. The current (December 1999) crisis in credit markets may yet turn out to be the exception.

33 It might have been more practical to make loans in baht *linked* to the dollar exchange rate.

34 It would also have had the benefit of compelling exporters to repatriate foreign currency earnings, without which it is almost impossible to maintain a fixed exchange rate for very long.

35 At least not analytically, although one could imagine a second- or third-generation model simple enough to make it possible to answer the timing question by numerical methods.

PART V

Conclusions

The last chapter looks back at the material covered in this book and discusses where we might go from here, in particular what look the most promising avenues for future research.

19 Conclusions

Introduction

In this book, I have tried to provide the determined reader with a fair summary of the state of our existing knowledge about exchange rates and an adequate foundation for getting to grips with the original literature, if so desired. The concluding chapter will briefly survey the material in the book and then go on to consider the question: where might research go from here?

19.1 Summary of the book

In the first chapter the reader was introduced to the working of a currency market under fixed and floating exchange rates, and the significance of the balance of payments was explained. As a background to the theory to follow, a brief history of the international monetary system was given, with particular emphasis on the prelude to today's floating exchange rates: the disintegration of the Bretton Woods regime and the series of attempts to reimpose fixed exchange rates, culminating in the ongoing experiment with currency unions.

There followed three chapters of essential preliminaries. In the first, it was shown how extending the law of one price to product markets in the open economy led to the conclusion that price levels ought to move in unison, once allowance was made for exchange rate movements. Unfortunately, however attractive it might look in theory, purchasing power parity turned out to fit the facts very poorly, if at all.

By contrast, extending the law of one price to the market for international securities looked more promising. Two conclusions emerged from Chapter 3. First, arbitrage ought to make the forward premium equal to the international interest differential – and, by and large, the evidence suggests it does. On the other hand, uncovered interest rate parity is much more difficult to test since it involves the unobservable *expected* rate of depreciation.

Finally in Part I, Chapter 4 extended the textbook aggregate demand and supply framework to accommodate an open economy.

The preliminaries completed, Part II examined a number of models of exchange rate determination, starting with the monetary model, a convenient benchmark for future reference. In essence it is an extension of the classical quantity theory to the open economy context. First, it predicts that increases in the money stock will be reflected in depreciation of the same proportion and, second, that (real) income growth will be associated with a rising international currency value. Both results automatically flow from the fact that the model is constructed out of two building blocks: PPP and the balance of supply and demand in the money market. Not surprisingly, given the failure of PPP to fit the facts, the monetary model also fares rather poorly in that respect.

By way of contrast, the Mundell–Fleming model (Chapter 6) goes to the opposite extreme of taking the price level as constant. Since it also ignores the role of expectations, its relevance to contemporary currency markets is limited, although it has been very influential, both on academic researchers and on the architects of macroeconomic policy, particularly in the UK and the USA.

The Dornbusch model (Chapter 7) represents a compromise, suspending PPP in the short run but acknowledging it as undeniable in the long run. The implication turns out to be that financial markets, which are still assumed to clear instantaneously, have to *over*adjust to disturbances.

In fact, this conclusion is quite general, as was seen in the next two chapters. In particular, overshooting is a feature of portfolio balance models (Chapter 8) in which investors are seen as allocating their wealth to three broad asset categories: domestic money and bonds and foreign currency bonds. It is also an implication of currency substitution models (Chapter 9) in which investors are assumed to focus more narrowly on the choice between domestic and foreign currency balances, shifting their relative money demand in response to changes in the rate of depreciation.

Both models make strong predictions, especially with regard to the link between the current account and the exchange rate. Neither fits the facts very closely and neither proves reliable for forecasting purposes. The same criticism could be made of the models outlined in Chapter 10, albeit for different reasons. In taking a general equilibrium approach, the Redux model and its successors try to relate exchange rate movements to the underlying structure of the economy and in particular to the utility-maximizing choices of agents in each country. The aim is laudable, but the outcome throws more light on international macroeconomics than on exchange rate behaviour. Part II ends with a chapter on a topic in what is sometimes called political economy: what does our understanding of exchange rates imply for the optimal size of a currency zone? In particular, what are the likely effects of the new European Monetary Union?

In Part III, the consequences of uncertainty, which had been avoided up to this point, were confronted under three headings. Start with an equation such as Equation 12.4, rewritten as follows:

$$s_t = \rho_{t-1} + f_{t-1}^t + u_t \tag{19.1}$$

Chapter 12 looked at the role of the forward rate in this equation and in the process introduced the important concepts of rational expectations and market efficiency. Chapter 13 concentrated on the innovation term, u_t, and showed that it ought to be explained by the intermittent arrival of new information – 'news' – about the fundamentals. In the next chapter, the risk premium, ρ_{t-1} was linked to the behaviour of individual decisionmakers faced with investment choices under conditions of uncertainty.

Examination of the evidence revealed something of a puzzle. On the one hand, unbiasedness could be ruled out with some confidence. In other words, the intercept term in Equation 12.15 was not zero. On the other hand, from several points of view, it was hard to credit that the risk premium could explain the gap between the spot and lagged forward rate. The same applied to 'news': the theory contributed to some extent to an explanation of the facts, but nowhere near enough. Finally in this section, readers were introduced to the microeconomic approach to exchange rate modelling, with a very brief overview of the use made of order flow data in the published research literature and an examination of a recent model that tries to explain the forward premium puzzle.

Chapter 16 pointed to a possible reconciliation of some of the recurrent themes in the book. It was shown there that in some cases non-linear models can generate predictions for exchange rate behaviour that cover almost every variety of conceivable pattern, ranging from almost mechanical cycles to fluctuations that are virtually indistinguishable from randomness. It remains to be seen whether this type of model will ultimately advance our understanding of how currency markets work.

Finally, Chapters 17 and 18 dealt with two aspects of fixed exchange rate regimes that have been extensively analysed in the literature of the past few years. Target zones are for all practical purposes a necessary concomitant of any fixed exchange rate regime. Following through their implications yielded theoretical predictions that were not quite what might have been expected in advance. The last chapter examined the way fixed exchange rate systems break down once they have lost their credibility. Again, the mechanism involves subtleties that might not have been obvious at first, notably the fact that a fixed rate can be shown to fail precisely at the point where its collapse results in no perceptible change.

19.2 Where do we go from here?

In the conclusion to the third edition of this book, I warned that the consequences for exchange rates of globalization and in particular of electronic trading in goods, services and securities were impossible to predict. In the intervening years, the same trends have continued and in some respects accelerated. None the less, it is still too soon to hazard a guess as to the overall impact of these developments, which, although rapid, must have much further to go. However, I remain convinced that the erosion of political and economic sovereignty implied by the new technologies will at some stage (possibly quite soon) start to weaken the link between currencies and nationalities. In some respects, this is already occurring, often for reasons that have nothing directly to do with globalization or technology. In addition to the obvious example of European Monetary Union, there is also the beginning of what could be a trend towards currency boards. But, as usual, a more powerful influence is likely to come from spontaneous market forces. In general, the phenomenon called currency substitution in Chapter 9 is likely to become far more widespread in the future, simply because the institutional and political constraints that in the past prevented its becoming a practical reality are quickly disappearing. For example, it is far easier today than it was even five years ago to hold deposits in foreign currencies or indeed a number of different currencies, switching at will between the two. It is increasingly difficult to pin a national flag on the banks that offer these facilities to corporates and individuals – they are not only multinational in the accepted sense of having subsidiaries in a number of countries but also increasingly located in cyberspace, offering services that are either Internet- or phone-based, with customers calling on local numbers in, say, Glasgow, being routed seamlessly to call centres in India or Malaysia. Once banks no longer have a home country, they no longer have a home currency. Their large corporate customers have for some time been in the same situation, often listing their shares on more than one major stock market and presenting their annual accounts in two or more currencies.

By this stage, it is only the individual household consumer who stands in the way of currency competition and he is likely to prove a very low hurdle indeed for a number of reasons. First, and most important, the decision about the vehicle currency for transactions is often taken out of the hands of the consumer, who sees (and cares about) only the currency in which the transaction is invoiced. Second, even where the consumer has a choice, the vehicle currency decision is often tied to other more important decisions. When I am choosing between two Internet offers on my motor insurance, a foreign holiday or a bundle of CDs, whether the quote is in dollars, pounds or euros is likely to be a minor consideration. The payment mechanism is the same in any case: an ordinary credit card makes it possible to convert funds painlessly (and at money centre exchange rates) into even the most obscure currencies.

Money evolved before the nation state and, in one form or another, it will outlive it. Originally, money was either privately issued, by bankers of good standing in their own right, or by kings or potentates whose nationality in the sense we understand the term today was more or less undefined, but who were none the less able to enjoy the benefits of seignorage. Most 'countries' – kingdoms, dukedoms, principalities, and so on – never attempted to issue their own money, making payments instead in either gold or whatever was the most commonly used local currency. Hence, currencies such as the Thaler (from which, incidentally, we get the word 'dollar') became widely used across western Europe by people who neither knew nor cared about its national provenance but were concerned only with its acceptability. It may well be that the twenty-first century will see a return to a high-tech version of that world. To some extent, it is already foreshadowed in the constraints that global currency markets are imposing on national governments. Countries are being forced as never before to compete for the favours of money holders. In terms of the Keynesian taxonomy of motives for holding money, while the speculative and precautionary demands have always been to a greater or lesser degree sensitive to international competitive pressures, technology has brought monetary competition into the transactions demand too.

The net effect of all these developments on exchange rates is difficult to foresee, except in so far as it threatens to make the already feeble link between national income and the value of a currency via the transactions demand for money completely invisible. In the meantime, humility seems to be required. The final paragraph of the first and second editions of this book ran as follows:

Perhaps the *worst* thing we could do would be to pretend that we know more than we actually do – an affliction which seems to affect academics occasionally and politicians, professional and amateur, very frequently – as witnessed by some of the arguments used in Britain to support the case for EMS membership.

Those words were written in 1988. The history of Britain's brief membership of EMS illustrated the point perfectly: politicians and many economists held out the promise in particular of lower interest rates to a gullible public. The outcome was, of course, the complete opposite. The indictment is hubris: getting the forecast wrong is, alas, one of the accepted perils of the trade, but the confidence with which the forecasts were sold in the first place was less forgivable. Some of the advocates of EMU are in this respect recidivists.

You have been warned.

Appendix: list of symbols*

$\tilde{X}$ Ratio of UK to US value of variable X, X/X^* (Section 5.1).

$\bar{X}$ The equilibrium, fixed or long-run value of an endogenous variable, X. Otherwise, denotes exogenous variable (Section 5.2).

$\dot{X}$ The change in the value of the variable S per unit of time, dX/dt (Section 9.1.2).

$\dot{x}$ The rate of change (growth rate) of the variable X per unit of time, $d(\log X)/dt$ (Section 7.3).

X^* The value of the variable X for the USA (Section 2.4).

A Investor's holding of forward contracts to buy dollars (Section 13.2.2).

B The surplus on the current account of the UK balance of payments (Section 6.1.2).

D Deposit liabilities of the commercial banks (Section 4.1.2).

DC Domestic credit (bank advances) (Section 4.1.2).

f The forward premium, $F/S - 1$ (Section 3.2).

F The stock of dollar-denominated securities held by the UK private sector (Section 8.1).

F_t The forward exchange rate at time t for currency to be delivered at time $t + 1$ (Section 3.2).

FX Gold and foreign currency reserves of the Bank of England (Section 4.1.2).

G Government spending on goods and service (Section 4.1.1).

K Net inflow of capital from the USA into the UK (Section 6.1.2).

L Lending by UK commercial banks to UK non-government sector (Section 4.1.2).

LG Lending by the Bank of England to the UK government (Section 4.1.2).

MB^b Monetary base in bank tills (Section 4.1.2).

MB^p Monetary base in circulation with public (Section 4.1.2).

MB Total monetary base: $MB = MB^b + MB^p$ (Section 4.1.2).

M^s The supply of money (Section 4.1.2).

* List excludes symbols used exclusively in Chapter 10.

M^d The demand for money (Section 4.1.2).

μ   The growth rate of the UK money stock (Section 9.1).

$$\frac{d \log M^s}{dt} = \frac{1}{M^s} \frac{dM^s}{dt}$$

$μ_X$ The mean of a random variable, X (Section 13.2.1).

P The (product) price level in the UK economy (Section 2.3).

Q The real exchange rate, SP^*/P (Section 2.4).

r A representative UK interest rate (Section 3.1.1).

R Real rate of interest (Section 3.6).

ρ   The risk premium on transactions in the forward market (Section 6.7).

S Exchange rate (£ price of $) (Section 1.1).

$\bar{S}$ A fixed exchange rate.

$σ_X$ The standard deviation of the variable, X (Section 13.2.1).

$σ_X^2$ The variance of the variable, X (Section 13.2.2).

V The value of UK oil revenues at any point (Section 7.4).

$\bar{V}$ The permanent-income value of UK oil revenues (Section 7.4).

W UK private sector financial wealth (Section 8.1).

Y Nominal national income (Section 4.1).

y Real national income, Y/P (Section 4.1).

Bibliography

Adler M. and Lehmann B. (1983). Deviations from purchasing power parity in the long run. *Journal of Finance*, **38** (5), 1471–87

Aliber R. Z. (1973). The interest rate parity theorems: a reinterpretation. *Journal of Political Economy*, **81** (6), 1451–59

Andersen T. G., Bollerslev T., Diebold F. X. and Vega C. (2003). Micro effects of macro announcements: real-time price discovery in foreign exchange. *American Economic Review*, **93** (1), 38–62

Anderson P. W., Arrow K. J. and Pines D. (1988). *The Economy as an Evolving Complex System*. Reading, MA: Addison-Wesley

Artis M. J. (1984). *Macroeconomics*. Oxford: Oxford University Press

Azariadis C. (1993). *Intertemporal Macroeconomics*. Oxford, UK, and Cambridge, MA: Blackwell

Bacchetta P. and van Wincoop E. (2006). Can information heterogeneity explain the exchange rate determination puzzle? *American Economic Review*, **96** (3), 552–76

Baillie R. T. and Bollerslev T. (2000). The forward premium anomaly is not as bad as you think. *Journal of International Money and Finance*, **19**, 471–88

Baillie R. T., Lippens R. E. and McMahon P. C. (1983). Testing rational expectations and efficiency in the foreign exchange market. *Econometrica*, **51**, 553–63

Baliño T. J. T. and Enoch C. (1997). Currency board arrangements: issues and experiences. IMF Occasional Paper No. 151

Bansal R. (1997). An exploration of the forward premium puzzle in currency markets. *Review of Financial Studies*, **10**, 369–403

Barnett W. A., Geweke J. and Shell K. (1989). *Economic Complexity: Chaos, Sunspots, Bubbles and Nonlinearity*. Cambridge: Cambridge University Press

Barro R. J. (1974). Are government bonds net worth? *Journal of Political Economy*, **82**, 1095–117

Barro R. J. (1977). Unanticipated money growth and unemployment in the United States. *American Economic Review*, **67**, 101–15

Barro R. J. (1984). *Macroeconomics*. New York: John Wiley & Sons

Baumol W. J. and Benhabib J. (1989). Chaos: significance, mechanism, and economic applications. *Journal of Economic Perspectives*, **3** (1), 77–105

Begg D. K. (1982). *The Rational Expectations Revolution in Macroeconomics*. Oxford: Philip Allan

Begg D. K., Dornbusch R. and Fischer S. (1987). *Macroeconomics*. Maidenhead: McGraw-Hill

Bertola G. and Caballero R. J. (1992). Target zones and realignments. *American Economic Review*, **82**, 520–36

Betts C. and Devereux M. B. (1996). The exchange rate in a model of pricing to market. *European Economic Review*, **40**, 1007–21

Betts C. and Devereux M. B. (2000). Exchange rate dynamics in a model of pricing to market. *Journal of International Economics*, **50**, 215–44

Bilson J. F. (1979). Recent developments in monetary models of exchange rate determination. *IMF Staff Papers*, **26** (2), 201–23

Bilson J. O. (1981). The speculative efficiency hypothesis. *Journal of Business*, **54** (3), 435–51

Black F. (1986). Noise. *Journal of Finance*, **41** (3), 529–43

Blanchard O. J. (2005). Macroeconomics, 4th edn. New York: Prentice-Hall

Blanchard O. J. and Katz L. F. (1992). Regional evolutions. *Brookings Papers on Economic Activity*, **1**, 1–75

Blanchard O. J. and Watson M. (1982). Bubbles, rational expectations and financial markets. In Wachtel P. (ed.) *Crises in the Economic and Financial Structure*. Lexington, MA: Lexington Books

Branson W. H. (1983). Macroeconomic determinants of real exchange risk. In Herring R. J. (ed.) *Managing Foreign Exchange Risk*. Cambridge: Cambridge University Press

Branson W. H. and Halttunen H. (1979). Asset market determination of exchange rates: initial empirical and policy results. In Martin J. P. and Smith A. (eds) *Trade and Payments Under Flexible Exchange Rates*. London: Macmillan

Branson W. H. and Henderson D. W. (1985). The specification and influence of asset markets. In Jones R. A. and Kenen P. B. (eds) *Handbook of International Economics* vol. II. Amsterdam: North-Holland

Branson W. H., Halttunen H. and Masson P. (1979). Exchange rates in the short run: the dollar–Deutschmark rate. *European Economic Review*, **10**, 303–24

Brock W. A., Hsieh D. A. and LeBaron B. (1991). *Nonlinear Dynamics, Chaos and Instability: Statistical Theory and Economic Evidence*. Cambridge, MA: MIT Press

Bruno M. and Sachs J. (1982). Input price shocks and the slowdown in economic growth: the case of UK manufacturing. *Review of Economic Studies*, **49**, 679–705

Buiter W. H. and Miller M. H. (1982). Monetary policy and international competitiveness. In Sinclair P. J. N. and Eltis W. A. (eds) *The Money Supply and the Exchange Rate*. Oxford: Oxford University Press

Buiter W. H. and Miller M. H. (1983). Real exchange rate overshooting and the output cost of bringing down inflation: some further results. In Frenkel J. (ed.) *Exchange Rates and International Macroeconomics*. Chicago, IL: University of Chicago Press

Buiter W. H. and Purvis D. D. (1983). Oil disinflation and export competitiveness: a model of the Dutch disease. In Bhandari J. S. and Putnam B. H. (eds) *Economic Interdependence and Flexible Exchange Rates*. Cambridge, MA: MIT Press

Burnside C., Eichenbaum M. S. and Rebelo S. (2007). Understanding the forward premium puzzle: a microstructure approach. National Bureau of Economic Research Working Paper No. 13278

Calvo G. and Rodriguez C. A. (1977). A model of exchange rate determination under currency substitution and rational expectations. *Journal of Political Economy*, **85** (3), 617–26

Cassel G. (1916). The present situation of the foreign exchanges. *Economic Journal*, **28**, 413–15

Chance D. (1998). *An Introduction to Derivatives*, 4th edn. San Diego, CA: Dryden Press/ Harcourt Brace

Cheung Y. W. and Lai K. S. (1993). A fractional cointegration analysis of purchasing power parity. *Journal of Business and Economic Statistics*, **11**, 103–12

Christou C. (1992). National monetary policies and the European Monetary Union. *Greek Economic Review*, **15** (1), 115–30

Chrystal A. (1977). Demand for international media of exchange. *American Economic Review*, **67**, 840–50

Copeland L. S. (1983). Public sector prices and the real exchange rate in the UK recession. *Bulletin of Economic Research*, **35** (2), 97–121

Copeland L. S. (1989). Exchange rates and 'news': a vector autoregression approach. In Macdonald R. and Taylor M. P. (eds) *Innovations in Open Economy Macroeconomics*. Oxford: Blackwell

Copeland T. E. and Weston J. F. (1983). *Financial Theory and Corporate Policy*, 2nd edn. Reading, MA: Addison-Wesley

Cox J., Ross S. and Rubinstein M. (1979). Option pricing: a simplified approach. *Journal of Financial Economics*, **7**, 229–64

Cvitanovic P. (1989). *Universality in Chaos*, 2nd edn. Bristol, UK, and New York: Adam Hilger

Daniel B. C. (1982). Monetary expansion and aggregate supply in a small open economy. *Economica*, **49** (195), 267–87

Deardorff A. V. (1979). One way arbitrage and its implications for the foreign exchange markets. *Journal of Political Economy*, **87** (2), 351–64

Delgado F. and Dumas B. (1991). Target zones big and small. National Bureau of Economic Research Working Paper No. 3601

Devaney R. L. (1989). *An Introduction to Chaotic Dynamical Systems*, 2nd edn. Redwood City, CA: Addison-Wesley

Diba B. T. and Grossman H. I. (1988). Rational inflationary bubbles. *Journal of Monetary Economics*, **21**, 35–46

Diebold F. X., Husted S. and Rush M. (1991). Real exchange rates under the gold standard. *Journal of Political Economy*, **99**, 1252–71

Dixit A. (1993). *The Art of Smooth Pasting*. Frankfurt: Harwood Academic Publishers GmbH

Dominguez K. M. E. and Panthaki F. (2006). What defines 'news' in foreign exchange markets? *Journal of International Money and Finance*, **25**, 168–98

Dooley M. P. (1997). A model of crises in emerging markets. National Bureau of Economic Research Working Paper No. 6300

Dooley M. P. and Shafer J. R. (1983). Analysis of short run exchange rate behavior: March 1973 to November 1981. In Bigman D. and Taya T. (eds) *Exchange Rate and Trade Instability*. Cambridge, MA: Ballinger

Dornbusch R. (1973). Devaluation, money and non-traded goods. *American Economic Review*, **63**, 871–80

Dornbusch R. (1976a). Expectations and exchange rate dynamics. *Journal of Political Economy*, **84**, 1161–76

Dornbusch R. (1976b). The theory of flexible exchange rate regimes and macroeconomic policy. *Scandinavian Journal of Economics*, **78** (2), 255–76

Dornbusch R. (1982). Equilibrium and disequilibrium exchange rates. In Lessard D. R. (ed.) *International Financial Management: Theory and Application*. Chichester: John Wiley & Sons

Dornbusch R. (1983). Exchange rate risk and the macroeconomics of exchange rate determination. In Hawkins R. G., Levich R. M. and Whilborg C. G. (eds) *The Internationalization of Financial Markets and National Economic Policy*. Greenwich, CT: JAI Press

Dornbusch R. and Fischer S. (1980). Exchange rates and the current account. *American Economic Review*, **70** (5), 960–71

Dunn R. M. (1983). The many disappointments of flexible exchange rates. *Princeton Essays in International Finance*, **154**

Eastwood R. K. and Venables A. J. (1982). The macroeconomic implications of a resource discovery in an open economy. *Economic Journal*, **92**, 285–99

Edison H. J., Luangaram P. and Miller M. (1998). Asset bubbles, domino effects and 'lifeboats': elements of the East Asian crisis. Centre for the Study of Globalisation and Regionalisation Working Paper No. 05/98

Edwards S. (1982). Exchange rates and news: a multi-currency approach. *Journal of International Money and Finance*, **1** (1), 211–24

Edwards S. (1983). Floating exchange rates, expectations and new information. *Journal of Monetary Economics*, **11**, 321–36

Engel C. (1999). Accounting for US real exchange rate changes. *Journal of Political Economy*, **107** (3), 507–38

Evans G. W. (1986). A test for speculative bubbles in the sterling–dollar exchange rate: 1981–1984. *American Economic Review*, **76** (4), 621–36

Evans M. D. D. (2006). Foreign exchange market microstructure. In *New Palgrave Dictionary of Economics*

Evans M. D. D. and Lyons R. K. (2006). *Myths About the Micro Approach to Exchange Rates*. Mimeo

Evans M. D. D. and Lyons R. K. (2007). Exchange rate fundamentals and order flow. National Bureau of Economic Research Working Paper No. 13151

Fama E. F. (1970). Efficient capital markets: a review of theory and empirical work. *Journal of Finance*, **25**, 383–417

Feldstein M. (1992). Europe's monetary union: the case against EMU. *The Economist*, 13 June 1992

Fleming J. M. (1962). Domestic financial policies under fixed and floating exchange rates. *IMF Staff Papers*, **9**, 369–77

Flood R. P. and Garber P. M. (1982). Bubbles, runs, and gold monetization. In Wachtel P. (ed.) *Crises in the Economic and Financial Structure*. Lexington, MA: Lexington Books

Flood R. P. and Garber P. M. (1984). Collapsing exchange rate regimes: some linear example. *Journal of International Economics*, **17**, 1–13

Frankel J. A. (1979). On the Mark: a theory of floating exchange rates based on real interest differentials. *American Economic Review*, **69**, 610–22

Frankel J. A. (1980). Tests of rational expectations in the forward exchange market. *Southern Economic Journal*, **46** (4), 1083–101

Frankel J. A. (1982). In search of the exchange rate premium: a six currency test assuming mean variance optimization. *Journal of International Money and Finance*, **1**, 255–74

Frankel J. A. (1983a). Monetary and portfolio-balance models of exchange rate determination. In Bhandari J. S. and Putnam B. H. (eds) *Economic Interdependence and Flexible Exchange Rates*. Cambridge, MA: MIT Press

Frankel J. A. (1983b). Estimation of portfolio-balance functions that are mean-variance optimizing: the Mark and the dollar. *European Economic Review*, **23**, 315–27

Frankel J. A. (1986). The implications of mean-variance optimization for four questions in international macroeconomics. *Journal of International Money and Finance*, **5**, 53–75

Frankel J. A. and Froot K. A. (1987). Using survey data to test standard propositions regarding exchange rate expectations. *American Economic Review*, **77** (1), 133–53

Frenkel J. A. (1976). A monetary approach to the exchange rate: doctrinal aspects and empirical evidence. *Scandinavian Journal of Economics*, **78** (2), 200–24

Frenkel J. A. (1977). The forward exchange rate, expectations and the demand for money: the German hyperinflation. *American Economic Review*, **67** (4), 653–70

Frenkel J. A. (1978). Purchasing power parity: doctrinal perspective and evidence from the 1920s. *Journal of International Economics*, **8** (2), 169–91

Frenkel J. A. (1980). The collapse of purchasing power parities during the 1970s. *European Economic Review*, **7**, 145–65

Frenkel J. A. (1981). Flexible exchange rates, prices and the role of news: lessons from the 1970s. *Journal of Political Economy*, **89**, 655–705

Frenkel J. A. and Levich R. M. (1975). Covered interest arbitrage: unexploited profits? *Journal of Political Economy*, **83** (2), 325–38

Frenkel J. A. and Razin A. (1980). Stochastic prices and tests of efficiency of foreign exchange markets. *Economics Letters*, **6**, 165–70

Frenkel J. A. and Razin A. (1988). The Mundell–Fleming model a quarter century later: a unified exposition. *IMF Staff Papers*, **35**, 567–620

Frenkel J. A. and Rodriguez C. A. (1982). Exchange rate dynamics and the overshooting hypothesis. *IMF Staff Papers*, **29**, 1–30

Friedman M. (1953). The case for flexible rates. *Essays in Positive Economics*. Chicago, IL: University of Chicago Press

Frömmel M., MacDonald R. and Menkhoff L. (2002). Markov-switching regimes in a monetary exchange rate model. Department of Economics, University of Hanover, Discussion Paper No. 26

Frömmel M., Mende A. and Menkhoff L. (2007). Order flows, news, and exchange rate volatility. *Journal of International Money and Finance*, **12** (1), 21–35

Froot K. A. and Thaler R. H. (1990). Anomalies: foreign exchange. *Journal of Economic Perspectives*, **4**, 179–92

Ghosh A. R., Gulde A.-M. and Wolf H. C. (1998). Currency boards: the ultimate fix? IMF Working Paper No. 98/8

Gleick J. (1987). *Chaos: Making A New Science*. London: Cardinal Books

Grabbe J. O. (1986). *International Financial Markets*. Amsterdam: Elsevier

Green H. A. (1976). *Consumer Theory*. London: Macmillan

Grossman S. F. and Shiller R. J. (1981). The determinants of the variability of stock market prices. *American Economic Review*, **71** (2), 222–7

Grossman S. and Stiglitz J. (1980). On the impossibility of informationally efficient markets. *American Economic Review*, **70**, 393–408

Grubel H. G. (1977). *International Economics*. Homewood, IL: Richard D. Irwin

Hamburger M. J. (1977). The demand for money in an open economy: Germany and the United Kingdom. *Journal of Monetary Economics*, **3**, 25–40

Hansen L. P. and Hodrick R. J. (1980). Forward exchange rates as optimal predictors of future spot rates: an econometric analysis. *Journal of Political Economy*, **88**, 829–53

Hansen L. P. and Hodrick R. J. (1983). Risk averse speculation in the forward foreign exchange market: an econometric analysis of linear models. In Frenkel J. (ed.) *Exchange Rates and International Macroeconomics*. Chicago, IL: University of Chicago Press

Hartley P. (1983). Rational expectations and the foreign exchange market. In Frenkel J. (ed.) *Exchange Rates and International Macroeconomics*. Chicago, IL: University of Chicago Press

Hau H., Killeen W. and Moore M. (2002). The euro as an international currency: explaining puzzling first evidence from the foreign exchange markets. *Journal of International Money and Finance*, **21**, 351–83

Hodrick R. J. and Srivastava S. (1986). The covariation of risk premiums and expected future spot exchange rates. *Journal of International Money and Finance*, **5**, s5–s22

Honohan P. and Peruga R. (1986). Exchange rates do not fail variance bound tests. *Manchester School of Economics and Social Studies*, **53** (3), 308–13

Hsieh D. A. (1993). Using nonlinear methods to search for risk premia in currency futures. *Journal of International Economics*, **35**, 113–32

Hull J. C. (1998). *Options, Futures and Other Derivatives*. Englewood Cliffs, NJ: Prentice-Hall

Hume D. (1741). Of the balance of trade. In *Essays: Moral, Political and Literary*. Oxford: Oxford University Press (reprinted 1963)

Iannizzotto M. and Taylor M. P. (1999). The target zone model, non-linearity and mean reversion: is the honeymoon really over? *Economic Journal*, **109**, C96–110

Isard P. (1977). How far can we push the law of one price? *American Economic Review*, **67**, 942–8

Johnson H. G. (1972). The monetary approach to balance of payments theory. In *Further Essays in Monetary Theory*. London: Allen & Unwin

Johnson H. G. (1977). The monetary approach to the balance of payments: a non-technical guide. *Journal of International Economics*, **7**, 251–68

Katseli-Papaefstratiou L. T. (1979). The re-emergence of the purchasing power parity doctrine in the 1970s. *Princeton Studies in International Finance*, **13**

Katz M. L. and Rosen H. S. (1998). *Microeconomics*. Homewood, IL: Richard D. Irwin

Kindleberger C. P. (1978). *Manias, Panics and Crashes*. London: Basic Books and Macmillan

Kindleberger R. and Lindert P. (1978). *International Economics*, 3rd edn. Homewood, IL: Richard D. Irwin

Kouri P. J. (1976). The exchange rate and the balance of payments in the short and in the long run: a monetary approach. *Scandinavian Journal of Economics*, **78**, 280–304

Kouri P. J. (1983). Balance of payments and the foreign exchange market: a dynamic partial equilibrium model. In Bhandari J. S. and Putnam B. H. (eds) *Economic Interdependence and Flexible Exchange Rates*. Cambridge, MA: MIT Press

Krasker W. (1980). The peso problem in testing the efficiency of forward exchange markets. *Journal of Monetary Economics*, **6**, 269–76

Kravis I. B. and Lipsey R. E. (1971). *Price Competitiveness in World Trade*. New York: Columbia University Press

Krugman P. (1979). A model of balance of payments crises. *Journal of Money, Credit and Banking*, **11**, 311–25

Krugman P. (1987). Pricing to market when the exchange rate changes. In Arndt S. W. and Richardson J. D. (eds) *Real Financial Linkages among Open Economies*. Cambridge, MA: MIT Press

Krugman P. (1991). Target zones and exchange rate dynamics. *Quarterly Journal of Economics*, **106**, 669–82

Krugman P. (1996). Are currency crises self-fulfilling? *NBER Macroeconomics Annual*, **11**

Kyle A. S. (1985). Continuous auctions and insider trading. *Econometrica*, **53**, 1315–35

Laidler D. E. (1985). *The Demand for Money: Theories, Evidence and Problems*. New York: Harper & Row

Lane P. (2001). The new open economy macroeconomics: a survey. *Journal of International Economics*, **54** (2), 235–66

Levich R. M. (1979a). On the efficiency of markets for foreign exchange. In Dornbusch R. and Frenkel J. A. (eds) *International Economic Policy: Theory and Evidence*. Baltimore, MD: Johns Hopkins University Press

Levich R. M. (1979b). *The International Money Market: An Assessment of Forecasting Techniques and Market Efficiency*. Greenwich, CT: JAI Press

Levich R. M. (1985). Empirical studies of exchange rates: price behavior, rate determination and market efficiency. In Jones R. W. and Kenen P. B. (eds) *Handbook of International Economics*. Amsterdam: North-Holland

Loisel O. and Martin P. (1999). Coordination, cooperation, contagion and currency crises. Centre for Economic Policy Research Discussion Paper No. 2075

Lyons R. K. (2001). *The Microstructure Approach to Exchange Rates*. Cambridge, MA: MIT Press

Macdonald R. (1988). *Floating Exchange Rates: Theory and Evidence*. London: Unwin Hyman

Macdonald R. and Taylor M. P. (1989). Economic analysis of foreign exchange markets: an expository survey. In Macdonald R. and Taylor N. P. (eds) *Innovations in Open Economy Macroeconomics*. Oxford: Blackwell

Mankiw N. G. (2007). *Principles of Macroeconomics*, 4th edn. New York: South-Western

Magee S. P. (1978). Contracting and spurious deviations from purchasing power parity. In Frenkel J. A. and Johnson H. G. (eds) *The Economics of Exchange Rates: Selected Studies*. Reading, MA: Addison-Wesley

Markowitz H. M. (1959). *Portfolio Selection: Efficient Diversification of Investments*. New York: John Wiley & Sons

Marston R. C. (1982). Wages, relative prices and the choice between fixed and flexible exchange rates. *Canadian Journal of Economics*, **15** (1), 87–103

May R. M. (1976). Simple mathematical models with very complicated dynamics. *Nature*, **261**, 459

McKinnon R. I. (1963). Optimum currency areas. *American Economic Review*, **53**, 717–65

McKinnon R. I. (1979). *Money in International Exchange*. Oxford: Oxford University Press

McKinnon R. I. (1982). Currency substitution and instability in the world dollar standard. *American Economic Review*, **72** (3), 320–33

Meade J. A. (1955). The case for variable exchange rates. *Three Banks Review*, **26**, 3–27

Meese R. A. (1986). Testing for bubbles in exchange markets: a case of sparkling rates? *Journal of Political Economy*, **94** (2), 345–73

Meese R. A. and Rogoff K. (1983). The out-of-sample failure of empirical exchange rate models: sampling error or misspecification? In Frenkel J. (ed.) *Exchange Rates and International Macroeconomics*. Chicago, IL: University of Chicago Press

Meese R. A. and Singleton K. J. (1983). On unit roots and the empirical modelling of exchange rates. *Journal of Finance*, **37**, 1029–35

Metzler L. A. (1951). Wealth, saving and the rate of interest. *Journal of Political Economy*, **2** (2), 93–116

Minford A. P. L. and Peel D. A. (2002). *Advanced Macroeconomics: A Primer*. Cheltenham: Edward Elgar

Mood A. M. and Graybill F. A. (1963). *Introduction to the Theory of Statistics*, 2nd edn. New York: McGraw-Hill

Mundell R. A. (1961). A theory of optimum currency areas. *American Economic Review*, **51**, 509–17

Mundell R. A. (1962). The appropriate use of monetary and fiscal policy under fixed exchange rates. *IMF Staff Papers*, **9**, 70–7

Mundell R. A. (1968). *International Economics*. New York: Macmillan

Mussa M. (1976). The exchange rate, the balance of payments and monetary policy under a regime of controlled floating. *Scandinavian Journal of Economics*, **78**, 228–48

Mussa M. (1979). Empirical regularities in the behaviour of exchange rates and theories of the foreign exchange market. In Brunner K. and Meltzer A. H. (eds) *Policies for Employment, Prices, and Exchange Rates* vol. 11. Rochester, NY: Carnegie Rochester Conference Series

Muth J. F. (1961). Rational expectations and the theory of price movements. *Econometrica*, **29**, 315–35

Obstfeld M. (1996). Models of currency crises with self-fulfilling features. *European Economic Review*, **40**, 1037–48

Obstfeld M. (2001). International macroeconomics: beyond the Mundell–Fleming model. *IMF Staff Papers*, **47** (special issue)

Obstfeld M. (2002). Exchange rates and adjustment: perspectives from the new open economy macroeconomics. National Bureau of Economic Research Working Paper No. 9118

Obstfeld M. and Rogoff K. (1995a). The mirage of fixed exchange rates. *Journal of Economic Perspectives*, **9** (4), 73–96

Obstfeld M. and Rogoff K. (1995b). Exchange rate dynamics Redux. *Journal of Political Economy*, **103**, 624–60

Obstfeld M. and Rogoff K. (1996). *Foundations of International Macroeconomics*. Cambridge, MA, and London: MIT Press

Obstfeld M. and Rogoff K. (1998). Risk and exchange rates. National Bureau of Economic Research Working Paper No. 6694

Obstfeld M. and Rogoff K. (2000a). The six major puzzles in international macroeoconomics: is there a common cause? Center for International and Development Economics Research, University of California, Berkeley, Paper C00-112

Obstfeld M. and Rogoff K. (2000b). New directions for stochastic open economy models. *Journal of International Economics*, **50**, 117–53

Officer L. H. (1976). The purchasing power parity theory of exchange rates: a review article. *IMF Staff Papers*, **23**, 1–60

Peitgen H.-O., Jurgens H. and Saupe D. (1992). *Chaos and Fractals: New Frontiers of Science*. New York: Springer-Verlag

Rime D. (2003). New electronic trading systems in foreign exchange markets. In Jones D. C. (ed.) *New Economy Handbook*. San Diego, CA: Academic Press

Rogoff K. (1996). The purchasing power parity puzzle. *Journal of Economic Literature*, **XXXIV**, 647–68

Roll R. (1979). Violations of purchasing power parity and their implications for efficient international commodity markets. In Sarnat M. and Szego G. P. (eds) *International Finance and Trade*. Cambridge MA: Bellinger

Rubinstein M. (1976). The valuation of uncertain income streams and the pricing of options. *Bell Journal of Economics*, **7** (2), 407–25

Sager M. J. and Taylor M. P. (2006). Aspects of foreign exchange market microstructure: editors' introduction, *International Journal of Finance and Economics*, **11**, 1–2

Sarkovskii A. N. (1964). Coexistence of cycles of a continuous map of a line into itself. *Ukrainian Mathematical Zeitung*, **16**, 61–71

Sarno L. and Taylor M. P. (2001). The microstructure of the foreign exchange market: a selective survey of the literature. *Princeton Studies in International Economics*, 89

Sarno L. and Taylor M. P. (2002). Purchasing power parity and the real exchange rate. *IMF Staff Papers*, **49** (1), 65–105

Sharpe W. F. (1985). *Investments*, 3rd edn. Englewood Cliffs, NJ: Prentice-Hall

Sheffrin S. S. (1983). *Rational Expectations*. Cambridge: Cambridge University Press

Stewart I. (1990). *Does God Play Dice?* London: Penguin Books

Svensson L. E. O. (1992). An interpretation of recent research on exchange rate target zones. *Journal of Economic Perspectives*, **6** (4), 119–44

Taylor M. P. (1987). Covered interest parity: a high-frequency, high-quality data study. *Economica*, **54**, 429–38

Taylor M. P. (1988). What do investment managers know? An empirical study of practitioners' predictions. *Economica*, **55** (218), 185–202

Taylor M. P., Peel D. A. and Sarno L. (2001). Nonlinear mean-reversion in real exchange rates: toward a solution to the purchasing power parity puzzles. *International Economic Review*, **42** (4), 1015–42

Tobin J. (1958). Liquidity preference as behavior towards risk. *Review of Economic Studies*, **25** (67), 65–86

Tobin J. (1965). Money and economic growth. *Econometrica*, **33**, 671–84

Tobin J. (1969). A general equilibrium approach to monetary theory. *Journal of Money Credit and Banking*, **1** (1), 15–29

Tsiang S. C. (1959). The theory of forward exchange and effects of government intervention on the forward exchange market. *IMF Staff Papers*, **7**, 75–106

Varian H. R. (2005). *Intermediate Microeconomics*, 7th edn. New York: Norton

Vitale P. (2004). A guided tour of the market microstructure approach to exchange rate determination. CEPR Discussion Paper No. 4530

Wachtel P. (ed.) (1982). *Crises in the Economic and Financial Structure*. Lexington, MA: Lexington Books

West K. D. (1987). A standard monetary model and the variability of the deutschemark–dollar exchange rate. *Journal of International Economics*, **23** (1/2), 57–76

Williamson J. (1983). *The Open Economy and the World Economy*. New York: Basic Books

Wilson C. A. (1979). Anticipated shocks and exchange rate dynamics. *Journal of Political Economy*, **87** (3), 639–47

Wonnacott R. J. and Wonnacott T. H. (1977). *Introductory Statistics*, 3rd edn. Chichester: John Wiley & Sons

Index